BRIEF EDITION

BUSINESS MATH

FOURTH EDITION

CHERYL CLEAVES
State Technical Institute at Memphis

MARGIE HOBBS
State Technical Institute at Memphis

Prentice Hall
Upper Saddle River, New Jersey 07458

Library of Congress Cataloging-in-Publication Data

Cleaves, Cheryl S., (date)
    Business math : practical applications / Cheryl Cleaves, Margie
Hobbs. — 4th ed., brief ed.
      p.   cm.
    Includes index.
    ISBN 0-13-365909-7.
    1. Business mathematics.   I. Hobbs, Margie J.
II. Title.
HF5691.C53   1995
650′.01′513—dc20   95-38735
                                                CIP

Acquisitions Editor: Catherine Rossbach
Editorial/production supervision: WordCrafters Editorial
   Services, Inc.
Cover design: Bruce Kenselaar
Cover illustration: created by Lauren Ling, Cliff Knecht
Prepress/manufacturing buyer: Ilene Sanford
Marketing manager: Frank Mortimer

This book was set in Times Roman by Clarinda
and was printed and bound by Banta Printing Company, Menasha.
The cover was also printed by Banta.

© 1996, 1993, 1990 by Prentice Hall, Inc.
A Simon & Schuster Company
Upper Saddle River, New Jersey 07458

Photo credits:
p. 39: © W. Salvatti/Photo '95; p. 271: © Photografx '94; p. 365: © Photografx '94; p. 389: photo
courtesy of Ford Motor Company.

Printed in the United States of America

10 9 8 7 6 5 4 3 2 1

ISBN 0-13-365909-7

Prentice-Hall International (UK) Limited, *London*
Prentice-Hall of Australia Pty, Limited, *Sydney*
Prentice-Hall Canada Inc., *Toronto*
Prentice-Hall Hispanoamericana, S.A., *Mexico*
Prentice-Hall of India Private Limited, *New Dehli*
Prentice-Hall of Japan, Inc., *Tokyo*
Simon & Schuster Asia Pte. Ltd., *Singapore*
Editora Prentice-Hall do Brasil, Ltda., *Rio de Janeiro*

CONTENTS

PREFACE

In almost any career you pursue, the business math you learn in this book will serve you well and help you get ahead. Anyone can learn to deal with a certain amount of math, even those who have avoided the formal study of mathematics. We have given much thought to the best way to teach business math. If you will follow the course of the book as we have laid it out, making use of the special features we have put in the text, you will get the most out of this book and out of this course. The following features are meant to help you learn business math procedures.

Learning Objectives. Each section begins with a statement of learning objectives, which lays out for you what you should look for and learn in that section. If you read and think about these before you begin the section, you will know what to look for as you go through the section.

Self-Checks. These short quizzes that are keyed to learning objectives appear at the end of each section throughout the chapter; they are a signal to you to check yourself to make sure that you understand what you have just read or worked out before you go on to the next section. The solutions are at the end of each chapter, so you can get immediate feedback on whether you have understood the material.

Decision Key Approach to Problem Solving. This format enables students to take a systematic approach to solving problems in the business world. Each chapter has an example of the decision key to problem solving. The student is asked to analyze and compare, and then to make a business decision based on the data.

How-To Boxes. These boxes appear throughout the text to help to introduce a new procedure. To make these procedures as clear as possible, we break them down for you into step-by-step instructions. Each box is then followed by an example. The chapter Overview repeats these procedures.

Good Decisions Through Teamwork. Each chapter opens with a suggested class project designed to promote the various facets of teamwork. The collection of projects incorporates a wide variety of team-building strategies. Each project involves students in a unique way. The various projects emphasize computational skills, interpersonal skills, oral or written communication skills, organizational skills, research skills, critical thinking, and/or decision-making skills. Students submit project reports to a variety of audiences including instructors, peers, employers, and immediate supervisors.

You may decide to use any or all of the projects, or you may organize teams within the class and have each team select a project from a different chapter.

Business and Mathematics in the News. These features incorporate and are based on newspaper and magazine articles. These articles demonstrate how widespread math applications are in business and the world around you. In addition to providing a "real world" problem solving opportunity, they are intended to increase your awareness of the relevance of mathematics to your everyday life and to demonstrate the ways in which you will regularly use the math concepts you are learning.

Around the Business World Boxes. This multicultural feature appears in each chapter and may serve as a catalyst for class discussion on complex business issues or may motivate some students to further investigation of the topic.

Calculator Boxes. The use of a calculator is essential in all types of math, and especially business math. In most chapters we have calculator boxes that introduce calculator strategies. They allow multiple calculations to be performed in a continuous series of keystrokes. The boxes discuss how to analyze the procedure and set up a problem for a calculator solution; this is followed by a sample series of keystrokes involved in the solution.

Tips and Traps Boxes. These boxes point out helpful hints or pitfalls involved in business math procedures. Often, looking at the right and wrong way of doing something can save you from a costly or time-consuming error down the line. We do not always have to learn from our own mistakes—sometimes we can learn from other people's experience and not make the same mistakes ourselves.

Overview Chart. Each chapter ends with a summary in the form of a chart. This chart summarizes the how-to boxes from that chapter, with new examples. The chart also contains the page numbers where each objective is covered in the chapter, so you can go back and check it if you have questions. This chart is an excellent tool to use to review a chapter.

End-of-Chapter Review. An extensive set of exercises appears at the end of each chapter to review all the procedures and objectives covered in the chapter. These exercises may be assigned by your instructor as homework, or you may want to work them on your own for extra practice. The answers to odd-numbered exercises are at the end of the book. Solutions to odd-numbered exercises appear in a separate Student Solutions Manual.

Practice Test. Take this to test yourself before you take the real one in class. Again, answers to odd-numbered exercises appear at the end of the book; your professor has the worked-out solutions to the entire test. Solutions to odd-numbered exercises appear in a separate Student Solutions Manual.

Glossary/Index. Part of learning business math is learning the basic vocabulary of business. This vocabulary is introduced in the text, and in the Glossary/Index the terms are repeated with definitions. Each key term appears in **boldface** in the text.

Student Solutions Manual. This manual can be purchased at your bookstore. It will give you extra "learning insurance" to help you master this course. The manual contains worked-out solutions to the odd-numbered exercises in the end-of-chapter review and the practice test from each chapter of the text. Answers to these exercises appear in the back of your text, but here in the manual you can study the full worked-out solutions.

How to Study Business Math. Your instructor has free copies of this booklet, which goes over the various learning techniques you can use in class and in preparation for class to make learning business math much more efficient.

Business Math Quick Reference Tables. Annual percentage rate, simple interest, compound interest, percent value tables and more are all bound into a free-standing manual to facilitate your homework preparation and in-class testing.

To the Instructor

We have tried to provide a text that your students will enjoy using and that you will find easy and helpful to teach from. In addition to the text, we have provided a complete supplements package to increase your teaching effectiveness.

The most important supplement is the Annotated Instructor's Edition, which contains the complete student text with answers to all exercises as well as teaching aids in the margins and lecture notes with points to stress in the front of the book. The rest of the supplements are described in full in the Annotated Instructor's Edition; for your convenience a short list is given here:

- Annotated Instructor's Edition • Test Item File and Computerized Test Item File • Achievement Tests • Transparency Masters • Transparencies on Power Point • Instructor Training Video Tape • Instructor's Overhead Calculator • Instructor's Solutions Manual • Spreadsheet Templates • Student Solutions Manual • How to Study Math Booklet • Business Math Quick Reference Tables

Acknowledgments

The following reviewers provided advice and insights we have valued through several editions. We are grateful for their interest and help.

Fay Armstrong, Houston Community College
Carol Baker, Napa Valley College
Corine Baker, South Seattle Community College
Jerome Baness, Illinois Valley Community College
Walter R. Bayless, Brown-Mackie College
Rex Bishop, Charles County Community College
Elizabeth Bliss, Trident Technical College
Marg Y. Blyth, Detroit College of Business
Don Boyer, Jefferson College
Lee Brainerd, Altadena, California
James Carey, Onondaga Community College
Charles Cheetham, County College of Morris
George Chiv, Technical Career Institutes
Janet Ciccarelli, Herkimer County Community College
Dick Clark, Portland Community College
J. Cluver, Rockford Business School
Kim Collier, State Technical Institute at Memphis
Rita Cross, Northland Community College
John Cuniffe, Northland Pioneer College
James F. Dowis, Des Moines Area Community College
Norm Dreisen, Essex Community College
William L. Drezdzon, Oakton Community College
Elise Earl, Tulsa Junior College
Glenda Echert, Rogers State College
Nell Edmundson, Miami Dade Community College

Chuck Ellison, Bessemer State Technical School
Susan Ellison, Bessemer, Alabama
Marsha Faircloth, Thomas Technical Institute
Cheryl H. Fante, Central Florida Community College
Margaret Ferguson, Houston Community College
Carol Flakus, Lower Columbia College
Robert Forbes, McIntosh College
Clark Ford, Middle Tennessee State University
Paul S. Franklin, DeVry Institute of Technology
John F. Galio, Cuyahoga Community College District
Frank Goulard, Portland Community College
Cecil Green, Riverside Community College
Stephen Griffin, Tarrant County Junior College
Vi Harrington, The Culinary Arts Institute of Louisiana
Suzanne Hawk, Chaparral College
Jackie Hedgpeth, Antelope Valley College
Joseph Hinsburg, Pima County Community College
Patricia Hirschy, Asnutuck Community Technical College
Mary Hjelter-Squire, Blackhawk Technical College
S. Hunt, San Diego Mesa College
Ilhan A. Izmirli, Strayer College

John Johnson, Seattle Central Community
College
Carolyn Karnes, Macomb Community
College
Kenneth Ketelhohn, Milwaukee Area
Technical College
Ed Laughbaum, Columbus State
Community College
S. Lee, Heald Business College
Barb Leonard, Skagit Valley College
Nolan Lickey, Westark Community
College
Rena Lombardi, The Huntington Institute
Jane Loprest, Bucks County Community
College
D. Maas, Lansing Community College
Lynn Mack, Piedmont Technical College
Robert Malena, Community College of
Allegheny County, South Campus
Gary Martin, DeVry Institute of
Technology, Atlanta
Paul Martin, Aims Community College
Roberta Miller, Indian River Community
College
Linda Morgren, DeKalb Technical Institute
at Memphis
Barbara Nasewicz, Blake Business
School
Nancy Nelson, Salish Kootenai College
Howard L. Newhouse, Berkeley College
James Page, Mountain View College
Mary Pretti, State Technical Institute at
Memphis
Nancy J. Priselac, Garrett Community
College
Dave Randall, Oakland Community
College

Louise Rickman, Redlands Community
College
Sam Robinson, NHTC-Manchester
Joan Ryan, Lane Community College
Janice C. Salles, Merced College
Lona P. Scala, Roberts-Walsh Business
School
Janet Schilling, Washington State
Community College
Lynn Schuster, Central Penn Business
School
Gerald W. Shields, Austin Community
College
Georgia N. Simpson, Robeson Community
College
Beverly Sisk, Gwinnett Technical Institute
Jim and Renee Smith, West Memphis
Debiruth Stanford, DeVry Institute of
Technology
Herbert Stein, Merritt College
Alice Steljes, Illinois Valley Community
College
Louise Stevens, Golden West College
Jack Stowers, Johnston Community
College
Scott Swearingen, Tulsa, Oklahoma
Kitty Tabers, Oakton Community College
Ron Trontuet, Northwest Technical
College—Thief River Falls
Joan Van Glaebeck, Edison Community
College
Rich Vitto, Abbie Business Institute
Keith Wilson, Oklahoma City Community
College
Chuck Wiseman, Oakland Community
College
Toby Wraye, Santa Rosa, California

Accuracy is always a concern in mathematics, and we were fortunate to have the help of several colleagues who worked with us to produce the level of accuracy needed in a college textbook. The reviewers mentioned were of course our first source of corrections and queries. We also had the help of Jim and Renée Smith, Paul Franklin, and Toby Wraye.

The production of a book would not come together without the help and input of many individuals. Although the list of persons who worked on this edition is extensive, we would like to single out a few key persons. We acknowledge first acquisitions editor Catherine Rossbach who guided this edition through the months of its preparations. We thank Laurie Golson, the developmental editor, for her contributions. We also thank Judy Casillo, the supplements editor; Marianne Frasco, cover director; and Craig Campanella, editorial assistant.

We appreciate the contribution of those who provided technical information on business procedures and forms. We acknowledge the reviewers and users of past editions, who made comments and suggestions for improvement and helped make this book successful.

Finally, we express our deepest gratitude to our families: Charles Cleaves and Allen and Holly Hobbs. Their support and encouragement were vital to the completion of this project.

Cheryl Cleaves
Margie Hobbs

CHAPTER 1

PROBLEM SOLVING WITH WHOLE NUMBERS AND DECIMALS

GOOD DECISIONS THROUGH TEAMWORK

Choose a specific job in your team's target career field, and investigate the job's net monthly pay. Based on this figure, create a monthly budget for a single person living in rented housing.

Begin by listing all categories of expenses, reflecting on everything a person might spend money on throughout a year's time. Obvious categories are rent, utilities, and food. Often overlooked categories are clothing, entertainment, and miscellaneous expenses such as dry cleaning.

Once your team has agreed on the categories, research various sources to determine monthly amounts for each category. Search the newspaper, for example, to determine local rental costs. Check with car dealers to determine monthly car payments. Try to use actual figures for each category.

Now balance the monthly expenses with the monthly pay, adjusting expenses as necessary. While some categories are essential to every good budget, other categories, or the amounts assigned to them, depend on the team's priorities. Setting priorities, then, is an important part of balancing expenses to fit an income.

CHAPTER 1 PROBLEM SOLVING—WHOLE NUMBERS & DECIMALS

1.1 Problem Solving with Whole Numbers

1 ▶ *Read and write whole numbers*

2 ▶ *Round whole numbers*

3 ▶ *Add whole numbers*

4 ▶ *Subtract whole numbers*

5 ▶ *Multiply whole numbers*

6 ▶ *Divide whole numbers*

1.2 Problem Solving with Decimals

1 ▶ *Read, write, and round decimals*

2 ▶ *Add and subtract decimals*

3 ▶ *Multiply and divide decimals*

Much of our world—especially the business part of our world—runs on numbers and calculations. We go to the store that advertises the sale, take out a CD at the bank with the highest rates, apply for mortgages at the bank with the best terms, and grumble about lower take-home pay when social security withholding goes up.

This course will prepare you to enter the business world with mathematical tools for a variety of career paths. The chapters on business topics build on your knowledge of mathematics, so it is important to begin the course with a review of the mathematics skills you will need in the chapters to come.

In most businesses, arithmetic computations are done on a calculator or computer. Even so, every businessperson needs a thorough understanding of mathematical concepts in order to make the best use of a calculator. A machine will only do what you tell it to do. Pressing a wrong key or performing the wrong operations on a calculator will result in a rapid but incorrect answer. If you understand the mathematics and know how to make reasonable estimates, you can catch and correct many errors.

1.1 Problem Solving with Whole Numbers

1 ▶ *Read and write whole numbers*

2 ▶ *Round whole numbers*

3 ▶ *Add whole numbers*

4 ▶ *Subtract whole numbers*

5 ▶ *Multiply whole numbers*

6 ▶ *Divide whole numbers*

We begin our review with *whole numbers,* that is, numbers like 0, 1, 2, 3, 4 . . . . . Most business calculations involving whole numbers involve one or more of four basic *mathematical operations:* addition, subtraction, multiplication, and division.

1 ▶ *Reading and Writing Whole Numbers*

Reading numbers is based on an understanding of the **place-value system** that is part of our decimal number system. The chart in Figure 1–1 shows that system applied to the number 381,345,287,369,021.

To apply this chart to any number, follow the steps in the How-To box. You'll find these boxes, and examples illustrating their use, throughout this text.

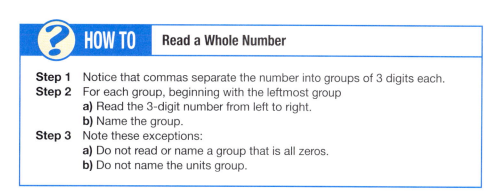

Figure 1–1 Place-Value Chart for Whole Numbers

 HOW TO | **Read a Whole Number**

Step 1 Notice that commas separate the number into groups of 3 digits each.
Step 2 For each group, beginning with the leftmost group
    a) Read the 3-digit number from left to right.
    b) Name the group.
Step 3 Note these exceptions:
    a) Do not read or name a group that is all zeros.
    b) Do not name the units group.

Example 1 Read the number 3,007,047,203.

3 007 047 203	Notice that commas separate the number into groups of 3 digits.
3	three billion
007	seven million
047	forty-seven thousand
203	two hundred three

The number is read: three billion, seven million, forty-seven thousand, two hundred three.

! TIPS & TRAPS

When reading numbers, first notice the commas that separate groups. The group name will be read at each comma. Since no comma follows the units group, that will serve as your reminder that the group name *units* is not read.

In 3,007,047,203 a group name is read at each comma: 3 billion, 7 million, 47 thousand, 203.

Other reminders: Hundreds is NOT a group name. Every group has a ones, tens, and hundreds *place*. The word *and* is NOT used when reading whole numbers. If a number has more than 4 digits, but no commas, like you see on a calculator display, insert commas when you write the number.

Translating Word Names to Numbers Suppose you are in a sales meeting and the marketing manager presents a report of the sales for the previous quarter, the projected sales for the current quarter, and the projected sales for the entire year. How would you record these figures in the notes you are taking for the meeting?

You will need to have a mental picture of the place-value structure of our numbering system. You begin recording digits, and when you hear the first group name, insert a comma. From this point, you can anticipate how many digits will follow. If a group name is skipped, three zeros are placed in that group followed by a comma. Look at the next example to see how this thinking process is used.

 Example 2 Write the number given its word name.

(a) Fifteen million, three hundred sixty-two thousand, five hundred thirty-eight
(b) Five hundred forty-two billion, five hundred thousand, twenty-nine

(a) 15, __ __ __ , __ __ __	**Record the first digits followed by a comma when the group name *millions* is heard (or read). Then roups to follow (thousands and units).**
15,362,538	**Fill in each remaining group as the digits and group names are heard (or read).**

The number is 15,362,538.

(b) 542, __ __ __ , __ __ __ , __ __ __ ,	**Record the first group and anticipate the groups to follow (millions, thousands, and units).**
542, __ __ __ , 500, __ __ __ ,	**The next group name you hear (or read) is *thousands,* so you place the 500 in the thousands group, saving space to place 3 zeros in the millions group.**
542,000,500,029	**Place 3 zeros in the *millions* group and listen for (read) the last 3 digits. You hear (read) twenty-nine, which is a 2-digit number. Thus, a 0 is placed in the hundreds place.**

The number is 542,000,500,029.

 ! **TIPS & TRAPS**

When writing the digits for a number that you hear or read, the group name always indicates that a comma should be used. One difficulty in writing the digits for a number that is spoken is that you delay writing the digits for a group until you hear a group name. Then while you are writing, the next digits are already being spoken. You can build skill through practice. Pair with a classmate and take turns reading and writing numbers.

2 ▶ *Rounding Whole Numbers*

Exact numbers are not always necessary or desirable. For example, the board of directors does not want to know to the penny how much was spent on office supplies (though the accounting staff should know). Approximate or **rounded** numbers are often used. In general, you should round a number to a specified place or to the first digit from the left in a number.

Occasionally, you may need to *round to the first digit*. The first digit is the leftmost digit.

HOW TO | Round a Whole Number to a Specified Place

Step 1 Find the digit in the specified place.
Step 2 Look at the next digit to the right.
  a) If this digit is less than 5, replace it and all digits to its right with zeros.
  b) If this digit is 5 or more, add 1 to the digit in the specified place, and replace all digits to the right of the specified place with zeros.

Example 3 Round 2,748 (a) to the nearest hundred (b) to the first digit.

(a) The specified place is the hundreds place.

2,748   **The digit in the hundreds place is 7.**

2,748   **The digit to the right of 7 is 4.**

2,700   **4 is less than 5, so step 2a applies: replace all digits to the right of 7 with zeros.**

2,748 rounded to the nearest hundred is 2,700.

(b) The specified place is the place of the first digit.

2,748   **The first digit is 2.**

2,748   **The digit to the right of 2 is 7.**

3,000   **7 is 5 or more, so step 2b applies: add 1 to 2 to get 3, and replace all digits to its right with zeros.**

2,748 rounded to the first digit is 3,000.

 Adding Whole Numbers

Numbers being added are called **addends.** The answer, or result of addition is called the **sum,** or **total.** Numbers can be added in any order without changing their sum.

$$\begin{array}{r} 2 \\ 3 \\ +4 \\ \hline 9 \end{array}$$ ← addends
← sum or total

HOW TO | Add Whole Numbers

Step 1 Write the numbers in a vertical column, aligning digits according to their places.
Step 2 For each *place* in turn, beginning with the ones place
  a) Add the *place* digits.
  b) Write the units digit of this sum directly below the *place* digit of the last addend.
  c) Write the remaining digits of the sum directly above the *next place* digit of the first addend.

Instructions for performing operations using a calculator are provided on the inside back cover. Look for the calculator icon throughout the text for additional tips for using a calculator.

Example 4 Add 452 + 83 + 3,256.

Write the numbers in a vertical column, aligning digits by place value.

$$
\begin{array}{r}
452 \\
83 \\
\underline{3,256} \\
3,791
\end{array}
$$

Add the ones place digits, carrying 1 to the tens place. Add the tens place digits, carrying 1 to the hundreds place. Add the hundreds place digits. Finally, add the thousands place digits.

The sum is 3,791.

Estimating for Accuracy   There are several ways to improve your accuracy for calculations. One is to recalculate a second time. A second way is to recalculate using a calculator. A third way is to **estimate** the result before or after you calculate.

A quick and often-used way to estimate a sum is to round each addend to its first digit, and add the rounded addends. In the previous example, if we round 452 to 500, 83 to 100, 3,256 to 3,000, the estimated sum is 3,600. You can use rounding to estimate other operations like division.

Example 5 Estimate the sum by rounding each addend to its first digit. Compare the estimate to the exact sum.

$$
\begin{array}{rcl}
885 & \text{rounds to} & 900 \\
569 & \text{rounds to} & 600 \\
343 & \text{rounds to} & 300 \\
231 & \text{rounds to} & 200 \\
\underline{+562} & \text{rounds to} & \underline{+600} \\
2,590 & & 2,600
\end{array}
$$

The estimate is 2,600; the exact sum is 2,590.

 A Decision Key for Problem-Solving   Decision making or problem solving is an important skill for the successful businessperson. The decision making process can be applied by either individuals or action teams. Many strategies have been developed to enable individuals and teams to *organize* the information given and to *develop* a plan for finding the information needed to make effective business decisions or to solve business-related problems.

The plan we have developed is a seven-step process. This feature of the text will be indicated throughout the text by the decision key located in the margin as shown here. The key words to identify each of the seven steps are:

1. **Decision needed** means "What decision do I need to make?" Sometimes the problem to be solved is to find an unknown fact. In problems of this type, the *decision needed* step is not required.
2. **Unknown fact(s)** means "What facts do I need to find to make a decision?" or in the case that no decision is required, "What facts am I trying to find?"
3. **Known fact(s)** means "What relevant facts are known or given?"
4. **Relationships** means "How are the known and unknown facts related?" and "What formulas or definitions are used to establish a model?"
5. **Estimation** means "Approximately, what should be the result of my calculation?"
6. **Calculation** means to perform the operations identified in the relationships.
7. **Decision made** means "Based upon the result of calculation to find unknown facts, what is my decision?" When the situation calls for determining unknown facts only, this step is not necessary.

In the following example, we apply the decision key.

Example 6 Holly Hobbs supervises the shipping department at AH Transportation and must schedule her employees to handle all shipping requests within a specified time frame while keeping the payroll amount within the amount budgeted. Complete the payroll report for the first quarter and decide if Holly has kept the payroll within the quarterly department payroll budget of $25,000.

Quarterly Payroll Report for the Shipping Department

Employee	Quarterly Payroll
Oluwatoyin, Adesipe	$6,463
Alexander, Karen	5,389
Burke, Tracie	5,781
Ores, Vincent	5,389
Department Total	

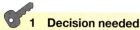

1 Decision needed Is the quarterly payroll within budget?

2 Unknown facts Quarterly total for the department

3 Known facts Quarterly total for each employee (in chart)
Quarterly department budget: $25,000

4 Relationships Quarterly department total = sum of quarterly total for each employee
Quarterly department total = 5,389 + 5,781 + 6,463 + 5,389

5 Estimation Round each employee quarterly total to its first digit; then add to estimate the sum:

$$
\begin{array}{ccc}
5,389 & \longrightarrow & 5,000 \\
5,781 & \longrightarrow & 6,000 \\
6,463 & \longrightarrow & 6,000 \\
5,389 & \longrightarrow & \underline{5,000} \\
& & 22,000
\end{array}
$$

The estimated quarterly department total is $22,000.

6 Calculation Calculate by hand or using a calculator the actual sum of employee quarterly totals.

$$
\begin{array}{l}
5,389 \quad \text{Add the digits for each place.} \\
5,781 \\
6,463 \\
\underline{5,389} \\
23,022
\end{array}
$$

The quarterly department total is $23,022.

7 Decision made Is the quarterly department total less than or equal to $25,000? The total $23,022 is less than the budgeted amount of $25,000. **Holly's department expenditure for payroll _is_ within the amount budgeted for the department.**

 Subtracting Whole Numbers

When subtracting one number from another, the number subtracted from is called the **minuend.** The number being subtracted is called the **subtrahend.** The result of subtraction is called the **difference.**

$$
\begin{array}{ccl}
135 & \longrightarrow & \text{minuend} \\
\underline{-\ 72} & \longrightarrow & \text{subtrahend} \\
63 & \longrightarrow & \text{difference}
\end{array}
$$

 **HOW TO** | **Subtract Whole Numbers**

Step 1 Write the numbers in a vertical column, the subtrahend below the minuend, aligning digits according to their places.

Step 2 For each *place* in turn, beginning with the ones place
    a) If the *place* digit of the minuend is less than the *place* digit of the subtrahend, add 10 to the *place* digit of the minuend and subtract 1 from the *next place* digit of the minuend.
    b) Subtract the *place* digits.
    c) Write this difference directly below the *place* digit of the subtrahend.

Step 3 Check the difference by adding the subtrahend and the difference. Their sum should be the same as the minuend.

Example 7 Subtract 27 from 64.

$$\begin{array}{r} 64 \\ -27 \\ \hline \end{array}$$

Arrange the numbers so that the places align.

$$\begin{array}{r} \cancel{6}\,4 \\ -2\,7 \\ \hline 3\,7 \end{array}$$

4 is smaller than 7, so you must "borrow" from the tens place (thus 6 becomes 5), and add 10 to the ones place. Subtract ones place digits, then subtract tens place digits.

Check:
$$\begin{array}{r} 37 \\ +27 \\ \hline 64 \end{array}$$

The sum of the subtrahend and difference equals the minuend. The difference is correct.

The difference of 64 and 27 is 37.

 Multiplying Whole Numbers

When multiplying one number by another, the number being multiplied is called the **multiplicand.** The number we multiply by is called the **multiplier.** Each number can also be called a **factor.** The result of multiplication is called the **product.** Numbers can be multiplied in any order without changing the product. When the multiplier has more than one digit, the product of each digit and the multiplicand is called a **partial product.**

$$\begin{array}{r} 75 \\ 32 \\ \hline 150 \\ 225 \\ \hline 2400 \end{array}$$
← multiplicand
← multiplier   ⎫ ← factors
← partial products ⎫
← product

 **HOW TO** | **Multiply Whole Numbers**

Step 1 Write the numbers in a vertical column, aligning digits according to their place.

Step 2 For each place of the multiplier in turn, beginning with the ones place
    a) Multiply the multiplicand by the *place* digit of the multiplier.
    b) Write the partial product directly below the multiplier (or the last partial product), aligning the ones digit of the partial product with the *place* digit of the multiplier (and aligning all other digits, to the left accordingly).

Step 3 Add the partial products.

Example 8 Multiply 127 by 53.

$$
\begin{array}{r}
127 \\
\times \quad 53 \\
\hline
381 \\
6\,35 \\
\hline
6{,}731
\end{array}
$$

⟵ multiplicand
⟵ multiplier
⟵ **first partial product: $3 \times 127 = 381$; 1 in 381 aligns with 3 in 53.**
⟵ **second partial product: $5 \times 127 = 635$: 5 in 635 aligns with 5 in 53.**
⟵ **product: add the partial products**

The product of 127 and 53 is 6,731.

 TIPS & TRAPS

When you multiply numbers that contain two or more digits, it is crucial to *place the partial products* properly. A common mistake in multiplying is to forget to "indent" the partial products that follow the first partial product.

$$
\begin{array}{r}
265 \\
\times \quad 23 \\
\hline
795 \\
5\,30 \\
\hline
6{,}095
\end{array}
$$

We get the second partial product, 530, by multiplying 265×2. Therefore, the 0 in 530 should be directly below the 2 in 23.

$$
\begin{array}{r}
265 \\
\times \quad 23 \\
\hline
795 \\
530 \\
\hline
1{,}325
\end{array}
$$

CORRECT   **INCORRECT**

As in addition, you can improve your multiplication accuracy by recalculating a second time, by recalculating using a calculator, or by estimating the product.

Zeros are used in many helpful shortcuts to multiplying. You must pay careful attention to the position of zeros in partial products. When one of the numbers being multiplied is 10, 100, 1,000, and so on, you can use a shortcut to find the product.

 HOW TO | **Multiply When Numbers End in Zero**

Step 1   Mentally eliminate zeros from the end of each number.
Step 2   Multiply the new numbers.
Step 3   Attach to the end of the product the total number of zeros mentally eliminated in step 1.

Example 9 Multiply 20,700 by 860.

$$
\begin{array}{r}
207\,00 \\
\times \quad 86\,0 \\
\hline
1\,242 \\
16\,56 \\
\hline
17{,}802\,000
\end{array}
$$

Mentally eliminate 3 zeros from the ends of 20,700 and 860. Multiply 207 by 86, aligning digits and finding partial products.

Attach the 3 zeros that were mentally eliminated in step 1.

The product of 20,700 and 860 is 17,802,000.

If the multiplier has a zero in the middle, such as 102, 507, or 1,306, for example, you can use another shortcut to multiplication.

Instead of writing a partial product consisting only of zeros, write a partial product of zero directly below the zero in the multiplier and then write the next partial product on the same line.

Example 10
Max Wertheimer works at the Wendy's warehouse and is processing store orders totaling 45,000 8-ounce cups. He found 303 packages of 8-ounce cups. Each package contains a gross of cups. Does Max need to order more cups from the manufacturer to fill the store orders if one gross is 144 items?

1 Decision needed

Should more cups be ordered?

2 Unknown facts

Total quantity of cups on hand

3 Known facts

Store orders: 45,000 cups

Packages of cups on hand: 303

Cups per package: 1 gross, or 144

4 Relationships

Total quantity of cups on hand = quantity of packages × cups per package

Total quantity of cups on hand = 303 × 144

5 Estimation

If each package contained 100 cups and there were 300 packages on hand, the total would be 100×300. This is easier to multiply mentally and gives us an estimate. $100 \times 300 = 30,000$. It appears there are not enough cups on hand. However, since both numbers were rounded down, we know that this estimate is less than the actual number of cups on hand.

6 Calculation

$$
\begin{array}{r}
303 \\
\times \quad 144 \\
\hline
1\,212 \\
12\,12 \\
30\,3 \\
\hline
43,632
\end{array}
$$

1 212   Partial product of 303 × 4
12 12   Partial product of 303 × 4
30 3   Partial product of 303 × 1
43,632   Add the partial products.

The total quantity of cups on hand is 43,632.

7 Decision made

There are 43,632 cups in the warehouse, but store orders totaled 45,000. Therefore, **Max needs to order more cups from the manufacturer to fill all the store orders.**

6 ▶ Dividing Whole Numbers

When dividing one number by another, the number being divided is called the **dividend.** The number divided by is called the **divisor.** The result of division is called the **quotient.** When the quotient is not a whole number, the quotient has a **whole number part** and a **remainder.** When a dividend has more digits than a divisor, parts of the dividend are called **partial dividends,** and the quotient of a partial dividend and the divisor is called a **partial quotient.**

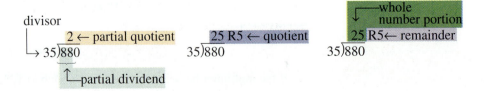

divisor
    2 ← partial quotient
35)880
    └─partial dividend

25 R5 ← quotient
35)880

        ┌─whole
        │   number portion
25 R5← remainder
35)880

Step 1   Beginning with its leftmost digit, identify the first group of digits of the dividend that is larger than or equal to the divisor. This group of digits is the first *partial dividend*.

Step 2   For each partial dividend in turn, beginning with the first;

     a) Divide the partial dividend by the divisor. Write this partial quotient above the rightmost digit of the partial dividend.

     b) Multiply the partial quotient by the divisor. Write the product below the partial dividend, aligning places.

     c) Subtract the product from the partial dividend. Write the difference below the product, aligning places. The difference must be less than the divisor.

     d) Next to the ones place of the difference, write the next digit of the dividend. This is the new partial dividend.

Step 3   When all the digits of the dividend have been used, write the final difference in step 2c as the remainder (unless the remainder is 0). The whole number part of the quotient is the number written above the dividend.

Step 4   To check, multiply the quotient by the divisor and add the remainder to the product. This sum equals the dividend.

 TIPS & TRAPS

Two types of common business problems require division. Both types involve distributing items equally into groups. In the first type, we distribute a specified total quantity of items so that each group gets a specific equal share. Division determines the number of groups. For example, you need to ship 78 crystal vases. With appropriate packaging to avoid breakage, only 5 vases fit in each box. How many boxes are required? You divide the total quantity of vases by the quantity of vases that will fit into one box to determine how many boxes are required.

In the second type of problem that requires division, we distribute a specified total quantity so that we have a specific number of groups. Division determines each group's equal share. For example, how many ounces will each of 4 cups contain if a carafe of coffee containing 32 ounces is poured equally into the cups? The capacity of the carafe is divided by the number of coffee cups: $32 \div 4 = 8$. Eight ounces of coffee are contained in each of the 4 cups.

Example 11   Leroy needs to ship 78 crystal vases. With standard packing to avoid damage, 5 vases fit in each available box. Does Leroy need to arrange for extra packing or will each box contain exactly 5 vases?

1 Decision needed   Is extra packing required?

2 Unknown facts   The quantity of boxes required to ship the vases

3 Known facts   Total quantity of vases to be shipped: 78
Quantity of vases per box without the extra packing: 5

4 Relationships   Quantity of boxes needed = total vases ÷ quantity of vases per box

Quantity of boxes needed = $78 \div 5$

5 Estimation

$$70 \div 5 = 14 \qquad \text{\textbf{\color{blue}Round down the dividend.}}$$

$$80 \div 5 = 16 \qquad \text{\textbf{\color{blue}Round up the dividend.}}$$

Since 78 is between 70 and 80, the number of boxes needed is between 14 and 16.

$$\begin{array}{r} 1 \\ 5\overline{)78} \end{array}$$

7 is the first partial dividend since it is at least as large as 5. Divide 7 by 5 and write the partial quotient 1 above 7.

$$\begin{array}{r} 1 \\ 5\overline{)78} \\ 5 \\ \hline 2 \end{array}$$

The product of 1 and 5 is 5, so write 5 below 7, and subtract.

The difference, 2, is less than the divisor, 5.

$$\begin{array}{r} 1 \\ 5\overline{)78} \\ 5 \\ \hline 28 \end{array}$$

The next digit of the dividend is 8, so write 8 next to 2.

$$\begin{array}{r} 15 \\ 5\overline{)78} \\ 5 \\ \hline 28 \\ 25 \\ \hline 3 \end{array}$$

Divide 28 by 5, and write the partial quotient 5 above 8. Multiply 5 by 5, and subtract the product 25 from 28.

$$\begin{array}{r} 15\,R3 \\ 5\overline{)78} \\ 5 \\ \hline 28 \\ 25 \\ \hline 3 \end{array}$$

The whole number part of the quotient is 15; the remainder is 3.

Check:
Check the quotient by multiplying the whole number part 15 by the divisor 5. Then add the remainder. The sum should equal the dividend 78.

$$\begin{array}{cc} 15 & 75 \\ \underline{5} & \underline{+3} \\ 75 & 78 \end{array}$$ **The result checks.**

The quantity of boxes needed is 15 boxes containing 5 vases, and 1 box containing 3 vases.

Fifteen boxes will have 5 vases each, needing no extra packing. One additional box is required to ship the remaining 3 vases. **Extra packing is needed to fill the additional box.**

⚠ TIPS & TRAPS

Be very careful in lining up the numbers in a division problem and in entering zeros in the quotient.

$$\begin{array}{r} 507 \\ 5\overline{)2,535} \\ 2\,5 \\ \hline 3 \\ \underline{0} \\ 35 \\ 35 \\ \hline 0 \end{array}$$

$$\begin{array}{r} 570 \\ 5\overline{)2,535} \\ 2\,5 \\ \hline 35 \\ 35 \\ \hline 0 \end{array}$$

CORRECT   **INCORRECT**

You will find Self-Check exercises throughout each chapter. These exercises give you a chance to review the material you have just read and see how well you understand the chapter so far. After you have done the exercises, check your answers against the solutions provided at the end of the chapter.

Self-Check 1.1

 Write the word name for the number.

1. 5,702,005

2. 317,000,171

3. 4,204,049,201

 Round 3,645 to the specified place.

4. hundreds

5. first digit

6. tens

 Add and check the sum.

7.
```
   328
   583
+  726
```

8.
```
   671
   982
+   57
```

9. $791 + 1000 + 52$

 Subtract and check the difference.

10.
```
   55
 −36
```

11.
```
   308
 −275
```

12. $5,409 − 2,176$

 Multiply and check the product.

13.
```
    730
 ×   60
```

14.
```
    904
 ×   24
```

15. 1,005 by 89

 Divide and check the quotient.

16. $96 ÷ 6$

17. $13,838 ÷ 34$

18. $3,808 ÷ 15$

19. The menswear department of Rich's Department Store has a sales goal of $40,000 for its Founder's Day Sale. Complete the following worksheet for the sales totals by salesperson and by days. Decide if the goal was reached. What is the difference between the goal and the actual total sales amount?

	W	Th	F	S	Su	Personal Total
Fletes, Raul	2,492	1,948	2,307	4,301	1,589	
Grimes, Selena	897	421	598	1,025	897	
Johnston, Margaret	1,708	2,096	3,222	1,507	2,801	
Keck, Neal	723	1,687	2,196	1,737	2,186	
Daily Sales Total						

20. Atkinson's Candy Company manufactures seven types of hard candy for its Family Favorites mixed candy which is packaged in three-pound bags. Brenda Jinkins, the floor supervisor, must supervise the repackaging of bulk candy from 84 containers that each contain 25 pounds of candy. The bulk candy will be bagged in three-pound bags, then packed in boxes for shipping. Each box will contain 12 of the bags of mixed candy. Wilma Jackson-Randle is responsible for inventory of containers for the company and reports that she currently has 1,000 three-pound bags on hand and 100 boxes of the size that will be used to ship this candy. Decide if enough materials are in inventory to complete the mixing and packaging process.

21. University Trailer Sales Company sold 352 utility trailers during a recent year. If the gross annual sales for the company was $324,800, what was the average selling price for each trailer?

22. An acre of ground is a square piece of land which is 210 feet on each of the four equal sides. Fencing can be purchased in 50-foot rolls for $49 per roll. You are giving a bid to install the fencing at a cost of $1 per foot of fencing plus the cost of materials. If the customer has bids of $1,700, $2,500, and $2,340 in addition to your bid, decide if your bid is the low bid for the job to determine if you will likely get the business.

23. If you are paying three employees $7 per hour and the fence installation in exercise 22 requires 21 hours when all three employees are working, determine how much you will be required to pay in wages. What will be your gross profit on the job?

24. The 7th Inning Baseball Card Shop buys cards from eight vendors. In the month of November the company purchased 8,832 boxes of cards. If an equal number of boxes were purchased from each vendor, how many boxes of cards were supplied by each vendor?

25. If you have 348 packages of Halloween candy to rebox for shipment to a discount store and you can pack 12 packages in each box, how many boxes will you need?

BUSINESS AND MATHEMATICS *IN THE NEWS*

Detroit has Best Year Since 1988

By Michael Clements
USA TODAY

Ford won the 1994 sales title Thursday for both cars and trucks as the auto industry closed the books on its best year since 1988.

Ford, Chrysler and General Motors and their foreign competitors sold nearly 15 million cars and light trucks in the USA last year, up more than 1 million from 1993 and best since 1988's 15.5 million.

Light trucks — pickups, minivans and sport-utilities — set a record at nearly 6.1 million sales, up 13%.

For the year, sales of cars and trucks rose 8%. Japanese makers gained market share as their sales rose 8.8% vs. a 7.4% gain for the Big Three.

Ford, whose sales gained 7%, won races for top seller in three big categories.
▶ The F-Series pickup was the best-selling truck.
▶ Taurus was the best-selling car, topping the Honda Ac-

cord for the third straight year.
▶ Explorer was the top-selling sport-utility vehicle for the fourth year in a row.

GM's 1994 sales increased 7% from a year earlier. GM's vehicle sales topped 5 million for the first time since 1989.

Chrysler Wednesday reported an 8% increase over '93.

Top sellers

U.S. top 10 vehicle sales:

Automaker	1994 sales
Ford F-series pickup	646,039
Chevy C/K pickup	551,849
Ford Taurus	397,037
Honda Accord	367,615
Ford Ranger pickup	344,744
Ford Escort	336,967
Toyota Camry	321,797
Saturn	286,003
Ford Explorer	278,065
Dodge Caravan	276,963

Source: Autodata

1. Round each of the top five 1994 sales to the nearest ten thousand.

2. Round each of the top ten vehicle sales to the nearest hundred thousand. Use your rounded numbers to help you estimate the approximate number of top ten vehicles sold in the U.S.

3. Use a calculator to find the exact number of top ten vehicles sold in the U.S.

4. Compare your answers in exercises 2 and 3. Was your estimate over or under the actual number of vehicles sold?

5. What are some advantages of using rounded numbers?

1 ▸ *Read, write, and round decimals*

2 ▸ *Add and subtract decimals*

3 ▸ *Multiply and divide decimals*

Decimal numbers allow us to write quantities smaller than one whole. We use decimals in some form or another every day—even our money system is based on decimals. Calculators use decimals, and decimals are the basis of percent, interest, markups, and markdowns.

1 ▸ ***Reading, Writing, and Rounding Decimals***

Our money system, which is based on the dollar, uses the **decimal system.** In the decimal system, as you move right to left from one digit to the next, the place value of the digit increases by 10 times (multiply by 10). As you move left to right from one digit to the next, the place value of the digit gets 10 times smaller (divide by 10). The place value of the digit to the right of the ones place is 1 divided by 10.

There are several ways for indicating 1 divided by 10. In the decimal system, we write 1 divided by 10 as 0.1. Other ways to write 1 divided by 10 are:

$$10)\overline{1} \quad 1 \div 10 \quad 0.1$$

Figure 1–2   1 whole divided into 10 parts. The shaded part is 0.1.

How much is 0.1? How much is 1 divided by 10? It is one part of a 10-part whole. We read 0.1 as one-tenth. Using decimal notation, we can extend our place-value chart to the right of the ones place and express quantities that are not whole numbers. When extending to the right of the ones place, a period called a **decimal point** separates the **whole number part** from the **decimal part.**

The names of the places to the right of the decimal are tenths, hundredths, thousandths, etc. These place names are similar to the place names for whole numbers but they all end in *ths*. In the chart below, we show the place names for the digits in the number 2,315.627432.

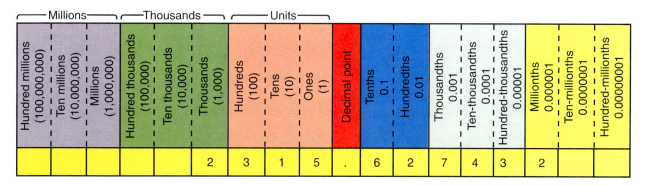

Millions			Thousands			Units											
Hundred millions (100,000,000)	Ten millions (10,000,000)	Millions (1,000,000)	Hundred thousands (100,000)	Ten thousands (10,000)	Thousands (1,000)	Hundreds (100)	Tens (10)	Ones (1)	Decimal point	Tenths 0.1	Hundredths 0.01	Thousandths 0.001	Ten-thousandths 0.0001	Hundred-thousandths 0.00001	Millionths 0.000001	Ten-millionths 0.0000001	Hundred-millionths 0.00000001
					2	3	1	5	.	6	2	7	4	3	2		

Figure 1–3   Place Value Chart for Decimals

HOW TO Read or Write a Decimal

Step 1 Read or write the whole number part (to the left of the decimal point) as you would read or write a whole number.
Step 2 Use the word *and* for the decimal point.
Step 3 Read or write the decimal part (to the right of the decimal point) as you would read or write a whole number.
Step 4 Read or write the place name of the rightmost digit.

TIPS & TRAPS

When reading decimal numbers that represent money amounts, we read whole numbers as *dollars*. $45 is read *forty-five dollars*. Decimal amounts are read as *cents*. $0.72 is read *seventy-two cents* rather than *seventy-two hundredths of a dollar*. Since one cent is one hundredth of a dollar, the words *cent* and *hundredth* have the same meaning. $38.21 is read *thirty-eight dollars and twenty-one cents*.

Example 1 Write the word name for the decimal: (a) 3.12 (b) 0.209 (c) $234.93

(a) three and twelve hundredths   **The rightmost digit, 2, is in the hundredths place.**

(b) two hundred nine thousandths   **The whole number part, 0, is not written.**

(c) two hundred thirty-four dollars
and ninety-three cents

You round decimals for the same reasons that you round whole numbers, and in a similar way.

HOW TO Round to a Specified Decimal Place

Step 1 Find the digit in the specified place.
Step 2 Look at the next digit to the right.
  a) If this digit is less than 5, eliminate it and all digits to its right.
  b) If this digit is 5 or more, add 1 to the digit in the specified place, and eliminate all digits to its right.

Example 2 Round the number to the specified place: (a) 17.3754 to the nearest hundredth (b) $193.48 to the nearest dollar (c) $17.375 to the nearest cent

(a) 17.3754   **The digit in the hundredths place is 7.**

17.3754   **The digit to the right of 7 is 5. Since 5 is 5 or more, step 2b applies; add 1 to 7 to get 8, and eliminate all digits to its right.**

17.38

17.3754 rounded to the nearest hundredth is 17.38.

(b) $19**3**.48   Rounding to the nearest dollar means rounding to the ones place. The digit in the ones places is 3.

$193.**4**8   The digit to the right of 3 is 4. Since 4 is less than 5, step 2a applies; eliminate 4 and all digits to its right.

$193

$193.48 rounded to the nearest dollar is $193.

(c) $17.3**75**   Rounding to the nearest cent means rounding to the nearest hundredth. The digit in the hundredths place is 7.

$17.37**5**   The digit to the right of 7 is 5. Since 5 is 5 or more, step 2b applies.

$17.38

$17.375 rounded to the nearest cent is $17.38.

 Adding and Subtracting Decimals

Some math skills are used more often than others. Adding and subtracting decimal numbers are regularly used in transactions involving money. To increase your awareness of the use of decimals, refer to your paycheck stub, grocery store receipt, fast food ticket, odometer on your car, the bills you receive each month, and your checking account statement balance.

 HOW TO   **Add or Subtract Decimals**

Step 1   Write the numbers in a vertical column, aligning digits according to their places.
Step 2   Attach extra zeros to the right end of each number so that each number has the same quantity of digits to the right of the decimal point.
Step 3   Add or subtract as though the numbers are whole numbers.
Step 4   Place the decimal point in the sum or difference to align with the decimal point in the addends or subtrahend and minuend.

Example 3 Add $32 + 2.55 + 8.85 + 0.625$.

$$
\begin{array}{r}
32 \\
2.55 \\
8.85 \\
\underline{0.625} \\
44.025
\end{array}
$$

A decimal point is understood to follow the 32.
Assume blank places to be zero.
All decimal points are aligned vertically.
Add the numbers as you would add whole numbers.
Place the decimal in the sum.

The sum is 44.025.

TIPS & TRAPS

A common mistake in adding decimals is to misalign the digits or decimal points.

```
  15        All digits and decimals          15      ← not aligned correctly
   4.28     points are aligned                4.28
   3.04     correctly.                        3.04
   0.735                                       0.7 35  ← not aligned correctly
 23.055                                        1.4 82
```

CORRECT   **INCORRECT**

Example 4 Subtract 26.3 − 15.84.

```
    5 1210
  2 6.3 0    Write the numbers so that the digits align according to their places.
− 1 5.8 4    Subtract the numbers, borrowing as you would in whole-number
  1 0.4 6    subtraction.
```

The difference of 26.3 and 15.84 is 10.46.

 Multiplying and Dividing Decimals

You are frequently called upon to calculate the amount of tip to add to a restaurant bill. A typical tip in the United States is 20 cents per dollar, which is 0.20 or 0.2 per dollar. To calculate the tip on a bill of $28.73 we multiply 28.73×0.2.

We multiply decimals as though they are whole numbers. Then we place the decimal point according to the quantity of digits in the decimal parts of the factors.

HOW TO Multiply Decimals

Step 1 Multiply the decimal numbers as though they are whole numbers.
Step 2 Count the digits in the decimal parts of both decimal numbers.
Step 3 Place the decimal point in the product so that there are as many digits in its decimal part as there are digits you counted in step 2. If necessary, attach zeros on the left end of the product so that you can place the decimal point accurately.

Example 5 Multiply (a) 3.5×3 (b) 2.35×0.015.

```
(a)      3.5     There is 1 digit to the right of the decimal point so the product has 1
      ×    3     digit to the right of the decimal point.
        10.5
```

The product of 3.5 and 3 is 10.5.

(b)
$$
\begin{array}{r}
2.35 \\
\times\ \ 0.015 \\
\hline
1175 \\
235 \\
\hline
0.03525
\end{array}
$$

There are 2 digits to the right of the decimal point in 2.35, and there are 3 digits to the right of the decimal point in 0.015. So the product must have 5 digits to the right of the decimal point. One 0 is attached on the left to accurately place the decimal point.

The product of 2.35 and 0.015 is 0.03525.

Note that the zero to the left of the decimal point in Example 5b is not necessary, but it helps to make the decimal point visible.

⚠ TIPS & TRAPS

A common mistake is to drop unnecessary zeros *before* placing the decimal point in the product.

$$
\begin{array}{r}
2.5 \\
\times\ \ 0.14 \\
\hline
100 \\
25 \\
\hline
0.350
\end{array}
$$

There is 1 digit to the right of the decimal point in 2.5, and there are 2 digits to the right of the decimal point in 0.14. There must be 3 digits to the right of the decimal point in the product.

$$
\begin{array}{r}
2.5 \\
\times\ \ 0.14 \\
\hline
100 \\
25 \\
\hline
0.0350
\end{array}
$$

CORRECT   **INCORRECT**

Example 6   Find the amount of tip you would pay on a restaurant bill of $28.73 if you tip 20 cents on the dollar (0.2) for the bill.

1 Decision needed   Decision not required

2 Unknown fact   Amount of tip

3 Known facts   Restaurant bill: $28.73
Rate of tip: 0.2 (20 cents on the dollar) of the bill

4 Relationships   Amount of tip = restaurant bill × rate of tip
Amount of tip = 28.73 × 0.2

5 Estimation   Round the restaurant bill to $30 and multiply by 0.2: $30 \times 0.2 = 6$

6 Calculation
$$
\begin{array}{r}
28.73 \\
\times\ \ 0.2 \\
\hline
5.746
\end{array}
$$

The tip is $5.75 when rounded to the nearest cent.

7 Decision made   Decision not required.

Division of decimals has many uses in the business world. For example, we are often given a portion and a total amount and divide to determine the relationship between the portion and the total. When this quotient is rounded to hundredths we say this represents the number of cents per dollar. In a later chapter we will show this relationship as a percent.

Step 1   Place a decimal point for the quotient directly above the decimal point in the dividend.

Step 2   Divide as though the decimal numbers are whole numbers.

Example 7   Divide 5.95 by 17.

```
       0.35
   17)5.95
      5 1
       85
       85
```

Place a decimal point for the quotient directly above the decimal point in the dividend.

The quotient of 5.95 and 17 is 0.35.

If the division does not come out even, you can continue it as far as you want by attaching zeros to the dividend. If you are planning to round a quotient to a specified place, carry the division to one place to the right of the specified place, and then round the quotient.

Example 8   Find the quotient of 37.4 ÷ 24 to the nearest hundredth.

```
      1.558    rounds to 1.56
  24)37.400
     24
     13 4
     12 0
      1 40
      1 20
       200
       192
         8
```

To be able to round the quotient to the nearest hundredth, carry the division out to the thousandths place, and then round.

The quotient is 1.56 to the nearest hundredth.

! **TIPS & TRAPS**

A common mistake is to attach zeros to the dividend without placing a decimal for the quotient first. Divide: 12 ÷ 8.

```
      1.5
   8)12.0
     8
     4 0
     4 0
```
←—The zero and decimal point are placed correctly in the dividend, and the decimal point in the quotient is in the correct place.

CORRECT

```
      1 5
   8)12 0
     8
     4 0
     4 0
```
←—The zero was attached, but the decimal point was left out.

INCORRECT

If the divisor is a decimal rather than a whole number, we make use of an important fact: Increasing both the divisor and the dividend by the same factor does not change their quotient. For instance, for each of the quotients

$$5.\overline{)10.} \qquad 50.\overline{)100.} \qquad 500.\overline{)1000.}$$

we've increased the divisor and the dividend both by a factor of 10, and then by a factor of 10 again. The quotient is always 2. Notice that increasing by a factor of 10 makes the decimal point move one place to the right.

? HOW TO | **Divide by a Decimal**

Step 1 Change the divisor to a whole number by moving the decimal point to the right, counting the places as you go.
Step 2 Move the decimal point in the dividend to the right as many places as you moved it in the divisor.
Step 3 Place the decimal point for the quotient directly above the *new* decimal point in the dividend.
Step 4 Divide as you would divide by a whole number.

You may find it helpful to mark the new location of the decimal point in both the divisor and dividend with a caret (∧).

Example 9 Find the quotient of 59.9 ÷ 0.39 to the nearest hundredth.

$$0.39\overline{)59.90} \longrightarrow 39\overline{)5,990}$$

Move the decimal point 2 places to the right in both the divisor and the dividend.

$$39\overline{)5,990.000}$$

Place the decimal point for the quotient directly above the decimal point in the dividend.

$$
\begin{array}{r}
153.589 \\
39\overline{)5,990.000} \\
\underline{39} \\
2\,09 \\
\underline{1\,95} \\
140 \\
\underline{117} \\
23\,0 \\
\underline{19\,5} \\
3\,50 \\
\underline{3\,12} \\
380 \\
\underline{351} \\
\end{array}
$$

Divide, carrying out the division to the thousandths place.

The quotient is 153.59 to the nearest hundredth.

AROUND THE BUSINESS WORLD

Can Business Ethics be Taught?

Résumés do not list a moral grade point average. So how can a corporation gauge the ethical grounding of potential hires? Can ethics be taught?

A growing number of business schools around the country are teaching ethics, a movement led not by academics but by the private sector. Business benefactors have endowed some 25 to 30 chairs in ethics, up from a mere handful a decade ago, estimates Prof. Tom Donaldson of Georgetown University's business school. Requirements and electives in ethics are growing apace. Harvard Business School, for example, which for eight years has required a nine-class Decision Making and ethical Values course for beginning MBA students, will nearly double the length of the class this fall. Charles Hickman of the American Assembly of Collegiate Schools of Business attributes the "boom industry" in business ethics education today to Wall Street's insider trading scandals of the 1980s.

Business school professors do not pretend that they can transform budding Gordon Gekkos into George Baileys—James Stewart's character in *It's a Wonderful Life*. Instead, they force students to confront ethical dilemmas from corporate case studies and come up with their own responses. Stanford University's Kirk Hanson presents his students with 25 "Unavoidable Ethical Dilemmas in a Business Career," such as "When you are tempted to oversell your product to close the deal."

Some lessons in ethics may be necessary to counteract the effects of other business school course work. Though he has not yet measured the impact of finance classes on MBA scholars, economist Robert Frank of Cornell University has tracked a disturbing pattern among economics students. In games that test moral reasoning, most noneconomics undergraduates make less selfish choices as they progress through four years of college, while economics students increasingly put themselves first. The reason perhaps: Economic theory stresses maximization of self-interest.

Example 10 Irene Maciol paid a tip of $8 on a restaurant bill of $43.17. How many cents per dollar (rounded to the nearest cent) of the bill did Irene pay as a tip?

🔑 1	**Decision needed**	No decision needed
2	**Unknown fact**	The number of cents per dollar of the bill as a tip
3	**Known facts**	Total bill: $43.17 Amount of tip: $8
4	**Relationships**	Cents per dollar of the bill as a tip = amount of tip ÷ total bill Cents per dollar of the bill as a tip = $8 ÷ $43.17
5	**Estimation**	Round the bill to $40.

$$\frac{0.20}{40)8.00}$$

The estimate is 20 cents per dollar.

6   Calculation

$$\begin{array}{r} 0.185 \\ 43.17\overline{)8.00\,000} \\ \underline{4\ 31\ 7} \\ 3\ 68\ 30 \\ \underline{3\ 45\ 36} \\ 22\ 940 \\ \underline{21\ 585} \\ 1\ 355 \end{array}$$

This decimal is 0.19 rounded to the nearest hundredth.

Irene paid 19 cents per dollar as a tip.

7   Decision made   No decision required

Self-Check 1.2

 Write the word name for the decimal.

1. 0.582

2. 1.0009

3. 782.07

Round to the nearest dollar.

4. $493.91

5. $785.03

6. $19.80

 Add.

7. 6.005 + 0.03 + 924 + 3.9

8. 82 + 5000.1 + 101.703

Subtract.

9. 407.96 − 298.39

10. 500.70 from 8097.125

 Multiply.

11. $\begin{array}{r} 19.7 \\ \times\ \ 4 \\ \hline \end{array}$

12. 0.0321 × 10

13. 73.7 by 0.02

Divide and round to the nearest hundredth.

14. 123.72 ÷ 12

15. $35\overline{)589.06}$

16. $0.35\overline{)0.0084}$

17. Laura Voight earns $8.43 per hour as a telemarketing employee. One week she worked 28 hours. What was her gross pay before any deductions?

18. Daniel Dawson is plant manager for a company that produces abrasive wheels as sharpening tools. Rubber and abrasive compounds are mixed and heated in molds to produce the abrasive wheels. One mold can produce 32 wheels from a sheet of material. If it takes nine hours to process 18 sheets of material, how many wheels are processed in nine hours?

19. Cassie James works a 26-hour week at a part-time job while attending classes at Shelby State Community College. Her weekly gross pay is $137.28. What is her hourly rate of pay?

---

20. Calculate the cost of 1,000 gallons of gasoline if it costs $1.17 per gallon.

21. All the employees in your department are splitting the cost of a celebratory lunch, catered at a cost of $142.15. If your department has 23 employees, will each employee be able to pay an equal share? How should the catering cost be divided?

SELF-CHECK SOLUTIONS

Self-Check 1.1

1. Five million, seven hundred two thousand, five   **2.** Three hundred seventeen million, one hundred seventy-one
3. Four billion, two hundred four million, forty-nine thousand, two hundred one   **4.** 3,<u>6</u>45   Since 4 is less than 5 we round to 3,600.   **5.** 3,6<u>4</u>5   Since 6 is 5 or more, we round to 4,000.   **6.** 3,6<u>4</u>5   Since 5 is 5 or more, we round to 3,650.

7.
```
  11
 328
 583
+726
─────
1,637
```
8.
```
  21
 671
 982
+ 57
─────
1,710
```
9.
```
   1
 791
1,000
+ 52
─────
1,843
```
10.
```
 4 15
 5 5
−3 6
────
 1 9
```
11.
```
 2 10
 3 0 8
−2 7 5
──────
  3 3
```
12.
```
 3 10
5,4 0 9
−2,1 7 6
────────
 3,2 3 3
```
13.
```
   730
×   60
──────
43,800
```
14.
```
   904
×   24
──────
 3 616
18 08
──────
21,696
```
15.
```
  1,005
×    89
───────
 9 045
80 40
───────
89,445
```

16.
```
    16
 6)96
    6
   ──
   36
   36
   ──
```
17.
```
      407
 34)13,838
    13 6
    ────
      23
       0
      ──
      238
      238
      ───
```
18.
```
      253 R13
 15)3,808
    3 0
    ──
     80
     75
     ──
     58
     45
     ──
     13
```

19. Personal Totals

Fletes	Grimes	Johnston	Keck
2,492	897	1,708	723
1,948	421	2,096	1,687
2,307	598	3,222	2,196
4,301	1,025	1,507	1,737
1,589	897	2,801	2,186
12,637	3,838	11,334	8,529

Total 12,637 + 3,838 + 11,334 + 8,529 = 36,338

Daily Sales Totals

W	Th	F	S	Su
2,492	1,948	2,307	4,301	1,589
897	421	598	1,025	897
1,708	2,096	3,222	1,507	2,801
723	1,687	2,196	1,737	2,186
5,820	6,152	8,323	8,570	7,473

Total 5,820 + 6,152 + 8,323 + 8,570 + 7,473 = 36,338

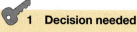

1 Decision needed

2 Unknown facts

3 Known facts

4 Relationships

20. Are enough materials available to mix and package the candy?

Number of three-pound bags needed for packaging

Number of boxes needed for shipping

84 containers each contain 25 pounds of candy. Bulk candy will be repackaged into three-pound bags. Twelve bags of candy will be packed into each box.

There are 5,000 three-pound bags on hand.

There are 400 boxes on hand.

Total pounds of candy = number of containers × pounds per container.

Number of bags of candy = total pounds ÷ pounds per bag (3)

Number of boxes of candy = number of bags of candy ÷ bags per box (12)

5   Estimation

Round to the first digit, then multiply 80 × 30 = 2,400. The estimated number of pounds of candy is 2,400 pounds.

6   Calculations

Total pounds of candy equals 84 × 25 = 2,100

Number of bags of candy = 2,100 ÷ 3 = 700

Number of boxes of candy = 700 ÷ 12 = 58 R4

There are 58 boxes of candy and 4 bags left so 59 boxes will be needed to ship all the candy.

7   Decision made

Enough bags and boxes are on hand to package.

21.
$$
\begin{array}{r}
922 \text{ R}256 \\
352\overline{)324,800} \\
316\,8 \\
\hline
8\,00 \\
7\,04 \\
\hline
960 \\
704 \\
\hline
256
\end{array}
$$
The average selling price of each trailer was nearly $923.

22. Total length of fencing needed = 210 × 4 = 840 feet
Number of rolls of fencing needed = 840 ÷ 50 = 16.8
Since a partial role of fencing cannot be purchased, 17 rolls are needed.
Cost of 17 rolls of fencing = $49 × 17 = $833
Cost of installing fence = $1 × 840 = $840
Total cost = $833 + $840 = $1,673
Your bid is the lowest bid and you are likely to get the business.

23. Wages = 3 × 7 × 21 = $441
Gross profit = total − cost of materials − cost of labor
Gross profit = $1,673 − $833 − $441 = $399

24. $8\overline{)8,832}$
Each vendor supplied 1,104 boxes of cards.

25.
$$
\begin{array}{r}
29 \\
12\overline{)348} \\
24 \\
\hline
108 \\
108
\end{array}
$$
You will need 29 boxes.

Self-Check 1.2

1. Five hundred eighty-two thousandths   **2.** One and nine ten-thousandths   **3.** Seven hundred eighty-two and seven hundredths

4. $49<u>3</u>.91
$494

5. $78<u>5</u>.03
$785

6. $1<u>9</u>.80
$20

7.
6.005
0.03
924
3.9
933.935

8.
82
5,000.1
101.703
5,183.803

9.
$$
\begin{array}{r}
3\,9\;17\,8\;16 \\
4\cancel{0}7.9\cancel{6} \\
-2\,9\,8.3\,9 \\
\hline
1\,0\,9\,.5\,7
\end{array}
$$

10.
$$
\begin{array}{r}
7\;10\;6\;11 \\
\cancel{8},\cancel{0}97.\cancel{1}25 \\
500.7 \\
\hline
7,596.425
\end{array}
$$

11.
19.7
× 4
78.8

12.
0.0321
× 10
0.3210

13.
73.7
× 0.02
1.474

14.
$$
\begin{array}{r}
10.31 \\
12\overline{)123.72} \\
12 \\
\hline
3 \\
0 \\
\hline
3\,7 \\
3\,6 \\
\hline
12 \\
12
\end{array}
$$

15.
$$
\begin{array}{r}
16.830 \text{ or } 16.83 \\
35\overline{)589.060} \\
35 \\
\hline
239 \\
210 \\
\hline
29\,0 \\
28\,0 \\
\hline
1\,06 \\
1\,05 \\
\hline
10 \\
0 \\
\hline
10
\end{array}
$$

16.
$$
\begin{array}{r}
0.\,024 \text{ or } 0.02 \\
0.35\overline{)0.00{}_{\wedge}840} \\
70 \\
\hline
140 \\
140
\end{array}
$$

17.
$8.43
× 28
67 44
168 6
$236.04

18. 32 wheels per sheet × 18 sheets = 576
576 wheels can be produced in nine hours.

19.
```
        $5.28
    26)$137.28
        130
          7 2
          5 2
          2 08
          2 08
```

20. $1.17 × 1,000 = $1,170
Shift the decimal 3 places to the right.

21.
```
        6.18
    23)142.15
        138
          4 1
          2 3
          1 85
          1 84
            1
```
Twenty-two employees pay $6.18
and one employee pays $6.19.

Section—Objective

Important Points with Examples

(page 2)

Read and write whole numbers

Step 1 Notice that commas separate the number into groups of 3 digits each. **Step 2** For each group, beginning with the leftmost group **a)** Read the 3-digit number from left to right. **b)** Name the group. **Step 3** Note these exceptions: **a)** Do not read or name a group that is all zeros. **b)** Do not name the units group.

The word *and* is never part of the word name for a whole number.

> 574 is read *five hundred seventy-four.*
>
> 3,804,321 is read *three million, eight hundred four thousand, three hundred twenty-one.*

(page 4)

Round whole numbers

Step 1 Find the digit in the specified place. **Step 2** Look at the next digit to the right. **a)** If this digit is less than 5, replace it and all digits to its right with zeros. **b)** If this digit is 5 or more, add 1 to the digit in the specified place, and replace all digits to the right of the specified place with zeros.

> 4,860 rounded to the nearest hundred is 4,900.
>
> 7,439 rounded to the nearest thousand is 7,000.
>
> 4,095 rounded to the first digit is 4,000.

(page 5)

Add whole numbers

Step 1 Write the numbers in a vertical column, aligning digits according to their places. **Step 2** For each *place* in turn, beginning with the ones place **a)** Add the *place* digits. **b)** Write the units digit of this sum directly below the *place* digit of the last addend. **c)** Write the remaining digits of the sum directly above the *next place* digit of the first addend.

1		1 21
364	Add: 2,074 + 485 + 12,592	2,074
+473		485
837		12,592
		15,151

Subtract whole numbers

(page 7)

Step 1 Write the numbers in a vertical column, the subtrahend below the minuend, aligning digits according to their places. **Step 2** For each *place* in turn, beginning with the ones place **a)** If the *place* digit of the minuend is less than the *place* digit of the subtrahend, add 10 to the *place* digit of the minuend and subtract 1 from the *next place* digit of the minuend. **b)** Subtract the *place* digits. **c)** Write this difference directly below the *place* digit of the subtrahend. **Step 3** Check the difference by adding the subtrahend and the difference. Their sum should be the same as the minuend.

4 14	7 10	8 99 10	0 9 17	0 9 99 10
75 4	8 0 7	9,00 0	1 0 7 9	10,00 0
−32 9	−3 2 1	−3,52 1	−2 9 8	−99 9
42 5	4 8 6	5,47 9	7 8 1	9,00 1

Multiply whole numbers

(page 8)

Step 1 Write the numbers in a vertical column, aligning digits according to their places. **Step 2** For each *place* of the multiplier in turn, beginning with the ones place **a)** Multiply the multiplicand by the *place* digit of the multiplier. **b)** Write this partial product directly below the multiplier (or the last partial product), aligning the ones digit of the partial product with the *place* digit of the multiplier (and aligning all other digits to the left accordingly.) **Step 3** Add the partial products.

543	509	8,100	18 × 10 = 180
× 32	× 87	× 300	18 × 100 = 1,800
1 086	3 563	2,430,000	18 × 1,000 = 18,000
16 29	40 72		
17,376	44,283		

1.1 — 6 *(page 10)*

Divide whole numbers

Step 1 Beginning with its leftmost digit, identify the first group of digits of the dividend that is larger than or equal to the divisor. This group of digits is the first *partial dividend*. **Step 2** For each partial dividend in turn, beginning with the first, **a)** Divide the partial dividend by the divisor. Write this partial quotient above the rightmost digit of the partial dividend. **b)** Multiply the partial quotient by the divisor. Write the product below the partial dividend, aligning places. **c)** Subtract the product from the partial dividend. Write the difference below the product, aligning places. The difference must be less than the divisor. **d)** Next to the ones place of the difference, write the next digit of the dividend. This is the new partial dividend. **Step 3** When all the digits of the dividend have been used, write the final difference in step 2c as the remainder (unless the remainder is 0). The whole number part of the quotient is the number written above the dividend. **Step 4** To check, multiply the quotient by the divisor and add the remainder to the product. This sum will equal the dividend.

Be sure the difference in step 2c is less than the divisor. If it isn't, the partial quotient in step 2b must be corrected.

```
  287 R1        804
3)862       56)45,024        21,000 ÷ 10 = 2,100
  6             44 8          21,000 ÷ 100 = 210
 26              22           21,000 ÷ 1,000 = 21
 24               0
 22             224
 21             224
  1
```

1.2 — 1 *(page 15)*

Read, write, and round decimals

Read or write a decimal   **Step 1** Read or write the whole number part (to the left of the decimal point) as you would read or write a whole number. **Step 2** Use the word *and* for the decimal point. **Step 3** Read or write the decimal part (to the right of the decimal point) as you would read or write a whole number. **Step 4** Name the place of the rightmost digit.

> 0.3869 is read "three thousand, eight-hundred sixty-nine ten-thousandths."

Round to a specified decimal place   **Step 1** Find the digit in the specified place. **Step 2** Look at the next digit to the right. **a)** If this digit is less than 5, eliminate it and all digits to its right. **b)** If this digit is 5 or more, add 1 to the digit in the specified place, and eliminate all digits to its right.

> 37.357 rounded to the nearest tenth is 37.4.

> 3.4819 rounded to the first digit is 3.

1.2 — 2 *(page 17)*

Add and subtract decimals

Step 1 Write the numbers in a vertical column, aligning digits according to their places. **Step 2** Attach extra zeros to the right end of each decimal number so that each number has the same quantity of digits to the right of the decimal point. **Step 3** Add or subtract as though the numbers are whole numbers. **Step 4** Place the decimal point in the sum or difference to align with the decimal point in the addends or subtrahend and minuend.

```
Add: 32.68 + 3.31 + 49      Subtract: 24.7 − 18.25
                                  1 14 6 10
 32.68                          2 4.7 0
  3.31                         −1 8.2 5
 49.                              6.4 5
 84.99
```

1.2 — 3 *(page 18)*

Multiply and divide decimals

Multiply decimals   **Step 1** Multiply the decimal numbers as though they are whole numbers. **Step 2** Count the digits in the decimal parts of both decimal numbers. **Step 3** Place the decimal point in the product so that there are as many digits in its decimal part as there are digits you counted in step 2. If necessary, attach zeros on the left end of the product so that you can place the decimal point accurately.

Multiply: 36.48×2.52	Multiply: 2.03×0.036	
$\begin{array}{r} 36.48 \\ \times \quad 2.52 \\ \hline 7296 \\ 18\ 240 \\ 72\ 96 \\ \hline 91.9296 \end{array}$	$\begin{array}{r} 2.03 \\ \times \quad 0.036 \\ \hline 1218 \\ 609 \\ \hline 0.07308 \end{array}$	$3.492 \times 10 = 34.92$ $3.492 \times 100 = 349.2$ $3.492 \times 1{,}000 = 3{,}492$

Divide a decimal by a whole number **Step 1** Place a decimal point for the quotient directly above the decimal point in the dividend. **Step 2** Divide as though the decimal numbers are whole numbers.

Divide: $58.5 \div 45$

$$\begin{array}{r} 1.3 \\ 45\overline{)58.5} \\ \underline{45} \\ 13\ 5 \\ \underline{13\ 5} \end{array}$$

$43.7 \div 10 = 4.37$
$43.7 \div 100 = 0.437$
$43.7 \div 1{,}000 = 0.0437$

Divide by a decimal **Step 1** Change the divisor to a whole number by moving the decimal point to the right, counting the places as you go. **Step 2** Move the decimal point in the dividend as many places as you moved it in the divisor. **Step 3** Place the decimal point for the quotient directly above the *new* decimal point in the dividend. **Step 4** Divide as you would divide by a whole number.

Divide: $0.770 \div 3.5$

$$\begin{array}{r} 0.22 \\ 3.5\overline{)0.7\wedge70} \\ \underline{70} \\ 70 \\ \underline{70} \end{array}$$

Divide: $0.485 \div 0.24$
Round to the nearest tenth.

$$\begin{array}{r} 2.02 = 2.0 \text{ rounded} \\ 0.24\overline{)0.48\wedge50} \\ \underline{48} \\ 50 \\ \underline{48} \\ 2 \end{array}$$

CHAPTER 1 REVIEW

Section 1.1

Write the word name for the number.
  1. 4,209   **2.** 97,168   **3.** 301,000,009   **4.** 5,200,000

Round to the specified place.
  5. 378 (nearest hundred)   **6.** 8,248 (nearest hundred)

  7. 9,374 (nearest thousand)   **8.** 348,218 (nearest ten thousand)

9. 834 (nearest ten)

10. 29,712 (nearest thousand)

11. 29,712 (nearest ten thousand)

12. 275,398,484 (nearest million)

13. 27,500,000,078 (nearest billion)

14. 897,284,017 (nearest ten million)

Round to the first digit.

15. 3,784,809

16. 2,063,948

17. 5,178

18. 17,295,183,109

19. 10,097,437

20. 5,475

21. 396

22. 18,924

23. 685,294

24. 7,098,764

Add and check the sum.

25.	**26.**	**27.**	**28.**	**29.**	**30.**
6	1	6	7	4	8
3	9	9	2	5	8
4	5	4	7	6	1
+7	8	9	7	1	2
	+2	6	7	3	4
		+1	+8	+9	+9

31.	**32.**
8,152	9,892
3,363	7,433
4,529	4,090
8,327	5,282
+6,416	+1,987

Add.

33. 47 + 385 + 87 + 439 + 874

34. 32,948 + 6,804 + 15,695 + 415 + 7,739

35.	**36.**	**37.**	**38.**
734	683	1,661	44,349
643	252	9,342	71,486
688	867	2,994	67,565
656	867	5,778	57,971
928	325	1,770	+48,699
197	274	5,445	
785	835	1,770	
527	713	2,656	
337	118	3,874	
+278	+627	+8,724	

Estimate the sum by rounding each number to the first digit. Then find the exact sum.

39. 74,374
     82,849
     72,494
    +89,219

40. 374
     847
     521
     873
    +482

41. 3,748
     9,409
     3,577
    +4,601

42. 3,470
     843
    3,872
     574

Estimate the sum by rounding each number to the nearest hundred. Then find the exact sum.

43. 747
     854
     324
    +687

44. 4,274
      643
    1,274
    +   97

45. Mary Luciana bought 48 pencils, 96 pens, 36 diskettes, and 50 bottles of correction fluid. How many items did she buy?

46. Jorge Englade has 57 baseball cards from 1978, 43 cards from 1979, 104 cards from 1980, 210 cards from 1983, and 309 cards from 1987. How many cards does he have in all?

47. Linda Cagle collects dolls. She has 12 antique dolls, 135 Barbie dolls, 35 Shirley Temple dolls, and 287 other dolls. How many dolls are there in all?

48. A furniture-manufacturing plant had the following labor-hours in one week: Monday, 483; Tuesday, 472; Wednesday, 497; Thursday, 486; Friday, 464; Saturday, 146; Sunday, 87. Find the total labor-hours worked during the week.

49. Lillie Lewis had the following test scores: 92, 87, 96, 85, 72, 84, 57, 98. What is the student's total number of points?

50. June Knox is planning to build a fence around her backyard. The sides of the yard measure 42 feet, 117 feet, 58 feet, and 119 feet. How many feet of fencing does June need to surround her yard?

Subtract and check the difference.

51. 75,184
    −65,428

52. 937,452
    −395,773

53. 2,090,684
    −224,943

54. 3,000,000
    −291,438

55. 19,000,000
    −14,284,394

56. 7,007,000
    −3,018,094

57. 9,010,000
    −3,687,429

58. 29,007,400
    −18,457,396

Estimate the difference by rounding each number to the first digit. Then find the exact difference.

59. 9,748
    −5,676

60. 370,408
    −187,506

61. 83,748,194
    −27,209,104

62. 12,748
    − 5,438

Estimate the difference by rounding each number to the nearest thousand. Then find the exact difference.

63.   84,378
        −28,746

64. 109,849
        −35,464

65. Sam Andrews has 42 packages of hamburger buns on hand but expects to use 130 packages. How many must he order?

66. Frieda Salla had 148 tickets to sell for a baseball show. If she has sold 75 tickets, how many does she still have to sell?

67. An inventory shows 596 fan belts on hand. If the normal in-stock count is 840, how many should be ordered?

68. Veronica McCulley weighed 132 pounds before she began a weight-loss program. After 8 weeks, she weighed 119 pounds. How many pounds did she lose?

Multiply and check the product.

69.   5,931
         ×   835

70.   5,565
         ×   839

71.   1,987
         ×   394

72.   78,626
         ×   87

73.   708
         × 59

74.   2,105
         ×   64

75.   70,803
         ×   98

76.   2,174
         ×   308

77.   1,700
         ×   507

78.   3,987
         ×   1,033

Multiply.

79. 33 × 500

80. 283 × 3,000

81. 160 × 300

82. 405 × 400

83. 50 × 600

84. 25 × 10,000

85. 7,870 × 6,000

86. 974 × 7,000

87. 270 × 600

88. 560 × 9,000

Estimate the product by rounding each number to the first digit. Then find the exact product.

89.   7,489
        ×   34

90.   378
        × 72

Estimate the product by rounding each number to the nearest hundred. Then find the exact product.

91.   3,128
         ×   478

92.   378
         ×546

93. An office has 15 printers. The supply coordinator is expected to keep 8 ribbons for each printer. How many ribbons should be kept on hand?

94. Collierville Florist has 152 orders for 12 red roses. How many roses are required to fill the orders?

95. A day-care center has 28 children. If each child eats one piece of fruit each day, how many pieces of fruit are required for a week (5 days)?

96. Auto Zone has a special on fuel filters. Normally, the price of one filter is $15, but with this sale, you can purchase 2 filters for only $27. How much can you save by purchasing 2 filters at the sale price?

Divide and check the quotient.

97. $7\overline{)315}$ **98.** $5\overline{)213}$ **99.** $9\overline{)216}$ **100.** $6\overline{)314}$

101. $1{,}232 \div 16$ **102.** $4{,}020 \div 12$ **103.** $1{,}247 \div 23$ **104.** $3{,}362 \div 32$

Estimate the quotient by rounding each number. Then find the exact quotient.

105. $85\overline{)748{,}431}$ **106.** $346\overline{)174{,}891}$

107. A parts dealer has 2,988 washers. The washers are packaged with 12 in each package. How many packages can be made?

108. A stack of countertops measures 238 inches. If each countertop is 2 inches thick, how many are in the stack?

109. If 127 employees earn $1,524 in one hour, what is the average hourly wage per employee?

110. Sequoia Brown has 15 New Zealand coins, 32 Canadian coins, 18 British coins, and 12 Australian coins in her British Commonwealth collection. How many coins does she have in this collection?

111. Jessica Lisker mailed 62 birthday cards, 6 get-well cards, 2 sympathy cards, and 5 graduation cards to the customers on her sales routes. How many cards did she mail?

112. John Chang ordered 48 paperback novels for his bookstore. When he received the shipment, he learned that 11 were on back order. How many novels did he receive?

113. Baker's Department Store sold 23 pairs of ladies' patent leather pumps. If the store's original inventory was 43 pairs of the shoes, how many pairs remain in inventory?

114. An oral communication textbook contains 3 pages of review at the end of each of its 16 chapters. What is the total number of pages devoted to review?

115. A sales clerk earns $5 an hour. If she works 32 hours a week, how much does she earn in a week?

116. Juan Mendez must fill a school order for 77 dozen pencils. Since a dozen is 12, how many pencils are needed for the order?

117. Galina makes $320 a week. If she works 40 hours a week, what is her hourly pay rate?

118. A garage has five cars to tune. If each car has 8 cylinders, and each cylinder requires one spark plug, how many spark plugs are needed to tune the cars?

119. Holding-tank deodorant for travel trailer and marine use is sold in packages containing six 8-ounce bottles. How many ounces are in each package of six bottles?

120. Jeff Mills has 15 boxes and needs to pack 118 wood carvings. Is he able to pack an equal quantity in each box? If so, how many? If not, give Jeff instructions for packing the boxes.

Write the word name for the decimal.

121. 0.5

122. 0.27

123. 0.108

124. 0.013

125. 0.00275

126. 0.120704

127. 17.8

128. 3.04

129. 128.23

130. 3,000.003

131. 500.0007

132. 184.271

Round to the specified place.

133. 0.1345 (nearest thousandth)

134. 384.72 (nearest tenth)

135. 384.73 (nearest ten)

136. 1,745.376 (nearest hundredth)

137. 1,745.376 (nearest hundred)

138. 32.57 (nearest whole number)

139. $175.24 (nearest dollar)

140. $5.333 (nearest cent)

Add.

141. $0.3 + 0.05 + 0.266 + 0.63$

142. $31.005 + 5.36 + 0.708 + 4.16$

143. $78.87 + 54 + 32.9569 + 0.0043$

144. $9.004 + 0.07 + 723 + 8.7$

145. A shopper purchased a cake pan for $8.95, a bath mat for $9.59, and a bottle of shampoo for $2.39. Find the total cost of the purchases.

146. Robert McNab ordered 18.3 square meters of carpet for his halls, 123.5 square meters of carpet for bedrooms, 28.7 square meters of carpet for the family room, and 12.9 square meters of carpet for the play room. Find the total number of square meters of carpet he ordered.

Subtract.

147. $500.05 - 123.31$

148. $815.01 - 335.6$

149. $125.35 - 67.8975$

150. $404.04 - 135.8716$

151. $423 - 287.4$

152. $807.38 - 529.79$

153. $482.073 - 62.97$

154. $5,003.02 - 689.23$

155. $\begin{array}{r} 486.57 \\ -160.83 \\ \hline \end{array}$

156. 1,423.97
    − 802.89

157. 21.0357
    −18.7289

158. 5.8376
    −2.9608

159. 0.02135
    −0.019876

160. 6.213502
    −3.098107

161. Four tires that retailed for $486.95 are on sale for $397.99. By how much are the tires reduced?

162. If two lengths of metal sheeting measuring 12.5 inches and 15.36 inches are cut from a roll of metal measuring 96 inches, how much remains on the roll?

163. Leon Treadwell's checkbook had a balance of $196.82 before he wrote checks for $21.75 and $82.46. What was his balance after he wrote the checks?

164. Janet Morris weighed 149.3 pounds before she began a weight-loss program. After 8 weeks she weighed 129.7 pounds. How much did she lose?

Multiply.

165. 27.63
    × 7

166.   384
    × 3.51

167. 6.42
    × 7.8

168.   0.0015
    × 6.003

169. 75.84
    × 0.28

170. 73.41
    × 15

171. 27.58×10

172. 1.394×100

173. $0.19874 \times 1,000$

174. 54×100

175. $27.3 \times 1,000$

176. $38.17 \times 10,000$

177. $1,745.4 \times 10$

178. $0.1754 \times 1,000,000$

179. $37 \times 10,000$

180. 0.004×10

181. Find the cost of 1,000 gallons of paint if 1 gallon costs $12.85.

182. Ernie Jones worked 37.5 hours at the rate of $5.97 per hour. Calculate his earnings.

Divide. Round to the nearest hundredth if division does not terminate.

183. $1.65 \div 11$

184. $0.105 \div 15$

185. $25 \overline{)54.68}$

186. $27 \overline{)365.04}$

187. $34 \overline{)291.48}$

188. $74 \overline{)85.486}$

189. $2.8 \overline{)94.546}$

190. $0.041 \overline{)8.897}$

191. $296.36 \div 0.19$

192. $0.0056 \overline{)0.4576}$

193. $0.68 \overline{)41,285}$

194. $923.19 \div 0.541$

195. 85.72 ÷ 10

196. 4.139 ÷ 100

197. 19.874 ÷ 1,000

198. 39 ÷ 10

199. 0.18 ÷ 100

200. 274.85 ÷ 10,000

201. 3,749,298 ÷ 100,000

202. 574 ÷ 10,000

203. 0.178 ÷ 10

204. 3,741.29 ÷ 100

205. If 100 gallons of gasoline costs $98.90, what is the cost per gallon?

206. If Dynamo Sugar costs $2.87 for 80 ounces, what is the cost per ounce, rounded to the nearest cent?

Challenge Problems

207. Comparative Budgeting. Terry Kelly has recorded the following financial information for 1995. She now wants to prepare a budget for 1996 to use as a guide.

INCOME	1995	1996
Gross income	32,720	
Interest income	141	
Dividend income	364	
Total	33,225	

EXPENSES		
Living	15,898	
Home maintenance	825	
Auto maintenance & repair	195	
Insurance premiums (medical, auto, home, life)	1,578	
Taxes (sales, income, FICA, real property, personal property)	10,630	
Medical (not covered by insurance)	450	
Planned investment	2,000	
Unspent income	1,649	
Total	33,225	

Terry is scheduled to receive a salary increase of $1,636 in 1996. She expects the dividend income to increase by 0.25 and the interest income to double. She hopes her living expenses will increase no more than $1,000. She hopes to decrease maintenance on her home and auto by 0.4. Her accountant estimates her taxes will increase by approximately $500. Her insurance premiums will increase by $200. No change in uncovered medical expenses is expected. Kelly will increase her planned investment by $500. Make the needed adjustments to prepare Kelly's budget for 1996. Adjust the unspent income category so that the total expenses equal total income.

208. Sales Quotas. A sales quota establishes a minimum amount of sales expected during a given period for a salesperson in some businesses, such as selling cars or houses. In setting sales quotas, sales managers take certain factors into consideration, such as the nature of the sales representative's territory, the experience of the salesperson, and the expectations expressed by the sales force. Such sales quotas enable a company to forecast the sales and future growth of the company for budget and profit purposes.

Try the following quota problem:

A sales representative for a timesharing company has a monthly sales quota of 500 units. The representative sold 120 units during the first week, 135 units during the second week, and 165 units during the third week of the month. How many units must be sold before the end of the month if the salesperson is to meet the quota?

Write the word name for the number.

1. 503

2. 12,056,039

Round to the specified place.

3. 84,321 (nearest hundred)

4. 58,967 (nearest thousand)

5. 80,235 (first digit)

6. 587,213 (first digit)

Estimate by rounding to hundreds. Then find the exact result.

7. $863 + 983 + 271 =$

8. $987 - 346 =$

Estimate by rounding to the first digit. Then find the exact result.

9. $892 \times 46 =$

10. $53\overline{)4{,}021}$

11. An inventory clerk counted the following items: 438 rings, 72 watches, and 643 pen and pencil sets. How many items were counted?

12. A warehouse is 31 feet high. Boxes that are each 2 feet high are to be stacked in the warehouse. How many boxes can be stacked one on top of the other?

13. Round 30.5375 to the first digit.

14. Write the word name for 24.1007.

Perform the indicated operation.

15. $39.17 - 15.078$

16. 27.418×100

17. $0.387 + 3.17 + 17 + 204.3$

18. $28.34 \div 50$ (nearest hundredth)

19. $\begin{array}{r} 324 \\ \times 1.38 \\ \hline \end{array}$

20. $0.138 \div 10$

21. $128 - 38.18$

22. $\begin{array}{r} 17.75 \\ \times 0.325 \\ \hline \end{array}$

23. $2{,}347 + 0.178 + 3.5 + 28.341$

24. $91.25 \div 12.5$

25. $317.24 - 138$

26. $374.17 \div 100$

27. What is the cost of 5.5 pounds of chicken breasts if they cost $3.49 per pound?

28. A patient's chart showed a temperature reading of 101.23 degrees Fahrenheit at 3 P.M. and 99.47 degrees Fahrenheit at 10 P.M. What was the drop in temperature?

BANK RECORDS

GOOD DECISIONS THROUGH TEAMWORK

Investigate and report on the advantages and disadvantages of using Automated Teller Machines (ATMs), including these and other aspects:

- convenience
- personal safety
- card theft or loss
- record of transactions
- machine locations
- alternative uses (e.g., service stations)
- code memorization

As a team, brainstorm ideas for other aspects, and then assign aspects to each team member. Individually, research your assigned aspects and prepare a brief report of your findings. Together, read, critique, and edit each member's findings. Then organize a final report. Be sure to include introductory and summary paragraphs, cover all aspects of using ATMs, and represent all viewpoints about their benefits and drawbacks.

CHAPTER 2 BANK RECORDS

2.1 Checking Account Forms

1 ▶ *Fill out a bank deposit ticket*
2 ▶ *Write a bank check*
3 ▶ *Fill out a check stub*
4 ▶ *Use an account register*
5 ▶ *Endorse a check*

2.2 Bank Statements

1 ▶ *Read a bank statement*
2 ▶ *Reconcile a bank statement with an account register*

When its time to pay the bills, whether personal or business related, most Americans turn to a checkbook. The specific forms, policies, and procedures for checking accounts vary from bank to bank, but once you know the reasoning behind these banking procedures, it is easy enough to understand the minor variations among banks. For business or personal use, it is important to use banking forms correctly, to keep accurate records, and to track financial transactions carefully.

2.1 Using Checking Account Forms

1 ▶ *Fill out a bank deposit ticket*
2 ▶ *Write a bank check*
3 ▶ *Fill out a check stub*
4 ▶ *Use an account register*
5 ▶ *Endorse a check*

In using a checking account for your personal or business financial matters, various checking account forms are needed. The bank must be able to account for all funds that flow into or out of your account, and written evidence of changes in your account is necessary.

1 ▶ Filling Out a Bank Deposit Ticket

When money is put into a checking account, this transaction is called a **deposit.** The bank refers to this transaction as a **credit.** A deposit or credit *increases* the amount of the account. One bank record for deposits made by the account holder is called the **deposit ticket.** Figure 2–1 shows a sample deposit ticket for a personal account. Figure 2–2 shows a sample deposit ticket for a business account. Deposit tickets are available to the person opening an account along with a set of preprinted checks. The bank's account number and the customer's account number are written at the bottom of the ticket in magnetic ink using specially designed characters and symbols to facilitate machine processing.

A deposit ticket has a place for the date and for listing the checks and cash to be deposited. Checks and cash are listed separately, and each individual check is listed. The amounts to be deposited are then added and the sum is written in the place marked "Total." If the bank discovers an error in the deposit transaction, it will notify you of

Figure 2–1 A Deposit Ticket for a Personal Account

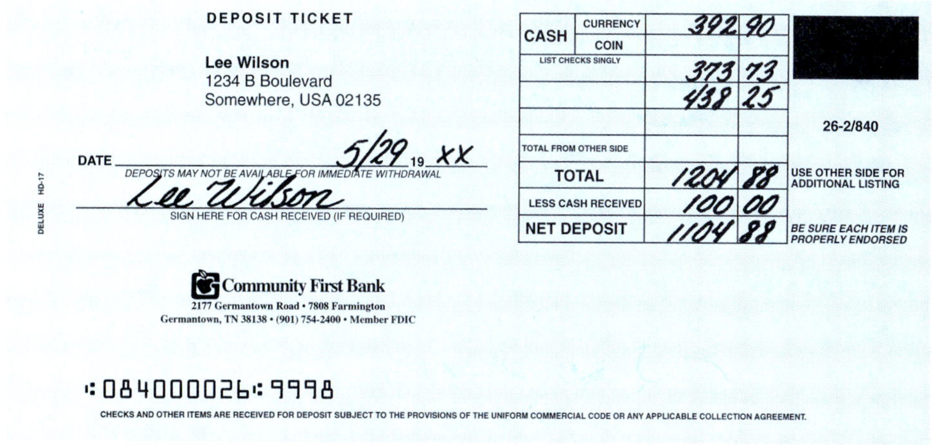

DEPOSIT TICKET

Lee Wilson
1234 B Boulevard
Somewhere, USA 02135

DATE _____ 5/29 19 XX

DEPOSITS MAY NOT BE AVAILABLE FOR IMMEDIATE WITHDRAWAL

Lee Wilson
SIGN HERE FOR CASH RECEIVED (IF REQUIRED)

CASH	CURRENCY	392	90
	COIN		
LIST CHECKS SINGLY		373	73
		438	25
TOTAL FROM OTHER SIDE			
TOTAL		1204	88
LESS CASH RECEIVED		100	00
NET DEPOSIT		1104	88

26-2/840

USE OTHER SIDE FOR ADDITIONAL LISTING

BE SURE EACH ITEM IS PROPERLY ENDORSED

Community First Bank
2177 Germantown Road • 7808 Farmington
Germantown, TN 38138 • (901) 754-2400 • Member FDIC

⑆084000026⑆ 9998

CHECKS AND OTHER ITEMS ARE RECEIVED FOR DEPOSIT SUBJECT TO THE PROVISIONS OF THE UNIFORM COMMERCIAL CODE OR ANY APPLICABLE COLLECTION AGREEMENT.

the correction through a **bank memo.** If the error correction increases your balance, the bank memo is called a **credit memo.** If the error decreases your balance, the bank memo is called a **debit memo.**

For a personal account, if the depositor wants to get some of the total deposit back in cash, the depositor writes this amount in the place marked *"Less cash received,"* and subtracts it from the total. The difference is entered in the place marked *"Net deposit."* Other notations and reminders vary from bank to bank. In general, banks will not honor requests for "less cash received" from business accounts. To receive cash, the company must write a check drawn on the company checking account.

Deposits to bank accounts can be made electronically. Individuals may request their employer to deposit their paycheck directly to their bank account by completing a form which gives the banking information, including the account number. The government encourages recipients of social security and other government funds to have these funds **electronically deposited.** Businesses who permit customers to use credit cards to charge merchandise may receive payment through electronic deposit from the credit-card company. These transactions are sometimes called **point-of-sale** transactions since the money is transferred electronically when the sale is made. VISA, Master Card, and Discover are some of the major credit-card companies that electronically transmit funds to business accounts. Transactions made electronically are called **Electronic Funds Transfers** (EFTs).

▶ Writing a Bank Check

When money is taken from a checking account, this transaction is called a **withdrawal.** The bank refers to this transaction as a **debit.** A withdrawal or debit *decreases* the amount of the account. One bank record for withdrawals made by the account holder is called a **check.** Figure 2–3 shows the basic features of a check.

Notice that, when the amount of the check is written in numerals, the number of cents is written as a fraction. But cents can be written in decimal form, too. When the amount of the check is written in words, however, the number of cents is still written in numerals, and always in fraction form. The word *and* separates the dollar amount from the cent amount.

Personal checks and some business checks have a line called "Memo" or "For" which provides space for the maker to describe what the check is for. Some business checks may need more space for noting the purpose of a check and have a special tear off portion for listing the information necessary for internal accounting procedures.

When a checking account is opened, those persons authorized to write checks on the account must sign a **signature card,** which is kept on record at the bank. When-

Figure 2–2 A Deposit Ticket for a Business Account

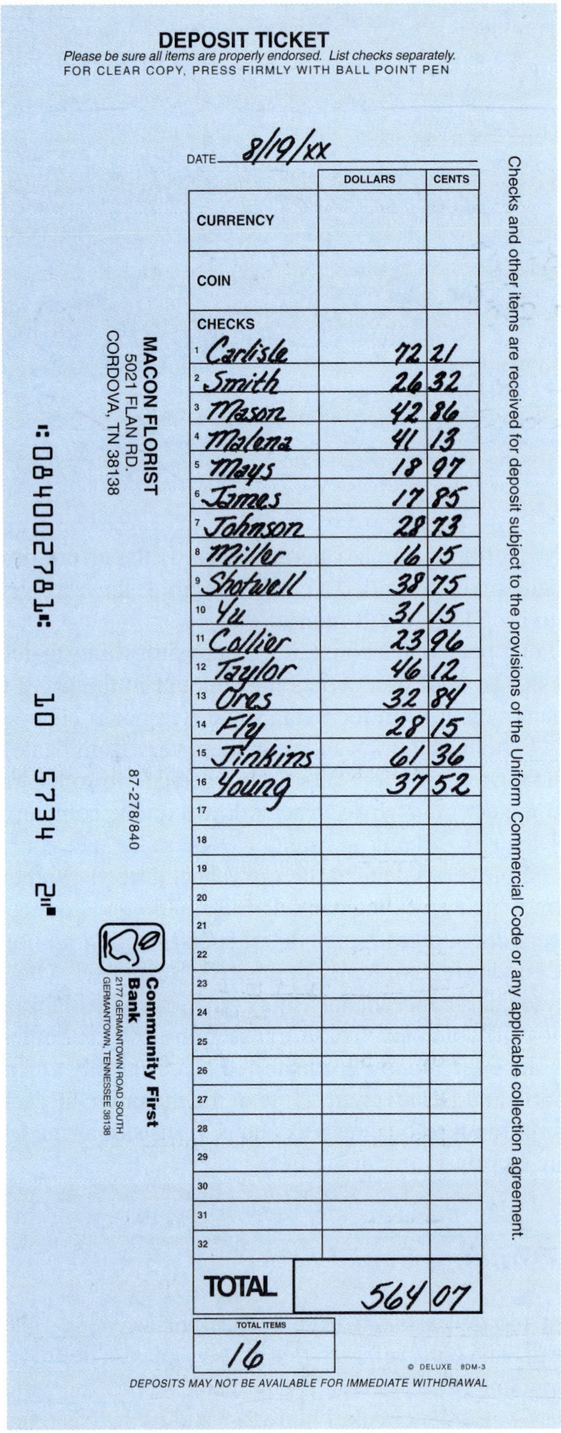

ever there is a question about a signature or whether or not a person is authorized to write checks on an account, the bank refers to the signature card to resolve the question.

Withdrawals from personal and business bank accounts can also be made electronically. Many persons elect to have regular monthly bills such as house note, rent, utilities, insurance, etc., paid electronically through **automatic drafts** from their bank account. The amount of the debit is shown on the monthly bank statement. Individuals may also use a **debit card** to pay for services and goods. The debit card works just like a check except the transaction is handled electronically at the time the transaction is made.

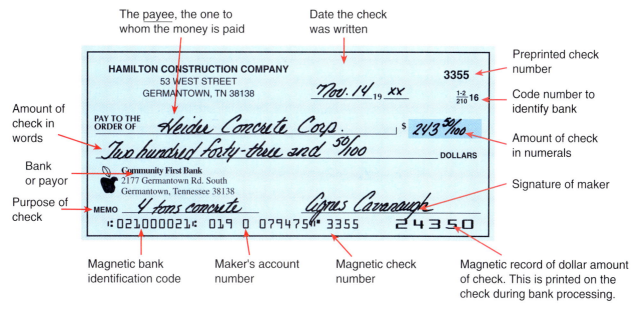

The payee, the one to whom the money is paid

Date the check was written

Preprinted check number

Code number to identify bank

Amount of check in words

Amount of check in numerals

Bank or payor

Signature of maker

Purpose of check

Magnetic bank identification code

Maker's account number

Magnetic check number

Magnetic record of dollar amount of check. This is printed on the check during bank processing.

Figure 2–3   A Bank Check

Example 1   Write a check dated April 8, 19XX, to Disk-O-Mania in the amount of $84.97, for computer diskettes.

Enter the date: 4/8/XX.

Write the name of the payee: Disk-O-Mania.

Enter the amount of the check in numerals: 84.97.

Enter the amount of the check in words. Note the fraction $\frac{97}{100}$ showing cents, or hundredths of dollars: eighty four and $\frac{97}{100}$.

Write the purpose of the check on the memo line: computer diskettes.

Sign your name.

The completed check is shown in Figure 2–4.

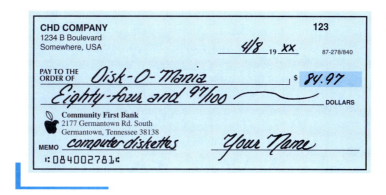

Figure 2–4   The Completed Check

▶ **Filling Out a Check Stub**

Most businesses and individuals who have checking accounts use either a check stub or a check register to record all the checks they write and all the deposits they make. Check stubs are provided by the bank, usually in a bound book with the perforated check attached to its stub.

A **check stub** has a place to list the check number (if it is not preprinted), the date, the amount of the check, the person to whom the check is made, and what the check is written for. There is also a place to record the balance forward (the balance after the previous check was written), the amount deposited since that time, the amount of the check, and the new balance.

When filling out the check stub, you add any deposits and subtract the amount of the check to get the new balance. It's a good idea to fill out the check stub *before* writing the check so that you won't forget to do it.

Example 2   Complete the stub for the check written in Example 1. The balance forward is $8,324.09. Deposits of $325, $694.30, and $82.53 were made after the previous check was written.

The check number, 123, is preprinted in this case.

Enter the date: 4/8/XX.

Enter the amount of this check: $84.97.

Enter the payee: Disk-O-Mania.

Enter the purpose: computer diskettes.

Enter the balance forward: $8,324.09

Enter the total of the deposits: $1,101.83.

Add the balance forward and the deposits to find the total: $9,425.92.

Enter the amount of this check: $84.97.

Subtract the amount of the check from the total to find the balance: $9,340.95.

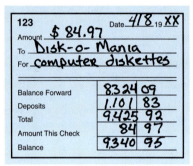

Figure 2–5   The Completed Stub

The completed stub is shown in Figure 2–5. Carry the balance to the next stub as the Balance Forward.

4 ▶ *Using an Account Register*

Like check stubs, an **account register** allows you to maintain a record of all transactions made to the account. Transactions that increase the account balance are called **credits.** Transactions that decrease the account balance are called **debits.** Most banks provide preprinted account registers for individual account holders. However, many businesses prefer to use more customized account registers. On the bank's preprinted account register, space is provided for entering the transaction number, the date, a description of the transaction, the amount of the transaction (be it a check, a deposit, or a fee), a check-mark $\checkmark$ (used to balance the account register), and the account balance. Figure 2–6 shows a sample account register page.

As banking becomes increasingly complex and more electronic and the penalty for overdrawing bank accounts escalates, it becomes more important to carefully maintain an account register of all transactions. Computer programs are available to individuals as well as businesses to keep bank account records.

> ## ⚠ TIPS & TRAPS
>
> Checks should be written and recorded in the account register in numerical order to make it easier to verify that all checks have been recorded in the account register or on the check stub.

Figure 2–6 An Account
Register

NUMBER	DATE	DESCRIPTION OF TRANSACTION	DEBIT	√	FEE	CREDIT	BALANCE
		RECORD ALL TRANSACTIONS THAT AFFECT YOUR ACCOUNT					6843 00
543	8/9	Golden Wheat Dist.	685 56				6157 44
544	8/9	Consolidated Berry Farms	89 78				6067 66
	8/9	Cash withdrawal	250 00				5817 66
	8/10	Deposit				1525 61	7343 27

5 ▶ *Endorsing a Check*

Before a check can be cashed, it must be **endorsed.** That is, the payee must sign or stamp the check on the back. There are several ways to endorse a check. The simplest way is for the payee to sign the back of the check exactly as the name is written on the front of the check. Banks generally cash checks drawn on their own bank or for payees who are account holders. Banks cashing checks drawn on their own bank may require the payee to present appropriate identification if they are not account holders at that bank. Banks will cash checks drawn on a different bank for payees who are account holders and require the payee's account number to be written below the signature.

While banking procedures are designed to prevent misuse of checks, it is a good idea to use a **restricted endorsement** for signing checks. One type of restricted endorsement changes the payee of the check. The original payee writes "pay to the order of," lists the name of the new payee, then signs the check. This choice would be used when you want to receive cash from the bank for the check or if you want to assign the check to someone else. Another type of restricted endorsement is used for depositing the check into the payee's bank account. The payee writes "for deposit only," lists the account number, then endorses the check. Many businesses imprint this type of endorsement on all checks using an electronic cash register or an ink stamp.

The Federal Reserve Board regulates the way endorsements can be placed on checks. As Figure 2–7 shows, the endorsement must be placed within $1\frac{1}{2}$ inches from the left edge of the check. The rest of the back of the check is reserved for bank endorsements. Many check-printing companies now mark this space and provide lines for endorsements.

Figure 2–7 The Back of a
Check Showing Areas for
Endorsements

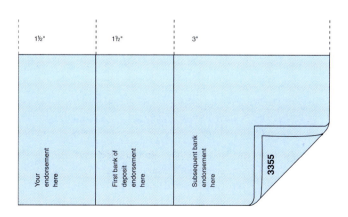

1. On April 29, 19XX, Mr. Yan Yu made a deposit to the account for Park's Oriental Grocery. He deposited $858.63 in cash and two checks, one in the amount of $157.38, the other in the amount of $32.49. Fill out Mr. Yu's deposit ticket for April 29, 19XX.

2. Complete the deposit ticket for Delectables Candies. The deposit is made on March 31, XX and includes the following items: Cash: 196.00; checks: Cavanaugh, $14.72; Bryan, $31.18; Wossum, $16.97; Wright, $28.46; Howell, $17.21; Coe, $32.17; Beulke, $17.84; Palinchak, $31.96; and Paszel, $19.16.

3. On April 29, 19XX, after Mr Yu made his deposit (see Exercise 1), he wrote a check to Green Harvest in the amount of $155.30 for fresh vegetables. Write a check as Mr. Yu wrote it.

4. Write a check dated June 20, 19XX, to Ronald H. Cox Realty in the amount of $596.30 for house repairs.

5. Before Mr. Yu made his deposit (see Exercise 1), the balance in the account was $7,869.40. Complete the check stub for the check you wrote in Exercise 3.

6. Complete the check stub for the check you wrote in exercise 4 if the balance brought forward is $2,213.56.

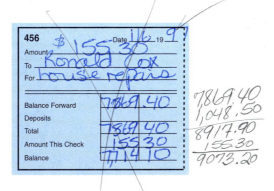

7. Enter in the account register all the transactions described in Exercises 1, 3, and 5, and find the ending balance.

		RECORD ALL TRANSACTIONS THAT AFFECT YOUR ACCOUNT						
NUMBER	DATE	DESCPRICTION OF TRANSACTION	DEBIT	√	FEE	CREDIT	BALANCE	
							7,869	40
456	4/29	Ronald Cox	155 30					
3215	6/20	Green Harvest	596 30					

8. On September 30 you deposited your payroll check of $932.15. You then wrote the following checks on the same day.

Check number	Payee	Amount
3176	Electric Coop.	$107.13
3177	Amoco	$ 47.15
3178	Visa	$ 97.00

Show these transactions in your account register and show the ending balance if your beginning balance was $435.97.

NUMBER	DATE	DESCPRICTION OF TRANSACTION	DEBIT	√	FEE	CREDIT	BALANCE 435.97
	9/30	Deposit	$			$ 932.15	1368.12
3176	9/30	Electric Coop.	107.13				1260.99
3177	9/30	Amoco.	47.15				1213.84
3178	9/30	Visa	97.00				1116.84

RECORD ALL TRANSACTIONS THAT AFFECT YOUR ACCOUNT

9. Show how the check in Exercise 4 would be endorsed for deposit to account number 26-8224021. What type of endorsement is this called?
For Deposit to 26-8224021 Ronald H. Cox Realty

10. If you were the owner of Green Harvest (Exercise 3), would you be able to exchange this check for cash? If so, show how you would endorse the check. If not, explain how you could handle the check.
No. It is a business. Can only be deposited.

Keeping Accounts in Check

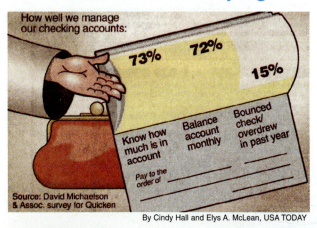

How well we manage our checking accounts:
73% Know how much is in account
72% Balance account monthly
15% Bounced check/ overdrew in past year
Pay to the order of

Source: David Michaelson & Assoc. survey for Quicken
By Cindy Hall and Elys A. McLean, USA TODAY

Copyright 1995, USA TODAY. Reprinted with permission.

For every 100 people surveyed, 73 of them know how much is in their checking account. This fact is represented by 73%.

1. For every 100 people surveyed, how many of them balance their checking account monthly?

2. For every 100 people surveyed, how many of them bounced a check or overdrew their account in the past year?

3. If 200 people were surveyed, how many would know how much is in their checking account?

4. For every 100 people surveyed, how many of them do not balance their checking account monthly?

1 ▶ *Read a bank statement*

2 ▶ *Reconcile a bank statement with an account register*

Each month, banks send statements to their checking account customers to enable account holders to reconcile any differences between that statement and the customer's own account register.

1 ▶ ### Reading a Bank Statement

The primary tool for reconciling an account is the monthly **bank statement,** a listing of all transactions that took place in the customer's account during the past month. It includes checks and other debits and deposits and other credits. A sample bank statement is shown in Figure 2–8.

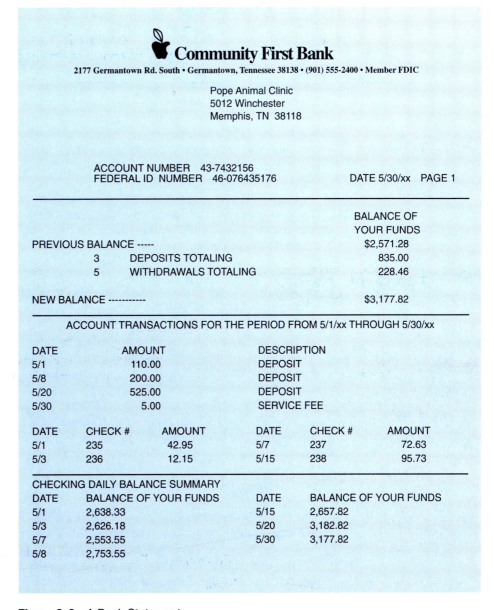

Figure 2–8   A Bank Statement

Most bank statements explain the various letter codes and symbols contained in the statement. One of the first steps to take when you receive a bank statement is to check this explanatory section for any terms that you do not understand in the statement.

One of the items that may appear on a bank statement is a **service charge.** This is a fee the bank charges for maintaining the checking account; it may be a standard monthly fee, a charge for each check, or some combination.

Another type of bank charge appearing on a bank statement is for checks that "bounce" (are not backed by sufficient funds). Suppose Joe writes you a check and you cash the check or deposit it. Later your bank is notified that Joe does not have enough money in his bank account to cover the check. So Joe's bank returns the check to your bank. Such a check is called a **returned check.** Your bank will deduct the amount of the returned check from your account. You bank may also deduct a **returned check fee** from your account to cover the cost of handling this transaction. If you write a check for which you do not have sufficient funds in your account, your bank will charge you a **nonsufficient funds fee (NSF).** The bank notifies you through a **debit memo** of the decrease in your account balance.

Your statement may also include a debit for **FDIC insurance premium.** The federal government set up the Federal Deposit Insurance Corporation to guarantee bank deposits against bank failure. To pay for this insurance, banks are charged an FDIC insurance fee.

All costs of FDIC insurance were assumed by most banks prior to 1991. In 1991, this insurance increased significantly due to the failure of several banks. As a result many banks began the practice of passing on all or part of the cost of FDIC insurance to customers. The cost of insurance to the financial institution was raised from 12 cents to 23 cents per hundred dollars. This increase of 11 cents per one hundred dollars is the same as 0.11 percent or 0.0011 per one dollar. Some banks pass only the increase along to customers, while other banks pass the entire cost of the insurance to customers.

Your bank statement also reflects electronic funds transfers such as withdrawals and deposits made using an **automatic teller machine (ATM)** and authorized electronic withdrawals and deposits.

What does *not* appear on the bank statement is the amount of any check you wrote or deposit you made that reaches the bank *after* the statement is printed. Such transactions may be called **outstanding checks or deposits.** This is one reason your bank statement and your account register may not agree initially.

> Re
> Returned checks are those given to you that bounced and are sent back to your bank
> *In doing so the amount of is deducted and posabley along with a fee along with

Example 1 Refer to the bank statement in Figure 2–8.
(a) How many deposits were made during the month?
(b) What amount of service charge was paid?
(c) On what day did check 237 clear the bank?
(d) Which of the following types of transactions are not illustrated in the bank statement: service charge, returned check, returned check fee, FDIC insurance premium, automatic teller transaction?

(a) 3 (b) $5.00 (c) 5/7 (d) returned check, returned check fee, FDIC insurance premium, automatic teller transaction

2▶ *Reconciling a Bank Statement with an Account Register*

When a bank statement and an account register do not initially agree, you need to take steps to make them agree. The process of making the bank statement agree with the account register is called **reconciling a bank statement** or **bank reconciliation.**

The first thing to do when you receive a bank statement is to go over it and compare its contents with your account register. You can check off all the checks and deposits listed on the statement by using the √ column in the account register (Figure 2–6) or by marking the check stub.

What? You Haven't Heard of MITAC?
It Makes Computers—a Lot of Them—Under Other Brand Names

Matthew Miau is resigned to being one of the computer world's least-known powers. As chairman of Mitac International Corp., the former Intel engineer has built his company into Taiwan's No. 2 computer maker, behind Acer Inc. But most PC users have never heard of Mitac. During the computer industry shakeout of the early 1990s, Miau pulled the plug on efforts to sell Mitac's brand-name computers and monitors in the U.S. "We weren't as daring as Acer," he says. "We lost a few million and decided to cut our losses."

At a time when the Taiwanese government wants local companies to publicize their own products, Mitac is content with the obscurity of being an original equipment manufacturer (OEM) for others. By focusing on production of PCs, notebooks, and monitors that bear other companies' brand names, Mitac has lifted itself out of the red and won contracts from some of the biggest names in the industry. Indeed, rather than pushing their own brands, other Taiwanese manufacturers might be better off with Mitac's back-to-the-future plan. "The changes in the computer industry have squeezed the room available for brand-name products," says Chen Hsiu-hsian, manager for Coopers & Lybrand Consultants Taiwan.

Deals-a-poppin'. Mitac won't reveal the names of its OEM customers. But industry sources report deals between the company and AT&T, Compaq, and Apple

Computer. To win this business, Mitac is providing not only design and manufacturing services but also final assembly and global distribution. That has helped Mitac become "increasingly important in the global marketplace," says Jennifer Wu, marketing research development manager with Dataquest Taiwan.

Even so, Mitac has a long way to go before it catches up with Acer, seventh among the world's PC makers. Chairman Stan Shih has revamped Acer's management, in particular giving more autonomy to overseas units. That, in addition to Shih's focus on brand-name marketing, has paid off well for Acer. In 1994, its sales topped $3 billion—compared with Mitac's $610 million.

To Mitac executives, though, Acer's success in marketing its own computers provides them with an opening. "Most of our customers are more comfortable with us than with a company like Acer, because they know we won't be competing against them," says Francis Tsai, Mitac's general manager. In some cases, Mitac even operates like a manufacturing and distribution arm of its customers, shipping goods directly to retail outlets. For example, Mitac ships PCs to Sears Roebuck & Co. outlets across the U.S. The company whose brand name appears on the computers never touches the product.

By Margaret Dawson in Taipei

 TIPS & TRAPS

While the bank statement does not have a √ column, it is helpful to verify that every transaction is recorded in the account register by checking each item on the bank statement as it is checked in the register.

The check method on both the bank statement and account register makes it easier to identify errors, omissions, and outstanding transactions.

Review this again

Step 1 Check off all matching transactions appearing on both the bank statement and the account register.

Step 2 Enter into the register the transactions appearing on the bank statement that have not been checked off. Check off these transactions in the register as they are entered. Update the register balance accordingly.

Step 3 Make a list of all the checks and other debits appearing in the register that have not been checked off. Add the amounts on the list to find the *total outstanding debits.*

Step 4 Make a list of all the deposits and other credits appearing in the register that have not been checked off in step 1. Add the amounts on the list to find the *total outstanding credits.*

Step 5 Calculate the *adjusted statement balance* by adding the statement balance and the total outstanding credits, and then subtracting the total outstanding debits. Adjusted statement balance = statement balance + total outstanding credits − total outstanding debits.

Step 6 Compare the adjusted statement balance with the register balance. These amounts should be equal.

Step 7 If the adjusted statement balance does not equal the register balance, locate the cause of the discrepancy and correct the register accordingly.

Step 8 Write *statement reconciled* on the next blank line in the account register and record the statement date.

 TIPS & TRAPS

When your adjusted statement balance does not equal your account register balance, you need to locate the cause of the discrepancy and correct the register accordingly.

To do so, first be sure you have calculated the adjusted statement balance accurately. Double check, for instance, that the list of outstanding debits is complete and their sum is accurate. Double check the list of outstanding credits, too. Double check that you correctly added the total outstanding credits and subtracted the total outstanding debits from the statement balance. If you are sure you have carried out all the reconciliation steps correctly, the discrepancy may be due to an error that you made in the account register or to an error made by the bank. Here are three common errors and strategies to locate them.

Error You entered a transaction in the register but you did not update the register balance.
Strategy To locate the transaction, calculate the difference of the adjusted statement balance and the register balance (subtract one from the other). Compare this difference with each transaction amount in the register to see if this difference matches a transaction amount exactly.

Error You transposed digits, for instance 39 was entered as 93, when entering the amount in the register or when listing outstanding items from the statement.
Strategy Divide the difference between the adjusted statement balance and the adjusted register balance by 9. If the quotient has no remainder, check the entries to find the transposed digits.

Error   You entered a transaction in the register but to update the register balance you added the transaction amount when you should have subtracted, or vice versa.

Strategy   To locate the transaction, calculate the difference of the adjusted statement balance and the adjusted register balance (subtract one from the other). Now calculate half of this difference (divide the difference by 2). Compare this half-difference with each transaction amount in the register to see if this half-difference matches a transaction amount exactly.

Error   You entered a transaction in the register but to update the register balance you added (or subtracted) the transaction amount incorrectly.

Strategy   To locate the transaction, begin with the first transaction in the register following the previous reconciliation. From this point on, redo your addition (or subtraction) for each transaction to see if you originally added (or subtracted) the transaction amount correctly.

RECORD ALL TRANSACTIONS THAT AFFECT YOUR ACCOUNT

NUMBER	DATE	DESCRIPTION OF TRANSACTION	DEBIT (−)		√T	FEE (IF ANY) (−)	CREDIT (+)		BALANCE	
									2,571	28
235	4/20	Pet Supply Company	42	95					2,528	33
Deposit	5/1	Customer Receipts					110	00	2,638	33
236	5/1	K-mart	12	15					2,626	18
237	5/1	Telephone Company	72	63					2,553	55
Deposit	5/8	Customer Receipts					200	00	2,753	55
238	5/10	Chickasaw Electric Co.	95	73					2,657	82
239	5/15	Protein Technologies Dog Food	117	28					2,540	54
240	5/15	Rand M Drug Co.	92	69					2,447	85
Deposit	5/20	Customer Receipts					525	00	2,972	85
Deposit	5/25	Customer Receipts					200	00	3,172	85

REMEMBER TO RECORD AUTOMATIC PAYMENTS/DEPOSITS ON DATE AUTHORIZED.

Figure 2–9   Pope Animal Clinic Account Register

A reconciliation form is usually printed on the back of the bank statement. The form leads you through a reconciliation process that may be different than the one given in this book, but the result is the same: a reconciled statement.

Many businesses and individuals use software programs to keep banking records. The user enters transaction amounts into the computer, and the program updates the register balance. At reconciliation time, the user enters information from the bank statement into the computer, and the program reconciles the bank statement with the account register.

These programs can also be useful for budgeting and tax purposes. Transactions can be categorized and tracked according to the user's specifications. Monthly and yearly budgets can be prepared accordingly, for both individuals and businesses. At tax time, these programs may even be used to generate and fill in tax forms.

Example 2 Pope Animal Clinic regularly transfers money from its checking account to a special account used for one-time expenditures such as equipment. The decision to transfer is made each month when the bank statement is reconciled. Money is transferred only if the adjusted statement balance exceeds $2500; all the excess is transferred. The bank statement is shown in Figure 2–8 and the register is shown in Figure 2–9. Should money be transferred? If so, how much?

1 Decision needed   Should money be transferred? If so, how much?

2 Unknown fact   The adjusted statement balance

3 Known facts   Bank statement transactions (Figure 2-8) and register transactions (Figure 2-9)

4 Relationships   Adjusted statement balance = statement balance + total outstanding credits − total outstanding debits

5 Estimation   Not appropriate for this situation

6 Calculations   Check off all matching transactions appearing on both the statement and the register (Figures 2-10 and 2-11).

Now enter into the register the transactions appearing on the bank statement that have not been checked off. The service fee is the only unchecked-off transaction. As you enter it into the register, check it off the bank statement and the register.

Now list the outstanding credits and debits: transactions appearing on the register that have not been checked off. The register is reconciled. The adjusted statement balance is $3,167.85.

Outstanding Credits		Outstanding Debits	
5/25	200.00	239	117.28
		240	92.69
Total	200.00	Total	209.97

Adjusted statement balance = statement balance + total outstanding credits − total outstanding debits
Adjusted statement balance = $3177.82 + $200.00 − $209.97
Adjusted statement balance = $3167.85

7 Decision made   The adjusted statement balance is more than $2,500. **Money should be transferred.** Since the excess over $2,500 should be transferred, **the amount transferred is** $3,167.85 − $2,500, or **$667.85.**

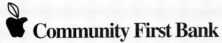
Community First Bank

2177 Germantown Rd. South • Germantown, Tennessee 38138 • (901) 555-2400 • Member FDIC

Pope Animal Clinic
5012 Winchester
Memphis, TN 38118

ACCOUNT NUMBER   43-7432156
FEDERAL ID NUMBER   46-076435176

DATE 5/30/xx   PAGE 1

		BALANCE OF YOUR FUNDS
PREVIOUS BALANCE -----		$2,571.28
3	DEPOSITS TOTALING	835.00
5	WITHDRAWALS TOTALING	228.46
NEW BALANCE -----------		$3,177.82

ACCOUNT TRANSACTIONS FOR THE PERIOD FROM 5/1/xx THROUGH 5/30/xx

DATE	AMOUNT	DESCRIPTION
5/1	110.00 ✓	DEPOSIT
5/8	200.00 ✓	DEPOSIT
5/20	525.00 ✓	DEPOSIT
5/30	5.00	SERVICE FEE

DATE	CHECK #	AMOUNT	DATE	CHECK #	AMOUNT
5/1	235	42.95 ✓	5/7	237	72.63 ✓
5/3	236	12.15 ✓	5/15	238	95.73 ✓

CHECKING DAILY BALANCE SUMMARY

DATE	BALANCE OF YOUR FUNDS	DATE	BALANCE OF YOUR FUNDS
5/1	2,638.33	5/15	2,657.82
5/3	2,626.18	5/20	3,182.82
5/7	2,553.55	5/30	3,177.82
5/8	2,753.55		

Figure 2–10   Matching Transactions Checked off the Bank Statement

RECORD ALL TRANSACTIONS THAT AFFECT YOUR ACCOUNT

NUMBER	DATE	DESCRIPTION OF TRANSACTION	DEBIT (−)		√T	FEE (IF ANY) (−)	CREDIT (+)		BALANCE	
									2,571	28
235	4/20	Pet Supply Company	42	95	√				2,528	33
Deposit	5/1	Customer Receipts			√		110	00	2,638	33
236	5/1	K-mart	12	15	√				2,626	18
237	5/1	Telephone Company	72	63	√				2,553	55
Deposit	5/8	Customer Receipts			√		200	00	2,753	55
238	5/10	Chickasaw Electric Co.	95	73	√				2,657	82
239	5/15	Protein Technologies Dog food	117	28					2,540	54
240	5/15	Rand M Drug Co.	92	69					2,447	85
Deposit	5/20	Customer Receipts			√		525	00	2,972	85
Deposit	5/25	Customer Receipts					200	00	3,172	85
	5/30	Service Fee	5	00	√				3,167	85
	5/30	Statement reconciled							—	

REMEMBER TO RECORD AUTOMATIC PAYMENTS/DEPOSITS ON DATE AUTHORIZED.

Figure 2–11 Reconciled Account Register

Self-Check 2.2

 Use Tom Deskin's bank statement (page 57) for exercises 1-3.

1. Does Tom pay bills through electronic funds transfer? If so, which ones?

2. Did Tom use the automatic teller during the month? If so, what transactions were made and for what amounts?

3. What were the lowest and highest daily bank balances for the month?

Community First Bank

2177 Germantown Rd. South • Germantown, Tennessee 38138 • (901) 555-2400 • Member FDIC

Tom Deskin
1234 South Street
Germantown, TN 38138

ACCOUNT NUMBER   13-2882139
SOCIAL SECURITY NUMBER   213-44-6688   DATE 9-29-xx   PAGE 1

		BALANCE OF YOUR FUNDS
PREVIOUS BALANCE -----		$2,472.86
3	DEPOSITS TOTALING	4,812.76
16	WITHDRAWALS TOTALING	4,685.04
NEW BALANCE ----------		$2,600.58

ACCOUNT TRANSACTIONS FOR THE PERIOD FROM 8-28-xx THROUGH 9-27-xx

DATE	AMOUNT	DESCRIPTION
9/1	2,401.32	DEPOSIT - SCHERING-PLOUGH PAYROLL 213446688
9/1	942.18	WITHDRAWAL - LEADER FEDERAL MTG PMT 314123
9/4	217.17	WITHDRAWAL - LG&W PMT 21814
9/15	2,401.32	DEPOSIT - SCHERING-PLOUGH PAYROLL 213446688
9/20	60.00	WITHDRAWAL - ATM KIRBY WOODS
9/27	.64	FDIC INSURANCE PREMIUM
9/27	10.12	INTEREST EARNED

DATE	CHECK #	AMOUNT	DATE	CHECK #	AMOUNT	DATE	CHECK #	AMOUNT
8/31	1094	42.37	9/10	1099	583.21	9/25	1106*	1,238.42
9/2	1095	12.96	9/16	1100	283.21	9/25	1107	500.00
9/5	1096	36.01	9/18	1102*	48.23			
9/5	1097	178.13	9/21	1103	71.16			
9/5	1098	458.60	9/23	1104	12.75			

CHECKING DAILY BALANCE SUMMARY

DATE	BALANCE OF YOUR FUNDS	DATE	BALANCE OF YOUR FUNDS
8/28	2,472.86	9/15	4,804.87
8/31	2,430.49	9/16	4,521.66
9/1	3,889.63	9/18	4,473.43
9/2	3,876.67	9/20	4,413.43
9/4	3,659.50	9/21	4,342.27
9/5	2,986.76	9/23	4,329.52
9/10	2,403.55	9/25	2,591.10
		9/27	2,600.58

4. A bank statement shows a balance of $12.32. The service charge for the month was $2.95. The account register shows deposits of $300, $100, and $250 that do not appear on the statement. Outstanding checks are in the amount of $36.52, $205.16, $18.92, $25.93, and $200. The register balance is $178.74. Find the adjusted statement balance.

5. Tom Deskin's account register is shown below. Reconcile the bank statement (see Exercise 1) with the account register.

		RECORD ALL TRANSACTIONS THAT AFFECT YOUR ACCOUNT							
NUMBER	DATE	DESCRIPTION OF TRANSACTION	DEBIT (−)		√T	FEE (IF ANY) (−)	CREDIT (+)	BALANCE	
								2472	86
1094	8/28	K-mart	42	37				2430	49
1095	8/28	Walgreen's	12	96				2417	53
Deposit	9/1	Payroll Schering-Plough					2401 32	4,818	85
A W	9/1	Leader Federal	942	18				3,876	67
A W	9/1	LG & W	217	17				3,659	50
1096	9/1	Kroger	36	01				3,623	49
1097	9/1	Texaco	178	13				3,445	36
1098	9/1	Univ. of Memphis	458	60				2,986	76
1099	9/15	GMAC Credit Corp	583	21				2,403	55
1100	9/18	VISA	283	21				2,120	34
1101	9/10	Radio Shack	189	37				1,930	97
1102	9/10	Auto Zone	48	23				1,882	74
Deposit	9/15	Payroll- Schering Plough					2401 32	4,284	06

REMEMBER TO RECORD AUTOMATIC PAYMENTS/DEPOSITS ON DATE AUTHORIZED.

		RECORD ALL TRANSACTIONS THAT AFFECT YOUR ACCOUNT							
NUMBER	DATE	DESCRIPTION OF TRANSACTION	DEBIT (−)		√T	FEE (IF ANY) (−)	CREDIT (+)	BALANCE	
								4,284	06
1103	9/15	Geoffrey Beane	71	16				4,212	90
1104	9/14	Heaven Scent Flowers	12	75				4,200	15
1105	9/20	Kroger	87	75				4,112	40
ATM	9/20	Kirby Woods	60	00				4,052	40
1106	9/21	Traveler's Insurance	1,238	42				2,813	98
1107	9/23	Nation's Bank-Savings	500	00				2,313	98

1.

DEPOSIT TICKET

Park's Oriental Grocery
1428 Central Ave.
Germantown, TN 38138

DATE 4/29 19 XX

DEPOSITS MAY NOT BE AVAILABLE FOR IMMEDIATE WITHDRAWAL

_____
SIGN HERE FOR CASH RECEIVED (IF REQUIRED)

Community First Bank
2177 Germantown Road • 7808 Farmington
Germantown, TN 38138 • (901) 754-2400 • Member FDIC

⑆084000063⑈1579⑈5

CHECKS AND OTHER ITEMS ARE RECEIVED FOR DEPOSIT SUBJECT TO THE PROVISIONS OF THE UNIFORM COMMERCIAL CODE OR ANY APPLICABLE COLLECTION AGREEMENT.

CASH	CURRENCY	850	00
	COIN	8	63
LIST CHECKS SINGLY		157	38
		32	49
TOTAL FROM OTHER SIDE			
TOTAL			
LESS CASH RECEIVED			
NET DEPOSIT		1,048	50

26-2/840

USE OTHER SIDE FOR ADDITIONAL LISTING

BE SURE EACH ITEM IS PROPERLY ENDORSED

2.

DEPOSIT TICKET

Please be sure all items are properly endorsed. List checks separately.
FOR CLEAR COPY, PRESS FIRMLY WITH BALL POINT PEN

DATE March 31, XX

DELECTABLES CANDIES
5981 POPLAR AVE.
MEMPHIS, TN 38121

87-278/840

Community First Bank
2177 GERMANTOWN ROAD SOUTH
GERMANTOWN, TENNESSEE 38138

⑆084007281⑈ 11 8116 3⑈

Checks and other items are received for deposit subject to the provisions of the Uniform Commercial Code or any applicable collection agreement.

	DOLLARS	CENTS
CURRENCY	196	00
COIN		
CHECKS		
1 Cavanaugh	14	72
2 Bryan	31	18
3 Wassum	16	97
4 Wright	28	46
5 Howell	17	21
6 Coe	32	17
7 Beville	17	84
8 Palinchak	31	96
9 Raszel	19	16
10		
11		
12		
13		
14		
15		
16		
17		
18		
19		
20		
21		
22		
23		
24		
25		
26		
27		
28		
29		
30		
31		
32		
TOTAL	405	67

TOTAL ITEMS
9

© DELUXE 8DM-3

DEPOSITS MAY NOT BE AVAILABLE FOR IMMEDIATE WITHDRAWAL

3.

Park's Oriental Grocery
1428 Central Ave.
Germantown, TN 38138

456

April 29, 19XX

87-278/840

PAY TO THE ORDER OF Green Harvest $ 155.30

One hundred fifty-five and 30/100 —————— DOLLARS

Community First Bank
2177 Germantown Rd. South
Germantown, Tennessee 38138

MEMO fresh vegetables   Yan Yu

⑆084002781⑆

4.

		RECORD ALL TRANSACTIONS THAT AFFECT YOUR ACCOUNT							
							BALANCE		
NUMBER	DATE	DESCPRICTION OF TRANSACTION	DEBIT	√	FEE	CREDIT	7,869	40	
	4/29	Deposit	$			$ 1,048 50	8,917	90	
456	4/29	Green Harvest	155 30				8,762	60	

5.

456   Date 4/29 19XX

Amount $155.30
To Green Harvest
For fresh vegetables

Balance Forward	7,869	40
Deposits	1,048	50
Total	8,917	90
Amount This Check	155	30
Balance	8,762	60

6.

3215   Date 6/20 19XX

Amount 596.13
To Ronald H. Cox Realty
For house repairs

Balance Forward	2,213	56
Deposits	0	
Total	2,213	56
Amount This Check	596	13
Balance	1,617	43

7.

		RECORD ALL TRANSACTIONS THAT AFFECT YOUR ACCOUNT							
							BALANCE		
NUMBER	DATE	DESCPRICTION OF TRANSACTION	DEBIT	√	FEE	CREDIT	7,869	40	
	4/29	Deposit	$			1,048 50	8,917	90	
456	4/29	Green Harvest	155 30				8,762	60	

8.

NUMBER	DATE	DESCRIPTION OF TRANSACTION	DEBIT		√	FEE	CREDIT	BALANCE	
								435	97
Dep.	9/30	Payroll Deposit	$				$ 932 15	1,368	12
3176	9/30	Electric Coop	107	13				1,260	99
3177	9/30	Amoco	47	15				1,213	84
3178	9/30	Visa	97	00				1,116	84

RECORD ALL TRANSACTIONS THAT AFFECT YOUR ACCOUNT

9.

For Deposit to
account 26-8224021
Ronald H. Cox Realty

3355

10. The check cannot be exchanged for cash because the payee is a business. It will need to be deposited into an account owned by Green Harvest.

Self-Check 2.2

1. Leader Federal: $942.18; LG & W: $217.17

2. Withdrawal: $60.00

3. Lowest balance: $2,403.55; Highest balance: $4,804.87

4. After entering the $2.95 service charge in the account register, the updated account balance is $175.79.

	Outstanding Credits		Outstanding Debits	
				36.52
		300.00		205.16
		100.00		18.92
		250.00		25.93
Total		650.00		200.00
			Total	486.53

Adjusted statement balance = statement balance + total outstanding credits − total outstanding debits

Adjusted statement balance = $12.32 + $650.00 − $486.53

Adjusted statement balance = $175.79

5. Below is Tom's account register after he has checked off transactions matching those on the bank statement, and after he has entered and checked-off transactions appearing on the bank statement that had not been checked off in the bank statement.

RECORD ALL TRANSACTIONS THAT AFFECT YOUR ACCOUNT

NUMBER	DATE	DESCRIPTION OF TRANSACTION	DEBIT (-)	√T	FEE (IF ANY) (-)	CREDIT (+)	BALANCE
							2,472 86
1094	8/28	K-Mart	42 37	√			2,430 49
1095	8/28	Walgreen's	12 96	√			2,417 53
Deposit	9/1	payroll Schering-Plough		√		2,401 32	4,818 85
AW	9/1	Leader Federal	942 18	√			3,876 67
AW	9/1	LG & W	217 17	√			3,659 50
1096	9/1	Kroger	36 01	√			3,623 49
1097	9/1	Texaco	178 13	√			3,445 36
1098	9/1	Univ. of Memphis	458 60	√			2,986 76
1099	9/5	GMAC Credit Corp	583 21	√			2,403 55
1100	9/8	VISA	283 21	√			2,120 34
1101	9/10	Radio Shack	189 37				1,930 97
1102	9/10	Auto Zone	48 23	√			1,882 74
Deposit	9/15	payroll Schering-Plough		√		2,401 32	4,284 06

REMEMBER TO RECORD AUTOMATIC PAYMENTS/DEPOSITS ON DATE AUTHORIZED.

RECORD ALL TRANSACTIONS THAT AFFECT YOUR ACCOUNT

NUMBER	DATE	DESCRIPTION OF TRANSACTION	DEBIT (-)	√T	FEE (IF ANY) (-)	CREDIT (+)	BALANCE
							4,284 06
1103	9/15	Geoffrey Beane	71 16	√			4,212 90
1104	9/14	Heaven Scent Flowers	12 75	√			4,200 15
1105	9/20	Kroger	87 75				4,112 40
ATM	9/20	Kirby Woods	60 00	√			4,052 40
1106	9/21	Traveler's Insurance	1238 42	√			2,813 98
1107	9/23	Nation's Bank-Savings	500 00	√			2,313 98
	9/27	FDIC Insurance		√	.64		2,313 34
	9/27	Interest Earned		√		10 12	2,323 46
	9/29	Statement reconciled					—

Outstanding Credits	Outstanding Debits		
None	1101	$189.37	
	1105	$ 87.75	
	Total	$277.12	

Adjusted statement balance = statement balance + total outstanding credits − total outstanding debits
Adjusted statement balance = $2,600.58 + $0 − $277.12
Adjusted statement balance = $2,323.46
Since the adjusted statement balance equals the updated account balance, the statement is reconciled.

Section—Objective	Important Points with Examples

2.1 — 1 *(page 40)*

Fill out a bank deposit ticket

A deposit ticket is a form that tells the bank which account should receive money (cash or checks) that is being deposited. The bank provides the account holder with deposit tickets that carry the name and address of the account holder and the account number. For every deposit, a deposit ticket must be filled out to describe each check and all the cash being deposited.

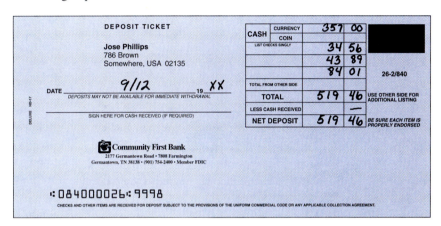

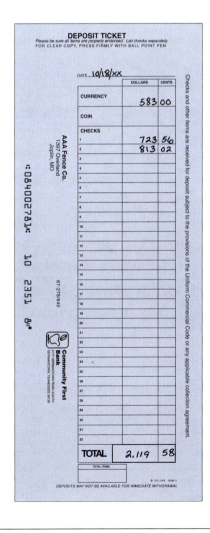

2.1 — **2** (page 41)

Write a bank check

A check is a form that authorizes the bank to pay someone money from an account. The bank provides an account holder with checks that carry the name and address of the account holder and the account number. A check must be filled out with the name of the person or company to whom money should be paid, and the amount of money to pay.

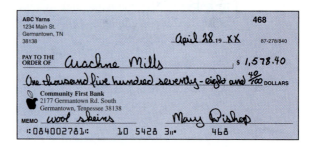

2.1 — **3** (page 43)

Fill out a check stub

A check stub is a form attached to a check. When a check is written, the stub is filled out to record information about the check. A check stub also has space to write information about deposits made between checks.

2.1 — **4** (page 44)

Use an account register

An account register is a form on which the account holder records every transaction made for an account. The register indicates the current balance brought forward and lists all checks, withdrawals, deposits, and other charges.

2.1 — **5** (page 45)

Endorse a check

To endorse a check means to sign or stamp the back of a check with the name of the payee, the person or company to whom the money should be paid. A bank ordinarily will not honor a check that is not endorsed. A check can be endorsed in more than one way.

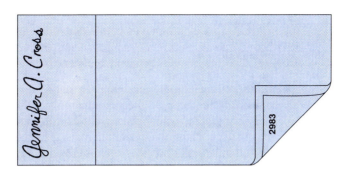

2.2 — 1 *(page 49)*

Read a bank statement

A bank statement is a monthly record that most banks send to each account holder. The statement shows all deposits, withdrawals, and service charges, and summarizes all other activity for the account. The account holder must compare the bank statement with the account register to make sure that both records are complete and accurate and that the records agree with each other.

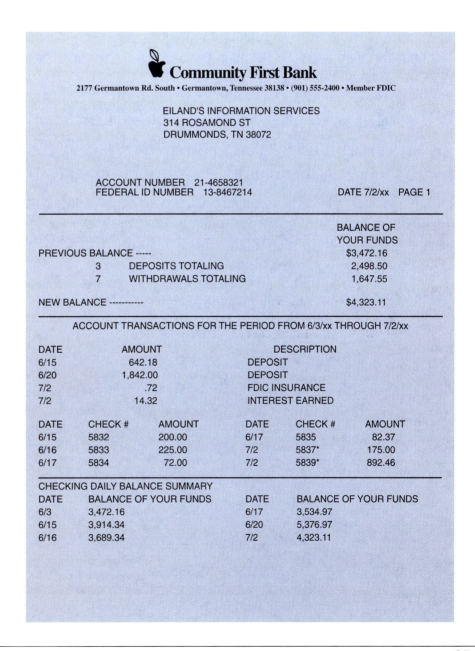

Community First Bank

2177 Germantown Rd. South • Germantown, Tennessee 38138 • (901) 555-2400 • Member FDIC

EILAND'S INFORMATION SERVICES
314 ROSAMOND ST
DRUMMONDS, TN 38072

ACCOUNT NUMBER   21-4658321
FEDERAL ID NUMBER   13-8467214   DATE 7/2/xx   PAGE 1

		BALANCE OF YOUR FUNDS
PREVIOUS BALANCE -----		$3,472.16
3	DEPOSITS TOTALING	2,498.50
7	WITHDRAWALS TOTALING	1,647.55
NEW BALANCE -----------		$4,323.11

ACCOUNT TRANSACTIONS FOR THE PERIOD FROM 6/3/xx THROUGH 7/2/xx

DATE	AMOUNT	DESCRIPTION
6/15	642.18	DEPOSIT
6/20	1,842.00	DEPOSIT
7/2	.72	FDIC INSURANCE
7/2	14.32	INTEREST EARNED

DATE	CHECK #	AMOUNT	DATE	CHECK #	AMOUNT
6/15	5832	200.00	6/17	5835	82.37
6/16	5833	225.00	7/2	5837*	175.00
6/17	5834	72.00	7/2	5839*	892.46

CHECKING DAILY BALANCE SUMMARY

DATE	BALANCE OF YOUR FUNDS	DATE	BALANCE OF YOUR FUNDS
6/3	3,472.16	6/17	3,534.97
6/15	3,914.34	6/20	5,376.97
6/16	3,689.34	7/2	4,323.11

2.2 — 2 *(page 50)*

Reconcile a bank statement with an account register

Reconciliation is the process of comparing the account register with the bank statement to make sure that both records are complete and accurate and that the records agree with each other.

Step 1 Check off all matching transactions appearing on both the bank statement and the account register. **Step 2** Enter into the register the transactions appearing on the bank statement that have not been checked off. Check off these transactions in the register as they are entered. Update the register balance accordingly. **Step 3** Make a list of all the checks and other debits appearing in the register that have not been checked off. Add the amounts on the list to find the *total outstanding debits*. **Step 4** Make a list of all the deposits and other credits appearing in the register that have not been checked off in Step 1. Add the amounts on the list to find the *total outstanding credits*. **Step 5** Calculate the *adjusted statement balance* by adding the statement balance and the total outstanding credits, and then subtracting the total outstanding debits: Adjusted statement balance = statement balance + total outstanding credits − total outstanding debits. **Step 6** Compare the adjusted statement balance with the register balance. These amounts should be equal. **Step 7** If the adjusted statement balance does not equal the register balance, locate the cause of the discrepancy and correct the register accordingly. **Step 8** Write *statement reconciled* on the next blank line in the account register and record the statement date.

Below is the account register and bank statement for Eiland's Information Services. Steps 1 and 2 of the reconciliation process have already been carried out: matching transactions have been checked off, and all transactions appearing on the bank statement have been entered in the register and checked off, including FDIC insurance of $0.72 and interest earned of $14.32. The updated register balance is $18,020.36.

Now we find the total outstanding debits and the total outstanding credits, transactions in the register that do not appear on the bank statement.

Outstanding Credits		Outstanding Debits	
6/15	20,000	5836	42.18
		5838	4,976.21
Total	20,000	Total	5,018.39

Adjusted statement balance = statement balance + total outstanding credits − total outstanding debits
Adjusted statement balance = 4,309.51 + 20,000 − 5,018.39
Adjusted statement balance = 19,304.72

The adjusted statement balance does not equal the register balance. To locate the error, first find the difference of the two amounts: $19,304.72 − 18,020.36 = 1,284.36$. This amount does not match any transaction exactly. So, divide the difference by 2: $1,284.36 ÷ 2 = 642.18$. This amount matches a deposit made on 6/15. The deposit was subtracted from the balance when it should have been added. Make an entry in the account register to offset the error: deposit $1,284.36, which is the amount that was subtracted in error plus the amount of the 6/15 deposit. Below is shown the reconciled register. Notice the entry "statement reconciled" dated 7/2.

RECORD ALL TRANSACTIONS THAT AFFECT YOUR ACCOUNT

NUMBER	DATE	DESCRIPTION OF TRANSACTION	DEBIT (-)		√ T	FEE (IF ANY) (-)	CREDIT (+)		BALANCE	
									3,472	16
5832	6/13	City of Chicago	200	00	√				3,272	16
5833	6/13	City of Phoenix	225	00	√				3,047	16
5834	6/14	City of Fresno	72	00	√				2,975	16
5835	6/15	Hardware house	82	37	√				2,892	79
Deposit	6/15	Can Com, Inc.	642	18	√				2,250	61
5836	6/18	Office Max copies	42	18					2,208	43
5837	6/20	City of New Orleans	175	00	√				2,033	43
Deposit	6/20	List purchases			√		1842	00	3,075	43
Deposit	6/25	Federal Credit Union Small business loan					20,000	00	23,875	43
5838	6/30	Hardware house computer	4,976	21					18,899	22
5839	6/30	Wade office Furniture Desk chair, file Cabinet	892	46	√				18,006	76
	7/2	FDIC Insurance			√	72			18,006	04
	7/2	Interest earned			√		14	32	18,020	36

REMEMBER TO RECORD AUTOMATIC PAYMENTS/DEPOSITS ON DATE AUTHORIZED.

RECORD ALL TRANSACTIONS THAT AFFECT YOUR ACCOUNT

NUMBER	DATE	DESCRIPTION OF TRANSACTION	DEBIT (-)	√ T	FEE (IF ANY) (-)	CREDIT (+)		BALANCE	
								18,020	36
	7/4	Correction to deposit on 6/15		√		1,284	36	19,304	72
	7/2	Statement Reconciled		√				———	

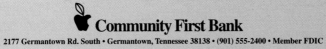

Community First Bank

2177 Germantown Rd. South • Germantown, Tennessee 38138 • (901) 555-2400 • Member FDIC

EILAND'S INFORMATION SERVICES
314 ROSAMOND ST
DRUMMONDS, TN 38072

ACCOUNT NUMBER   21-4658321
FEDERAL ID NUMBER   13-8467214   DATE 7/2/xx   PAGE 1

		BALANCE OF YOUR FUNDS
PREVIOUS BALANCE -----		$3,472.16
3	DEPOSITS TOTALING	2,498.50
7	WITHDRAWALS TOTALING	1,647.55
NEW BALANCE ----------		$4,323.11

ACCOUNT TRANSACTIONS FOR THE PERIOD FROM 6/3/xx THROUGH 7/2/xx

DATE	AMOUNT	DESCRIPTION
6/15	642.18 ✓	DEPOSIT
6/20	1,842.00 ✓	DEPOSIT
7/2	.72 ✓	FDIC INSURANCE
7/2	14.32 ✓	INTEREST EARNED

DATE	CHECK #	AMOUNT	DATE	CHECK #	AMOUNT
6/15	5832	200.00 ✓	6/17	5835	82.37 ✓
6/16	5833	225.00 ✓	7/2	5837*	175.00 ✓
6/17	5834	72.00 ✓	7/2	5839*	892.46 ✓

CHECKING DAILY BALANCE SUMMARY

DATE	BALANCE OF YOUR FUNDS	DATE	BALANCE OF YOUR FUNDS
6/3	3,472.16	6/17	3,534.97
6/15	3,914.34	6/20	5,376.97
6/16	3,689.34	7/2	4,323.11

Section 2.1

1. Write a check dated June 13, 19XX, to Byron Johnson in the amount of $296.83 for a washing machine.

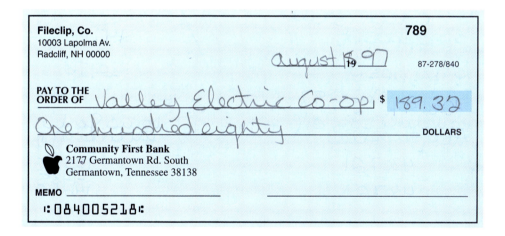

2. Write a check dated August 18, 19XX, to Valley Electric Co-op in the amount of $189.32 for utilities.

3. Complete a deposit slip to add checks in the amounts of $136.00 and $278.96, and $480 cash on May 8, 19XX.

4. Complete a deposit slip on November 11, 19XX, to show the deposit of $100 in cash, checks in the amounts of $87.83, $42.97, and $106.32, with a $472.13 total from the other side of the deposit slip. Your account number is 8021346.

5. Complete the stub for check 786, written on May 10, 19XX, to Jacqueline Voss Office Supplies in the amount of $28.97 for office supplies. The amount brought forward is $4,307.21.

6. Complete the stub for check 1021, written on September 30, 19XX, to Louis Jenkins Plumbing Service for plumbing repairs. The amount brought forward is $1,021.03 and the amount of the check is $65. Deposits of $146 and $297.83 were made before the check was written.

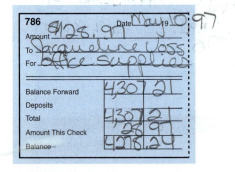

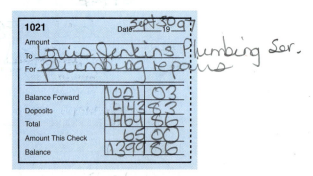

7. Enter the following information and transactions in the check register for Happy Center Day Care. On July 10, 19XX, with an account balance of $983.47, check 1213 was written to Linens Inc. for $220 for laundry services, and check 1214 was written to Bugs Away for $65 for extermination services. On July 11, $80 was withdrawn from an automatic teller machine, and on July 12, checks in the amount of $123.86, $123.86, and $67.52 were deposited. Show the balance after these transactions.

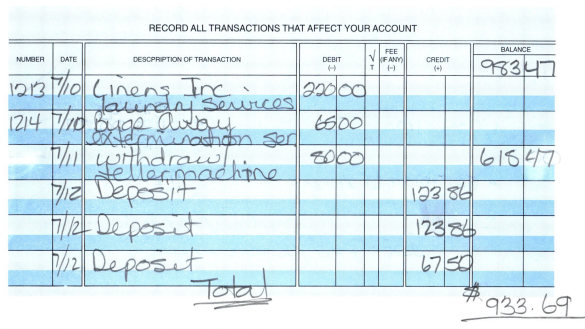

NUMBER	DATE	DESCRIPTION OF TRANSACTION	DEBIT (−)	√T	FEE (IF ANY) (−)	CREDIT (+)	BALANCE
							983 47
1213	7/10	Linens Inc. Laundry Services	220 00				
1214	7/10	Bugs Away Extermination ser.	65 00				
	7/11	Withdrawl Teller machine	80 00				618 47
	7/12	Deposit				123 86	
	7/12	Deposit				123 86	
	7/12	Deposit				67 50	
		Total					$ 933.69

8. Fill out a deposit slip to show a check for $524.75 and $75 cash deposited on April 7, 19XX, to the CHD Company account.

9. Write a check dated June 12, 19XX, to Alpine Industries in the amount of $85.50 for building supplies.

10. Fill out the check stub for a check payable to Turner Wallcoverings for wallpaper installation in the amount of $145. The amount brought forward is $37.43. A cash deposit of $200 was made May 3.

110	Date_____19___
Amount _____	
To ~~Turner Wallcovering~~	
For _____	

Balance Forward	37	43
Deposits	200	00
Total	237	43
Amount This Check	145	00
Balance	92	43

11. Enter the following information and transactions in the check register for Sloan's Tree Service. On May 3, 19XX, with an account balance of $876.54, check 234 was written to Organic Materials for $175 for fertilizer and check 235 was written to Klean Kuts in the amount of $524.82 for a chain saw. On May 5, checks in the amount of $147.63 and $324.76 were deposited. Show the balance after these transactions.

RECORD ALL TRANSACTIONS THAT AFFECT YOUR ACCOUNT

NUMBER	DATE	DESCRIPTION OF TRANSACTION	DEBIT (−)	√T	FEE (IF ANY) (−)	CREDIT (+)	BALANCE
							876 54
234	5/3	Organic Materials Fertilizer	175 00				
235	5/4	Klean Cuts chain saw	524 82				176 72
	5/5	Deposit				147 63	
	5/5	Deposit				324 76	
							649 11

12. Show how Byron Johnson would endorse the check in Exercise 1 if he wanted the bank to give him cash for it.

Byron Johnson

13. How would the check in Exercise 2 be endorsed if it was to be deposited to account number 15-271 3140 which is held by Valley Electric Coop? What type of endorsement is this?

Valley Electric Coop
 # 15-271-3140

14. Discuss the use of the deposit ticket in maintaining a checking account.

15. Discuss the advantages and disadvantages of having your paycheck electronically deposited to your account.

Tree Top Landscape Service's bank statement is shown below.

16. How many deposits were made during the month?

4

17. What amount of service charge was paid?

$21.17

18. What was the amount of the largest check written?

$238.00

19. How many checks appear on the bank statement?

5

20. What is the balance at the beginning of the statement period?

4,782.96

21. What is the balance at the end of the statement period?

$4,975.50

22. What is the amount of check 718?

$29.36

23. On what date did check 717 clear the bank?

7/7

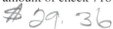

Community First Bank

2177 Germantown Rd. South • Germantown, Tennessee 38138 • (901) 555-2400 • Member FDIC

Tree Top Landscape Service
31125 Forest Hill-Irene Rd
Collierville, TN 38017

ACCOUNT NUMBER   25-39042
FEDERAL ID NUMBER   32-1186387

DATE 8/2/xx   PAGE 1

		BALANCE OF YOUR FUNDS
PREVIOUS BALANCE -----		$4,782.96
	DEPOSITS TOTALING	725.00
	WITHDRAWALS TOTALING	532.46
NEW BALANCE -----------		$4,975.50

ACCOUNT TRANSACTIONS FOR THE PERIOD FROM 7/3/xx THROUGH 8/2/xx

DATE	AMOUNT	DESCRIPTION
7/3	200.00	Deposit
7/5	175.00	Deposit
7/9	50.00	Deposit
7/15	300.00	Deposit
7/20	80.00	Withdrawal - ATM 5172 Poplar Ave
7/25	21.17	Check Order

DATE	CHECK #	AMOUNT	DATE	CHECK #	AMOUNT
7/5	716	90.23	7/15	719	238.00
7/7	717	42.78	7/22	720	30.92
7/12	718	29.36			

CHECKING DAILY BALANCE SUMMARY

DATE	BALANCE OF YOUR FUNDS	DATE	BALANCE OF YOUR FUNDS
7/3	4,982.96	7/15	5,107.59
7/5	5,067.73	7/20	5,027.59
7/7	5,024.95	7/22	4,996.67
7/9	5,074.95	7/25	4,975.50
7/12	5,045.59	8/2	4,975.50

Enrique Anglade's bank statement is shown below.

24. How many deposits were made during the month?

3

25. What amount of service charge was paid?

$12.50

26. What was the amount of the smallest check written?

$82.75

27. How many checks appear on the bank statement?

3

28. What is the balance at the beginning of the statement period?

1,034.10

29. What is the balance at the end of the statement period? $2,583.87

30. What is the amount of check 5375?

$82.75

31. On what date did check 5376 clear the bank?

4/8

Community First Bank

2177 Germantown Rd. South • Germantown, Tennessee 38138 • (901) 555-2400 • Member FDIC

Enrique Anglade
1901 Jones Drive
Miami, FL

ACCOUNT NUMBER   32-123-32
SOCIAL SECURITY NUMBER   123-34-5634

DATE 4/30/xx   PAGE 1

		BALANCE OF YOUR FUNDS
PREVIOUS BALANCE -----		1,034.10
3	DEPOSITS TOTALING	2,500.00
4	WITHDRAWALS TOTALING	962.73
NEW BALANCE -----------		2,571.37

ACCOUNT TRANSACTIONS FOR THE PERIOD FROM 4/1/xx THROUGH 4/30/xx

DATE	AMOUNT	DESCRIPTION
4/1	850.00	Deposit - Walgreens 237875
4/3	800.00	Deposit - Walgreens 237875
4/15	850.00	Deposit - Walgreens 237875
4/30	12.50	Service Fee

DATE	CHECK #	AMOUNT
4/5	5374	647.53
4/5	5375	82.75
4/8	5376	219.95

CHECKING DAILY BALANCE SUMMARY

DATE	BALANCE OF YOUR FUNDS	DATE	BALANCE OF YOUR FUNDS
4/1	1,884.10	4/8	1,733.87
4/3	2,684.10	4/15	2,583.87
4/5	1,953.92	4/30	2,571.37

The bank statement for Tracie Burke's Apparel Shop is shown below.

32. How many deposits were made during the month?

3

33. What amount of interest was earned?

$5.83

34. How much were the total deposits?

$8213.00

35. How many checks appear on the bank statement?

5

36. What is the balance at the beginning of the statement period?

$700.81

37. What is the balance at the end of the statement period?

$3,485.73

38. What is the amount of check 8214?

$490.00

39. On what date did check 8219 clear the bank?

6/20

Community First Bank

2177 Germantown Rd. South • Germantown, Tennessee 38138 • (901) 555-2400 • Member FDIC

TRACIE BURKE'S APPAREL SHOP
1396 MALL OF AMERICA
MINNEAPOLIS, MN

ACCOUNT NUMBER   12-324134523
FEDERAL ID NUMBER   33-35462445   DATE 6/30/XX   PAGE 1

			BALANCE OF YOUR FUNDS
PREVIOUS BALANCE -----			700.81
	4	DEPOSITS TOTALING	8,218.83
	6	WITHDRAWALS TOTALING	5,433.91
NEW BALANCE ----------			3,485.73

ACCOUNT TRANSACTIONS FOR THE PERIOD FROM 6/1/XX THROUGH 6/30/XX

DATE	AMOUNT	DESCRIPTION
6/1	1,830.00	DEPOSIT
6/5	2,583.00	DEPOSIT
6/15	3,800.00	DEPOSIT
6/30	.83	FDIC INSURANCE
6/30	5.83	INTEREST EARNED

DATE	CHECK #	AMOUNT	DATE	CHECK #	AMOUNT
6/2	8213	647.93	6/12	8217*	416.83
6/3	8214	490.00	6/20	8219*	3,150.00
6/5	8215	728.32			*2000.00*

CHECKING DAILY BALANCE SUMMARY

DATE	BALANCE OF YOUR FUNDS	DATE	BALANCE OF YOUR FUNDS
6/1	2,530.81	6/12	2,830.73
6/2	1,882.88	6/15	6,630.73
6/3	1,392.88	6/20	3,480.73
6/5	3,247.56	6/30	3,485.73

6/5 –2000.00
148573

40. Tree Top Landscape's account register is shown below. Reconcile the bank statement (see Exercises 16–23) with the account register.

RECORD ALL TRANSACTIONS THAT AFFECT YOUR ACCOUNT

NUMBER	DATE	DESCRIPTION OF TRANSACTION	DEBIT (-)	√ T	FEE (IF ANY) (-)	CREDIT (+)	BALANCE
							4,782 96
716	7/1	Dabney Nursery	90 23	√			4,692 73
717	7/3	Office Max	42 78	√			4,649 95
Deposit	7/3	Louis Lechlerter	-			200 00	4,849 95
Deposit	7/5	Tony Trim				175 00	5,024 95
Deposit	7/9	Dale Crosby				50 00	5,074 95
718	7/10	Texaco Gas	29 36	√			5,045 59
719	7/10	Nation's Bank	238 00	√			4,807 59
Deposit	7/15	Bobby Cornelius				300 00	5,107 59
ATM	7/20	Withdrawl Branch	80 00	√			5,027 59
720	7/20	AT&T	30 92	√			4,996 67
	7/25	Check order					21.17
		bank Reconciled					4975.50

REMEMBER TO RECORD AUTOMATIC PAYMENTS/DEPOSITS ON DATE AUTHORIZED.

41. Enrique Anglade's account register is shown below. Reconcile the bank statement (see Exercises 24–31) with the account register.

RECORD ALL TRANSACTIONS THAT AFFECT YOUR ACCOUNT

NUMBER	DATE	DESCRIPTION OF TRANSACTION	DEBIT (-)	√ T	FEE (IF ANY) (-)	CREDIT (+)	BALANCE
							1,034 10
Deposit	4/1	Payroll				850 00	1,884 10
Deposit	4/3	Payroll - Bonus				800 00	2,684 10
5374	4/3	First Union Mortgage Co.	647 53	√			2,036 57
5375	4/3	South Florida Utility	82 75	√			1,953 82
5376	4/5	First Federal Credit Union	219 95	√			1,733 87
5377	4/15	Banc Boston	510 48				1,223 39
Deposit	4/15	Payroll				850 00	2,073 39
5378	4/20	Northwest Air lines	403 21				1,670 18
5379	4/26	Auto Zone	18 97				1,651 21
ATM	5/4	Cordova Branch	100 00				1,551 21
	4/30	Service fee	12.50	√			1538.71
		bank Reconciled					1538.71

REMEMBER TO RECORD AUTOMATIC PAYMENTS/DEPOSITS ON DATE AUTHORIZED.

42. The account register for Tracie Burke's Apparel Shop is shown below. Reconcile the bank statement (see Exercises 32–39) with the account register.

NUMBER	DATE	DESCRIPTION OF TRANSACTION	DEBIT (−)	√T	FEE (IF ANY) (−)	CREDIT (+)	BALANCE 700	81
8213	5/28	Lands End	647 93	√			52	88
Deposit	6/1	Receipts		√		1,830 00	1,882	88
8214	6/1	Collier Management Co.	490 00	√			1,392	88
8215	6/3	Jinkins Wholesale	728 32	√			664	56
Deposit	6/5	Receipts		√		2583 00	3,247	56
8216	6/5	Minneapolis Utility Co.	257 13	√			2,990	43
8217	6/10	State of MN	416 83	√			2,573	60
8218	6/15	Receipts				3,800 00	6,373	60
8219	6/15	Tracie Burke Salary	2,000 00				4,373	60
8220	6/20	Brown's Wholesale	3,150 00	√			1,223	60
Deposit	7/2	Receipts				1,720 00	2,943	60
	6/30	FDIC Insurance		√	83		2,942	77
	6/30	Interest Earned				5 83	2,948	60
	6/30	Statement Reconciled						

RECORD ALL TRANSACTIONS THAT AFFECT YOUR ACCOUNT

REMEMBER TO RECORD AUTOMATIC PAYMENTS/DEPOSITS ON DATE AUTHORIZED.

43. The July bank statement for A & H Iron Works shows a balance of $37.94 and a service charge of $8.00. The account register shows deposits of $650 and $375.56 that do not appear on the statement. Checks in the amounts of $217.45, $57.82, $17.45, and $58.62 are outstanding. The register balance before reconciliation is $720.16. Reconcile the bank statement with the account register.

44. The September bank statement for Dixon Fence Company shows a balance of $275.25 and a service charge of $7.50. The account register shows deposits of $120.43 and $625.56 that do not appear on the statement. Checks in the amounts of $144.24, $154.48, $24.17, and $18.22 are outstanding. A $100 ATM withdrawal does not appear on the statement. The register balance before reconciliation is $587.63. Reconcile the bank statement with the account register.

45. Taylor Flowers' bank statement shows a balance of $135.42 and a service charge of $8.00. The account register shows deposits of $112.88 and $235.45 that do not appear on the statement. The register shows outstanding checks in the amounts of $17.42 and $67.90 and two cleared checks recorded in the account register as $145.69 and $18.22. The two cleared checks actually were written for and shown on the statement as $145.96 and $18.22. The register balance before reconciliation is $406.70. Reconcile the bank statement with the account register.

46. The bank statement for Randazzo's Market shows a balance of $1,102.35 and a service charge of $6.50. The account register shows a deposit of $265.49 that does not appear on the statement. The account register shows outstanding checks in the amounts of $617.23 and $456.60 and two cleared checks recorded as $45.71 and $348.70. The two cleared checks actually were written for $45.71 and $384.70. The register balance before reconciliation is $336.51. Reconcile the bank statement with the account register.

47. Terry Kelly (whom we met in Chapter 1) talked with her investment counselor. She was advised to calculate her current net worth and to project her 1997 net worth to determine if her 1997 budget would accomplish her objective of increasing her net worth. She listed the following assets and liabilities for 1996. To calculate her net worth she found the difference between total assets and total liabilities.

ASSETS:

Checking Account	2,099	
Savings Account	2,821	
Auto	10,500	
Home and Furnishings	65,000 × .04	
Stocks and Bonds	4,017	
Other Personal Property	3,200	
Total assets	*87,637*	

LIABILITIES:

Car Loan	8,752	6,652
Home mortgage	54,879	53,992
Personal loan	1,791	0
Total liabilities	*65,422*	*60,644*

Terry's home appreciated (increased) in value by 0.04 times the 1996 value while her car depreciated (decreased) in value by 0.125 times the 1996 value. Her car loan decreased by $2,100 while her home mortgage balance decreased by $887. Kelly plans to pay her personal loan in full by the end of 1997. Of her $2,000 planned investment, she will place $1,000 in savings and $1,000 in stocks and bonds. She also plans to reinvest the interest income of $141 (in savings) and the dividend income of $364 (in stocks and bonds) earned in 1996. She projects her checking account balance will be $1,500 at year-end for 1997.

Calculate Terry's total assets and total liabilities for 1996. Then calculate her net worth for 1996. Use the information given to project Terry's assets and liabilities for 1997. Then project her 1997 net worth. How much does Terry expect her net worth to increase (or decrease) from 1996 to 1997?

CHAPTER 2 PRACTICE TEST

1. Fill out the check stub provided. The balance brought forward is $2,301.42, deposits were made for $200 on May 12 and $83.17 on May 20, and check 195 was written on May 25 to Lon Associates for $152.50 for supplies.

0195	Date_____ 19____
Amount _____	
To _____	
For _____	

Balance Forward		
Deposits		
Total		
Amount This Check		
Balance		

D. G. Hernandez Equipment's bank statement is shown below.

2. What is the balance at the beginning of the statement period?

3. How many checks cleared the bank during the statement period?

4. What was the service charge for the statement period?

5. Check 3786 was written for what amount?

6. On what date did check 3788 clear the account?

7. What was the total of the deposits?

8. What was the balance at the end of the statement period?

9. What was the total amount for all checks written during the period?

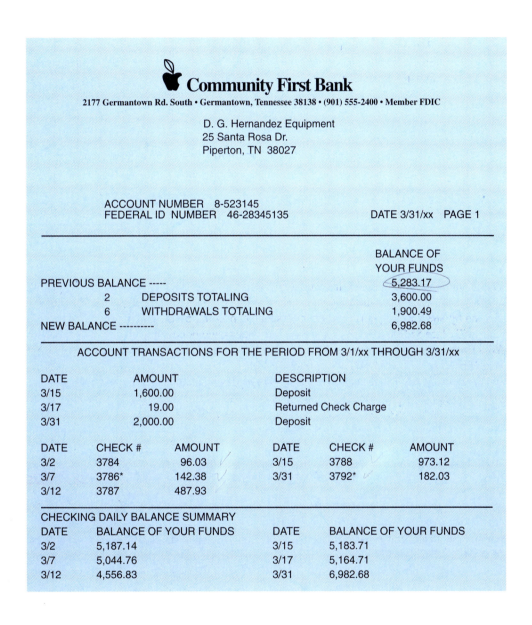

Community First Bank

2177 Germantown Rd. South • Germantown, Tennessee 38138 • (901) 555-2400 • Member FDIC

D. G. Hernandez Equipment
25 Santa Rosa Dr.
Piperton, TN 38027

ACCOUNT NUMBER   8-523145
FEDERAL ID NUMBER   46-28345135   DATE 3/31/xx   PAGE 1

		BALANCE OF YOUR FUNDS
PREVIOUS BALANCE -----		5,283.17
2	DEPOSITS TOTALING	3,600.00
6	WITHDRAWALS TOTALING	1,900.49
NEW BALANCE ---------		6,982.68

ACCOUNT TRANSACTIONS FOR THE PERIOD FROM 3/1/xx THROUGH 3/31/xx

DATE	AMOUNT	DESCRIPTION
3/15	1,600.00	Deposit
3/17	19.00	Returned Check Charge
3/31	2,000.00	Deposit

DATE	CHECK #	AMOUNT	DATE	CHECK #	AMOUNT
3/2	3784	96.03	3/15	3788	973.12
3/7	3786*	142.38	3/31	3792*	182.03
3/12	3787	487.93			

CHECKING DAILY BALANCE SUMMARY

DATE	BALANCE OF YOUR FUNDS	DATE	BALANCE OF YOUR FUNDS
3/2	5,187.14	3/15	5,183.71
3/7	5,044.76	3/17	5,164.71
3/12	4,556.83	3/31	6,982.68

10. Hernandez Equipment's account register is shown below. Reconcile the bank statement (see test question 9) with the account register.

		RECORD ALL TRANSACTIONS THAT AFFECT YOUR ACCOUNT						
NUMBER	DATE	DESCRIPTION OF TRANSACTION	DEBIT (−)	√ T	FEE (IF ANY) (−)	CREDIT (+)	BALANCE 5,283 17	
3784	2/27		96 03 √				5,187	14
3785	3/5		346 18				4,840	95
3786	3/5		142 38 √				4,698	58
3787	3/11		487 93 √				4,210	65
3788	3/11		973 12 √				3,237	53
3789	3/15		72 83				3,164	70
Dep.	3/15					1,600 00	4,764	70
3790	3/17		146 17				4,618	53
3791	3/20		152 03				4,466	50
3792	3/31		182 08				4,284	42
Deposit	3/31					2,000 00	6,284	42
		returned √ crg.	19.00					
			.10				626.47	

REMEMBER TO RECORD AUTOMATIC PAYMENTS/DEPOSITS ON DATE AUTHORIZED.

11. Before reconciliation, an account register balance is $1,817.93. The bank statement balance is $860.21. A service fee of $15 and one returned item of $213.83 were charged against the account. Deposits in the amounts of $800 and $412.13 are outstanding. Checks written for $243.17, $167.18, $13.97, $42.12, and $16.80 are outstanding. Reconcile the bank statement with the account register.

2424.26   860.21   1,817.93

Deposits   800.00   Fee   15.00
          +412.13   213.83
          1,212.13   228.83

        √'s 243.17
             167.18
             13.97
             42.12
             16.80
             483.24
           1,941.02

PROBLEM SOLVING WITH FRACTIONS AND PERCENTS

GOOD DECISIONS THROUGH TEAMWORK

Over the course of one week, each time you see a fraction or percent being used outside of the classroom, take note of it, describing the situation and the use being made of percent or fraction. For instance, you notice a grocery store advertises a half-off sale; or you see that your bank charges $9\frac{1}{2}\%$ interest on car loans; or you prepare a recipe calling for $4\frac{1}{2}$ tablespoons of sugar.

With your team, make a master list of situations, eliminating duplications. For each situation on your master list, discuss why a fraction or percent is used rather than a whole number. Discuss too why a fraction is used rather than a percent, or a percent rather than a fraction.

On the basis of your discussion, identify major categories of the use of fractions and percents. How many of these categories could apply to a business setting? Give a business-related example for each category your team judges to be business-related. Choose a team member to share the results of your discussion with the class.

CHAPTER 3 PROBLEM SOLVING WITH FRACTIONS AND PERCENTS

3.1 Problem Solving with Fractions

1. *Identify types of fractions*
2. *Change a fraction to an equivalent fraction*
3. *Add and subtract fractions and mixed numbers*
4. *Multiply and divide fractions and mixed numbers*
5. *Write a decimal as a fraction and write a fraction as a decimal*

3.2 Problem Solving with Percents

1. *Write a whole number, fraction, or decimal as a percent*
2. *Write a percent as a whole number, fraction, or decimal*
3. *Use the percentage formula to find the percentage*
4. *Use the percentage formula to find the base*
5. *Use the percentage formula to find the rate*

3.1 Problem Solving with Fractions

1. *Identify types of fractions*
2. *Change a fraction to an equivalent fraction*
3. *Add and subtract fractions and mixed numbers*
4. *Multiply and divide fractions and mixed numbers*
5. *Write a decimal as a fraction and write a fraction as a decimal*

In Chapter 1 we represented parts of whole items by using decimal notation. While decimal notation is the most common way to represent fractional parts in the business world, fraction notation is also used for some applications.

1 *Identifying Types of Fractions*

We use fractions as another way to represent numbers. The fraction format is also used to represent two relationships between numbers. The first relationship is the relationship between a part and a whole. If one whole quantity has four equal parts, then 1 of the four parts is represented by the fraction $\frac{1}{4}$.

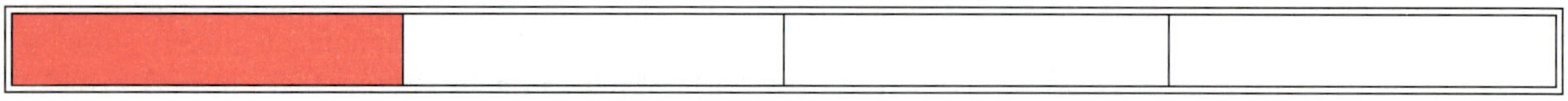

Figure 3–1 One part out of 4 parts is $\frac{1}{4}$ of the whole.

Another relationship represented by fractions is the relationship of division. The fraction $\frac{1}{4}$ can be interpreted as $1 \div 4$ which is 0.25.

In the fraction $\frac{1}{4}$, 4 represents the number of parts contained in one whole quantity and is called the **denominator.** When the fraction is interpreted as division, the denominator is the divisor. The 1 in the fraction $\frac{1}{4}$ represents the number of parts under consideration and is called the **numerator.** When the fraction is interpreted as division, the numerator is the dividend.

The line separating the numerator and denominator may be written as a horizontal line (—) or as a slash (/) and is called the **fraction line.** When the fraction is interpreted as division, the fraction line is interpreted as the division symbol.

When a fraction has a value less than one it is called a **proper fraction.**

Example 1 Visualize the fraction to identify whether it is a proper fraction. Describe the relationship between the numerator and denominator of proper fractions.

a. $\frac{2}{5}$ b. $\frac{3}{2}$ c. $\frac{4}{4}$ d. $\frac{1}{3}$

a. 2 parts out of 5 parts

The fraction $\frac{2}{5}$ is a proper fraction since it is less than one whole quantity.

b. 3 parts when the one whole quantity contains 2 parts

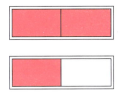

The fraction $\frac{3}{2}$ represents more than one whole quantity. It is not a proper fraction.

c. 4 parts when the whole contains 4 parts

The fraction $\frac{4}{4}$ represents one whole quantity. It is not a proper fraction.

d. 1 part when the whole contains 3 parts

The fraction $\frac{1}{3}$ is a proper fraction since it represents less than one whole quantity.

The fractions $\frac{2}{5}$ and $\frac{1}{3}$ are proper fractions. In a proper fraction, the numerator is *less than* **the denominator.**

Proper fractions are used in various business situations. For example, Dobbs Ford dealership has 125 cars on their lot. Of these, 12 are Crown Victoria cars. The number 125 is the number of items (cars) contained in one whole quantity (dealership). The number 12 is the number of items (Crown Victoria cars) being considered or used. The fraction showing the relationship between the number of Crown Victoria cars and the total number of cars on the lot is $\frac{12}{125}$.

When a fraction has a value equal to or more than one, it is called an **improper fraction.**

Example 2 Which fractions in Example 1 are improper fractions? Describe the relationship between the numerator and denominator of improper fractions.

The fractions $\frac{3}{2}$ and $\frac{4}{4}$ are improper fractions. In an improper fraction, the numerator is equal to or more than the denominator.

In Example 1b, the fraction $\frac{3}{2}$ was shown as one whole quantity and $\frac{1}{2}$ of a second quantity. This amount, $\frac{3}{2}$, can also be written as $1\frac{1}{2}$. When an amount is written as a combination of a whole number and a fraction, it is called a **mixed number.** Thus, numbers like $1\frac{1}{2}$ are called mixed numbers. Every mixed number can also be written as an improper fraction.

Improper fractions are used as a convenience in making some calculations. To interpret the meaning of an improper fraction, we would use its whole number or mixed number equivalent. Thus, it is important to be able to convert between these two forms.

HOW TO	**Write an Improper Fraction as a Whole or Mixed Number**

Step 1 Divide the numerator of the improper fraction by the denominator.
Step 2 Examine the remainder.
    a) If the remainder is 0, the quotient is a whole number: The improper fraction is equivalent to this whole number.
    b) If the remainder is not 0, the quotient is not a whole number: The improper fraction is equivalent to a mixed number. The whole number part of this mixed number is the whole-number part of the quotient. The fraction part of the mixed number has a numerator and a denominator. The numerator is the remainder; the denominator is the divisor (the denominator of the improper fraction).

Example 3 Write $\frac{139}{8}$ as a whole or mixed number.

$$
\begin{array}{r}
17 \text{ R3, or } 17\frac{3}{8} \\
8\overline{)139} \\
\underline{8} \\
59 \\
\underline{56} \\
3
\end{array}
$$

Divide 139 by 8. The quotient is 17 R3, which equals $17\frac{3}{8}$.

$$\frac{139}{8} = 17\frac{3}{8}$$

A mixed number can be written as an improper fraction by "reversing" the steps you use to write an improper fraction as a mixed number. For example, to write $3\frac{1}{5}$ as an improper fraction, imagine starting with the improper fraction and dividing to get $3\frac{1}{5}$:

$$\frac{?}{5} = 5\overline{)?}\,^{3 \text{ R1}} = 3\frac{1}{5}$$

The ? is the numerator of the improper fraction. The numerator must be 16, since $3 \times 5 + 1 = 16$:

$$
\begin{array}{r}
3 \text{ R1} \\
5\overline{)16} \\
\underline{15} \\
1
\end{array}
$$

The improper fraction is $\frac{16}{5}$. But how do we get 16? We multiply the whole number 3 by the denominator 5 and add 1.

$$3\frac{1}{5} = \frac{3 \times 5 + 1}{5} = \frac{16}{5}$$

Example 4   Write $2\frac{3}{4}$ as an improper fraction.

$$2\frac{3}{4} = \frac{(4 \times 2) + 3}{4} = \frac{11}{4}$$ For the numerator, multiply 4 by 2 and add 3.

Thus, $2\frac{3}{4}$ is $\frac{11}{4}$

A whole number can be written as an improper fraction by writing the whole number as the numerator and 1 as the denominator:

$$8 = \frac{8}{1}$$

② ▶ Equivalent Fractions

Many fractions represent the same portion of a whole. Such fractions are called **equivalent fractions.** For example, $\frac{1}{2}, \frac{2}{4}$, and $\frac{4}{8}$ are equivalent fractions.

Figure 3–2 Equivalent Fractions

Equivalent Fractions in Lowest Terms   To be able to recognize equivalent fractions, we often reduce fractions to lowest terms. A fraction in **lowest terms** has a numerator and denominator that can not be evenly divided by the same number except 1.

Step 1 Inspect the numerator and denominator to find any whole number that they both can be evenly divided by.

Step 2 Divide both the numerator and denominator by that number, and inspect the new fraction to find any other number that the numerator and denominator can be evenly divided by.

Step 3 Repeat steps 1 and 2 until there are no more numbers other than 1 that the numerator and denominator can be evenly divided by.

Example 5 Reduce $\frac{30}{36}$ to lowest terms.

$$\frac{30}{36} = \frac{30 \div 2}{36 \div 2} = \frac{15}{18}$$

Both the numerator and denominator can be divided evenly by 2.

$$\frac{15}{18} = \frac{15 \div 3}{18 \div 3} = \frac{5}{6}$$

Both the numerator and denominator of the new fraction can be divided evenly by 3.

Thus, $\frac{30}{36}$ in lowest terms is $\frac{5}{6}$.

There are no other numbers except 1 that both the numerator and denominator can be evenly divided by. The fraction is now in lowest terms.

The fastest way to reduce a fraction to lowest terms is to divide the numerator and denominator by the **greatest common divisor (GCD),** which is the greatest number by which both parts of a fraction can be evenly divided. Let's look at a helpful short-cut to finding the GCD.

Step 1 Divide the larger number by the smaller number.

Step 2 Divide the divisor from step 1 by the remainder from step 1.

Step 3 Divide the divisor from step 2 by the remainder from step 2.

Step 4 Continue this division process until the remainder is 0. The current divisor is the greatest common divisor.

Example 6 Use the GCD to write $\frac{168}{198}$ in lowest terms. First find the GCD.

$$168\overline{)198}\quad 1\ R\ 30$$

Divide the numerator into the denominator.

$$30\overline{)168}\quad 5\ R\ 18$$

Divide the original divisor by the original remainder.

$$18\overline{)30}\quad 1\ R\ 12$$

Divide the divisor of each previous division by the remainder of that division.

$$12\overline{)18}\quad 1\ R\ 6$$

$$6\overline{)12}\quad 2$$

When the remainder is 0, the divisor is the greatest common divisor.

Now reduce using the GCD.

$$\frac{168}{198} = \frac{168 \div 6}{198 \div 6} = \frac{28}{33}$$ Divide the numerator and denominator by the GCD.

Thus, $\frac{168}{198}$ in lowest terms is $\frac{28}{33}$.

Equivalent Fractions in Higher Terms   Just as you can reduce a fraction to lowest terms by dividing the numerator and denominator by the same number, you can build a fraction to *higher* terms by *multiplying* the numerator and denominator by the same number. This is important in addition and subtraction of fractions, as you shall see later in this chapter.

 **HOW TO**   **Build a Fraction to Higher Terms Given the New Denominator**

Step 1   Divide the *new* denominator by the *old* denominator.
Step 2   Multiply *both* the old numerator and denominator by the quotient from step 1.

Example 7   Rewrite $\frac{5}{8}$ as a fraction with a denominator of 72.

$$\frac{5}{8} = \frac{?}{72}$$ State the problem clearly.

$$8\overline{)72}^{\,9}$$ Divide the new denominator (72) by the old denominator (8) to find the number by which the old numerator and denominator must be multiplied. That number is 9.

$$\frac{5}{8} = \frac{5 \times 9}{8 \times 9} = \frac{45}{72}$$ Multiply the numerator and denominator by 9 to get the new fraction with a denominator of 72.

Thus, $\frac{5}{8} = \frac{45}{72}$.

 Adding and Subtracting Fractions and Mixed Numbers

Adding Fractions and Mixed Numbers   The statement that 3 calculators plus 4 typewriters is the same as 7 calculators is not true. The reason this is not true is that calculators and typewriters are *unlike* terms, and we can only add *like* terms. What *is* true is that 3 calculators plus 4 typewriters is the same as 7 office machines. What we have done is to *rename* calculators and typewriters using a like term. Both a calculator and a typewriter are office machines. In the same way, to add fractions that have different denominators, we must rename the fractions using a like, or common, denominator. When fractions have like denominators, we can write their sum as a single fraction.

| ? | **HOW TO** | **Add Fractions with Like Denominators** |

Step 1 Find the numerator of the sum: Add the numerators of the addends.
Step 2 Find the denominator of the sum: Use the like denominator of the addends.
Step 3 Reduce to lowest terms and/or write as a whole or mixed number.

Example 8 Find the sum: $\frac{1}{4} + \frac{3}{4} + \frac{4}{4}$.

$$\frac{1}{4} + \frac{3}{4} + \frac{4}{4} = \frac{1+3+4}{4} = \frac{8}{4}$$

The sum of the numerators is the numerator of the sum. The original like denominator is the denominator of the sum.

$$\frac{8}{4} = 2$$

Convert the improper fraction to a whole number.

The sum is 2.

To add fractions with different denominators, first find their **least common denominator (LCD)**—the smallest number that can be divided evenly by each original denominator.

To find a common denominator, you can use *prime numbers*. A **prime number** is a number greater than 1 that can be divided evenly only by itself and 1. The first ten prime numbers are 2, 3, 5, 7, 11, 13, 17, 19, 23, and 29.

| ? | **HOW TO** | **Find the Least Common Denominator of Two or More Fractions** |

Step 1 Write the denominators in a row and divide each one by the smallest prime number that any of the numbers can be evenly divided by.
Step 2 Write a new row of numbers using the quotients from step 1 and any numbers in the first row that cannot be evenly divided by the first prime number.
Step 3 Continue this process until you have a row of 1s.
Step 4 Multiply all the prime numbers you used to divide by. The product is the least common denominator.

Example 9 Find the least common denominator of $\frac{5}{6}$, $\frac{5}{8}$, and $\frac{1}{12}$.

$$
\begin{array}{r}
2\overline{)6 \quad 8 \quad 12} \\
2\overline{)3 \quad 4 \quad 6} \\
2\overline{)3 \quad 2 \quad 3} \\
3\overline{)3 \quad 1 \quad 3} \\
1 \quad 1 \quad 1
\end{array}
$$

Find the LCD: Write the denominators in a row and divide by 2, which is the smallest prime number.

Repeat the division with 2 until none of the numbers can be evenly divided by 2. 3 is not evenly divisible by 2, so we bring 3 down to the next row, and use the next prime number, 3.

$$2 \times 2 \times 2 \times 3 = 24$$ The LCD is the product of all the prime numbers used.

The LCD is 24.

Now that you know how to find a common denominator, we can add fractions with different denominators.

	HOW TO	Add Fractions with Different Denominators

Step 1 Find the least common denominator.
Step 2 Change each fraction to an equivalent fraction using the least common denominator.
Step 3 Add the new fractions with like denominators.

Example 10 Find the sum of $\frac{5}{6}$, $\frac{5}{8}$, and $\frac{1}{12}$.

We saw in Example 9 that the least common denominator for these fractions is 24. Change each fraction to an equivalent fraction that has a denominator of 24.

$$\frac{5}{6} = \frac{5 \times 4}{6 \times 4} = \frac{20}{24}$$

$$\frac{5}{8} = \frac{5 \times 3}{8 \times 3} = \frac{15}{24}$$

$$\frac{1}{12} = \frac{1 \times 2}{12 \times 2} = \frac{2}{25}$$

$$\frac{20}{24} + \frac{15}{24} + \frac{2}{24} = \frac{20 + 15 + 2}{24} = \frac{37}{24}$$

Add the fractions with like denominators: add numerators and use the common denominator.

$$\frac{37}{24} = 1\frac{13}{24}$$

Change the improper fraction to a mixed number.

The sum is $1\frac{13}{24}$.

Example 11 Add $3\frac{2}{5} + 10\frac{3}{10} + 4\frac{7}{15}$.

Add the fraction parts first.

Step 1

Find the LCD.

Step 2

Change the fractions to equivalent fractions using the LCD.

Step 3

Add the fractions with like denominators.

$$\begin{array}{r} 2\overline{)5 \quad 10 \quad 15} \\ 3\overline{)5 \quad 5 \quad 15} \\ 5\overline{)5 \quad 5 \quad 5} \\ 1 \quad 1 \quad 1 \end{array}$$

$$\frac{2}{5} = \frac{?}{30} \quad 5\overline{)30}^{\,6}$$

$$\frac{2}{5} = \frac{2 \times 6}{5 \times 6} = \frac{12}{30}$$

$$\frac{12}{30} + \frac{9}{30} + \frac{14}{30} = \frac{35}{30}$$

$$2 \times 3 \times 5 = 30$$

$$\frac{3}{10} = \frac{?}{30} \quad 10\overline{)30}^{\,3}$$

$$\frac{3}{10} = \frac{3 \times 3}{10 \times 3} = \frac{9}{30}$$

$$\frac{35}{30} = \frac{7}{6} = 1\frac{1}{6}$$

The LCD is 30.

$$\frac{7}{15} = \frac{?}{30} \quad 15\overline{)30}^{\,2}$$

$$\frac{7}{15} = \frac{7 \times 2}{15 \times 2} = \frac{14}{30}$$

Now add the whole number parts.

$$3 + 10 + 4 = 17$$

Finally, add the whole number sum and the fraction sum:

$$17$$
$$+ \ 1\frac{1}{6}$$
$$\overline{18\frac{1}{6}}$$

The sum is $18\frac{1}{6}$.

Subtracting Fractions and Mixed Numbers   In subtracting fractions, just as in adding fractions, you need to find a common denominator.

 HOW TO   **Subtract Fractions**

With like denominators
Step 1   Find the numerator of the difference: Subtract the numerators of the fraction.
Step 2   Find the denominator of the difference: Use the like denominator.
Step 3   Reduce to lowest terms and/or write as a whole or mixed number.
With different denominators
Step 1   Find the least common denominator.
Step 2   Change each fraction to an equivalent fraction using the least common denominator.
Step 3   Subtract the new fractions with like denominators.

Example 12   Subtract: $\frac{5}{12} - \frac{4}{15}$.

The denominators are different.

Step 1	**Step 2**	**Step 3**
Find the LCD.	Change the fractions to equivalent fractions using the LCD.	Subtract numerators, and use the like denominator. Reduce to lowest terms.

Step 1:
$$\begin{array}{r|rr} 2 & 12 & 15 \\ 2 & 6 & 15 \\ 3 & 3 & 15 \\ 5 & 1 & 5 \\ & 1 & 1 \end{array}$$

$2 \times 2 \times 3 \times 5 = 60$

The LCD is 60.

Step 2:
$$\frac{5}{12} = \frac{5 \times 5}{12 \times 5} = \frac{25}{60}$$
$$\frac{4}{15} = \frac{4 \times 4}{15 \times 4} = \frac{16}{60}$$

Step 3:
$$\frac{25}{60} - \frac{16}{60} = \frac{9}{60}$$
$$\frac{9}{60} = \frac{3}{20}$$

The difference is $\frac{3}{20}$.

Subtracting mixed numbers is like subtracting fractions. First, be sure the fraction parts of the mixed numbers have like denominators.

? HOW TO	Subtract Mixed Numbers

Step 1 If the fractions have different denominators, find the LCD and change the fractions to equivalent fractions using the LCD.
Step 2 If necessary, borrow (subtract) 1 from the whole number in the minuend, and add 1 (in the form of LCD/LCD) to the fraction in the minuend.
Step 3 Subtract the fractions and the whole numbers.
Step 4 Reduce to lowest terms.

Example 13

Subtract $10\frac{1}{3} - 7\frac{3}{5}$.

$$10\frac{1}{3} = 10\frac{5}{15}$$

Convert both fractions to equivalent fractions with denominators of 15, the LCD.

$$-7\frac{3}{5} = 7\frac{9}{15}$$

$$10\frac{5}{15} = 9\frac{20}{15}$$

We cannot subtract $\frac{9}{15}$ from $\frac{5}{15}$, so we borrow 1 from 10, leaving 9. Write the borrowed 1 as $\frac{15}{15}$, and add it to $\frac{5}{15}$. Rewrite the problem to show the borrowing, and then subtract the whole numbers and the fractions.

$$-7\frac{9}{15} = 7\frac{9}{15}$$

$$2\frac{11}{15}$$

The fraction is already in lowest terms, so you do not have to reduce it.

The difference is $2\frac{11}{15}$.

4 ▶ *Multiplying and Dividing Fractions and Mixed Numbers*

Multiplying Fractions and Mixed Numbers Robert Palinchak has three Domino's Pizza stores. His distributor shipped only $\frac{3}{4}$ of a cheese order which Robert had expected to distribute equally among his three stores. What fractional part of the original order will each store receive?

Each store will receive $\frac{1}{3}$ of the *shipment*, but the shipment is only $\frac{3}{4}$ of the *original order*. Each store, then, will receive only $\frac{1}{3}$ of $\frac{3}{4}$ of the original order. Finding $\frac{1}{3}$ of $\frac{3}{4}$ illustrates the use of multiplying fractions, because—just as "2 boxes **of** 3 cans each" amounts to 2 × 3, or 6 cans, so too $\frac{1}{3}$ **of** $\frac{3}{4}$ amounts to $\frac{1}{3}$ × $\frac{3}{4}$.

We can visualize $\frac{1}{3} \times \frac{3}{4}$ or $\frac{1}{3}$ **of** $\frac{3}{4}$, by first visualizing $\frac{3}{4}$ of a whole.

Figure 3–3   3 parts out of 4 parts = $\frac{3}{4}$ of a whole

Now visualize $\frac{1}{3}$ of $\frac{3}{4}$ of a whole.

Figure 3–4   1 part out of 3 parts in $\frac{3}{4}$ of a whole = 1 part out of 4 parts or $\frac{1}{4}$ of a whole

Chapter 3   Problem Solving with Fractions and Percents   **91**

$$\frac{1}{3} \quad \text{of} \quad \frac{3}{4} \quad \text{is} \quad \frac{1}{4}$$

$$\frac{1}{3} \quad \times \quad \frac{3}{4} \quad = \quad \frac{1}{4}$$

❓ HOW TO — Multiply Fractions

Step 1 Find the numerator of the product: Multiply the numerators of the fractions.

Step 2 Find the denominator of the product: Multiply the denominators of the fractions.

Step 3 Reduce to lowest terms.

---

1 Decision needed

2 **Unknown fact**

3 **Known facts**

4 **Relationships**

5 **Estimation**

6 **Calculation**

7 **Decision made**

Example 14 What fraction of the original cheese order will each of Robert's three stores receive equally if $\frac{9}{10}$ of the original order is shipped?

Fraction of original shipment that each store will receive equally

Fraction of shipment each store can receive: $\frac{1}{3}$
Fraction of original order received for all the stores $= \frac{9}{10}$

Fraction of original order each store can receive = fraction of shipment each store can receive × fraction of original order received. Fraction of original order each store can receive $= \frac{1}{3} \times \frac{9}{10}$.

Since the shipment is slightly less than the original order, each stores receives slightly less than $\frac{1}{3}$ of the original order. Thus, the fraction of the original order that each store will receive is slightly less than $\frac{1}{3}$.

$$\frac{1}{3} \times \frac{9}{10} = \frac{1 \cdot 9}{3 \cdot 10} = \frac{9}{30}$$ **Multiple numerators; multiply denominators.**

$$\frac{9}{30} = \frac{3}{10}$$ **Reduce to lowest terms.**

Each store will receive $\frac{3}{10}$ of the original order.

⚠ TIPS & TRAPS

When you multiply fractions, you save time by reducing fractions *before* you multiply them. If *any* numerator and *any* denominator can be divided evenly by the same number, divide both the numerator and the denominator by that number. You can then multiply the reduced numbers faster and with greater accuracy than you could multiply the larger numbers.

$$\frac{1}{3} \times \frac{3}{4} = \frac{1}{4}$$ **A numerator and a denominator can be divided evenly by 3.**

Chapter 3   Problem Solving with Fractions and Percents

To multiply mixed numbers and whole numbers, change the mixed numbers and whole numbers to fractions.

> **? HOW TO** | **Multiply Mixed Numbers and Whole Numbers**
>
> **Step 1** Write the mixed numbers and whole numbers as improper fractions.
> **Step 2** Reduce numerators and denominators as appropriate.
> **Step 3** Multiply the fractions.
> **Step 4** Reduce to lowest terms and/or write as a whole or mixed number.

Example 15 Multiply $2\frac{1}{3} \times 3\frac{3}{4}$.

$$2\frac{1}{3} \times 3\frac{3}{4} = \frac{(3 \times 2) + 1}{3} \times \frac{(4 \times 3) + 3}{4} =$$

Write the mixed numbers as improper fractions.

$$\frac{7}{3} \times \frac{\overset{5}{15}}{4} = \frac{35}{4}$$

Divide both 3 and 15 by 3, reducing to 1 and 5. Multiply the numerators and denominators.

$$\frac{35}{4} = 8\frac{3}{4}$$

Write as a mixed number.

The product is $8\frac{3}{4}$.

> **⚠ TIPS & TRAPS**
>
> A product is not always greater than the factors being multiplied.
>   When the multiplier is a proper fraction, the product is *less than* the original number. This is true when the multiplicand is a whole number, fraction, or mixed number.
>
> $$5 \times \frac{3}{5} = 3 \qquad \text{3 is less than 5}$$
>
> $$\frac{3}{4} \times \frac{4}{9} = \frac{1}{3} \qquad \frac{1}{3} \text{ is less than } \frac{3}{4}$$
>
> $$2\frac{1}{2} \times \frac{1}{2} = \frac{5}{2} \times \frac{1}{2} = \frac{5}{4} = 1\frac{1}{4} \qquad 1\frac{1}{4} \text{ is less than } 2\frac{1}{2}$$

Dividing Fractions and Mixed Numbers Division of fractions is related to multiplication. *Total amount = number of units of a specified size times (×) the specified size.* If you know the total amount and the number of equal units, you can find the size by dividing the total amount by the number of equal units. If you know the total amount and the specified size, you can find the number of equal units by dividing the total amount by the specified size.

Central Hardware has a stack of plywood that is 32 inches high. If each sheet of plywood is $\frac{1}{2}$ inch, how many sheets of plywood are in the stack? We are trying to determine how many equal units of plywood are contained in the total stack, so we divide the height of the stack (total amount) by the thickness of each sheet (specified size).

$$32 \div \frac{1}{2}$$

Another way of approaching the problem is to think of the number of sheets of plywood in one inch of height. If each sheet of plywood is $\frac{1}{2}$ inch, then two sheets of plywood are one inch thick. If there are 2 sheets of plywood for each inch, there will be 64 pieces of plywood in the stack.

$$32 \div \frac{1}{2} = 32 \times \frac{2}{1} = 64$$

The relationship between multiplication and division of fractions involves a concept called **reciprocals.** Two numbers are reciprocals if their product is 1. Thus, $\frac{2}{3}$ and $\frac{3}{2}$ are reciprocals ($\frac{2}{3} \times \frac{3}{2} = 1$) and $\frac{7}{8}$ and $\frac{8}{7}$ are reciprocals ($\frac{7}{8} \times \frac{8}{7} = 1$).

? HOW TO   Find the Reciprocal of a Number

Step 1 Write the number as a fraction.
Step 2 Interchange the numerator and denominator.

Example 16 Find the reciprocal of   a. $\frac{7}{9}$ b. 5   c. $4\frac{1}{2}$

a. The reciprocal of $\frac{7}{9}$ is $\frac{9}{7}$.

b. Write 5 as the fraction $\frac{5}{1}$. The reciprocal of $\frac{5}{1}$ is $\frac{1}{5}$.

c. Write $4\frac{1}{2}$ as the fraction $\frac{9}{2}$. The reciprocal of $\frac{9}{2}$ is $\frac{2}{9}$.

In the Central Hardware discussion, we reasoned that $32 \div \frac{1}{2}$ is the same as 32×2. That is, to divide by a fraction, we *multiply* by the *reciprocal* of the divisor.

? HOW TO   Divide Fractions or Mixed Numbers

Step 1 Write numbers as fractions.
Step 2 Find the reciprocal of the divisor.
Step 3 Multiply the dividend by the reciprocal of the divisor.
Step 4 Reduce to lowest terms and/or write as a whole or mixed number.

Example 17 Madison Duke makes appliqués from brocade fabric. A customer has ordered five appliqués. Can Madison fill the order without buying more fabric? She has $\frac{3}{4}$ yard of fabric and each appliqué requires $\frac{1}{6}$ of a yard.

1 Decision needed

Can Madison fill the order?

2 Unknown fact

The number of appliqués that can be made from the fabric.

3 Known facts

Total length of fabric: $\frac{3}{4}$ yard
Length of fabric needed for each appliqué: $\frac{1}{6}$ yard

4 Relationships

Number of appliqués = total length of fabric ÷ length of fabric needed for each appliqué

$$\text{Number of appliqués} = \frac{3}{4} \div \frac{1}{6}$$

5 Estimation

It takes $\frac{1}{6}$ yard to make one appliqué, so one yard makes six appliqués. Since she has less than one yard, she can make fewer than six appliqués.

Chapter 3   Problem Solving with Fractions and Percents

6 Calculation

Number of appliqués $= \dfrac{3}{4} \div \dfrac{1}{6}$

$$= \dfrac{3}{4} \times \dfrac{6}{1}$$

$$= \dfrac{18}{4} = \dfrac{9}{2} = 4\dfrac{1}{2}$$

Madison can make 4 complete appliqués from the $\frac{3}{4}$ yard of fabric.

7 Decision made

Since the order is five appliqués, **Madison cannot fill the order without buying more fabric.**

Example 18 Find the quotient: $5\frac{1}{2} \div 7\frac{1}{3}$

$5\dfrac{1}{2} = \dfrac{(2 \times 5) + 1}{2} = \dfrac{11}{2}$ **Write the numbers as fractions.**

$7\dfrac{1}{3} = \dfrac{(3 \times 7) + 1}{3} = \dfrac{22}{3}$ **The divisor is $\frac{22}{3}$. Its reciprocal is $\frac{3}{22}$.**

$\dfrac{11}{2} \div \dfrac{22}{3} =$

$\dfrac{\overset{1}{\cancel{11}}}{2} \times \dfrac{3}{\underset{2}{\cancel{22}}} = \dfrac{1 \cdot 3}{2 \cdot 2} = \dfrac{3}{4}$ **Multiply $\frac{11}{2}$ by the reciprocal of the divisor, $\frac{3}{22}$.**

The quotient is $\frac{3}{4}$.

5▶ *Writing a Decimal as a Fraction and a Fraction as a Decimal*

As we discussed in Chapter 1, decimals can represent parts of a whole, just as fractions can. We can write a decimal as a fraction, or a fraction as a decimal.

❓ HOW TO	Write a Decimal as a Fraction

Step 1 Find the denominator: Write 1 followed by as many zeros as there are places to the right of the decimal point.
Step 2 Find the numerator: use the digits without the decimal point.
Step 3 Reduce to lowest terms and/or write as a whole or mixed number.

Example 19 Change 0.38 to a fraction.

$\dfrac{38}{100}$ **The digits without the decimal point form the numerator. There are 2 places to the right of the decimal point, so the denominator is 1 followed by 2 zeros.**

$\dfrac{38}{100} = \dfrac{19}{50}$ **Reduce the fraction to lowest terms.**

Thus, 0.38 written as a fraction is $\frac{19}{50}$.

Fractions indicate division. Therefore, to write a fraction as a decimal, divide the numerator by the denominator, as you would divide decimals.

Step 1 Write the numerator as the dividend and the denominator as the divisor.
Step 2 Divide the numerator by the denominator, taking the division out as many places as necessary.

Example 20   Change $\frac{1}{4}$ to a decimal number.

$$
\begin{array}{r}
0.25 \\
4\overline{)1.00} \\
\underline{8} \\
20 \\
\underline{20}
\end{array}
$$

Divide the numerator by the denominator, adding zeros to the right of the decimal point as needed.

When the division comes out even (that is, there is no remainder), we say that the division terminates, and the quotient is called a **terminating decimal.** If, however, the division *never* comes out even (there is always a remainder), we call the number a **nonterminating** or **repeating decimal.** If the quotient is a repeating decimal, either write the quotient as a mixed decimal or rounded decimal.

Example 21   Write $\frac{2}{3}$ as a decimal number.

$$
\begin{array}{r}
0.66\frac{2}{3} \text{ or } 0.67 \text{ (rounded)} \\
3\overline{)2.00} \\
\underline{1\ 8} \\
20 \\
\underline{18} \\
2
\end{array}
$$

Thus, $\frac{2}{3} = 0.67$.

Self Check 3.1

1 ▶ *Classify the fractions as proper or improper.*

1. $\frac{5}{9}$ **2.** $\frac{12}{7}$ **3.** $\frac{7}{7}$ **4.** $\frac{1}{12}$

Write the fraction as a whole or mixed number.

5. $\frac{12}{7}$ **6.** $\frac{7}{7}$ **7.** $\frac{16}{8}$ **8.** $\frac{388}{16}$

Write the whole or mixed number as an improper fraction.

9. 6 **10.** $3\frac{4}{5}$ **11.** $1\frac{5}{8}$ **12.** $6\frac{2}{3}$

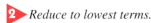

2 *Reduce to lowest terms.*

13. $\dfrac{12}{15}$

14. $\dfrac{18}{36}$

Change the fraction to an equivalent fraction with the given denominator.

15. $\dfrac{3}{8}, \dfrac{}{16}$

16. $\dfrac{5}{9}, \dfrac{}{27}$

3 *Perform the indicated operation. Write the sum as a fraction, whole number, or mixed number in lowest terms.*

17. $\dfrac{1}{9} + \dfrac{2}{9} + \dfrac{5}{9}$

18. $\dfrac{5}{8} + \dfrac{7}{12}$

19. $4\dfrac{5}{6} + 7\dfrac{1}{2}$

$$\dfrac{24}{\cancel{\;}}\qquad \dfrac{109}{15}\qquad \dfrac{15}{\;}$$
$$\dfrac{29}{6} + \dfrac{15}{2}\qquad \dfrac{124}{8} = 8\overline{\smash{)}124}$$
$$\dfrac{44}{40}$$
$$\dfrac{4}{8} \;\; 12\dfrac{1}{2}$$

20. Loretta McBride is decorating a house and determining the amount of fabric required for window treatments. She finds that a single window requires $11\dfrac{3}{4}$ yards and a double window requires $18\dfrac{5}{8}$ yards of fabric. If she has two single windows and one double window, how much fabric will be required?

Find the difference.

21. $\dfrac{8}{9} - \dfrac{2}{9}$

22. $\dfrac{3}{4} - \dfrac{5}{7}$

23. $9\dfrac{1}{2} - 6\dfrac{2}{3}$

$$\dfrac{19}{2}\qquad \dfrac{6}{6}\; \dfrac{9}{\;}$$
$$\dfrac{19}{2}\;20\qquad 9\dfrac{1}{2} = \dfrac{3+}{6}$$
$$6\dfrac{2}{3} = \dfrac{4}{6}\;\; \dfrac{5}{6}$$

24. The fabric Loretta McBride has selected for the window treatment in Exercise 20 has only 45 yards on the only roll available. Will she be able to use the fabric or must she make an alternate selection? If she can use the fabric, will she have enough left for throw pillows?

4 *Find the product.*

25. $\dfrac{5}{7} \times \dfrac{1}{6}$

26. $5\dfrac{3}{4} \times 3\dfrac{8}{9}$

27. $\dfrac{3}{8} \times 24$

28. Carl Heinrich has six lateral filing cabinets which need to be placed on one wall of a storage closet. The filing cabinets are each $3\dfrac{1}{2}$ feet wide and the wall is 21 feet long. Decide if all the cabinets can be placed on the wall.

Find the reciprocal.

29. $\dfrac{3}{5}$

30. 9

31. $3\dfrac{3}{8}$

Find the quotient.

32. $\frac{5}{8} \times \frac{3}{4}$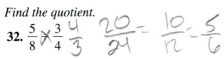

33. $5\frac{1}{4} \div 2\frac{2}{3}$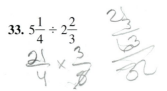

34. Terry Kelly is handling the estate of a prominent businesswoman. The will states that the surviving spouse is to receive $\frac{1}{4}$ of the estate and the remaining $\frac{3}{4}$ of the estate will be divided equally among five surviving children. What fraction of the estate does each child receive?

 35. Write 0.68 as a fraction in lowest terms.

36. Write 1.4 as a mixed number in lowest terms.

Write the number as a decimal. Round to hundredths if necessary.

37. $\frac{3}{4}$

38. $\frac{7}{8}$

39. $1\frac{3}{5}$

40. $\frac{3}{7}$

3.2 Problem Solving with Percents

1 ▸ *Write a whole number, fraction, or decimal as a percent*

2 ▸ *Write a percent as a whole number, fraction, or decimal*

3 ▸ *Use the percentage formula to find the percentage*

4 ▸ *Use the percentage formula to find the base*

5 ▸ *Use the percentage formula to find the rate*

With fractions and decimals, we compare only like quantities; that is fractions with common denominators and decimals with the same number of decimal places. We can standardize our representation of quantities so that they can be more easily compared. We standardize by expressing quantities in relation to a standard unit of 100. This relationship, called a **percent,** is used to solve many different types of business problems.

The word *percent* means *hundredths* or *out of 100* or *per 100* or *over 100* (in a fraction). That is, 44 percent means 44 hundredths, or 44 out of 100, or 44 per 100, or 44 over 100. We can write 44 hundredths as 0.44 or $\frac{44}{100}$.

The symbol for *percent* is %. You can write 44 percent using the percent symbol: 44%; using fractional notation: $\frac{44}{100}$; or using decimal notation: 0.44. 44% = 44 percent = 44 hundredths = $\frac{44}{100}$ = 0.44.

Percents can contain whole numbers, decimals, fractions, mixed numbers, or mixed decimals. Percents with mixed numbers and mixed decimals are often referred to as **mixed percents.** Examples are $33\frac{1}{3}\%$, 0.05%, and $0.23\frac{1}{3}\%$.

1 ▸ *Writing Numbers as Percents*

The businessperson must be able to write whole numbers, decimals, or fractions as percents, and to write percents as whole numbers, decimals, or fractions. First we examine writing whole numbers, decimals, and fractions as percents.

Hundredths and percent have the same meaning: per hundred. Just as 100 cents is the same as 1 dollar, 100 percent is the same as 1 whole quantity.

$$100\% = 1$$

We use this fact to write percent equivalents of numbers, and to write numerical equivalents of percents. We also use this fact to calculate markups, markdowns, discounts, and numerous other business applications.

When we multiply a number by 1, the product has the same value as the original number. N × 1 = N. We have used this concept to change a fraction to an equivalent fraction with a higher denominator. For example,

$$1 = \frac{2}{2} \text{ and } \frac{1}{2} \times \frac{2}{2} = \frac{2}{4}$$

$$1 = \frac{3}{3} \text{ and } \frac{1}{2} \times \frac{3}{3} = \frac{3}{6}$$

We can also use the fact, N × 1 = N, to change numbers to equivalent percents.

$$1 = 100\% \text{ and } \frac{1}{2} \times 100\% = \frac{1}{\underset{1}{2}} \times \frac{\overset{50}{100\%}}{1} = 50\%$$

$$1 = 100\% \text{ and } 0.5 \times 100\% = 050.\% = 50\%$$

In each case when we multiply by 1 in some form, the value of the product is equivalent to the value of the original number even though the product looks different.

❓ HOW TO   Write a Number as Its Percent Equivalent

Multiply the number by 1 in the form of 100%.

❗ TIPS & TRAPS

To write a number as its percent equivalent, identify the number as a fraction, whole number, or decimal. If the number is a fraction, multiply it by 1 in the form of $\frac{100\%}{1}$. If the number is a whole number or decimal, multiply by 100% by using the shortcut rule for multiplying by 100. In each case, the percent equivalent will be expressed with a percent symbol.

Example 1 Write the decimal or whole number as a percent.

   a. 0.27   b. 0.875   c. 1.73   d. 0.004   e. 2

   a. $0.27 = 0.27 \times 100\% = 0\,27.\% = 27\%$
      0.27 as a percent is 27%.

      Multiply 0.27 by 100% (move the decimal point two places to the right).

   b. $0.875 = 0.875 \times 100\% = 0\,87.5\% = 87.5\%$
      0.875 as a percent is 87.5%.

      Multiply 0.875 by 100% (move the decimal point two places to the right).

   c. $1.73 = 1.73 \times 100\% = 1\,73.\% = 173\%$
      1.73 as a percent is 173%.

      Multiply 1.73 by 100% (move the decimal point two places to the right).

   d. $0.004 = 0.004 \times 100\% = 0\,00.4\% = 0.4\%$
      0.004 as a percent is 0.4%

      Multiply 0.004 by 100% (move the decimal point two places to the right).

   e. $2 = 2 \times 100\% = 2\,00.\% = 200\%$
      2 as a percent is 200%.

      Multiply 2 by 100% (move the decimal point two places to the right).

As you can see, the procedure is the same regardless of the number of decimal places in the number and regardless of whether the number is more than, equal to, or less than 1.

Example 2 Write the fraction as a percent.

a. $\dfrac{67}{100}$　b. $\dfrac{1}{4}$　c. $3\dfrac{1}{2}$　d. $\dfrac{7}{4}$　e. $\dfrac{2}{3}$

a. $\dfrac{67}{100} = \dfrac{67}{100} \times 100\% = 67\%$

b. $\dfrac{1}{4} = \dfrac{1}{4} \times \dfrac{\overset{25}{\cancel{100}}}{1} = 25\%$

c. $3\dfrac{1}{2} = 3\dfrac{1}{2} \times \dfrac{100\%}{1} = \dfrac{7}{2} \times \dfrac{\overset{50}{\cancel{100\%}}}{1} = 350\%$

d. $\dfrac{7}{4} = \dfrac{7}{4} \times \dfrac{\overset{25}{\cancel{100\%}}}{1} = 175\%$

e. $\dfrac{2}{3} = \dfrac{2}{3} \times \dfrac{100\%}{1} = \dfrac{200\%}{3} = 66\dfrac{2}{3}\%$

▶ *Writing Percents as Numbers*

When we divide a number by 1 the quotient has the same value as the original number. $N \div 1 = N$ or $\dfrac{N}{1} = N$. We have used this concept to reduce fractions. For example,

$$1 = \dfrac{2}{2} \text{ and } \dfrac{2}{4} \div \dfrac{2}{2} = \dfrac{1}{2}$$

$$1 = \dfrac{3}{3} \text{ and } \dfrac{3}{6} \div \dfrac{3}{3} = \dfrac{1}{2}$$

We can also use the fact $N \div 1 = N$ or $\dfrac{N}{1} = N$ to change percents to numerical equivalents.

$$50\% \div 100\% = \dfrac{50\%}{100\%} = \dfrac{50}{100} = \dfrac{1}{2}$$

$$50\% \div 100\% = 50 \div 100 = 0.50 = 0.5$$

 HOW TO　**Write a Percent as a Number**

Divide by 1 in the form of 100%.

TIPS & TRAPS

To write a percent as its numerical equivalent, first decide what form (whole number, decimal, or fraction) you want.

To get a whole number or decimal equivalent, write the number in front of the percent symbol in decimal form. Then divide by 1 in the form of 100% by using the short-cut rule for dividing by 100. To get a fraction equivalent, write the number in front of the percent symbol in fraction form. Then divide by 1 in the form of $\frac{100\%}{1}$. This means we will multiply by $\frac{1}{100\%}$.

Example 3 Write the percent as a decimal.

a. 37%   b. 26.5%   c. 127%   d. 7%   e. 0.9%   f. $2\frac{19}{20}\%$ g. $167\frac{1}{3}\%$

a. $37\% = 37\% \div 100\% = .37 = 0.37$

b. 26.5% $= 26.5\% \div 100\% = .26\,5 = 0.265$

c. $127\% = 127\% \div 100\% = 1.27 = 1.27$

d. $7\% = 7\% \div 100\% = .07 = 0.07$

e. $0.9\% = 0.9\% \div 100\% = .00\,9 = 0.009$

f. $2\dfrac{19}{20}\% = 2.95\% \div 100\% = 0.02\,95 = 0.0295$ **Write the mixed number in front of the percent symbol as a mixed decimal before dividing by 100%.**

g. $167\dfrac{1}{3}\% = 167.3\overline{3}\% \div 100\% =$ **Write the mixed number in front of the percent symbol as a repeating mixed decimal before dividing by 100.**
$1.67\,3\overline{3} = 1.673\overline{3}$ or 1.673 (rounded)

Example 4 Write the percent as a fraction or mixed number.

a. 65%   b. $\frac{1}{4}\%$ c. 250%   d. $83\frac{1}{3}\%$ e. 12.5%

a. $65\% = 65\% \div 100\% = \dfrac{\overset{13}{65\%}}{1} \times \dfrac{1}{\underset{20}{100\%}} = \dfrac{13}{20}$

b. $\dfrac{1}{4}\% = \dfrac{1}{4}\% \div 100\% = \dfrac{1\%}{4} \times \dfrac{1}{100\%} = \dfrac{1}{400}$

c. $250\% = 250\% \div 100\% = \dfrac{\overset{5}{250\%}}{1} \times \dfrac{1}{\underset{2}{100\%}} = \dfrac{5}{2} = 2\dfrac{1}{2}$

d. $83\dfrac{1}{3}\% = 83\dfrac{1}{3}\% \div 100\% = \dfrac{\overset{5}{250\%}}{3} \times \dfrac{1}{\underset{2}{100\%}} = \dfrac{5}{6}$

e. $12.5\% = 12\dfrac{1}{2}\% = 12\dfrac{1}{2}\% \div 100\% = \dfrac{\overset{1}{25\%}}{2} \times \dfrac{1}{\underset{4}{100\%}} = \dfrac{1}{8}$

Using the Percentage Formula to Find the Percentage

A formula expresses a relationship among quantities. When you use the decision key in this book, step 4, Relationships, is a formula written in words and letters.

The percentage formula, *Percentage = Rate × Base*, can be written as $P = R \times B$. The letters or words represent numbers. When the numbers are put in place of the letters, the formula guides you through the calculations.

In the formula $P = R \times B$, the *base* (B) represents the original number or entire quantity. The *percentage* (P) represents a portion of the base. The *rate* (R) is a percent that tells us how the base and percentage are related. In the statement "50 is 20% of 250," 250 is the base (the entire quantity), 50 is the percentage (part), and 20% is the rate (percent).

When a formula shows that two numbers are multiplied to get a product, if you know the product and one of the numbers being multiplied, you can find the missing number (factor) by division. So

Missing factor = product ÷ known factor

For example, if $24 = 3 \times N$, then $N = 24 \div 3$. In other words, the missing number (N) is $24 \div 3$, or 8.

Using the percentage formula, we can determine alternate formulas by a similar strategy.

$$\text{Since } P = R \times B, \text{ then } B = P \div R \text{ or } \mathbf{B = \frac{P}{R}}$$

$$\text{Since } P = R \times B, \text{ then } R = P \div B \text{ or } \mathbf{R = \frac{P}{B}}$$

Normally, we put the letter that represents the missing number on the left and the letters and other symbols that represent known numbers on the right. Then, the right side of the formula guides you to make the appropriate calculations.

The three percentage formulas are

Percentage = Rate × Base	$P = R \times B$	for finding the percentage
Base = $\dfrac{\text{Percentage}}{\text{Rate}}$	$B = \dfrac{P}{R}$	for finding the base
Rate = $\dfrac{\text{Percentage}}{\text{Base}}$	$R = \dfrac{P}{B}$	for finding the rate

Figure 3–5 shows circles that will help us visualize these formulas. The part of the circle that is shaded represents the missing amount. The unshaded parts represent the known amounts. If the unshaded parts are side-by-side, multiply their corresponding numbers to find the missing number.

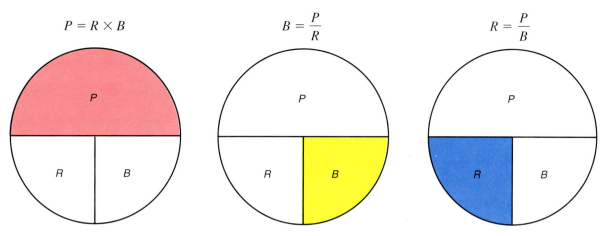

$$P = R \times B \qquad B = \frac{P}{R} \qquad R = \frac{P}{B}$$

Figure 3–5 Percentage Formulas

If the unshaded parts are one on top of the other, then divide the corresponding numbers to find the missing number.

? HOW TO   Use the Percentage Formula to Find the Percentage

Step 1 Write the formula **P = R × B.**
Step 2 Replace R and B by the known numbers for rate (R) and base (B).
Step 3 Write R as a decimal or fraction.
Step 4 Multiply R by B.

Example 5 Find the percentage if the rate is 6% and the base is $20.

$P = R \times B$ **The percentage is unknown.**

$P = 6\% \times \$20$ **The rate (R) is 6%; the base (B) is $20.
Write 6% as a decimal.**

$P = 0.06 \times \$20$ **Multiply 0.06 by $20.**

$P = \$1.20$

The percentage is $1.20.

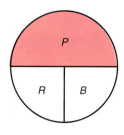

! TIPS & TRAPS

It is important to change the rate (percent) to a decimal or a fraction *before* you make any calculations. Look at what might happen in Example 5 if you do not change the rate to a decimal number.

$P = 0.06 \times \$20 = \$1.20$ $\qquad\qquad$ $P = 6\% \times \$20 = \$120$

CORRECT $\qquad\qquad\qquad\qquad\qquad$ **INCORRECT**

Very few percentage problems that you encounter in business tell you the values of *P, R,* and *B* directly. Percentage problems are usually written in words that must be interpreted before you can tell which form of the percentage formula you should use.

Example 6 During a special one-day sale, 600 customers bought the on-sale pizza. Of these customers, 20% used coupons. The manager will run the sale again the next day if more than 100 coupons were used. Should she run the sale again?

1 Decision needed Should the manager run the sale again?

2 Unknown fact Quantity of coupon-using customers

3 Known facts Total customers: 600
Coupon-using customers as a percent of total customers: 20%

4 Relationships The quantity of coupon-using customers is a *percentage* of the *base* of total customers, at a *rate* of 20%.

$$P = R \times B$$

Quantity of coupon-using customers = 20% × 600

5 Estimation 20% is less than 50%, or $\frac{1}{2}$. Half of 600 is 300, so the quantity of coupon-using customers is less than 300. Also, 20% is more than 10%. 10% × 600 = 60, so more than 60 customers used coupons.

6 Calculation Quantity of coupon-using customers = 20% × 600

$$= 0.2 \times 600 = 120$$

The quantity of coupon-using customers is 120.

7 Decision made **Since 120 is more than 100, the manager should run the sale again.**

Example 7 If $66\frac{2}{3}$% of the 900 employees in a company choose the B-Healthy insurance plan, how many people from that company are enrolled in the plan?

First, identify the terms. The rate is the percent, and the base is the total number of employees. The percentage is the quantity of employees enrolled in the plan.

$P = R \times B$ **The percentage is the unknown.**

$P = 66\dfrac{2}{3}\% \times 900$ **The rate is $66\frac{2}{3}$%; the base is 900.**

$P = \dfrac{2}{\underset{1}{\cancel{3}}} \times \dfrac{\overset{300}{\cancel{900}}}{1} = 600$ **Write $66\frac{2}{3}$% as a fraction.**

The quantity of employees enrolled in the plan is 600.

Paying for Health Care

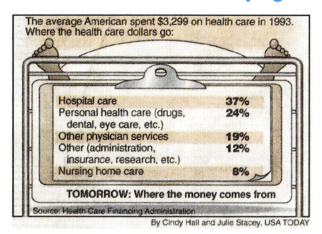

The average American spent $3,299 on health care in 1993. Where the health care dollars go:

Hospital care	37%
Personal health care (drugs, dental, eye care, etc.)	24%
Other physician services	19%
Other (administration, insurance, research, etc.)	12%
Nursing home care	8%

TOMORROW: Where the money comes from

Source: Health Care Financing Administration

By Cindy Hall and Julie Stacey, USA TODAY

1. Dave Williamson spent a total of $3,299 on health care in 1993. If his expenses matched the average American's expenses, how much did he spend on hospital care and personal health care?

2. Rhonda claims that she spent $\frac{6}{25}$ of her health care dollars on personal health care. How does this compare to the average American in 1993?

3. Joe Reyes spent $3,299 on health care in 1993. Of that, he spent $1,650 for hospital care. Compared to the average American, did Joe spend more for hospital care?

▶ **4** *Using the Percentage Formula to Find the Base*

Using the percentage formula form $B = P/R$, you can find the base if the percentage and rate are known.

❓ HOW TO | **Use the Percentage Formula to Find the Base**

Step 1 Write the formula $B = \dfrac{P}{R}$.

Step 2 Replace P and R by the known numbers for percentage (P) and rate (R).
Step 3 Write R as a decimal or fraction.
Step 4 Divide P by R.

Example 8 Find the base if the percentage is 42 and the rate is $33\frac{1}{3}\%$.

$B = \dfrac{P}{R}$ *The base, or entire quantity, is unknown.*

$B = \dfrac{42}{33\frac{1}{3}\%}$ *The percentage (P) is 42; the rate is $33\frac{1}{3}\%$. Write $33\frac{1}{3}\%$ as a fraction.*

$B = \dfrac{42}{\frac{1}{3}}$ *Divide 42 by $\frac{1}{3}$.*

$B = 42 \div \dfrac{1}{3} = \dfrac{42}{1} \times \dfrac{3}{1} = 126$

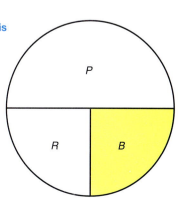

The base is 126.

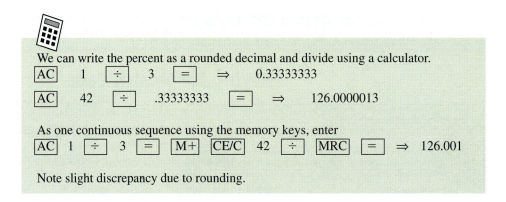

We can write the percent as a rounded decimal and divide using a calculator.

AC   1   ÷   3   =   ⇒   0.33333333

AC   42   ÷   .33333333   =   ⇒   126.0000013

As one continuous sequence using the memory keys, enter

AC   1   ÷   3   =   M+   CE/C   42   ÷   MRC   =   ⇒   126.001

Note slight discrepancy due to rounding.

Example 9 Stan sets aside 25% of his weekly income for rent. If he sets aside $50 each week, what is his weekly income?

Identify the terms: The rate is the number written as a percent. The percentage is given, $50; it is a portion of his weekly income, the unknown base.

$$B = \frac{P}{R}$$ **The base is the weekly income and the unknown to be found.**

$$B = \frac{\$50}{25\%}$$ **The percentage is $50; the rate is 25%.**

$$B = \frac{\$50}{0.25} = \$200$$ **Write 25% as a decimal.**

Stan's weekly income is $200.

Example 10 Thirty percent of Hill Community College graduates continued their education at four-year colleges. If 60 people continued their education, how many Hill Community College graduates were there?

Identify the terms: You might not recognize the rate immediately because it is written in words, thirty percent. The base is the total number of graduates, so 60 is the percentage of the graduates who continued their education.

$$B = \frac{P}{R}$$ **The base is the total number of graduates and the unknown to be found.**

$$B = \frac{60}{30\%}$$ **The percentage is 60; the rate is 30%.**

$$B = \frac{60}{0.3} = 200$$ **Write 30% as a decimal.**

There were 200 Hill Community College graduates.

5▶ *Using the Percentage Formula to Find the Rate*

Like solving for the base, to solve for the rate we use an alternate form of the percentage formula:

$$R = \frac{P}{B}$$

Step 1   Write the formula $R = \dfrac{P}{B}$.

Step 2   Replace P and B by the known values for percentage (P) and base (B).

Step 3   Write the fraction $\dfrac{P}{B}$ as a percent: Multiply by 100%.

Example 11   Find the rate if the percentage is 20 and the base is 200.

$$R = \dfrac{P}{B}$$ The rate, or percent, is the unknown to find.

$$R = \dfrac{20}{200}$$ The percentage is 20 and the base is 200.

Write $\frac{20}{200}$ as a percent.

$$R = \dfrac{\overset{10}{\cancel{20}}}{\underset{1}{\cancel{200}}} \times \dfrac{\overset{1}{\cancel{100\%}}}{1} = 10\%$$

The rate is 10%.

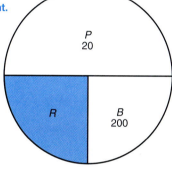

Example 12   If 20 cars were sold from a lot that had 50 cars, what percent of the cars were sold?

When you identify the terms in a percent problem, look for the rate, or the number written as a percent, first. In this problem, you can see that the rate is unknown. The base is the entire lot of cars, 50; the percentage, 20, is a portion of the base.

$$R = \dfrac{P}{B}$$ The rate is the unknown to find.

$$R = \dfrac{20}{50}$$ The percentage is 20; the base is 50.

$$R = \dfrac{20}{\underset{1}{\cancel{50}}} \times \dfrac{\overset{2}{\cancel{100\%}}}{1} = 40\%$$ Write $\frac{20}{50}$ as a percent.

Of the cars on the lot, 40% were sold.

TIPS & TRAPS

The following descriptions may help you recognize the rate, base, or percentage more quickly:

Rate is usually written as a percent, but it may be a decimal or fraction.

Base is the total amount, original amount, entire amount, and so on; it is the amount that the *percentage* is a portion of.

Percentage is called part, partial amount, portion, amount of increase or decrease, amount of change, and so on; it is a portion of the *base*.

AROUND THE BUSINESS WORLD

Dancing for Fast-Food Dollars

On a heady day in May, John M. Cranor III, president and chief executive officer of Kentucky Fried Chicken, watched 110 Shanghai schoolchildren dressed in white wigs, fake goatees and string ties perform the "Colonel Sanders Chicken Dance" for influential local officials and businessmen. Cranor cut the ribbon at the grand opening of KFC's 9,000th outlet worldwide and announced that in the next four years KFC will spend $200 million in China to expand from 28 outlets to at least 200.

The hoopla was designed to convey how bullish KFC is on China. Timothy Lane, KFC's president for Asia/Pacific, says that in 10 years China will be one of KFC's 10 largest markets. The Chinese, who have often been wary about granting foreigners access to their markets, are almost as eager as KFC to see the U.S. chicken chain spread its wings. One reason for the enthusiasm: KFC has inspired domestic competitors and helped create a fast-growing fast-food sector in China, now expanding at about 20 percent a year.

Glorious competition. Growth has been particularly fast in Beijing and Shanghai. Since KFC entered Shanghai five years ago, 300 fast-food restaurants have opened, most of them explicitly crediting KFC for their existence. "After KFC entered our market, we felt we wanted to do our own version, but with characteristics of the Chinese people," says

Hua Yuanming, Shanghai general manager of Glory China Chicken Snack Co., which considers itself KFC's chief local competitor.

KFC's outlets in China are clean, cool and brightly lit. Cranor describes the chain's well-dressed Chinese customers as "aspirational consumers" with enough disposable income to spend $2.50 to $3.50 on a fast-food meal. Glory China Chicken attracts a different clientele. Meals cost an average of $1.50, the walls are often spattered with grease and the floors are strewn with chicken bones.

Other parts of Asia may soon see a more upscale entrant into the rapidly expanding fast-food chicken market. Loy Weston, the 65-year-old entrepreneur who initially brought KFC to Asia in 1969, is back with Kenny Rogers Roasters, a pricier rotisserie restaurant. Weston and his partners are currently targeting 14 countries—from South Korea to New Zealand. The group hopes to capitalize on East Asia's emerging middle class. These consumers, like so many Chinese, are obviously developing a growing appetite for eating out American-style.

BY SUSAN V. LAWRENCE
IN SHANGHAI WITH MIKE THARP

Copyright July 18, 1994, U.S. News & World Report.

Write the decimal as a percent.

1. 0.39   **2.** 0.693   **3.** 2.92   **4.** 0.0007

Write the fraction as a percent.

5. $\dfrac{39}{100}$ **6.** $5\dfrac{1}{4}$ **7.** $\dfrac{9}{4}$

 Write the percent as a decimal.

8. $15\dfrac{1}{2}\%$ **9.** $\dfrac{1}{8}\%$ **10.** $125\dfrac{1}{3}\%$ **11.** $\dfrac{3}{7}\%$

Write the percent as a fraction.

12. 45%   **13.** 180%   **14.** $\dfrac{3}{4}\%$ **15.** $33\dfrac{1}{3}\%$

 Use the percentage formula or one of its forms.

16. Find *P* if *R* = 25% and *B* = 300.   **17.** Find 40% of 160.   **18.** What number is $33\dfrac{1}{3}\%$ of 150?

19. What number is 154% of 30?

20. At the Evans Formal Wear department store, all suits are reduced 20% from the retail price. If Charles Stewart purchased a suit that originally retailed for $258.30, how much did he save?

21. Joe Passarelli earns $8.67 per hour working for Dracken International. If Joe earns a merit raise of 12%, how much will he earn per hour?

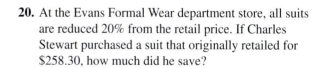

22. An ice cream truck began its daily route with 95 gallons of ice cream. The truck driver sold 78% of the ice cream. How many gallons of ice cream were sold?

23. Find *B* if *P* = 36 and *R* = $66\dfrac{2}{3}\%$.

24. Jenny sold 80% of the tie-dyed T-shirts she took to the Green Valley Music Festival. If she sold 42 shirts, how many shirts did she take?

25. A stockholder sold her shares and made a profit of $1,466. If this is a profit of 23%, how much were the shares worth when she originally purchased them?

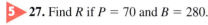

26. The Drammelonnie Department Store sold 30% of its shirts in stock. If the department store sold 267 shirts, how many shirts did the store have in stock?

27. Find *R* if *P* = 70 and *B* = 280.

28. Ali gave correct answers to 23 of the 25 questions on the driving test. What percent of the questions did he get correct?

29. A soccer stadium in Manchester, England, has a capacity of 78,753 seats. If 67,388 seats were filled, what percent of the stadium seats were vacant? Round to the nearest tenth of a percent.

Self-Check 3.1

1. proper   **2.** improper   **3.** improper   **4.** proper

5. $7\overline{)12}$ gives $1\frac{5}{7}$, $\frac{7}{5}$

6. $7\overline{)7}$ gives 1

7. $8\overline{)16}$ gives 2

8. $16\overline{)388}$ gives $24\frac{4}{16} = 24\frac{1}{4}$
$$\begin{array}{r}32 \\ \overline{68} \\ 64 \\ \overline{4}\end{array}$$

9. $\frac{6}{1}$

10. $\frac{(5 \times 3) + 4}{5} = \frac{19}{5}$

11. $\frac{(8 \times 1) + 5}{8} = \frac{13}{8}$

12. $\frac{(3 \times 6) + 2}{3} = \frac{20}{3}$

13. $\frac{12}{15} \div \frac{3}{3} = \frac{4}{5}$

14. $\frac{18}{36} \div \frac{18}{18} = \frac{1}{2}$

15. $\frac{3}{8} \times \frac{2}{2} = \frac{6}{16}$

16. $\frac{5}{9} \times \frac{3}{3} = \frac{15}{27}$

17. $\frac{1}{9}$ $\frac{2}{9}$ $+\frac{5}{9}$ $= \frac{8}{9}$

18.
$$\begin{array}{r}\frac{5}{8} \times \frac{3}{3} = \frac{15}{24} \\ +\frac{7}{12} \times \frac{2}{2} = \frac{14}{24} \\ \hline \frac{29}{24} = 1\frac{5}{24}\end{array}$$

19.
$$\begin{array}{r}4\frac{5}{6} = 4\frac{5}{6} \\ + 7\frac{1}{2} = 7\frac{3}{6} \\ \hline 11\frac{8}{6} = 12\frac{2}{6} = 12\frac{1}{3}\end{array}$$

20.
$$\begin{array}{r}11\frac{3}{4} = 11\frac{6}{8} \\ 11\frac{3}{4} = 11\frac{6}{8} \\ + 18\frac{5}{8} = 18\frac{5}{8} \\ \hline 40\frac{17}{8} = 42\frac{1}{8}\end{array}$$

21.
$$\begin{array}{r}\frac{8}{9} \\ -\frac{2}{9} \\ \hline \frac{6}{9} = \frac{2}{3}\end{array}$$

22.
$$\begin{array}{r}\frac{3}{4} \times \frac{7}{7} = \frac{21}{28} \\ -\frac{5}{7} \times \frac{4}{4} = \frac{20}{28} \\ \hline \frac{1}{28}\end{array}$$

23.
$$\begin{array}{r}9\frac{1}{2} = 9\frac{3}{6} = 8\frac{9}{6} \\ -6\frac{2}{3} = 6\frac{4}{6} = 6\frac{4}{6} \\ \hline 2\frac{5}{6}\end{array}$$

24. She only needs $42\frac{1}{8}$ yards so she can use the fabric.
$$\begin{array}{r}45 = 44\frac{8}{8} \\ -42\frac{1}{8} = 42\frac{1}{8} \\ \hline 2\frac{7}{8}\end{array}$$

$2\frac{7}{8}$ yards will make at least one very large pillow and may be enough fabric to make two or three pillows.

25. $\frac{5}{7} \times \frac{1}{6} = \frac{5}{42}$

26. $5\frac{3}{4} \times 3\frac{8}{9} = \frac{23}{4} \times \frac{35}{9} = \frac{805}{36} = 22\frac{13}{36}$

27. $\frac{3}{8} \times \frac{24}{1} = 9$ (with 3 and 1 shown as cancellations)

28. $3\frac{1}{2} \times 6 = \frac{7}{2} \times \frac{6}{1} = 21$ (with 3 and 1 shown as cancellations)

29. $\frac{5}{3}$

30. $9 = \frac{9}{1}$, so reciprocal is $\frac{1}{9}$

31. $3\frac{3}{8} = \frac{27}{8}$, so reciprocal is $\frac{8}{27}$

32. $\frac{5}{8} \div \frac{3}{4} = \frac{5}{8} \times \frac{4}{3} = \frac{5}{6}$ (with 2 shown as cancellation)

33. $5\frac{1}{4} \div 2\frac{2}{3} = \frac{21}{4} \div \frac{8}{3} = \frac{21}{4} \times \frac{3}{8} = \frac{63}{32} = 1\frac{31}{32}$

34. $\frac{3}{4} \div \frac{5}{1} = \frac{3}{4} \times \frac{1}{5} = \frac{3}{20}$

35. $\frac{68}{100} = \frac{17}{25}$

36. $1\frac{4}{10} = 1\frac{2}{5}$

37.
$$\begin{array}{r}0.75 \\ 4\overline{)3.00} \\ 2\ 8 \\ \hline 20 \\ 20 \\ \hline\end{array}$$

38.
$$\begin{array}{r}0.875 \\ 8\overline{)7.000} \\ 6\ 4 \\ \hline 60 \\ 56 \\ \hline 40 \\ 40 \\ \hline\end{array}$$

39. $1\frac{3}{5} = \frac{8}{5}$
$$\begin{array}{r}1.6 \\ 5\overline{)8.0} \\ 5 \\ \hline 30 \\ 30 \\ \hline\end{array}$$

40.
$$\begin{array}{r}0.428 \approx 0.43 \\ 7\overline{)3.000} \\ 2\ 8 \\ \hline 2\ 0 \\ 14 \\ \hline 60 \\ 56 \\ \hline 4\end{array}$$

1. $0.39 = 0.39 \times 100\% = 39\%$ **2.** $0.693 = 0.693 \times 100\% = 69.3\%$ **3.** $2.92 = 2.92 \times 100\% = 292\%$

4. $0.0007 = 0.0007 \times 100\% = 0.07\%$ **5.** $\dfrac{39}{100} = \dfrac{39}{\underset{1}{100}} \times \dfrac{100\%}{1} = 39\%$ **6.** $5\dfrac{1}{4} = 5\dfrac{1}{4} \times \dfrac{100\%}{1} = \dfrac{21}{\underset{1}{4}} \times \dfrac{\overset{25}{100}}{1}\% = 525\%$

7. $\dfrac{9}{4} = \dfrac{9}{\underset{1}{4}} \times \dfrac{\overset{25}{100\%}}{1} = 225\%$ **8.** $15\dfrac{1}{2}\% = 15.5\%$
$= 15.5\% \div 100\% = 0.155$

9. $8\overline{)1.000}$ $\overset{0.125}{}$ $\dfrac{1}{8}\% = 0.125\% = 0.125\% \div 100\% = 0.00125$
$\dfrac{80}{20}$
$\dfrac{16}{40}$
$\dfrac{40}{}$

10. $125\dfrac{1}{3}\% = 125.\overline{3}\%$
$= 125.\overline{3}\% \div 100\%$
$= 1.253$ (rounded)

11. $7\overline{)3.0000000}$ $\overset{0.4285714}{}$ $\dfrac{3}{7}\% = 0.428\% \div 100\% = 0.004$ (rounded)
$\dfrac{2\ 8}{20}$
$\dfrac{14}{60}$
$\dfrac{56}{40}$
$\dfrac{35}{50}$
$\dfrac{49}{10}$
$\dfrac{7}{30}$
$\dfrac{28}{2}$

12. $45\% = \dfrac{45\%}{100\%} = \dfrac{9}{20}$

13. $180\% = \dfrac{180\%}{100\%} = \dfrac{18}{10} = \dfrac{9}{5} = 1\dfrac{4}{5}$

14. $\dfrac{3}{4}\% = \dfrac{3}{4}\% \div 100\% = \dfrac{3}{4}\% \times \dfrac{1}{100\%} = \dfrac{3}{400}$

15. $33\dfrac{1}{3}\% = 33\dfrac{1}{3}\% \div 100\% = 33\dfrac{1}{3}\% \times \dfrac{1}{100\%} = \dfrac{100}{3} \times \dfrac{1}{\underset{1}{100}} = \dfrac{1}{3}$

16. $P = R \times B$
$P = 25\% \times 300$
$P = 0.25 \times 300$
$P = 75$

17. $P = R \times B = 40\% \times 160 = 0.40 \times 160 = 64$

18. $P = R \times B = 33\dfrac{1}{3}\% \times 150 = \dfrac{1}{\underset{1}{3}} \times \dfrac{\overset{50}{150}}{1} = 50$

19. $P = R \times B = 154\% \times 30 = 1.54 \times 30 = 46.2$

20. $P = R \times B = 20\% \times \$258.30 = 0.20 \times \$258.30$
$= \$51.66$ saved

21. $P = R \times B = 12\% \times \$8.67 = 0.12 \times \$8.67 = \$1.04$ increase
$\$8.67 + \$1.04 = \$9.71$ new pay per hour

22. $P = R \times B = 78\% \times 95 = 0.78 \times 95$
$= 74.1$ gallons or 74 gallons (rounded)

23. $B = \dfrac{P}{R} = \dfrac{36}{66\frac{2}{3}\%} = \dfrac{36}{\frac{2}{3}} = \dfrac{\overset{18}{36}}{1} \times \dfrac{3}{\underset{1}{2}} = 54$

24. $B = \dfrac{P}{R} = \dfrac{42}{80\%} = \dfrac{40}{0.8} = 52.5$, or 53 shirts

25. $B = \dfrac{P}{R} = \dfrac{\$1,466}{23\%} = \dfrac{\$1,466}{0.23} = \$6,373.91$ original cost

26. $B = \dfrac{P}{R} = \dfrac{267}{30\%} = \dfrac{267}{0.3} = 890$ shirts

27. $R = \dfrac{P}{B} = \dfrac{70}{280} = \dfrac{\overset{1}{70}}{\underset{4}{280}} \times \dfrac{\overset{25}{100\%}}{1} = 25\%$

28. $R = \dfrac{P}{B} = \dfrac{23}{25} = \dfrac{23}{\underset{1}{25}} \times \dfrac{\overset{4}{100\%}}{1} = 92\%$

29. $R = \dfrac{P}{B} = \dfrac{11,365}{78,753} = \dfrac{11,365}{78,753} \times \dfrac{100\%}{1} = \dfrac{1,136,500}{78,753}\% = 14.43\%$

Section—Objective   **Important Points with Examples**

3.1 — 1 (page 82)

Identify types of fractions

Write an improper fraction as a whole or mixed number   **Step 1** Divide the numerator of the improper fraction by the denominator. **Step 2** Examine the remainder: **a)** If the remainder is 0, the quotient is a whole number: The improper fraction is equivalent to this whole number. **b)** If the remainder is not 0, the quotient is not a whole number: The improper fraction is equivalent to a mixed number. The whole number part of this mixed number is the whole-number part of the quotient. The fraction part of the mixed number has a numerator and a denominator: The numerator is the remainder; the denominator is the divisor (the denominator of the improper fraction).

$$\frac{150}{3} \;\rightarrow\; 3\overline{)150}^{\,50\,R0} \;\rightarrow\; 50 \qquad \frac{152}{3} \;\rightarrow\; 3\overline{)152}^{\,50\,R2} \;\rightarrow\; 50\frac{2}{3}$$

Write a mixed number as an improper fraction   **Step 1** Find the numerator of the improper fraction. **a)** Multiply the denominator of the mixed number by the whole-number part. **b)** Add the product from step 1a to the numerator of the mixed number. **Step 2** Find the denominator of the improper fraction: use the denominator of the mixed number.

$$5\frac{5}{8} = \frac{(8 \times 5) + 5}{8} = \frac{40 + 5}{8} = \frac{45}{8} \qquad 7 = \frac{7}{1}$$

3.1 — 2 (page 85)

Change a fraction to an equivalent fraction

Reduce a fraction to lowest terms   **Step 1** Inspect the numerator and denominator to find any whole number that they both can be evenly divided by. **Step 2** Divide both the numerator and denominator by that number and inspect the new fraction to find any other number that the numerator and denominator can be divided by. **Step 3** Repeat steps 1 and 2 until there are no more numbers other than 1 that the numerator and denominator can be evenly divided by.

$$\frac{12}{36} = \frac{12}{36} \div \frac{2}{2} = \frac{6}{18} \qquad \text{or} \qquad \frac{12}{36} \div \frac{12}{12} = \frac{1}{3} \qquad \frac{100}{250} = \frac{100}{250} \div \frac{50}{50} = \frac{2}{5}$$

$$= \frac{6}{18} \div \frac{2}{2} = \frac{3}{9}$$

$$= \frac{3}{9} \div \frac{3}{3} = \frac{1}{3}$$

Find the greatest common divisor of two numbers   **Step 1** Divide the larger number by the smaller. **Step 2** Divide the divisor from step 1 by the remainder from step 1. **Step 3** Divide the divisor from step 2 by the remainder from step 2. **Step 4** Continue this division process until the remainder is 0. The current divisor is the greatest common divisor.

Find the GCD of 27 and 36.

$$
\begin{array}{r} 1\ R9 \\ 27\overline{)36} \\ \underline{27} \\ 9 \end{array}
\qquad
\begin{array}{r} 3 \\ 9\overline{)27} \\ \underline{27} \end{array}
$$

The GCD is 9.

Find the GCD of 28 and 15.

$$
\begin{array}{r} 1\ R13 \\ 15\overline{)28} \\ \underline{15} \\ 13 \end{array}
\qquad
\begin{array}{r} 1\ R2 \\ 13\overline{)15} \\ \underline{13} \\ 2 \end{array}
\qquad
\begin{array}{r} 6\ R1 \\ 2\overline{)13} \\ \underline{12} \\ 1 \end{array}
\qquad
\begin{array}{r} 2 \\ 1\overline{)2} \\ \underline{2} \end{array}
$$

The GCD is 1.

Build a fraction to higher terms, given the new denominator   **Step 1** Divide the *new* denominator by the *old* denominator. **Step 2** Multiply both the old numerator and denominator by the quotient from step 1.

$$
\frac{3}{4} = \frac{?}{20}
\qquad\qquad\qquad
\frac{2}{3} = \frac{?}{60}
$$

$$
\begin{array}{r} 5 \\ 4\overline{)20} \end{array}
\qquad\qquad\qquad
\begin{array}{r} 20 \\ 3\overline{)60} \end{array}
$$

$$
\frac{3}{4} = \frac{3}{4} \times \frac{5}{5} = \frac{15}{20}
\qquad\qquad
\frac{2}{3} \times \frac{20}{20} = \frac{40}{60}
$$

3.1 — 3 (page 87)

Add and subtract fractions and mixed numbers

Add fractions with like denominators   **Step 1** Find the numerator of the sum: Add the numerators of the addends. **Step 2** Find the denominator of the sum: Use the like denominator of the addends. **Step 3** Reduce to lowest terms and/or write as a whole or mixed number.

$$
\frac{3}{5} + \frac{7}{5} + \frac{5}{5} = \frac{15}{5} = 3
\qquad\qquad
\frac{82}{109} + \frac{13}{109} = \frac{95}{109}
$$

Find the least common denominator of two or more fractions   **Step 1** Write the denominators in a row and divide each one by the smallest prime number that any of the numbers can be evenly divided by. **Step 2** Write a new row of numbers using the quotients from step 1 and any numbers in the first row that cannot be evenly divided by the first prime number. **Step 3** Continue this process until you have a row of 1s. **Step 4** Multiply all the prime numbers you used to divide by. The product is the least common denominator.

Find the least common denominator of $\frac{5}{6}$, $\frac{6}{15}$, and $\frac{7}{20}$.

```
2)6  15  20
2)3  15  10
3)3  15   5
5)1   5   5
   1   1   1
```

LCD = 2 × 2 × 3 × 5 = 60

Find the least common denominator of $\frac{4}{5}$, $\frac{3}{10}$, and $\frac{1}{6}$.

```
2)5  10  6
3)5   5  3
5)5   5  1
   1   1  1
```

LCD = 2 × 3 × 5 = 30

Add fractions with different denominators   **Step 1** Find the least common denominator. **Step 2** Change each fraction to an equivalent fraction using the least common denominator. **Step 3** Add the new fractions with like denominators.

Add $\frac{5}{6} + \frac{6}{15} + \frac{7}{20}$.

The LCD is 60.

$$\frac{5}{6} = \frac{5}{6} \times \frac{10}{10} = \frac{50}{60}$$

$$\frac{7}{20} = \frac{7}{20} \times \frac{3}{3} = \frac{21}{60}$$

$$\frac{6}{15} = \frac{6}{15} \times \frac{4}{4} = \frac{24}{60}$$

$$\frac{5}{6} + \frac{6}{15} + \frac{7}{20} = \frac{50}{60} + \frac{21}{60} + \frac{24}{60}$$

$$\frac{95}{60} = \frac{19}{12} = 1\frac{7}{12}$$

Add $\frac{4}{5} + \frac{3}{10} + \frac{1}{6}$.

The LCD is 30.

$$\frac{4}{5} \times \frac{6}{6} = \frac{24}{30}$$

$$\frac{3}{10} \times \frac{3}{3} = \frac{9}{30}$$

$$\frac{1}{6} \times \frac{5}{5} = \frac{5}{30}$$

$$\frac{4}{5} + \frac{3}{10} + \frac{1}{6} = \frac{24}{30} + \frac{9}{30} + \frac{5}{30} = \frac{38}{30}$$

$$= \frac{19}{15} = 1\frac{4}{15}$$

Subtract fractions   **With like denominators**   **Step 1** Find the numerator of the difference: Subtract the numerators of the fractions. **Step 2** Find the denominator of the difference: Use the like denominator. **Step 3** Reduce to lowest terms and/or write as a whole or mixed number. **With different denominators**   **Step 1** Find the least common denominator. **Step 2** Change each fraction to an equivalent fraction using the least common denominator. **Step 3** Subtract the new fractions with like denominators.

$$\frac{10}{81} - \frac{7}{81} = \frac{3}{81} = \frac{1}{27}$$

$$\frac{7}{8} - \frac{1}{3} = \frac{21}{24} - \frac{8}{24} = \frac{13}{24}$$

Subtract mixed numbers   **Step 1** If the fractions have different denominators, find the LCD and change the fractions to equivalent fractions using the LCD. **Step 2** If necessary, borrow (subtract) 1 from the whole number in the minuend, and add 1 (in the form of LCD/LCD) to the fraction in the minuend. **Step 3** Subtract the fractions and the whole numbers. **Step 4** Reduce to lowest terms.

$$24\frac{1}{2} = 24\frac{2}{4} = 23\frac{6}{4}$$
$$-11\frac{3}{4} = -11\frac{3}{4} = -11\frac{3}{4}$$
$$12\frac{3}{4}$$

$$53 = 53\frac{0}{5} = 52\frac{5}{5}$$
$$-37\frac{4}{5} = 37\frac{4}{5} = 37\frac{4}{5}$$
$$15\frac{1}{5}$$

3.1 — 4 (page 91)

Multiply and divide fractions and mixed numbers

Multiply fractions **Step 1** Find the numerator of the product: Multiply the numerators of the fractions. **Step 2** Find the denominator of the product: Multiply the denominators of the fractions. **Step 3** Reduce to lowest terms.

$$\frac{3}{2} \times \frac{12}{17} = \frac{36}{34} = 1\frac{2}{34} = 1\frac{1}{17} \qquad \frac{7}{\overset{3}{\cancel{9}}} \times \frac{\overset{5}{\cancel{15}}}{\underset{4}{\cancel{28}}} = \frac{5}{12}$$

or

$$\frac{3}{\underset{1}{\cancel{2}}} \times \frac{\overset{6}{\cancel{12}}}{17} = \frac{18}{17} = 1\frac{1}{17}$$

Multiply mixed numbers and whole numbers **Step 1** Write the mixed numbers and whole numbers as improper fractions. **Step 2** Reduce numerators and denominators as appropriate. **Step 3** Multiply the fractions. **Step 4** Reduce to lowest terms and/or write as a whole or mixed number.

$$3\frac{3}{4} \times 3\frac{2}{3} = \frac{15}{4} \times \frac{11}{3} = \frac{165}{12} = \frac{55}{4} = 13\frac{3}{4} \qquad 5\frac{7}{8} \times 3 = \frac{47}{8} \times \frac{3}{1} = \frac{141}{8} = 17\frac{5}{8}$$

or

$$\frac{\overset{5}{\cancel{15}}}{4} \times \frac{11}{\underset{1}{\cancel{3}}} = \frac{55}{4} = 13\frac{3}{4}$$

Find the reciprocal of a number **Step 1** Write the number as a fraction. **Step 2** Interchange the numerator and denominator.

The reciprocal of 6 is $\frac{1}{6}$. $\quad 6 = \frac{6}{1}$ $\quad$ The reciprocal of 0.25 is 4. $\quad 0.25 = \frac{1}{4}$

The reciprocal of $\frac{2}{3}$ is $\frac{3}{2}$. $\quad$ The reciprocal of 3.2 is $\frac{5}{16}$. $\quad 3.2 = 3\frac{2}{10} = 3\frac{1}{5} = \frac{16}{5}$

The reciprocal of $1\frac{1}{2}$ is $\frac{2}{3}$. $\quad 1\frac{1}{2} = \frac{3}{2}$

Divide fractions or mixed numbers **Step 1** Write the numbers as fractions. **Step 2** Find the reciprocal of the divisor. **Step 3** Multiply the dividend by the reciprocal of the divisor. **Step 4** Reduce to lowest terms and/or write as a whole or mixed number.

$$\frac{55}{68} \div \frac{11}{17} = \frac{\overset{5}{\cancel{55}}}{\underset{4}{\cancel{68}}} \times \frac{\overset{1}{\cancel{17}}}{\underset{1}{\cancel{11}}} = \frac{5}{4} = 1\frac{1}{4} \qquad 3\frac{1}{4} \div 1\frac{1}{2} = \frac{13}{4} \div \frac{3}{2}$$

$$= \frac{13}{\underset{2}{\cancel{4}}} \times \frac{\overset{1}{\cancel{2}}}{3} = \frac{13}{6} = 2\frac{1}{6}$$

Write a decimal as a fraction and write a fraction as a decimal

(page 95)

Write a decimal as a fraction **Step 1** Find the denominator: Write 1 followed by as many zeros as there are places to the right of the decimal point. **Step 2** Find the numerator: Use the decimal without the decimal point. **Step 3** Reduce to lowest terms and/or write as a whole or mixed number.

$$0.05 = \frac{5}{100} = \frac{1}{20} \qquad 0.584 = \frac{584}{1,000} = \frac{73}{125}$$

Write a fraction as a decimal **Step 1** Write the numerator as the dividend and the denominator as the divisor **Step 2** Divide the numerator by the denominator, taking the division out as many places as necessary.

$$\frac{5}{8} = 8\overline{)5.000} = 0.625 \qquad \frac{57}{76} = 76\overline{)57.00} = 0.75$$

$$
\begin{array}{r}
0.625 \\
8\overline{)5.000} \\
\underline{4\ 8} \\
20 \\
\underline{16} \\
40 \\
\underline{40}
\end{array}
\qquad
\begin{array}{r}
0.75 \\
76\overline{)57.00} \\
\underline{53\ 2} \\
3\ 80 \\
\underline{3\ 80}
\end{array}
$$

Write a whole number, fraction, or decimal as a percent

(page 98)

Write a number as its percent equivalent. Multiply the number by 1 in the form of 100%.

$$6 = 6 \times 100\% = 600\% \qquad \frac{3}{5} = \frac{3}{\underset{1}{\cancel{5}}} \times \frac{\overset{20}{\cancel{100}}}{1}\% = 60\%$$

$$0.075 = 0.075 \times 100\% = 7.5\%$$

3.2 — 2 (page 100)

Write a percent as a whole number, fraction, or decimal

Write a percent as a number. Divide by 1 in the form of 100%.

$$48\% = 48\% \div 100\% = 0.48 \qquad 20\% = 20\% \div 100\% = \frac{\overset{1}{\cancel{20}}}{\underset{5}{\cancel{100}}} = \frac{1}{5}$$

$$157\% = 157\% \div 100\% = 1.57 \qquad 33\frac{1}{3}\% = 33\frac{1}{3}\% \div 100\% = 0.33\frac{1}{3}$$

$$\text{or } 0.3\overline{3}$$

 **(page 102)**

Step 1 Write the formula $P = R \times B$. **Step 2** Replace R and B by the known numbers for rate (R) and base (B). **Step 3** Write R as a decimal or fraction. **Step 4** Multiply R by B.

Use the percentage formula to find the percentage

Find P if $B = 20$ and $R = 15\%$

$$P = R \times B$$

$$P = 15\% \times 20 = 0.15 \times 20$$

$$= 3$$

Find P if $B = 81$ and $R = 33\frac{1}{3}\%$

$$P = R \times B$$

$$P = 33\frac{1}{3}\% \times 81 = \frac{1}{3} \times 81$$

$$= \frac{81}{3} = 27$$

 **(page 105)**

Step 1 Write the formula $B = P/R$. **Step 2** Replace P and R by the known numbers for percentage (P) and rate (R). **Step 3** Write R as a decimal or fraction. **Step 4** Divide P by R.

Use the percentage formula to find the base

Find B if $P = 36$ and $R = 9\%$

$$B = \frac{P}{R}$$

$$B = \frac{36}{9\%} = \frac{36}{0.09}$$

$$= 400$$

Find B if $P = 22$ and $R = 66\frac{2}{3}\%$

$$B = \frac{P}{R}$$

$$B = \frac{22}{66\frac{2}{3}\%} = \frac{22}{\frac{2}{3}}$$

$$= \frac{\overset{11}{\cancel{22}}}{1} \times \frac{3}{\underset{1}{\cancel{2}}} = 33$$

 **(page 106)**

Step 1 Write the formula $R = P/B$. **Step 2** Replace P and B by the known numbers for percentage (P) and base (B). **Step 3** Write the fraction P/B as a percent: Multiply by 1 in the form of 100%.

Use the percentage formula to find the rate

Find R if $P = 4$ and $B = 5$

$$R = \frac{P}{B}$$

$$R = \frac{4}{5} = \frac{4}{\underset{1}{\cancel{5}}} \times \frac{\overset{20}{\cancel{100}}}{1}\%$$

$$= 80\%$$

Find R if $P = 75$ and $B = 50$

$$R = \frac{P}{B}$$

$$R = \frac{75}{50} = \frac{75}{\underset{1}{\cancel{50}}} \times \frac{\overset{2}{\cancel{100}}}{1}\%$$

$$= 150\%$$

Section 3.1

1. Give five examples of fractions whose value is less than 1. What are these fractions called?

2. Give five examples of fractions whose value is greater than or equal to 1. What are these fractions called?

Write the improper fraction as a whole or mixed number.

3. $\dfrac{124}{6}$ 4. $\dfrac{52}{15}$ 5. $\dfrac{84}{12}$ 6. $\dfrac{83}{4}$ 7. $\dfrac{17}{2}$

8. $\dfrac{77}{11}$ 9. $\dfrac{62}{5}$ 10. $\dfrac{19}{10}$ 11. $\dfrac{372}{25}$ 12. $\dfrac{904}{9}$

Write the mixed number as an improper fraction.

13. $5\dfrac{5}{6}$ 14. $7\dfrac{3}{8}$ 15. $4\dfrac{1}{3}$

16. $10\dfrac{1}{5}$ 17. $33\dfrac{1}{3}$ 18. $66\dfrac{2}{3}$

Reduce to lowest terms. Try to use the greatest common divisor.

19. $\dfrac{25}{40}$ 20. $\dfrac{18}{20}$ 21. $\dfrac{15}{18}$ $\dfrac{5}{3}$ $\dfrac{3}{6}$ $\dfrac{1}{2}$ 22. $\dfrac{20}{30}$

23. $\dfrac{21}{24}$ $\cdot$ $\dfrac{7}{6}$ $\dfrac{3}{4}$ 24. $\dfrac{30}{48}$ 25. $\dfrac{21}{56}$ $\cdot$ $\dfrac{7}{7}$ $=$ $\dfrac{3}{8}$ 26. $\dfrac{27}{36}$

27. $\dfrac{48}{64}$ $=$ $\dfrac{4}{8}$ $=$ $\dfrac{1}{2}$ 28. $\dfrac{16}{48}$ 29. $\dfrac{24}{60}$ $\dfrac{12}{12}$ $=$ $\dfrac{2}{5}$ 30. $\dfrac{18}{63}$

31. $\dfrac{56}{72}$ $\cdot$ $\dfrac{8}{8}$ $=$ $\dfrac{7}{9}$ 32. $\dfrac{54}{84}$ 33. $\dfrac{120}{144}$ $\dfrac{12}{12}$ $=$ $\dfrac{10}{12}$ $\dfrac{5}{6}$ 34. $\dfrac{78}{104}$ 35. $\dfrac{75}{125}$ $\dfrac{3}{5}$

36. $\dfrac{78}{96}$ 37. $\dfrac{32}{48}$ $\cdot$ $\dfrac{16}{12}$ $=$ $\dfrac{2}{4}$ 38. $\dfrac{220}{242}$ 39. $\dfrac{65}{120}$ 40. $\dfrac{30}{140}$

Rewrite as a fraction with the indicated denominator.

41. $\dfrac{3}{4} = \dfrac{}{72}$ **42.** $\dfrac{7}{9} = \dfrac{}{81}$ **43.** $\dfrac{5}{6} = \dfrac{}{12}$ **44.** $\dfrac{5}{8} = \dfrac{}{32}$ **45.** $\dfrac{2}{3} = \dfrac{}{15}$

46. $\dfrac{4}{7} = \dfrac{}{49}$ **47.** $\dfrac{9}{11} = \dfrac{}{77}$ **48.** $\dfrac{3}{14} = \dfrac{}{56}$ **49.** $\dfrac{9}{11} = \dfrac{}{143}$ **50.** $\dfrac{4}{15} = \dfrac{}{105}$

51. A company employed 105 people. If 15 of the employees left the company in a three-month period, what fractional part of the employees left?

52. If 8 students in a class of 30 earned grades of A, what fractional part of the class earned As?

Find the least common denominator for these fractions.

53. $\dfrac{1}{4}, \dfrac{1}{12}, \dfrac{11}{16}$ **54.** $\dfrac{7}{8}, \dfrac{1}{20}, \dfrac{13}{16}$ **55.** $\dfrac{2}{1}, \dfrac{1}{5}, \dfrac{1}{10}, \dfrac{5}{6}$

56. $\dfrac{1}{8}, \dfrac{5}{9}, \dfrac{7}{12}, \dfrac{9}{24}$ **57.** $\dfrac{5}{56}, \dfrac{7}{24}, \dfrac{7}{12}, \dfrac{5}{42}$ **58.** $\dfrac{5}{12}, \dfrac{3}{15}$

Add.

59. $\dfrac{3}{5} + \dfrac{4}{5}$ **60.** $\dfrac{7}{8} + \dfrac{1}{8}$ **61.** $\dfrac{2}{5} + \dfrac{2}{3}$

62. $\dfrac{3}{4} + \dfrac{7}{8}$ **63.** $\dfrac{5}{6} + \dfrac{17}{18}$ **64.** $\dfrac{1}{4} + \dfrac{11}{12} + \dfrac{7}{16}$

65. $\dfrac{1}{6} + \dfrac{7}{8} + \dfrac{5}{12}$ **66.** $\dfrac{7}{9} + \dfrac{13}{16} + \dfrac{2}{3}$ **67.** $\dfrac{5}{6} + \dfrac{1}{12} + \dfrac{4}{9}$

68. $\dfrac{3}{4} + \dfrac{7}{15} + \dfrac{5}{6} + \dfrac{3}{5} + \dfrac{3}{20}$ **69.** $7\dfrac{1}{2} + 4\dfrac{3}{8}$ **70.** $11\dfrac{5}{6} + 8\dfrac{2}{3}$

71. $15\dfrac{1}{2} + 9\dfrac{3}{4}$ **72.** $7\dfrac{2}{3} + 3\dfrac{5}{6} + 4\dfrac{1}{2}$ **73.** $8\dfrac{7}{10} + 9\dfrac{1}{5} + 5\dfrac{1}{2}$

74. $3\dfrac{1}{4} + 2\dfrac{1}{3} + 3\dfrac{5}{6}$ **75.** $\begin{aligned} 73\dfrac{1}{2} \\ +18\dfrac{1}{3} \\ \hline \end{aligned}$ **76.** $\begin{aligned} 36\dfrac{2}{3} \\ +28\dfrac{1}{2} \\ \hline \end{aligned}$

77. $96\dfrac{5}{6}$
$+57\dfrac{4}{7}$

78. $20\dfrac{7}{12}$
$27\dfrac{5}{8}$
$+\ 7\dfrac{5}{6}$

79. $54\dfrac{1}{2}$
$37\dfrac{2}{3}$
$+15\dfrac{5}{6}$

80. $11\dfrac{2}{3}$
$68\dfrac{1}{5}$
$+57\dfrac{5}{8}$

81. Two types of fabric are needed for curtains. The lining requires $12\dfrac{3}{8}$ yards and the curtain fabric needed is $16\dfrac{5}{8}$ yards. How many yards of fabric are needed?

82. Three pieces of lumber measure $5\dfrac{3}{8}$ feet, $7\dfrac{1}{2}$ feet, and $9\dfrac{3}{4}$ feet. What is the total length of the lumber?

Subtract. Borrow when necessary. Reduce the difference to lowest terms.

83. $\dfrac{5}{12}-\dfrac{1}{4}$

84. $\dfrac{2}{3}-\dfrac{1}{6}$

85. $\dfrac{1}{2}-\dfrac{1}{3}$

86. $\dfrac{6}{7}-\dfrac{5}{14}$

87. $\dfrac{13}{16}-\dfrac{2}{3}$

88. $\dfrac{11}{15}-\dfrac{1}{6}$

89. $7\dfrac{4}{5}-4\dfrac{1}{2}$

90. $4\dfrac{1}{2}-3\dfrac{6}{7}$

91. $4\dfrac{5}{6}-3\dfrac{1}{3}$

92. $8\dfrac{2}{3}-2\dfrac{1}{2}$

93. $4\dfrac{5}{12}-1\dfrac{1}{3}$

94. $3\dfrac{1}{2}-1\dfrac{1}{4}$

95. $7\dfrac{5}{9}$
$-5\dfrac{1}{2}$

96. $564\dfrac{5}{9}$
$-317\dfrac{5}{6}$

97. $232\dfrac{2}{15}$
$-189\ \dfrac{2}{5}$

98. $83\dfrac{1}{9}$
$-46\dfrac{1}{3}$

99. $9\dfrac{3}{7}$
$-7\dfrac{3}{5}$

100. $106\ \dfrac{1}{4}$
$-\ 37\dfrac{9}{24}$

101. $38\frac{1}{2}$

$-26\frac{1}{3}$

102. $182\frac{9}{12}$

$-90\frac{5}{6}$

103. A board $3\frac{5}{8}$ feet long must be sawed from a 6-foot board. How long is the remaining piece?

104. George Mackie worked the following hours during a week: $7\frac{3}{4}$, $5\frac{1}{2}$, $6\frac{1}{4}$, $9\frac{1}{4}$, and $8\frac{3}{4}$. Maxine Ford worked 40 hours. Who worked the most hours? How many more?

Multiply and reduce to lowest terms, or write as whole or mixed numbers.

105. $\frac{1}{4} \times \frac{7}{8}$

106. $\frac{9}{10} \times \frac{3}{4}$

107. $\frac{5}{6} \times \frac{1}{3}$

108. $\frac{1}{8} \times \frac{7}{8}$

109. $\frac{3}{5} \times \frac{3}{4}$

110. $\frac{1}{2} \times \frac{1}{2}$

111. $5 \times \frac{2}{3}$

112. $\frac{3}{7} \times 8$

113. $\frac{7}{8} \times 3$

114. $6 \times \frac{4}{5}$

115. $\frac{5}{6} \times \frac{2}{3}$

116. $\frac{3}{4} \times \frac{4}{5}$

117. $\frac{3}{4} \times \frac{8}{9} \times \frac{7}{12}$

118. $\frac{2}{5} \times \frac{5}{6} \times \frac{7}{8}$

119. $\frac{9}{10} \times \frac{8}{5} \times \frac{7}{15}$

120. $\frac{9}{10} \times \frac{2}{5} \times \frac{5}{9} \times \frac{3}{7}$

121. $\frac{5}{9} \times \frac{8}{21} \times \frac{9}{10} \times \frac{6}{7}$

122. $\frac{15}{25} \times \frac{13}{20} \times \frac{14}{30}$

123. $\frac{1}{8} \times \frac{3}{5} \times \frac{40}{41}$

124. $3\frac{1}{3} \times 4\frac{1}{4}$

125. $4\frac{1}{5} \times 8\frac{5}{6}$

126. $6\frac{2}{9} \times 4\frac{1}{2}$

127. $7\frac{5}{8} \times 9\frac{5}{6}$

128. $8\frac{2}{5} \times 9\frac{4}{9}$

129. $9\frac{1}{6} \times 10\frac{2}{7}$

130. $10\frac{1}{2} \times 1\frac{5}{7}$

131. Katrina Kimble received $\frac{3}{4}$ of a regular day's pay as a tribute to her birthday. If she regularly earns $64 a day, how much birthday pay did she receive?

132. A recipe for pecan pralines calls for the following.

$\frac{3}{4}$ cup brown sugar $\frac{1}{4}$ teaspoon vanilla

$\frac{3}{4}$ cup white sugar   2 tablespoons margarine

$\frac{1}{2}$ cup evaporated milk   1 cup pecans

Brenda Lewis is making treats for her second-grade class, so she must make $2\frac{1}{2}$ times as many pralines as this recipe yields. How much of each ingredient is needed?

133. The price of computers has fallen by $\frac{2}{5}$. If the original price of a computer was $10,275, by how much has the price fallen?

134. After a family reunion, $10\frac{2}{3}$ cakes were left. If Shirley McCool took $\frac{3}{8}$ of these cakes, how many did she take?

Find the reciprocal of the numbers.

135. $\frac{5}{8}$

136. $\frac{2}{3}$

137. $\frac{1}{4}$

138. 8

139. $3\frac{1}{4}$

140. $2\frac{3}{8}$

141. $1\frac{3}{5}$

142. $2\frac{5}{9}$

Divide and reduce to lowest terms.

143. $\frac{3}{4} \div \frac{1}{4}$

144. $\frac{5}{6} \div \frac{1}{8}$

145. $\frac{15}{36} \div \frac{7}{8}$

146. $\frac{3}{8} \div 3$

147. $\frac{3}{10} \div 6$

148. $15 \div \frac{3}{4}$

149. $7\frac{1}{2} \div 2$

150. $7\frac{1}{2} \div 1\frac{2}{3}$

151. $3\frac{1}{7} \div 5\frac{1}{2}$

152. $6\frac{4}{5} \div 8\frac{5}{6}$

153. A board 244 inches long is cut into pieces that are each $7\frac{5}{8}$ inches. How many pieces can be cut?

154. A stack of $1\frac{5}{8}$-inch plywood measures 91 inches. How many pieces of plywood are in the stack?

155. If city sales tax is $5\frac{1}{2}\%$ and state sales tax is $2\frac{1}{4}\%$, what is the total sales tax rate on purchases made in the city?

156. Sue Parsons has three lengths of $\frac{3}{4}$-inch PVC pipe: $1\frac{1}{5}$ feet, $2\frac{3}{4}$ feet, and $1\frac{1}{2}$ feet. What is the total length of pipe?

157. Bill New placed a piece of $\frac{5}{8}$-inch plywood and a piece of $\frac{3}{4}$-inch plywood on top of one another to create a spacer between two 2 × 4's, but the spacer was $\frac{1}{8}$ inch too thick. How thick should the spacer be?

158. Brienne Smith must trim $2\frac{3}{16}$ feet from a board 8 feet long. How long will the board be after it is cut?

159. Certain financial aid students must pass $\frac{2}{3}$ of their courses each term in order to continue their aid. If a student is taking 18 hours, how many hours must be passed?

160. Wallboard measuring $\frac{5}{8}$ inch thick is in a stack $62\frac{1}{2}$ inches high. How many sheets of wallboard are in the stack?

161. Sol's Hardware and Appliance Store is selling electric clothes dryers for $\frac{1}{3}$ off the regular price of $288. What is the sales price of the dryer?

162. A recipe for French toast that serves six calls for $\frac{3}{4}$ cup granulated sugar, 1 cup evaporated milk, $\frac{1}{3}$ teaspoon vanilla, and 12 thick slices of French bread. How much of each ingredient is needed to serve only three?

163. Chair rail molding 144 inches long must be cut into pieces of $35\frac{1}{2}$ inches each. How many pieces can be cut from the molding?

164. A farmer wants to stock several ponds with 500 catfish fingerlings. If the farmer expects to lose $\frac{1}{6}$ of the fingerlings, would ordering 560 be enough to expect 500 to survive?

Section 3.2

Write the decimal as a percent.

165. 0.23

166. 0.675

167. 0.82

168. 2.63

169. 0.03

170. 0.007

171. 0.34

172. 3.741

173. 0.601

174. 0.0004

175. 1

176. 0.6

177. 3

178. 0.242

179. 0.37   **180.** 0.811   **181.** 0.2

182. 2.54   **183.** 4   **184.** 0.03

Write the fraction or mixed number as a percent. Round to the nearest hundredth percent if necessary.

185. $\dfrac{17}{100}$ **186.** $\dfrac{99}{100}$ **187.** $\dfrac{6}{100}$ **188.** $\dfrac{20}{100}$

189. $\dfrac{52}{100}$ **190.** $\dfrac{13}{20}$ **191.** $\dfrac{1}{10}$ **192.** $3\dfrac{2}{5}$

193. $\dfrac{5}{4}$ 125%   **194.** $7\dfrac{1}{2}$ **195.** $\dfrac{39}{100}$ **196.** $\dfrac{2}{5}$
$4\overline{)5.00}$

197. $\dfrac{1}{3}$ **198.** $1\dfrac{5}{8}$ **199.** $\dfrac{3}{100}$ **200.** $\dfrac{1}{12}$

Write the percent as a decimal.

201. 98%   **202.** 84.6%   **203.** 256%   **204.** 52%

205. 91.7%   **206.** 3%   **207.** 0.5%   **208.** 0.02%

209. 6%   **210.** 9%   **211.** 36%   **212.** 274%

213. 6%   **214.** 30%

Write the percent as a whole number, mixed number, or fraction, reduced to lowest terms.

215. 10%   **216.** 20%   **217.** 6%

218. 170%   **219.** 89%   **220.** 361%

221. 45%   **222.** 25%   **223.** 225%   **224.** $12\frac{1}{2}\%$

	Percent	Fraction	Decimal
225.	$33\frac{1}{3}$	_____	_____
226.	_____	$\frac{2}{5}$	_____
227.	_____	_____	0.125
228.	50%	_____	_____
229.	_____	_____	0.8
230.	$87\frac{1}{2}\%$	_____	_____

Find P, R, or B using the percentage formula or one of its forms.

231. $B = 300$, $R = 27\%$ **232.** $B = \$1,900$, $R = 106\%$

233. $B = 1,000$, $R = 2\frac{1}{2}\%$ **234.** $B = \$500$, $R = 7.25\%$

235. $P = 25$, $B = 100$ **236.** $P = 170$, $B = 85$

237. $P = 2$, $B = 6$ **238.** $P = \$600$, $R = 5\%$

239. $P = 26$, $R = 6\frac{1}{2}\%$ **240.** $P = \$15.50$, $R = 7.75\%$

Round decimals to the nearest hundredth and percents to the nearest whole-number percent.

241. $B = 36$, $R = 42\%$ **242.** $P = 68$, $B = 85$ **243.** $P = \$835$, $R = 3.2\%$

244. $R = 72\%$, $B = 16$ **245.** $R = 136\%$, $B = 834$ **246.** $P = 397$, $B = 200$

247. $P = 52$, $R = 17\%$ **248.** $P = 512$, $B = 128$ **249.** $P = 125$, $B = 50$

250. $B = 892$, $R = 63\%$ **251.** $B = 643$, $R = 8\%$ **252.** $P = 803$, $B = 4,015$

Use the percentage formula or one of its forms.

253. Find 30% of 80.   **254.** Find 150% of 20.

255. 30% of 27 equals what number?   **256.** What number is 70% of 300?

257. 90% of what number is 27?   **258.** 82% of what number is 94.3?

259. $33\frac{1}{3}\%$ of what number is 60?   **260.** 112 is 14% of what number?

261. 97 is what percent of 100?   **262.** What percent of 54 is 36?

263. 51.52 is what percent of 2,576?

264. What percent of 180 is 60?

265. 42 is what percent of 21?

266. 27 is what percent of 9?

267. Eighty percent of one store's customers paid with credit cards. Forty customers came in that day. How many customers paid for their purchases with credit cards?

268. If a picture frame costs $30 and the tax on the frame is 6% of the cost, how much is the tax on the picture frame?

1.80 taxes

269. Seventy percent of the town's population voted in an election. If 1,589 people voted, what is the population of the town?

270. Five percent of a batch of fuses were found to be faulty during an inspection. If 27 fuses were faulty, how many fuses were inspected?

540 fuses

271. Thirty-seven of the 50 shareholders attended the meeting. What percent of the shareholders attended the meeting?

272. In Memphis the sales tax is $8\frac{1}{4}$%. How much tax is paid on a purchase of $20.60? (Round to the nearest cent.)

1.72 tax

273. A business math student answered 60 questions correctly on a 75-question test. What percent of the questions were answered correctly?

274. A football stadium has a capacity of 53,983. If 47,892 fans attended a game, what percent of the seats were filled?

88.72% seats

275. A large university campus has 197 restrooms. If 38 of these are designed to accommodate persons with disabilities, what percent can accommodate persons with disabilities?

276. The United Way expects to raise $63 million in the current drive. The chairperson projects that 60% of the funds will be raised in the first 12 weeks. How many dollars are expected to be raised in the first 12 weeks?

$37,800,000

277. The financial officer for an accounting firm allows $3,400 for supplies in the annual budget. After three months, $898.32 has been spent on supplies. Is this figure within 25% of the annual budget?

278. An accountant who is currently earning $42,380 annually expects a 6.5% raise. What is the amount of the expected raise?

$2,754.70

Challenge Problems

279. A room is $25\frac{1}{2}$ feet by $32\frac{3}{4}$ feet wide. How much will it cost to cover the floor with carpet costing $12.50 a square yard (9 square feet), if 4 extra square yards are needed for matching? If a portion of a square yard is needed, an entire square yard must be purchased.

280. Brian Sangean has been offered a job in which he will be paid strictly on a commission basis. He will receive a 2% commission on all sales of computer hardware he closes. Brian's goal for a gross yearly salary is $30,000. How much computer hardware must Brian sell in order to meet his target salary?

281. If you have considered renting or buying a home, you may want to think about the following rule of thumb used in many real estate offices: Your rent or house payment should not be more than 25% of your monthly gross pay. If your gross pay is $1,000 a month, then your rent payment should not be more than $250 month.

$$\$1,000 \times 25\% = \$1,000 \times 0.25 = \$250$$

Example: You are interested in renting an apartment for $325 a month. Your monthly gross pay is $1,050. Should you be able to afford this payment, based on this rule of thumb?

$$\frac{\$325}{\$1,050} = 0.3095 = 31\%$$

Since $325 is about 31% of your monthly salary, you may find this apartment too expensive.

In looking for an apartment, you see an advertisement for an apartment that rents for $405 a month. If your monthly salary is $1,625, is this apartment affordable for you?

If your gross pay is $1,250 a month, what is the approximate rent you should be able to pay?

If your house payment is $375 a month and your monthly gross pay is $1,115, what percent of your pay is your house payment?

282. If you own a business that occupies space in a shopping center or mall, your lease may require you to pay a percent of the common area maintenance (CAM). This fee pays for parking lot maintenance, grounds contracts, garbage collection, taxes, sign maintenance, and other expenses that are part of the operating expenses of such a project. The amount each business pays depends on the size of the building. Each percent is based on the square footage per building or space and the total square footage of the mall or shopping center.

If your building is 8,640 square feet and the shopping center has a total of 69,590 square feet, then you occupy 12.42% of the space and must pay 12.42% of the CAM.

$$\frac{8,640}{69,590} = 0.1242 = 12.42\%$$

The total common area maintenance is $9,519.34; your share of the CAM is 12.42% of this total, or $1,182.30.

$$12.42\% \times \$9,519.34 = 0.1242 \times \$9,519.34$$

$$= \$1,182.30$$

If your business occupies 1,400 square feet in a mall containing 88,260 square feet, what percent of the mall do you occupy? If the total common area maintenance is $15,621.88, what is your share of the expense?

A lease requires the owner of a business occupying 2,000 square feet of a 78,900-square-foot shopping center to pay a percent of the yearly taxes based on space occupied. If the taxes for the year are $18,789, how much must the business owner pay?

CHAPTER 3 PRACTICE TEST

Perform the indicated operation. Reduce results to lowest terms.

1. $\dfrac{5}{6} - \dfrac{4}{6}$

2. $\dfrac{5}{8} + \dfrac{9}{10}$

3. $\dfrac{5}{8} \times \dfrac{7}{10}$

4. $\dfrac{5}{6} \div \dfrac{3}{4}$

5. $10\dfrac{1}{2} \div 5\dfrac{3}{4}$

6. $56 \times 32\dfrac{6}{7}$

7. $2\dfrac{1}{2} + 3\dfrac{1}{3}$

8. $137 - 89\dfrac{4}{5}$

9. Dale Burton ordered $\frac{3}{4}$ truckload of merchandise. If approximately $\frac{1}{3}$ of the $\frac{3}{4}$ truckload of merchandise has been unloaded, how much remains to be unloaded?

10. A company that employs 580 people expects to lay off 87 workers. What fractional part of the workers are expected to be laid off?

Write the decimal as a percent.

11. 0.24

12. 0.925

13. 0.6

Write the fraction or mixed number as a percent.

smaller/bigger

14. $\frac{21}{100}$

15. $\frac{3}{8}$ $\frac{3}{8} \times 100\%$

$8\overline{)3.00}$

16. Write $\frac{1}{4}$% as a fraction.

$\frac{1}{4}\% \div 100\%$

$\frac{1}{4} \times \frac{1}{100}\%$

Use the percentage formula or one of its forms.

17. Find 30% of $240.

$P = .30 \times 240 = 72$

18. 50 is what percent of 20?

$\frac{50}{20} \div 2.50\%$

19. What percent of 8 is 7?

$\frac{8}{7} =$

20. What is the sales tax on an item that costs $42 if the tax rate is 6%?

$P = R \times B$

$6\% \times \$42$

21. If 100% of 22 rooms are full, how many rooms are full?

22. Twelve employees at a meat packing plant were sick on Monday. If the plant employs 360 people, what percent of the employees were sick on Monday?

$\frac{12}{360}$

23. A department store had 15% turnover in personnel last year. If the store employs 600 people, how many employees were replaced last year?

$P = R \times B$

$.15 \times 600 =$

24. The Dawson family left a 15% tip for a restaurant check. If the check totaled $19.47, find the amount of the tip. What was the total cost of the meal, including the tip?

$B = R \times P$

$.15 \times 19.47$

25. A certain make and model of automobile was projected to have a 3% rate of defective autos. If the number of defective automobiles was projected to be 1,698, how many automobiles were to be produced?

26. Of the 26 questions on this practice test, 12 are word problems. What percent of the problems are word problems? (Round to the nearest whole number percent.)

$\frac{26}{12} =$

STATISTICS, TABLES, AND GRAPHS

GOOD DECISIONS THROUGH TEAMWORK

Your team has been hired to conduct market research for a major consumer magazine. Your assignment is to choose an area of interest, conduct a survey, and prepare a report of your findings.

Begin by determining a suitable multiple-choice survey question. For example, "Which soft drink do you prefer?" Then identify five to ten possible responses, including "None of the above."

Next, determine your team's survey methods: How many survey responses will you try to get? Twenty responses per team member may be realistic, but keep in mind that the more responses you get, the more reliable your results will be. Where and when will you get the responses? On campus? At a mall? Discuss how location and time of day can affect survey results.

Conduct the survey, recording your responses. Then tabulate, calculating the number of respondents choosing each possible response. Construct a circle, bar, and line graph illustrating the results.

Write a report documenting your methods, results, and conclusions, including the tabulation of responses and the summary graphs. Keep in mind: a high quality report could mean another high paying market research assignment for your team!

CHAPTER 4 STATISTICS, TABLES, AND GRAPHS

4.1 Statistics

1 ▶ *Find the range*

2 ▶ *Find the mean*

3 ▶ *Find the median*

4 ▶ *Find the mode*

5 ▶ *Put statistics to work*

4.2 Tables and Graphs

1 ▶ *Read and construct a table*

2 ▶ *Read and construct a bar graph*

3 ▶ *Read and construct a line graph*

4 ▶ *Read and construct a circle graph*

5 ▶ *Put tables and graphs to work*

Galileo once said that mathematics is the language of science. In the 21st century, he might have said that mathematics is also the language of business. Through numbers, businesspeople communicate their business history, status, and goals. And statistics, tables, and graphs are three important tools with which to do so.

4.1 Statistics

1 ▶ *Find the range*

2 ▶ *Find the mean*

3 ▶ *Find the median*

4 ▶ *Find the mode*

5 ▶ *Put statistics to work*

All through the year, a business records its daily sales. At the end of the year, 365 values—one for each day—are on record. These values are a **data set.** With this data set, and using the right *statistical* methods, we may calculate manageable and meaningful information; this information is called **statistics.** Recording the statistics, we should be able to reconstruct—well enough—the original data set, or make predictions about a future data set. Statistical methods and statistical results are the domain of the science called **statistics.**

1 ▶ *Range*

One of the first statistics we can calculate for a data set is its **range**, also called its **spread**. The range of a data set is the difference of the largest value and the smallest value. A small range indicates that the values in the data set are very similar to each other, whereas a large range indicates at least some variety.

HOW TO | **Find the Range of a Data Set**

Step 1 Identify the largest value and the smallest value of the set.
Step 2 Subtract the smallest value from the largest.

Range = largest value − smallest value

Table 4–1 Prices of Used Automobiles Sold in Tyreville Over the Weekend of May 1–2

$1,850	$ 5,600
$2,300	$ 6,100
$4,600	$ 5,800
$2,750	$ 9,400
$4,800	$11,500
$5,200	$ 5,450

Example 1 Find the range in the used automobile prices in Table 4–1. Inspection shows that the lowest price is $1,850 and the highest price is $11,500.

Range = largest value − smallest value   **Subtract the smallest from the largest to find the range.**

= $11,500 − $1,850

= $9,650

The range is $9,650, which is quite large. That is, the smallest price and the largest price are very different.

 Mean

A second statistic we may calculate for a data set is its mean. The **mean** is the statistical term for the ordinary arithmetic average. To find the mean, or arithmetic average, we divide the sum of the values by the total number of values.

HOW TO | **Find the Mean of a Data Set**

Step 1 Find the sum of the values.
Step 2 Divide the sum by the total number of values.

$$\text{Mean} = \frac{\text{sum of values}}{\text{number of values}}$$

Example 2 Find the mean used car price for the prices in Table 4–1. First find the sum of the values.

$1,850   **Add all the prices.**
2,300
4,600
2,750
4,800
5,200
5,600
6,100
5,800
9,400
11,500
+   5,450
———
$65,350

$65,350 ÷ 12 = $5,445.8\overline{3}   **There are 12 prices listed, so find the mean by dividing the sum of values by 12.**

The mean price is $5,450, rounded to the nearest ten dollars.

Median

Another kind of average is a statistic called the **median.** To find the median of a data set, we arrange the values in order from the smallest to the largest or from largest to smallest and select the value in the middle. If the data set has an even number of values, then there are two values "in the middle." In this case, the median of the data set is the mean of the middle two values. This middle value is the median.

> **? HOW TO** | **Find the Median of a Data Set**
>
> **Step 1** Arrange the values in order from smallest to largest or largest to smallest.
> **Step 2** Count the number of values.
>   **a)** If the number of values is odd, identify the value in the middle.
>   **b)** If the number of values is even, find the mean of the middle two values.
>
>   Median = middle value or mean of middle two values

Example 3   Find the median price of used cars in Table 4–1.

      $11,500   **Arrange the values from largest to smallest. There are 12**
        9,400   **prices, an even number; so there are two "middle" prices.**
        6,100
        5,800
        5,600
        5,450 ←   **There are two "middle" values: 5 values above and 5**
        5,200 ←   **values below the pair.**
        4,800
        4,600
        2,750
        2,300
        1,850

$$\frac{5,450 + 5,200}{2} = 5,325$$ **Find the mean of the middle two values by dividing their sum by 2.**

The median price is $5,325.

 Mode

A third kind of average is the **mode.** The mode is the value or values that occur most frequently in a data set. If no value occurs most frequently, then there is no mode for that data set. Since no used car price in Table 4–1 occurs more than once, there is no mode for that set of prices.

> **? HOW TO** | **Find the Mode(s) of a Data Set**
>
> **Step 1** For each value, count the number of times the value occurs.
> **Step 2** Identify the value or values that occur most frequently.
>
>   Mode = Most frequent value(s)

Example 4 Find the mode(s) for this set of test grades in a mathematics class:

76, 83, 94, 76, 53, 83, 74, 76, 97, 83, 65, 77, 76, 83

The grade of 76 occurs four times. The grade of 83 also occurs four times. All other grades occur once each. Therefore, both 76 and 83 occur the same number of times and are modes.

Both 76 and 83 are modes for this set of test grades.

 Putting Statistics to Work

The range of a data set describes the spread of values. The mean, median, and mode may each be called an *average*. Taken together, the mean, median, and mode describe the tendencies of a data set to cluster between the smallest and largest values. Sometimes it is useful to know all three of these statistical averages, since each represents a different way of describing the data set. It is like looking at the same thing from three different points of view.

To look at just one statistic for a set of numbers often distorts the total picture. It is advisable to find the range, mean, median, and mode and then analyze the results.

⚠ TIPS & TRAPS

When the range for a set of data is small, the mean, median, and mode usually have values that are very similar. When the range is very large, it is especially important to examine each of the three averages—mean, median, and mode—to determine which is most representative of the data. The mean can be greatly affected by extreme values in a set of data. In this case the mean is less descriptive of the set.

Example 5 A real estate agent told a prospective buyer that the average cost of a home in Tyreville was $71,000 during the past three months. The agent based this statement on this list of selling prices: $170,000, $150,000, $50,000, $50,000, $50,000, $50,000, $49,000, $45,000, $25,000.

Which statistic—the mean, the median, or the mode—gives the most realistic picture of how much a home in Tyreville is likely to cost?

1 Decision needed

Which statistic gives the most realistic picture of how much a home in Tyreville is likely to cost?

2 Unknown facts

The range, mean, median, and mode

3 Known facts

Houses sold during the period: 9
Prices of these houses: $170,000, $150,000, $50,000, $50,000, $50,000, $50,000, $49,000, $45,000, and $25,000.

4 Relationships

Range = largest value − smallest value
Mean = sum of values ÷ number of values
Median = middle value when values are arranged in order
Mode = most frequent value

---

5 Estimation	The mean, median, and mode are between $25,000 (smallest value) and $170,000 (largest value). To estimate the mean, group values that total approximately 100,000 or 200,000, then add the estimates and divide by 9. $170,000 + 25,000$ is approximately 200,000. $150,000 + 50,000$ is 200,000; $50,000 + 50,000 + 50,000 + 49,000$ is approximately 200,000. $200,000 + 200,000 + 200,000 + 45,000 = 645,000$; $645,000 \div 9$ is approximately 70,000. Thus, the estimated mean is $70,000. Estimation of the range, median, and mode is not appropriate.
6 Calculations	Range = largest value − smallest value $= \$170,000 - \$25,000$ $= \$145,000$ Mean = sum of values ÷ number of values $= \$639,000 \div 9$ $= \$71,000$ The values are listed in order from largest to smallest, and the middle value is $50,000. Median = middle value = $50,000 Mode = most frequent amount = $50,000 The range is $145,000. The mean is $71,000. The median is $50,000. The mode is $50,000.
7 Decision made	The large range indicates extremes in prices, so the mean is probably not the most useful statistic. **The median and mode give a more realistic picture of how much a home is likely to cost: about $50,000.**

Self-Check 4.1

1. Find the range of the numbers: 3,850; 5,300; 8,550; 4,200; 5,350.

2. Salaries for the research and development department of Richman Chemical were given as: $48,397, $27,982, $42,591, $19,522, $32,400, and $37,582. Find the range.

3. Sales in thousand dollars for men's suits for a major department store chain for a twelve-month period were: 127, 215, 135, 427, 842, 687, 321, 512, 351, 742, 482, 305. Find the range.

4. Find the range for the following prices of cars sold by AutoWonderland Cars on the given Friday: $17,485; $14,978; $13,592; $14,500; and $18,540.

5. Find the mean of the numbers: 3,850; 5,300; 8,550; 4,200; 5,350.

6. Find the mean for the salaries given in Exercise 2.

7. Find the mean for the men's suits sales in Exercise 3.

8. Find the mean price of cars sold in Exercise 4.

3 ▶ 9. Find the median of the numbers: 3,850; 5,300; 8,550; 4,200; 5,350.

10. Find the median for the salaries in Exercise 2.

11. Find the median for the men's suits sales in Exercise 3.

12. Find the median for the price of cars sold in Exercise 4.

4 ▶ 13. Find the mode for the numbers: 86, 94, 73, 94, 84, 86, 94.

14. Find the mode for the test scores of students who took the test on Chapter 3: 85, 92, 72, 80, 43, 97, 86, 99, 86, 93, 75, 86, 92, 100, 49, 85

15. The recorded temperatures for a seven-day period were: 83, 78, 85, 79, 82, 82, 80. What is the mode?

16. The following scores are recorded by a researcher: 109, 83, 89, 89, 83, 89, 95, 93, 83, 79, 106. What is the mode?

5 ▶ 17. Last Saturday, Autowonderland sold cars for the prices: $15,300, $17,500, $11,400, $14,500, and $13,500. Find the range, the mean, the median, and the mode for these car prices. What do these prices tell us about the cost of cars sold last Saturday? Which statistic(s) would give the most realistic description of Autowonderland's prices on Saturday?

18. Accountants often use the median when studying salaries for various businesses. What is the median of the following salary list? $32,084, $21,983, $27,596, $43,702, $38,840, $25,997.

19. What is the range of the salaries given in Exercise 18?

20. Weather forecasters sometimes give the average (mean) temperature for a particular city. The following temperatures were recorded as highs on June 30 of the last 10 years in a certain city: 89°, 88°, 90°, 92°, 95°, 89°, 93°, 98°, 93°, 97°. What is the mean high temperature for June 30 for the last 10 years?

21. What is the range of temperatures in Exercise 20?

22. What is the median temperature on June 30 for the city in Exercise 20?

23. What is the mode(s) temperature(s) in Exercise 20?

1 ▶ *Read and construct a table*

2 ▶ *Read and construct a bar graph*

3 ▶ *Read and construct a line graph*

4 ▶ *Read and construct a circle graph*

5 ▶ *Put tables and graphs to work*

Scan a newspaper, a magazine, or a business report, and you are likely to see tables and graphs. Tables and graphs do more than present sets of data. They make visual the relationship between the sets. The relationship between data sets might be visualized by a table, a bar graph, a line graph, or a circle graph. Depending on "what you want to see," one of these forms helps you to see the relationship more meaningfully.

1 ▶ *Tables*

A **table** displays data in rows and columns. Each place that a row and column intersects is called an **entry** or a **cell** of the table. It is important to give a meaningful title to a table, and to label the columns and rows according to what each measures. In this way, data can be accurately read and interpreted.

A table may be a simple correspondence or a complex one. Table 4–2 displays membership data for the Feel Good Fitness Club. This simple table relates the months of 1995 to the numbers of men registered as members of the club at the end of each month.

Table 4–2   1995 Monthly Male Membership for the Feel Good Fitness Club

Month	Jan	Feb	March	April	May	June	July	Aug	Sep	Oct	Nov	Dec
Members Joining	169	176	151	153	154	152	150	148	151	157	159	166

A table with just two rows, or two columns, is easy to read, but only a little more useful than a simple list. The more data you pack into a table, the more useful it may be. Naturally, reading the table becomes more difficult. Table 4–3 adds to the data in Table 4–2, and displays not only male membership, but female.

Table 4–3   1995 Monthly Membership for the Feel Good Fitness Club, Male and Female

Month	Jan	Feb	March	April	May	June	July	Aug	Sep	Oct	Nov	Dec
Male	169	176	151	153	154	152	150	148	151	157	159	166
Female	173	179	154	155	156	158	156	155	159	163	165	172

Reading Table 4–3, we can compare male and female membership for the same month. Reading the July column, for instance, we see that the male July entry is 150, and the female July entry is 156: At the end of July there were 150 men and 156 women in the club.

Table 4–4 is a more complicated table still: not only does the table display male/female membership for 1995; it does so for 1991, 1992, 1993, and 1994 as well. Reading Table 4–4 requires more attention: looking for a particular cell we must find the year, month, and male or female data.

A Crunch for Cereal Makers

Breakfast will never be the same in Micheal Miller's household. To cut his family's $420-a-month grocery bill, the 40-year-old beverage distributor from Rices Landing, Pa., has zeroed in on a pricey target: cereals. Instead of purchasing Cheerios at the local Giant Eagle supermarket, Miller now brings home a store brand called Food Club's Toasted Oats. Cheerios costs almost $4 a box, while Toasted Oats sells for $1.79. Says Miller: "We don't notice a quality difference but we notice a big difference in value."

Like Miller, many frugal Americans are turning away from name-brand cereals, which can cost nearly $5 a box. Last month, the Kellogg Co. increased prices an average of 2.6 percent across its product line. The increase represented the company's fourth price hike in the last 13 months. As a result, Corn Flakes will cost 7 percent more and Frosted Mini-Wheats an additional 4 percent. After Kellogg's increase, Quaker Oats raised cereal prices an average of 2.2 percent and Kraft General Foods upped prices on some cereals an average of 3.1 percent.

The escalating cost of cereal is an anomaly in the supermarket. Since 1990, cereal prices have climbed 15.6 percent, compared with the 5.9 percent price increase for all grocery store food. The price hikes appear to be eating into brand-name cereal sales. Seven of the top-10-selling cereals lost market share last year. A loss of just one share point is equivalent to $80 million in annual sales.

The big cereal makers are trying to hold on to customers by issuing a blizzard of coupons. According to Chicago-based Promotion Information Management, cereal coupon expenditures climbed from $785.1 million to $963.2 million last year. During the same period, the average face value of cereal coupons increased from 79 cents to 86.1 cents, well above the grocery store average of 59.5 cents. These growing

marketing expenditures seem to be hurting cereal companies' earnings. Operating net income at Kellogg declined 0.3 percent in 1993, for example, and was flat in General Mills' consumer food division for the first nine months of the current fiscal year. Says John Breuer, president of Quaker's U.S. cereals operation: "This business is a dogfight."

Kellogg, which invented Corn Flakes in 1898, has tried to aggressively defend its franchise. In one new advertising campaign, the company seeks to demonstrate that it is in sync with today's cost-conscious consumers. The TV commercials show men and women who are surprised to learn that one serving of Corn Flakes costs less than 25 cents.

General Mills has tried to break away from the cereal industry's pricing policy. When the recent round of price increases was announced, "Big G" did not follow suit. But like Kellogg, General Mills is focusing on value. It recently added 25 percent more ingredients to five popular adult cereals. And like Kellogg, General Mills is couponing aggressively. Retail and consumer promotions represent 26 percent of the company's cereal sales, up from 20 percent in fiscal 1991.

Cereal makers are increasingly shifting dollars from advertising to couponing. Industry advertising declined 1.5 percent last year, while coupon expenditures jumped 22.7 percent. This marketing mix could present problems because most discounts are matched or exceeded by competitors.

Despite the potential downside, there probably won't be a cease-fire in the cereal wars anytime soon. Still, Kellogg officials say they would like to increase advertising and cut back on couponing for existing products. But many analysts doubt that the market will allow Kellogg this luxury.

—Warren Cohen

Table 4–4   Monthly Membership for the Feel Good Fitness Club, 1991–1995

Month	Jan	Feb	Mar	April	May	June	July	Aug	Sep	Oct	Nov	Dec
1991												
Male	82	84	21	29	35	38	49	53	59	65	71	79
Female	29	32	8	12	14	15	15	17	20	23	25	28
1992												
Male	101	108	87	88	89	89	86	88	88	91	95	98
Female	66	70	33	39	43	44	44	45	47	51	58	61
1993												
Male	129	135	108	110	111	109	107	107	109	113	118	127
Female	105	115	74	76	78	79	78	77	79	86	92	101
1994												
Male	148	148	138	141	140	135	132	133	135	138	140	143
Female	147	151	117	125	126	125	125	127	132	137	142	144
1995												
Male	169	176	151	153	154	152	150	148	151	157	159	166
Female	173	179	154	155	156	158	156	155	159	163	165	172

Example 1   How many men belonged to the Feel Good Fitness Club by the end of November 1992?

We find the 1992 rows, then the male row, then the November column. The column and row intersect at the cell whose entry is 95

1992   Nov
Male   101   108   87   88   89   89   86   88   88   91   95   98

By the end of November 1992, 95 men belonged to the club.

Constructing a table, we must decide on the most convenient and revealing arrangement. The data in Table 4–4, for instance, can be constructed in a new table by reversing the rows and columns.

Example 2   Construct a table of membership data for the Feel Good Fitness Club using months as the first column.

Since months are to be the first column, we reverse the data in Table 4–4. Data for each year, then, run vertically rather than horizontally.

Table 4–5   Monthly* Membership for the Feel Good Fitness Club, 1991–1995

Month	1991 Male	1991 Female	1992 Male	1992 Female	1993 Male	1993 Female	1994 Male	1994 Female	1995 Male	1995 Female
January	82	29	101	66	129	105	148	147	169	173
February	84	32	108	70	135	115	148	151	176	179
March	21	8	87	33	108	74	138	117	151	154
April	29	12	88	39	110	76	141	125	153	155
May	35	14	89	43	111	78	140	126	154	156
June	38	15	89	44	109	79	135	125	152	158
July	49	15	86	44	107	78	132	125	150	156
August	53	17	88	45	107	77	133	127	148	155
September	59	20	88	47	109	79	135	132	151	159
October	65	23	91	51	113	86	138	137	157	163
November	71	25	95	58	118	92	140	142	159	165
December	79	28	98	61	127	101	143	144	166	172

*Number of members at the end of each month.

Notice that Table 4–5 is more compact than Table 4–4, and that columns are clearly labeled.

▶ Bar Graphs

Like tables, **bar graphs** are used to make visual the relationship between data. As its name implies, a bar graph uses horizontal or vertical bars to show relative quantities. Figure 4–1 is a bar graph of the 1995 membership data for the Feel Good Fitness Club, as originally given in Table 4–3.

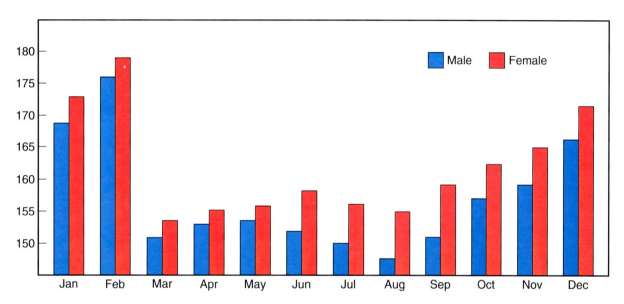

Figure 4–1 1995 Monthly Membership for the Feel Good Fitness Club, Male and Female

Along the bottom of the bar graph are the months, which correspond to the first row of Table 4–3. Along the left side of the bar graph is a scale from 150 to 180. In relation to the scale, each bar corresponds to the cells of Table 4–3. The colors of the bars distinguish data for males and females. The height of each bar corresponds to the numbers of female or male members in the club at the end of the month.

Figure 4–1 demonstrates why bar graphs are so useful: we can easily grasp the rise and fall of membership throughout the year, and see at a glance how male and female membership compare. Figure 4–1 also demonstrates a disadvantage of bar graphs, compared to tables: we lose precision. For instance, the height of the bar for female members in October looks to be between 160 and 165, but Table 4–3 tells us the precise value is 163.

In constructing a bar graph, we need to establish appropriate scales and labels.

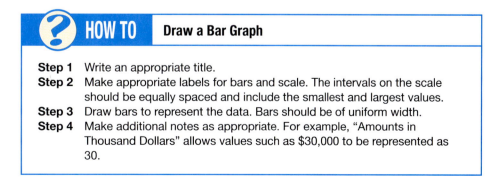

? HOW TO   **Draw a Bar Graph**

Step 1   Write an appropriate title.
Step 2   Make appropriate labels for bars and scale. The intervals on the scale should be equally spaced and include the smallest and largest values.
Step 3   Draw bars to represent the data. Bars should be of uniform width.
Step 4   Make additional notes as appropriate. For example, "Amounts in Thousand Dollars" allows values such as $30,000 to be represented as 30.

Example 3 The data show Corky's Barbecue Restaurant sales during January through June.

Draw a bar graph that represents the data.

January	$37,734	April	$52,175
February	$43,284	May	$56,394
March	$58,107	June	$63,784

The title of the graph is "Corky's Barbecue Restaurant Sales, January–June."

The smallest value is $37,734 and the largest value is $63,784. Therefore, the graph should show values from $30,000 to $70,000. To avoid using very large numbers, indicate on the graph that the numbers represent dollars in thousands. Therefore, 65 on the graph would represent $65,000. The bars can be either horizontal or vertical and we choose to make the bars horizontal. Months are labeled along the vertical line, and the dollar scale is labeled along the horizontal line. For each month, the length of the bar corresponds to the sales for the month.

Figure 4–2 Corky's Barbecue Restaurant Sales, January–June

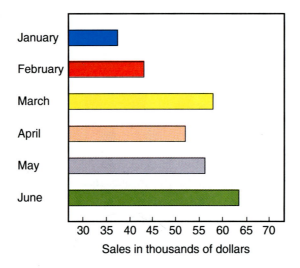

Figure 4–3 Corky's Barbecue Restaurant Sales, January–June

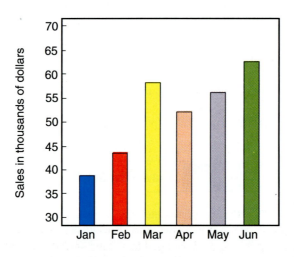

We can also use vertical bars, label months along the horizontal line and label the dollar scale along the vertical line (see Figure 4–3).

3▶ *Line Graphs*

Line graphs are very similar to vertical bar graphs. The difference is that a line graph uses a single dot to represent height, rather than a whole bar. When the dots are in place, they are connected by a line. Line graphs make even more apparent the rising and falling trends of the data. Figure 4–4 is a line graph of the vertical bar graph in Figure 4–3.

Figure 4–4 Corky's Barbecue Restaurant Sales, January–June

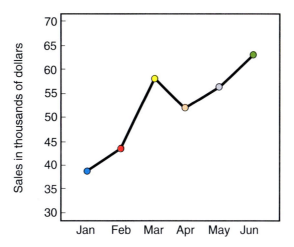

Line graphs may have enough points that connecting them yields a curve rather than angles. Figure 4–5 shows such a line graph, relating how long film must be developed to the degree of contrast achieved in the developed film. To read the graph, we locate a specific degree of contrast on the vertical scale, then move horizontally until we intersect the curve. From that point, we move down to locate the corresponding number of minutes on the horizontal scale.

Figure 4–5 Developing Time Required for Degrees of Contrast

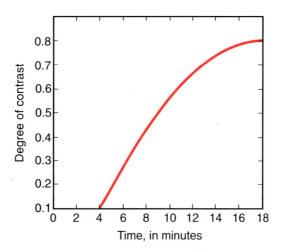

Example 4   Use Figure 4–5 to answer the questions.
a. If the film is to be developed to a contrast of 0.5, how long must it be developed?
b. If the film is developed for 13 min, what is its degree of contrast?

a. Find 0.5 on the vertical scale, then move horizontally until you intersect the curve. From the point of intersection, move down to locate the corresponding number of minutes on the horizontal scale. **Figure 4–6 shows the minutes are 9.**

---

b. Find 13 minutes on the horizontal scale, move up until you intersect the curve. From the point of intersection, move across to locate the corresponding degree of contrast. **Figure 4–6 shows the degree of contrast is 0.7.**

Figure 4–6 Developing Time Required for Degrees of Contrast

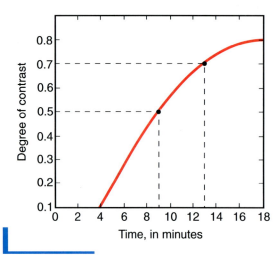

As in drawing bar graphs, drawing line graphs often means using approximations of the given data.

 HOW TO | **Draw a Line Graph**

Step 1 Write an appropriate title.
Step 2 Make and label appropriate horizontal and vertical scales, each with equally spaced intervals. Often, the horizontal scale represents time.
Step 3 Use points to locate data on the graph.
Step 4 Connect data points with line segments.

Example 5 Draw a line graph to represent the data in Table 4–6.

The smallest and greatest values in the table are $1,237 and $1,984, respectively, so the graph may go from $1,000 to $2,000 in $100 intervals. Do not label every interval. This would crowd the side of the graph and make it harder to read. The

Figure 4–7 Neighborhood Grocery Daily Sales for Week Beginning Monday, June 21

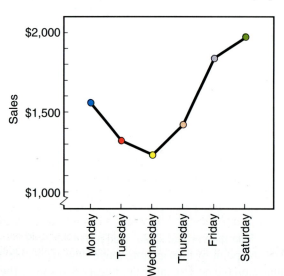

Table 4–6 Neighborhood Grocery Daily Sales for Week Beginning Monday, June 21

Monday	$1,567
Tuesday	$1,323
Wednesday	$1,237
Thursday	$1,435
Friday	$1,848
Saturday	$1,984

purpose of any graph is to give information that is quick and easy to understand and interpret.

The horizontal side of the graph will show the days of the week, and the vertical side will show the daily sales. Plot each day's sales by placing a dot directly above the appropriate day of the week across from the approximate value. For example, the sales for Monday totaled $1,567. Place the dot above Monday in the interval between $1,500 and $1,600. After each amount has been plotted, connect the dots with straight lines.

Figure 4–7 shows the resulting graph.

4 ▶ *Circle Graph*

A **circle graph** is a circle divided into sections to give a visual picture of *how some whole quantity* (represented by the whole circle) *is being divided*. Each section represents a portion of the total amount. Figure 4–8 shows a circle graph illustrating how different portions of a family's total income are spent on nine categories of expenses: food, housing, contributions, savings, clothing, insurance, education, personal items, and miscellaneous items.

Figure 4–8 Distribution of Family Monthly Take-home Pay

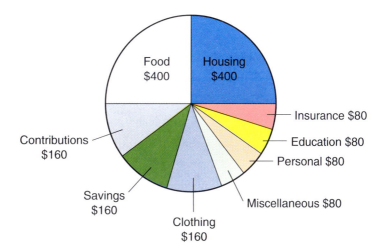

Circle graphs are relatively easy to read, and they make it easy to compare categories. The more difficult aspect of circle graphs is drawing them, because each value in the data set must be represented as a fraction of the sum of all the values. We must calculate these fractions, and then draw the graph.

❓ HOW TO | **Draw a Circle Graph**

Step 1 Write an appropriate title.

Step 2 Find the sum of the values in the data set.

Step 3 Represent each value as a fractional or decimal part of the sum of values.

Step 4 For each fraction or decimal, find the number of degrees in the sector of the circle to be represented by the fraction or decimal: Multiply the fraction or decimal by 360 degrees. The sum of the degrees for all sectors should be 360 degrees.

Step 5 Use a compass (a tool for drawing circles) to draw a circle. Indicate the center of the circle and a starting point on the circle.

Step 6 For each degree value, draw a sector: Use a protractor (a measuring instrument for angles) to measure the number of degrees for the sector of the circle to be represented by the value. Where the first sector ends, the next sector begins. The last sector should end at the starting point.

Step 7 Label each sector of the circle and make additional explanatory notes as necessary.

Example 6 Construct a circle graph showing the budgeted operating expenses for one month for Silver's Spa: Salary, $25,000; Rent, $8,500; Depreciation, $2,500; Miscellaneous, $2,000; Taxes and Insurance, $10,000; Utilities, $2,000; Advertising, $3,000. The title of the graph is "Silver's Spa Monthly Budgeted Operating Expenses." Since several calculations are required, it is helpful to organize the calculation results in a chart.

Table 4–7 Calculating Silver's Spa Circle Graph

Type of Expense	Amount of Expense	Expense as Fraction of Total Expenses	Degrees in Sector: Fraction × 360
Salary	$25,000	$\frac{25,000}{53,000}$ or $\frac{25}{53}$	$\frac{25}{53} \times 360$, or 170
Rent	$ 8,500	$\frac{8,500}{53,000}$ or $\frac{85}{530}$	$\frac{85}{530} \times 360$, or 58
Depreciation	$ 2,500	$\frac{2,500}{53,000}$ or $\frac{25}{530}$	$\frac{25}{530} \times 360$, or 17
Miscellaneous	$ 2,000	$\frac{2,000}{53,000}$ or $\frac{2}{53}$	$\frac{2}{53} \times 360$, or 14
Taxes and insurance	$10,000	$\frac{10,000}{53,000}$ or $\frac{10}{53}$	$\frac{10}{53} \times 360$, or 68
Utilities	$ 2,000	$\frac{2,000}{53,000}$ or $\frac{2}{53}$	$\frac{2}{53} \times 360$, or 14
Advertising	$ 3,000	$\frac{3,000}{53,000}$ or $\frac{3}{53}$	$\frac{3}{53} \times 360$, or 20
Total	$53,000		361*

*Extra degree due to rounding

Use a compass to draw a circle. Then measure the sectors of the circle with a protractor, using the calculations you just made. **The finished circle graph is shown in Figure 4–9.**

Figure 4–9 Monthly Budgeted Operating Expenses for Silver's Spa

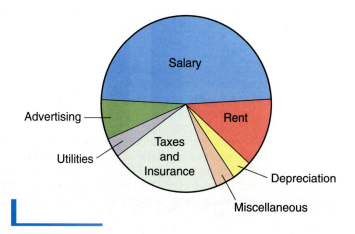

Job Picture Brightens

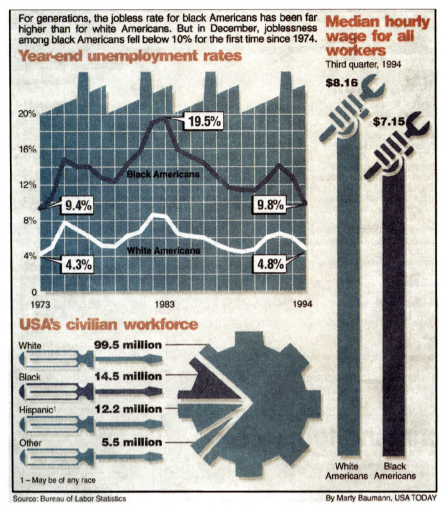

For generations, the jobless rate for black Americans has been far higher than for white Americans. But in December, joblessness among black Americans fell below 10% for the first time since 1974.

Year-end unemployment rates

19.5%
Black Americans
9.4%   9.8%
White Americans
4.3%   4.8%
1973   1983   1994

USA's civilian workforce

White   99.5 million
Black   14.5 million
Hispanic¹   12.2 million
Other   5.5 million

1 – May be of any race

Source: Bureau of Labor Statistics

Median hourly wage for all workers
Third quarter, 1994

$8.16
$7.15

White Americans   Black Americans

By Marty Baumann, USA TODAY

1. Identify the types of graphs in the article.

2. Find the total number of people in the United States civilian workforce.

3. Find the percent of White, Black, Hispanic, and Other employed in the USA's civilian workforce. Round each answer to the nearest whole percent.

4. What would a graph of the mean hourly wage for all workers represent?

5. What would a graph of the mode of hourly wage for all workers represent?

 Putting Tables and Graphs to Work

Being able to read tables and graphs allows us to pull out data and make calculations to get new data. Doing so is often referred to as *analyzing* the data. For instance, let's look again at the table of membership data for the Feel Good Fitness Club.

Example 7 How many males joined the Feel Good Fitness Club between the end of April 1991 and the end of May 1991? (See Table 4-8.)

$$\begin{array}{r} 35 \\ -\ 29 \\ \hline 6 \end{array}$$

(male members at the end of May, 1991)
(male members at the end of April, 1991)

Subtract the number of male club members in April 1991 from the number of male club members in May 1991.

Six men joined during May 1991.

Table 4–8 Monthly* Membership for the Feel Good Fitness Club, 1991–1995

Month	1991 Male	1991 Female	1992 Male	1992 Female	1993 Male	1993 Female	1994 Male	1994 Female	1995 Male	1995 Female
January	82	29	101	66	129	105	148	147	169	173
February	84	32	108	70	135	115	148	151	176	179
March	21	8	87	33	108	74	138	117	151	154
April	29	12	88	39	110	76	141	125	153	155
May	35	14	89	43	111	78	140	126	154	156
June	38	15	89	44	109	79	135	125	152	158
July	49	15	86	44	107	78	132	125	150	156
August	53	17	88	45	107	77	133	127	148	155
September	59	20	88	47	109	79	135	132	151	159
October	65	23	91	51	113	86	138	137	157	163
November	71	25	95	58	118	92	140	142	159	165
December	79	28	98	61	127	101	143	144	166	172

*Number of members at the end of each month.

Comparing data in a graph or table may involve the concept of *ratio*. The **ratio** of one number to another is a fraction whose numerator is the one number and whose denominator is the other number. When we say, for instance, that the ratio of 15 to 20 is $\frac{3}{4}$ we mean that $\frac{15}{20}$ is $\frac{3}{4}$ in reduced form. The ratio 15 to 20 can also be written as 15:20, or 3:4.

Example 8 Find the ratio of men to women in the Feel Good Fitness Club at the end of June 1994.

Make a fraction of the values.

$$\frac{135}{125} \frac{\text{men}}{\text{women}}$$ **The numerator is the number of men; the denominator is the number of women.**

$$\frac{135}{125} = \frac{27}{25}$$ **Reduce.**

The ratio of men to women at the end of June 1994 is $\frac{27}{25}$ or 27 to 25, or 27:25.

Comparing data in a table or graph may also involve the concept of *rate of change*.

Change, or the difference between two amounts, is often expressed in terms of a percent. When the change is from a smaller amount to a larger amount, the difference in the two amounts is an *increase*. Likewise, when the change is from a larger amount to a smaller amount, the difference in the two amounts is a *decrease*. Whether an increase or a decrease, this amount of change is a *percentage* of the original amount, the *base*. The **rate of change** (increase or decrease) is the *percent*. We can find the rate of change, then, using the percentage formula $R = \frac{P}{B}$.

❓ HOW TO **Find Percent or Rate of Change (Increase or Decrease)**

Step 1 Find the amount of change: subtract the larger of the original amount and new amount from the smaller of the two.

Step 2 Write the percentage formula $R = \frac{P}{B}$.

Step 3 Replace P by the amount of change, and replace B by the original amount.

Step 4 Write the fraction $\frac{P}{B}$ as a percent: multiply by 100%.

Example 9 What is the rate of change in female membership at the Feel Good Fitness Club for the year 1992?

On the table, we locate female membership at the end of Dec 1991: 28. Then we locate female membership at the end of December 1992: 61.

$$\begin{array}{r} 61 \\ -\ 28 \\ \hline 33 \end{array}$$ Subtract the larger amount from the smaller amount, to find the amount of change.

$$R = \frac{P}{B}$$ The percentage formula

$$R = \frac{33}{28}$$ Replace *P* by the amount of change and *B* by the original amount.

$$\frac{33}{28} \times 100\% = 118\%$$ Write $\frac{33}{28}$ as a percent, rounded to the nearest whole percent.

The rate of change is 118%.

Another way to find the rate of change is to write the fraction $\frac{\text{new amount}}{\text{original amount}}$ as a percent. If the percent is more than 100%, subtract 100% from it. Otherwise, subtract the percent from 100%. In either case, the difference is the rate of change.

Example 10 Find the rate of change in male membership from January to February 1993.

$$\frac{135}{129} \quad \begin{array}{l} \text{new amount} \\ \text{original amount} \end{array}$$ Write the fraction $\frac{\text{new amount}}{\text{original amount}}$.

$$\frac{135}{129} = \frac{135}{129} \times 100\%$$ Write the fraction as a percent.

$$= 105\% \text{ rounded to nearest percent}$$ 105% is more than 100%, so subtract 100% from it.

$$105\% - 100\% = 5\%$$

The rate of change is 5%.

We can find ratios and rates of change analyzing data from a line or bar graph, too. Because of their visual form, bar or line graphs lend themselves to other kinds of analysis as well.

Example 11 Use Figure 4–10 to answer the questions.

Figure 4–10 Corky's Barbecue Restaurant Sales, January–June

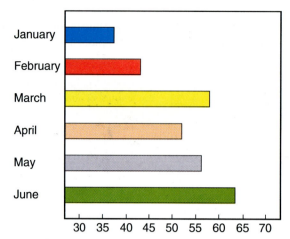

a. Which month had the highest sales? b. Estimate the total sales for the three-month period from January through March. c. Find the ratio of January sales to June sales.

a. The longest bar is for the month of June; therefore, **the sales were highest for June.**

b. January sales are estimated at $38,000; February sales are estimated at $43,000; March sales are estimated at $58,000. The estimated total sales for the three-month period is the sum of the estimated monthly sales:

$$\$38,000 + \$43,000 + \$58,000 = \$139,000.$$

The estimated sales for the three-month period are $139,000.

c. January sales are estimated at $38,000, June sales at $64,000.

$$\frac{38,000}{64,000} = \frac{38}{64} = \frac{19}{32}$$

The ratio of January sales to June sales is 19 to 32.

Circle graphs show portions of a whole, so it is natural to interpret the data in percent form. Recalling Figure 4–8, we can calculate the percent (rate) of take-home pay for any of the nine categories of expenses. Again using the formula $R = \frac{P}{B}$, we identify the amount of any category as the percentage, and the sum of all the categories as the base.

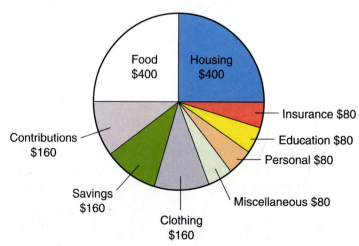

Example 12 Use Figure 4–8 to find the percent of total take-home pay spent for food.

Use the formula $R = \frac{P}{B}$. The total take-home pay is the base B; the amount spent on food is the percentage P.

$$\$400 + \$400 + \$80 + \$80$$
$$+ \$80 + \$80 + \$160 + \$160$$
$$+ \$160 = \$1,600$$

Add the amounts for each section of the graph to find the total take-home pay. Write the formula.

$$R = \frac{\text{Food}}{\text{Take-home pay}} = \frac{400}{1,600} = \frac{4}{16}$$

Divide the amount spent on food by the total take-home pay.

$$= \frac{1}{4}$$

$$\frac{1}{4} = \frac{1}{4} \times 100\% = 25\%$$

Convert $\frac{1}{4}$ to a percent.

25% of the family's take-home pay is spent on food.

Example 13 Find the percent of take-home pay available for a vacation if the family's savings and education expenses for one month are used.

Savings $160   Add savings and education costs for one month.
Education   + 80
          $240

(Part) $\rightarrow \dfrac{240}{1,600} = \dfrac{3}{20} = 0.15 = 15\%$

Write a fraction with the part as the numerator and the whole as the denominator. Multiply by 100%.

The calculator sequence is

$$\boxed{AC} \;\; 160 \;\; \boxed{+} \;\; 80 \;\; \boxed{=} \;\;\; \boxed{\div} \;\; 1600 \;\; \boxed{\times} \;\; 100 \;\; \boxed{=} \;\; \Rightarrow 15$$

The percent is 15%.

    Many calculators have a "percent" key $\boxed{\%}$ that functions similar to the "equal" key and **is used in place of the "equal" key.** The "percent" key automatically changes the numerical result of division to a percent when finding the rate. The "percent" key automatically changes a percent to its numerical equivalent when finding the percentage or base.

    Using the "percent" key, the calculator sequence is:

$$\boxed{AC} \;\; 160 \;\; \boxed{+} \;\; 80 \;\; = \;\; \boxed{\div} \;\; 1600 \;\; \boxed{\%} \;\; \Rightarrow \; 15$$

    Since changing percents to decimal equivalents and vice versa is most often done mentally, many persons choose not to use the percent key at all when using the calculator.

Use Table 4–9 for Exercises 1–4.

Table 4–9 Sales by Salesperson at Happy's Gift Shoppe

Salesperson	Sales						Total
	Mon.	Tues.	Wed.	Thurs.	Fri.	Sat.	
Brown	Off	$110.25	$114.52	$186.42	$126.81	$315.60	$853.60
Jackson	$121.68	Off	$118.29	Off	$125.42	Off	$365.39
Ulster	$112.26	$119.40	$122.35	$174.51	$116.78	Off	$645.30
Young	Off	$122.90	Off	$181.25	Off	$296.17	$600.32
Totals	$233.94	$352.55	$355.16	$542.18	$369.01	$611.77	$2,464.61

1. What day of the week had the highest amount in sales? What day had the lowest amount in sales?

2. Which day did Ulster have higher sales than any other salesperson?

3. Which salesperson made the most sales for the week? Which salesperson made the second highest amount in sales?

4. Construct a new table so that the days of the week are the first column and the names of the salespersons are the first row.

 Use Figure 4-11 for Exercises 5–7.

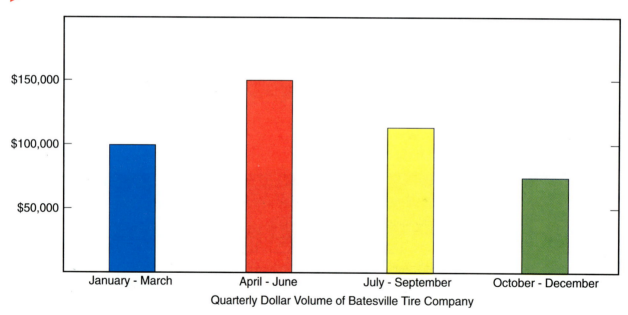

Figure 4–11 Quarterly Dollar Volume of Batesville Tire Company

5. Which quarter had the highest dollar volume?

6. What percent of the yearly sales was the sales for October-December?

7. What was the percent of increase in sales from the first to the second quarter?

8. Draw a bar graph comparing the quarterly sales of the Oxford Company: January–March, $280,000; April–June, $310,000; July–September, $250,000; October–December, $400,000.

3▶ *Use Figure 4–12 for Exercises 9–12.*

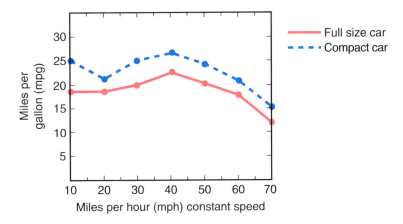

Figure 4–12 Automobile Gasoline Mileage Comparisons

9. What speed gave the highest gasoline mileage for both types of automobiles? 40

10. What speed gave the lowest gasoline mileage for both types of automobiles? 70

11. At what speed did the first noticeable decrease in gasoline mileage occur? Which car showed this decrease?

12. Identify factors other than gasoline mileage that should be considered when deciding which type of car to purchase, full size or compact.

4▶ *Use Figure 4–8 (repeated here) for Exercise 13.*

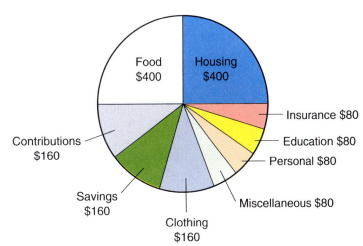

13. The family budget does not include transportation expenses. Redistribute the budget to include expenses for a vehicle. Draw a circle graph to represent the redistributed budget.

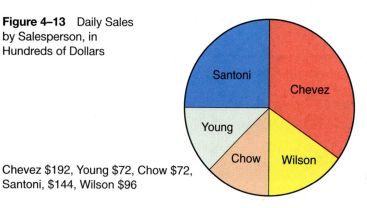

Figure 4–13 Daily Sales by Salesperson, in Hundreds of Dollars

Chevez $192, Young $72, Chow $72, Santoni, $144, Wilson $96

14. Match the dollar values with the names in the circle graph of Figure 4–13: $192, $144, $96, $72, $72

5 ▶ Use Table 4–5 on page 138 for Exercises 15–17.

15. How many more women members than men members were there in October of 1995?

16. Find the ratio of men to women in the club as of the end of December 1994.

17. What percent of the increase in club members between December 1994 and December 1995 was men?

Use Table 4–9 on page 150 for Exercises 18 and 19.
18. What percent of the week's sales was made on Thursday? What percent was made on Monday? (Round to the nearest whole percent.)

19. What percent of the day's sales for Saturday did Young make? (Round to the nearest whole percent.)

Use Figure 4–8 on page 143 for Exercises 20 and 21.
20. What percent of take-home pay is spent for contributions?

21. What percent of take-home pay is spent for education if education, savings, and miscellaneous funds are used for education?

Use Figure 4–14 for Exercises 22–25.
22. What is the percent of increase in Dale's salary from 1991 to 1992?

23. Calculate the amount and percent of increase in Dale's salary from 1993 to 1994.

24. Calculate the amount and percent of increase in Dale's salary from 1994 to 1996.

25. If the cost-of-living increase was 10% from 1990 to 1995, determine if Dale's salary for this period of time kept pace with inflation.

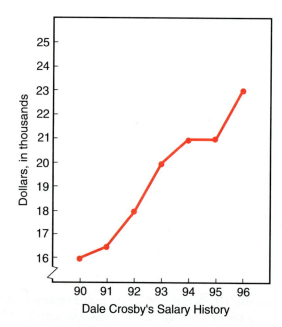

Figure 4–14

Chapter 4   Statistics, Tables, and Graphs

Self-Check 4.1

1. Range = 8,550 − 3,850 = 4,700   **2.** Range = $48,397 − $19,522 = $28,875   **3.** Range = 842 − 127 = 715 thousand dollars, or $715,000

4. Range = $18,540 − $13,592 = $4,948   **5.** Mean = (3,850 + 5,300 + 8,550 + 4,200 + 5,350) ÷ 5 = $\dfrac{27,250}{5}$ = 5,450   **6.** Mean = ($48,397 + $27,982 + $42,591 + $19,522 + $32,400 + $37,582) ÷ 6 = $\dfrac{\$208,474}{6}$ = $34,745.67

7. Mean = (127 + 215 + 135 + 427 + 842 + 687 + 321 + 512 + 351 + 742 + 482 + 305) ÷ 12 = $\dfrac{5,146}{12}$ = 428.833 thousand dollars, or $428,833   **8.** Mean = ($17,485 + $14,978 + $13,592 + $14,500 + $18,540) ÷ 5 = $\dfrac{\$79,095}{5}$ = $15,819

9. Arrange the numbers from smallest to largest:

3,850   4,200   5,300   5,350   8,550

↑
middle number

Median: 5,300

10. $19,522; $27,982; $32,400; $37,582; $42,591; $48,397

Median: $\dfrac{\$32,400 + \$37,582}{2}$ = $34,991

11. 127, 135, 215, 305, 321, 351, 427, 482, 512, 687, 742, 842

Median: $\dfrac{351 + 427}{2}$ = 389 thousand dollars, or $389,000

12. $13,592; $14,500; $14,978; $17,485; $18,540

Median: $14,978

13. Arrange the numbers from smallest to largest:

73, 84, 86, 86, 94, 94, 94

Mode: 94

14. 43, 49, 72, 75, 80, 85, 85, 86, 86, 86, 92, 92, 93, 97, 99, 100

Mode: 86

15. 78, 79, 80, 82, 82, 83, 85

Mode: 82

16. 79, 83, 83, 83, 83, 89, 89, 89, 93, 95, 106, 109

Mode: 83

17. Arrange the prices in order from smallest to largest:

$11,400 $13,500 $14,500 $15,300 $17,500

Range = $17,500 − $11,400 = $6,100

Mean = ($11,400 + $13,500 + $14,500 + $15,300 + $17,500) ÷ 5

= $72,200 ÷ 5 = $14,440

Median: = $14,500

No mode.

Since the mean and median are close but the range is large, we can use the mean and median to get a realist picture of the cost of an automobile in this area.

18. $21,983, $25,997, $27,596, $32,084, $38,840, $43,702

Median: $\dfrac{\$27,596 + \$32,084}{2}$ = $29,840

19. Range = $43,702 − $21,983 = $21,719

20. Mean = (89 + 88 + 90 + 92 + 95 + 89 + 93 + 98 + 93 + 97) ÷ 10 = 92.4

21. Range = 98 − 88 = 10 degrees   **22.** 88, 89, 89, 90, 92, 93, 93, 95, 97, 98. Median: $\dfrac{92 + 93}{2}$ = 92.5

23. Modes: 89 and 93

1. Saturday highest ($611.77); Monday lowest ($233.94)   **2.** Wednesday ($122.35)   **3.** Most sales: Brown ($853.60); Second highest sales: Ulster ($645.30)

4. Sales by Salesperson at Happy's Gift Shoppe

Day	Salesperson				Total
	Brown	**Jackson**	**Ulster**	**Young**	
Mon	Off	$121.68	$112.26	Off	$233.94
Tue	$110.25	Off	$119.40	$122.90	$352.55
Wed	$114.52	$118.29	$122.35	Off	$355.16
Thur	$186.42	Off	$174.51	$181.25	$542.18
Fri	$126.81	$125.42	$116.78	Off	$369.01
Sat	$315.60	Off	Off	$296.17	$611.77
Total	$853.60	$365.39	$645.30	$600.32	$2,464.61

5. April–June   **6.** $100,000 + $150,000 + $125,000 + $80,000 = $455,000

$$\frac{\$80,000}{\$455,000} = 17.6\%$$

7. $150,000 − $100,000 = $50,000

$$\frac{\$50,000}{\$100,000} = 50\%$$

8.

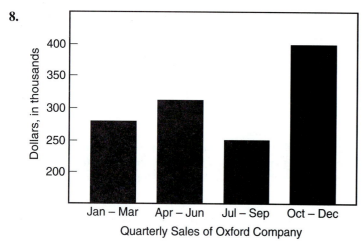

Quarterly Sales of Oxford Company

9. 40 mph   **10.** 70 mph   **11.** 20 mph, compact car   **12.** Answers will vary; consider price, safety, room or space, comfort.

13. Answers will vary.   **14.** Chevez, $192; Young, $72; Chow, $72; Santoni, $144; Wilson, $96

15. 163 − 157 = 6   **16.** $\dfrac{\text{Men}}{\text{Women}} = \dfrac{143}{144}$ **17.** Total club members at the end of December 1994 = 143 + 144 = 287
Total club members at the end of December 1995 = 166 + 172 = 338
New club members in 1995 = 338 − 287 = 51
New male club members in 1995 = 166 − 143 = 23

Male percent of new club members $= \dfrac{P}{B} = \dfrac{23}{51} = \dfrac{23}{51} \times 100\% = 45\%$

18. Percent of week's sales made on Thursday $= \dfrac{P}{B} = \dfrac{\$542.18}{\$2,464.61} = 0.2199861 = 22\%$

Percent of week's sales made on Monday $= \dfrac{P}{B} = \dfrac{\$233.94}{\$2,464.61} = 0.0949196 = 9\%$

19. Percent of day's sales made by Young on Saturday $= \dfrac{P}{B} = \dfrac{\$296.17}{\$611.77} = 0.4841198 = 48\%$

20. Percent of total take-home pay spent for contributions $= \dfrac{P}{B} = \dfrac{\$160}{\$1600} = \dfrac{\$160}{\$1600} \times 100\% = 10\%$

21. Percent of total take-home pay spent for education if education, savings, and miscellaneous funds are used =

$$\frac{P}{B} = \frac{\$80 + \$160 + \$80}{\$1600} = \frac{\$320}{\$1600} = \frac{\$320}{\$1600} \times 100\% = 20\%$$

22. $18,000 − $16,500 = $1,500   **23.** $21,000 − $20,000 = $1,000   **24.** $23,000 − $21,000 = $2,000

$$\frac{\$1,500}{\$16,000} \times 100\% = 9.1\%$$ $$\frac{\$1,000}{\$20,000} \times 100\% = 5\%$$ $$\frac{\$2,000}{\$21,000} \times 100\% = 9.5\%$$

25. $21,000 − $16,000 = $5,000

$$\frac{\$5,000}{\$16,000} \times 100\% = 31\%$$

Yes, the percent of increase was 31% and it exceeded rate of inflation.

CHAPTER 4 OVERVIEW

Section—Objective

Important Points with Examples

4.1 — 1 (page 130)

Find the range

Step 1 Identify the largest value and the smallest value of the set. **Step 2** Subtract the smallest value from the largest.

$$\text{Range} = \text{largest value} - \text{smallest value}$$

> A survey of computer stores in a large city shows that a certain printer was sold for the following prices: $435, $398, $429, $479, $435, $495, and $435. Find the range.
>
> $$\text{Range} = \text{largest value} - \text{smallest value} = \$495 - \$398 = \$97$$

4.1 — 2 (page 131)

Find the mean

Step 1 Find the sum of the values. **Step 2** Divide the sum by the total number of values.

$$\text{Mean} = \frac{\text{sum of values}}{\text{number of values}}$$

> Find the median price of the printers (see example above).
>
> $$\text{Mean} = \frac{\text{sum of values}}{\text{number of values}}$$
>
> $$= \frac{\$435 + \$398 + \$429 + \$479 + \$435 + \$495 + \$435 = \$3106}{7}$$
>
> $$= \$443.71$$

4.1 — 3 (page 132)

Find the median

Step 1 Arrange the values in order from smallest to largest or largest to smallest. **Step 2** Count the number of values: **a)** If the number of values is odd, identify the value in the middle. **b)** If the number of values is even, find the mean of the middle two values.

$$\text{Median} = \text{middle value or mean of middle two values}$$

Find the median price of the printers (see example above).

Median = middle value of $495, $479, $435, $435, $435, $429, $398

= $435

Find the mode

(page 132)

Step 1 For each value, count the number of times the value occurs. **Step 2** Identify the value or values that occur most frequently.

Mode = most frequent value(s)

Find the mode price of the printers (see example above).

Mode = most frequent value

= $435

Put statistics to work

(page 133)

When the range for a set of data is small, the mean, median, and mode usually have values that are very similar. When the range is very large, it is especially important to examine each of the three averages—mean, median, and mode—to determine which is most representative of the data. The mean can be greatly affected by extreme values in a set of data. In this case, the mean is less descriptive of the set.

Find the range, mean, median, mode for the scores: 95, 97, 98, 95, 92, 93, 97, 95, 98, 93

range = 98 − 92 = 6

$$\text{mean} = \frac{95 + 97 + 98 + 95 + 92 + 93 + 97 + 95 + 98 + 93}{10} = \frac{953}{10} = 95.3$$

arranged from smallest to largest: 92, 93, 93, 95, 95, 95, 97, 97, 98, 98

median = 95

mode = 95 since 95 occurs three times

Since the range is small, the mean, median, and mode are very close.

Read and construct a table

(page 136)

A table consists of sets of data grouped horizontally in rows and vertically in columns. In this way, values of one data set are corresponded to values of another data set.

		M	T	W	T	F	S	S	Total
	Payroll Register								
Brown		8	8	8	8	8			40
James		8	6	8	8	8	4		42
Warwick		8	8	8	8	0	8		40
Zedick		8	0	8	8	8	0		32

How many hours did James work on Tuesday?   6
Which employee worked the least number of hours for the week?   Zedick

 **(page 139)**

Read and construct a bar graph

Draw a bar graph Step 1 Write an appropriate title. **Step 2** Make appropriate labels for bars and scale. The intervals on the scale should be equally spaced and include the smallest and largest values. **Step 3** Draw bars to represent the data. Bars should be of uniform width. **Step 4** Make additional notes as appropriate. For example, "Amounts in Thousand Dollars" allows values such as $30,000 to be represented by 30.

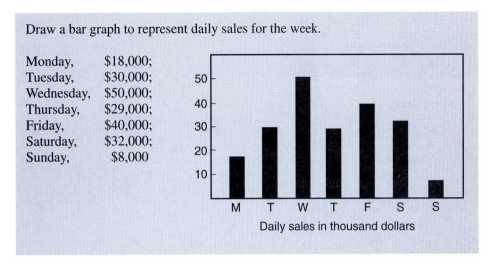

Draw a bar graph to represent daily sales for the week.

Monday, $18,000;
Tuesday, $30,000;
Wednesday, $50,000;
Thursday, $29,000;
Friday, $40,000;
Saturday, $32,000;
Sunday, $8,000

Daily sales in thousand dollars

 **(page 141)**

Read and construct a line graph

Draw a line graph **Step 1** Write an appropriate title. **Step 2** Make and label appropriate horizontal and vertical scales, each with equally spaced intervals. Often, the horizontal scale represents time. **Step 3** Use points to locate data on the graph. **Step 4** Connect data points with line segments.

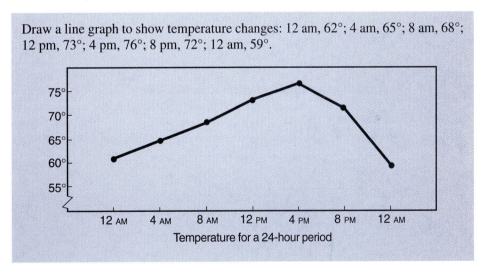

Draw a line graph to show temperature changes: 12 am, 62°; 4 am, 65°; 8 am, 68°; 12 pm, 73°; 4 pm, 76°; 8 pm, 72°; 12 am, 59°.

Temperature for a 24-hour period

 **(page 143)**

Read and construct a circle graph

Draw a circle graph Step 1 Write an appropriate title. **Step 2** Find the sum of the values in the data set. **Step 3** Represent each value as a fractional or decimal part of the sum of values. **Step 4** For each fraction or decimal, find the number of degrees in the sector of the circle to be represented by the fraction or decimal: Multiply the fraction or decimal by 360 degrees. The sum of the degrees for all sectors should be 360 degrees. **Step 5** Use a compass (a tool for drawing circles) to draw a circle. Indicate the center of the circle and a starting point on the circle. **Step 6** For each degree value, draw a sector: Use a protractor (a measuring instrument for angles) to measure the number of degrees for the sector of the circle to be represented by the value. Where the first sector ends, the next sector begins. The last sector should end at the starting point. **Step 7** Label each sector of the circle and make additional explanatory notes as necessary.

Draw a circle graph to represent the data.

Total salary: $28,000
Housing: $8,000
Food: $6,000
Clothing: $1,000
Transportation: $2,000
Taxes: $5,000
Insurance: $1,800
Utilities: $1,200
Savings: $3,000

Housing: $\dfrac{\$8,000}{\$28,000} \times 360° = 103°$

Food: $\dfrac{\$6,000}{\$28,000} \times 360° = 77°$

Clothing: $\dfrac{\$1,000}{\$28,000} \times 360° = 13°$

Transportation: $\dfrac{\$2,000}{\$28,000} \times 360° = 26°$

Taxes: $\dfrac{\$5,000}{\$28,000} \times 360° = 64°$

Insurance: $\dfrac{\$1,800}{\$28,000} \times 360° = 23°$

Utilities: $\dfrac{\$1,200}{\$28,000} \times 360° = 15°$

Savings: $\dfrac{\$3,000}{\$28,000} \times 360° = 39°$

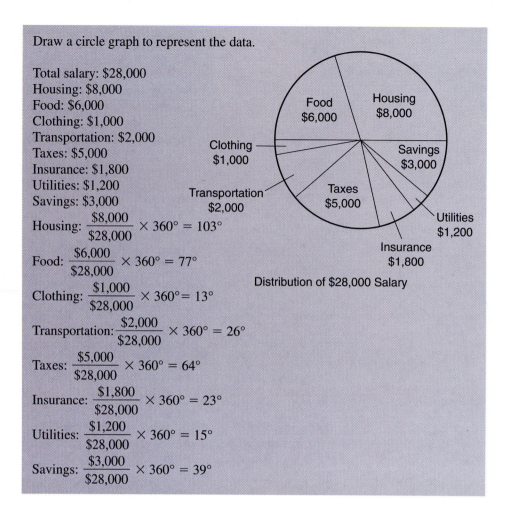

Distribution of $28,000 Salary

4.2 — 5 (page 145)

Put tables and graphs to work

Find Percent or Rate of Change (Increase or Decrease) Step 1 Find the amount of change: Subtract the larger of the original amount and new amount from the smaller of the two. **Step 2** Write the percentage formula $R = \frac{P}{B}$ **Step 3** Replace P by the amount of change and replace B by the original amount. **Step 4** Write the fraction $\frac{P}{B}$ as a percent: Multiply by 100%.

Mario's salary increased from $53,840 to $62,500. What was the percent increase?

$62,500 - \$53,840 = \$8,660$ increase

$\dfrac{\$8,660}{\$53,840} \times 100\% = 16.1\%$ increase

Section 4.1

Find the range, mean, median, and mode for the following. Round to the nearest hundredth if necessary.

1. New car mileages
   17 mi/gal
   16 mi/gal
   25 mi/gal
   22 mi/gal
   30 mi/gal

2. Test scores
   61
   72
   63
   70
   93
   87

3. Sandwiches
   $0.95
   $1.65
   $1.27
   $1.97
   $1.65
   $1.15

4. Credit hours
   16
   12
   18
   15
   16
   12
   12

5. Find the range, mean, median, and mode of the hourly pay rates for the employees.

Thompson	$13.95	Cleveland	$ 5.25
Chang	$ 5.80	Gandolfo	$ 4.90
Jackson	$ 4.68	DuBois	$13.95
Smith	$ 4.90	Serpas	$13.95

6. Find the range, mean, median, and mode of the weights of the metal castings after being milled.

Casting A	1.08 kg	Casting D	1.1 kg
Casting B	1.15 kg	Casting E	1.25 kg
Casting C	1.19 kg	Casting F	1.1 kg

7. During the past year, Piazza's Clothiers sold a certain sweater at different prices: $42.95, $36.50, $40.75, $38.25, and $43.25. Find the range, mean, median, and mode of the selling prices.

8. Which statistic in Exercise 7 best represents the price of the sweater?

Section 4.2

Use Table 4–10 for Exercises 9–17.

Table 4–10   Class Enrollment by Period and Days of the First Week for the Second Semester

Period	Mon.	Tues.	Wed.	Thur.	Fri.	Sat.
1. 7:00– 7:50 A.M.	277	374	259	340	207	0
2. 7:55– 8:45 A.M.	653	728	593	691	453	361
3. 8:50– 9:40 A.M.	908	863	824	798	604	361
4. 9:45–10:35 A.M.	962	782	849	795	561	361
5. 10:40–11:30 A.M.	914	858	795	927	510	361
6. 11:35–12:25 P.M.	711	773	375	816	527	182
7. 12:30– 1:20 P.M.	686	734	696	733	348	161
8. 1:25– 2:15 P.M.	638	647	659	627	349	85
9. 2:20– 3:10 P.M.	341	313	325	351	136	78
10. 3:15– 4:05 P.M.	110	149	151	160	45	0
11. 4:10– 5:00 P.M.	46	72	65	67	11	0
12. 5:05– 5:55 P.M.	37	91	68	48	0	0
13. 6:00– 6:50 P.M.	809	786	796	705	373	0
14. 6:55– 7:45 P.M.	809	786	796	705	373	0
15. 7:50– 8:40 P.M.	565	586	577	531	373	0
16. 8:45– 9:35 P.M.	727	706	817	758	373	0
17. 9:40–10:30 P.M.	702	706	817	758	27	0
18. 10:35–11:25 P.M.	76	70	46	98	0	0

9. How many students were enrolled in class on Wednesday during the fifth period?

10. How many students were enrolled in class on Monday during the eleventh period?

11. What is the total class enrollment for the third period Monday through Friday?

12. What is the total class enrollment for the ninth period Monday through Friday?

13. How many more people are enrolled in third period Monday through Friday than in ninth period?

14. Find the total class enrollment by periods Monday through Friday.

Period	Students
1	
2	
3	
4	
5	
6	
7	
8	
9	
10	
11	
12	
13	
14	
15	
16	
17	
18	

15. What period has the highest enrollment during the day (periods 1 to 12)?

16. What period has the highest enrollment at night (periods 13 to 18)?

17. If 1,768 day students were enrolled during the second semester, what percent of the students were enrolled in a fourth-period class on Monday? Round to the nearest tenth of a percent.

18. Complete Table 4–11, calculating day enrollment (periods 1 to 12) and night enrollment (periods 13 to 18).

Table 4–11 Day and Night Class Enrollment Second Semester

	Periods	Mon.	Tues.	Wed.	Thurs.	Fri.	Sat.
Day	1–12						
Night	13–18						

Use Table 4–12 for Exercises 19–20 and 25–26.

Table 4–12 Sales for The Family Store, 1995–1996

	1995	1996
Girls' clothing	$ 74,675	$ 81,534
Boys' clothing	$ 65,153	$ 68,324
Women's clothing	$125,115	$137,340
Men's clothing	$ 83,895	$ 96,315

19. What is the least value for 1995 sales? For 1996 sales?

20. What is the greatest value for 1995 sales? For 1996 sales?

Use Figure 4–15 for Exercises 21–24.

Figure 4–15 Distribution of Tax Dollars

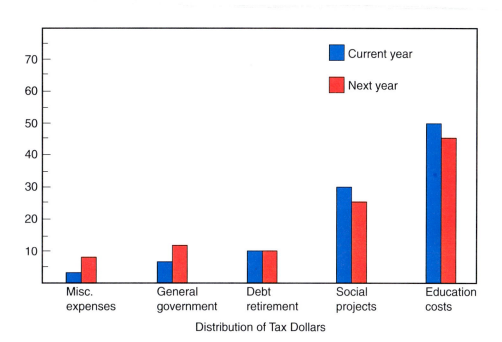

Distribution of Tax Dollars

21. What expenditure is expected to be the same next year as this year?

22. What two expenditures are expected to increase next year?

23. What two expenditures are expected to decrease next year?

24. What is the percent of decrease in the education costs?

25. Using the values in Table 4–11, which of the following interval sizes would be more appropriate in making a bar graph? Why?
   a. $1,000 intervals ($60,000, $61,000, $62,000, . . .)
   b. $10,000 intervals ($60,000, $70,000, $80,000, . . .)

26. Draw a comparative bar graph to show both the 1995 and 1996 values for The Family Store (see Table 4–12). Be sure to include a title, explanation of the scales, and any additional information needed.

Use Figure 4–16 for Exercises 27–30.

Figure 4–16 Monthly Sales for 7th Inning Sports Memorabilia

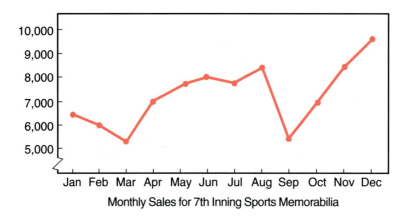

Monthly Sales for 7th Inning Sports Memorabilia

27. What three-month period maintained a fairly constant sales record?

28. Calculate the approximate annual sales.

29. What are some factors that could contribute to the dramatic drop in sales for the month of September?

30. What are some factors that could contribute to the high sales in December?

Use the information below for Exercises 31–34. The temperatures were recorded at 2-hour intervals June 24.

12 A.M.	76°	8 A.M.	70°	2 P.M.	84°	8 P.M.	82°
2 A.M.	75°	10 A.M.	76°	4 P.M.	90°	10 P.M.	79°
4 A.M.	72°	12 P.M.	81°	6 P.M.	90°	12 A.M.	77°
6 A.M.	70°						

31. What is the smallest value?

32. What is the greatest value?

33. Which interval size is most appropriate when making a line graph? Why?
   a. 1°   b. 5°   c. 50°   d. 100°

34. Draw a line graph representing the data. Be sure to include the title, explanation of the scales, and any additional information needed.

35. Which of the following terms would describe this line graph?
   a. Continually increasing   b. Continually decreasing   c. Fluctuating

Use Figure 4–17 for Exercises 36–39.

Figure 4–17 Distribution of Gross Pay ($350)

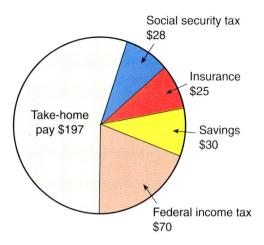

Social security tax
$28

Insurance
$25

Savings
$30

Take-home
pay $197

Federal income tax
$70

36. What percent of the gross pay goes into savings? Round to tenths.

37. What percent of the gross pay is federal income tax? Round to tenths.

38. What percent of the gross pay is the take-home pay? Round to tenths.

39. What are the total deductions for this payroll check?

Use Figure 4–18 for Exercises 40–42.

40. What percent of the overall cost does the lot represent? (Round to the nearest tenth.)

41. What is the cost of the lot with landscaping? What percent of the total cost does this represent? (Round to the nearest tenth.)

42. What is the cost of the house with furnishings? What percent of the total cost does this represent? (Round to the nearest tenth.)

Figure 4–18 Distribution of Costs for an $86,000 Home

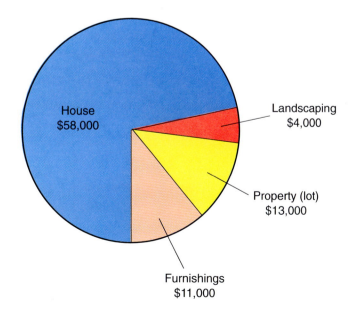

House
$58,000

Landscaping
$4,000

Property (lot)
$13,000

Furnishings
$11,000

Use the Automobile Dealership table for Exercises 43–46.

43. What was the total number of cars sold?

44. How many degrees should be used to represent the new business on the circle (to the nearest whole degree)?

45. How many degrees should be used to represent the repeat business on the circle (to the nearest whole degree)?

46. Construct a circle graph for these data. Label the parts of the graph as "New" and "Repeat." Be sure to include a title and any additional information needed.

47. What are some advertising strategies that could be used to increase repeat business?

Automobile Dealership's
New and Repeat Business

Customer	Cars Sold
New	920
Repeat	278

Find the range, mean, median, and mode for each set of data. Round to the nearest hundredth if necessary.

48. New car mileages

17 mi/gal
16 mi/gal
25 mi/gal
22 mi/gal
30 mi/gal

49. Test scores

61
72
63
70
93
87

Challenge Problem

50. Have the computers made a mistake? You have been attending Northeastern State College (which follows a percentage grading system) for two years. You have received good grades, but after four semesters have not made the Dean's List which requires an overall average of 90% for all accumulated credits or 90% for any given semester. Below are your grade reports:

First Semester Fall			Second Semester Spring			Third Semester Fall			Fourth Semester Spring		
Course	Cr Hr	Gr.	Course	Cr Hr	Gr.	Course	Cr Hr	Gr.	Course	Cr Hr	Gr.
BUS MATH	4	90	SOC.	3	92	FUNS.	4	88	CAL. I	4	89
ACC I	4	89	PSYC.	3	91	ACC II	4	89	ACC IV	4	90
ENG I	3	91	ENG II	3	90	ENG 888	3	95	ENG IV	3	96
HISTORY	3	92	ACC II	4	88	PURCH.	3	96	ADV.	3	93
ECON	5	85	ECON II	4	86	MGMT. I	5	84	MGMT. II	5	83

To find the grade point average for a semester, multiply each grade by the credit hours. Add the products and then divide by the total number of credit hours for the semester. To calculate the overall grade point average, proceed similarly, but divide the sum of the products for all semesters by the total accumulated credit hours.

What is the grade point average for each semester? What is your overall grade point average for the four semesters? If you take 15 credits in the *fifth* semester, what minimum semester grade point average must you earn in order to achieve an overall grade point average of 90%?

CHAPTER 4 PRACTICE TEST

Use the following data for Exercises 1–4.

42	86	92	15	32	67	48	19	87	63
15	19	21	17	53	27	21	15	82	15

1. What is the range? **2.** What is the mean? **3.** What is the median? **4.** What is the mode?

Use the following data for Exercises 5–8.

105	215	165	172	138
198	165	170	165	146
187	170	165	146	200

5. What is the range? **6.** What is the mean? **7.** What is the median? **8.** What is the mode?

The costs of producing a piece of luggage at ACME Luggage Company are: labor, $45; materials, $40; overhead, $35. Use this information for Exercises 9–14.

9. What is the total cost of producing a piece of luggage?

10. What percent of the total cost is attributed to labor?

11. What percent of the total cost is attributed to materials?

12. What percent of the total cost is attributed to overhead?

13. Compute the number of degrees for labor, materials, and overhead needed for a circle graph.

14. Construct a circle graph for the cost of producing a piece of luggage.

Katz Florist recorded the sales for a six-month period for fresh and silk flowers in Table 4–13. Use the table for Exercises 15–18.

Table 4–13 Sales for Katz Florist, Jan–June

	January	February	March	April	May	June
Fresh	$11,520	$22,873	$10,380	$12,562	$23,712	$15,816
Silk	$8,460	$14,952	$5,829	$10,621	$17,892	$7,583

15. What is the greatest value of fresh flowers? Of silk flowers?

16. What is the smallest value for fresh flowers? Of silk flowers?

17. What interval size would be most appropriate when making a bar graph? Why?
a. $100 b. $1,000 c. $5,000 d. $10,000

18. Construct a bar graph for the sales at Katz Florist.

Use the following data for Exercises 19–20. The totals of the number of laser printers sold in the years 1990 through 1995 by Smart Brothers Computer Store are as follows:

1990	1991	1992	1993	1994	1995
983	1,052	1,117	615	250	400

19. What is the smallest value? The greatest value?

20. Draw a line graph representing the data. Use an interval of 250. Be sure to include a title and explanation of the scales.

Use Figure 4–19 for Exercises 21–24.

Figure 4–19 Comparison of Sick Days for Men and Women

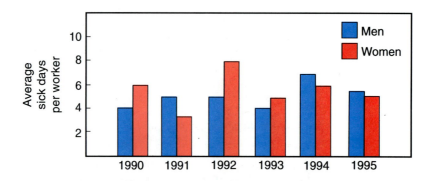

21. In what year(s) did women use more sick days than men?

22. In what year(s) did men use five sick days?

23. In what year(s) did men use more sick days than women?

24. What was the greatest number of sick days for men?

PROBLEM SOLVING WITH FORMULAS AND EQUATIONS

GOOD DECISIONS THROUGH TEAMWORK

Form teams in which team members have an interest in a similar type of business. With your team, find samples of spreadsheets used to perform a specific function in the selected business. Examples of types of businesses to investigate are retail sales, insurance, accounting, transportation, manufacturing, hospitality, catering, tourism, and health-related services.

Gather examples of the spreadsheets used in the selected business from library research, interviews with professionals or business educators, or other appropriate sources. Select one of the spreadsheets to analyze further. This analysis should include the purpose of the spreadsheet, how the information is collected, what additional information is derived through calculations, and what formulas are used to make these calculations.

Present your team's findings to the class and be prepared to answer questions from class members.

5.1 **Formulas**

1 ▸ *Evaluate formulas*
2 ▸ *Write a formula to find an unknown value*

5.2 **Equations**

1 ▸ *Solve equations using multiplication or division*
2 ▸ *Solve equations using addition or subtraction*
3 ▸ *Solve equations using more than one operation*
4 ▸ *Solve equations containing multiple unknown terms*
5 ▸ *Solve equations containing parentheses*

5.3 **Using Equations to Solve Problems**

1 ▸ *Use the decision key approach to analyze and solve word problems*

Many business problems—determining an employee's wages, for example, or determining inventory levels or profits—involve answering the question "How much?" One way to answer the question is to write relationships as *formulas or equations*. Equations and formulas are similar in that they both use letters, numbers, and mathematical symbols to express a relationship. In this chapter you will see how to use both formulas and equations to solve various business problems.

5.1 **Formulas**

1 ▸ *Evaluate formulas*
2 ▸ *Write a formula to find an unknown value*

In the problem-solving techniques we have used so far, we have written the relationships among the known and unknown facts of a problem. These relationships could also be called *formulas*. A **formula** is a mathematical shorthand for expressing the process of finding an unknown value. For example, when the rate R and base B are known and the percentage P is unknown, the formula $P = R \times B$ tells us we must multiply R and B to find P. Similarly, when the percentage P and base B are known and the rate R is unknown, the formula $R = P/B$ tells us we must divide P by B to find R.

For a formula to be meaningful, we must know what each letter in the formula represents. For example, in the percent formulas, we must know that P represents the percentage or part, R represents the fractional or decimal equivalent of the rate or percent, and B represents the total or original amount.

 ▸ *Evaluating Formulas*

Finding an unknown value in a formula when all the other values are known is called **evaluating** the formula. Remember from our work with the percentage formula that, to find an unknown value in the formula—that is, to *evaluate* the formula—we chose one of three variations of the formula, depending on which value, *P, B,* or *R,* was unknown. We always chose the variation in which the unknown was "isolated" on the left side of the formula.

? HOW TO — Evaluate a Formula

Step 1 Replace letters in the formula with their known values.
Step 2 Perform the operations indicated by the formula.
Step 3 Interpret the result.

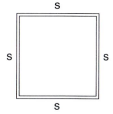

Example 1 Evaluate the formula $P = 4s$ to find the perimeter (P) of a square when we know the length of one side (s) is 8 feet.

To understand this formula, we first must know the meaning of the words *square* and *perimeter*. A **square** is a four-sided shape with all four sides equal and all four corner angles equal. The **perimeter** of a square is the distance around the edges of the square.

We must also know the meaning of the *expression* "4s." In the mathematical shorthand of formulas, a letter written next to a number means *multiply*. So $4s$ means 4 times s, or 4 times the value of s. The formula $P = 4s$, then, means "The perimeter of a square is equal to 4 times the length of one side."

Now we are ready to evaluate the formula.

$P = 4s$

$P = 4(8)$ **Replace letters in the formula with their known values: the known value of s is 8.**

$P = 32$ **Perform the indicated operations: multiply 4 by 8.**

The perimeter of the square is 32 feet.

! TIPS & TRAPS — Notation Used in Formulas

Multiplication	Division
$2A = 2 \times A$	$\dfrac{A}{B} = A \div B$
$2 \cdot A = 2 \times A$	$A/B = A \div B$
$2 * A = 2 \times A$	
$AB = A \times B$	
$A = 1 \times A$	
$3(7) = 3 \times 7$	

When a formula indicates more than one operation to be performed, we must proceed according to a particular **standard order of operations**. This order of operations is agreed upon by all those who write and use formulas. It requires us to work from **left to right,** performing **first** all multiplications and divisions as they occur in the formula and **second** all additions and subtractions as they occur in the formula. To show exceptions to this standard order, you need to use parentheses. Operations within parentheses are performed first. In the following example, we illustrate the use of the standard order of operations, and parentheses.

Example 2 Find the perimeter of a rectangle that is 7 inches long and 5 inches wide using two versions of the rectangle perimeter formula: $P = 2(l + w)$ and $P = 2l + 2w$.

Chapter 5   Problem Solving with Formulas and Equations   **169**

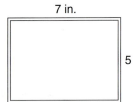

7 in.

5

A rectangle, like a square, is a four-sided shape with equal corner angles. Unlike the square, all sides of a rectangle may not be equal. But opposite sides *are* equal. Each of the two longest sides is called the *length* of the rectangle. Length is represented by l. Each of the two shortest sides is called the *width* of the rectangle. Width is represented by w. Again, P represents the perimeter or distance around the shape.

$$P = 2(l + w) \qquad P = 2l + 2w$$ **Two versions of the rectangle perimeter formula.**

$$P = 2(7 + 5) \qquad P = 2(7) + 2(5)$$ **Substitute known values.**

$$P = 2(12) \qquad P = 14 + 10$$ **Perform operations according to the order of operations: operations within parentheses are done first. Then multiply. Then add.**

$$P = 24 \qquad P = 24$$

The perimeter of the rectangle is 24 inches.

 Writing a Formula to Find an Unknown Value

Any relationship involving numbers and operations can be expressed as a formula. Some formulas are common formulas, frequently used in the business world. For example, Selling Price = Cost + Markup is a common business formula. However, common or not, any relationship involving calculations may be expressed as a formula. We have already expressed many relationships using our decision key to solve problems.

Quarterly department totals = sum of quarterly total for each employee	Section 1.1 Ex. 6, p. 7
Total quantity of cups on hand = quantity per package × cups per package	Section 1.1 Ex. 10, p. 10
Quantity of boxes needed = total number of vases ÷ vases per box	Section 1.1, Ex. 11, p. 11
Amount of tip = restaurant bill × rate of tip	Section 1.2, Ex. 6, p. 19
Adjusted statement balance = statement balance + outstanding deposits and other credits − outstanding checks and other debits	Section 2.2, Ex. 2, p. 54
Percentage = rate × base	Section 3.2, Ex. 6, p. 104
Range = largest value − smallest value	Section 4.3, Ex. 5, p. 133
Mean = sum of values ÷ number of values	Section 4.3, Ex. 5, p. 133

While formulas written in words may be easy to understand, it is cumbersome to continually write them in words. So we use single letters in place of words. Using single letters and operation symbols, we translate relationships into mathematical shorthand.

? HOW TO   Write a Formula to Find an Unknown Value

Step 1 Represent the unknown value with a letter.
Step 2 Represent each known value with a letter.
Step 3 Write the unknown-value letter on the left side of an equal sign and the known-value letters with appropriate operation symbols on the right side of the equal sign.

Example 3 Write a formula to find the perimeter of a five-sided figure if each of the five sides are equal.

We let P represent perimeter, the unknown value. Let s represent the length of a side.

One version of the formula could be $P = s + s + s + s + s$. Another version could be $P = 5s$, since, $s + s + s + s + s$ is the same as 5 times s.

Writing Computer or Calculator Instructions as Formulas A programmable calculator or a computer software program can make series of calculations. The person using the calculator or computer gives the instructions through a formula. The known facts are then entered and the calculator or computer performs the calculations. Examples of computer software packages that can evaluate formulas are DERIVE, Converge, Mathematica, and MathCad. Spreadsheet programs such as Lotus 123, Excel, and Quatro also can evaluate formulas. While each software package or programmable calculator has unique requirements for entering formulas, the basic concept for evaluating formulas with an electronic tool is the same.

Using an appropriate electronic tool, a formula for finding the perimeter of a rectangle, such as $P = 2l + 2w$, can be entered. Most of these applications require that the formula be written with the unknown value on the left of the equal sign and all known values on the right. When values for l and w are known, say, l is 12 in. and w is 7 in., these values are assigned to the respective letters. Then, the program can be instructed to evaluate the formula and display the results. The specific format of the instructions depends on the particular electronic tool. One possible sequence of instructions and results is:

1. $P = 2l + 2w$ The formula is entered.
2. $l = 12$ The known value l is entered.
3. $w = 7$ The known value of w is entered.
4. $P = 38$.   The resulting value of P is displayed.

Once the formula $P = 2l + 2w$ is entered, the formula can be evaluated for different values of l and w by reassigning l and w. For instance, let $l = 15$ and $w = 9$. The sequence of instructions that follows illustrates how different values can be used in the same formula.

1. $P = 2l + 2w$
2. $l = 12$
3. $w = 7$
4. $P = 38$
5. $l = 15$
6. $w = 9$
7. $P = 48$

The perimeter of the rectangle with a length of 15 in. and a width of 9 in. is 48 in.

An **electronic spreadsheet** is a computer program that displays information in the rows and columns of a table called a **spreadsheet.** In building a spreadsheet, data are entered into some of the cells, and formulas are entered into other cells. The spreadsheet program evaluates the formulas and displays the results in the same cells in which the formulas were entered.

The feature that makes spreadsheets so attractive in the business world is that key information can be changed while retaining the basic formulas of the spreadsheet. As new key data are entered, the program automatically updates the results in the spreadsheet. This process allows the business person to quickly see how various changes in the key data impact the results.

To illustrate the power of an electronic spreadsheet, we use the data given in Example 6 in Section 4.2, budgeted amounts for each expense category of Silver's Spa.

The spreadsheet program calculates the total budgeted amount using a formula to add the amounts in expense categories.

Figure 5–1 Silver's Spa Spreadsheet, Data Entered

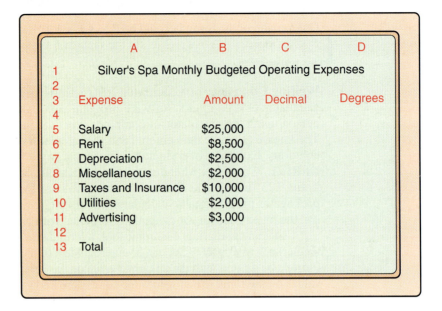

	A	B	C	D
1	Silver's Spa Monthly Budgeted Operating Expenses			
2				
3	Expense	Amount	Decimal	Degrees
4				
5	Salary	$25,000		
6	Rent	$8,500		
7	Depreciation	$2,500		
8	Miscellaneous	$2,000		
9	Taxes and Insurance	$10,000		
10	Utilities	$2,000		
11	Advertising	$3,000		
12				
13	Total			

As shown in Figure 5–1, the spreadsheet program labels columns with the letters A, B, C, D, and rows with numbers 1–13. The user enters the spreadsheet title, which is displayed as row 1, data set labels, which are displayed as row 3, and the known data, which are displayed in rows 5–11, columns A and B. The program identifies each cell by its column letter and row number.

For example, cell B5 is the cell in column B and row 5 ($25,000). The Total amount cell (B13) is calculated by adding the entries for cells B5, B6, B7, B8, B9, B10, and B11. The formula is written as B13 = B5+B6+B7+B8+B9+B10+B11. Each cell in the Decimal column is calculated as a decimal rate of the total expense. For instance, cell C5 is calculated by dividing B5 by B13. The formula is written as C5 = B5/B13. Each cell in the Degrees column is calculated as a percentage of the total degrees in a circle graph. For instance, cell D5 is calculated by multiplying C5 by 360. The formula is written as D5 = C5 * 360.

In a spreadsheet program it is very important to have all formulas written correctly. Since the results of one calculation may be used in another calculation, one incorrect formula can result in many mistakes on the spreadsheet. The formulas used in this spreadsheet are:

B13 = B5 + B6 + B7 + B8
      + B9 + B10 + B11
	C5 = B5/B13
	C6 = B6/B13
	C7 = B7/B13
	C8 = B8/B13
	C9 = B9/B13
	C10 = B10/B13
	C11 = B11/B13
	C13 = C5 + C6 + C7
	      + C8 + C9
	      + C10 + C11
		D5 = C5*360
		D6 = C6*360
		D7 = C7*360
		D8 = C8*360
		D9 = C9*360
		D10 = C10*360
		D11 = C11*360
		D13 = D5 + D6 + D7
		      + D8 + D9
		      + D10 + D11

When using some spreadsheet programs, formulas can be examined by highlighting the cell location and entering the appropriate instruction code. Figure 5–2 shows the completed spreadsheet for the budgeted expenses.

Figure 5–2 Silver's Spa Spreadsheet, Results Calculated

	A	B	C	D
1	Silver's Spa Monthly Budgeted Operating Expenses			
2				
3	Expense	Amount	Decimal	Degrees
4				
5	Salary	$25,000	0.4716981	170
6	Rent	$8,500	0.1603774	58
7	Depreciation	$2,500	0.0471698	17
8	Miscellaneous	$2,000	0.0377358	14
9	Taxes and Insurance	$10,000	0.1886792	68
10	Utilities	$2,000	0.0377358	14
11	Advertising	$3,000	0.0566038	20
12				
13	Total	$53,000	1.0000000*	360*

*Total is sum before rounding.

Because his spreadsheet uses formulas, as Mr. Silver's expense amounts change, he can use the same spreadsheet to determine total expenses, decimal cell values, and degree cell values.

Figure 5–3 Silver Spa's Spreadsheet, New Data and New Results

	A	B	C	D
1	Silver's Spa Operating Expenses for April			
2				
3	Expense	Amount	Decimal	Degrees
4				
5	Salary	$33,823	0.5487807	198
6	Rent	$8,500	0.1379131	50
7	Depreciation	$2,500	0.0405627	15
8	Miscellaneous	$3,542	0.0574692	21
9	Taxes and Insurance	$8,532	0.1384323	50
10	Utilities	$2,157	0.0349975	13
11	Advertising	$2,579	0.0418445	15
12				
13	Total	$61,633	1.0000000*	360*

*Total is sum before rounding.

Figure 5–3 illustrates the same spreadsheet and formulas but with actual amounts for April rather than budgeted amounts. This spreadsheet was generated by entering only new amount data. The spreadsheet program calculated all the other entries. This enables Mr. Silver to compare his actual expenses with his budgeted or anticipated expenses. Also, this spreadsheet can be used for subsequent months; comparisons can be made and trends observed. It is common to use tables, graphs, and statistics in examining these trends.

The formula S = C + M *is used to find the selling price* S *when the cost* C *and markup* M *are given.*

1. Evaluate the formula $S = C + M$ if the cost of a blouse is $13.98 and the markup is $12.50.

2. Evaluate the formula $S = C + M$ if the cost of a refrigerator is $700 and the markup is $859.

The formula I = Prt *is used to find the Interest* I *earned on money called the Principal* P *invested at an annual interest rate* r *for some number* t *of years.*

3. Find the interest if $8,000 is invested at an annual interest rate of 7% for 2 years.

4. Find the interest on $12,000 invested at $5\frac{1}{2}\%$ for three years.

5. Use the formula $P = 2l + 2w$ to find the perimeter of a rectangle if the length is 12 inches and the width is 8 inches.

 6. Write a formula to find the perimeter of a regular hexagon. A regular hexagon is a figure that has six equal sides.

The gross pay of an hourly worker is calculated by multiplying the number of hours worked by the pay earned per hour.

7. Write a formula to find the gross pay of an hourly worker.

8. Find the gross pay for Lou Ferrante if he worked 40 hours and earned $6.25 per hour.

9. A markdown on merchandise is a percentage of the selling price. Write a formula to find the markdown when the selling price and markdown rate are given.

10. Find the markdown on a suit that has a selling price of $259 if the markdown rate is 25%.

11. The reduced price of an item is found by subtracting the markdown from the selling price. Write a formula to find the reduced price of an item.

12. Find the reduced price of the item in Exercise 10.

Sales tax on an item is found by multiplying the price of the item by the sales tax rate.

13. Write a formula to find the sales tax.

14. Find the sales tax on a calculator if its price is $12.95 and the sales tax rate is 6 percent.

To find the total cost of an item, we add the price and the sales tax.

15. Write a formula to find the total price.

16. Find the total cost of the calculator in Exercise 14.

17. Use the formulas in the Silver's Spa Spreadsheet (page 172) to complete the table for operating expenses for May.

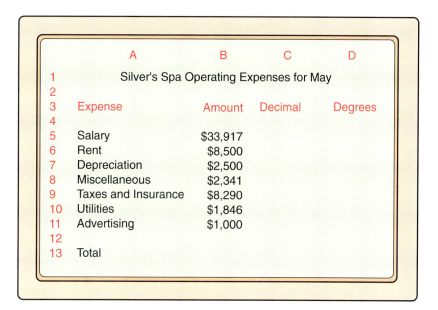

	A	B	C	D
1	Silver's Spa Operating Expenses for May			
2				
3	Expense	Amount	Decimal	Degrees
4				
5	Salary	$33,917		
6	Rent	$8,500		
7	Depreciation	$2,500		
8	Miscellaneous	$2,341		
9	Taxes and Insurance	$8,290		
10	Utilities	$1,846		
11	Advertising	$1,000		
12				
13	Total			

AROUND THE BUSINESS WORLD

A Woman's Place? In Charge

Women are better bosses. That's the verdict from a survey of more than 9,000 managers who graded male and female superiors on 20 skills ranging from communicating to decisiveness. According to Lawrence A. Pfaff & Associates, the Kalamazoo (Mich.) consulting firm that did the study, women are rated the best in every category.

The gap is the biggest on planning, making changes, and evaluating employee performance, where females outshine males by 10 points. Ratings are like school grades, from 0 to 100. So, for example, women score 56 on planning, vs. 46 for men. The sexes come the closest on delegating authority, 55–54.

Why would women make better chiefs than men? Says Larry Pfaff, the firm's president: "Women are still brought up to be more social. Those skills pay off in the workplace."

This survey certainly seems to dispute old notions that "male" qualities make for better leaders. But other surveys indicate no real differences exist between genders. Jeffrey Sonnenfeld, director of Emory University's Center for Leadership and Career Studies, says these studies show a greater gap between individuals than between sexes. He decries "creating a cartoon character of gender differences."

Reprinted from February 27, 1995 issue of Business Week by special permission, copyright © 1995 by the McGraw-Hill Companies.

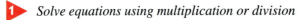

> 1▶ *Solve equations using multiplication or division*
> 2▶ *Solve equations using addition or subtraction*
> 3▶ *Solve equations using more than one operation*
> 4▶ *Solve equations containing multiple unknowns*
> 5▶ *Solve equations containing parentheses*

In the previous section we saw how formulas are used in many business applications. However, in each formula we used, the unknown value was on the left side of the equal sign and the known values were on the right side. Variations of formulas were used to ensure that the unknown value would be on the left. In this section we look at methods for evaluating a formula no matter where the unknown value occurs in the formula. Why are these methods important? The simplest answer is: efficiency! With the methods you learn in this section, you need only remember one variation of the percentage formula, not three. Remembering, or finding a reference for, just one variation is enough to allow you to evaluate the formula for *P, R,* or *B*.

To be able to evaluate a formula no matter where the unknown value occurs, we must know how to *solve equations*.

1▶ *Solving Equations Using Multiplication or Division*

An **equation** is a mathematical statement in which two quantities are equal. Like formulas, equations are represented by mathematical shorthand that uses numbers, letters, and operational symbols. In fact, *formula* is the special name we use for an equation that has at least two letters. $P = R \times B$, then, is an equation. If we replace *R* by 0.5, for instance, and *P* by, say, 10, we get an equation with just one letter: $10 = 0.5 \times B$. *Solving an equation* like $10 = 0.5 \times B$ means finding the value of *B* so that 0.5 times this value is the same as 10.

To begin our examination of equations, we look at equations that involve multiplication or division, and one unknown value.

 HOW TO   **Solve an Equation with Multiplication or Division**

Step 1   Isolate the unknown value:
     a) If the equation contains the *product* of the unknown value and a number, then *divide* both sides of the equation by the number.
     b) If the equation contains the *quotient* of the unknown value and a number, then *multiply* both sides of the equation by the number.
Step 2   Identify the solution: the solution is the number on the side opposite the isolated unknown-value letter.
Step 3   Check the solution: In the original equation, replace the unknown-value letter with the solution, perform the indicated operations, and verify that both sides of the equation are the same number.

Example 1   Solve the equation $2A = 18$. (A number multiplied by 2 is 18.)

$$2A = 18$$ **The equation shows multiplication by 2; so you do the opposite: divide both sides of the equation by 2.**

$$\frac{2A}{2} = \frac{18}{2}$$

$$A = \boxed{9}$$ **The solution is 9.**

Check:

$$2A = 18 \quad \text{Replace A with the solution 9 and see if both sides are equal.}$$

$$2\,(9) \stackrel{?}{=} 18$$

$$18 = 18$$

The solution of the equation is 9.

Example 2 Find the value of A if $\frac{A}{4} = 5$. (A number divided by 4 is 5.)

$$\frac{A}{4} = 5 \quad \text{The equation shows division by 4, so you do the opposite: multiply both sides of the equation by 4.}$$

$$4\left(\frac{A}{4}\right) = 5(4)$$

$$A = \boxed{20} \quad \text{The solution is 20.}$$

Check:

$$\frac{A}{4} = 5 \quad \text{Replace } A \text{ with the solution 20 and see if both sides are equal.}$$

$$\frac{20}{4} \stackrel{?}{=} 5$$

$$5 = 5$$

The solution of the equation is 20.

 Solving Equations Using Addition or Subtraction

Suppose 15 of the 25 people who work at Carton Manufacturers work on the day shift. How many people work there in the evening? You know that 15 people work there during the day, that 25 people work there in all, and that some unknown quantity work there in the evening. Assign the letter N to the unknown number of night-shift workers. The information from the problem can then be written in words as "the night-shift workers plus the day-shift workers equal 25" and in symbols: $N + 15 = 25$. This equation is one that can be solved with subtraction.

? HOW TO	Solve an Equation with Addition or Subtraction

Step 1 Isolate the unknown value:
   a) If the equation contains the *sum* of the unknown value and another number, then *subtract* the number from both sides of the equation.
   b) If the equation contains the *difference* of the unknown value and another number, then *add* the number to both sides of the equation.
Step 2 Identify the solution: the solution is the number on the side opposite the isolated unknown-value letter.
Step 3 Check the solution: In the original equation, replace the unknown-value letter with the solution, perform the indicated operations, and verify that both sides of the equation are the same number.

Example 3 Solve the equation $N + 15 = 25$. (A number increased by 15 is 25.)

$$
\begin{array}{r}
N + 15 = 25 \\
-\,15 \quad -\,15 \\
\hline
N = 10
\end{array}
$$

15 is added, so you do the opposite: subtract 15 from both sides.

$N =$ 10   **The solution is 10.**

Check:

$N + 15 = 25$ **Replace N with the solution 10 and see if both sides are equal.**

$10 + 15 \overset{?}{=} 25$

$25 = 25$

The solution is 10.

Example 4 Find the value of A if $A - 5 = 8$. (A number decreased by 5 is 8.)

$$
\begin{array}{r}
A - 5 = 8 \\
+\,5 \quad +\,5 \\
\hline
A = 13
\end{array}
$$

The equation shows 5 is subtracted, so you do the opposite: add 5 to both sides.

$A = $ 13   **The solution is 13.**

Check:

$A - 5 = 8$ **Replace A with the solution 13 and see if both sides are equal.**

$13 - 5 \overset{?}{=} 8$

$8 = 8$

The solution is 13.

 TIPS & TRAPS

In general, unknowns are isolated in an equation by "undoing" all operations associated with the unknown. Use addition to undo subtraction. Use subtraction to undo addition. Use multiplication to undo division. Use division to undo multiplication. To keep the equation in balance, we perform the same operation on both sides of the equation.

▶ Solving Equations Using More Than One Operation

Many business equations contain more than one operation. To solve such equations, we undo each operation in turn. Just as we follow the standard order of operations to *perform* operations, to *undo* operations we must follow the standard order *in reverse:* working from left to right, we first undo all additions or subtractions, and then undo all multiplications or divisions. Our goal is still to isolate the unknown.

? HOW TO	Solve an Equation with More Than One Operation

Step 1 Isolate the unknown value.
  a) Working from left to right, add or subtract as necessary *first*.
  b) Working from left to right, multiply or divide as necessary *second*.
Step 2 Identify the solution: the solution is the number on the side opposite the isolated unknown-value letter.
Step 3 Check the solution: In the original equation, replace the unknown-value letter with the solution, perform the indicated operations according to the standard order, and verify that both sides of the equation are the same number.

Example 5 Find A if $2A + 1 = 15$. (Two times a number increased by 1 is 15.)

The equation contains both addition and multiplication. Subtract first, and then divide.

$$2A + 1 = 15$$ The equation contains addition of 1, so subtract 1 from both sides.
$$\frac{-1 \quad -1}{2A \quad = \quad 14}$$

$$2A = 14$$ The equation shows multiplication by 2, so divide both sides by 2.

$$\frac{2A}{2} = \frac{14}{2}$$

$$A = \boxed{7}$$ The solution is 7.

Check:

$$2A + 1 = 15$$ Replace A with 7 in the original equation and see if both sides are equal.
$$2\,\boxed{(7)} + 1 \overset{?}{=} 15$$

$$14 + 1 \overset{?}{=} 15$$

$$15 = 15$$

The solution is 7.

Example 6 Solve the equation $\dfrac{A}{5} - 3 = 1$. (A number divided by 5 and decreased by 3 is 1.)

The equation contains both subtraction and division: add first and then multiply.

$$\frac{A}{5} - 3 = 1$$ The equation shows subtraction of 3, so add 3 to both sides.
$$\frac{+3 \quad +3}{\dfrac{A}{5} \quad = \quad 4}$$

$$\frac{A}{5} = 4$$

$$5\left(\frac{A}{5}\right) = 4(5)$$ The equation shows division by 5, so multiply both sides by 5.

$$A = \boxed{20}$$ The solution is 20.

Check:

$$\frac{A}{5} - 3 = 1$$ Replace *A* with 20 in the original equation and see if both sides are equal.

$$\frac{20}{5} - 3 \stackrel{?}{=} 1$$

$$4 - 3 \stackrel{?}{=} 1$$

$$1 = 1$$

The solution is 20.

4 ▶ *Solving Equations Containing Multiple Unknowns*

In some equations, the unknown value may occur more than once. The simplest instance is when the unknown value occurs in two addends. We solve such equations by first combining these addends. Remember that $5A$, for instance, means 5 times A, or $A + A + A + A + A$. To combine $2A + 3A$, we add 2 and 3, to get 5, and then multiply 5 by A, to get $5A$. Thus, $2A + 3A$ is the same as $5A$.

 HOW TO | **Solve an Equation When the Unknown Value Occurs in Two Addends**

Step 1 Combine the unknown-value addends:
  a) Add the numbers in each addend.
  b) Multiply their sum by the unknown value.
Step 2 Solve the resulting equation.

Example 7 Find *A* if $A + 3A - 2 = 14$.

$$A + 3A - 2 = 14$$ First, combine the unknown-value addends. Remember that *A* is the same as 1*A*, so $A + 3A = 4A$.

$$\begin{aligned} 4A - 2 &= 14 \\ +2 \quad &+ 2 \\ \hline 4A \quad &= 16 \end{aligned}$$ The equation shows subtraction of 2, so add 2 to both sides.

$$\frac{4A}{4} = \frac{16}{4}$$ The equation shows multiplication by 4, so divide both sides by 4. The solution is 4.

$$A = 4$$

Check:

$$A + 3A - 2 = 14$$ Replace *A* with 4 and see if both sides are the same.

$$4 + 3(4) - 2 \stackrel{?}{=} 14$$

$$4 + 12 - 2 \stackrel{?}{=} 14$$

$$16 - 2 \stackrel{?}{=} 14$$

$$14 = 14$$

The solution is 4.

TIPS & TRAPS

Remember that *A* is the same as 1*A*. When combining unknown-value addends, and one of the addends is *A,* it may help you to write *A* as 1*A* first.

$$A + 5A = 1A + 5A = 6A$$

 Solving Equations Containing Parentheses

To solve an equation containing parentheses, we first write the equation in a form that contains no parentheses. Remember the perimeter formula $P = 2(l + w)$? The formula written without parentheses is $P = 2l + 2w$. In this instance, writing the formula without parentheses means writing $2(l + w)$ as $2l + 2w$: we multiply 2 by each addend inside the parentheses, and then add the resulting products $2l$ and $2w$.

? HOW TO   Solve an Equation Containing Parentheses

Step 1   Eliminate the parentheses:
      a) Multiply the number just outside the parentheses by each addend inside the parentheses.
      b) Show the resulting products as addition.
Step 2   Solve the resulting equation.

Example 8   Solve the equation $5(A + 3) = 25$.

$5(A + 3) = 25$ **First eliminate the parentheses. Multiply 5 by *A*, multiply 5 by 3,**
$5A + 15 = 25$ **then show the products as addition.**

$$\begin{array}{rr} 5A + 15 = & 25 \\ -15 & -15 \\ \hline 5A \quad\;\; = & 10 \end{array}$$ **The equation shows addition of 15, so subtract 15 from both sides.**

$$\frac{5A}{5} = \frac{10}{5}$$ **The equation shows multiplication by 5, so divide both sides by 5.**

$$A = \boxed{2}$$ **The solution is 2.**

Check:

$$5(A + 3) = 25$$ **Replace A with 2 and see if both sides are equal.**
$$5(\boxed{2} + 3) \overset{?}{=} 25$$
$$10 + 15 \overset{?}{=} 25$$
$$25 = 25$$

The solution is 2.

TIPS & TRAPS

Parentheses in an equation should grab your attention, because they say ELIMINATE ME FIRST. You need to eliminate the parentheses before you do anything else in the equation. Trying to solve an equation *without* eliminating parentheses can lead to an incorrect solution, as shown here.

Find X if $5(X - 2) = 45$.

$$5(X - 2) = 45$$

$$5X - 10 = 45$$
$$\underline{+ 10 \quad + 10}$$
$$5X \quad = 55$$

$$\frac{5X}{5} = \frac{55}{5}$$

$$X = 11$$

CORRECT

$$5(X - 2) = \quad 45$$
$$\underline{+ 2 \quad + 2}$$
$$5X \quad = 47$$

$$\frac{5X}{5} = \frac{47}{5}$$

$$X = 9\frac{2}{5}$$

INCORRECT

Self-Check 5.2

1. Solve the equation $5A = 20$.

$5A = 20$

2. Find the value of B if $\frac{B}{7} = 4$.

3. Solve the equation $7C = 56$.

4. Solve the equation $4M = 48$.

5. Find the value of R if $\frac{R}{12} = 3$.

$(12)\frac{R}{12}$ $3(12)$ $R = 36$

6. Solve the equation $\frac{P}{5} = 8$.

$(5)\frac{P}{5} = 8(5)$ $P = 40$

7. Solve the equation for B if $B + 7 = 12$.

8. Find the value of A if $A - 9 = 15$.

$+9 \quad +9$
$A = 20$

9. Find the value of R if $R + 7 = 28$.

$-7 \quad -7$
$R = 21$

10. Solve the equation for A if $A - 16 = 3$.

11. Find the value of X if $X - 48 = 36$.

86
$+48 \quad +48$
$X = 84$

12. Solve the equation for C if $C + 5 = 21$.

$-5 \quad -5$
$C = 16$

13. Solve the equation $4A + 3 = 27$.

14. Solve the equation $\frac{B}{3} + 2 = 7$.

15. Solve the equation $3B - 1 = 11$.

16. Find K if $\frac{K}{4} - 5 = 3$.

17. Find K if $\frac{K}{2} + 3 = 5$.

$(2)\frac{K}{2} = 2(2)$
$-3 = 3$
$\frac{}{2}$ $K = 4$

18. Solve the equation $7B - 1 = 6$.

19. Find C if $\frac{C}{2} - 1 = 9$.

$(2)\frac{C}{2} = 10(2)$
$+1 \quad +1$
10 $C = 20$

20. Solve the equation $8A - 1 = 19$.

$8A - 1 = 19$
$8A + 1 = 19$
9

21. Find A if $2A + 5A = 35$.

22. Find B if $B + 2B = 27$.

23. Find K if $5K - 3K = 40$.

24. Find K if $8K - 2K = 42$.

25. Find J if $3J + J = 28$.

26. Find J if $2J - J = 21$.

27. Find B if $3B + 2B - 6 = 9$.

28. Find C if $8C - C + 6 = 48$.

5 ▶ 29. Solve the equation $2(X - 3) = 6$.

30. Solve the equation $4(A + 3) = 16$.

31. Solve the equation $3(B - 1) = 21$.

32. Solve the equation $6(B + 2) = 30$.

5.3   Using Equations to Solve Problems

1 ▶ *Use the decision key approach to analyze and solve word problems*

Equations are powerful business tools because equations use mathematical shorthand for expressing relationships. As we know from using the decision key to solve problems, identifying relationships is a critical step. In this section, we practice how to identify relationships, and how to write these relationships as equations.

1 ▶ *Relationships, Equations, and Solving Problems*

Certain key words in a problem give you clues as to whether a certain quantity is added to, subtracted from, or multiplied or divided by another quantity. For example, if a word problem tells you that Carol's salary in 1996 *exceeds* her 1995 salary by $2,500, you know that you should *add* $2,500 to her 1995 salary to find her 1996 salary. Many times, when you see the word *of* in a problem, the problem involves multiplication. Table 5–1 summarizes important key words and what they generally imply when they are used in a word problem. This list should help you analyze the information in word problems and write the information in symbols.

Writing Equations   If you are able to express a relationship among quantities, say,

$$\text{Tax} = \text{tax rate} \times \text{price}$$

then you are able to write an equation, because an equation uses letters rather than words:

$$t = r \times p$$

Table 5–1   Key Words and What They Generally Imply in Word Problems

Addition	Subtraction	Multiplication	Division	Equality
The sum of	Less than	Times	Divide(s)	Equals
Plus/total	Decreased by	Multiplied by	Divided by	Is/was/are
Increased by	Subtracted from	Of	Divided into	Is equal to
More/more than	Difference between	The product of	Half of (divided by two)	The result is
Added to	Diminished by	Twice (two times) as	Third of ($\frac{1}{3}$ times)	What is left
Exceeds	Take away	Double (two times) many	Per	What remains
Expands	Reduced by	Triple (three times)		The same as
Greater than	Less/minus	Half ($\frac{1}{2}$ times)		Gives/giving
Gain/profit	Loss			Makes
Longer	Lower			Leaves
Older	Shrinks			
Heavier	Smaller than			
Wider	Younger			
Taller	Slower			

Chapter 5   Problem Solving with Formulas and Equations

183

You practiced writing equations in section 5.2 when you wrote formulas that used letters rather than words. You can apply the same skill using the decision key to solve problems. Identify the **unknown fact** (value) in words, and assign a letter to it. Identify the **known facts.** Write the **relationship** using the known facts and the unknown-value *letter:* this is the equation. Solve the equation with the appropriate **calculations** and check your solution.

Example 1 Full-time employees at Charlie's Steakhouse work more hours per day than part-time employees. If the difference of working hours is four per day, and if part-timers work six hours per day, how many hours per day do full-timers work?

1 Decision needed

2 Unknown fact   Hours per day that full-timers work: n

3 Known facts   Hours per day that part-timers work: 6.

Difference between hours worked by full-timers and hours worked by part-timers: 4

4 Relationship   The word *difference* implies subtraction. Full-time hours − part-time hours = difference of hours

$$n - 6 = 4$$

5 Estimation   Full-time workers work *more* hours than part-time workers so we anticipate that n is more than 6.

6 Calculation
$$
\begin{array}{rl}
n - 6 = & 4 \\
+ 6 \quad + & 6 \quad \text{Add 6 to both sides.} \\
\hline
n \quad = & 10 \quad \text{The solution is 10.}
\end{array}
$$

Check:

$$10 - 6 \stackrel{?}{=} 4 \quad \text{Replace } n \text{ with 4.}$$

$$4 = 4 \quad \text{The sides are equal.}$$

The hours per day that full-timers work is 10.

7 Decision made

Because we want to focus on using equations, in the examples that follow we have modified the decision key to leave out Decision needed, Estimation, and Decision made.

Example 2 Wanda plans to save $\frac{1}{10}$ of her salary each week. If her weekly salary is $350, how much will she save each week?

1 Decision needed

2 Unknown fact   Amount to be saved: S

3 Known facts   Salary = $350

Rate of saving: $\dfrac{1}{10}$

4 Relationship   The word *of* implies multiplication. (Also, the relationship is the percentage formula.)

Amount to be saved = rate of saving $\times$ salary

$$S = \frac{1}{10}(\$350)$$

6   Calculation

$$S = \frac{1}{\cancel{10}} (\$\cancel{350}) \quad \textbf{Multiply.}$$

with 35 above 350 and 1 below 10

$$S = \$35 \qquad \textbf{The solution is 35.}$$

Check:

$$\$35 \stackrel{?}{=} \frac{1}{\cancel{10}} (\$\cancel{350}) \quad \textbf{Replace S with \$35 and see if the sides are equal.}$$

with 35 above 350 and 1 below 10

$$\$35 = \$35$$

Wanda will save \$35 per week.

7   Decision made

! TIPS & TRAPS

It's a good idea to read a word problem several times. With each reading a different aspect of the problem is analyzed.

1. Read for a general understanding of the problem.
2. Read to determine what you want to find: the unknown fact.
3. Read to locate the given and implied facts: the known facts.
4. Read to relate the known and unknown facts: the relationship, the equation.
5. After solving the equation, read to see if the solution satisfies the conditions of the problem. Does it make sense?

Many times a problem requires finding more than one unknown value. Our strategy will be to choose just one unknown value to represent with a letter. Using known facts, we should then be able to express all other unknown values *in terms of* the one letter. For instance, if we know that twice as many men as women attended a conference, then we might represent the number of men as M, and the number of women as $2M$, twice as many as M.

Example 3   At Alexander's Cafe last Wednesday, there were twice as many requests for seats in the nonsmoking section as there were requests for seats in the smoking section. If 342 customers came to the Cafe that day, how many requested the smoking section? How many requested the nonsmoking section?

1   Decision needed

2   Unknown fact

Both the number of smokers and the number of nonsmokers are unknown, but we choose one—smokers—to be represented by a letter, S.

Number of smokers: S

3   Known facts

Since the number of nonsmokers is *twice* the number of smokers, we represent the number of nonsmokers as $2S$, or 2 times S.

Number of nonsmokers: $2S$
Total customers: 342

4   Relationships

5   Estimation

Smokers + nonsmokers = total customers

$$S + 2S = 342$$

---

6 Calculation

$$S + 2S = 342$$

$$3S = 342 \qquad \text{Combine addends.}$$

$$\frac{\cancel{3}S}{\cancel{3}} = \frac{\overset{114}{\cancel{342}}}{\cancel{3}} \qquad \text{Divide both sides by 3.}$$

$$S = 114 \qquad \text{The solution is 114 which represents the number of smokers.}$$

$$2S = 2(114)$$

$$2S = 228 \qquad \text{Twice } S \text{ is twice 114, or 228 nonsmokers.}$$

Check:

$$114 + 228 \overset{?}{=} 342$$

$$342 = 342$$

7 Decision made

There were 114 smokers and 228 nonsmokers.

Example 4 Juana supervises six times as many data entry clerks as Millie. There are ten fewer clerks working for Millie than for Juana. How many clerks are working for Millie? How many clerks are working for Juana?

1 Decision needed

2 Unknown fact   Number of Millie's clerks: M

3 Known facts   Since the number of Juana's clerks is *six times* the number of Millie's clerks, we represent the number of Juana's clerks as $6M$, or 6 times M. Also we know that the difference of Juana's clerks and Millie's clerks is 10, since *10 fewer* work for Millie than for Juana.

Number of Juana's clerks: $6M$
Difference of Juana's clerks and Millie's clerks: 10

4 Relationships
5 Estimation   Juana's clerks $-$ Millie's clerks $=$ difference

$$6M - M = 10$$

6 Calculation

$$6M - M = 10 \qquad \text{Since } 6M \text{ represents the larger amount, it should come first in the subtraction.}$$

$$5M = 10 \qquad \text{Combine.}$$

$$\frac{\cancel{5}M}{\cancel{5}} = \frac{\overset{2}{\cancel{10}}}{\cancel{5}} \qquad \text{Divide both sides by 5.}$$

$$M = 2 \qquad \text{The solution is 2, which represents Millie's clerks.}$$

$$6M = 6(2)$$

$$6M = 12 \qquad \text{6 times } M \text{ is 6(2), or 12, Juana's clerks.}$$

Check:

$$12 - 2 \overset{?}{=} 10$$

$$10 = 10$$

7 Decision made

Millie supervises 2 clerks; Juana supervises 12 clerks.

Many problems give a *total* number of two types of items. You want to know the number of each of the two types of items. The next example illustrates this type of problem.

Example 5  The Cheerful Card Shop spent a total of $950 orderin
Wit's End Co., whose humorous cards cost $1.75 each and whose
$1.50 each. How many of each style card did the card shop order?

1 Decision needed

2 Unknown fact
There are two unknown facts, but we choose one—the number of hur
be represented by a letter, H.

Number of humorous cards: H

3 Known facts
Knowing that the total number of cards is 600, we represent the number of nature
cards as 600 minus the humorous cards, or $600 - H$.

Total cost of cards: $950
Number of nature cards: $600 - H$
Cost per humorous card: $1.75
Cost per nature card: $1.50

4 Relationship
Total cost = (cost per humorous card)(number of humorous cards) +
(cost per nature card)(number of nature cards)

5 Estimation

$$950 = (1.75)(H) + (1.50)(600 - H)$$

$$950 = 1.75H + 1.50(600 - H)$$

6 Calculations
$$950 = 1.75H + (1.50)(600) - 1.50H$$ **Eliminate parentheses showing grouping.**

$$950 = 1.75H + 900 - 1.50H$$

$$950 = 0.25H + 900$$ **Combine letter terms.**
$$-900 \qquad\qquad -900$$

$$50 = 0.25H$$ **Subtract 900 from both sides.**

$$\frac{50}{0.25} = \frac{0.25H}{0.25}$$ **Divide both sides by 0.25.**

$$200 = H$$ **The solution is 200, which represents the number of humorous cards.**

$$600 - H = 600 - 200$$ **Subtract H, or 200, from 600 to find 600 − H, or 400, the number of nature cards.**

$$600 - H = 400$$

Check:

$$950 \overset{?}{=} (1.75)(200) + (1.50)(600 - 200)$$

$$950 \overset{?}{=} 350 + (1.50)(400)$$

$$950 \overset{?}{=} 350 + 600$$

$$950 = 950$$

7 Decision made   **The card shop ordered 200 humorous cards and 400 nature cards.**

Equations that are Proportions   Many problems encountered daily involve a
relationship known as a *proportion*.
   A proportion is an equation in which each side is a ratio. For example, using two
ounces out of a four-gallon bottle of cleaning fluid is proportional to using four ounces
out of an eight-gallon bottle. Expressed as a proportion, this example would be

$$\frac{2 \text{ oz}}{4 \text{ gal}} = \frac{4 \text{ oz}}{8 \text{ gal}}$$

Foreign Office Rents

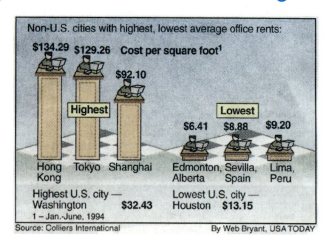

Non-U.S. cities with highest, lowest average office rents:

$134.29 $129.26 Cost per square foot[1]

$92.10

Highest

Lowest

$6.41 $8.88 $9.20

Hong Kong   Tokyo   Shanghai   Edmonton, Alberta   Sevilla, Spain   Lima, Peru

Highest U.S. city —
Washington   **$32.43**

Lowest U.S. city —
Houston   **$13.15**

1 – Jan.-June, 1994

Source: Colliers International   By Web Bryant, USA TODAY

1. A company rents office space in Tokyo, Japan, and Lima, Peru. If they rent the same amount of space in each city and spend $138,460 per month, how many square feet do they rent in each city?

2. A+ Microchips rents twice as much office space in Sevilla, Spain, as they rent in Hong Kong. The company spends a total of $121,640 per month for rent. Find the number of square feet A+ Microchips rents in Sevilla, Spain, and the number of square feet it rents in Hong Kong.

3. A company is considering international expansion into Hong Kong, China, and Lima, Peru. The company has a maximum of $200,000 per month to spend on rent, and would prefer to rent 1,500 square feet in each new location. What advice would you offer the company?

The fractions $\frac{2}{4}$ and $\frac{4}{8}$ are equivalent. If one of the four numbers in the proportion is an unknown value, you can solve the equation by using *cross-multiplication:*

$$\frac{3}{x} = \frac{7}{5}$$

$$7 \cdot x = 3 \cdot 5$$

$$7x = 15$$

$$\frac{7x}{7} = \frac{15}{7}$$

$$x = 2\frac{1}{7}$$

Cross-multiplication amounts to multiplying both sides of the equation by each of the denominators, in this case x and 5. The shortcut is to "cross-multiply"—left numerator times right denominator = right numerator times left denominator.

In solving a word problem by this method, it is helpful to write in words the units being compared. There are usually three known values and two different units. Write a comparison of the two units and solve the problem.

Example 6 Your car gets 23 miles to a gallon of gas. How far can you go on 16 gallons of gas?

Distance traveled using 16 gallons: x miles

Distance traveled using 1 gallon: 23 miles

Miles traveled per 16 gallons is proportional to miles traveled per 1 gallon.

$$\frac{x \text{ miles}}{16 \text{ gallons}} = \frac{23 \text{ miles}}{1 \text{ gallon}}$$

$$\frac{x}{16} = \frac{23}{1}$$

$1x = (16)(23)$ **Cross multiply.**

$x = 368$

Check:

$$\frac{368}{16} \overset{?}{=} \frac{23}{1}$$

$$(1)(368) \overset{?}{=} (16)(23)$$

$$368 = 368$$

You can travel 368 miles using 16 gallons of gas.

Example 7 The label on a container of concentrated weed killer gives directions to mix three ounces of week killer with every two gallons of water. For five gallons of water, how many ounces of weed killer should you use?

Amount of weed killer for five gallons of water: x ounces

Amount of weed killer for two gallons of water: three ounces

Amount of weed killer per five gallons is proportional to amount of weed killer per two gallons.

$$\frac{x \text{ ounces}}{5 \text{ gallons}} = \frac{3 \text{ ounces}}{2 \text{ gallons}}$$

$$\frac{x}{5} = \frac{3}{2}$$

$2x = (5)(3)$ **Cross multiply.**

$2x = 15$

$$\frac{2x}{2} = \frac{15}{2}$$ **Divide both sides by 2.**

$x = 7\frac{1}{2}$ **The solution is $7\frac{1}{2}$.**

Check:

$$\frac{7\frac{1}{2}}{5} \overset{?}{=} \frac{3}{2}$$

$$(2)(7\tfrac{1}{2}) \overset{?}{=} (5)(3)$$

$$\left(\frac{\cancel{2}}{1}\right)\left(\frac{15}{\cancel{2}}\right) \overset{?}{=} 15$$

$$15 = 15$$

7 Decision made

You should use $7\frac{1}{2}$ ounces of weed killer.

Another format that is handy for using the decision-key approach to solving word problems is a table format. Examine the solution to Example 7 using this format.

Unknown	Knowns	Relationship	Calculation
Weed killer for 5 gallons of water: x	Weed killer for 2 gallons of water: 3 ounces	x ounces weed killer per 5 gallons water is proportional to 3 ounces weed killer per 2 gallons water $\dfrac{x \text{ ounces}}{5 \text{ gallons}} = \dfrac{3 \text{ ounces}}{2 \text{ gallons}}$	$\dfrac{x}{5} = \dfrac{3}{2}$ $2x = (5)(3)$ $2x = 15$ $\dfrac{2x}{2} = \dfrac{15}{2}$ $x = 7\dfrac{1}{2}$

You should use $7\frac{1}{2}$ ounces of weed killer.

Check
$7\dfrac{1}{2} \overset{?}{=} \dfrac{3}{2}$ $2\left(7\dfrac{1}{2}\right) = (5)(3)$ $\dfrac{2}{1}\left(\dfrac{15}{2}\right) = 15$ $15 = 15$

Self-Check 5.3

 1. The difference in hours between full-timers and the part-timers who work five hours a day is four hours. How long do full-timers work?

2. Manny plans to save $\frac{1}{12}$ of his salary each week. If his weekly salary is $372, find the amount he will save each week.

3. Last week at the Sunshine Valley Rock Festival, Joel sold three times as many tie-dyed T-shirts as silk-screened shirts. He sold 176 shirts altogether. How many tie-dyed shirts did he sell?

4. Elaine sold three times as many magazine subscriptions as Ron did. Ron sold 16 fewer subscriptions than Elaine did. How many subscriptions did each sell?

5. Will ordered two times as many boxes of ballpoint pens as boxes of felt-tip pens. Ballpoint pens cost $3.50 per box, and felt-tip pens cost $4.50. If Will's order of pens totaled $46, how many boxes of each type of pen did he buy?

6. A real-estate salesperson bought promotional calendars and date books to give to her customers at the end of the year. The calendars cost $0.75 each and the date books cost $0.50 each. She ordered a total of 500 promotional items and spent $300. How many of each item did she order?

7. A scale drawing of an office building is not labeled, but indicates $\frac{1}{4}'' = 5'$. On the drawing, one wall measures two inches. How long is the wall?

8. A recipe uses three cups of flour to $1\frac{1}{4}$ cups of milk. If you have two cups of flour, how much milk should you use?

9. For 32 hours of work, you are paid $241.60. How much would you receive for 37 hours?

SELF-CHECK SOLUTIONS

Self-Check 5.1

1. $S = C + M$
$S = 13.98 + 12.50$
$S = 26.48$
The blouse sells for $26.48.

2. $S = C + M$
$S = 700 + 859$
$S = 1,559$
The refrigerator sells for $1,559.

3. $I = Prt$
$I = 8,000(0.07)(2)$
$I = 1,120$
The interest is $1,120.

4. $I = Prt$
$I = 12,000(0.055)(3)$
$I = 1,980.$
The interest is $1,980.

5. $P = 2l + 2w$
$P = 2(12) + 2(8)$
$P = 24 + 16$
$P = 40$
The perimeter is 40 inches.

6. $P = s + s + s + s + s + s$ or $P = 6s$

7. $P = hr$, where P is gross pay, h is hours worked, and r is pay per hour

8. $P = 40(6.25)$
$p = \$250$
The gross pay is $250.

9. $m = rs$, where m is markdown, r is markdown rate, and s is selling price

10. $m = (0.25)(259)$
$m = \$64.75$
The markdown is $64.75.

11. $p = s - m$, where p is reduced price, s is selling price, and m is markdown.

12. $p = 259 - 64.75$
$p = \$194.25$
The reduced price is $c = \$194.25.$

13. $t = rp$, where t is sales tax, p is price, and r is sales tax rate.

14. $t = (0.06)12.95$
$t = 0.777$ or 0.78 (rounded)
The sales tax is $0.78.

15. $c = p + t$, where c is total cost, p is price, and t is sales tax.

16. $c = 12.95 + 0.78$
$c = \$13.73$
The total cost of the calculator is $13.73.

17.

	A	B	C	D
1	Silver's Spa Operating Expenses for May			
2				
3	Description	Amount	Decimal	Degrees
4				
5	Salary	$33,917	0.5808302	209
6	Rent	$8,500	0.1455629	52
7	Depreciation	$2,500	0.0428126	15
8	Miscellaneous	$2,341	0.0400897	14
9	Taxes and Insurance	$8,290	0.1419666	51
10	Utilities	$1,846	0.0316128	11
11	Advertising	$1,000	0.0171250	6
12				
13	Total	$58,394	0.9999998	358

Total = $33,917 + 8,500 + 2,500 + 2,341 + 8,290 + 1,846 + 1,000 = 58,394$

Salary decimal $= \dfrac{33,917}{58,394} = 0.5808302$

Salary degrees $= 0.5808302 \times 360 = 209$

Rent decimal $= \dfrac{8,500}{58,394} = 0.1455629$

Rent degrees = 0.1455629 × 360 = 52

Depreciation decimal = $\dfrac{2,500}{58,394}$ = 0.0428126

Depreciation degrees = 0.0428126 × 360 = 15

Miscellaneous decimal = $\dfrac{2,341}{58,394}$ = 0.0400897

Miscellaneous degrees = 0.0400897 × 360 = 14

Taxes and insurance decimal = $\dfrac{8,290}{58,394}$ = 0.1419666

Taxes and insurance degrees = 0.1419666 × 360 = 51

Utilities decimal = $\dfrac{1,846}{58,394}$ = 0.0316128

Utilities degrees = 0.0316128 × 360 = 11

Advertising decimal = $\dfrac{1,000}{58,394}$ = 0.0171250

Advertising degrees = 0.0171250 × 360 = 6
Total degrees = 209 + 52 + 15 + 14 + 51 + 11 + 6 = 358

Self-Check 5.2

1. $\dfrac{5A}{5} = \dfrac{20}{5}$
$A = 4$

2. $(7)\dfrac{B}{7} = 4(7)$
$B = 28$

3. $\dfrac{7C}{7} = \dfrac{56}{7}$
$C = 8$

4. $\dfrac{4M}{4} = \dfrac{48}{4}$
$M = 12$

5. $(12)\dfrac{R}{12} = 3(12)$
$R = 36$

6. $(5)\dfrac{P}{5} = 8(5)$
$P = 40$

7. $B + 7 = 12$
$\underline{ -7 \quad -7}$
$B = 5$

8. $A - 9 = 15$
$\underline{ +9 \quad +9}$
$A = 24$

9. $R + 7 = 28$
$\underline{ -7 \quad -7}$
$R = 21$

10. $A - 16 = 3$
$\underline{ +16 \quad +16}$
$A = 19$

11. $X - 48 = 36$
$\underline{ +48 \quad +48}$
$X = 84$

12. $C + 5 = 21$
$\underline{ -5 \quad -5}$
$C = 16$

13. $4A + 3 = 27$
$\underline{ -3 \quad -3}$
$4A = 24$
$\dfrac{4A}{4} = \dfrac{24}{4}$
$A = 6$

14. $\dfrac{B}{3} + 2 = 7$
$\underline{ -2 \quad -2}$
$\dfrac{B}{3} = 5$
$(3)\dfrac{B}{3} = 5(3)$
$B = 15$

15. $3B - 1 = 11$
$\underline{ +1 \quad +1}$
$3B = 12$
$\dfrac{3B}{3} = \dfrac{12}{3}$
$B = 4$

16. $\dfrac{K}{4} - 5 = 3$
$\underline{ +5 \quad +5}$
$\dfrac{K}{4} = 8$
$(4)\dfrac{K}{4} = 8(4)$
$K = 32$

17. $\dfrac{K}{2} + 3 = 5$
$\underline{ -3 \quad -3}$
$\dfrac{K}{2} = 2$
$(2)\dfrac{K}{2} = 2(2)$
$K = 4$

18. $7B - 1 = 6$
$\underline{ +1 \quad +1}$
$7B = 7$
$\dfrac{7B}{7} = \dfrac{7}{7}$
$B = 1$

19. $\dfrac{C}{2} - 1 = 9$
$\underline{ +1 \quad +1}$
$\dfrac{C}{2} = 10$
$(2)\dfrac{C}{2} = 10(2)$
$C = 20$

20. $8A - 1 = 19$
$\underline{ +1 \quad +1}$
$8A = 20$
$\dfrac{8A}{8} = \dfrac{20}{8}$
$A = \dfrac{20}{8} = 2\dfrac{4}{8} = 2\dfrac{1}{2}$

21. $2A + 5A = 35$
$7A = 35$
$\dfrac{7A}{7} = \dfrac{35}{7}$
$A = 5$

22. $B + 2B = 27$
$3B = 27$
$\dfrac{3B}{3} = \dfrac{27}{3}$
$B = 9$

23. $5K - 3K = 40$
$2K = 40$
$\dfrac{2K}{2} = \dfrac{40}{2}$
$K = 20$

24. $8K - 2K = 42$
$6K = 42$
$\dfrac{6K}{6} = \dfrac{42}{6}$
$K = 7$

25. $3J + J = 28$
$4J = 28$
$\dfrac{4J}{4} = \dfrac{28}{4}$
$J = 7$

26. $2J - J = 21$
$J = 21$

27. $3B + 2B - 6 = 9$
$5B - 6 = 9$
$\underline{ +6 \quad +6}$
$5B = 15$
$\dfrac{5B}{5} = \dfrac{15}{5}$
$B = 3$

28. $8C - C + 6 = 48$
$7C + 6 = 48$
$\underline{ -6 \quad -6}$
$7C = 42$
$\dfrac{7C}{7} = \dfrac{42}{7}$
$C = 6$

29.
$$2X - 6 = 6$$
$$\underline{+6 \quad +6}$$
$$2X = 12$$
$$\frac{2X}{2} = \frac{12}{2}$$
$$X = 6$$

30.
$$4A + 12 = 16$$
$$\underline{-12 \quad -12}$$
$$4A = 4$$
$$\frac{4A}{4} = \frac{4}{4}$$
$$A = 1$$

31.
$$3B - 3 = 21$$
$$\underline{+3 \quad +3}$$
$$3B = 24$$
$$\frac{3B}{3} = \frac{24}{3}$$
$$B = 8$$

32.
$$6B + 12 = 30$$
$$\underline{-12 \quad -12}$$
$$6B = 18$$
$$\frac{6B}{6} = \frac{18}{6}$$
$$B = 3$$

Self-Check 5.3

1.

Unknown	Knowns	Relationship	Calculation
Number of full time hours: N	Number of part time hours worked: 5 Difference of full-time hours and part-time hours: 4	Full-time hours − part time hours = difference $N - 5 = 4$	$N - 5 = 4$ $\underline{+5 \quad +5}$ $N \quad = 9$

The number of full-time hours is 9.

Check
$9 - 5 \overset{?}{=} 4$ $4 = 4$

2.

Unknown	Knowns	Relationship	Calculations
Amount saved: S	Salary = \$372 Rate of saving: $\frac{1}{12}$	Amount saved = Rate × Salary $S = \frac{1}{12} \times 372$	$S = \frac{1}{12}(372)$ $S = \frac{1}{\overset{}{12}} \cdot \frac{\overset{31}{372}}{\underset{1}{1}}$ $S = 31$

Manny will save \$31 each week.

Check
$\frac{1}{\overset{}{12}} \cdot \frac{\overset{31}{372}}{\underset{1}{1}} \overset{?}{=} 31$ $31 = 31$

3.

Unknown	Knowns	Relationship	Calculations
Number of silk-screened shirts sold: N	Number of tie-dyed shirts sold: $3N$ (three times as many) Total number of shirts sold: 176	Number of silk-screened shirts sold + number of tie-dyed shirts sold = total number sold $N + 3N = 176$	$N + 3N = 176$ $4N = 176$ $\frac{4N}{4} = \frac{176}{4}$ $N = 44$ $3N = 132$

There were 44 silk-screened and 132 tie-dyed shirts sold.

Check
$44 + 3(44) \overset{?}{=} 176$ $44 + 132 \overset{?}{=} 176$ $176 = 176$

4.

Unknown	Knowns	Relationship	Calculations
Number of subscriptions Ron sold: M	Number of subscriptions Elaine sold: $3M$ (three times as many) Difference of Elaine's subscriptions and Ron's subscriptions: 16	Elaine's subscriptions − Ron's subscriptions = difference $3M - M = 16$	$3M - M = 16$ $2M = 16$ $\dfrac{2M}{2} = \dfrac{16}{2}$ $M = 8$ $3M = 24$

Ron sold 8 magazine subscriptions and Elaine sold 24.

Check
$3(8) - 8 \overset{?}{=} 16$ $24 - 8 \overset{?}{=} 16$ $16 = 16$

5.

Unknown	Knowns	Relationship	Calculations
Number of boxes of felt-tip pens: N	Number of boxes of ballpoint pens: $2N$ Total value of felt-tip pens: $\$4.50N$ Total value of ballpoint pens: $\$3.50 (2N)$ Total order: $46	Total value of felt-tip pens + total value of ballpoint pens = total order $4.50N + 3.50(2N) = 46$	$4.50N + (3.50 \times 2N) = 46$ $4.50N + 7.00N = 46$ $11.50N = 46$ $\dfrac{11.50N}{11.50} = \dfrac{46}{11.50}$ $N = 4$ $2N = 8$

Will ordered 4 boxes of felt-tip pens and 8 boxes of ballpoint pens.

Check
$4.50(4) + (3.50 \times 8) \overset{?}{=} 46$ $18 + 28 \overset{?}{=} 46$ $46 = 46$

6.

Unknown	Knowns	Relationship	Calculations
Number of calendars: C	Number of date books: $500 - C$ Total cost of calendars: $\$0.75C$ Total cost of date books: $\$0.50(500 - C)$ Total order: $300	Cost of calendars + cost of the date books = total order $0.75C + 0.50(500 - C) = 300$	$0.75C + 0.50(500 - C) = 300$ $0.75C + 250 - 0.50C = 300$ $0.25C + 250 = 300$ $\underline{-250 \quad -250}$ $0.25C = 50$ $\dfrac{0.25C}{0.25} = \dfrac{50}{0.25}$ $C = 200$ $500 - C = 300$

200 calendars and 300 date books were ordered.

Check
$0.75(200) + 0.50(500 - 200) \overset{?}{=} 300$ $150 + 0.50(300) \overset{?}{=} 300$ $300 = 300$

7.

Unknown	Known	Relationship	Calculations
Number of feet represented by 2 inches: x	Number of feet represented by $\frac{1}{4}$ inch: 5	2 in. per x ft is proportional to $\frac{1}{4}$ in. per 5 ft $\dfrac{2 \text{ inches}}{x \text{ feet}} = \dfrac{\frac{1}{4} \text{ inch}}{5 \text{ feet}}$	$\dfrac{2 \text{ in.}}{x \text{ ft}} = \dfrac{\frac{1}{4} \text{ in.}}{5 \text{ ft}}$ $\frac{1}{4}x = 2(5)$ $\frac{1}{4}x = 10$ $4 \cdot \frac{1}{4}x = 10 \cdot 4$ $x = 40$

Check
$\dfrac{2}{40} \stackrel{?}{=} \dfrac{\frac{1}{4}}{5}$
$\dfrac{1}{\cancel{4}} \cdot \dfrac{\overset{10}{\cancel{40}}}{1} \stackrel{?}{=} 2(5)$
$10 = 10$

2 inches represents 40 feet.

8.

Unknown	Known	Relationship	Calculations
Number of cups of milk for 2 cups of flour: x	Number of cups of milk for 3 cups of flour: $1\frac{1}{4}$	2 cups flour per x cups milk is proportional to 3 cups flour per $1\frac{1}{4}$ cups milk. $\dfrac{2 \text{ cups flour}}{x \text{ cups milk}} = \dfrac{3 \text{ cups flour}}{1\frac{1}{4} \text{ cups milk}}$	$\dfrac{2 \text{ c flour}}{x \text{ c milk}} = \dfrac{3 \text{ c flour}}{1\frac{1}{4} \text{ c milk}}$ $3x = 2(1\frac{1}{4})$ $3x = \dfrac{\cancel{2}}{1} \cdot \dfrac{5}{\cancel{4}}$ $\dfrac{\cancel{3}x}{\cancel{3}} = \dfrac{\frac{5}{2}}{3}$ $x = \frac{5}{2} \div 3$ $x = \frac{5}{2} \cdot \frac{1}{3}$ $x = \frac{5}{6}$

Check
$\dfrac{2}{\frac{5}{6}} \stackrel{?}{=} \dfrac{3}{1\frac{1}{4}}$
$3 \cdot \frac{5}{6} \stackrel{?}{=} 2 \cdot 1\frac{1}{4}$
$\dfrac{\cancel{3}}{1} \cdot \dfrac{5}{\cancel{6}} \stackrel{?}{=} \dfrac{\cancel{2}}{1} \cdot \dfrac{5}{\cancel{4}}$
$\dfrac{5}{2} = \dfrac{5}{2}$

$\frac{5}{6}$ cups of milk is used for 2 cups of flour.

9.

Unknown	Known	Relationship	Calculations
Pay for 37 hours of work: x	Pay for 32 hours of work: $241.60	Pay per 37 hours of work is proportional to pay per 32 hours of work. $$\frac{x \text{ dollars}}{37 \text{ hours}} = \frac{\$241.60}{32 \text{ hours}}$$	$$\frac{x \text{ dollars}}{37 \text{ hours}} = \frac{\$241.60}{32 \text{ hours}}$$ $$32x = 37(241.60)$$ $$\frac{32x}{32} = \frac{8,939.20}{32}$$ $$x = \$279.35$$

Check

$$\frac{37}{279.35} \overset{?}{=} \frac{32}{241.60}$$
$$32(279.35) \overset{?}{=} 37(241.60)$$
$$8,939.20 = 8,939.20$$

$279.35 would be received for 37 hours of work.

CHAPTER 5 OVERVIEW

Section—Objective

Important Points with Examples

5.1 — 1 (page 168)

Evaluate formulas

Step 1 Replace letters in the formula with their known values. **Step 2** Perform the operations indicated by the formula. **Step 3** Interpret the result.

> Evaluate the formula $I = Prt$ when P is $2,000, r is 5%, and t is 2 years.
>
> $I = Prt$
> $I = 2,000(0.05)(2)$
> $I = 200$
>
> The interest is $200.

5.1 — 2 (page 170)

Write a formula to find an unknown value

Step 1 Represent the unknown value with a letter. **Step 2** Represent each known value with a letter. **Step 3** Write the unknown-value letter on the left side of an equal sign and the known-value letters with appropriate operation symbols on the right side of the equal sign.

> Write a formula to find the net pay (take-home pay) if net pay is equal to the total deductions subtracted from the gross pay.
>
> $N = G - D$, where N is net pay, G is gross pay, and D is deductions.

 $ex.\ N = 500 - 300$
$N = 200$

 $G = 500$
$D = 300$

5.2 — 1 (page 176)

Solve equations using multiplication or division

Step 1 Isolate the unknown value: **a)** If the equation contains the *product* of the unknown value and a number, then *divide* both sides of the equation by the number. **b)** If the equation contains the *quotient* of the unknown value and a number, then *multiply* both sides of the equation by the number. **Step 2** Identify the solution: the solution is the number on the side opposite the isolated unknown-value letter. **Step 3** Check the solution: In the original equation, replace the unknown-value letter with the solution, perform the indicated operations, and verify that both sides of the equation are the same number.

Find the value of A.

$$4A = 36$$

$$\frac{4A}{4} = \frac{36}{4} \qquad \text{Divide both sides by 4.}$$

$$A = 9$$

$$\frac{A}{7} = 6$$

$$\frac{A}{7} \times 7 = 6 \times 7 \qquad \text{Multiply both sides by 7.}$$

$$A = 42$$

Solve equations using addition or subtraction

(page 177)

Step 1 Isolate the unknown value: **a)** If the equation contains the *sum* of the unknown value and another number, then *subtract* the number from both sides of the equation. **b)** If the equation contains the *difference* of the unknown value and another number, then *add* the number to both sides of the equation. **Step 2** Identify the solution: the solution is the number on the side opposite the isolated unknown-value letter. **Step 3** Check the solution: In the original equation, replace the unknown-value letter with the solution, perform the indicated operations, and verify that both sides of the equation are the same number.

Find the value of A.

$$
\begin{array}{lll}
A - 7 = & 12 & \\
\underline{+7} & \underline{+7} & \text{Add 7 to both sides.}\\
A \;\;= & 19 &
\end{array}
\qquad
\begin{array}{lll}
A + 5 = & 32 & \\
\underline{-5} & \underline{-\;5} & \text{Subtract 5 from}\\
A \;\;= & 27 & \text{both sides.}
\end{array}
$$

Solve equations using more than one operation

(page 178)

Step 1 Isolate the unknown value: **a)** Working from left to right, add or subtract as necessary *first*. **b)** Working from left to right, multiply or divide as necessary *second*. **Step 2** Identify the solution: the solution is the number on the side opposite the isolated unknown-value letter. **Step 3** Check the solution: In the original equation, replace the unknown-value letter with the solution, perform the indicated operations according to the standard order, and verify that both sides of the equation are the same number.

Find the value of A.

$$
\begin{array}{lll}
4A + 4 = & 20 & \\
\underline{-4} & \underline{-\;4} & \text{Undo addition first.}\\
4A \;\;= & 16 &
\end{array}
$$

$$
\begin{array}{lll}
\frac{4A}{4} = & \frac{16}{4} & \text{Then undo multiplication.}\\
A = & 4 &
\end{array}
$$

$$
\begin{array}{lll}
\frac{A}{3} - 5 = & 17 & \\
\underline{+5} & \underline{+\;5} & \text{Undo subtrac-}\\
\frac{A}{3} = & \cancel{22}\;17 & \text{tion first.}
\end{array}
$$

$$\frac{A}{3} \times 3 = \cancel{17}\;22 \times 3 \qquad \text{Then undo division}$$

$$A = \cancel{51}\; A = 66$$

Solve equations containing a multiple unknown

(page 180)

Solve an equation when the unknown value occurs in two addends Step 1 Combine the unknown-value addends: **a)** Add the numbers in each addend. **b)** Multiply their sum by the unknown value. **Step 2** Solve the resulting equation.

Find the value of A.

$A - 5 + 5A = 25$

$$6A - 5 = 25 \quad \text{Combine addends.}$$
$$\underline{+5 \quad +5} \quad \text{Add 5 to both sides.}$$
$$6A = 30$$

$$\frac{6A}{6} = \frac{30}{6} \quad \text{Divide both sides by 6.}$$

$$A = 5$$

Solve equations containing parentheses

(page 181)

Step 1 Eliminate the parentheses: **a)** Multiply the number just outside the parentheses by each addend inside the parentheses. **b)** Show the resulting products as addition. **Step 2** Solve the resulting equation.

Find the value of A.

$3(A + 4) = 27$

$$3A + 12 = 27 \quad \text{Eliminate parentheses first.}$$
$$\underline{-12 \quad -12} \quad \text{Subtract 12 from both sides.}$$
$$3A = 15$$

$$\frac{3A}{3} = \frac{15}{3} \quad \text{Divide both sides by 3.}$$

$$A = 5$$

Use the decision key approach to analyze and solve word problems

(page 183)

Key words and what they imply in word problems

Key Words and What They Generally Imply in Word Problems

Addition	Subtraction	Multiplication	Division	Equality
The sum of	Less than	Times	Divide(s)	Equals
Plus/total	Decreased by	Multiplied by	Divided by	Is/was/are
Increased by	Subtracted from	Of	Divided into	Is equal to
More/more than	Difference between	The product of	Half of (divided by two)	The result is
Added to	Diminished by	Twice (two times)	Third of ($\frac{1}{3}$ times)	What is left
Exceeds	Take away	Double (two times)	Per	What remains
Expands	Reduced by	Triple (three times)		The same as
Greater than	Less/minus	Half ($\frac{1}{2}$ times)		Gives/giving
Gain/profit	Loss			Makes
Longer	Lower			Leaves
Older	Shrinks			
Heavier	Smaller than			
Wider	Younger			
Taller	Slower			

Section 5.1

Evaluate the formulas.

1. Use the formula $P = RB$ to find P when $R = 12\%$ and $B = \$1,000$.
$P = RB$
$P = .12(1,000)$
$P = 120$

2. Use the formula $P = RB$ to find P when $R = 8\%$ and $B = \$2,500$.
$P = RB$
$P = .08(2500)$
$P = 200$

3. Use the formula $P = 2l + 2w$ to find the perimeter P, when $l = 42$ feet and $w = 29$ feet.

4. Use the formula $P = 2l + 2w$ to find the perimeter P when $l = 96$ inches and $w = 82$ inches.
$P = 2l + 2w$
$P = 2(96) + 2(82)$
$P = 356$

5. Use the formula $I = Prt$ to find I when $P = \$4,500$, $r = 9\%$, and $t = 5$ years.

6. Use the formula $I = Prt$ to find I when $P = \$8,250$, $r = 8\%$, and $t = 2$ years.

7. Write the formula to find the perimeter (P) of a regular octagon. A regular octagon is a figure that has eight equal sides(s).

8. Write a formula to find the amount of social security (S) that is withheld from a paycheck if the gross pay (G) is multiplied by the withholding rate (R).
$S = G \times R$

9. Use the formula in Exercise 7 to find the perimeter of an octagon if the length of a side is 17 inches.

10. Use the formula in Exercise 8 to find the amount of Social Security withheld from a gross pay of $\$4,322.00$ if the rate is 5.85%.
$S = 4,322 \times 5.85\%$
$S = \$252.84$

Section 5.2

Find the value of the variable.

11. $5N = 35$

12. $3N = 27$ $N = 9$

13. $\dfrac{A}{6} = 2$

14. $\dfrac{A}{2} = 3$
$\dfrac{A}{2} \times \dfrac{2}{1} = \dfrac{3}{1} \times \dfrac{2}{1}$
$A = 6$

15. $N - 5 = 12$

16. $N + 8 = 20$

17. $2N + 4 = 12$

18. $3N - 5 = 10$
$+5 \quad +5$
$3N = 15$

19. $\dfrac{A}{3} + 4 = 12$

20. $\dfrac{A}{2} - 5 = 1$

21. $2(x - 3) = 8$

22. $5(A - 9) = 10$
$5A - 45 = 10$
$+45 \quad +45$
$A = 55$

23. $3(x - 1) = 30$

24. $7(B - 2) = 21$

25. $8A - 3A = 40$

26. $4A - A = 3$

27. $4X - X = 21$

28. $3X - 4 + 2X = 11$
$5X - 4 = 11$
$+4 \quad +4$
$\dfrac{15}{5}$ $X = 3$

Section 5.3

29. Ace Motors sold a total of 15 cars and trucks during one promotion sale. Six of the vehicles sold were trucks. What is the number of cars that were sold?

30. Edna's Book Carousel ordered several cookbooks and received 12. The shipping invoice indicated that 6 books would be shipped later. What is the number of books that was ordered?
$X = 12 + 6$
$X = 18$

31. The Queen of Diamonds Card Shop ordered an equal number of 12 different cards. If a total of 60 cards were ordered, how many of each type of card were ordered?

32. The Stork Club is a chain of baby clothing stores. The owner of the chain divided a number of Easter bonnets by the seven stores in the chain. If each store got nine bonnets, what was the number of bonnets distributed by the owner of the chain?

$$x = 7 \times 9$$
$$x = 63$$

33. An electrician pays $\frac{2}{5}$ of the amount he charges for a job for supplies. If he was paid $240 for a certain job, how much did he spend on supplies?

34. Liz Bliss spends 18 hours on a project and estimates that she has completed $\frac{1}{3}$ of the project. How many hours does she expect the project to take?

35. An inventory clerk is expected to have 2,000 fan belts in stock. If the current count is 1,584 fan belts, how many more should be ordered?

36. A personal computer costs $4,000, and a postscript printer costs $1,500. What is the total cost of the equipment?

37. Carrie McConnel spends $\frac{1}{6}$ of her weekly earnings on groceries. How much does she spend on groceries if her weekly earnings are $345?

38. A purse that sells for $68.99 is reduced by $25.50. What is the price of the purse after the reduction?

39. Shaquita Davis earns $350 for working 40 hours. How much does she make for each hour of work?

40. Wilson's Auto, Inc., has 37 employees and a weekly payroll of $10,878. If each employee makes the same amount, how much does each make?

41. Molly McWherter earns $7.36 per hour. How much would she make for 37 hours of work?

42. An imprint machine makes 1,897 imprints per hour. How many imprints can be made in 12 hours?

43. Wallpaper costs $12.97 per roll and a kitchen requires 9 rolls. What is the cost of the wallpaper needed to paper the kitchen?

44. Mack Construction Co. was billed for plasterboard installation. If the job required 3,582 square feet of plasterboard and cost $2,435.76, what was the cost per square foot?

45. Allen Brent purchased 250 pounds of tomatoes, 400 pounds of potatoes, 50 pounds of broccoli, and 130 pounds of birdseed for his chain stores. If all items are placed on the same shipment, what is the total weight of the shipment?

46. Harks Manufacturer is negotiating a waste-removal contract. A study indicates that, in general, 304 pounds of waste are produced on Monday, 450 pounds are produced on Tuesday, 483 pounds are produced on Wednesday, 387 pounds are produced on Thursday, and 293 pounds are produced on Friday. The plant is closed on Saturday and Sunday. How many pounds of waste are produced per week?

47. Cecil Hastings was overstocked with men's shirts and reduced the price from $18.99 to $15.97. By how much was each shirt reduced?

48. Cecil (Exercise 47) counted 216 shirts to be reduced. What was the total amount of reduction for 216 shirts?

49. The wholesale cost of an executive desk is $375, and the wholesale cost of a secretarial desk is $300. Allen Furniture Company filled an order for 40 desks, costing a total of $12,825. How many desks of each type were ordered?

50. A computer store sold 144 cases of two grades of computer paper. Microperforated paper cost $15.97 per case, and standard perforated paper cost $9.75 per case. If the store had paper sales totaling $1,715, how many cases of each type were sold? What was the dollar value of each type sold?

51. Bright Ideas purchased 1,000 light bulbs. Headlight bulbs cost $13.95 each, and taillight bulbs cost $7.55 each. If Bright Ideas spent $9,342 on light bulb stock, how many headlights and how many taillights did it get? What was the dollar value of the headlights ordered? What was the dollar value of the taillights ordered?

52. If a delivery van travels 252 miles on 12 gallons of gas, how many gallons are needed to travel 378 miles?

53. If five dozen roses can be purchased for $62.50, how much will eight dozen cost?

Challenge Problem

54. Find a variation of the formula $P = 2L + 2W$ so that W is alone on the left. When would you use this formula? Explain some of the advantages that are gained from using formulas and equations to solve problems.

CHAPTER 5 PRACTICE TEST

1. Evaluate the formula $S = C + M$ for S if $C = \$296$ and $M = \$150$.

2. Evaluate the formula $G = hr$ if $h = 40$ hours and $r = \$9.83$.

3. Write a formula for the relationship. The markup (M) on an item is the difference between the Selling Price (S) and the cost (C).

4. Write a formula to find the sales-tax rate (r) if it is the amount of tax (t) divided by the price of an item (p).

Solve.

5. $N + 7 = 18$

6. $5N = 45$

7. $\dfrac{A}{3} = 6$

8. $B - 8 = 7$

9. $3A - 5 = 10$

10. $5A + 8 = 33$

11. $2(N + 1) = 14$

12. $5A + A = 30$

13. An employee who was earning $249 weekly received a raise of $36. How much is the new salary?

14. An inventory clerk is expected to keep 600 filters on hand. A physical count shows there are 298 filters in stock. How many filters should be ordered?

15. A container of oil holds 585 gallons. How many containers each holding 4.5 gallons will be needed if all the oil is to be transferred to the smaller containers?

16. The buyer for a speciality gift store purchased an equal number of two types of designer telephones for a total cost of $7,200. The top-quality phones cost $120 each, and the plastic phones cost $80 each. How many of each type of phone were purchased and what was the total dollar value of each type?

17. A discount store sold plastic cups for $3.50 each and ceramic cups for $4 each. If 400 cups were sold for a total of $1,458, how many cups of each type were sold? What was the dollar value of each type of cup sold?

18. An appliance dealer sold nine more washing machines than dryers. Washing machines sell for $480 and dryers sell for $350. If total dollar sales were $21,750, how many of each appliance were sold? What was the dollar value of washing machines sold and the dollar value of dryers sold?

19. Find the cost of 200 suits if 75 suits cost $10,200.

20. Lashonna Harris is a buyer for Plough. She can purchase 100 pounds of chemical for $97. At this same rate, how much would 2,000 pounds of the chemical cost?

CHAPTER 6

PAYROLL

Divide into three investigative teams. Team one will explore the payroll process for hourly employees in a business that has fewer than 5 hourly employees. Team two will explore the payroll process for hourly employees in a business with more than 5 but fewer than 100 hourly employees. Team three will explore the payroll process for hourly employees in a company with more than 100 hourly employees.

Include in a team report how the time is recorded; what pay periods are used; who validates the time worked; how the pay is calculated; how the withholding, FICA, and Medicare taxes are derived; what other deduction options are available to hourly employees; and what payroll records are kept by the company. Present your team's report orally to the class. Compare and contrast the findings of each team through class discussions.

CHAPTER 6 PAYROLL

6.1 Gross Pay

▶ **1** *Find the gross pay per paycheck based on salary*

▶ **2** *Find the gross pay per weekly paycheck based on hourly wage*

▶ **3** *Find the gross pay per paycheck based on piecework wage*

▶ **4** *Find the gross pay per paycheck based on commission*

6.2 Payroll Deductions

▶ **1** *Find federal withholding tax per paycheck using IRS tax tables*

▶ **2** *Find federal withholding tax per paycheck using IRS percentage method tables*

▶ **3** *Find FICA tax and Medicare tax per paycheck*

▶ **4** *Find net earnings per paycheck*

6.3 The Employer's Payroll Taxes

▶ **1** *Find an employer's total deposit for withholding tax, FICA tax, and Medicare tax per pay period*

▶ **2** *Find an employer's SUTA tax and FUTA tax due for a quarter*

Pay is an important concern of employees and employers alike. If you have worked and received a paycheck, you know that part of your earnings are taken out of your paycheck before you ever see it. Your employer *withholds* (deducts) taxes, union dues, medical insurance payments, and so on. Thus there is a difference between **gross earnings (gross pay)**, the amount earned before deductions, and **net earnings (net pay)**—*take home pay*—the amount in the paycheck.

This chapter considers payroll issues from the point of view of the employee and the employer. Employers have the option of paying their employees in salary or in wages and of distributing these earnings at various intervals. Employers are required to withhold taxes and pay them to the federal, state, and local governments.

6.1 Gross Pay

▶ **1** *Find the gross pay per paycheck based on salary*

▶ **2** *Find the gross pay per weekly paycheck based on hourly wage*

▶ **3** *Find the gross pay per paycheck based on piecework wage*

▶ **4** *Find the gross pay per paycheck based on commission*

Employees may be paid according to a yearly salary, an hourly wage, a *piecework* rate, or a *commission* rate. Companies differ in how often they pay employees, which determines how many paychecks an employee receives in a year. If employees are paid **weekly**, they receive 52 paychecks a year; if they are paid **biweekly** (every other week), they receive 26 paychecks a year. **Semimonthly** (twice a month) paychecks are issued 24 times a year, and **monthly** paychecks come 12 times a year. This section shows what all these possibilities mean to the employee earning the paycheck.

▶ *Gross Pay Based on Salary*

Salary is usually stated as a certain amount of money paid each year. Salaried employees are paid the agreed-upon salary whether they work fewer or more than the usual number of hours. To find the amount of a salaried employee's paycheck before deductions, divide the salary per year by the number of paychecks the employee receives in the course of a year.

| HOW TO | **Find the Gross Pay Per Paycheck Based on Annual Salary** |

Step 1 Identify the number of pay periods per year:
       Monthly—12 pay periods per year
       Semimonthly—24 pay periods per year
       Biweekly—26 pay periods per year
       Weekly—52 pay periods per year
Step 2 Divide the annual salary by the number of pay periods per year.

Example 1 Charles Demetriou earns a salary of $30,000 a year. (a) If Charles is paid biweekly, how much is his paycheck before taxes are taken out? (b) If Charles is paid semimonthly, how much would his paycheck be before taxes?

(a) $30,000 ÷ 26 = $1,153.85
   Charles earns $1,153.85 biweekly before deductions.

              Biweekly paychecks are issued 26 times a year, so divide Charles's salary by 26.

(b) $30,000 ÷ 24 = $1,250
   Charles earns $1,250 semimonthly before deductions.

              Semimonthly paychecks are issued 24 times a year, so divide Charles's salary by 24.

 Gross Pay Based on Hourly Wage

Some jobs pay according to an *hourly wage*. The **hourly rate**, or **hourly wage**, is the amount of money paid for each hour the employee works in a standard 40 hour week. The Fair Labor Standards Act of 1938 set the standard work week at 40 hours. When hourly employees work more than 40 hours in a week, they earn the hourly wage for the first 40 hours, and they earn an **overtime rate** for the remaining hours. The overtime rate is often called **time and a half**. By law it must be at least 1.5 (one and one-half) times the hourly wage. Earnings based on the hourly wage are called **regular pay**. Earnings based on the overtime rate are called **overtime pay**. An hourly employee's gross pay is the sum of his or her regular pay and his or her overtime pay.

| HOW TO | **Find the Gross Pay Per Week Based on Hourly Wages** |

Step 1 Find the regular pay:
     a) If the hours worked in the week are 40 or less, multiply the hours worked by the hourly wage.
     b) If the hours worked are more than 40, multiply 40 hours by the hourly wage.
Step 2 Find the overtime pay:
     a) If the hours worked are 40 or less, the overtime pay is $0.
     b) If the hours worked are more than 40, subtract 40 from the hours worked and multiply the difference by the overtime rates.
Step 3 Add the regular pay and the overtime pay.

Example 2 Marcia Scott, whose hourly wage is $7.25, worked 46 hours last week. Find her gross pay for last week if she earns time and a half for overtime.

$40 \times \$7.25 = \boxed{\$290}$ **Find the regular pay for 40 hours of work at the hourly wage.**

$\underbrace{6 \times \$7.25 \times 1.5}_{\text{overtime rate}} = \$65.25$ **Find the overtime pay by multiplying the overtime hours by the overtime rate, which is the hourly wage times 1.5. Round to the nearest cent.**

$\boxed{\$290} + \$65.25 = \$355.25$ **Add the regular pay and the overtime pay to find Marcia's total gross earnings.**

Marcia's gross pay is $355.25.

 Gross Pay Based on Piecework Wage

Some employers motivate employees to produce more by paying according to the quantity of acceptable work done. Such **piecework rates** are typically offered in production or manufacturing jobs. Garment makers and some other types of factory workers, agricultural workers, and employees who perform repetitive tasks such as stuffing envelopes or packaging parts may be paid by this method. In the simplest cases the gross earnings of such workers are calculated by multiplying the number of items produced by the **straight piecework rate**.

Sometimes employees earn wages at a **differential piece rate**, also called an **escalating piece rate**. As the number of items produced by the worker increases, so does the pay per item. This method of paying wages offers employees an even greater incentive to complete more pieces of work in a given period of time.

Example 3 A shirt manufacturer pays a worker $0.27 for each acceptable shirt completed under the prescribed job description. If the worker had the following work record, find the gross earnings for the week: Monday, 250 shirts; Tuesday, 300 shirts; Wednesday, 178 shirts; Thursday, 326 shirts; Friday, 296 shirts.

$250 + 300 + 178 + 326 + 296$ **Find the total number of shirts made.**
$= \boxed{1,350}$ shirts

$\boxed{1,350} \times \$0.27 = \$364.50$ **Multiply the number of shirts by the piecework rate.**

The gross earnings are $364.50.

HOW TO	Find the Gross Pay Per Paycheck Based on Piecework Wage

Step 1 If a *straight piecework rate* is used, multiply the number of items completed by the straight piecework rate.

Step 2 If a *differential piecework rate* is used:
    a) For each rate category, multiply the number of items produced for the category by the rate for the category.
    b) Add the pay for all rate categories.

Example 4 Last week, Jorge Sanchez assembled 317 microchip boards. Find Jorge's gross earnings for the week if the manufacturer pays at the following differential piece rates.

Boards Assembled per Week	Pay per board
1–100	$1.32
101–300	$1.42
301 and over	$1.58

Find how many boards were completed at each pay rate, multiply the number of boards by the rate, and add the amounts.

First 100 items: $100 \times 1.32 = \$132.00$
Next 200 items: $200 \times 1.42 = \$284.00$
Last 17 items: $\ \ 17 \times 1.58 = \underline{\$\ \ 26.86}$
$\qquad\qquad\qquad\qquad\qquad \$442.86$

Jorge's gross earnings were $442.86.

BUSINESS AND MATHEMATICS *IN THE NEWS*

Longer Workweek

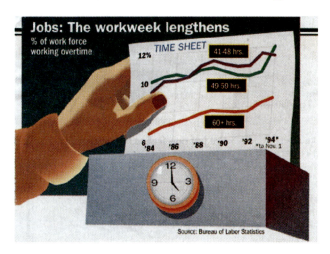

1. Which category showed the greatest increase from 1984 to 1994? Approximate the percent increase.

2. If the trend continues for the next ten years, what percent of the workforce will be working 60 or more hours per week in the year 2004?

3. If you were offered a job and knew these trends toward increasing employee overtime, discuss whether you would ask to be salaried, paid hourly, or paid on a piece-work rate.

Excerpted by permission from the January 1995 issue of *Kiplinger's Personal Finance Magazine*. Copyright © 1995 The Kiplinger Washington Editors, Inc.

4 ▸ *Gross Pay Based on Commission*

Many salespeople earn a **commission**, a percentage based on sales. Those whose entire pay is commission are said to work on **straight commission**. Those who receive a salary in addition to a commission are said to work on a **salary plus commission** basis.

A **commission rate** can be a percent of total sales, or a percent of sales greater than a specified **quota** of sales.

? HOW TO | **Find the Gross Pay Per Paycheck Based on Commission**

Step 1 Find the commission:
    a) If the commission is *commission based on total sales,* multiply the commission rate by the total sales for the pay period.
    b) If the commission is *commission based on quota,* subtract the quota from the total sales and multiply the difference by the commission rate.

Step 2 Find the salary:
    a) If the wage is *straight commission,* the salary is $0.
    b) If the wage is *commission-plus-salary,* use the How-To steps for finding gross pay based on salary.

Step 3 Add the commission and the salary.

Example 5 Shirley Dozier is a restaurant-supplies salesperson and receives 5% of her total sales as commission. Her sales totaled $15,000 during a given week. Find her gross earnings.

Use the percentage formula $P = R \times B$.

$P = 0.05 \times \$15,000 = \$750$ **Change the rate of 5% to a decimal and multiply it times the base of $15,000.**

The gross earnings are $750.

Example 6 Ms. Jones is paid on a salary-plus-commission basis. She receives $150 weekly in salary and 3% of all sales over $2,000. If she sold $6,000 worth of goods, find her gross pay.

$\$6,000 - \$2,000 = \$4,000$ **Subtract the quota from total sales to find the salary on which commission is paid.**

$P = R \times B$

$P = 0.03 \times 4,000$ **Change the rate of 3% to a decimal. Multiply the rate by the base of $4,000. Ms. Jones's commission is $120.**

$P = \boxed{\$120}$ (commission)

$\boxed{\$120} + \$150 = \$270$ **Add the commission and salary to find gross pay.**

Ms. Jones' gross earnings are $270.

Self-Check 6.1

1. If Timothy Oaks earns a salary of $19,000 a year and is paid weekly, how much is his weekly paycheck before taxes?

2. If Nita McMillan earns a salary of $27,988 a year and is paid biweekly, how much is her biweekly paycheck before taxes are taken out?

3. Gregory Maksi earns a salary of $52,980 annually and is paid monthly. How much is his gross monthly income?

4. Amelia Mattix is an accountant and is paid semimonthly. Her annual salary is $38,184. How much is her gross pay per period?

2▶5. William Melton worked 47 hours in one week. His regular pay was $7.60 per hour with time and a half for overtime. Find his gross earnings for the week.

6. Peter Moffatt, whose regular rate of pay is $8.25 per hour, with time and a half for overtime, worked 44 hours last week. Find his gross pay for the week.

7. Carlos Espinosa earns $15.90 per hour with time and a half for overtime and worked 47 hours during a recent week. Find his gross pay for the week.

3▶8. A belt manufacturer pays a worker $0.84 for each buckle she correctly attaches to a belt. If Yolanda Jackson had the following work record, find the gross earnings for the week: Monday, 132 buckles; Tuesday, 134 buckles; Wednesday, 138 buckles; Thursday, 134 buckles; Friday, 130 buckles.

9. Last week, Laurie Golson packaged 189 boxes of Holiday Cheese Assortment. Find her gross weekly earnings if she is paid at the following differential piece rate.

Cheese Boxes Packaged Per Week	Pay Per Package
1–100	$1.48
101–300	$1.58
301 and over	$1.68

10. Joe Thweatt makes icons for a major distributor. He is paid $8.13 for each icon and records the following number of completed icons: Monday, 9; Tuesday, 11; Wednesday, 10; Thursday, 12; Friday, 4. How much will he be paid for his work for the week?

4▶11. Raul Fletes is a paper mill sales representative who receives 6% of his total sales as commission. His sales last week totaled $8,972. Find his gross earnings for the week.

12. Mary Lee Strode is paid a straight commission on sales as a real estate salesperson. In one pay period she had a total of $452,493 in sales. What is her gross pay if the commission rate is $3\frac{1}{2}\%$?

13. Karen Farris is paid on a salary-plus-commission basis. She receives $275 weekly in salary and a commission based on 5% of all weekly sales over $2,000. If she sold $7,821 in merchandise in one week find her gross earnings for the week.

14. Vincent Ores sells equipment to receive satellite signals. He earns a 3% commission on monthly sales above $2,000. One month his sales totaled $145,938. What is his commission for the month?

6.2 **Payroll Deductions**

1▶ *Find federal withholding tax per paycheck using IRS tax tables*

2▶ *Find federal withholding tax per paycheck using IRS percentage method tables*

3▶ *Find FICA tax and Medicare tax per paycheck*

4▶ *Find net earnings per paycheck*

As anyone who has ever drawn a paycheck knows, many deductions may be deducted from gross pay. Deductions include federal, state, and local income or payroll taxes, FICA (Social Security) and Medicare taxes, union dues, medical insurance, credit union payments, and a host of others. By law, employers are responsible for withholding and paying their employee's taxes. In fact, the bookkeeping involved in payroll provides a major source of employment for many people in the business world.

The largest deduction from an employee's paycheck usually comes in the form of *income tax*. The tax paid to the federal government is called **federal withholding tax (FWT)**. The tax withheld is based on three things: the employee's gross earnings, the employee's tax filing status, and the number of *withholding allowances* the person claims. A **withholding allowance**, called an **exemption**, is a portion of gross earnings that is not subject to tax. Each employee is permitted one withholding allowance for himself, or herself, one for a spouse, and one for each dependent (such as a child or elderly parent). [A detailed discussion on eligibility for various allowances can be found in several IRS publications such as Publication 15 (Circular E, Employer's Tax Guide), Publication 505 (Tax Withholding and Estimated Tax), and Publication 17 (Your Federal Income Tax For Individuals).] Each employee fills out a *W-4 form* showing how many withholding allowances or exemptions he or she claims. The employer uses this information to figure how much tax to deduct from the employee's paycheck. Figure 6–1 shows a 1994 W-4 form.

There are several ways to figure the withholding tax for an employee. The most common methods are using tax tables and tax rates. These and other methods are referenced in IRS Publication 15 (Circular E, Employer's Tax Guide).

TIPS & TRAPS

The IRS provides recorded tax information on numerous topics that answer many individual and business tax topics. Touch-tone service is available 24 hours a day, seven days a week using the toll-free number 1-800-TAX-IIRS or 1-800-829-4477.

 Federal Withholding Tax Tables

To calculate federal withholding tax using IRS tax tables, an employer must know the employee's filing status (single, married, and so on), the number of withholding allowances the employee claims, the type of pay period (weekly, biweekly, and so on), and the employee's *adjusted gross income*.

In many cases, adjusted gross income is the same as gross pay. However, earnings contributed to funds such as IRAs, tax-sheltered annuities, 401Ks, or employee-sponsored child care and medical plans are called *adjustments* to income, and are subtracted from gross pay to determine the **adjusted gross income**.

Figures 6–2 and 6–3 show two IRS tax tables.

 **HOW TO** | **Find Federal Withholding Tax Per Paycheck Using the IRS Tax Tables**

Step 1 Find the adjusted gross pay by subtracting the total qualified adjustments from the gross pay per pay period. Select the appropriate table according to the employee's filing status (single, married, and so on), and according to the type of pay period (weekly, biweekly, and so on).

Step 2 Find the income row: In the rows labeled "If the wages are —", select the "At least" and "But less than" interval that includes the employee's adjusted gross pay for the pay period.

Step 3 Find the allowances column: In the columns labeled "And the number of withholding allowances claimed is —", select the number of allowances the employee claims.

Step 4 Find the cell where the income row and allowance column intersect. The correct tax is given in this cell.

Form W-4 (1995)

Want More Money In Your Paycheck?
If you expect to be able to take the earned income credit for 1995 and a child lives with you, you may be able to have part of the credit added to your take-home pay. For details, get Form W-5 from your employer.

Purpose. Complete Form W-4 so that your employer can withhold the correct amount of Federal income tax from your pay.

Exemption From Withholding. Read line 7 of the certificate below to see if you can claim exempt status. *If exempt, complete line 7; but do not complete lines 5 and 6.* No Federal income tax will be withheld from your pay. Your exemption is good for 1 year only. It expires February 15, 1996.

Note: *You cannot claim exemption from withholding if (1) your income exceeds $650 and includes unearned income (e.g., interest* and dividends) and (2) another person can claim you as a dependent on their tax return.

Basic Instructions. Employees who are not exempt should complete the Personal Allowances Worksheet. Additional worksheets are provided on page 2 for employees to adjust their withholding allowances based on itemized deductions, adjustments to income, or two-earner/two-job situations. Complete all worksheets that apply to your situation. The worksheets will help you figure the number of withholding allowances you are entitled to claim. However, you may claim fewer allowances than this.

Head of Household. Generally, you may claim head of household filing status on your tax return only if you are unmarried and pay more than 50% of the costs of keeping up a home for yourself and your dependent(s) or other qualifying individuals.

Nonwage Income. If you have a large amount of nonwage income, such as interest or dividends, you should consider making estimated tax payments using Form 1040-ES. Otherwise, you may find that you owe additional tax at the end of the year.

Two Earners/Two Jobs. If you have a working spouse or more than one job, figure the total number of allowances you are entitled to claim on all jobs using worksheets from only one Form W-4. This total should be divided among all jobs. Your withholding will usually be most accurate when all allowances are claimed on the W-4 filed for the highest paying job and zero allowances are claimed for the others.

Check Your Withholding. After your W-4 takes effect, you can use **Pub. 919,** Is My Withholding Correct for 1995?, to see how the dollar amount you are having withheld compares to your estimated total annual tax. We recommend you get Pub. 919 especially if you used the Two Earner/Two Job Worksheet and your earnings exceed $150,000 (Single) or $200,000 (Married). Call 1-800-829-3676 to order Pub. 919. Check your telephone directory for the IRS assistance number for further help.

Personal Allowances Worksheet

A   Enter "1" for **yourself** if no one else can claim you as a dependent . . . .   **A** _____

B   Enter "1" if:
- You are single and have only one job; or
- You are married, have only one job, and your spouse does not work; or
- Your wages from a second job or your spouse's wages (or the total of both) are $1,000 or less.

. . **B** _____

C   Enter "1" for your **spouse.** But, you may choose to enter -0- if you are married and have either a working spouse or more than one job (this may help you avoid having too little tax withheld) . . . .   **C** _____

D   Enter number of **dependents** (other than your spouse or yourself) you will claim on your tax return . . . .   **D** _____

E   Enter "1" if you will file as **head of household** on your tax return (see conditions under **Head of Household** above) .   **E** _____

F   Enter "1" if you have at least $1,500 of **child or dependent care expenses** for which you plan to claim a credit . .   **F** _____

G   Add lines A through F and enter total here. **Note:** This amount may be different from the number of exemptions you claim on your return ▶   **G** _____

For accuracy, do all worksheets that apply.
- If you plan to **itemize or claim adjustments to income** and want to reduce your withholding, see the Deductions and Adjustments Worksheet on page 2.
- If you are **single** and have **more than one job** and your combined earnings from all jobs exceed $30,000 OR if you are **married** and have a **working spouse or more than one job,** and the combined earnings from all jobs exceed $50,000, see the Two-Earner/Two-Job Worksheet on page 2 if you want to avoid having too little tax withheld.
- If **neither** of the above situations applies, **stop here** and enter the number from line G on line 5 of Form W-4 below.

--------------------- **Cut here and give the certificate to your employer. Keep the top portion for your records.** ---------------------

Form **W-4** Department of the Treasury Internal Revenue Service	**Employee's Withholding Allowance Certificate** ▶ **For Privacy Act and Paperwork Reduction Act Notice, see reverse.**	OMB No. 1545-0010 **1995**

1	Type or print your first name and middle initial	Last name		2	Your social security number

Home address (number and street or rural route)	3 ☐ Single ☐ Married ☐ Married, but withhold at higher Single rate. **Note:** *If married, but legally separated, or spouse is a nonresident alien, check the Single box.*
City or town, state, and ZIP code	4 If your last name differs from that on your social security card, check here and call 1-800-772-1213 for a new card . . . . . ▶ ☐

5   Total number of allowances you are claiming (from line G above or from the worksheets on page 2 if they apply) .   **5** _____

6   Additional amount, if any, you want withheld from each paycheck . . . .   **6** $_____

7   I claim exemption from withholding for 1995 and I certify that I meet **BOTH** of the following conditions for exemption:
- Last year I had a right to a refund of **ALL** Federal income tax withheld because I had **NO** tax liability; **AND**
- This year I expect a refund of **ALL** Federal income tax withheld because I expect to have **NO** tax liability.

If you meet both conditions, enter "EXEMPT" here . . . . ▶   **7** _____

Under penalties of perjury, I certify that I am entitled to the number of withholding allowances claimed on this certificate or entitled to claim exempt status.

Employee's signature ▶ _____   Date ▶ _____ , 19___

8	Employer's name and address (Employer: Complete 8 and 10 only if sending to the IRS)	9 Office code (optional)	10 Employer identification number

Cat. No. 10220Q

Figure 6–1   Employee's Withholding Allowance Certificate

SINGLE Persons—SEMIMONTHLY Payroll Period
(For Wages Paid in 1995)

If the wages are—		And the number of withholding allowances claimed is—										
At least	But less than	0	1	2	3	4	5	6	7	8	9	10
		The amount of income tax to be withheld is—										
$820	$840	108	93	77	61	46	30	15	0	0	0	0
840	860	111	96	80	64	49	33	18	2	0	0	0
860	880	114	99	83	67	52	36	21	5	0	0	0
880	900	117	102	86	70	55	39	24	8	0	0	0
900	920	120	105	89	73	58	42	27	11	0	0	0
920	940	123	108	92	76	61	45	30	14	0	0	0
940	960	126	111	95	79	64	48	33	17	1	0	0
960	980	129	114	98	82	67	51	36	20	4	0	0
980	1,000	132	117	101	85	70	54	39	23	7	0	0
1,000	1,020	135	120	104	88	73	57	42	26	10	0	0
1,020	1,040	138	123	107	91	76	60	45	29	13	0	0
1,040	1,060	144	126	110	94	79	63	48	32	16	1	0
1,060	1,080	149	129	113	97	82	66	51	35	19	4	0
1,080	1,100	155	132	116	100	85	69	54	38	22	7	0
1,100	1,120	160	135	119	103	88	72	57	41	25	10	0
1,120	1,140	166	138	122	106	91	75	60	44	28	13	0
1,140	1,160	172	143	125	109	94	78	63	47	31	16	0
1,160	1,180	177	148	128	112	97	81	66	50	34	19	3
1,180	1,200	183	154	131	115	100	84	69	53	37	22	6
1,200	1,220	188	159	134	118	103	87	72	56	40	25	9
1,220	1,240	194	165	137	121	106	90	75	59	43	28	12
1,240	1,260	200	171	141	124	109	93	78	62	46	31	15
1,260	1,280	205	176	147	127	112	96	81	65	49	34	18
1,280	1,300	211	182	153	130	115	99	84	68	52	37	21
1,300	1,320	216	187	158	133	118	102	87	71	55	40	24
1,320	1,340	222	193	164	136	121	105	90	74	58	43	27
1,340	1,360	228	199	169	140	124	108	93	77	61	46	30
1,360	1,380	233	204	175	146	127	111	96	80	64	49	33
1,380	1,400	239	210	181	151	130	114	99	83	67	52	36
1,400	1,420	244	215	186	157	33	117	102	86	70	55	39
1,420	1,440	250	221	192	163	136	120	105	89	73	58	42
1,440	1,460	256	227	197	168	139	123	108	92	76	61	45
1,460	1,480	261	232	203	174	145	126	111	95	79	64	48
1,480	1,500	267	238	209	179	150	129	114	98	82	67	51
1,500	1,520	272	243	214	185	156	132	117	101	85	70	54
1,520	1,540	278	249	220	191	161	135	120	104	88	73	57
1,540	1,560	284	255	225	196	167	138	123	107	91	76	60
1,560	1,580	289	260	231	202	173	143	126	110	94	79	63
1,580	1,600	295	266	237	207	178	149	129	113	97	82	66
1,600	1,620	300	271	242	213	184	155	132	116	100	85	69
1,620	1,640	306	277	248	219	189	160	135	119	103	88	72
1,640	1,660	312	283	253	224	195	166	138	122	106	91	75
1,660	1,680	317	288	259	230	201	171	142	125	109	94	78
1,680	1,700	323	294	265	235	206	177	148	128	112	97	81
1,700	1,720	328	299	270	241	212	183	153	131	115	100	84
1,720	1,740	334	305	276	247	217	188	159	134	118	103	87
1,740	1,760	340	311	281	252	223	194	165	137	121	106	90
1,760	1,780	345	316	287	258	229	199	170	141	124	109	93
1,780	1,800	351	322	293	263	234	205	176	147	127	112	96
1,800	1,820	356	327	298	269	240	211	181	152	130	115	99
1,820	1,840	362	333	304	275	245	216	187	158	133	118	102
1,840	1,860	368	339	309	280	251	222	193	164	136	121	105
1,860	1,880	373	344	315	286	257	227	198	169	140	124	108
1,880	1,900	379	350	321	291	262	233	204	175	146	127	111
1,900	1,920	384	355	326	297	268	239	209	180	151	130	114
1,920	1,940	390	361	332	303	273	244	215	186	157	133	117
1,940	1,960	396	367	337	308	279	250	221	192	162	136	120
1,960	1,980	401	372	343	314	285	255	226	197	168	139	123
1,980	2,000	407	378	349	319	290	261	232	203	174	144	126
2,000	2,020	412	383	354	325	296	267	237	208	179	150	129
2,020	2,040	418	389	360	331	301	272	243	214	185	156	132
2,040	2,060	424	395	365	336	307	278	249	220	190	161	135
2,060	2,080	429	400	371	342	313	283	254	225	196	167	138
2,080	2,100	435	406	377	347	318	289	260	231	202	172	143
2,100	2,120	440	411	382	353	324	295	265	236	207	178	149

$2,120 and over   Use Table 3(a) for a **SINGLE person** on page 32. Also see the instructions on page 30.

Figure 6–2   IRS Tax Table for Single Persons Paid Semimonthly

MARRIED Persons—WEEKLY Payroll Period
(For Wages Paid in 1995)

If the wages are—		And the number of withholding allowances claimed is—										
At least	But less than	0	1	2	3	4	5	6	7	8	9	10
		The amount of income tax to be withheld is—										
$0	$125	0	0	0	0	0	0	0	0	0	0	0
125	130	1	0	0	0	0	0	0	0	0	0	0
130	135	1	0	0	0	0	0	0	0	0	0	0
135	140	2	0	0	0	0	0	0	0	0	0	0
140	145	3	0	0	0	0	0	0	0	0	0	0
145	150	4	0	0	0	0	0	0	0	0	0	0
150	155	4	0	0	0	0	0	0	0	0	0	0
155	160	5	0	0	0	0	0	0	0	0	0	0
160	165	6	0	0	0	0	0	0	0	0	0	0
165	170	7	0	0	0	0	0	0	0	0	0	0
170	175	7	0	0	0	0	0	0	0	0	0	0
175	180	8	1	0	0	0	0	0	0	0	0	0
180	185	9	2	0	0	0	0	0	0	0	0	0
185	190	10	2	0	0	0	0	0	0	0	0	0
190	195	10	3	0	0	0	0	0	0	0	0	0
195	200	11	4	0	0	0	0	0	0	0	0	0
200	210	12	5	0	0	0	0	0	0	0	0	0
210	220	14	7	0	0	0	0	0	0	0	0	0
220	230	15	8	1	0	0	0	0	0	0	0	0
230	240	17	10	2	0	0	0	0	0	0	0	0
240	250	18	11	4	0	0	0	0	0	0	0	0
250	260	20	13	5	0	0	0	0	0	0	0	0
260	270	21	14	7	0	0	0	0	0	0	0	0
270	280	23	16	8	1	0	0	0	0	0	0	0
280	290	24	17	10	3	0	0	0	0	0	0	0
290	300	26	19	11	4	0	0	0	0	0	0	0
300	310	27	20	13	6	0	0	0	0	0	0	0
310	320	29	22	14	7	0	0	0	0	0	0	0
320	330	30	23	16	9	1	0	0	0	0	0	0
330	340	32	25	17	10	3	0	0	0	0	0	0
340	350	33	26	19	12	4	0	0	0	0	0	0
350	360	35	28	20	13	6	0	0	0	0	0	0
360	370	36	29	22	15	7	0	0	0	0	0	0
370	380	38	31	23	16	9	2	0	0	0	0	0
380	390	39	32	25	18	10	3	0	0	0	0	0
390	400	41	34	26	19	12	5	0	0	0	0	0
400	410	42	35	28	21	13	6	0	0	0	0	0
410	420	44	37	29	22	15	8	1	0	0	0	0
420	430	45	38	31	24	16	9	2	0	0	0	0
430	440	47	40	32	25	18	11	4	0	0	0	0
440	450	48	41	34	27	19	12	5	0	0	0	0
450	460	50	43	35	28	21	14	7	0	0	0	0
460	470	51	44	37	30	22	15	8	1	0	0	0
470	480	53	46	38	31	24	17	10	2	0	0	0
480	490	54	47	40	33	25	18	11	4	0	0	0
490	500	56	49	41	34	27	20	13	5	0	0	0
500	510	57	50	43	36	28	21	14	7	0	0	0
510	520	59	52	44	37	30	23	16	8	1	0	0
520	530	60	53	46	39	31	24	17	10	3	0	0
530	540	62	55	47	40	33	26	19	11	4	0	0
540	550	63	56	49	42	34	27	20	13	6	0	0
550	560	65	58	50	43	36	29	22	14	7	0	0
560	570	66	59	52	45	37	30	23	16	9	1	0
570	580	68	61	53	46	39	32	25	17	10	3	0
580	590	69	62	55	48	40	33	26	19	12	4	0
590	600	71	64	56	49	42	35	28	20	13	6	0
600	610	72	65	58	51	43	36	29	22	15	7	0
610	620	74	67	59	52	45	38	31	23	16	9	2
620	630	75	68	61	54	46	39	32	25	18	10	3
630	640	77	70	62	55	48	41	34	26	19	12	5
640	650	78	71	64	57	49	42	35	28	21	13	6
650	660	80	73	65	58	51	44	37	29	22	15	8
660	670	81	74	67	60	52	45	38	31	24	16	9
670	680	83	76	68	61	54	47	40	32	25	18	11
680	690	84	77	70	63	55	48	41	34	27	19	12
690	700	86	79	71	64	57	50	43	35	28	21	14
700	710	87	80	73	66	58	51	44	37	30	22	15
710	720	89	82	74	67	60	53	46	38	31	24	17
720	730	90	83	76	69	61	54	47	40	33	25	18
730	740	92	85	77	70	63	56	49	41	34	27	20

Figure 6–3   IRS Tax Table for Married Persons Paid Weekly

Example 1

Lynn Fly has a gross semimonthly income of $840, is single, and claims three withholding allowances. Find the amount of federal withholding tax to be deducted from his gross earnings by using Figure 6–2.

The amount $840 is seen in *both* the "At least" and "But less than" columns. Since $840 is not in the range "At least $820 but less than $840," choose the row "At least $840 but less than $860." Now choose the column for three withholding allowances. The withholding tax is $64.

Example 2

Gaynell Dudenhefer is married, has a gross weekly salary of $515, and claims two withholding allowances. Find the amount of withholding tax to be deducted from her gross salary.

In Figure 6–3, find the $510–$520 income row, and withholding allowance column 2.

The amount of withholding tax is $44.

▶ *Federal Withholding Tax Rates and the Percentage Method*

Instead of using the tax tables, many companies calculate federal withholding tax using *tax rates*. In order to use tax rates, the employer must deduct from the employee's adjusted gross income a tax-exempt amount based on the number of withholding allowances the employee claims. The resulting amount we will call the **percentage method income**.

Figure 6–4 shows how much of an employee's adjusted gross income is exempt for each withholding allowance claimed, according to the type of pay period—weekly, biweekly, and so on. The table in Figure 6–4 is available from the IRS, which calls this table a part of the **percentage method** for figuring employees' withholding taxes.

❓ HOW TO — Find the Percentage Method Income Per Paycheck

Step 1 Find the exempt-per-allowance amount: From the withholding allowance table (in Figure 6–4), identify the amount exempt for one withholding allowance according to the type of pay period.

Step 2 Find the total exempt amount: Multiply the number of withholding allowances the employee claims by the exempt-per-allowance amount.

Step 3 Subtract the total exempt amount from the employee's adjusted gross income for the pay period.

Example 3

Find the percentage-method income on Dollie Calloway's semi-monthly gross earnings of $3,150. She has no adjustments to income, is single, and claims two withholding allowances on her W-4 form.

Since Dollie has no adjustments to income, her gross earnings of $3,150 is her adjusted gross income. From the table in Figure 6–4, the amount exempt for one withholding allowance in a semimonthly pay period is $104.17.

$2 \times \$104.17 = \$208.34$ **Multiply the number of withholding allowances by the exempt-per-allowance amount.**

$\$3,150 - \$208.34 = \$2,941.66$ **Subtract the total exempt amount from the adjusted gross income.**

The percentage method income is $2,941.66.

Figure 6–4 IRS Table for Figuring Withholding Allowance According to the Percentage Method

Payroll period	One withholding allowance
Weekly	$48.08
Biweekly	96.15
Semimonthly	104.17
Monthly	208.33
Quarterly	625.00
Semiannually	1,250.00
Annually.	2,500.00
Daily or miscellaneous (each day of the payroll period)	9.62

Once an employee's percentage method income is found, the employer consults the percentage method tables, also available from the IRS, to know how much of this income should be taxed at which tax rate, according to the employee's marital status and the type of pay period. Figure 6–5 shows the IRS percentage method tables.

HOW TO — **Find Federal Withholding Tax Per Paycheck Using the IRS Percentage Method Tables**

Step 1 Select the appropriate table according to the employee's filing status and the type of pay period.

Step 2 Find the income row: In the rows labeled "If the amount of wages is . . .", select the "Over-" and "But not over-" interval that includes the employee's percentage method income for the pay period.

Step 3 Find the cell where the income row and the column labeled "of excess over-" intersect, and subtract the amount given in this cell from the employee's percentage method income for the pay period.

Step 4 Multiply the difference from step 3 by the percent given in the income row.

Step 5 Add the product from step 4 to the amount given with the *percent* in the income row and amount of tax column.

Example 4 Find the federal withholding tax that will be deducted from Dollie's income in Example 3.

From Figure 6–5 select Table 3(a) for single employees paid semimonthly. We found Dollie's percentage method income to be $2,941.66 for the pay period. Table 3(a) tells us that the tax for that income is $455.97 plus 31% of the income in excess of $2,165.

$2,941.66 − $2,165.00 = $776.66 — Subtract $2,165.00 from the percentage method income to find the amount in excess of $2,165.

$776.66 × 0.31 = $240.76 — Find 31% of the income in excess of $2,165.

$455.97 + $240.76 = $696.73 — Add $240.76 to $455.97 to find the withholding tax.

The federal withholding tax is $696.73 for the pay period.

Withholding tax calculated by the percentage method may differ slightly from the withholding tax given in the tax table. The tax table amounts are rounded to the nearest dollar.

Tables for Percentage Method of Withholding
(For Wages Paid in 1995)

TABLE 1—WEEKLY Payroll Period

(a) SINGLE person (including head of household)—

If the amount of wages (after subtracting withholding allowances) is:		The amount of income tax to withhold is:	
Not over $50.		$0	
Over—	**But not over—**		**of excess over—**
$50	—$476 . . .	15%	—$50
$476	—$999 . . .	$63.90 plus 28%	—$476
$999	—$2,295 . .	$210.34 plus 31%	—$999
$2,295	—$4,960 . .	$612.10 plus 36%	—$2,295
$4,960.		$1,571.50 plus 39.6%	—$4,960

(b) MARRIED person—

If the amount of wages (after subtracting withholding allowances) is:		The amount of income tax to withhold is:	
Not over $123		$0	
Over—	**But not over—**		**of excess over—**
$123	—$828 . . .	15%	—$123
$828	—$1,664 . .	$105.75 plus 28%	—$828
$1,664	—$2,839 . .	$339.83 plus 31%	—$1,664
$2,839	—$5,011 . .	$704.08 plus 36%	—$2,839
$5,011		$1,486.00 plus 39.6%	—$5,011

TABLE 2—BIWEEKLY Payroll Period

(a) SINGLE person (including head of household)—

If the amount of wages (after subtracting withholding allowances) is:		The amount of income tax to withhold is:	
Not over $100		$0	
Over—	**But not over—**		**of excess over—**
$100	—$952 . . .	15%	—$100
$952	—$1,998 . .	$127.80 plus 28%	—$952
$1,998	—$4,590 . .	$420.68 plus 31%	—$1,998
$4,590	—$9,919 . .	$1,224.20 plus 36%	—$4,590
$9,919.		$3,142.64 plus 39.6%	—$9,919

(b) MARRIED person—

If the amount of wages (after subtracting withholding allowances) is:		The amount of income tax to withhold is:	
Not over $246		$0	
Over—	**But not over—**		**of excess over—**
$246	—$1,656 . . .	15%	—$246
$1,656	—$3,329 . .	$211.50 plus 28%	—$1,656
$3,329	—$5,679 . .	$679.94 plus 31%	—$3,329
$5,679	—$10,021 .	$1,408.44 plus 36%	—$5,679
$10,021.		$2,971.56 plus 39.6%	—$10,021

TABLE 3—SEMIMONTHLY Payroll Period

(a) SINGLE person (including head of household)—

If the amount of wages (after subtracting withholding allowances) is:		The amount of income tax to withhold is:	
Not over $108		$0	
Over—	**But not over—**		**of excess over—**
$108	—$1,031 . .	15%	—$108
$1,031	—$2,165 . .	$138.45 plus 28%	—$1,031
$2,165	—$4,973 . .	$455.97 plus 31%	—$2,165
$4,973	—$10,746 . .	$1,326.45 plus 36%	—$4,973
$10,746		$3,404.73 plus 39.6%	—$10,746

(b) MARRIED person—

If the amount of wages (after subtracting withholding allowances) is:		The amount of income tax to withhold is:	
Not over $267		$0	
Over—	**But not over—**		**of excess over—**
$267	—$1,794 . . .	15%	—$267
$1,794	—$3,606 . . .	$229.05 plus 28%	—$1,794
$3,606	—$6,152 . .	$736.41 plus 31%	—$3,606
$6,152	—$10,856 .	$1,525.67 plus 36%	—$6,152
$10,856.		$3,219.11 plus 39.6%	—$10,856

TABLE 4—MONTHLY Payroll Period

(a) SINGLE person (including head of household)—

If the amount of wages (after subtracting withholding allowances) is:		The amount of income tax to withhold is:	
Not over $217		$0	
Over—	**But not over—**		**of excess over—**
$217	—$2,063 . .	15%	—$217
$2,063	—$4,329 . .	$276.90 plus 28%	—$2,063
$4,329	—$9,946 . .	$911.38 plus 31%	—$4,329
$9,946	—$21,492 . .	$2,652.65 plus 36%	—$9,946
$21,492		$6,809.21 plus 39.6%	—$21,492

(b) MARRIED person—

If the amount of wages (after subtracting withholding allowances) is:		The amount of income tax to withhold is:	
Not over $533		$0	
Over—	**But not over—**		**of excess over—**
$533	—$3,588 . . .	15%	—$533
$3,588	—$7,213 . . .	$458.25 plus 28%	—$3,588
$7,213	—$12,304 . . .	$1,473.25 plus 31%	—$7,213
$12,304	—$21,713 . .	$3,051.46 plus 36%	—$12,304
$21,713.		$6,438.70 plus 39.6%	—$21,713

Figure 6–5 IRS Tables for Percentage Method of Withholding

FICA and Medicare Tax

The second-largest amount withheld from an employee's paycheck is usually the deduction for FICA tax. **FICA (Federal Insurance Contributions Act) tax** is also referred to as **Social Security (SS) tax.** It comes from an emergency measure passed by Congress during the depression of the 1930s. The money from this tax goes into a fund that pays monthly benefits to retired and disabled workers. Prior to 1991, funds collected under the Social Security tax act were used for both Social Security and Medicare benefits. Beginning in 1991, funds were collected separately for these two programs.

The FICA tax rate and the income subject to FICA tax change periodically as the Congress passes new legislation. In a recent year, the FICA tax rate was 6.2% (0.062) of the first $61,200 gross earnings. This means that after a person has earned $61,200 in a year, no FICA tax will be withheld on any additional money he or she earns during that year. A person who earns $61,200 in a year pays exactly the same FICA tax as a person who earns $100,000. In this same year, the rate for Medicare was 1.45% (0.0145). Initially, there was a maximum income subject to Medicare tax; however, all wages earned are now subject to Medicare tax, unless the employee participates in a flexible benefits plan which is exempt.

> ## ⓘ TIPS & TRAPS
>
> Under certain conditions employers may provide *flexible benefits plans* for employees. These plans are written to provide employees with a choice or "menu" of benefits such as health insurance, child care, etc. In some instances the wages used to pay for these benefits are subtracted from gross earnings to give an adjusted gross income which is used as the basis for withholding tax, FICA tax, and Medicare tax.

Employers also pay a share of FICA and Medicare tax: The employer contributes the same amount as the employee contributes to an employee's Social Security account and Medicare account. Employers can figure FICA tax for employees and themselves by multiplying 6.2% by the employee's accumulated gross pay for the period as long as the employee's gross pay for the year does not exceed $61,200. Similarly, employers figure Medicare tax, both the employee contribution and the employer contribution, by multiplying 1.45% by the employee's gross pay for the period.

Example 5   Ralph Foster has a gross weekly income of $267. How much FICA and Medicare tax should be withheld?

FICA tax on $267 = 267 × 0.062 = $16.55

Medicare tax on $267 = 267 × 0.0145 = $3.87

The FICA tax withheld should be $16.55 and the Medicare tax withheld should be $3.87.

Example 6   John Friedlander, vice-president of marketing for Golden Sun Enterprises, earns $62,920 annually, or $1,210 per week. Find the amount of FICA and Medicare taxes that should be withheld for the 51st week.

At the end of the 51st week, John will have earned a total gross salary for the year of $61,710. Since FICA tax is withheld only on the first $61,200 annually, he does not pay FICA on $510 of his 51st week's earnings. We subtract $510 from his weekly gross of $1,210 to find that he pays FICA on only $700 of his earnings that week.

$$\$700 \times 0.062 = \$43.40 \quad \text{Multiply \$700 by the 6.2\% tax rate to find the FICA tax for the 51st week.}$$

Since Medicare tax is paid on the entire salary, John must pay the Medicare tax on the full week's salary of $1,210.

$$\$1,210 \times 0.0145 = \$17.55$$

The FICA tax for the 51st week is $43.40 and the Medicare tax is $17.55. No additional FICA tax would be withheld for the remainder of the year.

 Net Earnings

In addition to federal taxes, a number of other deductions may be made from an employee's paycheck. Often state and local income taxes must also be withheld by the employer. Other deductions are made at the employee's request, such as insurance or union dues. Some retirement plans and insurance are tax exempt; others are not. When all these deductions have been made, the amount left is called *net earnings*, *net pay*, or *take-home* pay.

 HOW TO | **Find Net Earnings Per Paycheck**

Step 1 Find the gross pay for the pay period.
Step 2 Find the adjustments-to-income deductions, such as tax exempt retirement, medical insurance, and so on.
Step 3 Find the FICA tax and Medicare tax based on gross pay.
Step 4 Find the federal withholding tax based on (a) or (b).
    a) adjusted gross income (gross pay minus adjustments to income) using IRS tax tables
    b) percentage method income (adjusted gross income minus amount exempt for withholding allowances) using IRS percentage method tables
Step 5 Find other withholding taxes, such as local or state taxes.
Step 6 Find the sum of all deductions from steps 2–4 and subtract the sum from the gross pay.

Example 7 Jeanetta Grandberry's gross weekly earnings are $376. She is married and claims two withholding allowances. Five percent of her gross earnings is deducted for her non-exempt retirement fund and $5.83 is deducted for non-exempt insurance. Find her net earnings.

Income tax withholding: | In Figure 6–3, find the amount of income tax to be withheld.
$23.00

FICA tax withholding: | Find the FICA tax by the percentage method.
$376 \times 0.062 = \$23.31$

Medicare tax withholding: | Find the Medicare tax by the percentage method.
$376 \times 0.0145 = \$5.45$

Retirement fund withholding: | Use the formula $P = R \times B$. Multiply rate (5% = 0.05)
$0.05 \times \$376 = \$18.80$ | by base (gross pay of $376).

Add all deductions:
Total deductions
= income tax + FICA tax + Medicare + insurance + retirement fund
= $23.00 + $23.31 + $5.45 + $5.83 + $18.80 = $76.39

$$\text{Gross earnings} - \text{total deductions} = \text{net earnings}$$
$$\$376 \quad - \quad \$76.39 \quad = \quad \$299.61$$

The net earnings are $299.61.

Self-Check 6.2

1. Khalid Khouri is married, has a gross weekly salary of $486 all of which is taxable, and claims three withholding allowances. Use the tax tables to find the federal withholding tax to be deducted from his weekly salary.

2. Mae Swift is married and has a gross weekly salary of $391. She has $32 in adjustments to income for tax exempt health insurance and claims two withholding allowances. Use the tax tables to find the federal withholding tax to be deducted from her weekly salary.

3. Paul Thomas is paid semimonthly an adjusted gross income of $1,431. He is single and claims two withholding allowances. Use the tax tables to find the federal withholding tax to be deducted from his salary.

4. Dieter Tillman earns a semimonthly salary of $1,698. He has a $100 adjustment to income flexible benefits package, is single, and claims three withholding allowances. Find the federal withholding tax to be deducted from his salary using the percentage method tables.

5. Mohammad Hajibeigy has a weekly adjusted gross income of $380, is single, and claims one withholding allowance. Find the federal withholding tax to be deducted from his weekly paycheck using the percentage method tables.

6. Margie Young is an associate professor at a major research university and earns $4,598 monthly with no adjustments to income. She is married and claims one withholding allowance. Find the federal withholding tax that is deducted from her monthly paycheck using the percentage method tables.

7. Dr. Josef Young earns an adjusted gross weekly income of $2,583. How much FICA tax should be withheld? How much Medicare tax should be withheld?

8. Dierdri Williams earns a gross biweekly income of $1,020 and has no adjustments to income. How much FICA tax should be withheld? How much Medicare tax should be withheld?

9. Rodney Whitaker earns $64,992 annually and is paid monthly. How much FICA tax will be deducted from his December earnings? How much Medicare tax will be deducted from his December earnings?

10. Pam Trim earns $5,291 monthly, is married, and claims four withholding allowances. Her company pays her retirement, but she pays $52.83 each month for nonexempt insurance premiums. Find her net earnings.

11. Shirley Riddle earns $1,319 biweekly. She is single and claims no withholding allowances. She pays 2% of her salary for retirement and $22.80 in nonexempt insurance premiums each pay period. What is her net earnings for each pay period?

12. Donna Wood's gross weekly earnings are $415. Three percent of her gross earnings is deducted for her nonexempt retirement fund and $4.79 is deducted for nonexempt insurance. Find the net earnings if Donna is married and claims two withholding allowances.

6.3 | **Calculating the Employer's Taxes**

 *Find an employer's total deposit for withholding tax, FICA tax, and Medicare tax per pay period*

2 *Find an employer's SUTA tax and FUTA tax due for a quarter*

1 ▶ *Employer's Contribution to FICA and Medicare Taxes*

The employer must deposit income tax withheld and both the employees' and employer's Social Security and Medicare taxes by mailing or delivering a check, money order, or cash to an authorized financial institution or Federal Reserve bank. If the employer's accumulated tax is less than $500, this payment may be made with the tax return (generally Form 941, Employer's Quarterly Federal Tax Return). Other circumstances create a different employer's deposit schedule. This schedule varies depending on the amount of tax liability and other criteria. IRS Publication 15 (Circular E, Employer's Tax Guide) and Publication 334 (Tax Guide for Small Business) give the criteria for depositing and reporting these taxes.

? HOW TO | **Find an Employer's Total Deposit for Withholding Tax, FICA Tax, and Medicare Tax Per Pay Period**

Step 1 Find the withholding tax deposit: From employee payroll records, find the total withholding tax for all employees for the period.

Step 2 Find the FICA tax deposit: Find the total FICA tax paid by all employees, and multiply this total by 2 to include the employer's matching tax.

Step 3 Find the Medicare tax deposit: Find the total Medicare tax for all employees for the pay period and mutiply the total by 2.

Step 4 Add the withholding tax deposit, FICA tax deposit, and Medicare tax deposit.

Example 1 Determine the employer's total deposit of withholding tax, FICA tax, and Medicare tax for the payroll register.

Payroll for June 1 through June 15, 1996

Employee	Gross Earnings	Withholding	FICA	Medicare	Net Earnings
Plumlee, C.	$1,050.00	$110.00	$65.10	$15.23	$ 859.67
Powell, M.	$2,085.00	$318.00	$129.27	$30.23	$1,607.50
Randle, M.	$1,995.00	$232.00	$123.69	$28.93	$1,610.38
Robinson, J.	$2,089.00	$260.00	$129.52	$30.29	$1,669.19

Total withholding = $110.00 + $318.00 + $232.00 + $260.00 = $920.00
Total FICA = $65.10 + $129.27 + $123.69 + $129.52 = $447.58
Total Medicare = $15.23 + $30.23 + $28.93 + $30.29 = $104.68
Total FICA and Medicare × 2 = ($447.58 + $104.68) × 2 = $552.26 × 2 = $1,104.52
Total employer's deposit = $920.00 + $1,104.52 = $2,024.52

The total amount of the employer's deposit for this payroll is $2,024.52.

Employer's Unemployment Taxes

The major taxes paid by employers are the employer's share of the FICA and Medicare taxes, which we have already discussed, and federal and state unemployment taxes. Federal and state unemployment taxes do not affect the paycheck of the employee. They are paid entirely by the employer. **Federal unemployment tax (FUTA)** is currently 6.2% of the first $7,000 earned by an employee in a year *minus* any amount that the employer has paid in **state unemployment tax (SUTA)**, up to a limit of 5.4% on the first $7,000. In most states SUTA is 5.4%. The SUTA rate may vary depending upon the company's unemployment record or the state's unemployment record. Thus, in most cases FUTA calculations are made using 0.8% (6.2% − 5.4%). FUTA tax is accumulated for all employees and is deposited quarterly if the amount exceeds $100. Amounts less than $100 are paid with the annual tax return that is due January 31 of the following year.

? HOW TO | **Find the SUTA Tax Due for a Quarter**

Step 1 For each employee, multiply 5.4% or the appropriate rate by the employee's cumulative earnings for the quarter (up to $7,000 annually).
Step 2 Add the SUTA tax owed on all employees.

? HOW TO | **Find the FUTA Tax Due for a Quarter**

Step 1 For each employee:
   a) If no SUTA tax is paid, multiply 6.2% by the employee's cumulative earnings for the quarter (up to $7,000 annually).
   b) If at least 5.4% of the employee's cumulative earnings for the quarter (up to $7,000 annually) is paid as SUTA tax, multiply 0.8% by the employee's cumulative earnings for the quarter (up to $7,000 annually).
Step 2 Add the FUTA tax owed on all employees for the quarter.
Step 3 If the total from step 2 is less than $100, no FUTA tax is due for the quarter, but the total from step 2 must be added to the amount due for the next quarter.

Example 2 Melanie McFarren earned $32,500 last year and over $7,000 in the first quarter of this year. If the state unemployment tax (SUTA) is 5.4% of the first $7,000 earned in a year, how much SUTA must Melanie's employer pay for her? Also, how much FUTA must be paid?

SUTA = tax rate × taxable wages   **$7,000 is subject to SUTA tax in the first quarter.**

SUTA = 5.4% × $7,000

SUTA = 0.054 × $7,000 = $378

FUTA = 0.8% × taxable wages   **$7,000 is subject to FUTA tax in the first quarter.**

0.008 × $7,000 = $56

The SUTA tax is $378 and FUTA is $56.

Example 3 AAA Plumbing Company has two employees who are paid semimonthly. One employee earns $1,040 per pay period and the other earns $985 per pay period. Based on the SUTA rate of 5.4%, the FUTA rate is 0.8% of the first $7,000 of each employee's annual gross pay. At the end of which quarter should the FUTA tax first be deposited?

1 Decision needed

At the end of which quarter should the FUTA tax first be deposited?

2 Unknown fact

The number of the quarter when cumulative FUTA owed first exceeds $100.

3 Known facts

Employee 1 pay: $1,040
Employee 2 pay: $985
Pay period: semimonthly
Cumulative FUTA owed per employee: 0.8% of employee's cumulative earnings, up to $7,000.

4 Relationships

FUTA tax per employee per pay period = employee salary × 0.008
FUTA tax for Employee 1 per pay period = $1,040 × 0.008 (on first $7,000 of salary)
FUTA tax for Employee 2 per pay period = $985 × 0.008 (on first $7,000 of salary)
Total FUTA tax per quarter = sum of quarterly FUTA tax for each employee

5 Estimation

Approximate annual FUTA tax per employee: $7,000 × 1% = 7,000 × 0.01 = $70
Approximate annual FUTA for two employees: $70 × 2 = $140
Thus, a deposit may need to be made before the end of the fourth quarter.

6 Calculations

Pay Period	Employee 1 Salary	Accumulated Salary Subject to FUTA	FUTA Tax	Employee 2 Salary	Accumulated Salary Subject to FUTA	FUTA Tax
Jan 15	1,040	1,040	8.32	985	985	7.88
Jan 31	1,040	2,080	8.32	985	1,970	7.88
Feb 15	1,040	3,120	8.32	985	2,955	7.88
Feb 28	1,040	4,160	8.32	985	3,940	7.88
Mar 15	1,040	5,200	8.32	985	4,925	7.88
Mar 31	1,040	6,240	8.32	985	5,910	7.88

First Quarter FUTA Totals   49.92 + 47.28 = $97.20
$97.20 is less than $100.00 so no deposit should be made at the end of the first quarter.

Pay Period	Employee 1 Salary	Accumulated Salary Subject to FUTA	FUTA Tax	Employee 2 Salary	Accumulated Salary Subject to FUTA	FUTA Tax
Apr 15	1,040	7,000	6.08*	985	6,895	7.88
Apr 31	1,040			985	7,000	0.84**
May 15	1,040			985		
May 28	1,040			985		
Jun 15	1,040			985		
Jun 31	1,040			985		

*$7,000 − $6,240 = $760; $760 × 0.008 = $6.08
**$7,000 − $6,895 = $105; $105 × 0.008 = $0.84

Second Quarter FUTA Totals $6.08 + $8.72 = $14.80
Total FUTA for first two quarters = $97.20 + $14.80 = $112.00

7 Decision made

FUTA tax should be deposited by the end of the month following the second quarter in the amount of $112.

1. Carolyn Luttrell owns Just the Right Thing, a small antique shop with four employees. For one payroll period the total withholding tax for all employees was $1,633. The total FICA tax was $482 and the total Medicare tax was $113. How much tax must Carolyn deposit as the employer's share of FICA and Medicare? What is the total tax that must be deposited?

2. Hughes' Trailer Manufacturer makes utility trailers and has seven employees who are paid weekly. For one payroll period the withholding tax for all employees was $1,661. The total FICA tax withheld from employees' paychecks was $608 and the total Medicare tax withheld was $142. What is the total tax that must be deposited by Hughes?

3. Determine the employer's deposit of withholding, FICA, and Medicare for the payroll register.

Employee	Gross Earnings	Withholding	FICA	Medicare	Net Earnings
Paszel, J.	$1,905	$384.00	$118.11	$27.62	$1,375.27
Thomas, P.	$1,598	$209.71	$ 99.08	$23.17	$1,266.04
Tillman, D.	$1,431	$192.00	$ 88.72	$20.75	$1,129.53

4. Heaven Sent Gifts, a small business that provides custom meals, flowers, and other speciality gifts, has three employees who are paid weekly. One employee earns $375 per week, is single, and claims one withholding allowance. Another employee earns $350 per week, is married, and claims two withholding allowances. The manager earns $925 per week, is married, and claims one withholding allowance. Calculate the amount of withholding tax, FICA tax, and Medicare tax which will need to be deposited by Heaven Sent Gifts.

Bruce Young earned $20,418 last year. His employer's SUTA rate is 5.4% of the first $7,000.

5. How much SUTA must Bruce's employer pay for him?

6. How much FUTA must Bruce's company pay for him?

7. Bailey Plyler has three employees in his carpet cleaning business. The payroll is semimonthly and the employees earn $745, $780, and $1,030 per pay period. Calculate when and in what amounts FUTA tax payments are to be made.

SELF-CHECK SOLUTIONS

Self-Check 6.1

1. $19,000 ÷ 52 = $365.38   **2.** $27,988 ÷ 26 = $1,076.46   **3.** $52,980 ÷ 12 = $4,415.00
4. $38,184 ÷ 24 = $1,591.00   **5.**   40 × $7.60 = $304   (regular pay)   **6.**   40 × $8.25 = $330
                                               7 × $7.60 × 1.5 = +$ 79.80 (overtime pay)   4 × $8.25 × 1.5 = +$ 49.50
                                                              $383.80 (gross earnings) $379.50

7. $40 \times \$15.90 \qquad = \qquad \$636.00$
$\quad 7 \times \$15.90 \times 1.5 = \underline{+ \$166.95}$
$\qquad\qquad\qquad\qquad\qquad \$802.95$

8. Total buckles $\; = 132 + 134 + 138 + 134 + 130 = 668$
$\qquad$ Gross earnings $= 668 \times \$0.84 = \$561.12$

9. First 100 boxes: $\$1.48 \times 100 = \qquad \$148$
$\quad$ Last 89 boxes: $\$1.58 \times 89 \; = \underline{+ \$140.62}$
$\qquad\qquad\qquad\qquad \$288.62$ (gross earnings)

10. $9 + 11 + 10 + 12 + 4 = 46$
$\qquad 46 \times \$8.13 = \$373.98$

11. $P = RB$
$\quad P = 0.06 \times \$8,972$
$\quad P = \$538.32$ (gross earnings)

12. $\$452,493 \times 0.035 = \$15,837.26$

13. $\$7,821 - \$2,000 = \$5,821$ (amount on which commission is paid)
$\quad P = RB$
$\quad P = 0.05 \times \$5,821$
$\quad P = \$291.05$
$\quad \$291.05 + \$275 = \$566.05$ (gross earnings)

14. $\$145,938 - \$2,000 = \$143,938$
$\qquad \$143,938 \times 0.03 = \$4,318.14$

Self-Check 6.2

1. Find the table for married persons. Move down the *at least* column to the amount $480. Then move across to the column marked 3 at the top. The amount is $33.

2. $391 − $32 = $359. Use the table for Married Persons—Weekly Payroll Period. Move down the *at least* column to $350. Move across to the column marked 2 at the top. The amount is $20.

3. Use the table for Single Persons—Semimonthly Payroll Period. Move down the *at least* column to $1,420. Move across to the column marked 2 at the top. The amount is $192.

4. $1,698 − $100 = $1,598 − adjusted gross income.
   Use Figure 6–4 to find the amount for one withholding allowance for a semimonthly payroll. The amount is $104.17.
   $104.17 × 3 = $312.51 (total withholding allowance).
   Percentage method income = $1,598.00 − $312.51 = $1,285.49
   Use Table 3a in the percentage method tables. The tax is $138.45 plus 28% of excess over $1,031.
   Excess over $1,031 = $1,285.49 − $1,031 = $254.49
   $254.49 × 0.28 = $71.26
   Withholding tax = $138.45 + $71.26 = $209.71

5. Using Figure 6–4 for a weekly salary of a single person with one withholding allowance, we see that the amount is $48.08. We subtract $48.08 from gross pay, $380, and get $331.92; this is the taxable income. Look at Table 1a in Figure 6–5: the tax is 15% of the excess amount over $50 so you subtract $50 from $331.92 and get $281.92, and multiply that times 15%: $281.92 × 0.15 = $42.29. The tax is $42.29.

6. From Figure 6–4 we get $208.33 for each withholding allowance. She has one allowance.
   Percentage method income = $4,598 − $208.33 = $4,389.67
   Use Table 4b in tables for percentage method. The tax is $458.25 plus 28% of excess over $3,588.
   $4,389.67 − $3,588 = $801.67
   $801.67 × 0.28 = $224.47
   Withholding tax = $458.25 + $224.47 = $682.72

7. FICA tax = $2,583 × 0.062 = $160.15
   Medicare tax = $2,583 × 0.0145 = $37.45

8. FICA tax = $1,020 × 0.062 = $63.24
   Medicare tax = $1,020 × 0.0145 = $14.79

9. FICA tax during this tax year is paid on the first $61,200 earned. Rodney's monthly salary is $64,992 ÷ 12 = $5,416. Earnings for first eleven months are $5,416 × 11 = $59,576. Rodney must pay FICA on the portion of his December check that would make his earnings equal $61,200. That is, $61,200 − $59,576 = $1,624
   FICA tax for December = $1,624 × 0.062 = $100.69
   Medicare tax for December = $5,416 × 0.0145 = $78.53

10. Use Figure 6–4 to find $208.33 for each withholding allowance for monthly payroll.
    Total withholding allowance = $208.33 × 4 = $833.32
    Percentage method income = $5,291 − $833.32 = $4,457.68
    Use Table 4b in tables for percentage method of withholding to find withholding tax. The tax is $458.25 plus 28% of excess over $3,588.
    Excess = $4,457.68 − $3,588 = $869.68
    $869.68 × 0.28 = $243.51

Total withholding tax = $458.25 + $243.51 = $701.76
FICA = $5,291 × 0.062 = $328.04
Medicare = $5,291 × 0.0145 = $76.72
Total deductions = $701.76 + $328.04 + $76.72 + $52.83 = $1,159.35
Net earnings = $5,291 − $1,159.35 = $4,131.65

11. Since Shirley claims zero withholding allowances we skip Figure 6–4 and use her full salary to calculate the amount of withholding. Use Table 2a of percentage method of withholding to find the withholding tax. The tax is $127.80 plus 28% of excess over $952.
Excess = $1,319 − $952 = $367
$367 × 0.28 = $102.76
Total withholding tax = $127.80 + $102.76 = $230.56
FICA = $1,319 × 0.062 = $81.78
Medicare = $1,319 × 0.0145 = $19.13
Retirement = $1,319 × 0.02 = $26.38
Total deductions = $230.56 + $81.78 + $19.13 + $26.38 + $22.80 = $380.65
Net earnings = $1,319 − $380.65 = $938.35

12. Use the withholding table for married persons—weekly payroll period. Move down the *at least* column to $410 then move to the right to the column for 2 deductions. The amount of tax is $29.
FICA = $415 × 0.062 = $25.73
Medicare = $415 × 0.0145 = $6.02
Nonexempt retirement = $415 × 0.03 = $12.45
Total deductions = $29 + $25.73 + $6.02 + $12.45 + $4.79 = $77.99
Net earnings = $415 − $77.99 = $337.01

Self-Check 6.3

1. Total FICA and Medicare = $482 + $113 = $595
Employer's share of FICA and Medicare = $595
Employer's tax deposit = $1,633 + (2 × $595) = $2,823
2. FICA and Medicare = $608 + $142 = $750
Employer's tax deposit = $1,661 + (2 × $750) = $3,161
3. Total withholding = $384.00 + $209.71 + $192.00 = $785.71
Total FICA = $118.11 + $99.08 + $88.72 = $305.91
Total Medicare = $27.62 + $23.17 + $20.75 = $71.54
Employer's deposit = $785.71 + [2 × ($305.91 + $71.54)] =
$785.71 + (2 × $377.45) = $1,540.61
4. Use the tax tables or percentage method tables to make a payroll chart for the employees.

	Gross earnings	Withholding	FICA	Medicare
Employee 1	$375	$41.54	$23.25	$5.44
Employee 2	$350	$19.63	$21.70	$5.08
Employee 3	$925	$119.45	$57.35	$13.41
Totals		$180.62	$102.30	$23.93

For Employee 1, use percentage method for withholding tax.
Figure 6–4 shows $48.08 for one withholding allowance.
Percentage method income = $375 − $48.08 = $326.92
Use Table 1a in percentage method tables. Tax is 15% of excess over $50.
$326.92 − $50.00 = $276.92
Withholding tax = $276.92 × 0.15 = $41.54
FICA = $375 × 0.062 = $23.25
Medicare = $375 × 0.0145 = $5.44
For employee 2, withholding allowances = $48.08 × 2 = $96.16.
Percentage method income = $350 − $96.16 = $253.84
Use Table 1b in percentage method tables. Tax is 15% of excess over $123.
$253.84 − $123 = $130.84
Withholding tax = $130.84 × 0.15 = $19.63
FICA = $350 × 0.062 = $21.70
Medicare = $350 × 0.0145 = $5.08

For Employee 3, withholding allowance = $48.08

Percentage method income = $925 − $48.08 = $876.92

Use Table 1a in percentage method tables. Tax is $105.75 plus 28% of excess over $828.

$876.92 − $828 = $48.92

$48.92 × 0.28 = $13.70

Withholding tax = $105.75 + $13.70 = $119.45

FICA = $925 × 0.062 = $57.35

Medicare = $925 × 0.0145 = $13.41

Employer's withholding tax deposit = $41.54 + $19.63 + $119.45 = $180.62

FICA tax deposit = 2 × ($23.25 + $21.70 + $57.35) = 2 × $102.30 = $204.60

Medicare tax deposit = 2 × ($5.44 + $5.08 + $13.41) = 2 × $23.93 = $47.86

5. $7,000 × 0.054 = $378.00   **6.** $7,000 × 0.008 = $56.00

7.

Pay Period	Employee 1 Accumulated Salary	FUTA Tax	Employee 2 Accumulated Salary	FUTA Tax	Employee 3 Accumulated Salary	FUTA Tax
Jan 15	745	5.96	780	6.24	1,030	8.24
Jan 31	1,490	5.96	1,560	6.24	2,060	8.24
Feb 15	2,235	5.96	2,340	6.24	3,090	8.24
Feb 28	2,980	5.96	3,120	6.24	4,120	8.24
Mar 15	3,725	5.96	3,900	6.24	5,150	8.24
Mar 31	4,470	5.96	4,680	6.24	6,180	8.24

First Quarter Totals = $35.76 + $37.44 + $49.44 = $122.64

Payment of $122.64 must be deposited by April 30.

Pay Period	Employee 1 Accumulated Salary	FUTA Tax	Employee 2 Accumulated Salary	FUTA Tax	Employee 3 Accumulated Salary	FUTA Tax
April 15	5,215	5.96	5,460	6.24	7,000	6.56
April 30	5,960	5.96	6,240	6.24		
May 15	6,705	5.96	7,000	6.08		
May 30	7,000	2.36				
June 15						
June 30						

7,000 − 6,705 = 295;   7,000 − 6,240 = 760;   7,000 − 6,180 = 820;

$295 × 0.008 = $2.36; $760 × 0.008 = $6.08; $820 × 0.008 = 6.56

Second Quarter Totals = $20.24 + $18.56 + $6.56 = $45.36

Payment of $45.36 must be deposited by January 31 of the next year since it does not exceed $100.

AROUND THE BUSINESS WORLD

Seattle Is on a (Cinnamon) Roll

First coffee bars, now bun shops. As it did with Starbucks, Seattle has launched another trendy chain, this one selling cinnamon buns. Like Starbucks, Cinnabon shops are popping up in cities across the land. Cinnabon sells huge, nine-ounce cinnamon rolls fresh from the oven, rich and sticky, dripping with margarine and spiced with Indonesian Korintji cinnamon. So what if a bun costs $1.89 and has 810 calories (a Minibon goes for $1.39, with 330 calories)? Long lines form outside Cinnabon shops.

Started in 1986, $100 million Cinnabon has averaged 25% annual sales growth. It now has 276 shops (about half franchised) in 37 states, Canada, and Mexico, with a 500-store goal by 2000. Its parent, Restaurants Unlimited, hopes to go public within three years.

The company calls its shops "bakeries" because customers can breathlessly watch the rolls being made. They come, says President Dennis Waldron, "for the emotional experience. . . . It's not a fuel stop." Oh, yes. Cinnabon also sells custom-blended coffee, called Rubymoon. After all, it's from Seattle.

Reprinted from February 27, 1995 issue of Business Week by special permission, coypright © 1995 The McGraw-Hill Companies.

Section—Objective	Important Points with Examples

Find the gross pay per paycheck based on salary

Step 1 Identify the number of pay periods per year: Monthly: 12; Semimonthly: 24; Biweekly: 26; Weekly: 52 **Step 2** Divide the annual salary by the number of pay periods per year.

If Barbara earns $23,500 per year, how much is her weekly gross pay?

$$\frac{\$23,500}{52} = \$451.92$$

Clemetee earns $32,808 annually and is paid twice a month. What is her gross pay per pay period?

$$\frac{\$32,808}{24} = \$1,367$$

6.1 — 2 (page 205)

Find the gross pay per weekly paycheck based on hourly wage

Step 1 Find the regular pay: **a)** If the hours worked in the week are 40 or less, multiply the hours worked by the hourly wage. **b)** If the hours worked are more than 40, multiply 40 hours by the hourly wage. **Step 2** Find the overtime pay: **a)** If the hours worked are 40 or less, the overtime pay is $0. **b)** If the hours worked are more than 40, subtract 40 from the hours worked and multiply the difference by the overtime rate. **Step 3** Add the regular pay and the overtime pay.

Aldo earns $6.25 per hour. He worked 38 hours this week. What is his gross pay?
$38 \times \$6.25 = \$237.50$

Belinda worked 44 hours one week. Her regular pay was $7.75 per hour and time and a half for overtime. Find her gross earnings.

$$40 \times \$7.75 = \$310$$

$$4 \times \$7.75 \times 1.5 = \$46.50$$

$$\$310 + \$46.50 = \$356.50$$

Find the gross pay per paycheck based on piecework wage

Step 1 If a *straight piecework* rate is used, multiply the number of items completed by the straight piecework rate. **Step 2** If a *differential piecework* rate is used: **a)** For each rate category, multiply the number of items produced for the category by the rate for the category. **b)** Add the pay for all rate categories.

Willy earns $0.30 for each widget he twists. He twisted 1,224 widgets last week. Find his gross earnings. $1,224 \times \$0.30 = \$367.20$

Nadine does piecework for a jeweler and earns $0.25 per piece for finishing 1 to 25 pins, $0.50 per piece for 26 to 50 pins, and $0.75 per piece for pins over 50. Yesterday she finished 70 pins. How much did she earn?

$(25 \times \$0.25) + (25 \times \$0.50) + (20 \times \$0.75) =$
$\quad \$6.25 \quad + \quad \$12.50 + \quad \$15 \quad = \$33.75$

 (page 208)

Find the gross pay per paycheck based on commission

Step 1 Find the commission: **a)** If the commission is *commission based on total sales*, multiply the commission rate by the total sales for the pay period. **b)** If the commission is *commission based on quota*, subtract the quota from the total sales and multiply the difference by the commission rate. **Step 2** Find the salary: **a)** If the wage is *straight commission*, the salary is $0. **b)** If the wage is *commission-plus-salary*, use the How-To steps for finding gross pay based on salary. **Step 3** Add the commission and the salary.

Bart earns a 4% commission on the appliances he sells. His sales last week totaled $8,000. Find his gross earnings.

0.04 × $8,000 = $320

Elaine earns $250 weekly plus 2% of all sales over $1,500. Last week she made $9,500 worth of sales. Find her gross earnings.

$$\$9,500 - \$1,500 = \$8,000$$
$$\text{Commission} = 0.02 \times \$8,000 = \$160$$
$$\$250 + \$160 = \$410$$

6.2 — 1 (page 210)

Find federal withholding tax per paycheck using IRS tax tables

Step 1 Find the adjusted gross pay by subtracting the total qualified adjustments from the gross pay per pay period. Select the appropriate table according to the employee's filing status (single, married, and so on), and according to the type of pay period (weekly, biweekly, and so on). **Step 2** Find the income row: In the rows labeled "If the wages are —", select the "At least" and "But less than" interval that includes the employee's adjusted gross pay for the pay period. **Step 3** Find the allowances column: In the columns labeled "And the number of withholding allowances claimed is —", select the number of allowances the employee claims. **Step 4** Find the cell where the income row and allowance column intersect. The correct tax is given in this cell.

Archy is married, has a gross weekly salary of $480, and claims two withholding allowances. Find his withholding tax.

Look in the first two columns of Figure 6–3 to find the range for $480. Move across to the column for two withholding allowances. The amount of federal tax to be withheld is $40.

Lexie Lagen is married and has a gross weekly salary of $655. He claims 3 withholding allowances and has $20 weekly deducted from his paycheck for a flexible benefits plan which is exempted from federal taxes. Find the amount of his withholding tax.

Adjusted gross income = $655 − $20 = $635

Find the range for $635 and three withholding allowances in Table 6–2. The tax is $55.

6.2 — 2 (page 214)

Find federal withholding tax per paycheck using IRS percentage method tables

Find the percentage method income **Step 1** Find the exempt-per-allowance amount: From the withholding allowance table (Figure 6–4), identify the amount exempt for one withholding allowance according to the type of pay period. **Step 2** Find the total exempt amount: Multiply the number of withholding allowances the employee claims by the exempt-per-allowance amount. **Step 3** Subtract the total exempt amount from the employee's adjusted gross income for the pay period.

228

Chapter 6   Payroll

Edith Sailor has weekly gross earnings of $890. Find her percentage method income if she has no adjustments to income, is married, and claims three withholding allowances.

Use Figure 6–4 to find one withholding allowance for weekly payroll period. Multiply by 3.

$48.08 × 3 = $144.24

Percentage method income = $890.00 − $144.24 = $745.76

Find the federal withholding tax per paycheck using the IRS percentage method tables **Step 1** Select the appropriate table according to the employee's filing status and the type of pay period. **Step 2** Find the income row: In the rows labeled "If the amount of wages is . . .", select the "Over—" and "But not over—" interval that includes the employee's percentage method income for the pay period. **Step 3** Find the cell where the income row and the column labeled "of excess over—" intersect, and subtract the amount given in this cell from the employee's percentage method income for the pay period. **Step 4** Multiply the difference from step 3 by the percent given in the income row. **Step 5** Add the product from step 4 to the amount given with the *percent* in the income row and amount of tax column.

Find the federal tax on Ruth's monthly income of $1,438. She is single and claims one exemption.

1 exemption = $208.33
$1,438 − $208.33 = $1,229.67
$1,229.67 is in the $217 to $2,063 range (Figure 6–5), so the amount of withholding tax is 15% of the amount over $217.

$1,229.67 − $217 = $1,012.67
$1,012.67 × $0.15 = $151.90

6.2 — 3 (page 217)

Find FICA tax and Medicare tax per paycheck

For FICA tax: Multiply 6.2% by the employee's gross pay, up to $61,200 annually. For Medicare tax: Multiply 1.45% by the employee's gross pay.

Find the FICA and Medicare tax for Abbas Laknahour, who earns $738 every two weeks.

FICA = $738 × 0.062 = $45.76
Medicare = $738 × 0.0145 = $10.70

Donna Shroyer earns $5,123 monthly. Find the FICA and Medicare tax that will be deducted from her December paycheck.

Pay for first 11 months = $5,123 × 11 = $56,353
December pay subject to FICA = $61,200 − $56,353 = $4,847
FICA tax = $4,847 × 0.062 = $300.51
Medicare tax = $5,123 × 0.0145 = $74.28

 (page 218)

Find net earnings per paycheck

Step 1 Find the gross pay for the pay period. **Step 2** Find the adjustments-to-income deductions, such as retirement, insurance, and so on. **Step 3** Find the FICA tax and Medicare tax based on gross pay. **Step 4** Find the federal withholding tax based on (a) or (b): **a)** adjusted gross income (gross pay minus adjustments to income) using IRS tax tables; **b)** percentage method income (adjusted gross income minus amount exempt for withholding allowances) using IRS percentage method tables. **Step 5** Find other withholding taxes, such as local or state taxes. **Step 6** Find the sum of all deductions from steps 2–5, and subtract the sum from the gross pay.

> Beth Cooley's gross weekly earnings are $388. Four percent of her gross earnings is deducted for her non-exempt retirement fund and $7.48 is deducted for insurance. Find her net earnings if Beth is married and claims three withholding allowances.
>
> Retirement fund = $388 × $0.04 = $15.52
> Withholding tax = $18 (from Figure 6-3)
> FICA = $388 × 0.062 = $24.06
> Medicare = $388 × 0.0145 = $5.63
> Total deductions = $15.52 + $7.48 + $18 + $24.06 + $5.63 = $70.69
> Net earnings = $388 − $70.69 = $317.31

6.3 — 1 (page 220)

Find an employer's total deposit for withholding tax, FICA tax, and Medicare tax per pay period

Step 1 Find the withholding tax deposit: From employee payroll records, find the total withholding tax for all employees for the pay period. **Step 2** Find the FICA tax deposit: Find the total FICA tax for all employees for the pay period, and multiply this total by 2 to include the employer's matching tax. **Step 3** Find the Medicare tax deposit: Find the total Medicare tax for all employees for the pay period, and multiply this total by 2. **Step 4** Add the withholding tax deposit, FICA tax deposit, and Medicare tax deposit.

> **Determine the Employer's Total Deposit**
>
> | Employee | Gross Earnings | Withholding | FICA | Medicare | Net Earnings |
> |---|---|---|---|---|---|
> | Davis, T. | $485.00 | $40.00 | $30.07 | $7.03 | $407.90 |
> | Dobbins, L. | $632.00 | $77.00 | $39.18 | $9.16 | $506.66 |
> | Harris, M. | $590.00 | $56.00 | $36.58 | $8.56 | $488.86 |
> | Totals | $1,707.00 | $173.00 | $105.83 | $24.75 | $1,403.42 |
>
> Employer's tax deposit = $173 + (2 × 105.83) + (2 × 24.75) = $434.16

6.3 — 2 (page 221)

Find an employer's SUTA tax and FUTA tax due for a quarter

Find the SUTA tax due for a quarter **Step 1** For each employee, multiply 5.4% or the appropriate rate by the employee's cumulative earnings for the quarter (up to $7,000 annually). **Step 2** Add the SUTA tax owed on all employees.

> Kim Brown has 3 employees who each earn $8,250 in the first 3 months of the year. How much SUTA tax should Kim pay for the first quarter if the SUTA rate is 5.4% of the first $7,000 earnings?
>
> $7,000 × 0.054 × 3 = $1,134
>
> Kim should pay $1,134 in SUTA tax for the first quarter.

Find the FUTA tax due for a quarter **Step 1** For each employee: **a)** If no SUTA tax is paid, multiply 6.2% by the employee's cumulative earnings for the quarter (up to $7,000 annually). **b)** If at least 5.4% of the employee's cumulative earnings for the quarter (up to $7,000 annually) is paid as SUTA tax, multiply 0.8% by the employee's cumulative earnings for the quarter (up to $7,000 annually). **Step 2** Add the FUTA tax owed on all employees for the quarter. **Step 3** If the total from step 2 is less than $100, no FUTA tax is due for the quarter, but the total from step 2 must be added to the amount due for the next quarter.

How much FUTA tax should Kim pay for the three employees?

$7,000 \times 0.008 \times 3 = \$168$

CHAPTER 6 REVIEW

Section 6.1

1. Brian Williams is a salaried employee who earns $95,256 and is paid monthly. What is his pay each payroll period?

2. Arsella Gallagher earns a salary of $63,552 and is paid semimonthly. What is her gross salary for each pay period?

3. Varonia Reed is paid a weekly salary of $1,036. What is her annual salary?

4. John Edmonds is paid a biweekly salary of $1,398. What is his annual salary?

5. Melanie Michael has a salaried job. She earns $425 a week. One week she worked 46 hours. Find her gross earnings for the week.

6. Fran Coley earns $896 biweekly on a salaried job. If she works 89 hours in one pay period, how much will she earn?

7. Glenda Chaille worked 27 hours in one week at $5.25 per hour. Find her gross earnings.

8. Robert Stout worked 40 hours at $12 per hour. Find his gross earnings for the week.

9. Susan Wood worked 52 hours in a week. She was paid at the hourly rate of $6.50 with time and a half for overtime. Find her gross earnings.

10. Leslie Jinkins worked a total of 58 hours in one week. Of these hours, he was paid for 8 hours at the overtime rate of 1.5 times his hourly wage, and for 10 hours at the holiday overtime rate of 2 times his hourly wage. Find his gross earnings for the week if his hourly wage is $14.95.

11. Ronald James is paid 1.5 times his hourly wage for all hours worked in a week exceeding 40. He worked 52 hours and earns $8.50 per hour. Calculate his gross pay.

12. Mike Kelly earns $21.30 per hour in his job as a chemical technician. One week he works 38 hours. What is his gross pay for the week?

Find the gross earnings of each employee.

Employee	Hours Worked M	T	W	T	F	S	S	Hourly Wage	Regular Hours	Regular Pay	Overtime Hours	Overtime Pay	Gross Pay
13. Allen, H.	8	9	8	7	10	4	0	$9.86					
14. Brown, J.	4	6	8	9	9	5	0	$4.97					
15. Pick, J.	8	8	8	8	8	4	0	$6.87					
16. Sayer, C.	9	10	8	9	11	9	0	$5.82					
17. Lovet, L.	8	8	8	8	0	0	0	$7.15					
18. Stacy, C.	8	8	8	8	8	0	0	$8.21					

Complete the following payroll records for employees who earn time and a half for more than 40 hours on Monday through Friday, time and a half on Saturday, and double time on Sunday.

Employee	Hours Worked M	T	W	T	F	S	S	Regular Hours	Hourly Wage	Regular Pay	Time and a Half Hours	Time and a Half Pay	Double Time Hours	Double Time Pay	Gross Earnings
19. Mitze, A.	8	8	4	3	8	2	4		$8.00						
20. James, Q.	8	8	8	8	8	0	4		$4.70						
21. Adams, A.	5	6	8	11	10	9	5		$6.75						
22. Smith, M.	8	8	8	8	8	8	8		$4.55						

23. For sewing buttons on shirts, employees are paid $0.08 a shirt. Marty Hughes completes an average of 500 shirts a day. Find her average gross weekly earnings for a five-day week.

24. Employees are paid $3.50 per piece for a certain job. In a week's time, Maria Sanchez produced a total of 78 pieces. Find her gross earnings for the week.

Use the following rates to find the gross weekly earnings for employees who twisted the following number of widgets in a week.

Widgets International pays widget twisters at the following differential piece rate for properly twisted widgets.

Widgets per week	Pay Per Widget
1–150	$1.85
151–300	$1.95
301 and over	$2.08

25. 117 widgets

26. 158 widgets

27. 257 widgets

28. 325 widgets

29. Patsy Hilliard is paid 5% commission on sales of $18,200. Find her gross salary.

30. Ada Shotwell, a computer salesperson, is paid 1% commission for all sales. If she needs a monthly income of $1,500, find the monthly sales volume she must meet.

31. Pamela Slagg sells produce and earns 5% commission on $8,000 in produce sales. Find her gross pay on this sale.

32. Find the gross pay of Minda Waller, a yarn company sales representative, who earns 5% of her total sales of $6,000.

33. Find the gross pay of Jerome Ware who is a salesperson who receives a 10% commission on $8,000 in sales.

34. Jewel Warner is a salesperson and is paid a salary of $200 plus 3% of all sales. Find her gross income if her sales are $8,000.

35. William Kelly is a real estate salesperson and receives a 6% commission on the sale of a piece of property for $130,000. Find his gross pay for this sale.

36. Debra Young sells $250,000 in equipment. At a 7% straight commission, calculate the gross earnings.

37. Vincent Ores is paid a salary of $400 plus 8% of sales. Calculate the gross income if new sales are $9,890.

38. Darrell Bright earns $150 plus 7% commission on all sales over $2,000. What are the gross earnings if sales for a week are $3,276?

39. Find the gross earnings if Juanita Wilson earns $275 plus 2% of all sales over $3,000 and the sales for a week are $5,982.

40. Dieter Tillman is paid $2,000 plus 5% of the total sales volume. If he sold $3,000 in merchandise, find the gross earnings.

Section 6.2

Use Figure 6–3 (weekly payroll period) to find the amount of federal withholding tax for the gross earnings of the following married persons with the indicated number of withholding allowances.

41. $225, 4 allowances

42. $238.50, 2 allowances

43. $475, 0 allowances

44. $295, 3 allowances

45. $395, 3 allowances

46. $725, 2 allowances

Use Figures 6–4 and 6–5 and the percentage method tables to find the amount of federal income tax to be withheld from the gross earnings of the following married persons who are paid weekly and have the indicated number of withholding allowances.

47. $273.96, 5 allowances

48. $620, 8 allowances

49. $875, 2 allowances

50. $1,020, 3 allowances

Use the percentage method tables to find the FICA and Medicare taxes for the following.

51. Weekly gross income of $157

52. Monthly gross income of $3,500

53. Yearly gross income of $24,000

54. Semimonthly gross income of $426

55. Yearly gross income of $18,225

56. Yearly gross income of $61,300

Complete the following payroll register. All employees are married and paid weekly and the number in parentheses is the number of withholding allowances that each person claims. Use Figure 6-3 to find the withholding tax.

Employee & Withholding Allowances	Gross Earnings	With-holding Tax	FICA	Medicare	Other Nonexempt Deductions	Total Deductions	Net Earnings
57. Abrams (3)	$145.00				$21.94		
58. Cowgill (0)	$139.25	2.00	8.63	2.02	$15.21		
59. Mason (4)	$165.00				$0		
60. Sachs (2)	$476.28		29.53	6.91	$19.38		

61. Irene Gamble earns $485 weekly. Deductions are as follows: withholding tax, $47; FICA tax, $30.07; Medicare, $7.03; nonexempt retirement, $24.95; nonexempt insurance, $8.45. Find the total deductions and net income.

62. Anita Loyd earns $883 semimonthly. She is single and claims no withholding allowances. She also pays $12.83 each pay period for nonexempt health insurance. What is her net pay?

63. Use the payroll register for Exercises 57–60 to determine the employer's withholding, FICA, and Medicare tax deposit.

64. How much tax should the employer deposit for Irene Gamble in Exercise 61?

Vince Brimaldi earned $32,876 last year. The state unemployment tax is 5.4% of the first $7,000 earned in a year.

65. How much SUTA must Vince's employer pay for him if the employer pays at the 5.4% rate?

66. How much FUTA must Vince's employer pay?

Does not reach 7,000

x 3   x 3   x 3

Elisa Marus has three employees who earn $2,500, $1,980, and $3,200 monthly.

67. How much SUTA will she need to pay at the end of the first quarter if the SUTA rate is 5.4%?

68. How much FUTA is due with the first payment and when must it be paid?

wrong answer in book.

First Quarter = 3 mo's.

Challenge Problem

69. Complete the following time card for Janice Anderson. She earns time-and-a-half overtime when she works more than eight hours on a weekday or on Saturday. She earns double time on Sundays and holidays. Calculate Janice's net pay if she is single and claims one allowance. *Book does not give hourly rate to figure out problem.*

pay per hr.?

WEEKLY TIME CARD
CHD Company

Name **Janice Anderson**   SS# **000-00-0000**

Pay for period ending

DATE	IN	OUT	IN	OUT	Total Regular Hours	Total Overtime Hours
M 8/4	7:00	11:00	11:30	7:30	8	4
Tu 8/5	8:00	12:00	12:30	4:30	8	0
W 8/6	8:00	12:00	12:30	4:30	8	0
Th 8/7	7:00	11:00	12:30	5:30	8	1
F 8/8	8:00	12:00	12:30	4:30	8	0
Sa 8/9	7:00	12:00			0	5
Su 8/10					0	0

	HOURS	RATE	PAY
Regular	40		
Overtime (1.5X)	10		
Overtime (2X)			
Total	50		

CHAPTER 6 PRACTICE TEST

1. Cheryl Douglas works 43 hours in a week for a salary of $354 per week. What are Cheryl's gross weekly earnings?

2. June Jackson earns $5.83 an hour. Find her gross earnings if she worked 46 hours (time and a half for overtime).

3. Willy Bell checks wrappers on cans in a cannery. He receives $0.07 for each case of cans. If he checks 750 cases on an average day, find his gross weekly salary. (A work week is 5 days.)

4. Stacey Ellis is paid at the following differential piece rate: 1–100, $1.58; 101–250, $1.72; 251–up, $1.94. Find her gross earnings for completing 475 pieces.

5. Dorothy Ford, who sells restaurant supplies, works on 3% commission. If her sales for a week are $4,200, find her gross earnings.

6. Carlo Mason works on 5% commission. If he sells $7,500 in merchandise, find his gross earnings.

7. Find the gross earnings of Sallie Johnson who receives a 9% commission and whose sales totaled $5,800.

8. Find the FICA tax (at 6.2%) and the Medicare tax (at 1.45%) for Anna Jones whose gross earnings are $213.86. Round to the nearest cent.

9. Find the FICA and Medicare tax for Michele Cottrell whose gross earnings are $361.25.

10. How much income tax should be withheld for Terry McLean, a married employee who earns $286 weekly and claims two allowances? (Use Figure 6–3.)

11. Use Figure 6–3 to find the federal income tax paid by Charlotte Jordan who is married with four exemptions, if her weekly gross earnings are $276.

12. Jo Ann Maxwell has gross earnings of $157. She has a 3% nonexempt retirement deduction and pays $21 for insurance. What is the total of these deductions?

13. If LaQuita White had net earnings of $177.58 and total deductions of $43.69, find her gross earnings.

14. Rita Rainey has a gross income of $258.21 and total deductions of $31.17. Find the net earnings.

Complete the weekly register for married employees. The number of each person's allowances is listed after each name. Round to the nearest cent. Use Figure 6-3.

Employee (Exemptions)	Gross Earnings	FICA	Medicare	Withholding Tax	Other Nonexempt Deductions	Net Earnings
15. Jackson (0)	$235.00				$25.12	
16. Love (1)	$173.80				$12.87	
17. Chow (2)	$292.17				$ 0	
18. Ferrante (3)	$ 77.15				$ 4.88	
19. Towns (4)	$210.13				$ 0	

20. How much SUTA tax must Anaston, Inc. pay to the state for a part-time employee who earns $5,290? The SUTA tax rate is 5.4% of the wages.

21. How much SUTA tax must University Dry Cleaners pay to the state for an employee who earns $38,200?

22. How much FUTA tax must University Dry Cleaners pay to the state for the employee in Exercise 21? The FUTA tax rate is 6.2% of the first $7,000 minus the SUTA tax.

23. How much SUTA tax does the employee in Exercise 21 pay?

24. How much withholding, FICA, and Medicare tax should the employer deposit for the payroll in Exercises 15–19?

TRADE AND CASH DISCOUNTS

GOOD DECISIONS THROUGH TEAMWORK

Ebony Products offers its customers credit terms of 4/14 n/30 with a 1.5% late payment fee. The customer pays all shipping charges. Of the $300,000 monthly sales, typically 25% are paid within the cash discount period and 10% are assessed the late fee.

A consulting firm has suggested that a free shipping incentive for all merchandise and cash discount terms of 2/15 n/30 would improve Ebony's cash flow (amount of money they receive each month). Reasearch shows that free shipping typically improves total sales by 10%.

With your team members, analyze the financial impact of changing the shipping and cash discount policies and decide what the company should do. Prepare a summary report and make an oral presentation to the class.

A discount is money deducted from money owed. Manufacturers and distributors give *trade discounts* as incentives for a sale, and *cash discounts* as incentives for paying promptly. Discounts are usually established by *discount rates,* given in percent or decimal form, of the money owed. The discount, then, is a percentage of the money owed. In learning about discounts, you will continually apply the percentage formula $P = RB$. You will also learn to interpret and apply *end-of-month* and *receipt-of-goods* terms of sale for determining the dates the cash discounts are allowed.

7.1 Net Price and the Trade Discount

1 ▶ *Find the trade discount using a single trade discount rate; find the net price using the trade discount*

2 ▶ *Find the net price using the complement of the single trade discount rate*

Most products go from the manufacturer to the consumer by way of the wholesale merchant (wholesaler or distributor) and the retail merchant (retailer).

Manufacturer
↓
Wholesaler
↓
Retailer
↓
Consumer

Manufacturers often describe each of their products in a book or catalog that is made available to wholesalers or retailers. In such catalogs, manufacturers suggest a price at which each product should be sold to the consumer. This price is called the **suggested retail price,** the **catalog price,** or, most commonly, the **list price.**

When a manufacturer sells an item to the wholesaler, the manufacturer deducts a certain amount from the list price of the item. The amount deducted is called the **trade discount.** The wholesaler pays the **net price,** which is the difference between the list price and the trade discount. Likewise, the wholesaler discounts the list price when selling to the retailer. The discount rate that the wholesaler gives the retailer is smaller than the discount rate that the manufacturer gives the wholesaler. The consumer pays the list price.

The trade discount is not usually stated in the published catalog. Instead, the wholesaler or retailer calculates it using the list price and the **discount rate.** The discount rate is a *percent* of the list price.

The manufacturer makes available lists of discount rates for all items in the catalog. The discount rates vary considerably depending on such factors as the customer class, the season, the condition of the economy, whether a product is being discontinued, and the manufacturer's efforts to encourage larger purchases. Each time the discount rate changes, the manufacturer updates the listing. Each new discount rate applies to the original list price in the catalog.

For a variety of reasons, manufacturers may establish "discounts on discounts." This situation, known as *discount series,* is covered in the next section. For now, we concentrate on the trade discount allowed by a **single discount rate.**

The Single Trade Discount Rate

To find the trade discount for an item when the list price and a single discount rate are given, we use

$$\text{Percentage (part)} = \text{rate (percent)} \times \text{base (whole) or } P = R \times B$$

In this case, percentage is the trade discount T, rate is the single trade discount rate R, and the base is the list price L.

$$P = R \times B$$
$$T = R \times L$$

HOW TO	Find the Trade Discount Using a Single Trade Discount Rate

Multiply the list price by the single trade discount rate.

$$\text{Trade discount} = \text{single trade discount rate} \times \text{list price}$$
$$T = RL$$

Since the trade discount is deducted from the list price to get the net price, once you know the trade discount, you can calculate the net price.

HOW TO	Find the Net Price Using the Trade Discount

Subtract the trade discount from the list price.

$$\text{Net price} = \text{list price} - \text{trade discount}$$
$$N = L - T$$

 Example 1 The list price of a refrigerator is $600. Young's Appliance Store can buy the refrigerator at the list price less 20%. (a) Find the trade discount. (b) Find the net price of the refrigerator.

a. Trade discount = single trade discount rate × list price

$$20\% \times \$600 = 0.20 \times \$600 \quad \text{Discount rate is 20\%; list price is \$600.}$$

$$= \boxed{\$120} \quad \text{Change the percent to a decimal. Multiply.}$$

The trade discount is $120.

b. Net price = list price − trade discount

$$= \$600 - \boxed{\$120} \quad \text{List price is \$600; trade discount is \$120.}$$

$$= \$480$$

The net price is $480.

2 ▶ *The Complements of the Single Trade Discount Rate*

Another method for calculating the net price uses the *complements* of percents. The **complement** of a percent is the difference between that percent and 100%. For example, the complement of 35% is 65%, since 100% − 35% = 65%. The complement of 20% is 80% because 100% − 20% = 80%.

The complement of the single trade discount rate can be used to find the net price. Here's why. Say the single trade discount rate is 25%. We know that

$$\text{Net price} = \text{list price} - \text{trade discount}$$

Because the trade discount is 25% of the list price, using percents we can write this formula as

$$\text{Net price} = 100\% \text{ of list price} - 25\% \text{ of list price}$$

The right side of this equation is the difference between two products, and each product includes the list price. An equivalent equation finds the difference between the two percents and then multiplies the difference by the list price.

$$\text{Net price} = (100\% - 25\%) \times \text{list price}$$

But 100% − 25% is the *complement* of the single trade discount rate. So

$$\text{Net price} = \text{complement of single trade discount rate} \times \text{list price}$$

This is the complement formula for finding the net price given the single trade discount rate, without having first to calculate the trade discount.

Since the complement is a percent, the complement is a rate. You might think of the complement as the "net price rate." The single trade discount rate is used to calculate the amount the retailer does *not* pay: the trade discount; the complement of the single trade discount rate is used to calculate the amount the retailer *does* pay: the net price.

HOW TO	**Find the Net Price Using the Complement of the Single Trade Discount Rate**

Step 1 Find the complement: Subtract the single trade discount rate from 100%.

Complement of single trade discount rate = 100% − single trade discount rate

Step 2 Multiply the list price by the complement of the single trade discount rate.

Net price = complement of single trade discount rate × list price

OR

Net Price = (100% − single trade discount rate) × list price

$N = CL$ or $N = (100\% - R)L$

If the single discount rate is the percentage of the list price that the retailer *does not* pay, then 100% minus the single discount rate, which equals the complement of the discount rate, is the portion of the list price the retailer *does* pay or the net price.

Example 2 Mays' Stationery Store buys 300 pens at $0.30 each, 200 legal pads at $0.60 each, and 100 boxes of paper clips at $0.90 each. The single trade discount rate for the order is 12%. Find the net price of the order.

$300 \times \$0.30 = \$\ 90$ **Find the list price of the pens.**

$200 \times \$0.60 = \$120$ **Find the list price of the legal pads.**

$100 \times \$0.90 = \underline{\$\ 90}$ **Find the list price of the paper clips.**
$\qquad\qquad\qquad \$300$ **Add to find the total list price.**

Net price = (100% − single trade discount rate) × list price

$= (100\% - 12\%) \times \boxed{\$300}$ **The single trade discount rate is 12%; the list price is $300.**

$= 88\% \times \$300$

$= 0.88 \times \$300$ **Write 88% as a decimal.**

$= \$264$ **Multiply.**

The net price is $264.

Self-Check 7.1

 1. Calculate the trade discount for 20 boxes of computer paper if the unit price is $14.67 and a single trade discount rate of 20% is allowed.

58.68

2. Calculate the trade discount for 30 cases of antifreeze coolant if each case contains six one-gallon units that cost $2.18 per gallon and a single trade discount rate of 18% is allowed.

 53.62

3. Calculate the net price for the 20 boxes of computer paper in Exercise 1.

4. Calculate the net price for the 30 cases of antifreeze coolant in Exercise 2.

5. Use the complement method to calculate the net price for the 20 boxes of computer paper in Exercise 1. Compare this net price with the net price found in Exercise 3.

6. Use the complement method to calculate the net price for the 30 cases of antifreeze coolant in Exercise 2. Compare this net price with the net price found in Exercise 4.

7. Which method of calculating net price do you prefer? Why?

8. If you were writing a spreadsheet program to calculate the net price for several items and you were not interested in showing the trade discount, which method would you be likely to use? Why?

9. Complete Invoice 2501 below, finding the net price using the single trade discount rate.

10. Verify that the net price calculated in Exercise 9 is correct by recalculating the net price using the complement of the single trade discount rate.

Invoice No. 2501
October 15, 19XX

Qty.	Item	Unit Price	List Price
15	Notebooks	$1.50	
10	Looseleaf paper	$0.89	
30	Ballpoint pens	$0.79	
		Total list price	
		40% trade discount	
		Net price	

Find the net price, applying a trade discount series and using the net decimal equivalent

 Find the trade discount, applying a trade discount series and using the single discount equivalent

Sometimes a manufacturer wants to promote a particular item or encourage additional business from a buyer. Also, buyers may be entitled to additional discounts as a result of buying large quantities. In such cases, the manufacturer may offer additional discounts that are deducted one after another from the list price. Such discounts are called a **trade discount series.** For example, a discount series would be written as $400 (list price) with a discount series of 20/10/5 (discount rates). That is, a discount of 20% is allowed off the list price, a discount of 10% is allowed off the amount that was left after the first discount, and a discount of 5% is allowed off the amount that was left after the second discount. It *does not* mean a total discount of 35% is allowed.

One way to calculate the net price is to make a series of calculations:

$400 × 0.2 = $80 $400 − $80 = $320   The first discount is taken on the list price of $400, which then leaves $320.

$320 × 0.1 = $32 $320 − $32 = $288   The second discount is taken on $320, which leaves $288.

$288 × 0.05 = $14.40 $288 − $14.40 = $273.60   The third discount is taken on $288, which leaves the net price of $273.60.

Thus, the net price of a $400 order with a discount series of 20/10/5 is $273.60.

As you can see, it is very time consuming to figure a trade discount series this way. The business world uses a faster way of calculating the net price of a purchase after a series discount has been taken.

 ## *The Net Decimal Equivalent*

Again, complements can be used to find net prices directly. For the $400 purchase with discounts of 20/10/5, using complements the net price after the first discount is 80% of $400.

$$0.8 × 400 = $320$$

The net price after the second discount is 90% of $320.

$$0.9 × $320 = $288$$

The net price after the third discount is 95% of $288.

$$0.95 × $288 = $273.60$$

To condense this process, the decimal equivalents of the complements of the discount rates can be multiplied to give a single decimal, the "net price rate." This single decimal is called the **net decimal equivalent.** Multiply the list price by the net decimal equivalent to get the net price.

HOW TO   Find Net Price Using the Net Decimal Equivalent of a Trade Discount Series

Step 1   Find the net decimal equivalent: Multiply the complements of the trade discounts, in decimal form, of all the rates in the series.

Net decimal equivalent = product of complements of the trade
discounts in decimal form.

Step 2   Multiply the list price by the net decimal equivalent.

Net price = net decimal equivalent × list price

$$N = DL$$

Example 1   Find the net price of an order with a list price of $600 and a trade discount series of 15/10/5. (*Remember:* To find the complement, you subtract the discount rate from 100%.)

$100\% - 15\% = 85\% = 0.85$ **Find the complement of each discount rate and write it as an equivalent decimal.**

$100\% - 10\% = 90\% = 0.9$

$100\% - 5\% = 95\% = 0.95$

$0.85 \times 0.9 \times 0.95 = \boxed{0.72675}$ **Multiply the complements to find the net decimal equivalent.**

Net price = net decimal equivalent × list price

$= \boxed{0.72675} \times \$600$ **The net decimal equivalent is 0.72675; the list price is $600.**

$= \$436.05$

The net price for a $600 order with a trade discount series of 15/10/5 is $436.05.

ⓘ TIPS & TRAPS

We have said that the trade discount series of 20/10/5 is *not* equivalent to the single discount rate of 35% (which is the *sum* of 20%, 10%, and 5%). Look at an example worked correctly and incorrectly.

Example: Find the net price of an article listed at $100 with a discount of 20/10/5.

Net price = net decimal equivalent × list price

$= (0.8 \times 0.9 \times 0.95) \times \$100$

$= 0.684 \times \$100$

$= \$68.40$

CORRECT

Net price = net decimal equivalent × list price

$= (100\% - 35\%) \times$ list price

$= 0.65 \times \$100$

$= \$65$

INCORRECT

Example 2 One manufacturer lists a desk at $700 with a discount series of 20/10/10. A second manufacturer lists the same desk at $650 with a discount series of 10/10/10. Which is the better deal?

1 Decision needed
Which deal on the desk is better?

2 Unknown facts
Net price for the first deal.
Net price for the second deal.

3 Known facts
List price for first deal: $700
Discount series for first deal: 20/10/10
List price for second deal : $650
Discount series for second deal: 10/10/10

4 Estimation
The net prices for both deals will be relatively close.

5 Relationship
Net Price = net decimal equivalent × list price

6 Calculations
Decimal equivalents of complements of 20%, 10%, and 10% are 0.8, 0.9, and 0.9 respectively.
Net decimal equivalent = 0.8(0.9)(0.9)
$\qquad$ = 0.648
Net Price for first deal = (0.648) $700
$\qquad$ = $453.60
Decimal equivalents of complements of 10%, 10%, and 10% are 0.9, 0.9, and 0.9 respectively.
Net decimal equivalent = 0.9(0.9)(0.9)
$\qquad$ = 0.729
Net Price for second deal = (0.729) $650
$\qquad$ = $473.85

7 Decision made
Since the net price for the first deal is $20.25 less than the net price for the second deal ($473.85 − $453.60), **the first deal—the $700 desk with the 20/10/10 discount series—is the better deal.**

The Single Discount Equivalent

If you want to know how much you have *saved* by using a discount series, you can calculate the savings—the trade discount—the long way, by finding the net price and then subtracting the net price from the list price. Or, you can apply another, quicker complement method. In percent form, the complement of the net decimal equivalent is the **single discount equivalent.** The product of the single discount equivalent and the list price is the trade discount.

> **HOW TO** | **Find the Trade Discount Using the Single Discount Equivalent**
>
> **Step 1** Find the single discount equivalent: Subtract the net decimal equivalent from 1.
>
> $\qquad$ Single discount equivalent = 1 − net decimal equivalent.
>
> **Step 2** Multiply the list price by the single discount equivalent.
>
> $\qquad$ Trade discount = single discount equivalent × list price
>
> $\qquad\qquad$ OR
>
> $\qquad$ Trade discount = (1 − net decimal equivalent) × list price

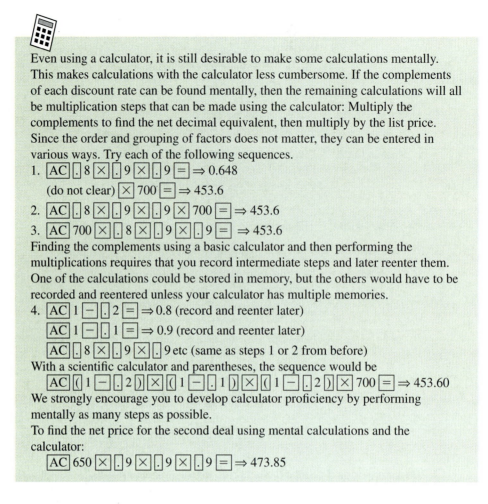

Even using a calculator, it is still desirable to make some calculations mentally. This makes calculations with the calculator less cumbersome. If the complements of each discount rate can be found mentally, then the remaining calculations will all be multiplication steps that can be made using the calculator: Multiply the complements to find the net decimal equivalent, then multiply by the list price. Since the order and grouping of factors does not matter, they can be entered in various ways. Try each of the following sequences.

1. $\boxed{\text{AC}}\;\boxed{.}\;8\;\boxed{\times}\;\boxed{.}\;9\;\boxed{\times}\;\boxed{.}\;9\;\boxed{=}\Rightarrow 0.648$

   (do not clear) $\boxed{\times}\;700\;\boxed{=}\Rightarrow 453.6$

2. $\boxed{\text{AC}}\;\boxed{.}\;8\;\boxed{\times}\;\boxed{.}\;9\;\boxed{\times}\;\boxed{.}\;9\;\boxed{\times}\;700\;\boxed{=}\Rightarrow 453.6$

3. $\boxed{\text{AC}}\;700\;\boxed{\times}\;\boxed{.}\;8\;\boxed{\times}\;\boxed{.}\;9\;\boxed{\times}\;\boxed{.}\;9\;\boxed{=}\Rightarrow 453.6$

Finding the complements using a basic calculator and then performing the multiplications requires that you record intermediate steps and later reenter them. One of the calculations could be stored in memory, but the others would have to be recorded and reentered unless your calculator has multiple memories.

4. $\boxed{\text{AC}}\;1\;\boxed{-}\;\boxed{.}\;2\;\boxed{=}\Rightarrow 0.8$ (record and reenter later)

   $\boxed{\text{AC}}\;1\;\boxed{-}\;\boxed{.}\;1\;\boxed{=}\Rightarrow 0.9$ (record and reenter later)

   $\boxed{\text{AC}}\;\boxed{.}\;8\;\boxed{\times}\;\boxed{.}\;9\;\boxed{\times}\;\boxed{.}\;9$ etc (same as steps 1 or 2 from before)

With a scientific calculator and parentheses, the sequence would be

$\boxed{\text{AC}}\;\boxed{(}\;1\;\boxed{-}\;\boxed{.}\;2\;\boxed{)}\;\boxed{\times}\;\boxed{(}\;1\;\boxed{-}\;\boxed{.}\;1\;\boxed{)}\;\boxed{\times}\;\boxed{(}\;1\;\boxed{-}\;\boxed{.}\;2\;\boxed{)}\;\boxed{\times}\;700\;\boxed{=}\Rightarrow 453.60$

We strongly encourage you to develop calculator proficiency by performing mentally as many steps as possible.

To find the net price for the second deal using mental calculations and the calculator:

$\boxed{\text{AC}}\;650\;\boxed{\times}\;\boxed{.}\;9\;\boxed{\times}\;\boxed{.}\;9\;\boxed{\times}\;\boxed{.}\;9\;\boxed{=}\Rightarrow 473.85$

Example 3   Use the single discount equivalent to calculate the trade discount on a $1,500 fax machine with a discount series of 30/20/10.

The single discount equivalent is the complement of the net decimal equivalent. So first find the net decimal equivalent.

$100\% - 30\% = 70\% = 0.7$ **Find the complement of each discount rate and write it as an equivalent decimal.**

$100\% - 20\% = 80\% = 0.8$

$100\% - 10\% = 90\% = 0.9$

$0.7(0.8)(0.9) = \boxed{0.504}$ **Multiply the decimals to find the net decimal equivalent.**

$1.000 - \boxed{0.504} = 0.496$ **Subtract the net decimals equivalent from 1 to find the single discount equivalent.**

Thus, the single discount equivalent for the trade discount series 30/20/10 is 0.496 or 49.6%.

trade discount = single discount equivalent $\times$ list price   **The single discount equivalent is 0.496; the list price is $1,500.**

$= 0.496 \times \$1,500$

$= \$744$

The trade discount on the $1,500 fax machine with a trade discount series of 30/20/10 is $744.

The calculator plan for finding the trade discount is to find the net decimal equivalent and store it in memory. Subtract the net decimal equivalent (which is in memory) from 1. Then, multiply the result by the net price.

$\boxed{AC}\ \boxed{MC}\ \boxed{.}7\ \boxed{\times}\ \boxed{.}8\ \boxed{\times}\ \boxed{.}9\ \boxed{=}\ \boxed{M^+}\ 1-\boxed{MR}\ \boxed{=}\ \boxed{\times}\ 1500\ \boxed{=}\Rightarrow 744.$

Self-Check 7.2

 1. Dianna Beulke manages an electronic equipment store and has ordered 100 color TVs with remote control for a special sale. The list price for each TV is $215 with a trade discount series of 7/10/5. Find the net price of the order by using the net decimal equivalent.

2. Robert Armstrong is purchasing an order of computers for his computer store. Find the net price of an order of 36 computers if each computer has a list price of $1,599 and a trade discount series of 5/5/10 is offered by the distributor.

3. Clair Berry needs to calculate the net price of an order with a list price of $800 and a trade discount series of 12/10/6. Use the net decimal equivalent to find the net price for Clair.

4. Thomas Atkins is responsible for Cummins Appliance Store's accounts payable department and has an invoice that shows a list price of $2,200 with a trade discount series of 25/15/10. Use the single discount equivalent to calculate the trade discount on the purchase.

5. Cynthia Calhoun is calculating the trade discount on a 6′ × 10′ × 10′ dog kennel that has a list price of $269 with a trade discount series of 10/10/10. What should she show as the trade discount? What is the net price for the kennel?

6. Christy Hodge manages a computer software distributorship and offers a desktop publishing software package for $395 with a trade discount series of 5/5/8. What is the trade discount on this package?

7. One distributor lists ink jet printers with 360 dpi and 6 scalable fonts that can print envelopes, labels, and transparencies for $189.97 with a trade discount series of 5/5/10. Another distributor lists the same brand and model printer at $210 with a trade discount series of 5/10/10. Which is the better deal if all other aspects of the deal such as shipping, time of availability, warranty, etc. are the same or equivalent.

8. Two distributors offer the same brand and model 586SX2/50 MHx PC computer with 8 MB RAM, 540 MB hard drive, 3.5″ floppy drive, CD-ROM drive, 1 MB video card, and manufacturer's warranty and toll-free help number. One of the distributors lists the computer at $1,899 with a trade discount series of 8/8/5 and the distributor will pay for shipping. The other distributor offers the computer at $2,000 with a trade discount series of 10/5/5 and $50 shipping cost. The shipping cost is added to the net price. Which computer is the better deal?

9. Stephen Black manages the furniture department in a large retail department store. He orders a large volume of merchandise from a particular furniture manufacturer in North Carolina and currently receives a trade discount series of 5/10/10 on merchandise purchased from the company. However, he is negotiating with another furniture manufacturer to purchase similar furniture of the same quality. The North Carolina company lists a dining room table and six chairs for $1,899. The other company lists a similar set of furniture for $1,800, and in an effort to develop this new customer, offers a trade discount series of 5/5/10. Considering just the cost factor, which deal should Mr. Black accept?

10. We have seen that the trade discount series 20/10/5 is *not* equal to a single trade discount rate of 35%. Does the trade discount series 20/10/5 equal the trade discount series 5/10/20? Use an item with a list price of $1,000 and calculate the trade discount for both series to justify your answer.

11. One distributor lists a dot-matrix printer at $460 with a trade discount series of 15/12/5. Another distributor lists the same printer at $410 with a trade discount series of 10/10/5. Which is the better deal?

BUSINESS AND MATHEMATICS *IN THE NEWS*

How Much Room to Bargain?

The table below lists the approximate percent of the manufacturer's suggested retail price (MSRP) that a dealer pays for a car.

Make	Cost factor(s)	Make	Cost factor(s)
Acura	86-88%	Land Rover	89%
Audi	88	Lexus	82-83
BMW	82-84	Lincoln	87
Buick	86-92	Mazda	86-93
Cadillac	86-92	Mercedes-Benz	85
Chevrolet	85-94	Mercury	89-92
Chrysler	90-94	Mitsubishi	80-90
Dodge	90-93	Nissan	87-89
Eagle	90-95	Oldsmobile	92-95
Ford	86-92	Plymouth	90-93
GMC	87-90	Pontiac	90-92
Geo	92-95	Saab	87-88
Honda	87-90	Saturn	87 [1]
Hyundai	88-90	Subaru	90-91
Infiniti	83-88	Suzuki	89-94
Isuzu	85-88	Toyota	84-92
Jaguar	82	Volkswagen	90-96
Jeep	91-96	Volvo	92-95

[1] *Dealer follows no-haggle policy.*

1. If an Infiniti has a sticker price of $25,000, what amounts does the table indicate the dealer could have paid for the car?

2. For the Infiniti in Exercise 1, find the corresponding discount rates.

3. Find the net price and the trade discount for a Lincoln that lists for $28,984.

4. Use your knowledge of complements to convert the first four cost factors to discount rates.

5. If you were interested in buying a car and you enjoyed bargaining with dealers, which make would you consider and why?

1▶ *Find the cash discount and the net amount using ordinary dating terms*

2▶ *Interpret and apply end-of-month (EOM) terms*

3▶ *Interpret and apply receipt-of-goods (ROG) terms*

4▶ *Find the amount credited and the outstanding balance from partial payments*

5▶ *Interpret freight terms*

To encourage prompt payment, many manufacturers and wholesalers allow buyers to take a **cash discount,** a reduction of the amount due on an invoice. The cash discount is a specified percentage of the price of the goods. Customers who pay their bills within a certain amount of time receive a cash discount. Many companies use computerized billing systems that compute the exact amount of a cash discount and show it on the invoice, so that the customer does not need to figure the discount and resulting net price. But the customer must still determine when the bill must be paid to receive the discount.

Bills are often due within 30 days from the date of the invoice. To figure out the exact day of the month the payment is due, you have to know how many days are in the month, 30, 31, or 28 in the case of February. There are two ways to help remember which months have 30 days and which have 31. The first method shown in Figure 7–1, is called the *knuckle method*. Each knuckle represents a month with 31 days and each space between knuckles represents a month with 30 days (except February, which has 28 days unless it is a leap year, when it has 29.

Figure 7–1 The knuckle months (Jan., March, May, July, Aug., Oct., and Dec.) have 31 days. The other months have 30 or fewer days.

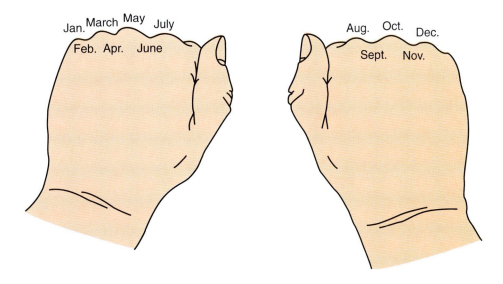

Another way to remember which months have 30 days and which have 31 is the following rhyme:

> Thirty days has September,
> April, June, and November,
> All the rest have 31,
> 'cept February has 28 alone.
> And leap year, that's the time
> When February has 29.

With this in mind, let's look at one of the most common credit terms and dating methods.

Ordinary Dating Terms

Many firms offer credit terms 2/10, n/30 (read "two ten, net thirty"). The 2/10 means a 2% cash discount rate may be applied if the bill is paid within 10 days of the invoice date. The n/30 means that the full amount or net amount of the bill is due within 30 days. After the 30th day, the bill is overdue, and the buyer may have to pay interest charges.

For example, say an invoice is dated January 4 with credit terms of 2/10, n/30. If the buyer pays on or before January 14, then a 2% cash discount rate is applied. If the buyer pays instead on or after January 15, no cash discount is allowed. Finally, since 30 days from January 4 is February 3, if the buyer pays on or after February 4, interest charges on the bill may be required.

⚠ TIPS & TRAPS   **Ordinary Dating Terms**

To find the last day to receive a discount, add to the invoice date the number of days specified in the terms. If this sum is greater than the number of days in the month the invoice is dated, subtract from the sum the number of days in the month the invoice is dated.

❓ HOW TO   **Find the Cash Discount**

Multiply the cash discount rate by the net price.

$$\text{Cash discount} = \text{cash discount rate} \times \text{net price}$$

Example 1 An invoice dated July 27 shows a net price of $450 with the terms 2/10, n/30. (a) Find the latest date the cash discount is allowed. (b) Find the cash discount.

a. The cash discount is allowed up to and including 10 days from the invoice date, July 27.

27th of July	**Invoice date.**
+10 days	**Days allowed according to terms 2/10.**
"37th of July"	**If July had 37 days . . .**
−31 days in July	**July has 31 days.**
6th of August	**Latest date allowed.**

August 6 is the latest date the cash discount is allowed.

b. Cash discount = Cash discount rate × net price

$$\text{Cash discount} = 2\% \times \$450$$
$$= 0.02\,(\$450)$$
$$= \$9.00$$

The cash discount is $9.00.

Once a cash discount is deducted from the list price, the amount remaining is called the **net amount.** The net amount, then, is the amount the buyer actually pays. Like the net price, there are two ways to calculate the net amount.

HOW TO Find the Net Amount

Using the cash discount Subtract the cash discount from the net price.

$$\text{Net amount} = \text{net price} - \text{cash discount}$$

OR

Using the complement of the cash discount rate Multiply the net price by the complement of the cash discount rate.

$$\text{Net amount} = \text{Complement of cash discount rate} \times \text{net price}$$

OR

$$\text{Net amount} = (100\% - \text{cash discount rate}) \times \text{net price}$$

Example 2 Find the net amount for the invoice in Example 1.

$$\text{Net amount} = \text{net price} - \text{cash discount}$$
$$= \$450 - \$9$$
$$= \$441$$

or

$$\text{Net amount} = \text{complement of cash discount rate} \times \text{net price}$$
$$= (100\% - 2\%)\,(\$450)$$
$$= 0.98\,(\$450)$$
$$= \$441$$

The net amount is $441.

Another common set of discount terms is 2/10, 1/15, n/30. These terms are read "two ten, one fifteen, net thirty." A 2% cash discount is allowed if the bill is paid within 10 days after the invoice date, a 1% cash discount is allowed if the bill is paid during the 11th through 15th days, and no discount is allowed during the 16th through the 30th days. Interest charges may accrue if the bill is paid after the 30th day from the date of the invoice.

For example, a bill dated September 2 with sales terms 2/10, 1/15, n/30 receives a 2% discount if paid on or before September 12. A 1% discount is allowed if the bill is paid on September 13 or any day up to and including September 17. The net amount is due if the bill is paid on September 18 through October 2. If the bill is paid on October 3 or any day after October 3, it is subject to interest charges.

 TIPS & TRAPS

The requirement for a bill to be paid on or before a specific date means that the payment must be received by the supplier on or before that date. For the payment to be postmarked by the due date does not generally count.

Example 3 Sycamore Enterprises received a $1,248 bill for computer supplies, dated September 2, with sales terms 2/10, 1/15, n/30. A 5% penalty is charged for payment after 30 days. Find the amount due if the bill is paid (a) on or before September 12; (b) on or between September 13 and September 17; (c) on or between September 18 and October 2; and (d) on or after October 3.

a. If the bill is paid on or before September 12 (within 10 days), the 2% discount applies:

$$\text{Cash discount} = 2\% \times \$1,248 = 0.02 \times \$1,248 = \boxed{\$24.96}$$

$$\text{Net amount} = \$1,248 - \boxed{\$24.96} = \$1,223.04$$

The net amount due on or before September 12 is $1,223.04.

b. If the bill is paid on or between September 13 and September 17 (within 15 days), the 1% discount applies:

$$\text{Cash discount} = 1\% \times \$1,248 = 0.01 \times \$1,248 = \boxed{\$12.48}$$

$$\text{Net amount} = \$1,248 - \boxed{\$12.48} = \$1,235.52$$

The net amount due on or between September 13 and September 17 is $1,235.52.

c. If the bill is paid on or between September 18 and October 2, no cash discount applies. **The net price of $1,248 is due.**

d. If the bill is paid on or after October 3, a 5% interest penalty is added:

$$\text{Interest} = 5\% \times \$1,248 = 0.05 \times \$1,248 = \boxed{\$62.40}$$

$$\text{Net amount} = \$1,248 + \boxed{\$62.40} = \$1,310.40$$

The net amount due on or after October 3 is $1,310.40.

2 ▶ End of Month (EOM) Terms

Included in the types of sales terms are **end-of-the-month (EOM)** terms. For example, the term might be 2/10 EOM, meaning that a 2% discount is allowed if the bill is paid during the first 10 days of the month *after* the month in the date of the invoice. Thus, if a bill is dated November 19, a 2% discount is allowed as long as the bill is paid on or before December 10.

Example 4 Newman, Inc., received a bill for cleaning services dated September 17 for $5,000 with terms 2/10 EOM. The invoice was paid on October 9. How much did Newman, Inc., pay?

Since the bill was paid within the first ten days of the next month, a 2% discount was allowed. The complement of 2% is 98%.

$$\text{Net amount} = 98\% \times \$5,000 = 0.98 \times \$5,000 = \$4,900$$

The net amount due on October 9 is $4,900.

An exception to this rule occurs when the invoice is dated *on or after the 26th of a month*. When this happens, the discount is allowed if the bill is paid during the first ten days of the month after the next month. Thus, if an invoice is dated May 28 with terms 2/10 EOM, a 2% discount is allowed as long as the bill is paid on or before *July* 10. This exception allows retailers adequate time to receive and pay the invoice.

Example 5 Archie's Shoes received a $200 bill for copying services dated April 27. The terms on the invoice were 3/10 EOM. The firm paid the bill on June 2. How much did it pay?

Since the bill was paid within the first ten days of the second month after the month on the invoice, a 3% discount was allowed. The complement of 3% is 97%.

Net amount = 97% × $200 = 0.97 × $200 = $194

The net amount paid was $194.

 Receipt-of-Goods (ROG) Terms

Sometimes sales terms hinge on the day the *goods are received* instead of the invoice date. In such cases, the terms may be written 1/10 *ROG*, where ROG stands for **receipt of goods.** These terms mean that a 1% discount is allowed on the bill if it is paid within ten days of the receipt of goods.

For instance, an invoice is dated September 6 but the goods do not arrive until the 14th. If the sales terms are 2/15 ROG, then a 2% discount is allowed if the bill is paid on any date up to and including September 29.

Example 6 An invoice for machine parts for $400 is dated November 9 and has sales terms 2/10 ROG. The machine parts arrive November 13. (a) If the bill is paid on November 21, what is the net amount due? (b) If the bill is paid on December 2, what is the net amount due?

a. Since the bill is being paid within ten days of the receipt of goods, a 2% discount is allowed. The complement of 2% is 98%.

Net amount = 98% × $400 = 0.98 × $400 = $392

The net amount due is $392.

b. No discount is allowed, since the bill is not being paid within ten days of the receipt of goods. **Thus, $400 is due.**

It is important to be able to distinguish types of payment terms as they appear on an invoice. For example, an invoice for $200 is dated September 28 but the merchandise arrives on October 15. The sales terms are 2/10 ROG, but the account manager thinks this means the bill can be paid within 10 days of the second month after the month in the date of the invoice (EOM) and pays the bill with a 2% discount on November 5. Does the discount apply? No, since the bill should have been paid within 10 days of the receipt of the goods. The last date to pay the bill and receive the discount is October 25th.

4 ▶ *Partial Payments*

A company sometimes cannot pay the full amount due in time to take advantage of cash discount terms. Most sellers allow buyers to make a **partial payment** and still get a **partial cash discount** off the net price if the partial payment is made within the time specified in the credit terms. The **amount credited** to the account, then, is the partial payment plus this partial cash discount. The **outstanding balance** is the amount still owed, and is expected to be paid within the time specified by the sales terms.

Calculating the amount credited and the outstanding balance is straightforward, but the explanation for these calculations we reserve for another course.

 HOW TO | **Find the Amount Credited and the Outstanding Balance from Partial Payments**

Step 1 Find the amount credited to the account: Divide the partial payment by the complement of the cash discount rate.

$$\text{Amount credited} = \frac{\text{partial payment}}{\text{complement of cash discount rate}}$$

Step 2 Find the outstanding balance: Subtract the amount credited from the net price.

$$\text{Outstanding balance} = \text{net price} - \text{amount credited}$$

OR

$$\text{Outstanding balance} = \text{net price} - \frac{\text{partial payment}}{\text{complement of cash discount rate}}$$

Example 7 The Semmes Corporation received an $875 invoice for cardboard cartons with terms of 3/10, n/30. The firm could not pay the entire bill within ten days but sent a check for $500. What amount was credited to Semmes' account?

$$\text{Amount credited} = \frac{\text{Partial payment}}{\text{complement of rate}} = \frac{\$500}{0.97}$$

$$= \$515.46$$

Divide the amount of the partial payment by the complement of the discount rate to find the amount credited.

$$\text{Outstanding balance} = \$875 - \$515.46 = \$359.54$$

Subtract the amount credited from the net price to find the outstanding balance.

A $515.46 payment was credited to the account and the outstanding balance was $359.54.

 Freight Terms

Manufacturers rely on a wide variety of carriers (truck, rail, ship, plane, and the like) to distribute their goods. The terms of freight shipment are indicated on a document called a **bill of lading** that is attached to each shipment. This document includes a description of the merchandise, the number of pieces, weight, name of consignee, destination, and method of payment of freight charges. Freight payment terms are usually specified on the *manufacturer's price list* so that purchasers clearly understand who is responsible for freight charges and under what circumstances before purchases are made. The cost of shipping may be paid by the buyer or seller. If the freight is paid by the buyer, the bill of lading is marked **FOB shipping point**—meaning "free on board" at the shipping point—or *freight collect*. For example, CCC Industries located in Tulsa purchased parts from Rawhide in Chicago. Rawhide ships FOB Chicago, so CCC Industries must pay the freight from Chicago to Tulsa. The freight company then collects freight charges from CCC upon delivery of the goods.

If the freight is paid by the seller, the bill of lading may be marked **FOB destination**—or *freight paid*. If Rawhide paid the freight in the preceding example, the term FOB Tulsa could also have been used. Many manufacturers pay shipping charges for shipments above some minimum dollar value. Some shipments of very small items may be marked *prepay and add*. That is, the seller pays the shipping charge and adds it to the invoice, so the buyer pays the shipping charge to the seller rather than to the freight company. Cash discounts do *not* apply to freight or shipping charges.

Example 8 Calculate the cash discount and the net amount paid for an $800 order of business forms with sales terms of 3/10, 1/15, n/30 if the cost of shipping was $40 (which is included in the $800). The invoice was dated June 13, marked *freight prepay and add,* and paid June 24.

Net price of merchandise

= Total invoice − shipping fee

= $800 − $40 = $760   **Apply the cash discount rate *only to* the net price of the merchandise.**

The net price is $760.

Cash discount

= $760 × 0.01 = $7.60   **The bill was paid within 15 days, so the 1% discount applies.**

Net amount

= $800 − $7.60 = $792.40   **Discount is taken from total bill.**

The cash discount was $7.60 and the net amount paid was $792.40 which included the shipping fee.

Self-Check 7.3

1 *Larry Blanton received an invoice dated March 9, with terms 2/10, n/30, amounting to $540. He paid the bill on March 12.*

1. How much was the cash discount?

2. What is the net amount Larry will pay?

James Champion gets an invoice for $450 with terms of 4/10, 1/15, n/30.

3. How much would James pay seven days after the invoice date?

4. How much would James pay 15 days after the invoice date?

5. How much would James pay 25 days after the invoice date?

Jana Turner, director of accounts, received a bill for $648, dated April 6, with sales terms 2/10, 1/15, n/30. A 3% penalty is charged for payment after 30 days.

6. Find the amount due if the bill is paid on or before April 16.

7. What amount is due if the bill is paid on or between April 17 and April 21.

8. What amount is due if Jana pays on or between April 22 and May 6?

9. If Jana pays on or after May 7, how much must she pay?

Grace Cox is an accounts payable officer for her company and must calculate cash discounts before paying invoices. She is paying bills on June 18 and has an invoice dated June 12 with terms 3/10, n/30.

10. If the net price of the invoice is $1,296.45, how much cash discount can she take?

11. What is the net amount Grace will need to pay?

2 **12.** Charlene Watson received a bill for $800 dated July 5, with sales terms of 2/10 EOM. She paid the bill on August 8. How much should Charlene pay?

13. An invoice for a camcorder that cost $1,250 is dated August 1, with sales terms of 2/10 EOM. If the bill is paid on September 8, how much is due?

14. Ruby Wossum received an invoice for $798.53 dated February 27 with sales terms of 3/10 EOM. How much should she pay if she pays the bill on April 15?

15. Sylvester Young received an invoice for a leaf blower for $493 dated April 15 with sales terms of 3/10 EOM. How much should he pay if he pays the bill on April 30?

3 *An invoice for $900 is dated October 15 and has sales terms of 2/10 ROG. The merchandise arrives October 21.*

16. How much is due if the bill is paid October 27?

17. How much is due if the bill is paid on November 3?

18. Sharron Smith is paying an invoice showing a total of $5,835 and dated June 2. The invoice shows sales terms of 2/10 ROG. The merchandise delivery slip shows a receiving date of 6/5. How much is due if the bill for the merchandise is paid on June 12?

19. Kariem Salaam is directing the accounts payable office and is training a new accounts payable associate. They are processing an invoice for a credenza which is dated August 19 in the amount of $392.34. The delivery ticket for the credenza is dated August 23. If the sales terms indicated on the invoice are 3/10 ROG, how much needs to be paid if the bill is paid on September 5?

4 20. Clordia Patterson-Nathanial handles all accounts payable for her company. She has a bill for $730 and plans to make a partial payment of $400 within the discount period. If the terms of the transaction were 3/10, n/30, find the amount credited to the account and find the outstanding balance.

21. Robert Penhollow has an invoice for a complete computer system for $3,982.48. The invoice shows terms of 3/10, 2/15, n/30. He can afford to pay $2,000 within ten days of the date on the invoice and the remainder within the 30-day period. How much should be credited to the account for the $2,000 payment, and how much is still due?

22. Ada Shotwell has been directed to pay all invoices in time to receive any discounts offered by vendors. However, she has an invoice with terms of 2/10, n/30 for $2,983 and the funds for accounts payable has a balance of $2,196.83. So she elects to pay $2,000 on the invoice within the ten-day discount period and the remainder within the 30-day period. How much should be credited to the account for the $2,000 payment and how much remains to be paid?

5 23. Dorothy Rogers' Bicycle Shop received a shipment of bicycles via truck from Better Bilt Bicycles. The bill of lading was marked FOB destination. Who paid the freight? To whom was the freight paid?

24. Mary Pretti is negotiating the freight payment for a large shipment of office furniture for her store and agrees to take a discount on the invoice offered by the vendor since the freight terms are FOB shipping point. Who is to pay the freight?

25. Phyllis Porter receives a shipment with the bill of lading marked "prepay and add." Who is responsible for freight charges? To whom are the shipping charges paid?

26. Explain the difference in the freight terms "FOB shipping point" and "prepay and add."

SELF-CHECK SOLUTIONS

Self-Check 7.1

1. $14.67 × 20 = $293.40 total cost
$293.40 × 0.2 = $58.68 trade discount

2. 30 × 6 = 180 one-gallon units
180 × $2.18 = $392.40
$392.40 × 0.18 = $70.63 trade discount

3. $293.40 - 58.68 = 234.72$ net price

4. $392.40 - 70.63 = 321.77$

5. Complement = $100\% - 20\% = 1 - 0.2 = 0.8$
$293.40 \times 0.8 = 234.72$ net price

6. Complement = $100\% - 18\% = 1 - 0.18 = 0.82$
$392.40 \times 0.82 = 321.77$

7. Answers will vary.

8. Complement method. The net price can be found using a direct series of calculations.

9. Notebooks: $15 \times \$1.50 = \$22.50$
Looseleaf paper: $10 \times \$0.89 = \$8.90$
Ballpoint pens: $30 \times \$0.79 = \$23.70$
Total list price = $\$22.50 + \$8.90 + \$23.70 = \$55.10$
40% trade discount = $\$55.10 \times 0.4 = \$22.04$
Net price = $\$55.10 - \$22.04 = \$33.06$

10. Complement = $100\% - 40\% = 1 - 0.4 = 0.6$
Net price = $\$55.10 \times 0.6 = \$33.06$

Self-Check 7.2

1. $100\% - 7\% = 93\% = 0.93$
$100\% - 10\% = 90\% = 0.9$
$100\% - 5\% = 95\% = 0.95$
$0.93 \times 0.9 \times 0.95 = 0.79515$
$100 \times \$215.00 = \$21,500$ list price of TVs
$\$21,500 \times 0.79515 = \$17,095.73$ total net price of TVs

2. $100\% - 5\% = 95\% = 0.95$
$100\% - 5\% = 95\% = 0.95$
$100\% - 10\% = 90\% = 0.90$
$(0.95)(0.95)(0.9) = 0.81225$
$36 \times \$1,599.00 = \$57,564$ total list price
$\$57,564 \times 0.81225 = \$46,756.36$

3. $100\% - 12\% = 88\% = 0.88$
$100\% - 10\% = 90\% = 0.9$
$100\% - 6\% = 94\% = 0.94$
$0.88 \times 0.9 \times 0.94 = 0.74448$
$\$800 \times 0.74448 = \$595.58$

4. $100\% - 25\% = 75\% = 0.75$
$100\% - 15\% = 85\% = 0.85$
$100\% - 10\% = 90\% = 0.90$
$0.75 \times 0.85 \times 0.90 = 0.57375$
$1.0000 - 0.57375 = 0.42625$
$\$2,200 \times 0.42625 = \$937.75$

5. $100\% - 10\% = 90\% = 0.9$
$100\% - 10\% = 90\% = 0.9$
$100\% - 10\% = 90\% = 0.9$
$0.9 \times 0.9 \times 0.9 = 0.729$ *trade*
$1 - 0.729 = 0.271$
$\$269 \times 0.271 = \$72.90$ *Net*
$\$269 - \$72.90 = \$196.10$

6. $100\% - 5\% = 95\% = 0.95$
$100\% - 5\% = 95\% = 0.95$
$100\% - 8\% = 92\% = 0.92$
$0.95 \times 0.95 \times 0.92 = 0.8303$
$1 - 0.8303 = 0.1697$
$\$395 \times 0.1697 = \$67.03$

7. $100\% - 5\% = 95\% = 0.95$
$100\% - 5\% = 95\% = 0.95$
$100\% - 10\% = 90\% = 0.90$
$0.95 \times 0.95 \times 0.9 = 0.81225$
$\$189.97 \times 0.81225 = \$154.30$
$100\% - 5\% = 95\% = 0.95$
$100\% - 10\% = 90\% = 0.9$
$100\% - 10\% = 90\% = 0.9$
$0.95 \times 0.9 \times 0.9 = 0.7695$
$\$210 \times 0.7695 = \$161.60$
The better deal is $189.97 with discounts 5/5/10.

8. $100\% - 8\% = 92\% = 0.92$
$100\% - 8\% = 92\% = 0.92$
$100\% - 5\% = 95\% = 0.95$
$0.92 \times 0.92 \times 0.95 = 0.80408$
$\$1,899 \times 0.80408 = \$1,526.95$
$100\% - 10\% = 90\% = 0.9$
$100\% - 5\% = 95\% = 0.95$
$100\% - 5\% = 95\% = 0.95$
$0.9 \times 0.95 \times 0.95 = 0.81225$
$\$2,000 \times 0.81225 = \$1,624.50$
The better deal is $1,899 with discounts of 8/8/5.

9. $100\% - 5\% = 95\% = 0.95$
$100\% = 10\% = 90\% = 0.9$
$100\% = 10\% = 90\% = 0.9$
$0.95 \times 0.9 \times 0.9 = 0.7695$
$\$1,899 \times 0.7695 = \$1,461.28$
$100\% - 5\% = 95\% = 0.95$
$100\% - 5\% = 95\% = 0.95$
$100\% - 10\% = 90\% = 0.9$
$0.95 \times 0.95 \times 0.9 = 0.81225$
$\$1,800 \times 0.81225 = \$1,462.05$
The better deal is $1,899 with discounts of 5/10/10.

10. $100\% - 20\% = 80\% = 0.8$
$100\% - 10\% = 90\% = 0.9$
$100\% - 5\% = 95\% = 0.95$
$0.8 \times 0.9 \times 0.95 = 0.684$
$1 - 0.684 = 0.316$ single discount equivalent for 20/10/5 series
Trade discount $= 0.316 \times \$1,000 = \$316$
$100\% - 5\% = 95\% = 0.95$
$100\% - 10\% = 90\% = 0.9$
$100\% - 20\% = 80\% = 0.8$
$0.95 \times 0.9 \times 0.8 = 0.684$
$1 - 0.684 = 0.316$ single discount equivalent for 5/10/20 series
Trade discount $= 0.316 \times \$1,000 = \$316$
Both series result in the same trade discount.

11. $100\% - 15\% = 85\%$
$100 - 12\% = 88\%$
$100\% - 5\% = 95\%$
$0.85 \times 0.88 \times 0.95 = 0.7106$
Net price $= \$460 \times 0.7106 = \$326.88$
$100\% - 10\% = 90\%$
$100\% - 10\% = 90\%$
$100\% - 5\% = 95\%$
$0.9 \times 0.9 \times 0.95 = 0.7695$
Net price $= \$410 \times 0.7695 = \$315.50$
The better deal is $410 with a discount series of 10/10/5.

Self-Check 7.3

1. Invoice paid within 2% discount period.
$\$540 \times 0.02 = \$10.80$ cash discount

2. $\$540 - \$10.80 = \$529.20$ net amount

3. Invoice paid within 4% discount period.
$1 - 0.04 = 0.96$ complement
$\$450 \times 0.96 = \$432$ net amount

4. Invoice paid within 1% discount period.
$1 - 0.01 = 0.99$ complement
$\$450 \times 0.99 = \$445.50$ net amount

5. No cash discount allowed.
$450 is due.

6. Bill paid within 2% discount period.
$1 - 0.02 = 0.98$ complement
$\$648 \times 0.98 = \$635.04$ net amount

7. Bill paid within 1% discount period.
$1 - 0.01 = 0.99$ complement
$\$648 \times 0.99 = \$641.52$ net amount

8. No cash discount allowed.
$648 is due.

9. 3% interest penalty charged
$\$648 \times 0.03 = \$19.44$ interest penalty
$\$648 + \$19.44 = \$667.44$ total bill

10. June 18 payment is within the 3% discount period.
$\$1,296.45 \times 0.03 = \$38.89$ discount

11. $\$1,296.45 - \$38.89 = \$1,257.56$ net amount

12. Bill paid within 2% discount period.
$1 - 0.02 = 0.98$ complement
$\$800 \times 0.98 = \$784$ net amount

13. Bill paid within 2% discount period.
$1 - 0.02 = 0.98$ complement
$\$1,250 \times 0.98 = \$1,225$ net amount

14. No cash discount allowed.
$798.53 is due.

15. April 30 is within the 3% discount period.
$1 - 0.03 = 0.97$ complement
$\$493 \times 0.97 = \$478.21$ net amount

16. October 27 is within the 2% discount period.
$1 - 0.02 = 0.98$ complement
$\$900 \times 0.98 = \$882$ net amount

17. No cash discount allowed.
$900 is due.

18. June 12 is within the 2% discount period.
$1 - 0.02 = 0.98$ complement
$\$5,835 \times 0.98 = \$5,718.30$ net amount

19. No cash discount allowed.
$392.34 is due.

20. $400 payment is within the 3% discount period.
$1 - 0.03 = 0.97$ complement
$\dfrac{400}{0.97} = \$412.37$ amount credited to account
$\$730 - \$412.37 = \$317.63$ outstanding balance

21. $2,000 payment is within the 3% discount period.
$1 - 0.03 = 0.97$ complement
$\dfrac{\$2,000}{0.97} = \$2,061.86$ amount credited to account
$\$3,982.48 - \$2,061.86 = \$1,920.62$ outstanding balance

22. $2,000 payment is within the 2% discount period.
$1 - 0.02 = 0.98$ complement
$\dfrac{\$2,000}{0.98} = \$2,040.82$ amount credited to account
$\$2,983 - \$2,040.82 = \$942.18$ outstanding balance

23. Better Bilt Bicycles paid the freight to the freight company.

25. The vendor pays the shipping company and adds the charge to Phyllis's invoice.

24. Mary Pretti pays the freight to the freight company.

26. FOB shipping point: Vendor pays shipping charges to the freight company.
Prepay and add: Vendor pays shipping charges to the freight company and adds these charges to the invoice. The receiving company pays shipping charges to the vendor.

CHAPTER 7 OVERVIEW

Section—Objective | **Important Points with Examples**

7.1 — 1 (page 239)

Find the trade discount using a single trade discount rate; find the net price using the trade discount

Find the trade discount using a single trade discount rate   Multiply the list price by the single trade discount rate.

$$\text{Trade discount} = \text{single trade discount rate} \times \text{list price}$$

> The list price of a laminating machine is $76 and the single trade discount rate is 25%. Find the trade discount.
>
> Trade discount = 25% $\times$ $76
>
>   = 0.25 $\times$ 76
>
>   = $19

Find the net price using the trade discount   Subtract the trade discount from the list price.

$$\text{Net price} = \text{list price} - \text{trade discount}$$

> Find the net price when the list price is $76 and the trade discount is $19.
>
> Net price = $76 − $19
>
>   = $57

7.1 — 2 (page 240)

Find the net price using the complement of the single trade discount rate

Step 1 Find the complement: Subtract the single trade discount rate from 100%.

$$\text{Complement of single trade discount rate} = 100\% - \text{single trade discount rate}$$

Step 2 Multiply the list price by the complement of the single trade discount rate.

$$\text{Net price} = \text{complement of single trade discount rate} \times \text{list price}$$

OR

$$\text{Net price} = (100\% - \text{single trade discount rate}) \times \text{list price}$$

> The list price is $480 and the single trade discount rate is 15%. Find the net price.
>
> Net price = (100% − 15%)($480)
>
>   = 0.85 ($480)
>
>   = $408

 (page 243)

Find the net price applying a trade discount series using the net decimal equivalent

Step 1 Find the net decimal equivalent: Multiply the complements of the trade discounts, in decimal form, of all the rates in the series.

Net decimal equivalent = product of complements of trade discounts,

in decimal form

Step 2 Multiply the list price by the net decimal equivalent.

Net price = net decimal equivalent × list price

> The list price is $960 and the discount series is 10/5/2. Find the net price.
>
> Net decimal equivalent = (0.9)(0.95)(0.98) = 0.8379 *(complements)*
>
> Net price = (0.8379)($960) *Complement × list price*
>
> = $804.38

 (page 245)

Find the trade discount applying a trade discount series using the single discount equivalent

Step 1 Find the single discount equivalent: Subtract the net decimal equivalent from 1.

Single discount equivalent = 1 − net decimal equivalent

Step 2 Multiply the list price by the single discount equivalent.

Trade discount = single discount equivalent × list price

OR   Trade discount = (1 − net decimal equivalent) × list price

> The list price is $2,800 and the discount series is 25/15/10. Find the trade discount.
>
> Net decimal equivalent = (0.75)(0.85)(0.9) = 0.57375
>
> Single decimal equivalent = 1 − 0.57375 = 0.42625
>
> Trade discount = (0.42625)($2,800)
>
> = $1,193.50

7.3 — 1 (page 250)

Find the cash discount and the net amount using ordinary dating terms

Interpret ordinary dating terms To find the last day to receive a discount, add to the invoice date the number of days specified in the terms. If this sum is greater than the number of days in the month the invoice is dated, subtract from the sum the number of days in the month the invoice is dated. The result is the last date the cash discount is allowed. Use the knuckle method to remember how many days are in each month, or use the days-in-a-month rhyme.

> By what date must an invoice dated July 10 be paid if it is due in ten days?
>
> July 10 + 10 days = July 20
>
> By what date must an invoice dated May 15 be paid if it is due in 30 days?
>
> May 15 + 30 = "May 45"
>
> May is a "knuckles" month, so it has 31 days.
>
> "May 45" − 31 days in May = June 14
>
> The invoice must be paid on or before June 14.

Step 1 Find the cash discount: Multiply the cash discount rate by the net price.

$$\text{Cash discount} = \text{cash discount rate} \times \text{net price}$$

Step 2 Find the net amount using the cash discount: Subtract the cash discount from the net price.

$$\text{Net amount} = \text{net price} - \text{cash discount}$$

Step 3 Find the net amount using the complement of the cash discount rate: Multiply the net price by the complement of the cash discount rate.

$$\text{Net amount} = \text{complement of cash discount rate} \times \text{net price}$$

OR

$$\text{Net amount} = (100\% - \text{cash discount rate}) \times \text{net price}$$

An invoice is dated July 17 with terms 2/10, n/30 on a $2,500 net price. What is the latest date a cash discount is allowed? What is the net amount due on that date? On what date may interest begin accruing? What is the net amount due one day earlier?

Sale terms 2/10, n/30 mean the buyer takes a 2% cash discount if he or she pays within ten days of the invoice date; interest may accrue after the 30th day.

Latest discount date = July 17 + 10 days = July 27

$$\text{Net amount} = (100\% - 2\%)(\$2,500)$$
$$= (0.98)(\$2,500)$$
$$= \$2,450$$

Latest no-interest date = July 17 + 30 = "July 47"

"July 47" − 31 days in July = Aug 16

Interest begins accruing Aug 17. On Aug 16 the amount due is the net price of $2,500.

7.3 — 2 (page 252)

Interpret and apply end-of-month (EOM) terms

To an invoice dated **before the 26th** date of the month: A cash discount is allowed when the bill is paid by the specified day of the *next month*. To an invoice dated **on or after the 26th** day of the month: A cash discount is allowed when the bill is paid by the specified day of the *month after the next month*.

An invoice dated November 5 shows terms of 2/10 EOM on a $880 net price. By what date does the invoice have to be paid in order to get the cash discount? What is the net amount due on that date?

Sale terms 2/10 EOM for an invoice dated on or before the 26th day of a month means a 2% cash discount is allowed if the invoice is paid on or before the 10th day of the next month.

Latest discount day = December 10

$$\text{Net amount} = (100\% - 2\%)(\$880)$$
$$= (0.98)(\$880)$$
$$= \$862.40$$

 **7.3 — 3** (page 253)

Interpret and apply receipt-of-goods (ROG) terms

A cash discount is allowed when the bill is paid within the specified number of days from the **receipt of goods,** not from the date of the invoice.

> What is the net amount due on April 8 for an invoice dated March 28 with terms of 1/10 ROG on a net price of $500? The shipment arrived April 1.
>
> Sales terms 1/10 ROG mean a 1% cash discount is allowed if the invoice is paid within ten days of the receipt of goods.
>
> April 8 is within ten days of April 1, the date the shipment is received, so the cash discount is allowed.
>
> Net amount = (100% − 1%)($500)
>
>   = (0.99)($500)
>
>   = $495

 **7.3 — 4** (page 254)

Find the amount credited and the outstanding balance from partial payments

Step 1 Find the amount credited to the account: Divide the partial payment by the complement of the cash discount rate.

$$\text{Amount credited} = \frac{\text{partial payment}}{\text{complement of cash discount rate}}$$

Step 2 Find the outstanding balance: Subtract the amount credited from the net price.

$$\text{Outstanding balance} = \text{net price} - \text{amount credited}$$

OR

$$\text{Outstanding balance} = \text{net price} - \frac{\text{partial payment}}{\text{complement of cash discount rate}}$$

> Estrada's Restaurant purchased carpet for $1,568 with sales terms of 3/10, n/30 and paid $1,000 on the bill within the ten days specified. How much was credited to Estrada's account and what balance remained?
>
> Amount credited to account = $1,000 ÷ 0.97 = $1,030.93
> Outstanding balance = $1,568 − $1,030.93 = $537.07

(handwritten in margin: 100% −3% .97)

7.3 — 5 (page 255)

Interpret freight terms

If the bill of lading is marked **FOB (free on board) shipping point,** or **freight collect,** the buyer is responsible for paying freight expenses directly to the freight company. If the bill of lading is marked **FOB destination** or **freight paid,** the shipper is responsible for paying freight expenses directly to the freight company. If the bill of lading is marked **prepay and add,** the buyer is responsible for paying the freight expenses to the seller, who pays the freight company. Cash discounts do not apply to freight charges.

> A shipment is sent from a manufacturer in Boston to a wholesaler in Dallas and is marked FOB destination. Who is responsible for the freight cost? The manufacturer is responsible and pays the shipper.

CHAPTER 7 REVIEW

Section 7.1

Complete the following table. Round results to the nearest cent.

List Price	Single Discount Rate	Trade Discount
1. $300	15%	_____
2. $48	10%	_____
3. $127.50	20%	_____
4. $100	12%	_____
5. $37.85	20%	_____
6. $425	15%	_____

7. Find the trade discount on a conference table listed at $1,025 less 10% (single discount rate).

8. The list price for velvet by Harris Fabrics is $6.25 per yard less 6%. What is the trade discount? Round to the nearest cent.

9. Find the trade discount on a suit listed at $165 less 12%.

10. Rocha Bros. offered a $12\frac{1}{2}$% trade discount on a tractor listed at $10,851. What was the trade discount? Round to the nearest cent.

11. Find the trade discount on an order of 30 lamps listed at $35 each less 9%.

12. The list price for a big screen TV is $1,480 and the trade discount is $301. What is the net price?

13. The list price on skirts is $22, and the list price on corduroy jumpers is $37. If Petitt's Clothing Store orders 30 skirts and 40 jumpers at a discount rate of 11%, what is the trade discount on the purchase?

14. A stationery shop bought 10 boxes of writing paper that were listed at $1 each and 200 greeting cards listed at $0.50 each. If the single discount rate for the purchase is 15%, find the trade discount.

Complete the following table. Round all results to the nearest cent.

List Price	Trade Discount	Net Price
15. $21	$3	_____
16. $24.62	$5.93	_____
17. $6.85	$0.72	_____
18. $0.89	$0.12	_____

19. A camera has a list price of $378.61 with a trade discount of $42.58. What is the net price?

20. The list price of carpeting from Marie's Mill Outlet is $19 per square yard. The trade discount is $2.50 per square yard. What is the net price per square yard?

X

Complete the following table. Round results to the nearest cent.

	List Price	Single Discount Rate	Trade Discount	Net Price
21.	$ 25	5%	_____	_____
22.	$1,263	12%	_____	_____
23.	$ 0.89	2%	_____	_____
24.	$ 27.50	3%	_____	_____
25.	$2,100	17%	_____	_____
26.	$8,952	18%	_____	_____

Complete the following table.

	List Price	Single Discount Rate	Complement	Net Price
27.	$ 15.97	4%	96%	15.33
28.	$ 421	5%	_____	_____
29.	$ 138.54	6%	_____	_____
30.	$ 721.18	3%	_____	_____
31.	$ 16.97	11%	_____	_____
32.	$3,983.00	8%	_____	_____

100% − .04 = 96%
15.97 × .96 = 15.33

Section 7.2

Complete the following table. Round results to the nearest cent.

	List Price	Trade Discount Series	Decimal Equivalents of Complements	Net Decimal Equivalent	Net Price
33.	$ 200	20/10	_____	_____	_____
34.	$ 50	10/7/5	(.9)(.93)(.95) =	.79515	53.76
35.	$1,500	20/15/10	_____	_____	_____
36.	$ 35	20/15/5	_____	_____	_____
37.	$ 400	15/5	_____	_____	_____
38.	$2,834	5/10/10	_____	_____	_____

① 100% − 10%
   100% − 7%
   100% − 5%
② (.9)(.93)(.95) =
③ .79515
   × 50

39. A trade discount series of 10/5 was allowed on ladies' scarves listed at $4. What was the net price of each scarf?

40. Find the net price of an item listed at $800 with a trade discount series of 25/10/5.

41. A trade discount series of 10/5/5 is offered on a typewriter, which is listed at $800. Also, a trade discount series of 5/10/5 is offered on a desk chair listed at $250. Find the total net price for the typewriter and the chair. Round to the nearest cent.

42. Five desks are listed at $400 each, with a trade discount series of 20/10/10. Also, ten bookcases are listed at $200 each, discounted 10/20/10. Find the total net price for the desks and bookcases.

Complete the following table. Round results to the nearest cent.

Net Decimal Equivalent	Net Decimal Equivalent in Percent Form	Single Discount Equivalent in Percent Form	
43. 0.765	_____	_____	
44. 0.82	*82%*	*18%*	*100% − 82% = .18*
45. 0.6835	_____	_____	
46. 0.6502	*65.02%*	*34.98%*	*100% − 65.02% = .3498*
47. 0.7434	_____	_____	
48. 0.758	_____	_____	

Find the single discount equivalent for the following discount series.

49. 20/10

50. 30/20/5

51. 10%, 5%, 2%

52. 10%, 10%, 5%

53. 10/5 *(.9)(.95)=85.5%*
100% − 85.5% = 14.5%

54. 20/15

55. A television set is listed at $400 less 20%. The same set is listed by another manufacturer for $425 less 24%. Which is the better deal?

56. A hutch is listed at $650 with a trade discount of $65. The same hutch is listed by another manufacturer for $595 with a trade discount of $25. Which is the better deal?

57. One manufacturer lists an aquarium for $58.95 with a trade discount of $5.90. Another manufacturer lists the same aquarium for $60 with a trade discount of $9.45. Which is the better deal?

58. One manufacturer lists a table at $200 less 12%. Another manufacturer lists the same table at $190 less 10%. Which is the better deal?

59. One manufacturer lists picture frames at $20 each, discounted 10/10/10. Another manufacturer lists the same picture frames at $19 with a trade discount series of 10/5/10. Which is the better deal?

60. A trunk is listed at $250 discounted 10/10/5. The same trunk is listed by another manufacturer for $260 discounted 10/10/10. Which is the better deal?

Section 7.3

61. Mr. Matthews received a bill dated March 1 with sales terms of 3/10, n/30. What percent discount will he receive if he pays the bill on March 5?

62. Ms. Wagner received a bill dated September 3 with sales terms of 2/10, n/30. Did she receive a discount if she paid the bill on September 15?

63. An invoice dated February 13 had sales terms of 2/10, n/30. The bill was paid February 19. Was a cash discount allowed?

64. Mr. Carruth received an invoice for $300 dated March 3 with sales terms of 1/10, n/30. He paid the bill on March 6. What was his cash discount?

65. Find the cash discount on an invoice for $270 dated April 17 with terms of 2/10, n/30 if the bill was paid April 22.

66. Find the cash discount on an invoice for $50 dated May 3 with terms 1/15, n/30 if the bill was paid May 14.

67. Ray Collings received an invoice dated June 5 for $70 with terms of 2/10, n/30. He paid the bill on June 9. What was his cash discount and how much did he pay?

68. Florence Randle received an invoice dated July 3 for $165 with terms of 2/10, n/30. She paid the bill on July 7. How much did she pay?

69. How much would have to be paid on an invoice for $350 with terms of 2/10, 1/15, n/30, if the bill is paid (a) 7 days after the invoice date; (b) 15 days after the invoice date; (c) 25 days after the invoice date?

70. How much would have to be paid on an invoice for $28 with terms of 3/10 EOM if the bill dated June 8 is paid (a) July 2; (b) July 20?

71. Susan Rains received an invoice for $650 dated January 26. The sales terms in the invoice were 2/10 EOM. She paid the bill on March 4. How much did Susan pay?

72. How much would have to be paid on an invoice for $328 with terms of 2/10 ROG if the merchandise invoice is dated January 3, the merchandise arrives January 8, and the invoice is paid (a) January 11; (b) January 15; (c) January 25?

73. An invoice for $5,298 has terms of 3/10 ROG and is dated March 15. The merchandise is received on March 20. How much should be paid if the invoice is paid on March 25?

74. Find the amount credited and the outstanding balance on an invoice dated August 19 if a partial payment of $500 is paid on August 25 and has terms of 3/10, 1/15, n/30. The amount of the invoice is $826.

75. An invoice for $1,200 is dated June 3, and terms of 3/10, n/30 are offered. A payment of $800 is made on June 12, and the remainder is paid on July 2. Find the amount remitted on July 2 and the total amount paid.

76. Campbell Sales purchased merchandise worth $745 and made a partial payment of $300 on day 13. If the sales terms were 2/15, n/30, how much was credited to the account? What was the outstanding balance?

77. Elmer Wilson purchased roll vinyl floor covering for $1,150 with sales terms of 3/15, n/30. He paid $800 on the bill within 15 days. How much was credited to his account? What was his outstanding balance after the payment?

78. A shipment of trailer parts has a bill of lading marked "FOB destination." Does the purchaser or vendor (seller) pay the freight? Who first receives the freight expense, the purchaser, vendor, or freight company?

79. Ultra Products Manufacturing Company places a shipment with a trucking company to be shipped "FOB shipping point." Who pays the freight?

80. Swift's Dairy Mart receives a shipment of refrigeration units totaling $2,386.50 including a shipping charge of $32. Swift's returns $350 worth of the units. Terms of the purchase are 2/10, n/30. If Swift's takes advantage of the discount, what is the net amount payable?

81. An important part of owning a business is the purchasing of equipment and supplies to run the office. Before paying an invoice, all items must be checked and amounts refigured before writing the check for payment. At this time the terms of the invoice can be applied.

Using the information on the invoice below, fill in the extended amount for each line, the merchandise total, the tax amount, and the total invoice amount. Locate the terms of the invoice and find how much you would write a check for to pay Harper on each of the following dates:

March 5, 19XX
March 12, 19XX
March 25, 19XX

INVOICE DATE	TERMS	DATE OF ORDER	ORDERED BY	PHONE NO.	REMIT TO ▶	HARPER General Accounting Office
02/27/XX	2/10, 1/15, n/30	02/27/XX		803-000-4488		

LINE NO.	MANUFACTURER PRODUCT NUMBER	QTY. ORD.	QTY. B.O.	QTY. SHP.	U/M	DESCRIPTION	UNIT PRICE	EXTENDED AMOUNT
001	REMYY370/02253	3	0	3	EA	TONER, F/ROYAL TA210 COP 1	11.90	
002	Sk 1230M402	5	0	3	EA	CORRECTABLE FILM RIBBON	10.95	
003	JRLM01023	10	0	10	EA	COVER-UP CORRECTION TAPE	9.90	
004	rTu123456	9	0	9	EA	PAPER, BOND, WHITE 8 1/2 x 11	58.23	

DATE REC'D.____	01460900001		5%		$0.00	TOTAL INVOICE AMOUNT ▶	
	OUR ORDER NO.	MDSE. TOTAL	TAX RATE	TAX AMOUNT	FREIGHT AMOUNT		

82. Mary Stone saved $15.98 by taking advantage of a $3\frac{1}{2}\%$ cash discount on an invoice. What was the amount of the invoice?

CHAPTER 7 PRACTICE TEST

1. The list price of a refrigerator is $550. The retailer can buy the refrigerator at the list price minus 20%. Find the trade discount.

2. The list price of a television is $560. The trade discount is $27.50. What is the net price?

3. A retailer can buy a lamp that is listed at $36.55 for 20% less than the list price. How much does the retailer have to pay for the lamp?

4. A manufacturer lists a dress at $39.75 with a trade discount of $3.60. Another manufacturer lists the same dress at $42 with a trade discount of $6.75. Which is the better deal?

5. One manufacturer lists a chair for $250 less 20%. Another manufacturer lists the same chair at $240 less 10%. Which manufacturer is offering the better deal?

6. Find the net price if a discount series of 20/10/5 is deducted from $70.

7. Find the net decimal equivalent of the series 20/10/5.

8. Find the single discount equivalent for the discount series 20/20/10.

9. What do the initials ROG represent?

10. A retailer buys 20 boxes of stationery at $4 each and 400 greeting cards at $0.50 each. The discount rate for the order is 15%. Find the trade discount.

11. A retailer buys 30 electric frying pans listed at $40 each for 10% less than the list price. How much does the retailer have to pay for the frying pans?

12. What is the complement of 15%?

13. What do the initials EOM represent?

14. Ms. Ryan received a bill dated September 1 with sales terms of 3/10, 1/15, n/30. What percent discount will she receive if she pays the bill on September 6?

15. Mr. Williams received an invoice for $200 dated March 6 with sales terms 1/10, n/30. He paid the bill on March 9. What was his cash discount?

16. Mrs. Montgomery received a bill for $300 dated April 7. The sales terms on the invoice were 2/10 EOM. If she paid the bill on May 2, how much did Mrs. Montgomery pay?

17. An invoice for $400 dated December 7 has sales terms of 2/10 ROG. The merchandise arrived December 11. If the bill is paid on December 18, what is the net amount due?

18. If the bill in Exercise 17 is paid on January 2, what is the amount due?

19. A trade discount series of 10% and 20% is offered on 20 dartboards that are listed at $14 each. Also, a trade discount series of 20% and 10% is offered on 10 bowling balls that are listed at $40 each. Find the total net price for the dartboards and bowling balls.

20. Zing Manufacturing lists artificial flower arrangements at $30 less 10% and 10%. Another manufacturer lists the same flower arrangements at $31 less 10%, 10%, and 5%. Which is the better deal?

21. The Dean Specialty Company purchased monogrammed items worth $895 and made a partial payment of $600 on day 12. If the sales terms were 3/15, n/30, how much was credited to the account? What was the outstanding balance?

22. The monogrammed items purchased by Dean Specialty Company are shipped by rail from the manufacturer. The bill of lading is marked "FOB destination." Who is responsible for paying freight expenses?

CHAPTER 8

MARKUP AND MARKDOWN

Choose a seasonal product and develop a pricing strategy to maximize profit. Begin by identifying and discussing the factors to consider in your strategy, including cost per unit, quantity purchased, typical markup, the effect of markdowns on quantity sold, and the period of time you can expect to sell the product. In judging the effect of markdowns, take into account the tendency of consumers to purchase products when they aren't necessary, or seasonal products when they aren't yet needed, to take advantage of a discount. Discuss the impact of offering a "percent off sale" versus a "dollars off" sale.

Interview local retailers of your chosen product about these pricing issues. Based on your team discussions and interviews, decide on your pricing strategy. Document for various dates the price, quantity sold, and profit from sale. Determine your total profit (or loss) from your initial purchase, and prepare a summary report for presentation to the class.

8.1 Markup

1 ▶ *Find the markup, cost, selling price, rate of markup, or rate of selling price when the markup is based on cost*

2 ▶ *Find the markup, cost, selling price, rate of markup, or rate of cost when the markup is based on selling price*

3 ▶ *Compare markup based on cost with markup based on selling price*

8.2 Markdown

1 ▶ *Find the markdown, cheaper price, original selling price, rate of markdown, or rate of cheaper price*

8.3 Markup and Markdown Series

1 ▶ *Find the final selling price for a series of markups and markdowns*

2 ▶ *Find the selling price to achieve a desired profit (markup)*

Any successful business must keep prices low enough to attract customers, yet high enough to pay expenses and make a profit.

The price at which a business purchases merchandise is called the **cost**. The merchandise is then sold at a higher price called the **selling price**. The difference between the selling price and the cost is the **markup** or **gross profit** or **margin**. Merchandise may also be reduced from the original selling price. The amount the selling price is reduced is called the **markdown**.

Markups and markdowns are an important part of operating a business.

8.1 Markup

1 ▶ *Find the markup, cost, selling price, rate of markup, or rate of selling price when the markup is based on cost*

2 ▶ *Find the markup, cost, selling price, rate of markup, or rate of cost when the markup is based on selling price*

3 ▶ *Compare markup based on cost with markup based on selling price*

The markup rate can be calculated as a percentage of either the cost or the selling price of an item. Most manufacturers calculate markup as a percentage of *cost*, since they typically keep their records in terms of cost. Some wholesalers and a few retailers also use this method. Most retailers, however, use the *selling price* as a base in computing markup, since they keep most of their records in terms of selling price.

Three basic formulas describe the relationship between cost, markup, and selling price, regardless of whether the markup rate is a percentage of cost or selling price. You can use these formulas to find the value of any one of the three amounts if you know the values of the other two.

$$\text{Selling price} = \text{cost} + \text{markup}, \qquad S = C + M$$

$$\text{Cost} = \text{selling price} - \text{markup}, \qquad C = S - M$$

$$\text{Markup} = \text{selling price} - \text{cost}, \qquad M = S - C$$

The first of the three formulas is the one that is referred to most often. The techniques we learned in solving equations can be applied in the first formula no matter which amount is unknown. Similarly, whether markup is based on cost or selling price, the *rate* of markup, the *rate* of selling price, and the *rate* of cost are related in the same way.

$$\text{Rate of } S = \text{rate of } C + \text{rate of } M$$

$$\text{Rate of } C = \text{rate of } S - \text{rate of } M$$

$$\text{Rate of } M = \text{rate of } S - \text{rate of } C$$

 Using Cost as a Base in Markup Applications

Most "markup problems" give you three facts and ask you to find additional facts. To organize the information you have and determine what you need to find, draw up a table using the cost (C) + markup (M) = selling price (S) formula.

When markup is based on cost, the rate of cost is always 100%, as noted in the table. The rest of the numbers, both percents and dollars, can be filled in according to the facts of the given situation.

> **(?) HOW TO**   **Find the Markup *M*, Cost *C*, Selling Price *S*, Rate of Markup, or Rate of Selling Price When the Markup is Based on Cost**
>
> **Step 1**   Place known information in the table.
>
> | | | | |
> |---|---|---|---|
> | C | $\$\underline{\quad}$ | rate of C | 100% |
> | $+M$ | $\$\underline{\quad}$ | + rate of M | $\underline{\quad}\%$ |
> | S | $\$\underline{\quad}$ | rate of S | $\underline{\quad}\%$ |
>
> **Step 2**   If one dollar value and and two rates are missing:
>
>   **a)** Use one of the markup formulas to find the missing dollar value:
>
> $$S = C + M \qquad \text{if } S \text{ is missing}$$
>
> $$C = S - M \qquad \text{if } C \text{ is missing}$$
>
> $$M = S - C \qquad \text{if } M \text{ is missing}$$
>
>   **b)** Use the percentage formula $R = \frac{P}{B}$ to find a missing rate. R is a missing rate, P is its corresponding dollar value, and B is the dollar value of the cost.
>
>   **c)** Use one of the rate-of-markup formulas to find the other missing rate.
>
> $$\text{Rate of } S = 100\% + \text{rate of } M \qquad \text{if rate of } S \text{ is missing}$$
>
> $$\text{Rate of } M = \text{rate of } S - 100\% \qquad \text{if rate of } M \text{ is missing}$$
>
> **Step 3**   If one rate and two dollar values are missing:
>
>   **a)** Do step 2c to find the missing rate.
>
>   **b)** Use one of the percentage formulas to find a missing dollar value. P is either markup M or selling price S, R is its corresponding rate, and B is cost C.
>
> $$P = RB \qquad \text{if } S \text{ or } M \text{ is missing but } C \text{ is not}$$
>
> $$B = \frac{P}{R} \qquad \text{if } C \text{ is missing}$$
>
>   **c)** Do step 2a to find the final dollar value.

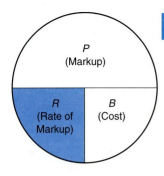

Figure 8–1 Percentage Formula Diagram

Example 1 The Van Dyke's Hat Shoppe buys hats from Carroll Millinery for $6 each and sells them for $10 each. Find the markup and the rate of markup based on cost. Check by using the rate of the selling price based on cost.

First, use a table to set up the problem. Remember, when doing a markup based on cost, the rate of cost is always 100%. Fill in the other two amounts you know from the problem: cost = $6 and selling price = $10.

C	$ 6	rate of C	100%
$+M$	$____	+ rate of M	____%
S	$10	rate of S	____%

Since M is what you are looking for, you need to use the formula $M = S - C$ (Markup = selling price − cost). The markup is $4, since $10 - 6 = 4$.

Next, use the percentage formula to find the *rate* of markup based on cost. As you saw in Chapter 3, the percentage formula may be written $P = R \times B$, $R = \frac{P}{B}$, or $B = \frac{P}{R}$. When finding the rate of markup based on cost, use the cost as the *base B*, the markup as the *percentage P*, and the rate of markup as the *rate R*. The percentage formula diagram is shown in Figure 8–1.

Use the form $R = \frac{P}{B}$ of the percentage formula to find the rate of markup based on the cost.

$$R = \frac{P}{B} = \frac{M}{C} = \frac{4}{6}$$

Divide the markup (percentage) by the cost (base) to find the rate of markup (rate).

$$= 0.6666, \text{ or } 67\% \text{ (rounded)}$$ The rate of markup based on cost is 67%.

Now use the relationship 100% + rate of markup = rate of selling price to find the rate of selling price:

C	$ 6	rate of C	100%
$+M$	$ 4	+ rate of M	67%
S	$10	rate of S	167%

Check:

$$P = R \times B$$

$$= 167\% \times 6 = 1.67 \times 6$$ Cost ($10) is still the *base.*

$$= \$10 \text{ (rounded)}$$ The answer is correct.

The markup is $4 and the percent of markup based on cost is 67%.

In most instances, you may know the cost and the rate of markup based on cost, and need to find the markup and the selling price. You can compute these amounts more easily if you use the table format.

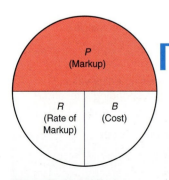

Figure 8–2 Markup = Rate of Markup × Cost

Example 2 A boutique pays $5 a pair for handmade earrings and sells them at a 50% markup rate based on cost. Find the markup and the selling price of the earrings.

Fill in the table with known data.

C	$5	rate of C	100%
$+M$	$____	+ rate of M	50%
S	$____	rate of S	____%

Add the cost rate (100%) and the markup rate (50%) to find the selling price rate (150%).

Use the percentage formula $P = R \times B$ (Figure 8–2) to find the markup:

$P = 0.5 \times 5$ **Multiply the rate of markup (rate) by the cost (base) to find the amount of markup (percentage).**

$P = \$2.50$

Now we add the cost and markup to find the selling price and complete the table:

C	$5	rate of C	100%
$+M$	$2.50	$+$rate of M	$+$ 50%
S	$7.50	rate of S	**150%** The selling price is $7.50.

Check:

$P = R \times B$

$= \boxed{150\%} \times 5 = \boxed{1.5} \times 5 = \$7.50$ **The answer is correct.**

The markup is $2.50 and the selling price is $7.50.

To enhance sales, sometimes items are marked down from the selling price. Before making the decision to mark down merchandise, you want to know how much the item costs. When researching the cost through invoices is impractical, you can calculate the cost and markup by using the selling price when you know the standard markup rate.

Example 3   A camera sells for $20. The markup rate is 50% of the cost. Find the cost of the camera and the markup.

Fill in the table with known data.

C	$13.33	rate of C	100%
M	$6.67	$+$ rate of M	50%
S	$20	rate of S	150%

Add the cost rate (100%) and the markup rate (50%) to find the selling price rate (150%).

Now find the missing cost. Use the formula $B = \frac{P}{B}$ (Figure 8–3), since B is the base, or cost.

$$B = \frac{P}{R} = \frac{\text{selling price}}{\text{rate of selling price}} = \frac{20}{\boxed{150\%}} = \frac{20}{\boxed{1.5}}$$

$$= \$13.33, \text{ rounded to the nearest cent}$$

Thus, the cost is $13.33. To find the markup, use the markup formula $M = S - C$.

$\$20 - \$13.33 = \$6.67.$

Complete the table and check:

C	$13.33	rate of C	100%
$+ M$	$6.67	$+$ rate of M	50%
S	$20.00	rate of S	**150%**

Check:

$P = R \times B$

$= \boxed{150\%} \times 13.33 = \boxed{1.5} \times 13.33 = \$20 \text{ (rounded)}$

The cost is $13.33 and the markup is $6.67.

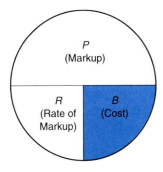

Figure 8–3   Cost $= \dfrac{\text{Markup}}{\text{Rate of Markup}}$

2▶ *Using the Selling Price as a Base in Markup Applications*

As noted earlier, most retailers base markup on the selling price because this method works best with their other records such as inventory. When the markup is based on *cost,* the *cost* is the *base,* and the rate of cost is 100%. Similarly, when the markup is based on *selling price,* the *selling price* is the *base,* and the rate of selling price is 100%.

? HOW TO **Find the Markup *M*, Cost *C*, Selling Price *S*, Rate of Markup, or Rate of Cost When the Markup is Based on Selling Price**

Step 1 Place known information in the table.

C	$___	rate of *C*	___%
+*M*	$___	+rate of *M*	___%
S	$___	rate of *S*	100%

Step 2 If one dollar value and two rates are missing:
   a) Use one of the markup formulas to find the missing dollar value.

$$S = C + M \quad \text{if } S \text{ is missing}$$

$$C = S - M \quad \text{if } C \text{ is missing}$$

$$M = S - C \quad \text{if } M \text{ is missing}$$

   b) Use the percentage formula $R = \frac{P}{B}$ to find a missing rate. *R* is a missing rate, *P* is its corresponding dollar value, and *B* is selling price.
   c) Use one of the rate-of-markup formulas to find the other missing rate.

$$\text{Rate of } C = 100\% - \text{rate of } M \quad \text{if rate of } C \text{ is missing}$$

$$\text{Rate of } M = 100\% - \text{rate of } C \quad \text{if rate of } M \text{ is missing}$$

Step 3 If one rate and two dollar values are missing:
   a) Do step 2c to find the missing rate.
   b) Use one of the percentage formulas to find a missing dollar value. *P* is either markup *M* or cost *C*, *R* is its corresponding rate, and *B* is selling price *S*.

$$P = RB \quad \text{if } C \text{ or } M \text{ is missing but } S \text{ is not}$$

$$B = \frac{P}{R} \quad \text{if } S \text{ is missing}$$

   c) Do step 2a to find the final dollar value.

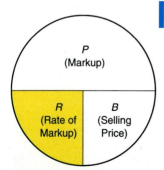

Figure 8–4 Rate of markup = $\dfrac{\text{Markup}}{\text{Selling Price}}$

Example 4 A calculator costs $5 and sells for $10. Find the rate of markup based on selling price.

Fill in the table with known data.

C	$ 5	rate of *C*	___%	**The markup is based on selling**
+ *M*	$___	+rate of *M*	___%	**price, so you know the rate of**
S	$10	rate of *S*	100%	**selling price is 100%.**

$\begin{array}{r} \$10 \\ -\$\ 5 \\ \hline \$\ 5 \end{array}$ **Use the formula *M* = *S* − *C*: Subtract the cost from the selling price to find the markup.**

Use the percentage formula $R = \frac{P}{B}$ (Figure 8-4) to find the rate of markup. The markup, $5, is the percentage *P*, and the selling price, $10, is the base *B*.

$$R = \frac{P}{B} = \frac{\text{markup}}{\text{selling price}} = \frac{5}{10} = 0.5 = \boxed{50\%}$$ The rate of markup based on selling price is 50%.

Complete the table as a check of your work. To complete the table, you still need the rate of cost.

C	$ 5	rate of C	50%
+ M	$ 5	+ rate of M	50%
S	$10	rate of S	100%

Subtract the markup rate (50%) from the selling price rate (100%) to find the cost rate: 100% − 50% = 50%.

Check:

$$P = R \times B$$

$$= \boxed{50\%} \times 10 = \boxed{0.5} \times 10 = \$5$$ The answer is correct.

The rate of markup based on selling price is 50%.

In some instances you may have records indicating the markup and the rate of markup but not the cost or the selling price. While the cost and selling price can be calculated from the markup and rate of markup, it is not likely that this situation will occur often.

Example 5 Find the cost and selling price if a textbook is marked up $5 with a 20% markup rate based on selling price.

If the selling price rate is 100% and the markup rate is 20%, then the cost rate equals 100% − 20%, or 80%.

C	$____	rate of C	80%
+ M	$5	+ rate of M	20%
S	$____	rate of S	100%

Use the formula $B = \frac{P}{R}$ to find the base or selling price (Figure 8–5). The markup, $5, is the percentage *P*, and the rate of markup, 20%, is the rate *R* or 0.2.

$$B = \frac{P}{R} = \frac{\text{markup}}{\text{rate of markup}} = \frac{\$5}{0.2} = \$25$$ The base or selling price is $25.

Use the formula $C = S - M$ to find the cost and complete the table.

C	$20	rate of C	80%
+ M	$ 5	+ rate of M	20%
S	$25	rate of S	100%

Check:

$$\boxed{80\%} \times 25 = \boxed{0.08} \times 25 = \$20$$ The answer is correct.

The cost is $20 and the selling price is $25.

Figure 8–5 Selling Price =

Markup
———————
Rate of Markup

Example 6 Find the markup and cost of a box of pencils that sells for $2.99 and is marked up 25% of the selling price.

The rate of cost is 100% − the rate of markup, or 100% − 25%, or 75%.

C	$____	rate of C	75%
+ M	$____	+ rate of M	25%
S	$2.99	rate of S	100%

Figure 8–6 Markup = Rate of Markup × Selling Price

Since you are looking for the markup, or percentage *P*, use the formula $P = RB$ (Figure 8–6). The selling price, or base *B*, is $2.99, and the rate of markup, or rate *R*, is 25%.

$$P = RB$$

$$P = \text{rate of markup} \times \text{selling price}$$

$$P = 0.25(2.99)$$

$$P = \$0.75$$

Round to the nearest cent. The markup is $0.75.

Complete the table. $C = S - M$.

$$C = \$2.99 - \$0.75 = \$2.24$$

C	$2.24	rate of *C*	75%
+ *M*	$0.75	+ rate of *M*	25%
S	$2.99	rate of *S*	100%

Check:

$$\fbox{75\%} \times 2.99 = \fbox{0.75} \times 2.99$$

$$= \$2.24 \text{ (rounded)} \quad \text{The answer is correct.}$$

The markup is $0.75 and the cost is $2.24.

Example 7 Find the selling price and markup for a pair of jeans that costs the retailer $28 and is marked up 30% of the selling price.

Since one of the known values is the cost, we should find the percent that the cost is of the selling price.

$$100\% - 30\% = 70\% \quad \text{Selling price rate minus markup rate equals cost rate.}$$

C	$28	rate of *C*	70%
+ *M*	$____	+ rate of *M*	30%
S	$____	rate of *S*	100%

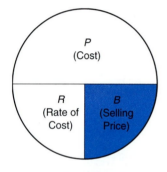

Figure 8–7 Selling Price = $\dfrac{\text{Cost}}{\text{Rate of Cost}}$

Use the formula $B = \frac{P}{R}$ (Figure 8–7) to find the selling price, or base *B*, given the cost, $28, as the percentage *P* and the rate of cost, 70%, as the rate *R*.

$$B = \frac{P}{R} = \frac{\text{cost}}{\text{rate of cost}} = \frac{\$28}{0.7} = \$40 \quad \text{The selling price is \$40.}$$

C	$28	rate of *C*	70%	($40 − $28 = $12)
+ *M*	$12	+ rate of *M*	30%	
S	$40	rate of *S*	100%	

Check:

$$\fbox{30\%} \times 40 = \fbox{0.3} \times 40 = \$12 \quad \text{The answer is correct.}$$

The selling price is $40 and the markup is $12.

 TIPS & TRAPS   **Finding the Rate of Markup**

To help remember a strategy for finding missing amounts or rates in markup problems, use these tips:

1. When the markup is based on cost, it means that the rate of the cost is given, and is 100%.

When the markup is based on selling price, it means that the rate of the selling price is given, and is 100%.

Thus, at least one rate is given in each instance.

2. If two dollar amounts and one rate are given, first find the third dollar amount. Then find the missing rates. See examples 1 and 4.

3. If two rates and one dollar amount are given, first find the missing rate. Then find the missing dollar amounts. See Examples 2, 3, 5, 6, and 7.

All markup problems are solved in basically the same way. The important thing to remember is that when the markup rate is based on selling price, the selling price is the base, so the selling price rate is 100%; when the markup rate is based on cost, the cost is the base, so the cost rate is 100%. You can then use the percentage formula or one of its variations, substitute in the known values, and solve for the missing value.

 TIPS & TRAPS

Look again at Examples 6 and 7 and Figures 8–6 and 8–7. When the *percentage* is the markup, the *rate* is the rate of markup. When the *percentage* is the *cost,* the *rate* is the rate of cost.

 Comparing Markup Based on Cost with Markup Based on Selling Price

If you go into a store and are told that the markup rate is 25%, you don't know whether that means markup based on cost or on selling price. What's the difference? Let's use a new computer as an example. The store pays \$1,500 for it and sells it for \$2,000. Here is the difference in rates of markup:

$$R = \frac{\$500 \text{ markup}}{\$2,000 \text{ selling price}} = 25\% \text{ markup based on selling price}$$

$$R = \frac{\$500 \text{ markup}}{\$1,500 \text{ cost}} = 33\frac{1}{3}\% \text{ markup based on cost}$$

There may be times when you need to switch from a markup based on selling price to a markup based on cost, or vice versa. Here is how to do it.

 **HOW TO** | **Convert a Markup Rate Based on Selling Price to a Markup Rate Based on Cost**

Step 1 Write the markup rate based on selling price in decimal form.
Step 2 Subtract the markup rate (decimal form) based on selling price from 1.
Step 3 Divide the markup rate (decimal form) based on selling price by the difference from step 2.

Markup rate (decimal form) based on cost
$$= \frac{\text{markup rate (decimal form) based on selling price}}{1 - \text{markup rate (decimal form) based on selling price}}$$

Example 8 A desk is marked up 25% based on selling price. What is the equivalent markup rate based on the cost?

$25\% = 0.25$ **Write the rate in decimal form.**

$$\text{Markup rate based on cost} = \frac{\text{markup rate based on selling price}}{1 - \text{markup rate of selling price}}$$

$$= \frac{0.25}{1 - 0.25} = \frac{0.25}{0.75} = 0.333 \text{ or } 33.3\%.$$

The markup rate based on cost is 33.3%.

Basic calculator using memory:

$$\boxed{AC}\ \boxed{MC}\ 1\ \boxed{-}\ .25\ \boxed{=}\ \boxed{M+}\ \boxed{C}\ .25\ \boxed{\div}\ \boxed{MR}\ \boxed{=}$$
Display 0.33333333

Scientific calculator using parenthesis:

$$\boxed{AC}\ .25\ \boxed{\div}\ \boxed{(}\ 1\ \boxed{-}\ .25\ \boxed{)}\ \boxed{=}$$
Display 0.33333333

 **HOW TO** | **Convert a Markup Rate Based on Cost to a Markup Rate Based on Selling Price**

Step 1 Write the markup rate based on cost in decimal form.
Step 2 Add the markup rate (decimal form) based on cost to 1.
Step 3 Divide the markup rate (decimal form) based on cost by the sum from step 2.

Markup rate (decimal form) based on selling price

$$= \frac{\text{markup rate (decimal form) based on cost}}{1 + \text{markup rate (decimal form) based on cost}}$$

Example 9 A VCR is marked up 40% based on cost. What is the markup percent based on selling price?

$$40\% = 0.4 \quad \textbf{Convert the percent to a decimal and use the formula.}$$

$$\text{Markup rate based on selling price} = \frac{\text{markup rate based on cost}}{1 + \text{markup rate based on cost}}$$

$$\frac{0.4}{1 + 0.4} = \frac{0.4}{1.4}$$

$$= 0.2857, \text{ or } 28.57\%$$

The markup rate based on selling price is 28.57%.

 TIPS & TRAPS

Here are some tips to help you remember the two formulas for converting between markup based on cost and markup based on selling price:

$$\text{Markup based on cost} = \frac{\text{original markup rate (M\%)}}{\text{original cost rate (C\%)}}$$

Since the original markup rate is based on the selling price, $S\% = 100\%$. The original

$$C\% = S\% - M\%.$$

$$= 100\% - M\%$$

$$= 1 - M\%$$

Similarly,

$$\text{Markup rate based on selling price} = \frac{\text{Original markup rate } (M\%)}{\text{Original selling price rate } (S\%)}$$

Since this original markup rate is based on the cost, $C\% = 100\%$.

$$\text{The original } S\% = C\% + M\%.$$

$$= 100\% + M\%$$

$$= 1 + M\%$$

AROUND THE BUSINESS WORLD

Big Macs Al Dente?

McDonald's is big all over the industrialized world—except in Italy. The burger chain boasts more than 1,000 outlets in Japan, 600 in Germany, 500 in Britain, and 294 in France. But devotion to traditional cooking has held the company to just 23 restaurants in Italy.

So, McDonald's is starting a major push to expand its Italian operations. The goal: 200 new outlets there over the next four years. Recently, the Golden Arches announced a deal to open 10 of them along superhighway rest stops, next to oil giant Agip Petroli's gas stations. McDonald's will be competing head-to-

head with Autogrill, a 322-store highway food chain that serves a rich menu including regional cuisine. Luigi Mele, head of McDonald's Italia, says his outfit's fast, efficient service and "much cleaner toilets" will win over motorists.

Indeed, the existing McDonald's restaurants in Italy are very popular, especially among the young, who are fascinated by Americana. In deference to local tastes, some outlets are built to blend in with the old surrounding buildings—and they serve espresso and cold pasta. Yet the primary fare is still highlighted by "un Big Mac."

Reprinted from November 28, 1994 issue of *Business Week* by special permission, copyright © 1994 by The McGraw-Hill Companies.

Self-Check 8.1

1. Bottoms Up buys mugs for $2 each and sells them for $6 each. Find the markup and the rate of markup based on cost.

2. It's a Cinch pays $4 each for handmade belts and sells them at a 60% markup rate based on cost. Find the markup and the selling price of the belts.

3. A compact disc player sells for $300. The markup rate is 40% of the cost. Find the cost of the CD player and the markup.

4. A compact disc costs $4 and sells for $12. Find the rate of markup based on the selling price.

5. Find the cost and selling price if a hard hat is marked up $5 with a 40% markup rate based on the selling price.

6. Find the markup and cost of a magazine that sells for $3.50 and is marked up 50% of the selling price.

7. Find the selling price and markup if a box of photocopier paper costs $40 and is marked up 60% of the selling price.

8. A chair is marked up 60% based on selling price. What is the rate of markup based on cost?

9. A surround sound audio system is marked up 75% based on selling price. What is the rate of markup based on cost?

10. A lamp is marked up 120% based on cost. What is rate of markup based on selling price?

11. A stereo TV is marked up 82% based on cost. What is the rate markup based on selling price?

8.2   Markdown

1 ▶ *Find the markdown, cheaper price, original selling price, rate of markdown, or rate of cheaper price*

Merchants often have to reduce the price of merchandise from the price at which it was originally sold. There are many reasons for this. Sometimes merchandise is marked too high to begin with. Sometimes it gets worn or dirty or goes out of style. Flowers, fruits, vegetables, and baked goods that have been around a day or two must be sold for less than fresh items because the quality of the items is not as good. Competition from other stores may also require that a retailer mark down prices.

1 ▶ ### *Using Markdown*

No matter what the reason for the reduction in price, you can determine the markdown by subtracting the cheaper price from the original selling price. You can then figure the rate of markdown by using a variation of the percentage formula, $R = \frac{P}{B}$. Unlike markups, which may be based on selling price *or* cost, markdowns, for all practical purposes, are always based on selling price. Applying the percentage formula, then, the base B is always the selling price.

The markup and rate of markup formulas we gave on page 272 actually apply to markdown situations, too. When we use the formulas for markdown situations, S is the original selling price, C is the cheaper price, and M is the markdown. The How-To box on page 276 applies as well. Here, too, S is the original selling price, C is the cheaper price, and M is the markdown. To reinforce these formulas and How-To steps, we repeat them here. Notice that the rate of the original selling price S is 100%, because the base for markdowns is the original selling price.

Original selling price = cheaper price + markdown $S = C + M$

Cheaper price = original selling price − markdown $C = S - M$

Markdown = original selling price − cheaper price $M = S - C$

100% = rate of C + rate of M

Rate of C = 100% − rate of M

Rate of M = 100% − rate of C

❓ **HOW TO**		**Find the Markdown, Cheaper Price, Original Selling Price, Rate of Markdown, or Rate of Cheaper Price**	

Step 1 Place known information in the table

		rate of C	
C	$____	rate of C	____%
+ M	$____	+ rate of M	____%
S	$____	rate of S	100%

Step 2 If one dollar value and two rates are missing:

a) Use one of the markdown formulas to find the missing dollar value:

$$S = C + M \quad \text{if } S \text{ is missing}$$
$$C = S - M \quad \text{if } C \text{ is missing}$$
$$M = S - C \quad \text{if } M \text{ is missing}$$

b) Use the percentage formula $R = \frac{P}{B}$ to find a missing rate. R is missing rate, P is its corresponding dollar value, and B is original selling price.

c) Use one of the rate-of-markdown formulas to find the other missing rate:

$$\text{Rate of } C = 100\% - \text{rate of } M \quad \text{if rate of } C \text{ is missing}$$
$$\text{Rate of } M = 100\% - \text{rate of } C \quad \text{if rate of } M \text{ is missing}$$

Step 3 If one rate and two dollar values are missing:

a) Do step 2c to find the missing rate.

b) Use one of the percentage formulas to find a missing dollar value. P is either markdown M or cheaper price C, R is its corresponding rate, and B is original selling price.

$$P = RB \quad \text{if } C \text{ or } M \text{ is missing but } S \text{ is not}$$
$$B = \frac{P}{R} \quad \text{if } S \text{ is missing}$$

c) Do step 2a to find the final dollar value.

▊ Example 1 A lamp originally sold for $36 and was marked down to sell for $30. Find the *markdown* and the *rate of markdown* (to the nearest hundredth).

Fill in the table with known data.

C	$30	rate of C	____%
+ M	$____	+ rate of M	____%
S	$36	rate of S	100%

Use the formula: Markdown = original selling price − cheaper price.

$$M = \$36 - \$30 = \$6$$

The markdown is $6.

Now use the formula $R = \frac{P}{B}$ to find the rate of markdown. The original selling price, $36, is the base B, and the markdown, $6, is the percentage P.

Figure 8–8 Rate of Markdown =
$$\frac{\text{Markdown}}{\text{Original Selling Price}}$$

$$R = \frac{P}{B} = \frac{\text{markdown}}{\text{original selling price}} = \frac{\$6}{\$36} = 0.1667 = 16.67\% \quad \textbf{(rounded)}$$

The lamp was marked down 16.67% of the original selling price.

To complete the table, the rate of cheaper price is 100% − 16.67% or 83.33%.

C	$30	rate of C	83.33%
+ M	$ 6	+ rate of M	16.67%
S	$36	rate of S	100 %

Check:

$$83.33\% \times \$36 = 0.8333 \times \$36 = \$30 \quad \text{The answer is correct.}$$

The amount of markdown is $6 and the rate of markdown is 16.67%.

Example 2

A wallet was originally priced at $12 and was reduced by 25%. Find the markdown and the sale price.

Fill in the table with known data.

C	$__	rate of C	__%
$+ M$	$__	+ rate of M	25%
S	$12	rate of S	100%

Use the formula: Rate of $C = 100\% -$ rate of M.

Rate of $C = 100\% - 25\% = 75\%$

The rate of the sale price, the cheaper price, is 75%.

Now use the percentage formula $P = RB$ (Figure 8-9) to find the markdown. The rate of markdown, 25%, is the rate R, and the original selling price, $12, is the base B.

$$P = RB = (\text{rate of markdown})(\text{selling price}) = 0.25 \times 12 = \$3$$

The markdown was $3.

Finally, to find the sale price, use the formula: Cheaper price = original selling price − markdown.

$$\text{Cheaper price} = \$12 - \$3 = \$9$$

The sale price was $9.

Figure 8–9 Markdown = Rate of Markdown × Original Price

C	$ 9	rate of C	75%
$+ M$	$ 3	+ rate of M	25%
S	$12	rate of S	100%

Check:

$$75\% \times \$12 = 0.75 \times \$12 = 9$$

The markdown is $3 and the sale price is $9.

Self-Check 8.2

1. A typewriter originally sold for $480 and was marked down to sell for $420. Find the markdown and the markdown rate.

2. A Sony handycam camcorder originally sold for $599.97 and was marked down to sell for $550. Find the markdown and the rate of markdown based on the original selling price.

3. An RCA 13″ TV with remote control originally sells for $169. It is marked down to sell for $139.97. Find the markdown and the rate of markdown.

4. Mickey Mania™ for Super Nintendo @ originally sells for $79.99. It is marked down to sell for $47.97. Find the markdown and the rate of markdown.

5. A Magnavox 4-head Hi-Fi Stereo VCR originally sells for $349.99 and is marked down to sell for $329.97. Find the markdown and the rate of markdown.

6. A calculator that was originally priced at $78 was reduced by 15%. Find the markdown and the sale price (reduced price).

7. A Maytag super capacity washer originally priced at $529.99 is reduced by 23%. Find the markdown and the sale price.

8. A Quasar microwave oven originally priced at $159.99 has been placed on sale with a 25% markdown. Find the markdown and the sale price.

9. An Amana 25.0 cu. ft. refrigerator with cubed ice and water dispenser was originally priced at $1,399.97 and is included in a Memorial Day sale at a 21% discount. Find the markdown and the sale price.

10. A Motorola flip portable cellular phone weighing only 9.9 ounces is included in a Memorial Day sale. It was originally priced at $59.99 and is marked down by 19%. What sale price should be listed for the phone?

8.3 Markup and Markdown Series

1 *Find the final selling price for a series of markups and markdowns*

2 *Find the selling price to achieve a desired profit (markup)*

Prices are in a continuous state of flux in the business world. Markups are made to cover increased costs. Markdowns are made to move merchandise more rapidly or to move dated or perishable merchandise.

 Finding the Final Selling Price for a Series of Markups and Markdowns

Every business expects to mark down the price of seasonal and slow-moving merchandise. Sometimes prices are marked down several times or marked up between markdowns before the merchandise is sold. Calculating each stage of prices, markups, markdowns, and rates, we use exactly the same markup/markdown formulas and How-To steps as before. To apply these formulas and How-To steps, though, we must be sure we understand that both the markup and the markdown are based on the *previous selling price* in the series. So:

- For a stage that requires a **markdown,** identify the previous selling price as the *original selling price S* for this stage. Then use the How-To steps for markdown to find *the cheaper price C.* This price is the selling price for this stage in the series.
- For a stage that requires a **markup,** identify the previous selling price as the *cost C* for this stage. Then use the How-To steps for markup *based on cost* to find the *selling price S.* This price is the selling price for this stage in the series.

 **HOW TO** | **Find the Final Selling Price for a Series of Markups and Markdowns**

Step 1 For the first stage in the series, find the first selling price, if it isn't known already, using the first markup/markdown facts and the How-To steps for markup or markdown.

Step 2 For each remaining stage in the series:
  a) If the stage requires a **markdown,** identify the previous selling price as the *original selling price S* for this stage. Use the How-To steps for markdown to find the *cheaper price C.* This price is the selling price for this stage.
  b) If the stage requires a **markup,** identify the previous selling price as the *cost C* for this stage. Use the How-To steps for markup *based on cost* to find the *selling price S.* This price is the selling price for this stage.

Step 3 Identify the selling price for the last stage as the *final selling price.*

Example 1 Belinda's China Shop paid a wholesale price of $800 for a set of imported china. August 8, Belinda marked up the china 50% based on the cost. On October 1, she marked the china down 25% for a special ten-day promotion. On October 11, she marked the china up 15%. The china was again marked down 30% for a pre-holiday sale. What was the final selling price of the china.

First Stage: August 8
Find the first selling price, using markup based on cost.

	C	$800	rate of C	100%
+ M		$____	+ rate of M	50%
S		$____	rate of S	____%

The rate of selling price is 150% (100% + 50%) of the cost. Since the cost is $800, find the selling price as a percentage P of the $800 base cost (Figure 8-10).

First selling price = RB = 150% × $800 = 1.5 × $800 = $1,200

The first selling price is $1,200.

Figure 8–10 Selling Price = Rate of Selling Price × Cost

Next Stage: October 1
The stage requires a 25% *markdown,* so identify the first selling price, $1,200, as the *original selling price S*. This is the base of the 25% markdown at this stage. Find the cheaper price C.

	C	$____	rate of C	____%
+ M		$____	+ rate of M	25%
S		$1,200	rate of S	100%

The rate of the cheaper price is the rate of the original selling price minus the rate of markdown, or 100% − 25%, or 75%. Use the formula $P = RB$ to find the cheaper price as a percentage P of the $1,200 base original selling price.

$P = RB$ = 75% × $1,200 = 0.75 × $1,200 = $900

The cheaper price is $900. This is the selling price at this stage.

Next Stage: October 11
The stage requires a 15% *markup,* so identify the previous selling price, $900, as the *cost C*. This is the base of the 15% markup at this stage. Find the selling price S.

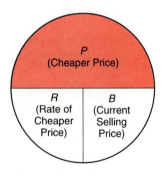

	C	$900	rate of C	100%
+ M		$____	+ rate of M	15%
S		$____	rate of S	____%

The rate of the selling price is 100% + 15%, or 115%. Use the formula $P = RB$ to find the selling price as a percentage P of the $900 base cost.

$P = RB$ = 115% × $900 = 1.15 × $900 = $1,035

The selling price at this stage is $1,035.

Figure 8–11 Cheaper Price = Rate of Cheaper Price × Current Selling Price

Last stage
For the 30% markdown, we identify the selling price, $1,035 as the *original selling price S* and the base of the markdown (Figure 8-11).

	C	$____	rate of C	____%
+ M		$____	+ rate of M	30%
S		$1,035	rate of S	100%

Rate of C = rate of S − rate of M = 100% − 30% = 70%

$P = RB$ = 70% × $1,035 = 0.7 × $1,035 = $724.50

The cheaper price is $724.50, and is the final price in the series.

Robinsons•May Sale Ad

HERE'S HOW IT WORKS:

ORIGINAL	$80
CURRENT	59.99
LESS 33%	-19.99
YOU PAY	**$40**

1. Using the original selling price of $80 and the current price of $59.99 as the sale price, find the amount of markdown and the percent of markdown to the nearest whole percent.

2. Compute the total markdown rate from the original selling price of $80 to the reduced price of $40 and the markdown rate from $59.99 to $40. Does the total markdown rate equal the sum of the markdown rates from $80 to $59.99 and from $59.99 to $40?

3. The identical $80 item is on sale at Hansen's. On Monday it was marked down 15%. On Wednesday it was marked down an additional 35%. What was the price after the markdown on Monday? on Wednesday?

4. Verify that 33% of $59.99 is $19.99. Discuss.

▶2 *Finding the Selling Price to Achieve a Desired Profit (Markup)*

Most businesses anticipate that some seasonal merchandise will have to be marked down from the original selling price. Stores that sell perishable or strictly seasonal items (fresh fruits, vegetables, swimsuits, or coats, for example) usually anticipate from past experience how much merchandise will have to be marked down or thrown out due to spoilage. For example, most retail stores mark down holiday items to 50% of the original price the day after the holiday. Thus, merchants set the original markup of such an item to obtain the desired profit level based on the projected number of items sold at "full price" (the original selling price).

❓ **HOW TO**	**Find the Selling Price to Achieve a Desired Profit**

Step 1 Establish the rate of profit (markup)—based on cost—desired on the sale of the merchandise.

Step 2 Find the total cost of the merchandise: Multiply the unit cost by the quantity of merchandise.

Step 3 Find the total profit (markup) based on cost: Multiply the rate of profit (markup) by the total cost.

Step 4 Find the total selling price: Add the total cost and the total profit.

Step 5 Establish the quantity expected to sell.

Step 6 Divide the total selling price by the expect-to-sell quantity.

$$\text{Selling price to achieve profit (markup)} = \frac{\text{total selling price}}{\text{expect-to-sell quantity}}$$

Example 2 Green's Grocery specializes in fresh fruits and vegetables. A portion of most merchandise must be reduced for quick sale, and some must be thrown out because of spoilage. Hardy Green, the owner, must mark the selling price of incoming produce high enough to make the desired amount of profit while taking expected markdowns and spoilage into account. Hardy receives 400 pounds of bananas, for which he pays $0.15 per pound. On the average, 8% of the bananas will spoil. Find the selling price per pound to obtain a 175% markup on cost.

The desired rate of profit (markup) is 175% based on cost.

$$C = \$0.15 \times 400 = \$60$$ **Find the total cost of the bananas.**

$$M = 1.75 \times \$60 = \$105$$ **Find the total profit (markup).**

$$S = C + M = \$60 + \$105 = \$165$$ **Find the total selling price.**

Hardy must receive $165 for the bananas he expects to sell. He expects 8% not to sell, or 92% to sell.

$$0.92 \times 400 = 368$$ **Establish how many pounds he can expect to sell.**

He can expect to sell 368 pounds of bananas.

$$\text{Selling price per pound} = \frac{\text{Total selling price}}{\text{Number of pounds expected to sell}}$$

$$= \frac{\$165}{368} = \$0.448 \text{ or } \$0.45$$

Hardy must sell the bananas for $0.45 per pound to receive the profit he desires. If he sells more than 92% of the bananas, he will receive additional profit.

Example 3   At the 7th Inning Sports Memorabilia Shop, Charlie has an opportunity to buy T-shirts with the 1996 University of Memphis basketball team imprinted on the shirt. The shirts will cost $6 each as long as he buys 200 shirts. He only expects to be able to sell 150 shirts before the end of the season and the other shirts will have little or no value. After doing marketing research, he thinks the shirts will sell only if they are priced at $10 or less. Of course more shirts are likely to be sold if the price is significantly less than $10. Since he must have a 50% markup based on cost to cover overhead expenses and desired profit, should Charlie buy the shirts?

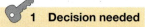

1   Decision needed   Should Charlie buy the University of Memphis T-shirts?

2   Known facts
Quantity of shirts to be purchased: 200 shirts
Quantity of shirts expected to be sold: 150 shirts
Cost per shirt: $6
Maximum selling price: $10 per shirt
Necessary rate of markup: 50% based on cost

3   Unknown facts   Selling price to achieve profit (markup)

4   Relationships
Total cost = cost per shirt × quantity purchased
Necessary markup = necessary rate of markup × total cost
Total selling price = total cost + necessary markup

$$\text{Selling price to achieve profit (markup)} = \frac{\text{total selling price}}{\text{expect-to-sell quantity}}$$

5   Estimate   If 150 shirts are sold at $10 each, the total selling price would be $1,500. If 200 shirts are purchased at $6 each, the total cost would be $1,200.

6   Calculations
Total cost = number of items × cost per item
Total cost = 200 × $6

Total cost = $1,200

Necessary markup = total cost × rate of necessary markup

Necessary markup = $1,200 × 50%

Necessary markup = $1,200 × 0.5

Necessary markup = $600

Total selling price = total cost + markup

Total selling price = $1,200 + $600

Total selling price = $1,800

$$\text{Selling price to achieve profit (markup)} = \frac{\text{total selling price}}{\text{expect-to-sell quantity}}$$

$$\text{Selling price} = \frac{\$1,800}{150 \text{ shirts}}$$

Selling price = $12 per shirt

7 Decision made **The shirts should not be purchased,** since Charlie would need to sell the shirts at $12 per shirt but, to sell, the shirts need to be priced at $10 or less.

Self-Check 8.3

1. The Splash Shop paid a wholesale price of $24 each for Le Paris swimsuits. On May 5 it marked up the suits 50% of this cost. On June 15, the swimsuits were marked down 15% for a two-day sale, and on June 17 they were marked up again by 10%. On August 30, the shop sold all remaining swimsuits for 40% off. What was the final selling price of a Le Paris swimsuit?

2. A ladies' suit selling for $135 is marked down 25% for a special promotion. It is later marked down 15% of the sale price. Since it still hasn't sold, it is marked down to a price 75% off the original selling price. What are the two sale prices of the suit? What is the final selling price of the suit?

3. Farmer Brown's fruit stand sells fresh fruits and vegetables. Becky Brown, the manager, must mark the selling price of incoming produce high enough to make the desired profit while taking expected markdowns and spoilage into account. Becky paid $0.35 per pound for 300 pounds of grapes. On the average, 12% of the grapes will spoil. Find the selling price per pound needed to achieve a 175% markup on cost.

4. Teddy Jeanfreau ordered 600 pounds of Red Delicious apples for the produce section of the supermarket. He paid $0.32 per pound for the apples and expected 15% of them to spoil. If the store wants to make a markup on cost of 90%, what should be the per-pound selling price?

5. The 7th Inning Sports Memorabilia Shop is considering buying T-shirts with the 1996 Atlanta Olympic emblem imprinted on them. The cost of the shirts, which includes permission fees paid to the Olympic Committee, will be $7.90 each if 1,000 shirts are purchased. Charlie projects that 800 shirts will sell before the Olympic games are over if he sells them at $15 each. However, Charlie calculates that he must have a 50% markup based on cost to justify handling them. Should Charlie buy the shirts?

Self-Check 8.1

1.

C	$2	rate of C	100%
+ M	$4	+ rate of M	200%
S	$6	rate of S	300%

Markup = $S - C$ = $6 - $2 = $4

Rate of markup based on cost = $\dfrac{P \text{ (markup)}}{B \text{ (cost)}} = \dfrac{\$4}{\$2} = 2 = 200\%$

2.

C	$4.00	rate of C	100%
+ M	$2.40	+ rate of M	60%
S	$6.40	rate of S	160%

Markup = R (rate of markup) $\times$ B (cost)

$= 0.6 \times \$4 = \$2.40$

Selling price = $C + M$ = $4 + $2.40 = $6.40

3.

C	$214.29	rate of C	100%
+ M	$ 85.71	+ rate of M	40%
S	$300.00	rate of S	140%

Rate of S = rate of C + rate of M

Rate of S = 100% + 40% = 140%

$$\text{Cost} = \dfrac{P \text{ (selling price)}}{R \text{ (rate of selling price based on cost)}}$$

$$= \dfrac{\$300}{1.4} = \$214.29 \text{ (rounded)}$$

Markup = $S - C$ = $300 - $214.29 = $85.71

4.

C	$ 4	rate of C	33.33%
+ M	$ 8	+ rate of M	66.67%
S	$12	rate of S	100 %

Find amount of markup first.

$M = S - C$ = $12 - $4 = $8

Rate of markup based on selling price = $\dfrac{P \text{ (markup)}}{B \text{ (selling price)}} = \dfrac{\$8}{\$12}$

$= 0.6667$

$= 66.67\%$

5.

C	$ 7.50	rate of C	60%
+ M	$ 5.00	+ rate of M	40%
S	$12.50	rate of S	100%

Rate of C = rate of S − rate of M

Rate of C = 100% − 40% = 60%

Selling price = $\dfrac{P \text{ (markup)}}{R \text{ (rate of markup based on selling price)}} = \dfrac{\$5}{0.4} = \$12.50$

$C = S - M$ = $12.50 − $5 = $7.50

6.

C	$1.75	rate of C	50%
+ M	$1.75	+ rate of M	50%
S	$3.50	rate of S	100%

Rate of C = rate of S − rate of M

Rate of C = 100% − 50% = 50%

Markup = R (rate of markup based on selling price) $\times$ B (selling price)

$= 0.5 \times \$3.50 = \$1.75$

Since the rate of markup and the rate of cost are the same, the markup and the cost are the same.

7.

C	$ 40	rate of C	40%
$+\, M$	$ 60	+ rate of M	60%
S	$100	rate of S	100%

Rate of C = rate of S − rate of M

Rate of C = 100% − 60% = 40%

$$\text{Selling price} = \frac{P \text{ (cost)}}{R \text{ (rate of cost based on selling price)}}$$

$$= \frac{\$40}{0.4} = \$100$$

$$M = S - C = \$100 - \$40 = \$60$$

8. Markup rate based on cost $= \dfrac{\text{markup rate based on selling price}}{1 - \text{markup rate based on selling price}} = \dfrac{0.6}{1 - 0.6} = \dfrac{0.6}{0.4} = 1.5,\ \text{or } 150\%$

9. Markup rate based on cost $= \dfrac{\text{markup rate based on selling price}}{1 - \text{markup percent based on selling price}} = \dfrac{0.75}{1 - 0.75} = \dfrac{0.75}{0.25} = 3,\ \text{or } 300\%$

10. Markup rate based on selling price $= \dfrac{\text{markup rate based on cost}}{1 + \text{markup percent based on cost}} = \dfrac{1.2}{1 + 1.2} = \dfrac{1.2}{2.2} = 0.5455,\ \text{or } 54.55\%$

11. Markup rate based on cost $= \dfrac{\text{markup rate based on cost}}{1 + \text{markup rate based on cost}} = \dfrac{0.82}{1 + 0.82} = \dfrac{0.82}{1.82} = 0.45 = 45\%$

Self-Check 8.2

1. Markdown = original selling price − cheaper price

$$= \$480 - \$420 = \$60$$

Rate of markdown $= \dfrac{P}{B} = \dfrac{\$60}{\$480} = 0.125 = 12.5\%$

2. Markdown = original selling price − cheaper price = $599.97 − $550 = $49.97

Rate of markdown $= \dfrac{P}{B} = \dfrac{\$49.97}{\$599.97} = 0.083 = 8.3\%$

3. Markdown = original selling price − cheaper price = $169.00 − $139.97 = $29.03

Rate of markdown $= \dfrac{P}{B} = \dfrac{\$29.03}{\$169.00} = 0.172 = 17.2\%$

4. Markdown = original selling price − cheaper price = $79.99 − $47.97 = $32.02

Rate of markdown $= \dfrac{P}{B} = \dfrac{\$32.02}{\$79.99} = 0.4 = 40.0\%$

5. Markdown = original selling price − cheaper price = $349.99 − $329.97 = $20.02

Rate of markdown $= \dfrac{P}{B} = \dfrac{\$20.02}{\$349.99} = 0.057 = 5.7\%$

6. Markdown = $R \times B$ = 0.15 × $78 = $11.70

Cheaper price = original selling price − markdown = $78 − $11.70 = $66.30

7. Markdown = markdown rate × original selling price = 0.23 × \$529.99 = \$121.90

Cheaper price = original selling price − markdown = \$529.99 − \$121.90 = \$408.09

8. Markdown = markdown rate × original selling price = 0.25 × \$159.99 = \$40.00

Cheaper price = original selling price − markdown = \$159.99 − \$40.00 = \$119.99

9. Markdown = markdown rate × original selling price = 0.21 × \$1,399.97 = \$293.99

Cheaper price = original selling price − markdown = \$1,399.97 − \$293.99 = \$1,105.98

10. Markdown = markdown rate × original selling price = 0.19 × \$59.99 = \$11.40

Cheaper price = original selling price − markdown = \$59.99 − \$11.40 = \$48.59

Self-Check 8.3

1. *May 5 markup:*
Markup = $R \times B$ = 0.5 × \$24 = \$12
$S = C + M$ = \$24 + \$12 = \$36 (original selling price)
June 15 markdown:
Markdown = $R \times B$ = 0.15 × \$36 = \$5.40
Cheaper price = \$36 − \$5.40 = \$30.60 = selling price at stage
June 17 markup:
Markup = $R \times B$ = 0.1 × \$30.60 = \$3.06
Selling price = \$30.60 + \$3.06 = \$33.66 = selling price at stage
August 30 markdown:
Markdown = $R \times B$ = 0.4 × \$33.66 = \$13.46
Cheaper price = \$33.66 − \$13.46 = \$20.20 = final selling price

2. Markdown = \$135 × 0.25 = \$33.75
Cheaper price = \$135 − \$33.75 = \$101.25 = first selling price
Markdown = \$101.25 × 0.15 = \$15.19
Cheaper price = \$101.25 − \$15.19 = \$86.06 = second selling price
Markdown = \$135 × 0.75 = \$101.25
Cheaper price = \$135 − \$101.25 = \$33.75 = final selling price

3.
Cost = 300 × \$0.35 = \$105
Markup = 1.75 × \$105 = \$183.75
Total selling price = $C + M$ = \$105 + \$183.75 = \$288.75
% of grapes expected to sell = 100% − 12% = 88%
Pounds of grapes expected to sell = 0.88 × 300 = 264 pounds
$$\text{Selling price} = \frac{\$288.75}{264 \text{ pounds}} = \$1.09 \text{ per pound}$$

4.
Cost = 600 × \$0.32 − \$192
Markup = \$192 × 0.9 = \$172.80
Total selling price = \$192 + \$172.80 = \$364.80
Percent of apples expected to sell = 100% − 15% = 85%
Pounds of apples expected to sell = 600 × 0.85 = 510
$$\text{Selling price} = \frac{\$364.80}{510 \text{ pounds}} = \$0.72 \text{ (rounded)}$$

5. Total cost = quantity of items × cost per item
Total cost = 1,000 × \$7.90 = \$7,900
Necessary markup = total cost × 50% = \$7,900 × 0.5 = \$3,950
Total selling price = total cost + markup = \$7,900 + \$3,950 = \$11,850

Selling price = total selling price ÷ quantity of items expected to sell = $\dfrac{\$11,850}{800 \text{ items}}$ = \$14.81 per item

Charlie should purchase the shirts and sell them for at least \$14.81 each.

CHAPTER 8 OVERVIEW

Section—Objective	Important Points with Examples

8.1 — 1 (page 272)

Find the markup, cost, selling price, rate of markup, or rate of selling price when the markup is based on cost

Step 1 Place known information in the table.

C	$____	rate of C	100%
+ M	$____	+ rate of M	____%
S	$____	rate of S	____%

Step 2 If one dollar value and two rates are missing: **a)** Use one of the markup formulas to find the missing dollar value:

$$S = C + M \qquad \text{if } S \text{ is missing}$$

$$C = S - M \qquad \text{if } C \text{ is missing}$$

$$M = S - C \qquad \text{if } M \text{ is missing}$$

b) Use the percentage formula $R = P/B$ to find a missing rate. R is missing rate, P is its corresponding dollar value, and B is the dollar value of the cost. **c)** Use one of the rate-of-markup formulas to find the other missing rate.

$$\text{Rate of } S = 100\% + \text{rate of } M \qquad \text{if rate of } S \text{ is missing}$$

$$\text{Rate of } M = \text{rate of } S - 100\% \qquad \text{if rate of } M \text{ is missing}$$

Step 3 If one rate and two dollar values are missing: **a)** Do step 2c to find the missing rate. **b)** Use one of the percentage formulas to find a missing dollar value. P is either markup M or selling price S, R is its corresponding rate, and B is cost C.

$$P = RB \qquad \text{if } S \text{ or } M \text{ is missing but } C \text{ is not}$$

$$B = P/R \qquad \text{if } C \text{ is missing}$$

c) Do step 2a to find the final dollar value.

> Find the markup and rate of markup based on a cost of $2 if the selling price is $4.
>
> | | | | |
> |---|---|---|---|
> | C | $2 | rate of C | 100% |
> | + M | $____ | + rate of M | ____% |
> | S | $4 | rate of S | ____% |
>
> Markup = $S - C$ = $4 − $2 = $2
>
> $$\text{Rate of markup} = \frac{P}{B} = \frac{\text{markup}}{\text{cost}} = \frac{2}{4} = 50\%$$

8.1 — 2 (page 275)

Find the markup, cost, selling price, rate of markup, or rate of cost when the markup is based on selling price

Step 1 Place known information in the table.

C	$____	rate of C	____%
+ M	$____	+ rate of M	____%
S	$____	rate of S	100%

Step 2 If one dollar value and two rates are missing: **a)** Use one of the markup formulas to find the missing dollar value:

$$S = C + M \qquad \text{if } S \text{ is missing}$$

$$C = S - M \qquad \text{if } C \text{ is missing}$$

$$M = S - C \qquad \text{if } M \text{ is missing}$$

b) Use the percentage formula $R = P/B$ to find a missing rate. R is a missing rate, P is its corresponding dollar value, and B is selling price. **c)** Use one of the rate-of-markup formulas to find the other missing rate.

$$\text{Rate of } C = 100\% - \text{rate of } M \qquad \text{if rate of } C \text{ is missing}$$

$$\text{Rate of } M = 100\% - \text{rate of } C \qquad \text{if rate of } M \text{ is missing}$$

Step 3 If one rate and two dollar values are missing: **a)** Do step 2c to find the missing rate. **b)** Use one of the percentage formulas to find a missing dollar value. P is either markup M or cost C, R is its corresponding rate, and B is selling price S.

$$P = RB \qquad \text{if } C \text{ or } M \text{ is missing but } S \text{ is not}$$

$$B = P/R \qquad \text{if } S \text{ is missing}$$

c) Do step 2a to find the final dollar value.

Find the cost and the selling price on an item marked up $50 if the rate of markup is 25% based on selling price.

C	$__	rate of C	__%
$+M$	$50	+ rate of M	25%
S	$__	rate of S	100%

$$\text{Selling price} = P/R = \frac{\text{markup}}{\text{rate of markup}} = \frac{50}{25\%} = \frac{50}{0.25} = \$200$$

$$\text{Cost} = \text{selling price} - \text{markup} = \$200 - \$50 = \$150$$

8.1 — 3 (page 279)

Compare markup based on cost with markup based on selling price

Convert a markup rate based on selling price to a markup rate based on cost
Step 1 Write the markup rate based on selling price in decimal form. **Step 2** Subtract the markup rate (decimal form) based on selling price from 1. **Step 3** Divide the markup rate (decimal form) based on selling price by the difference from step 2.

Markup rate (decimal form) based on cost

$$= \frac{\text{markup rate (decimal form) based on selling price}}{1 - \text{markup rate (decimal form) based on selling price}}$$

A fax machine is marked up 30% based on selling price. What is the rate of markup based on cost?

$$\text{Markup rate based on cost} = \frac{\text{markup rate based on selling price}}{1 - \text{markup rate based on selling price}}$$

$$= \frac{0.3}{1 - 0.3} = \frac{0.3}{0.7} = 0.429 = 42.9\%$$

Convert a markup rate based on cost to a markup rate based on selling price
Step 1 Write the markup rate based on cost in decimal form. **Step 2** Add the markup rate (decimal form) based on cost to 1. **Step 3** Divide the markup rate (decimal form) based on cost by the sum from step 2.

Markup rate (decimal form) based on selling price

$$= \frac{\text{markup rate (decimal form) based on cost}}{1 + \text{markup rate (decimal form) based on cost}}$$

A CD-ROM player is marked up 80% based on cost. What is the rate of markup based on selling price?

$$\text{Markup rate based on selling price} = \frac{\text{markup rate based on cost}}{1 + \text{markup rate based on cost}}$$

$$= \frac{0.8}{1 + 0.8} = \frac{0.8}{1.8} = 0.444 = 44.4\%$$

8.2 — 1 (page 282)

Find the markdown, cheaper price, original selling price, rate of markdown, or rate of cheaper price

Step 1 Place known information in the table.

C	$____	rate of C	____%
+ M	$____	+ rate of M	____%
S	$____	rate of S	100%

Step 2 If one dollar value and two rates are missing: **a)** Use one of the markdown formulas to find the missing dollar value:

$$S = C + M \quad \text{if } S \text{ is missing}$$

$$C = S - M \quad \text{if } C \text{ is missing}$$

$$M = S - C \quad \text{if } M \text{ is missing}$$

b) Use the percentage formula $R = P/B$ to find a missing rate. R is missing rate, P is its corresponding dollar value, and B is original selling price. **c)** Use one of the rate-of-markdown formulas to find the other missing rate:

$$\text{Rate of } C = 100\% - \text{rate of } M \quad \text{if rate of } C \text{ is missing}$$

$$\text{Rate of } M = 100\% - \text{rate of } C \quad \text{if rate of } M \text{ is missing}$$

Step 3 If one rate and two dollar values are missing: **a)** Do step 2c to find the missing rate. **b)** Use one of the percentage formulas to find a missing dollar value. P is either markdown M or cheaper price C, R is its corresponding rate, and B is original selling price.

$$P = RB \quad \text{if } C \text{ or } M \text{ is missing but } S \text{ is not}$$

$$B = P/R \quad \text{if } S \text{ is missing}$$

c) Do step 2a to find the final dollar value.

Find the markdown and rate of markdown if the original selling price is $4.50 and the sale price is $3.

C	$3.00	rate of C	____%
+ M	$____	+ rate of M	____%
S	$4.50	rate of S	100%

Markdown $= S - C = \$4.50 - \$3 = \$1.50$

$$\text{Rate of markdown} = \frac{P}{B} = \frac{\text{markdown}}{\text{original selling price}} = \frac{\$1.50}{\$4.50} = 0.33\frac{1}{3} = 33\frac{1}{3}\%$$

8.3 — 1 (page 285)

Find the final selling price for a series of markups and markdowns

Step 1 For the first stage in the series, find the first selling price, if it isn't known already, using the first markup/markdown facts and the How-To steps for markup or markdown. **Step 2** For each remaining stage in the series: **a)** If the stage requires a **markdown,** identify the previous selling price as the *original selling price S* for this stage. Use the How-To steps for markdown to find the *cheaper price C*. This price is the selling price for this stage. **b)** If the stage requires a **markup,** identify the previous selling price as the *cost C* for this stage. Use the How-To steps for markup *based* *on cost* to find the *selling price S*. This price is the selling price for this stage. **Step 3** Identify the selling price for the last stage as the *final selling price*.

An item costing $7 was marked up 70% on cost, then marked down 20%, marked up 10%, and finally marked down 20%. What was the final selling price?

First stage: Rate of selling price = 100% + 70% = 170%
$$\text{Selling price} = 170\% \times \$7 = 1.7 \times 7 = \$11.90$$

Second stage: Rate of cheaper price = 100% − 20% = 80%
$$\text{Cheaper price} = 80\% \times 11.90 = 0.8 \times 11.90 = \$9.52$$

Third stage: Rate of selling price = 100% + 10% = 110%
$$\text{Selling price} = 110\% \times \$9.52 = 1.1 \times 9.52 = \$10.47$$

Last stage: Rate of cheaper price = 100% − 20% = 80%
$$\text{Cheaper price} = 80\% \times \$10.47 = 0.8 \times 10.47 = \$8.38$$

The final selling price is $8.38.

8.3 — 2 (page 287)

Find the selling price to achieve a desired profit (markup)

Step 1 Establish the rate of profit (markup)—based on cost—desired on the sale of the merchandise. **Step 2** Find the total cost of the merchandise: Multiply the unit cost by the quantity of merchandise. **Step 3** Find the total profit (markup) based on cost: Multiply the rate of profit (markup) by the total cost. **Step 4** Find the total selling price: Add the total cost and the total profit. **Step 5** Establish the quantity expected to sell. **Step 6** Divide the total selling price by the expect-to-sell quantity.

$$\text{Selling price to achieve profit (markup)} = \frac{\text{total selling price}}{\text{expect-to-sell quantity}}$$

At a total cost of $25, 25% of 400 lemons are expected to rot before being sold. A 75% rate of profit (markup) on cost is needed. At what selling price must the lemons be sold to achieve the needed profit?

Total profit (markup) based on cost = 75% × $25 = 0.75 × 25 = $18.75

Total selling price = $18.75 + $25 = $43.75

Expect-to-sell quantity = (100% − 25%) × 400 = 0.75 × 400 = 300 lemons

$$\text{Selling price} = \frac{\$43.75}{300 \text{ lemons}} = \$0.15 \text{ per lemon}$$

CHAPTER 8 REVIEW

Section 8.1

Find the missing numbers in the table if the markup is based on the cost.

 Adding

1.

C	$50	rate of C	100%
+ M	$25	+ rate of M	50%
S	$____	rate of S	____%

2.

C	$4	rate of C	____%
+ M	$1	+ rate of M	25%
S	$____	rate of S	____%

3.	C	$41	rate of C	____%
	$+ M$	$____	$+$ rate of M	100%
	S	$____	rate of S	____%

4.	C	$25	rate of C	100%
	$+ M$	$5	$+$ rate of M	20%
	S	$30	rate of S	120%

Find the missing numbers in the table if the markup is based on the selling price.

5.	C	$38	rate of C	42%
	$+ M$	$____	$+$ rate of M	____%
	S	$____	rate of S	100%

6.	C	$86	rate of C	50%
	$+ M$	$86	$+$ rate of M	50%
	S	$172	rate of S	100%

$$86 \quad 50|100$$
$$8 \div 50 \times 100 = 172$$

7.	C	$____	rate of C	____%
	$+ M$	$8	$+$ rate of M	15%
	S	$____	rate of S	____%

8.	C	$16	rate of C	42%
	$+ M$	$22.10	$+$ rate of M	58%
	S	$38.10	rate of S	100%

$$16/42 \times 100 = 38.10$$

Solve the problems. Be careful to notice whether markup is based on the cost or the selling price.

9. A hairdryer costs $15 and is marked up 40% of the cost. Find the markup and selling price.

10. A hairbrush costs $3 and is marked up 40% of the cost. Find the markup and selling price.

11. A blender is marked up $9 and sells for $45. Find the cost and rate of markup if the markup is based on cost.

12. A package of cassette tapes costs $12 and is marked up $7.20. Find the selling price and rate of markup based on the cost.

13. A computer table sells for $198.50 and costs $158.70. Find the markup and rate of markup based on the cost. Round to the nearest tenth percent.

14. Find the cost and markup on an office chair if the selling price is $75 and this item is marked up 100% of the cost.

15. If a flower arrangement is marked up $12, which is 50% of the cost, find the cost and selling price.

16. A toaster sells for $28.70 and has a markup rate of 50% based on selling price. Find the markup and the cost.

17. A briefcase is marked up $15.30, which is 30% of the selling price. Find the cost and selling price of the item.

18. A three-ringed binder costs $4.60 and is marked up $3.07. Find the selling price and the rate of markup based on selling price. Round percents to the nearest hundredth.

19. A hole punch costs $40 and sells for $58.50. Find the rate of markup based on selling price and the markup. Round percents to the nearest hundredth.

20. A pair of bookends sells for $15. Its cost is $10. Find the rate of markup based on selling price.

21. A desk organizer sells for $35, which includes a markup rate of 60% of the selling price. Find the cost and markup.

22. A pair of athletic shoes cost $38 and is marked up $20. Find the selling price, rate of markup based on cost and rate of markup based on selling price.

Fill in the blanks in Exercises 23 through 32. Round rates to the nearest hundredth percent.

	Cost	Markup	Selling Price	Rate of Markup Based on Cost	Rate of Markup Based on Selling Price
23.	_____	$ 32	$ 89	_____	_____
24.	$486	_____	_____	_____	30%
25.	$ 1.56	_____	$ 2	_____	_____
26.	_____	$ 5.89	_____	15%	_____
27.	_____	$ 27.38	_____	40%	_____
28.	$ 25	_____	_____	_____	48%
29.	_____	_____	$124	150%	_____
30.	_____	$ 28	_____	_____	27%
31.	_____	_____	$ 18.95	_____	15%
32.	$ 16.28	$ 15.92	_____	_____	_____

33. Find the rate of markup based on cost of a textbook that is marked up 12% based on selling price.

34. A desk has an 83% markup based on selling price. What is the rate of markup based on cost?

35. A chest is marked up 63% based on cost. What is the rate of markup based on selling price?

36. A dining room suite is marked up 45% based on cost. What is the rate of markup based on selling price?

Section 8.2

37. A fiberglass shower surround originally sold for $379.98 and was marked down to sell for $341.98. Find the markdown and the rate of markdown.

38. A three-speed fan originally sold for $29.88 and was reduced to sell for $25.40. Find the markdown and the rate of markdown.

39. An area rug originally sold for $89.99 and was reduced to sell for $65. Find the markdown and the rate of markdown.

40. A room air conditioner that originally sold for $509.99 was reduced to sell for $400. Find the markdown and the rate of markdown.

41. A portable CD player was originally priced at $249.99 and was reduced by 20%. Find the markdown and the sale price (cheaper price).

42. A set of rollers was originally priced at $39.99 and was reduced by 30%. Find the markdown and the sale price.

43. A set of stainless steel cookware was originally priced at $79 and was reduced by 25%. Find the markdown and the sale price.

44. A down comforter was originally priced at $280 and was reduced by 64%. Find the markdown and the sale price.

45. Crystal stemware originally marked to sell for $31.25 was reduced 20% for a special promotion. The stemware was then reduced an additional 30% to turn inventory. What were the markdown and the sale price for each reduction?

46. A camcorder that originally sold for $1,199 was reduced to sell for $999. It was then reduced an additional 40%. What were the markdown and markdown rate for the first reduction, and what was the final selling price for the camcorder?

47. James McDonell operates a vegetable store. He purchases 800 pounds of potatoes at a cost of $0.18 per pound. If he anticipates a spoilage rate of 20% of the potatoes and wishes to make a profit of 140% of the cost, for how much must he sell the potatoes per pound?

48. Elena Jimenez received a shipment of oranges that was shipped after a severe frost, so she expects losses to be high. She paid $0.26 per pound for the 500 pounds and expects to lose 35% of the oranges. If she wishes to make 125% markup on cost, find the selling price per pound.

Challenge Problems

49. Pro Peds, a local athletic shoe manufacturer, makes a training sneaker at a cost of $8.40 per pair. A check of previous factory runs indicates that 10% of the sneakers will be defective and must be sold to Odd Tops, Inc. as irregulars for $12 per pair. If Pro Peds produces 1,000 pairs of the sneakers and desires a markup of 100% on cost, find the selling price per pair of the regular shoes.

50. Pro Peds has implemented a quality improvement initiative that has reduced the percentage of defective sneakers by 6%. Recalculate the selling price per pair based on this new information.

CHAPTER 8 PRACTICE TEST

1. A calculator sells for $23.99 and costs $16.83. What is the markup?

2. A mixer sells for $109.98 and has a markup of $36.18. Find the cost.

3. A cookbook has a 34% markup rate based on cost. If the markup is $5.27, find the cost of the cookbook.

4. A computer stand sells for $385. What is the markup if it is 45% of the selling price?

5. A box of computer paper costs $16.80. Find the selling price if there is a 35% markup rate based on cost.

6. The reduced price of a dress is $54.99. Find the original selling price if a reduction of 40% has been taken.

7. A daily organizer that originally sold for $86.90 was marked down by 30%. What is the markdown?

8. What is the sale price of the organizer in Exercise 7?

9. If a television cost $87.15 and was marked up $39.60, what is the selling price?

10. A refrigerator that sells for $387.99 was marked down $97. What is the sale price?

11. What was the rate of markdown for the refrigerator in Exercise 10?

12. A wallet cost $16.05 to produce. The wallet sells for $25.68. What is the rate of markup based on cost?

13. A lamp costs $88. What is the selling price if the markup is 45% of the selling price?

14. A file cabinet originally sold for $215 but was damaged and had to be reduced. If the reduced cabinet sold for $129, what was the rate of markdown based on the original selling price?

15. A bookcase desk originally sold for $129.99 was marked down 25%. During the sale it was damaged and had to be reduced by 50% more. What was the final selling price of the desk?

16. Donald Byrd, the accountant for Quick Stop Shop, calculates the selling price for all produce. If 400 pounds of potatoes were purchased for $0.13 per pound and 18% of the potatoes were expected to rot before being sold, determine the price per pound that the potatoes must sell for if a profit of 120% of the purchase price is desired.

17. Loose-leaf paper in a college bookstore is marked up 30% of its cost. Find the cost if the selling price is $2.34 per package.

18. A $5\frac{1}{4}$-inch double-sided, double-density floppy disk costs $0.90 and sells for $1.50. Find the rate of markup based on selling price. Also find the rate of markup based on cost.

19. A radio sells for $45, which includes a markup rate of 65% of the selling price. Find the cost and the markup.

20. Laura Kee purchased a small refrigerator for her dorm room for $95.20, which included a markup of $27.20 based on the cost. Find the cost and the rate of markup based on cost.

CHAPTER

SIMPLE INTEREST AND SIMPLE DISCOUNT

GOOD DECISIONS THROUGH TEAMWORK

With members of your team, investigate loan deals by researching the options available for the purchase of an engraving machine that costs $15,000 if the loan can be repaid in a lump sum in 18 months. List types of lending institutions that provide business loans and find local examples of each through newspapers and phone directories. Specify aspects of each institution's lending policies that should be compared in order to make the best decision for acquiring the loan, including:

- Rate. Is the rate simple interest or simple discount? What is the rate? Is the rate affected by any factors such as length of finance contract or the company's or owner's credit rating?
- Requirements for loan. What information must be provided to the institution in order to obtain a loan? Is a cosigner required? Is collateral in addition to the machine required?

Individually, select a type of lending institution and obtain the comparative information by reading published brochures or interviewing loan officers of selected institutions. After comparing the resulting information, as a team calculate the total cost of financing the purchase using two of the financing sources selected by team members. Select the deal that is the wisest choice for the loan. Prepare an oral report employing visual aids in which all team members participate.

CHAPTER 9 SIMPLE INTEREST AND SIMPLE DISCOUNT

Every business and every person at some time borrows or invests money. A person (or business) who borrows money must pay for the use of the money. A person who invests money must be paid by the person or firm who uses the money. The price paid for using money is called **interest.**

In the business world, we encounter two basic kinds of interest, *simple* and *compound*. **Simple interest** applies when a loan or investment is repaid in a lump sum. The person using the money has use of the full amount of money for the entire time of the loan or investment. **Compound interest,** which is explained in Chapter 10, most often applies to savings accounts, installment loans, and credit cards.

Both types of interest take into account three factors: the principal, the interest rate, and the time period involved. **Principal** is the amount of money borrowed or invested. **Rate** is the percent of the principal paid as interest per time period. **Time** is the number of days, months, or years that the money is borrowed or invested.

9.1 The Simple Interest Formula

1 ▶ *Find simple interest using the simple interest formula*

2 ▶ *Find the maturity value of a loan*

3 ▶ *Convert months to a fractional or decimal part of a year*

4 ▶ *Find the principal, rate, or time using the simple interest formula*

1 ▶ *Simple Interest*

The interest formula shows how interest, principal, rate, and time are related and gives us a way of figuring one of these values if the other three values are known.

❓ HOW TO | Find Simple Interest Using the Simple Interest Formula

Multiply the principal by the rate and time.

$$\text{Interest} = \text{Principal} \times \text{Rate} \times \text{Time}$$

$$I = PRT$$

The rate of interest is a percent for a given time period, usually one year. The time in the interest formula must be expressed in the same unit of time as the rate. If the rate is a percent per year, the time must be expressed in years or a decimal or fractional part of a year. Similarly, if the rate is a percent per month, the time must be expressed in months.

Example 1 Find the interest paid on a loan of $1,500 for 1 year at a simple interest rate of 12% per year.

$I = PRT$ **Use the simple interest formula.**

$I = (\$1,500)(12\%)(1)$ **Principal *P* is $1,500, rate *R* is 12% per year, time *T* is one year.**

$I = (\$1,500)(0.12)(1)$ **Write 12% as a decimal.**

$I = \$180$

The interest on the loan is $180.

Example 2 Kanette's Salon borrowed $5,000 at $12\frac{1}{2}\%$ per year simple interest for two years to buy new hair dryers. How much interest must be paid?

$I = PRT$ **Use the simple interest formula.**

$I = (\$5,000)(12\frac{1}{2}\%)(2)$ **Principal *P* is $5,000, rate *R* is $12\frac{1}{2}\%$ per year, time *T* is 2 years.**

$I = (\$5,000)(0.125)(2)$ **Write $12\frac{1}{2}\%$ as a decimal.**

$I = \$1,250$

Kanette's Salon will pay $1,250 interest.

 The Maturity Value of a Loan

The *total* amount of money due by the end of a loan period—the amount of the loan *and* the interest—is called the **maturity value** of the loan. When the principal and interest of a loan are known, the maturity value is found by adding the principal and the interest. The maturity value can also be found directly from the principal, rate, and time.

HOW TO — Find the Maturity Value of a Loan

Step 1 If the principal and interest are known, add them.

$$\text{Maturity values} = \text{principal} + \text{interest}$$

$$MV = P + I$$

Step 2 If the principal, rate, and time are known:
  a) Add 1 to the product of rate and time.
  b) Multiply the principal by the sum from step 2a.

$$\text{Maturity value} = \text{principal} (1 + \text{rate} \times \text{time})$$

$$MV = P(1 + RT)$$

The formula for finding the maturity value when the principal, rate, and time are known requires that the operations be performed according to the standard order of operations. To review briefly, when more than one operation is to be performed, perform operations within parentheses first. Perform multiplications and divisions before additions and subtractions. Perform additions and subtractions last.

Example 3 How much money will Kanette's Salon (Example 2) pay at the end of 2 years?

$$\text{Maturity value} = \text{principal} + \text{interest}$$

$$MV = P + I$$

$$= \$5{,}000 + \$1{,}250 = \$6{,}250$$

or, using the second formula given in the How-To box,

$$\text{Maturity value} = \text{principal} (1 + \text{rate} \times \text{time})$$

$$MV = P(1 + \boxed{RT})$$

$$MV = \$5{,}000(1 + \boxed{0.125 \times 2}) \quad \text{Follow the standard order of operations.}$$

$$MV = \$5{,}000(1 + \boxed{0.25}) \quad \text{Multiply } 0.125 \times 2.$$

$$MV = \$5{,}000(1.25) \quad \text{Add } 1 + 0.25.$$

$$MV = \$6{,}250$$

Kanette's Salon will pay $6,250 at the end of the loan period.

TIPS & TRAPS

Be careful to use the standard order of operations. In Example 3, the maturity value formula $MV = P(1 + RT)$ requires that the operations within the parentheses be done first. However, within the parentheses both addition and multiplication are indicated. Within the parentheses, perform the multiplication, then the addition.

$$MV = \$5{,}000(1 + 0.125 \times 2)$$

$$MV = \$5{,}000(1 + 0.25) \quad \text{Multiply within parentheses.}$$

$$MV = \$5{,}000(1.25) \quad \text{Add within parentheses.}$$

Finally, the multiplication that is indicated from outside the parentheses is performed.

$$MV = \$6{,}250$$

Using a basic calculator, you enter calculations as they should be performed according to the standard order of operations.

$$\boxed{\text{AC}}\ .125\ \boxed{\times}\ 2 = \boxed{+}\ 1\ \boxed{=}\boxed{\times}\ 5000\ \boxed{=} \Rightarrow 6250$$

Using an office calculator the calculations are still entered as they should be performed according to the standard order of operations, but using a different key sequence.

$$\boxed{\text{AC}}\ .125\ \boxed{\times}\ 2 = \boxed{1}\ +\ \boxed{\times}\ 5000\ \boxed{=} \Rightarrow 6250$$

Using a scientific calculator with parentheses keys allows you to enter values for the maturity value formula as they appear. The calculator is programmed to perform the operations in the standard order.

$$\boxed{\text{AC}}\ 5000\ \boxed{\times}\ \boxed{(}\ 1\ \boxed{+}\ .125\ \boxed{\times}\ 2\ \boxed{)}\ \boxed{=} \Rightarrow 6250$$

▶ 3 *Fractional Parts of a Year*

Not all loans or investments are made for a whole number of years, but when the interest rate is per year, then time must also be expressed in years.

? HOW TO	**Convert Months to a Fractional or Decimal Part of a Year**

Step 1 Write the number of months as the numerator of a fraction.
Step 2 Write 12 as the denominator of the fraction.
Step 3 Reduce the fraction to lowest terms.
Step 4 Divide the numerator by the denominator to get the decimal equivalent of the fraction.

Example 4 Convert (a) 5 months and (b) 15 months to years, expressed in decimal form.

a. 5 months $= \dfrac{5}{12}$ year   **5 months equal $\frac{5}{12}$ year.**

$$\begin{array}{r} 0.4166666 \text{ year} = 0.42 \text{ year} \\ 12\overline{)5.0000000} \end{array}$$

To write the fraction as a decimal, divide the number of months (the numerator) by the number of months in a year (the denominator).

5 months = 0.42 year (rounded)

b. 15 months $= \dfrac{15}{12}$ years $= \dfrac{5}{4}$ **15 months equal $\frac{15}{12}$ years.**

$$\begin{array}{r} 1.25 \text{ years} \\ 4\overline{)5.00} \end{array}$$

To write the fraction as a decimal, divide the number of months (the numerator) by the number of months in a year (the denominator).

15 months = 1.25 years

Example 5 To save money for a shoe repair shop, Stan Upright invested $2,500 for 45 months at $12\frac{1}{2}\%$ interest per year. How much interest did he earn?

$$T = \boxed{45 \text{ months}} = \frac{45}{12} \text{ years} = \boxed{3.75} \text{ years} \qquad \text{Write the time in terms of years.}$$

$$I = PRT \qquad \text{Use the simple interest formula.}$$

$$I = \$2,500(0.125)(\boxed{3.75}) \qquad \text{Principal } P \text{ is \$2,500, rate } R \text{ is 0.125, and time } T \text{ is } \frac{45}{12}.$$

$$I = \$1,171.88$$

Stan Upright earned $1,171.88 in interest.

When time is expressed in months, the calculator sequence is the same as when time is expressed in years, except that we do not enter a whole number for the time. Months can be changed to years in the sequence rather than as a separate calculation. All other steps are the same. To solve the equation using a calculator without the percent key, use the decimal equivalent of $12\frac{1}{2}\%$.

$$\boxed{\text{AC}} \ 2500 \ \boxed{\times} \ .125 \ \boxed{\times} \ 45 \ \boxed{\div} \ 12 \ \boxed{=} \ \Rightarrow 1171.875$$

The percent key on a calculator serves as an equal key *and* changes the percent to a decimal equivalent.

To solve the equation using a calculator with a percent key, enter

$$\boxed{\text{AC}} \ 2500 \ \boxed{\times} \ 12.5 \ \boxed{\%} \ \boxed{\times} \ 45 \ \boxed{\div} \ 12 \Rightarrow 1171.875$$

4 *Finding the Principal, Rate, or Time Using the Simple Interest Formula*

So far in this chapter, we have used the formula $I = PRT$ to find the simple interest on a loan. However, sometimes you need to find the principal or the rate or the time instead of the interest. You can remember the different forms of this formula with a circle diagram (see Figure 9–1) like the one used for the percentage formula. Cover the unknown term to see the form of the simple interest formula needed to find the missing value:

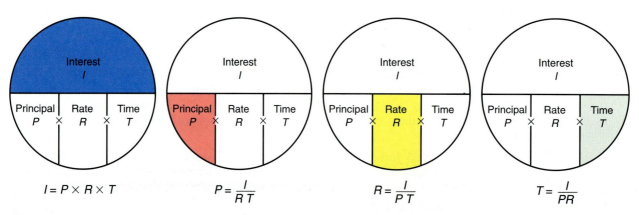

Figure 9–1 Various Forms of the Simple Interest Formula

HOW TO
Find the Principal, Rate, or Time Using the Simple Interest Formula

Step 1 Select the appropriate form of the formula.
a) If the principal is unknown, use

$$P = \frac{I}{RT}$$

b) If the rate is unknown, use

$$R = \frac{I}{PT}$$

c) If the time is unknown, use

$$T = \frac{I}{PR}$$

Step 2 Replace letters with known values, and perform the indicated operations.

AROUND THE BUSINESS WORLD

The Cola Wars Go to College

In the face of funding cuts, what's a cash-parched university to do to raise money? Here's one idea that worked for Rutgers University: Have a Coke, and smile all the way to the bank.

On Aug. 31, Rutgers inked a $10 million, 10-year contract giving Coca-Cola Co. exclusive rights to sell soft drinks and juices to the 48,000 students at New Brunswick and two other campuses in New Jersey. "This is one innovative way to help lessen the impact of cuts," Rutgers President Francis L. Lawrence said at a press conference announcing the pact. Under the deal, any campus-sponsored group has to sell Coke—and even campus restaurants and convenience stores that normally sell Pepsi will have to switch.

Rutgers is the latest example of a growing trend. Ever since Pennsylvania State University signed a beverage deal with Pepsi-Cola Co. in 1992 that is expected to earn it $14 million over 10 years, universities have been auctioning off rights to sell on their campuses in multiyear contracts. The University of Cincinnati, the University of Oregon, and others have also signed deals.

In jousting for campus business, says Jesse Meyer, publisher of *Beverage Digest,* Coke and Pepsi run the risk of "whomping up the bidding until you know whoever is the winner is in fact the financial loser." Coke and Pepsi won't comment on the profitability of the pacts, but both admit they highly value having a strong franchise with young cola quaffers.

The bargain that Rutgers cut shows just how adept universities have become at playing the companies off against each other. Coke already controlled 90% of the school's soft-drink business through a contract covering Rutgers' cafeterias, student centers, and fountain machines. Rutgers threw in its vending-machine business—which had belonged to Pepsi—plus special promo opportunities and the promise of exclusivity and got Coke and Pepsi to bid. Coke had to up Pepsi's offer of about $7.5 million or lose its spot on campus.

Brad Choate, a Penn State associate vice-president, predicts that universities will cut "more and more" such deals. He says Penn State already has similar agreements with AT&T and bookseller Barnes & Noble Inc. The lesson: The great campus cola wars may soon broaden out to include all sorts of businesses.

Example 6 To buy new knives for his restaurant, Mr. Cooke borrowed $800 for $3\frac{1}{2}$ years and paid $348 simple interest on the loan. What rate of interest did he pay?

$R = \dfrac{I}{PT}$ **R is unknown. Select the correct form of the simple interest formula.**

$I =$ $348

$P =$ $800

$T = 3.5$ years

$R = \dfrac{348}{(800)(3.5)}$ **Replace letters with known values: I is $348, P is $800, T is 3.5 years. Perform the operations.**

$R = 0.124$ **Write the rate in percent form by moving the decimal point two places to the right and attaching a % symbol.**

$R = 12.4\%$

He paid 12.4% interest.

There are several efficient ways to perform the calculations in Example 6.

1. Using memory: Multiply 800×3.5, store the result in memory and clear display, enter 348 and divide by the stored product:

    $\boxed{\text{AC}}$ 800 $\boxed{\times}$ 3.5 $\boxed{=}$ $\boxed{\text{M}^+}$ $\boxed{\text{CE/C}}$ 348 $\boxed{\div}$ $\boxed{\text{MRC}}$ $\boxed{=}$ $\Rightarrow 0.1242857$

2. Using repeated division: Divide 348 by both 800 and 3.5:

    $\boxed{\text{AC}}$ 348 $\boxed{\div}$ 800 $\boxed{\div}$ 3.5 $\boxed{=}$ $\Rightarrow 0.1242857$

3. Using a scientific calculator and parentheses: Group the calculations in the denominator using parentheses:

    $\boxed{\text{AC}}$ 348 $\div$ $\boxed{(}$ 800 $\boxed{\times}$ 3.5 $\boxed{)}$ $\boxed{=}$ $\Rightarrow 0.1242857$

Example 7 Ms. Cox wanted to borrow some money to expand her egg farm. She was told she could borrow a sum of money for 18 months at 18% simple interest per year and pay $540 in interest charges. How much money could she borrow?

$P = \dfrac{I}{RT}$ **P is unknown. Select the correct form of the simple interest formula.**

$T = 18$ months $= \dfrac{18}{12}$ **The interest rate is per year, so write 18 months as 1.5 years.**

$\phantom{T = 18 \text{ months}} = 1.5$ years

$P = \dfrac{540}{0.18(1.5)}$ **Replace letters with known values: I is $540, R is 0.18, T is 1.5.**

$P = $2,000$ **Perform the operations.**

The principal is $2,000.

1. Using memory: Multiply 0.18×1.5, store the result in memory and clear the display, and divide 540 by the stored product:

$$\boxed{\text{AC}} \quad .18 \quad \boxed{\times} \quad 1.5 \quad \boxed{=} \quad \boxed{\text{M}^+} \quad \boxed{\text{CE/C}} \quad 540 \quad \boxed{\div} \quad \boxed{\text{MRC}} \quad \boxed{=} \quad \Rightarrow 2000$$

2. Using repeated division: Divide 540 by both 0.18 and 1.5:

$$\boxed{\text{AC}} \quad 540 \quad \boxed{\div} \quad .18 \quad \boxed{\div} \quad 1.5 \quad \boxed{=} \quad \Rightarrow 2000$$

3. Using a scientific calculator and parentheses: Group the calculation in the denominator using parentheses:

$$\boxed{\text{AC}} \quad 540 \quad \boxed{\div} \quad \boxed{(} \quad .18 \times 1.5 \quad \boxed{)} \quad \boxed{=} \quad \Rightarrow 2000$$

Example 8 Lee's Tree Service borrowed $2,400 at 14% simple interest per year to repair its tree-topper. If it paid $840 interest, what was the duration of the loan?

$$T = \frac{I}{PR}$$

T is unknown. Select the correct form of the simple interest formula.

$$T = \frac{840}{2,400(0.14)} = 2.5 \text{ years}$$

Replace letters with known values: *I* = $840, *P* = $2,400, *R* = 0.14. Perform the operations.

The duration of the loan is 2.5 years.

Self-Check 9.1

1. Find the interest paid on a loan of $2,400 for one year at a simple interest rate of 11% per year.

2. Find the interest paid on a loan of $800 at $8\frac{1}{2}$% annual simple interest for two years.

3. How much interest will have to be paid on a loan of $7,980 for two years at a simple interest rate of 6.2% per year?

4. Find the total amount of money (maturity value) that the borrower will pay back on a loan of $1,400 at $12\frac{1}{2}$% annual simple interest for 3 years.

5. Find the maturity value of a loan of $2,800 after three years. The loan carries a simple interest rate of 7.5% per year.

6. Susan Duke borrowed $20,000 for four years to purchase a car. The simple interest loan has a rate of 8.2% per year. What is the maturity value of the loan?

Convert to years, expressed in decimal form.

7. 8 months

8. 40 months

9. A loan is made for 18 months. Convert the time to years.

10. Express 28 months in decimal form.

11. Ben Duke took out a $42,000 construction loan to remodel a house. The loan rate is 8.3% simple interest per year and will be repaid in six months. How much is paid back?

12. Madison Duke needed start-up money for her bakery. She borrowed $1,200 for 30 months and paid $360 simple interest on the loan. What interest rate did she pay?

13. Raul Fletes needed money to buy lawn equipment. He borrowed $500 for seven months and paid $53.96 in interest. What was the rate of interest?

14. Linda Davis agreed to lend money to Alex Luciano at a special interest rate of 9% per year, on the condition that he borrow enough that he would pay her $500 in interest over a two-year period. What was the minimum amount Alex could borrow?

15. Rob Thweatt needed money for college. He borrowed $6,000 at 12% simple interest per year. If he paid $360 interest, what was the duration of the loan?

16. Keaton Smith borrowed $25,000 to purchase stock for his baseball card shop. He repaid the simple interest loan after three years. He paid interest of $6,750. What was the interest rate?

9.2	**Ordinary and Exact Time and Interest**

 Find ordinary and exact time

 Find the due date

 Find the ordinary and exact interest rates

4 *Find simple interest using a table*

Sometimes the time period of a loan is indicated by the beginning date and the due date of the loan rather than by a specific number of months or days. In such cases, you

Table 9–1 Sequential Numbers for Dates of the Year

Day of Month	Jan.	Feb.	Mar.	Apr.	May	Jun.	Jul.	Aug.	Sept.	Oct.	Nov.	Dec.
1	1	32	60	91	121	152	182	213	244	274	305	335
2	2	33	61	92	122	153	183	214	245	275	306	336
3	3	34	62	93	123	154	184	215	246	276	307	337
4	4	35	63	94	124	155	185	216	247	277	308	338
5	5	36	64	95	125	156	186	217	248	278	309	339
6	6	37	65	96	126	157	187	218	249	279	310	340
7	7	38	66	97	127	158	188	219	250	280	311	341
8	8	39	67	98	128	159	189	220	251	281	312	342
9	9	40	68	99	129	160	190	221	252	282	313	343
10	10	41	69	100	130	161	191	222	253	283	314	344
11	11	42	70	101	131	162	192	223	254	284	315	345
12	12	43	71	102	132	163	193	224	255	285	316	346
13	13	44	72	103	133	164	194	225	256	286	317	347
14	14	45	73	104	134	165	195	226	257	287	318	348
15	15	46	74	105	135	166	196	227	258	288	319	349
16	16	47	75	106	136	167	197	228	259	289	320	350
17	17	48	76	107	137	168	198	229	260	290	321	351
18	18	49	77	108	138	169	199	230	261	291	322	352
19	19	50	78	109	139	170	200	231	262	292	323	353
20	20	51	79	110	140	171	201	232	263	293	324	354
21	21	52	80	111	141	172	202	233	264	294	325	355
22	22	53	81	112	142	173	203	234	265	295	326	356
23	23	54	82	113	143	174	204	235	266	296	327	357
24	24	55	83	114	144	175	205	236	267	297	328	358
25	25	56	84	115	145	176	206	237	268	298	329	359
26	26	57	85	116	146	177	207	238	269	299	330	360
27	27	58	86	117	147	178	208	239	270	300	331	361
28	28	59	87	118	148	179	209	240	271	301	332	362
29	29	*	88	119	149	180	210	241	272	302	333	363
30	30		89	120	150	181	211	242	273	303	334	364
31	31		90		151		212	243		304		365

*See the discussion on leap year. For centennial years (those at the turn of the century), leap years occur only when the number of the year is divisible by 400. Thus, 2000 will be a leap year (2000/400 divides exactly), but 1700, 1800, and 1900 were not leap years.

must first determine the number of days of the loan. If you count 30 days in each month, the time is **ordinary time.** If you count the exact number of days in a month, the time is **exact time.** Interest is called **ordinary interest** when 360 days per year is used. Interest is called **exact interest** when 365 (or 366 in a leap year) days per year is used.

Suppose you take out a loan on July 12 that is due September 12. If you use ordinary time, you figure each of the two months to have 30 days, so the total days are 2 × 30, or 60 days. If you use the exact time, you must figure the exact number of days from July 12 to Sept 12: add the 19 days remaining in July, the 31 days in August, and the 12 days in September to get the total of 62 days. This calculation is much quicker if you use Table 9–1, which numbers each day of the year in sequence beginning with Jan 1.

 *Ordinary and Exact Time*

To use Table 9–1 to find the exact time of a loan from July 12 to September 12, note that July 12 is the 193rd day of the year and September 12 is the 255th day. Subtract 193 from 255 to find the total number of days.

$$\begin{array}{r} 255 \\ \underline{193} \\ 62 \text{ days} \end{array}$$ Sequence number for September 12
Sequence number for July 12

If the period of a loan includes February, count it as 30 days for ordinary time but 28 days for exact time. In leap years, February has 29 days, so the exact time is determined by counting 28 days and adding 1 to the total number of days if February 29 is within the loan period.

To determine if a year is a leap year, see if the year is divisible by 4. (Remember the rule for divisibility by 4: If the last *two* digits form a number that is divisible by 4, th entire number is divisible by 4). The year 1996 is a leap year because 96 is divisible by 4; thus, 1996 is divisible by 4.

 HOW TO **Change Months and Years to Ordinary or Exact Time in Days**

Step 1 For ordinary time use:

1 month = 30 days

1 year = 360 days

Step 2 For exact time use:

1 month = exact number of days in the month

1 year = 365 days (or 366 days in a leap year)

HOW TO **Find the Exact Time of a Loan Using the Sequential Numbers Table (Table 9–1)**

Step 1 If the beginning and due dates of the loan fall within the same year, subtract the beginning date's sequential number from the due date's sequential number.

Step 2 If the beginning and due dates of the loan do not fall within the same year:
  a) Subtract the beginning date's sequential number from 365.
  b) Add the due date's sequential number to the difference from step 2a.

Step 3 If February 29 is between the beginning and due dates, add 1 to the difference from step 1 or the sum from step 2b.

Example 1 A loan made on September 5 is due July 5 of the *following year*. Find (a) the ordinary time, (b) the exact time for the loan in a non-leap year, and (c) the exact time in a leap year.

a. *Ordinary time*

There are 10 months from September to July.
10 months × 30 days/month = 300 days

b. *Exact time in a non-leap year*

From Table 9–1, September 5 is the 248th day.

$$\begin{array}{r} 365 \\ \underline{248} \\ 117 \end{array} \text{ days}$$ **Subtract 248 from 365.**

from September 5 through December 31

July 5 is the 186th day.

117 + 186 = 303 days   **Add 117 and 186 find the exact time of the loan.**

c. *Exact time in a leap year*

303 + 1 = 304 days   **Since Feb. 29 is between the beginning and due dates, add 1 to the non-leap year total.**

Ordinary time is 300 days. Exact time is 303 days in a non-leap year and 304 days in a leap year.

 Due Dates

Sometimes the beginning date of a loan and the time period of the loan are known, and the due date must be determined.

 HOW TO | **Find the Due Date of a Loan Given the Beginning Date and the Time Period in Days**

Step 1 For ordinary time:
  a) Determine the number of months of the loan, counting each month as 30 days.
  b) Count forward from the beginning date the number of months from step 1a. Add extra days for a part of a month if necessary.
Step 2 For exact time:
  a) Add the sequential number of the beginning date to the number of days in the time period.
  b) If the sum is less than or equal to 365, find the date (Table 9–1) corresponding to the sum.
  c) If the sum is more than 365, subtract 365 from the sum. Then find the date (Table 9–1) in the following year corresponding to the difference.
  d) Adjust for February 29 on a leap year if appropriate by subtracting one from the result in step 2b or 2c.

Example 2 Figure the due date using (a) ordinary time and (b) exact time for a 90-day loan made on November 15.

a. *Ordinary time*

In ordinary time, there are 30 days in a month, and 90 days is the same as 3 months.

Count 3 months from November 15 to find a due date of February 15.

b. *Exact time*

From Table 9–1, November 15 is the 319th day.

319   **Add 319 to 90 days in the time period.**
+ 90
———
409

409 is greater than 365, so the loan is due in the following year.

409   **Subtract 365 from 409.**
−365
———
44

In Table 9–1, day 44 corresponds to February 13.

The loan using ordinary time is due February 15 and using exact time is due February 13.

TIPS & TRAPS

When the number of days in ordinary time is not a multiple of 30, the extra days are used to adjust the due date. For a time period of 100 days, 90 days are three months in ordinary time. The extra ten days advance the due date by ten days. If the beginning date on a 100-day loan is July 25, three months advance the due date to October 25. Five of the extra days advance the due date to the end of the month (30 days). Then, the remaining extra five days advance the due date to November 5.

 Ordinary and Exact Interest Rates

An interest rate is normally given as a rate *per year*. But if the time period of the loan is in days, then using the simple interest formula requires that the rate *also* be expressed as a rate *per day*. We convert a rate per year to a rate per day in two different ways, depending on whether the rate per day is to be an **ordinary interest** rate or an **exact interest** rate. An ordinary interest rate assumes 360 days per year; an exact interest rate assumes 365 days per year. Thus:

$$\text{Ordinary interest rate per day} = \frac{\text{interest rate per year}}{360}$$

$$\text{Exact interest rate per day} = \frac{\text{interest rate per year}}{365}$$

 HOW TO   **Find the Ordinary Interest Rate and the Exact Interest Rate**

Step 1   For ordinary interest, divide the annual interest rate by 360.

$$\text{Ordinary interest rate per day} = \frac{\text{interest rate per year}}{360}$$

Step 2   For exact interest, divide the annual interest rate by 365.

$$\text{Exact interest rate per day} = \frac{\text{interest rate per year}}{365}$$

Example 3 Use ordinary time to find the ordinary interest on a loan of $500 at 17% annual interest rate. The loan was made on March 15 and is due May 15.

$$\text{Ordinary interest rate per day} = \frac{17\%}{360}$$ **Divide the annual rate by 360.**

$$\text{Ordinary time} = 2 \times 30 = 60 \text{ days}$$ **Multiply the number of days per month by 2.**

$$I = PRT$$

$$I = \$500\left(\frac{0.17}{360}\right)60$$ **Replace with known values.**

$$I = \$14.17$$ **Perform the operations.**

The interest is $14.17.

Example 4 Find the ordinary interest using exact time for the loan in Example 3.

$$\text{Ordinary interest rate per day} = \frac{17\%}{360}$$

$$\text{Exact time} = 135 - 74 = 61$$ **Find each date's sequential number in Table 9–1 and subtract.**

$$I = PRT$$

$$I = \$500\left(\frac{0.17}{360}\right)61$$ **Replace with known values.**

$$I = \$14.40$$ **Perform the operations.**

The interest is $14.40.

Example 5 Find the exact interest using exact time on the loan in Example 3.

$$\text{Exact interest} = \frac{17\%}{365}$$ **Divide the annual rate by 365.**

$$\text{Exact time} = 61 \text{ days}$$

$$I = PRT$$

$$I = \$500\left(\frac{0.17}{365}\right)61$$ **Replace with known values.**

$$I = \$14.21$$ **Perform the operations.**

The interest is $14.21.

Examples 3, 4, and 5 can be calculated and compared using a basic calculator:

Ex 3: [AC] 500 [×] .17 [=] [M+] [×] 60 [÷] 360 [=] $\Rightarrow$ 14.166666

Ex 4: [AC] [MR] [×] 61 [÷] 360 [=] $\Rightarrow$ 14.402777

Ex 5: [AC] [MR] [×] 61 [÷] 365 [=] $\Rightarrow$ 14.205479

Note that the interest varies in each case. The second method illustrated, *ordinary interest using exact time,* is most often used by bankers when they are *lending* money because it yields a slightly higher amount of interest. It is sometimes called the **banker's rule.** On the other hand, when bankers *pay* interest on savings accounts, they normally use a 365-day year—an exact interest rate—which yields a slightly lower amount of interest.

Example 6 Borrowing money to pay cash for large purchases is sometimes profitable when a cash discount is allowed on the purchases. Joann Jimanez purchased a computer and printer for her typing service that regularly sold for $5,999 during a special promotion for $5,890, with cash terms of 3/10, n/90. She does not have the cash to pay the bill now but she will within the next three months. She finds a bank that will loan her the money for the equipment at 13% (using ordinary interest) for 80 days. Should she take out the loan to take advantage of the special promotion and cash discount?

 1 Decision needed Should Joann Jimanez take out the loan?

2 Unknown fact Cash discount on special price, compared with interest on loan

3 Known facts Since Joann would have the money by the 90-day net period, she can take advantage of the special price with either choice.
Special price: $5,890
Cash discount rate: 0.03
Ordinary interest rate of loan: $\dfrac{0.13}{360}$ per day

Exact term of loan: 80 days

4 Relationships Cash discount = special price × discount rate
Cash discount = $5,890 × 0.03
Interest on loan = principal × rate × time

The principal is the net amount Joann would pay, once the cash discount is allowed. Net amount is the special price, $5,890, multiplied by the complement of the cash discount rate.

Interest on loan = ($5,890 × 0.97) × $\dfrac{0.13}{360}$ × 80

5 Estimate Both the cash discount and the interest on the loan are a percentage of the special price. That is, both are $5,890 multiplied by some factor.

Cash discount = $5,890 × 0.03

Interest on loan = $5,890 × $0.97 \times \dfrac{0.13}{360} \times 80$

One way to compare the interest and cash discount, then, is to compare these factors. We estimate

Cash discount factor = 0.03 = $\dfrac{3}{100} \approx \dfrac{1}{33}$

Interest factor ≈ $1 \times \dfrac{0.12}{360} \times 100 = \dfrac{12}{360} = \dfrac{1}{30}$

The cash discount factor looks to be slightly smaller than the interest factor, so that the cash discount may not be large enough to offset the interest on the loan. In any case, whatever dollar benefit there may be is likely to be small.

6 Calculate Cash discount = $5,890 × 0.03

= $176.70

$$\text{Interest on loan} = \$5{,}890 \times 0.97 \times \frac{0.13}{360} \times 80$$

$$= \$165.05$$

The interest on the loan is $165.05, slightly less than the cash discount of $176.70.

7   Decision made   Since the cash discount is about $10 more than the interest on the loan, Joann will not lose money by borrowing to take advantage of the discount terms of sale. But other factors—the time she spends to take out the loan, for example—may weigh her decision against the loan. Instead she may settle for paying a slightly higher price, foregoing the cash discount.

 Simple Interest Tables

Many tables are available for finding ordinary and exact interest. Notes on the table will explain how to interpret table values. The values in Table 9–2 give the exact interest for $100 for a specific number of days.

 HOW TO   **Find Simple Interest Using a Table**

Step 1   Identify the amount of money that the table uses as the principal. (A typical table principal is $1, $100, or $1,000.)
Step 2   Divide the loan principal by the table principal.
Step 3   Select the days row corresponding to the time period (in days) of the loan.
Step 4   Select the annual rate column corresponding to the annual interest rate of the loan.
Step 5   Locate the value in the cell where the annual rate column intersects the days row.
Step 6   Multiply the quotient from step 2 by the value from step 5.

Example 7   Find the exact interest on a loan of $6,500 at 11.75% annually for 45 days.

Use Table 9–2 (on page 317) to find the interest for $100. Move across the 45 days row to the $11\frac{3}{4}$% column. The number 1.448630 is the interest on $100 for 45 days. The interest on $6,500 is

$$\frac{\$6{,}500}{\$100} \times 1.448630 = 65 \times 1.448630 = \$94.16 \text{ (to nearest cent)}$$

To check this answer, we use the formula $I = PRT$.

Check:

$$I = PRT$$

$$I = \$6{,}500 \times \left(\frac{0.1175}{365}\right) \times 45 = \$94.16$$

The interest is $94.16.

Table 9–2 Simple Interest on $100 (Exact Time, Exact Interest Basis)

Days	11.5%	11.75%	12.00%	12.25%	12.50%	12.75%
1	0.031507	0.032192	0.032877	0.033562	0.034247	0.034932
2	0.063014	0.064384	0.065753	0.067123	0.068493	0.069863
3	0.094521	0.096575	0.098630	0.100685	0.102740	0.104795
4	0.126027	0.128767	0.131507	0.134247	0.136986	0.139726
5	0.157534	0.160959	0.164384	0.167808	0.171233	0.174658
6	0.189041	0.193151	0.197260	0.201370	0.205479	0.209589
7	0.220548	0.225342	0.230137	0.234932	0.239726	0.244521
8	0.252055	0.257534	0.263014	0.268493	0.273973	0.279452
9	0.283562	0.289726	0.295890	0.302055	0.308219	0.314384
10	0.315068	0.321918	0.328767	0.335616	0.342466	0.349315
11	0.346575	0.354110	0.361644	0.369178	0.376712	0.384247
12	0.378082	0.386301	0.394521	0.402740	0.410959	0.419178
13	0.409589	0.418493	0.427397	0.436301	0.445205	0.454110
14	0.441096	0.450685	0.460274	0.469863	0.479452	0.489041
15	0.472603	0.482877	0.493151	0.503425	0.513699	0.523973
16	0.504110	0.515068	0.526027	0.536986	0.547945	0.558904
17	0.535616	0.547260	0.558904	0.570548	0.582192	0.593836
18	0.567123	0.579452	0.591781	0.604110	0.616438	0.628767
19	0.598630	0.611644	0.624658	0.637671	0.650685	0.663699
20	0.630137	0.643836	0.567534	0.671233	0.684932	0.698630
21	0.661644	0.676027	0.690411	0.704795	0.719178	0.733562
22	0.693151	0.708219	0.723288	0.738356	0.753425	0.768493
23	0.724658	0.740411	0.756164	0.771918	0.787671	0.803425
24	0.756164	0.772603	0.789041	0.805479	0.821918	0.838356
25	0.787671	0.804795	0.821918	0.839041	0.856164	0.873288
26	0.819178	0.836986	0.854795	0.872603	0.890411	0.908219
27	0.850685	0.869178	0.887671	0.906164	0.924658	0.943151
28	0.882192	0.901370	0.920548	0.939726	0.958904	0.978082
29	0.913699	0.933562	0.953425	0.973288	0.993151	1.013014
30	0.945205	0.965753	0.986301	1.006849	1.027397	1.047945
31	0.976712	0.997945	1.019178	1.040411	1.061644	1.082877
32	1.008219	1.030137	1.052055	1.073973	1.095890	1.117808
33	1.039726	1.062329	1.084932	1.107534	1.130137	1.152740
34	1.071233	1.094521	1.117808	1.141096	1.164384	1.187671
35	1.102740	1.126712	1.150685	1.174658	1.198630	1.222603
36	1.134247	1.158904	1.183562	1.208219	1.232877	1.257534
37	1.165753	1.191096	1.216438	1.241781	1.267123	1.292466
38	1.197260	1.223288	1.249315	1.275342	1.301370	1.327397
39	1.228767	1.255479	1.282192	1.308904	1.385616	1.362329
40	1.260274	1.287671	1.315068	1.342466	1.369863	1.397260
41	1.291781	1.319863	1.347945	1.376027	1.404110	1.432192
42	1.323288	1.352055	1.380822	1.409589	1.438356	1.467123
43	1.354795	1.384247	1.413699	1.443151	1.472603	1.502055
44	1.386301	1.416438	1.446575	1.476712	1.506849	1.536986
45	1.417808	1.448630	1.479452	1.510274	1.541096	1.571918
46	1.449315	1.480822	1.512329	1.543836	1.575342	1.606849
47	1.480822	1.513014	1.545205	1.577397	1.609589	1.641781
48	1.512329	1.545205	1.578082	1.610959	1.643836	1.676712
49	1.543836	1.577397	1.610959	1.644521	1.678082	1.711644
50	1.575342	1.609589	1.643836	1.678082	1.712329	1.746575

1. 1. A loan made on March 10 is due September 10 of the *following year*. Find the ordinary time and exact time for the loan in a non-leap year and a leap year.

2. Find the ordinary and exact time of a loan made on March 25 and due on November 15 of the same year.

3. A loan is made on January 15 and has a due date of October 20 during a leap year. Find the ordinary time and the exact time of the loan.

2. 4. Find the due date using ordinary time and exact time for a loan made on October 15 for 120 days.

5. A loan is made on March 20 for 180 days. Find the due date using ordinary time and exact time.

6. Use exact time to find the due date of a loan that is made on February 10 of a leap year and is due in 60 days.

3. *Exercises 7–9: A loan for $3,000 with a simple annual interest rate of 15% was made on June 15 and was due on August 15.*

7. Use ordinary time to find the ordinary interest on the loan.

8. Find the exact interest using exact time.

9. Find the ordinary interest using exact time.

4. *For Exercises 10–12, use Table 9–2.*

10. Find the exact interest on a loan of $3,500 at $12\frac{1}{2}\%$ annual simple interest for 45 days.

11. Find the exact interest on a loan of $1,000 at 12% annual simple interest for 10 days.

BUSINESS AND MATHEMATICS *IN THE NEWS*

Savings Rates Across the USA Last Week

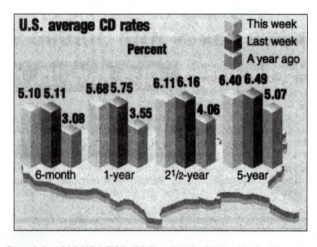

Copyright 1995 USA TODAY, Reprinted with permission.

The graph shown at left depicts the savings rates for certificates of deposit (CD) in the United States for the week of May 15, 1995 (labeled This week in the graph), last week, and a year ago.

1. What time periods are represented in the graph? Give your answers in decimal form in years.

2. What was the highest interest rate available, according to the graph?

3. In general, what time period gave the highest interest rate?

4. Compare interest rates for CDs a year ago to interest rates for CDs this week (May 15, 1995).

12. Find the exact interest on a loan of $1,850 at $11\frac{1}{2}\%$ annual simple interest for 21 days.

13. Discuss the practicality of using tables versus a calculator for finding interest.

 Find the bank discount and proceeds for a simple discount note

 Find the bank discount and proceeds for a third-party discount note

When a business or individual borrows money, it is customary for the borrower to sign a legal document promising to repay the loan. The document is called a **promissory note.** The note includes all necessary information about the loan. The **maker** is the person borrowing the money. The **payee** is the person loaning the money. The **term** of the note is the length of time for which the money is borrowed; the **maturity date** is the date on which the loan is due to be repaid. The **face value** of the note is the amount borrowed. Figure 9–2 shows a sample promissory note signed by Mary Fisher of Fisher's Tackle Shop.

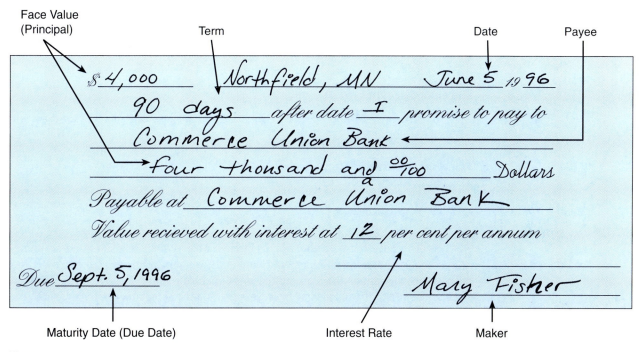

Figure 9–2 A Promissory Note

 Finding Bank Discount and Proceeds for a Simple Discount Note

If money is borrowed from a bank at a simple interest rate, the bank often collects the interest, which is also called the **bank discount,** at the time the loan is made. Thus, the maker receives the face value of the loan minus the bank discount. This difference is called the **proceeds.** Such a loan is called a **simple discount note.** Loans of this type allow the bank or payee of the loan to receive all fees and interest at the time the loan is made. This increases the yield on the loan. Besides increased yields, a bank may require this type of loan when the maker of the loan has an inadequate or poor credit history. This decreases the amount of risk to the bank or lender.

Step 1 For the bank discount use:

$$\text{Bank discount} = \text{face value} \times \text{discount rate} \times \text{time}$$

$$I = PRT$$

Step 2 For the proceeds use:

$$\text{Proceeds} = \text{face value} - \text{bank discount}$$

$$A = P - I$$

Example 1 Find the (a) bank discount and (b) proceeds using ordinary interest and ordinary time on the promissory note shown in Figure 9–2. It is a loan to Mary Fisher of $4,000 at 12% annual simple interest from June 5 to September 5.

(a) Bank discount $= P \times R \times T$

$$= \$4,000 \times \frac{0.12}{360} \times 90$$

$$= \$120$$

The bank discount is $120.

(b) Proceeds $= \$4,000 - \$120$ Subtract the bank discount from the face value of the note.

$$= \$3,880$$

The proceeds are $3,880.

The difference between the simple interest note (which is also called an undiscounted note) and the simple discount note is the amount of money the borrower has use of for the length of the loan, and also the maturity value of the loan, the amount owed at the end of the loan term. Interest is paid on the same amount for the same period of time in both cases. In the simple interest note, the borrower has use of the full principal of the loan, but the maturity value is principal plus interest. In the simple discount note the borrower has use of only the proceeds (face value − discount), but the maturity value is just the face value, since the interest (the discount) was paid "in advance." Thus, if Bill borrows $5,000 with a discount (interest) rate of 18%, the discount is 18% × $5,000, or $900, so he gets the use of only $4,100, though the bank charges interest on the full $5,000. The maturity value is $5,000.

Here is a comparison of simple interest notes versus simple discount notes:

	Simple Interest Note	Simple Discount Note
Face value	$5,000	$5,000
Discount or interest	900	900
Proceeds or amount available to borrower	5,000	4,100
Maturity value	5,900	5,000

2 *Third-Party Discount Notes*

Many businesses agree to be the payee for a promissory note as payment for the sale of goods. If these businesses in turn need cash, they may sell such a note to a bank who is the **third-party** of the note. Selling a note to a bank in return for cash is called discounting a note. The note is called a **third-party discount note.**

When the third-party bank discounts a note, it gives the business owning the note the maturity value of the note minus a bank discount. The bank's discount is based on how long it holds the note, called the **discount period.** The bank receives the full maturity value of the note from the maker when it comes due. From the standpoint of the note maker (the borrower), the term of the note is the same because the maturity (due) date is the same, and the maturity value is the same.

The following diagram shows how the discount period is figured:

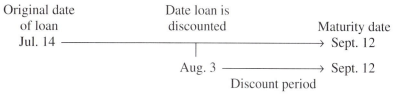

Original date
of loan
Jul. 14 ———————————————————→ Sept. 12

Date loan is
discounted

Maturity date

Aug. 3 ———————→ Sept. 12
Discount period

? HOW TO | **Find the Bank Discount and Proceeds for a Third-Party Discount Note**

Step 1 For the bank discount use:

Bank discount = maturity value of original note × discount rate
× discount period

$$I = PRT$$

Step 2 For the proceeds use:

Proceeds = maturity value of original note − bank discount

$$A = P - I$$

Example 2 Alpine Pleasures, Inc., delivers ski equipment to retailers in July but does not expect payment until mid-September, so the retailers agree to sign promissory notes for the equipment. These notes are based on exact interest and exact time, with a 10% annual simple interest rate. One promissory note held by Alpine is for $8,000, was made on July 14, and is due September 12. Alpine needs cash, so it takes the note to its bank. On August 3, the bank agrees to buy the note at a 12% discount rate using the banker's rule (ordinary interest, exact time). Find the proceeds for the note.

A table can help you organize the facts:

Date of Original Note	Principal of Note	Simple Interest Rate	Date of Discount Note	Bank Discount Rate	Maturity Date
July 14	$8,000	10%	Aug. 3	12%	Sept. 12

Calculate the time and maturity value of the original note. From Table 9–1, September 12 is the 255th day of the year, July 14 is the 195th day.

255
195
———
60 days

$$I = P \times R \times T$$

Use the simple interest equation to find exact interest using exact time.

$$= \$8{,}000 \times \frac{0.1}{365} \times 60$$

Ordinary interest rate is $\frac{10\%}{360}$.

$$= \$131.51 \text{ (rounded)}$$

The simple interest for the original loan is \$131.51.

To find the maturity value, add the principal and interest.

Maturity value

$$= \text{principal} + \text{interest}$$

$$= \$8{,}000 + \$131.51$$

$$= \boxed{\$8{,}131.51}$$

The maturity value of the original loan is \$8,131.51. Now calculate the discount period.

Discount period

$$= \text{number of days from}$$
$$\text{August 3 to September 12}$$

August 3 is the 215th day.

$$\begin{array}{r} 255 \\ \underline{215} \\ 40 \text{ days} \end{array}$$

The discount period for the discount note is 40 days. Now calculate the bank discount based on the banker's rule (ordinary interest using exact time).

Bank discount

$$= \text{maturity value} \times \text{bank discount rate} \times \text{discount period}$$

$$= \$8{,}131.51 \times \frac{0.12}{360} \times 40$$

Ordinary interest (discount) rate is $\frac{12\%}{360}$.

$$= \$108.42$$

The bank discount is \$108.42. Now calculate the proceeds that will be received by Alpine.

$$\text{Proceeds} = \text{maturity value} - \text{bank discount}$$

$$= \$8{,}131.51 - \$108.42$$

$$= \$8{,}023.09$$

The proceeds to Alpine are \$8,023.09.

TIPS & TRAPS

A non-interest-bearing note is very uncommon but sometimes available. This means that you borrow a certain amount and pay that same amount back later. The note itself carries no interest, and the maturity value of the note is the same as the face value or principal. The payee or person loaning the money only wants the original amount of money at the maturity date.

322   Chapter 9   Simple Interest and Simple Discount

What happens if a non-interest-bearing note is discounted? Use the information from Example 2, without the simple interest on the original loan.

$$\text{Bank discount} = \text{maturity value} \times \text{discount rate} \times \text{discount period}$$

$$\text{Bank discount} = \$8,000 \times \frac{0.12}{360} \times 40$$

The maturity value is the face value, or $8,000, rather than $8,131.51, which included interest.

$$= \$106.67$$

The bank discount is $106.67.

$$\text{Proceeds} = \text{maturity value} - \text{bank discount}$$

$$\text{Proceeds} = \$8,000 - \$106.67$$ **The maturity value is $8,000.**

$$= \$7,893.33$$

The proceeds are $7,893.33.

The original payee loans $8,000 and receives $7,893.33 in cash from the third-party bank.

Self-Check 9.3

Use the Banker's Rule unless otherwise specified.

1. José makes a simple discount note with a face value of $2,500, a term of 120 days, and a 16% discount rate. Find the discount.

2. Find the proceeds for Problem 1.

3. Find the discount and proceeds on a $3,250 face-value note for six months if the discount rate is 9.2%.

4. Find the maturity value of the undiscounted promissory note shown here.

5. Carter Manufacturing holds a note of $5,000 that has an interest rate of 11% annually. The note was made on March 18 and is due November 13. Carter sells the note to a bank on June 13 at a discount rate of 14% annually. Find the proceeds on the third-party discount note.

$ 3,000   Rockville, M.D. Aug. 5,   19 96

Nine Months   after date I promise to pay to

City Bank

three thousand and 00/100   Dollars

Payable at City Bank

Value recieved with interest at 16½ per cent per annum

Due May 5, 1997   Phillip Esterez

6. Discuss some reasons why a payee might agree to a non-interest-bearing note.

7. Discuss some reasons why a payee would sell a note to a bank and lose money in the process.

SELF-CHECK SOLUTIONS

Self-Check 9.1

1. $I = PRT$
$I = \$2,400 \times 0.11 \times 1$
$I = \$264$

2. $I = PRT$
$I = \$800 \times 0.085 \times 2$
$I = \$136$

3. $I = PRT$
$I = \$7,980 \times 0.062 \times 2$
$I = \$989.52$

4. $MV = P(1 + RT)$
$MV = \$1,400\,(1 + 0.125 \times 3)$
$MV = \$1,925$

5. $MV = P(1 + RT)$
$MV = \$2,800\,(1 + 0.075 \times 3)$
$MV = \$3,430$

6. $MV = P(1 + RT)$
$MV = \$20,000\,(1 + 0.082 \times 4)$
$MV = \$26,560$

7. 8 months $= \dfrac{8}{12}$ year
$= 0.6666666$, or 0.67 year

8. 40 months $= \dfrac{40}{12}$ years
$= 3.333333$, or 3.33 years

9. $18 \div 12 = 1.5$ years

10. $28 \div 12 = 2.333. . .$

11. $MV = P(1 + RT)$
$MV = \$42,000\,(1 + 0.083 \times 0.5)$
$MV = \$43,743$

12. $R = \dfrac{I}{PT}$ $T = 30$ months $= \dfrac{30}{12}$ years $= 2.5$ years

$R = \dfrac{\$360}{\$1,200 \times 2.5}$

$R = \dfrac{360}{3,000}$

$R = 0.12$, or 12% per year

13. $R = \dfrac{I}{PT}$ $T = \dfrac{7}{12}$ year

$R = \dfrac{\$53.96}{\$500 \times \frac{7}{12}}$ $\left(\$500 \times \dfrac{7}{12} = \$291.6667\right)$

$R = \dfrac{\$53.96}{\$291.6667}$

$R = 0.185$, or 18.5% per year

14. $P = \dfrac{I}{RT}$

$P = \dfrac{\$500}{0.09 \times 2}$

$P = \dfrac{\$500}{0.18}$

$P = \$2,777.78$

15. $T = \dfrac{I}{PR}$

$T = \dfrac{\$360}{\$6,000 \times 0.12}$

$T = \dfrac{360}{720}$

$T = 0.5 = \dfrac{1}{2}$ year, or 6 months

16. $R = \dfrac{I}{PT}$

$R = \dfrac{\$6,750}{\$25,000 \times 3}$

$R = 0.09$ or 9% per year

Self-Check 9.2

1. *Non-leap year*
Ordinary time: March 10 to March 10 is 12 months, or 12×30 days $= 360$ days.
March 10 to September 10 is 6 months, or 6×30 days $= 180$ days.
360 days $+$ 180 days $= 540$ days
Exact time: March 10 to March 10 of the following year is 1 year, or 365 days.

September 10 $=$ day 253
March 10 $=$ day $\underline{69}$
              184 days

$365 + 184 = 549$ days
Leap year
$1 + 549$ days $= 550$ days

2. Ordinary time: March 25 to November 25 is 8×30 days $= 240$ days.

November 15 = November 25 $- 10$ days

$$= 240 - 10$$
$$= 230 \text{ days}$$

Exact time: November 15 = day 319

$$\text{March 25} = \underline{\text{day } 84}$$
$$235 \text{ days}$$

3. Ordinary time: January 15 to October 15 is 9×30 days $= 270$ days.

October 20 = October 15 $+ 5$ days

$$= 270 + 5$$
$$= 275 \text{ days}$$

Exact time: October 20 = day 293

$$\text{January 15} = \underline{\text{day } 15}$$
$$278 \text{ days}$$

$$278 + \text{leap day} = 279 \text{ days}$$

4. Ordinary time: 120 days is $\frac{120}{30}$ months, or 4 months.

4 months from October 15 is February 15.

Exact time: October 15 = day 288

$$\underline{+120}$$
$$408$$

$408 - 365 = 43$ days

The 43rd day is February 12.

5. Ordinary time:

$180 \div 30 = 6$ months

Six months from March 20 is September 20.

Exact time:

March 20 = day 79

$$\underline{+180}$$
$$259$$

Day 259 is September 16.

6. Exact time:

February 10 = day 41

$$\underline{+60}$$
$$101$$

Day 101 is April 11, but adjusting for one leap day makes this April 10.

7. Ordinary time $= 2$ months, or 2×30 days $= 60$ days

$$I = \$3{,}000 \times \frac{0.15}{360} \times 60 = \$75$$

8. Exact time: August 15 = day 227

$$\text{June 15} = \underline{\text{day } 166}$$
$$61 \text{ days}$$

$$I = \$3{,}000 \times \frac{0.15}{365} \times 61 = \$75.21$$

9. $I = \$3{,}000 \times \dfrac{0.15}{360} \times 61 = \$76.25$

10. $I = \dfrac{\$3{,}500}{100} \times 1.541096 = \$53.94$

11. $I = \dfrac{\$1{,}000}{100} \times 0.328767 = \$3.29$

12. $I = \dfrac{\$1{,}850}{100} \times 0.661644 = \$12.24$

13. Answers will vary.

1. $I = \$2,500 \times \dfrac{0.16}{360} \times 120 = \$133.33$

2. Proceeds $= \$2,500 - \$133.33 = \$2,366.67$

3. $I = \$3,250 \times \dfrac{0.092}{360} \times 180$

$I = \$149.50$
Proceeds $= \$3,250 - \$149.50 = \$3,100.50$

4. Calculate time: December 31 = day 365
August 5 = day 217
148 days
May 5 = day 125
273 days

$I = \$3,000 \times \dfrac{0.165}{360} \times 273 = \$375.38$

Maturity value of note $= \$3,000 + \$375.38 = \$3,375.38$

5. Time: November 13 = day 317
March 18 = day 77
240 days

$I = \$5,000 \times \dfrac{0.11}{360} \times 240 = \$366.67$

Maturity value $= \$5,000 + \$366.67 = \$5,366.67$
Bank discount: November 13 = day 317
June 13 = day 164
153 days

$I = \$5,366.67 \times \dfrac{0.14}{360} \times 153 = \$319.31$

Proceeds $= \$5,361.64 - \$319.31 = \$5,042.33$

6. Answers will vary.

7. Answers will vary.

CHAPTER 9 OVERVIEW

Section—Objective

Important Points with Examples

9.1 — 1 (page 302)

Find simple interest using the simple interest formula

Multiply the principal by the rate and time.

$$\text{Interest} = \text{principal} \times \text{rate} \times \text{time}$$

$$I = PRT$$

Find the interest paid on a loan of \$8,400 for one year at $9\frac{1}{2}\%$ annual simple interest rate.	Find the interest paid on a loan of \$4,500 for two years at a simple interest rate of 12% per year.
Interest = principal × rate × time = \$8,400 × 0.095 × 1 = \$798	Interest = principal × rate × time = \$4,500 × 0.12 × 2 = \$1,080

 (page 303)

Find the maturity value of a loan

Step 1 If the principal and interest are known, add them.

$$\text{Maturity value} = \text{principal} + \text{interest}$$
$$MV = P + I$$

Step 2 If the principal, rate, and time are known: **a)** Add 1 to the product of the rate and time. **b)** Multiply the principal by the sum from step 2a.

$$\text{Maturity value} = \text{principal} \times (1 + \text{rate} \times \text{time})$$
$$MV = P(1 + RT)$$

Find the maturity value of a loan of \$8,400 with \$798 interest	Find the maturity value of a loan of \$4,500 for two years at a single interest rate of 12% per year.
$MV = P + I$ $\quad = \$8,400 + \$798$ $\quad = \$9,198$	$MV = P(1 + RT)$ $\quad = \$4,500(1 + 0.12 \times 2)$ $\quad = \$4,500(1.24)$ $\quad = \$5,580$

 (page 305)

Convert months to a fractional or decimal part of a year

Step 1 Write the number of months as the numerator of a fraction. **Step 2** Write 12 as the denominator of the fraction. **Step 3** Reduce the fraction to lowest terms. **Step 4** Divide the numerator by the denominator to get the decimal equivalent of the fraction.

Convert 42 months to years.	Convert 3 months to years.
$\dfrac{42}{12} = \dfrac{7}{2} = 3.5$ years	$\dfrac{3}{12} = \dfrac{1}{4} = 0.25$ years

 (page 306)

Find the principal, rate, or time using the simple interest formula

Step 1 Select the appropriate form of the formula. **a)** If the principal is unknown, use

$$P = \frac{I}{RT}$$

b) If the rate is unknown, use

$$R = \frac{I}{PT}$$

c) If the time is unknown, use

$$T = \frac{I}{PR}$$

Step 2 Replace letters with known values, and perform the indicated operations.

Jenny borrowed \$6,000 for $3\frac{1}{2}$ years and paid \$2,800 simple interest. What was the annual interest rate?

R is unknown.

$$R = \frac{I}{PT}$$

$$= \frac{\$2,800}{(\$6,000)(3.5)}$$

$$= 0.133$$

$$= 13.3\% \text{ annually}$$

Francesa paid $675 interest on an 18-month loan at 18% annual simple interest. What was the principal?

P is unknown.

$$P = \frac{I}{RT}$$

$$= \frac{\$675}{0.18(1.5)}$$

$$= \$2,500$$

Leon borrowed $1,500 at 16.5% annual simple interest. If he paid $866.25 interest, what was the time period of the loan?

T is unknown.

$$T = \frac{I}{PR}$$

$$= \frac{\$866.25}{\$1,500(0.165)}$$

$$= 3.5 \text{ years}$$

(page 311)

Find ordinary and exact time

Change months and years to ordinary or exact time in days **Step 1** For ordinary time use:

$$1 \text{ month} = 30 \text{ days}$$

$$1 \text{ year} = 360 \text{ days}$$

Step 2 For exact time use:

$$1 \text{ month} = \text{exact number of days in the month}$$

$$1 \text{ year} = 365 \text{ days (or 366 days in a leap year)}$$

Find the ordinary time of a loan made on October 1 and due May 1 (non-leap year).	Find the exact time of a loan made October 1 and due May 1 (non-leap year)
October 1 to May 1 = 7 months	October, December, January, and March have 31 days. November and April have 30 days. February has 28 days.
7 months = 7 × 30 days	
= 210 days	4(31) + 2(30) + 28 = 212 days

Find the exact time of a loan using the Sequential Numbers Table (Table 9–1) **Step 1** If the beginning and due dates of the loan fall within the same year, subtract the beginning date's sequential number from the due date's sequential number. **Step 2** If the beginning and due dates of the loan do not fall within the same year: **a)** Subtract the beginning date's sequential number from 365. **b)** Add the due date's sequential number to the difference from step 2a. **Step 3** If February 29 is between the beginning and due dates, add 1 to the difference from step 1 or to the sum from step 2b.

<table>
<tr><td>

Find the exact time of a loan
made on March 25 and
due on October 10.

October 10 = day 283
March 25 = <u>day 84</u>
             199 days

The loan is made for 199 days.

</td><td>

Find the exact time of a loan made
on June 7 and due the following
March 7 in a non-leap year.

December 31 = day 365
June 7 = <u>day 158</u>
            207 days
March 7 = <u>+ 66 days</u>
             273 days

The loan is made for 273 days in all.

</td></tr>
</table>

 (page 312)

Find the due date

Find the due date of a loan given the beginning date and the time period in days
Step 1 For ordinary time: **a)** Determine the number of months of the loan, counting each month as 30 days. **b)** Count forward from the beginning date the number of months from step 1a. Add extra days for a part of a month if necessary. **Step 2** For exact time: **a)** Add the sequential number of the beginning date to the number of days in the time period. **b)** If the sum is less than or equal to 365, find the date (Table 9–1) corresponding to the sum. **c)** If the sum is more than 365, subtract 365 from the sum. Then find the date (Table 9–1) in the following year corresponding to the difference. **d)** Adjust for February 29 on a leap year if appropriate.

Figure the due date using ordinary time and exact time for a 60-day loan made on August 12.

Ordinary time: Exact time:
60 days is two   August 12 = day 224
months. Two months   <u>+60</u>
from August 12 is   284
October 12.   Day 284 is October 11.

 (page 313)

Find the ordinary and exact interest rates

Step 1 For ordinary interest, divide the annual interest rate by 360.

$$\text{Ordinary interest rate per day} = \frac{\text{interest rate per year}}{360}$$

Step 2 For exact interest, divide the annual interest rate by 365.

$$\text{Exact interest rate per day} = \frac{\text{interest rate per year}}{365}$$

On May 15, Nora borrowed $6,000 at 12.5% annual simple interest. The loan was due on November 15. Use ordinary time to find the ordinary interest due on the loan.

Time is 6 months, 30 days each, or 6×30 days. Interest rate is $\frac{12.5\%}{360}$ per day.

$$I = PRT$$

$$= (\$6,000)\left(\frac{0.125}{360}\right)(6 \times 30)$$

$\times 180 = 6800$

$$= \$375$$

Use exact interest and exact time to find the interest due on Nora's loan (see above).

Use Table 9–1 to find exact time. November 15 is day 319. May 15 is day 135. So time is $319 - 135$ days. Interest is $\frac{12.5\%}{365}$ per day.

$$I = PRT$$

$$= (\$6,000)\left(\frac{0.125}{365}\right)(319 - 135)$$

$$= \$378.08$$

(page 316)

Find simple interest using a table

Step 1 Identify the amount of money that the table uses as the principal. (A typical table principal is $1, $100, or $1,000.) **Step 2** Divide the loan principal by the table principal. **Step 3** Select the days row corresponding to the time period (in days) of the loan. **Step 4** Select the annual rate column corresponding to the annual interest rate of the loan. **Step 5** Locate the value in the cell where the annual rate column intersects the days row. **Step 6** Multiply the quotient from step 2 by the value from step 5.

Use Table 9–2 to find the exact interest on a loan of $2,500 at a 12.5% annual interest rate for 40 days

$$\text{Interest} = \frac{\$2,500}{\$100} \times 1.369863$$

$$= \$34.25$$

Use Table 9–2 to find the exact interest on a loan of $4,875 at an annual rate of 12.75% for 30 days.

$$\text{Interest} = \frac{\$4,875}{\$100} \times 1.047945$$

$$= \$51.09$$

9.3 — 1 (page 319)

Find the bank discount and proceeds for a simple discount note

Step 1 For the bank discount, use:

$$\text{Bank discount} = \text{face value} \times \text{discount rate} \times \text{term}$$
$$I = PRT$$

Step 2 For the proceeds, use:

$$\text{Proceeds} = \text{face value} - \text{bank discount}$$
$$A = P - I$$

The bank charged Daniel a 16.5% annual discount rate on a bank note of $1,500 for 120 days. Find the proceeds of the note using banker's rule.

First find the discount, then subtract the discount from the face value of $1,500.

$$\text{Discount} = I = PRT$$

$$= \$1,500\left(\frac{0.165}{360}\right)(120) \quad \textcolor{blue}{\textbf{Rate is ordinary, time is exact.}}$$

$$= \$82.50$$

$$\text{Proceeds} = \$1,500 - \$82.50$$

$$= \$1,417.50$$

Chapter 9   Simple Interest and Simple Discount

Find the bank discount and proceeds for a third-party discount note

Step 1 For the bank discount, use:

Bank discount = maturity value of original note × discount rate × discount period

$$I = PRT$$

Step 2 For the proceeds, use:

Proceeds = maturity value of original note − bank discount

$$A = P - I$$

Brown Trailer Sales made a note of $10,000 with Robert Brown, company owner, at 9% simple interest based on exact interest and exact time. The note is made on August 12 and due on November 10. However, Brown Trailer Sales needs cash so the note is taken to the bank on September 5. The bank agrees to accept the note with a 13% annual discount rate using banker's rule. Find the proceeds of the rate.

To find the proceeds, we first find the bank discount. To find the bank discount, we first find the maturity value of the original note. Exact time is 90 days (314−224). Exact interest rate is $\frac{9\%}{365}$.

$$\text{Maturity value} = P(I + RT)$$

$$= \$10{,}000\left(1 + \frac{0.09}{365} \times 90\right)$$

$$= \$10{,}221.92$$

Exact time of the discount period is 66 days (314 − 248). Ordinary discount rate is $\frac{13\%}{360}$.

$$\text{Bank discount} = \$10{,}221.92\left(\frac{0.13}{360}\right)(66)$$

$$= \$243$$

$$\text{Proceeds} = \$10{,}221.92 - \$243$$

$$= \$9{,}978.92$$

CHAPTER 9 REVIEW

Section 9.1

Find the simple interest. Round to the nearest cent when necessary.

	Principal	Annual Rate	Time	Interest
1.	$500	12%	2 years	_____
2.	$1,000	$9\frac{1}{2}\%$	3 years	_____
3.	$3,575	21%	3 years	_____
4.	$2,975	$12\frac{1}{2}\%$	2 years	_____
5.	$800	18%	1 year	_____
6.	$25,000	6.9%	2 years	_____

7. Capco, Inc., borrowed $4,275 for 3 years at 15% interest. (a) How much simple interest did the company pay? (b) What is the maturity value?

8. Legan Company borrowed $15,280 at $16\frac{1}{2}\%$ for 12 years. How much simple interest did the company pay? What was the total amount paid back?

Find the rate of annual simple interest in each of the following problems.

	Principal	Interest	Time	Rate
9.	$800	$124	1 year	_____
10.	$1,280	$256	2 years	_____
11.	$1,000	$375	3 years	_____
12.	$40,000	$64,000	10 years	_____
13.	$175	$52.50	2 years	_____
14.	$423	$355.32	4 years	_____

Find the time period of the loan using the formula for simple interest.

	Principal	Annual Rate	Interest	Time
15.	$450	10%	$135	_____
16.	$700	18%	$252	_____
17.	$1,500	$21\frac{1}{2}$%	$483.75	_____
18.	$2,000	$16\frac{1}{2}$%	$825	_____
19.	$800	$15\frac{3}{4}$%	$252	_____
20.	$3,549	9.2%	$979.52	_____

21. Madewell Manufacturing paid back a loan of $7,500 at $16\frac{1}{2}$% annual rate with $618.75 simple interest. How long was the loan outstanding?

22. Ronald Cox received $1,440 on a loan of $12,000 at 16% annual simple interest rate. How long was the money invested?

In each of the following problems, find the principal, based on simple interest.

	Interest	Annual Rate	Time	Principal
23.	$100	10%	2 years	_____
24.	$281.25	$12\frac{1}{2}$%	3 years	_____
25.	$90	9%	1 year	_____
26.	$180	11.25%	2 years	_____
27.	$661.50	8.82%	5 years	_____
28.	$304.64	$13\frac{3}{5}$%	4 years	_____

29. A loan for three years with an annual simple interest rate of 18% cost $486 interest. Find the principal.

30. An investor earned $1,530 interest on funds invested at $12\frac{3}{4}$% annual simple interest for four years. How much was invested?

Write a fraction expressing each amount of time as a part of a year (12 months = 1 year).

31. 7 months

32. 18 months

33. 16 months

34. 9 months

35. 3 months

36. 42 months

37. Draw the circle showing the four parts of an interest problem.

38. Write the formula for finding each part of the interest formula.

39. Robert Ellis made a car loan for $2,500 to be paid off in $3\frac{1}{2}$ years. The simple interest rate for the loan was 12% annually. How much interest did he pay?

40. Jill Jones bought a dining room suite and paid for the furniture in full after one month, with a finance charge of $18.75. If she was charged 18% annual interest, how much did the suite cost?

41. Sue Jackson invested $500 at 8% annual for six months. How much interest did she receive?

42. Mark Hammer borrowed $500 for three months and paid $12.50 interest. What was the annual rate of interest?

43. Find the interest paid on a loan of $1,200 for 60 days at a simple interest rate of 6% annually.

44. Find the interest paid on a loan of $2,100 for 90 days at a simple interest rate of 4% annually.

45. Find the interest paid on a loan of $800 for 120 days at a simple interest rate of 6% annually.

46. Find the interest paid on a loan of $15,835 for 45 days at a simple interest rate of 8.1% annually.

Section 9.2

47. Time figured using 30 days per month is called what kind of time?

48. When the exact number of days in each month is used to figure time, it is called what kind of time?

Use Table 9–1 to find the exact time from the first date to the second date for non-leap years unless leap year is identified.

49. March 15 to July 10

50. April 12 to November 15

51. January 18 to October 6

52. November 12 to April 15 of the next year

53. January 5 to June 7

54. April 7, 1997, to August 15, 1997

55. January 12, 1998, to June 28, 1998

56. February 3, 1996, to August 12, 1996

57. January 27, 1996, to September 30, 1996

58. February 15, 1997, to June 15, 1998

59. April 5, 1996 to September 15, 1996

If a loan is made on the given date, find the date it is due, using both ordinary time and exact time.

60. March 15 for 30 days

61. January 10 for 210 days

62. May 30 for 240 days

63. August 12 for 60 days

64. June 13 for 90 days

65. December 28 for 60 days

For each of the following problems, find (a) the ordinary interest using ordinary time, (b) the exact interest using exact time, and (c) the ordinary interest using exact time. Round answers to the nearest cent.

66. $5,000 at 17% annually for 90 days

67. $3,500 at 18% annually for 60 days

68. A loan of $4,225 at 8% annually made on March 5, and due on May 5 of the same year

69. A loan of $1,200 at 10% annually made on October 15, and due on March 20 of the following year

Section 9.3

Use the following note for Exercises 70–76.

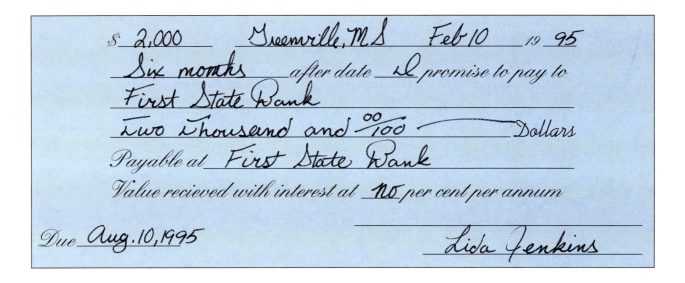

70. Who is the maker of the note shown here?

Lida Jenkins

71. Who is the payee?

72. What is the face value of the note?

2,000

73. What is the due date?

74. If the bank charged 9%, find the discount on the note.

90.50

75. Find the proceeds of the note.

76. If the bank charged 14% annually, find the discount on the note. Find the proceeds of the note. Compare the proceeds at 14% annual interest with the proceeds at 9% (Exercise 75).

Use Table 9–2.

77. Find the exact interest on a loan of $3,700 at $12\frac{1}{4}$% annually for 15 days.

78. Find the exact interest on a loan of $2,100 at $11\frac{1}{2}$% annual interest for 40 days.

79. Find the exact interest on a loan of $3,600 at 12.75% annual interest for 18 days.

80. Find the exact interest on a loan of $8,972 at 12% annually for 45 days.

81. MAK, Inc., accepted an interest-bearing note for $10,000 with 9% annual interest. The note was made on April 10 and was due December 6. MAK needed cash and took the note to First United Bank, which offered to buy the note at a discount rate of $12\frac{1}{2}$%. The transaction was made on July 7. How much cash did MAK receive for the note?

82. Allan Stojanovich can purchase an office desk for $1,500 with cash terms of 2/10, n/30. If he can borrow the money at 12% annual simple interest for 20 days, will he save money by taking advantage of the cash discount offered?

Challenge Problems

83. A data entry clerk at Third Federal Savings and Loan spilled coffee on a diskette, wiping out some critical loan data for several of S&L's customers. Your assignment, as chief accounting department troubleshooter, is to reconstruct the missing data from the data fragment below. Express all dollar amounts correct to the nearest cent, interest rates to one decimal place, and time to the nearest day.

What methods do banks use to protect themselves from the loss of vital financial data?

Customer	Interest	Principal	Annual Rate	Time (Ordinary)
Rocky's Market	$ 7.00		10%	30 days
David's Art Gallery	85.00		12%	100 days
Fortune Hardware	209.00	5,500		180 days
M. Converse & Son	22.63	1,460		90 days
Sun Twins Jai Alai	72.00	2,560	13.5%	
Sun Coast Brokerage	1,711.11	28,000	11%	

84. Are you interested in buying a "new" used car or installing a pool? A simple interest loan with a low monthly payment sounds good, but be sure you understand what this monthly payment means.

A simple interest loan with a final "balloon payment" can be a good deal for both the consumer and the banker. For the banker, this loan reduces the rate risk, since the loan rate is actually locked in for a short period of time. For the consumer, this loan allows you to make lower monthly payments.

Example: You borrow $5,000 at 13% simple interest rate for a year.

For 12 monthly payments:

$$\$5,000 \times 13\% \times 1 = \$650 \text{ interest}$$

$$\frac{\$5,650}{12} = \$470.83 \text{ monthly payment}$$

Your banker will offer to make the loan as if it is to be extended over five years, or 60 monthly payments. This means a much lower monthly payment.

For 60 monthly payments:

$$\frac{\$5,650}{60} = \$94.17 \text{ monthly payment}$$

The lower monthly payment is tempting! The banker will expect you to make these lower payments for a year. You will actually make 11 payments of $94.17: $94.17 × 11 = $1,035.87 amount paid during the first 11 months.
The 12th and final payment, the *balloon payment,* is the *remainder* of the loan.

$$\$5,650 - \$1,035.87 = \$4,614.13$$

At this time you are expected to pay the balance of the loan in the balloon payment shown above. Don't panic! Usually the loan is refinanced for another year. But beware—you may have to pay a higher interest rate for the next year.

a) Find the monthly payment for a $2,500 loan at 12% interest for one year extended over a three-year period.

b) What is the amount of the final balloon payment for a $1,000 loan at 10% interest for one year, extended over five years?

c) You need a loan of $5,000 at 10% interest for one year. What is the amount of the monthly payment?

d) If your banker agrees to extend the monthly payments over two years for the loan described in part c) above, how much will your monthly payments be? How much will the final balloon payment be?

CHAPTER 9 PRACTICE TEST

1. Find the simple interest on $500 invested at 14% annually for three years.

2. How much money was borrowed at 17% annually for six months if the interest was $85?

3. A loan of $3,000 was made for 210 days. If ordinary interest is $350, find the rate.

4. A loan of $5,000 at 16% annually requires $1,200 interest. For how long is the money borrowed?

5. Find the exact time from February 13 to November 27 in a non-leap year.

6. Find the exact time from October 12 to March 28 of the following year (a leap year).

7. Find the exact time from January 28, 1996, to July 5, 1996.

8. Find the ordinary time from April 5 to December 20.

9. Find the simple interest on a loan of $20,000 at 21% annual interest for two years.

10. Use ordinary time to find the ordinary interest on a loan of $2,800 at 10% annually made on March 15 for 270 days.

11. Find the interest on a loan of $469 if the simple interest rate charged is 12% annually for six months.

12. A bread machine with a cash price of $188 can be purchased with a one-year loan at 10% annual simple interest. Find the total amount to be repaid.

13. An investment of $7,000 is made for six months at the rate of 19% annual simple interest. How much interest will the investor earn?

14. A copier that originally cost $300 was purchased with a loan for 12 months at 15% annual simple interest. What was the *total* cost of the copier?

15. Find the ordinary interest on a loan of $850 at 15% annually. The loan was made January 15 and was due March 15. Use ordinary time.

16. Find the exact interest in Exercise 15. Use exact time in a non-leap year. Round to the nearest cent.

17. Find the duration of a loan of $3,000 if the loan required interest of $416.25 and was at a rate of $18\frac{1}{2}$% annual simple interest.

18. Find the simple interest on a loan of $165 if the interest rate is 16% annually over a three-month period.

19. Find the rate of simple interest on a $1,200 loan that requires the borrower to repay a total of $1,440 after one year.

20. Find the rate of simple interest on a $600 loan with total interest of $40.50 if the loan is paid in 6 months.

21. A promissory note has a face value of $5,000 and is discounted by the bank at the rate of $18\frac{1}{2}\%$. If the note is made for 180 days, find the discount of the note.

22. A promissory note with a face value of $3,500 is discounted by the bank at the rate of $19\frac{1}{2}\%$. The term of the note is six months. Find the proceeds of the note.

23. Find the ordinary interest paid on a loan of $1,600 for 90 days at a simple interest rate of 16% annually.

24. Jerry Brooks purchases office supplies totaling $1,890. He can take advantage of cash terms of 2/10, n/30 if he obtains a short-term loan. If he can borrow the money at $10\frac{1}{2}\%$ annual simple ordinary interest for 20 days, will he save money if he borrows to take advantage of the cash discount? How much will he save?

25. Find the exact interest on a loan of $25,000 at $11\frac{3}{4}\%$ annually for 21 days.

26. Find the exact interest on a loan of $1,510 at $12\frac{3}{4}\%$ annual interest for 27 days.

27. Find the exact interest on a loan of $4,300 at 11.75% annual interest for 32 days.

CHAPTER **10**

COMPOUND INTEREST, FUTURE VALUE, AND PRESENT VALUE

GOOD DECISIONS THROUGH TEAMWORK

With your team members, select several financial institutions in your area. Individually, contact one company to determine that lender's policies related to investing. Determine the types of investment opportunities available, the restrictions that apply, the risks involved, and the rate of interest for each type of investment.

With members of your team, analyze the information gathered by each team member from the various financial institutions and use the information to calculate the maximum amount of interest that could be earned on $5,000 invested for 5 years. Make a presentation to the class explaining how the team selected the best investment option for the $5,000.

10.1 Compound Interest and Future Value

1▶ *Use the simple interest formula to find the future value*

2▶ *Find the future value using a $1.00 future value table*

3▶ *Find the effective interest rate*

4▶ *Find the interest compounded daily using a table*

10.2 Present Value

1▶ *Find the present value based on annual compounding for one year*

2▶ *Find the present value using a $1.00 present value table*

For most loans made on a short-term basis, interest is computed once, using the simple interest formula. For longer-term loans, interest may be *compounded*: interest is calculated more than once during the term of the loan or investment and this interest is added to the principal. This sum (principal + interest) then becomes the principal for the next calculation of interest, and interest is charged or paid on this new amount.

This process of adding interest to the principal before interest is calculated for the next period is called *compounding interest*. Compounding interest has several uses in the business world. The one with which you are probably familiar is used in a savings account, where you "earn interest on your interest."

10.1 Compound Interest, Future Value, and Present Value

1▶ *Use the simple interest formula to find the future value*

2▶ *Find the future value using a $1.00 future value table*

3▶ *Find the effective interest rate*

4▶ *Find the interest compounded daily using a table*

Whether the interest rate is simple or compound, interest is calculated for each **interest period.** When the interest rate is simple, there is only one interest period: the entire period of the loan is the single, simple interest period. When the interest rate is compound, there are two or more interest periods, each of the same duration. The interest period may be one year long, for instance, or one day long. The greater the number of interest periods in the time period of the loan or investment, the greater the total interest that accumulates during the time period. The total interest that accumulates is called the **compound interest.** The sum of the compound interest and the original principal is called the **future value** or **maturity value** or **compound amount** in the case of an investment, or the **compound amount** in the case of a loan. In this chapter we may use the term *future value* to mean future value *or* compound amount, depending on whether the principal is an investment or a loan.

1▶ *Using the Simple Interest Formula to Find the Future Value*

We can calculate the future value of principal using the simple interest formula method. The terms of a loan or investment indicate the annual number of interest periods and the annual interest rate. Dividing the annual interest rate by the annual number of interest periods gives us the **period interest rate** or interest rate per period. We can use the period interest rate to calculate the interest that accumulates for each period using the familiar simple interest formula: $I = P \times R \times T$. I is the interest for the period, P is the principal at the beginning of the period, R is the period interest rate, and T is the length of the period. Notice, though, that since we are just now calculating the interest for the period, the length of time is one period. So the value of T in the formula is one period, and the formula is simplified to $I = P \times R \times 1$, or $I = P \times R$. Notice, too, that the value of P is different for each period in turn, because the principal at the beginning of each period includes the original principal and all the interest so far accumulated. Calculating the principal for each interest period in turn is our goal in calculating the future value of a loan or investment.

 HOW TO | **Find the Period Interest Rate**

Divide the annual interest rate by the number of interest periods per year.

$$\text{Period interest rate} = \frac{\text{annual interest rate}}{\text{number of interest periods per year}}$$

 HOW TO | **Find the Future Value Using the Simple Interest Formula Method**

Step 1 Find the first end-of-period principal: Multiply the original principal by the sum of 1 and the period interest rate.

First end-of-period principal = original principal × (1 + period interest rate)

$$A = P + (1 + R)$$

Step 2 For each remaining period in turn, find the next end-of-period principal: Multiply the previous end-of-period principal by the sum of 1 and the period interest rate.

End-of-period principal = previous end-of-period principal × (1 + period interest rate)

Step 3 Identify the last end-of-period principal as the future value.

Future value = last end-of-period principal

 HOW TO | **Find the Compound Interest**

Subtract the original principal from the future value.

Compound interest = future value − original principal

Example 1 A loan of $800 at 13% annually is made for three years, compounded annually. Find (a) the future value (compound amount) and (b) the compound interest paid on the loan. (c) Compare the compound interest with simple interest for the same loan period, original principal, and annual interest rate.

$$\text{Period interest rate} = \frac{\text{rate per year}}{\text{number of interest periods per year}}$$

a. Since the loan is compounded annually, there is just one interest period per year. So the period interest rate is $\frac{13}{100}$, or 0.13. Notice that there are a total of three interest periods, one for each of the three years.

First end-of-period principal = $800(1 + 0.13)   800(1.13) = 904

= $904

$$\text{Next end-of-period principal} = \$904(1 + 0.13)$$

904(1.13) = 1,021.52

$$= \$1,021.52$$

$$\text{Third end-of-period principal} = \$1,021.52(1 + 0.13)$$

1,021.52(1.13) = 1,154.32

$$= \$1,154.32$$

The future value is $1,154.32.

b. Compound interest is compound amount minus original principal.

$$
\begin{array}{rl}
\$1,154.32 & \text{Compound amount} \\
- \ 800 & \text{Original principal} \\
\hline
\$ \ \ 354.32 & \text{Compound interest}
\end{array}
$$

The compound interest is $354.32.

c. Use the simple interest formula to find the simple interest on $800 at 13% annually for three years.

$$I = PRT$$

$$I = \$800 \times 0.13 \times 3$$

$$I = \$312$$

The simple interest is $312, which is $42.32 less than the compound interest. This difference would be even greater if the interest were compounded more frequently.

Example 2 Find the future value of a $10,000 investment at 8% annual interest compounded semiannually for three years.

$$\text{Period interest rate} = \frac{8\% \text{ annually}}{2 \text{ periods annually}} = \frac{0.08}{2} = 0.04$$

$$\text{First end-of-period principal} = \$10,000(1 + 0.04)$$

10,000(1.04) = 10,400

$$= \$10,400$$

$$\text{Second end-of-period principal} = \$10,400(1 + 0.04)$$

10,400(1.04) = 10,816

$$= \$10,816$$

$$\text{Third end-of-period principal} = \$11,248.64$$

10,816(1.04) = 11,248.64

$$\text{Fourth end-of-period principal} = \$11,698.59$$

11,248.64(1.04) = 11,698.59

$$\text{Fifth end-of-period principal} = \$12,166.53$$

11,698.59(1.04) = 12,166.53

$$\text{Sixth end-of-period principal} = \$12,653.19$$

12,166.53(1.04) = 12,653.19

Since there are two interest periods for each of the three years, the sixth period (2 × 3) is the last.

The future value is $12,653.19.

 Finding the Future Value

As you may have guessed from Examples 1 and 2, compounding interest for a large number of periods is very time consuming. This task is done more quickly if you use a compound interest table, as shown in Table 10–1.

Table 10–1 gives the future value of $1.00, depending on the number of interest periods per year and the period interest rate.

AROUND THE BUSINESS WORLD

Pizza Hut: Out to Tempt the Italians

Coals to Newcastle, pizza to Parma. That's the gamble Pizza Hut is taking, aiming to sell its pies to the Italians, who invented the stuff. Wichita-based Pizza Hut plans to open by yearend its first Italian franchise, on Piazza Picelli in Parma's historical center, and later to expand throughout Italy. Already, Pizza Hut is in 88 other countries.

The company admits Parma will be a litmus test. The home of prosciutto and Parmesan cheese, this city is known for its discriminating tastes, both gastronomical and otherwise. Parma is where internationally renowned opera stars get booed right off the stage. Pizza Hut spokesman Robert Doughty contends that the chain will overcome resistance by adopting the decor of an Italian café and tailoring the menu to Italian tastes. "In Japan, for example, we offer pizza with squid."

Trouble is, company menu planners have yet to come up with a strategy to rival the Italian pie. Faith Heller Willinger, a food-service expert in Florence, says Pizza Hut's famous thick, doughy crust laden with cheese and pepperoni won't appeal to Italians, who prefer a thin, crispy crust and spare toppings.

Beyond that, the question turns on whether Italians will see Pizza Hut as homogenized fast food, which they dislike. But Romeo Medici, director of statistics research at Parma's Chamber of Commerce, says convenience and cheap prices work in Pizza Hut's favor. Italy, too, he says, is "becoming a culture of mass consumption."

Table 10–1 Future Value of $1.00

| Periods | \multicolumn{11}{c}{Rate per Period} |
	1%	1.5%	2%	2.5%	3%	4%	5%	6%	8%	10%	12%
1	1.01000	1.01500	1.02000	1.02500	1.03000	1.04000	1.05000	1.06000	1.08000	1.10000	1.12000
2	1.02010	1.03023	1.04040	1.05063	1.06090	1.08160	1.10250	1.12360	1.16640	1.21000	1.25440
3	1.03030	1.04568	1.06121	1.07689	1.09273	1.12486	1.15763	1.19102	1.25971	1.33100	1.40493
4	1.04060	1.06136	1.08243	1.10381	1.12551	1.16986	1.21551	1.26248	1.36049	1.46410	1.57352
5	1.05101	1.07728	1.10408	1.13141	1.15927	1.21665	1.27628	1.33823	1.46933	1.61051	1.76234
6	1.06152	1.09344	1.12616	1.15969	1.19405	1.26532	1.34010	1.41852	1.58687	1.77156	1.97382
7	1.07214	1.10984	1.14869	1.18869	1.22987	1.31593	1.40710	1.50363	1.71382	1.94872	2.21068
8	1.08286	1.12649	1.17166	1.21840	1.26677	1.36857	1.47746	1.59385	1.85093	2.14359	2.47596
9	1.09369	1.14339	1.19509	1.24886	1.30477	1.42331	1.55133	1.68948	1.99900	2.35795	2.77308
10	1.10462	1.16054	1.21899	1.28008	1.34392	1.48024	1.62889	1.79085	2.15892	2.59374	2.10585
11	1.11567	1.17795	1.24337	1.31209	1.38423	1.53945	1.71034	1.89830	2.33164	2.85312	3.47855
12	1.12683	1.19562	1.26824	1.34489	1.42576	1.60103	1.79586	2.01220	2.51817	3.18343	3.89598
13	1.13809	1.21355	1.29361	1.37851	1.46853	1.66507	1.88565	2.13293	2.71962	3.45227	4.36349
14	1.14947	1.23176	1.31948	1.41297	1.51259	1.73168	1.97993	2.26090	2.93719	3.79750	4.88711
15	1.16097	1.25023	1.34587	1.44830	1.55797	1.80094	2.07893	2.39656	3.17217	4.17725	5.47357
16	1.17258	1.26899	1.37279	1.48451	1.60471	1.87298	2.18287	2.54035	3.42594	4.59497	6.13039
17	1.18430	1.28802	1.40024	1.52162	1.65284	1.94790	2.29202	2.69277	3.70002	5.05447	6.86604
18	1.19615	1.30734	1.42825	1.55966	1.70243	2.02582	2.40662	2.85434	3.99602	5.55992	7.68997
19	1.20811	1.32695	1.45681	1.59865	1.75351	2.10685	2.52695	3.02560	4.31570	6.11591	8.61276
20	1.22019	1.34686	1.48595	1.63862	1.80611	2.19112	2.65330	3.20714	4.66096	6.72750	9.64629
21	1.23239	1.36706	1.51567	1.67958	1.86029	2.27877	2.78596	3.39956	5.03383	7.40025	10.80385
22	1.24472	1.38756	1.54598	1.72157	1.91610	2.36992	2.92526	3.60354	5.43654	8.14027	12.10031
23	1.25716	1.40838	1.57690	1.76461	1.97359	2.46472	3.07152	3.81975	5.87146	8.95430	13.55235
24	1.26973	1.42950	1.60844	1.80873	2.03279	2.56330	3.22510	4.04893	6.34118	9.84973	15.17863
25	1.28243	1.45095	1.64061	1.85394	2.09378	2.66584	3.38635	4.29187	6.84848	10.83471	17.00006
26	1.29526	1.47271	1.67342	1.90029	2.15659	2.77247	3.55567	4.54938	7.39635	11.91818	19.04007
27	1.30821	1.49480	1.70689	1.94780	2.22129	2.88337	3.73346	4.82235	7.98806	13.10999	21.32488
28	1.32129	1.51722	1.74102	1.99650	2.28793	2.99870	3.92013	5.11169	8.62711	14.42099	23.88387
29	1.33450	1.53998	1.77584	2.04641	2.35657	3.11865	4.11614	5.41839	9.31727	15.86309	26.74993
30	1.34785	1.56308	1.81136	2.09757	2.42726	3.24340	4.32194	5.74349	10.06266	17.44940	29.95992

Note: The values listed in the table have been rounded.
Table shows future value (*FV*) of $1 compounded for *N* periods at *R* rate per period.
Table values can be generated using the formula $FV = \$1(1 + R)^N$.

Step 1   Find the number of interest periods: Multiply the time period, number of years, by the number of interest periods per year.

Interest periods = number of years × number of interest periods per year

Step 2   Find the period interest rate: Divide the annual interest by the number of interest periods per year.

$$\text{Period interest rate} = \frac{\text{annual interest rate}}{\text{number of interest periods per year}}$$

Step 3   Select the periods row corresponding to the number of interest periods.

Step 4   Select the rate-per-period column corresponding to the period interest rate.

Step 5   Locate the value in the cell where the periods row intersects the rate-per-period column.

Step 6   Multiply the original principal by the value from step 5.

Example 3   Use Table 10–1 to compute the compound interest on a $500 loan for six years compounded annually at 4%.

Interest periods = years × interest periods per year

= 6 × 1 = 6 periods

$$\text{Period interest rate} = \frac{\text{annual interest rate}}{\text{interest periods per year}}$$

$$= \frac{4\%}{1} = 4\% = 0.04$$

Find period row 6 of the table and the 4% rate column. The value in the intersecting cell is 1.26532. This means that $1 would be worth $1.26532 or $1.27 rounded, compounded annually at the end of six years.

$500 × 1.26532 = **$632.66**   The loan is for $500, so multiply $500 by 1.26532 to find the future value of the loan.

The compound amount is $632.66.

$632.66 − $500 = $132.66   The compound amount minus the principal is the compound interest.

The compound interest on $500 for six years compounded annually at 4% is $132.66.

Example 4   An investment of $300 at 8% annually is compounded *quarterly* (four times a year) for three years. Find the future value and the compound interest.

Interest periods = number of years × number of interest periods per year

= 3 × 4 = 12   The investment is compounded four times a year for three years.

$$\text{Period interest rate} = \frac{\text{annual interest rate}}{\text{number of interest periods per year}}$$

$$= \frac{8\%}{4} = 2\% = 0.02$$

Divide the annual rate of 8% by the number of periods per year to find the period interest rate.

Future value of $1 = 1.26824

Find the 12 periods row in Table 10–1. Move across to the 2% column.

$300 × 1.26824 = $380.47

The principal times the future value per dollar equals the total future value.

$380.47 is the future value.

$$\text{Compound interest} = \text{future value} - \text{original principal}$$

$$= \$380.47 - \$300$$

$$= \$80.47$$

The compound interest is $80.47.

Example 5   Alan Ruscyk can invest $10,000 at 8% compounded quarterly for two years. Or he can invest the same $10,000 at 8.2% compounded annually for the same two years. If all other conditions (such as early withdrawal penalty, etc.) are the same, which deal should he take?

1   Decision needed

Which deal should Alan take?

2   Unknown facts

Future value for each investment

3   Known facts

Principal: $10,000
Time period: 2 years
Deal 1 annual rate: 8%
Deal 1 interest periods per year: 4
Deal 2 annual rate: 8.2%
Deal 2 interest periods per year: 1

4   Relationships

Number of interest periods = number of years × number of interest periods per year
Deal 1 interest periods = 2 × 4
Deal 2 interest periods = 2 × 1

$$\text{Period interest rate} = \frac{\text{annual interest rate}}{\text{number of interest periods per year}}$$

$$\text{Deal 1 period interest rate} = \frac{8\%}{4}$$

$$\text{Deal 2 period interest rate} = \frac{8.2\%}{1}$$

5   Estimate

Not appropriate

6   Calculations

Deal 1: Use the table method.
Interest periods = 4 × 2 = 8

$$\text{Period interest rate} = \frac{8\%}{4} = 2\% = 0.02$$

The Table 10–1 value is 1.17166.
Future value = $10,000 × 1.17166 = $11,716.60
Deal 1 future value is $11,716.60.

Deal 2: Use the simple interest formula method.

Interest periods = $2 \times 1 = 2$

Period interest rate = $\dfrac{8.2\%}{1} = 8.2\% = 0.082$

First end-of-period principal = $\$10,000 \times (1 + 0.082) = \$10,820$
Second end-of-period principal = $\$10,820 \times (1.082) = \$11,707.24$
Deal 2 future value is $\$11,707.24$.

7 Decision made

Deal 1, the lower interest rate of 8% compounded more frequently (quarterly), is a slightly better deal because it yields the greater future value.

 TIPS & TRAPS

Table 10–1 is generated using the formula $FV = \$1(1 + R)^N$, where FV represents the future value, R represents the rate per period, and N represents the number of periods. Using a scientific calculator and the general power key, , you can calculate these table values and other values not on the table.
Find the future value for $1 at 3% per period for five periods.

$$FV = \$1(1 + 0.03)^5 = 1(1.03)^5 = \$1.15927 \text{ (rounded)}$$

For any amount of money, substitute P for $1 in the formula, $FV = P(1 + R)^N$. Find the future value of $250 at 3% interest per year for five years.

$$FV = \$250(1 + 0.03)^5 = 250(1.15927) = \$289.82.$$

If you have access to a scientific calculator, results from manual or table calculations can be verified using the calculator and the formula.

 Finding the Effective Interest Rate

If the investment in Example 4 were compounded annually instead of quarterly for three years—three periods at 8% per period—the future value would be $377.91 (using table value 1.25971), and the compound interest would be $77.91. If the interest on the investment were simple interest, at the end of three years the interest would be $300 × 8% × 3, or $72. You can see from these comparisons that a loan or investment with an interest rate of 8%, compounded quarterly, carries higher interest than a loan with an interest rate of 8% compounded annually, or a loan with an annual simple interest rate of 8%. When you compare interest rates, you need to know the actual or **effective rate** of interest. The effective rate of interest equates compound interest rates to equivalent simple interest rates so that comparisons can be made.

? HOW TO | **Find the Effective Interest Rate of a Compound Interest Rate**

Step 1 Using the simple interest formula method: Divide the compound interest for the first year by the principal.

$$\text{Effective interest rate} = \frac{\text{compound interest for first year}}{\text{principal}}$$

Step 2 Using the table method: Subtract $1.00 from the future value of $1.00 after one year, and remove the dollar sign.

$$\text{Effective interest rate} = \frac{\text{future value of } \$1.00 \text{ after 1 year} - \$1.00}{\$1.00}$$

Example 6 Marcia borrowed $600 at 10% compounded semiannually. What is the effective interest rate?

Using the simple interest formula method

$$\text{Period interest rate} = \frac{10\%}{2} = 5\% = 0.05$$

$$\text{First end-of-period principal} = \$600(1 + 0.05)$$

$$= \$630$$

$$\text{Second end-of-period principal} = \$630(1 + 0.05)$$

$$= \$661.50$$

$$\text{Interest compounded after first year} = \$661.50 - \$600 = \$61.50$$

$$\text{Effective interest rate} = \frac{\$61.50}{\$600}$$

$$= 0.1025$$

$$= 10.25\%$$

Using the table method

10% compounded semiannually means two periods in the first (and every) year, and a period interest rate of 5%. The Table 10–1 value is 1.10250. Subtract 1.00.

$$\text{Effective interest rate} = 1.10250 - 1.00$$

$$= 0.10250$$

$$= 10.25\%$$

The effective interest rate is 10.25%.

The effective interest rate also can be calculated using a calculator or computer program that is capable of finding powers of numbers. Use the formula $E = \left(1 + \dfrac{R}{N}\right)^N - 1$ where E is the effective interest rate, R is the stated rate per year,

and N is the number of periods per year. Using this formula for the compound interest rate in Example 5, we have $E = \left(1 + \dfrac{0.08}{4}\right)^4 - 1$.

$$= (1 + 0.02)^4 - 1 = (1.02)^4 - 1 = 1.082432159 - 1 = 0.082432159 \text{ or } 8.24\%.$$

$$\boxed{AC}\,\boxed{(}\,1 + .08\,\boxed{\div}\,4\,\boxed{)}\,\boxed{x^y}\,4\,\boxed{-}\,1\,\boxed{=} \Rightarrow 0.082432159$$

4▸ *Finding the Interest Compounded Daily*

Some banks compound interest daily and others use continuous compounding to compute interest on savings accounts. There is no significant difference in the interest earned on money using interest compounded daily and compounded continuously. A computer is generally used in calculating interest if either daily or continuous compounding is used.

Table 10–2 gives compound interest on $100 compounded daily (using 365 days as a year). Notice that this table gives the *compound interest* on the principal rather than the future value, as is given in Table 10–1.

Using Table 10–2 is exactly like using Table 9–2, which gives the *simple* interest, rather than the compound interest, on $100: Locate the value in the cell where the applicable days row intersects the applicable annual rate column. This value is the interest on $100, so multiply this value by the quotient $\frac{principal}{100}$, which is the number of $100-units of principal.

Table 10–2 Compound Interest on $100, Compounded Daily (365 Days) (Exact Time, Exact Interest Basis)

Days	12%	12.25%	12.5%	12.75%	13%	13.25%	13.5%	13.75%	14%
					Annual Rate				
1	0.032876	0.033561	0.034246	0.034931	0.305616	0.306301	0.036986	0.037671	0.038356
2	0.065764	0.067134	0.068504	0.069875	0.071245	0.072615	0.073986	0.075356	0.076727
3	0.098662	0.100718	0.102774	0.104831	0.106887	0.108943	0.110999	0.113056	0.115112
4	0.131571	0.134314	0.137056	0.139799	0.142541	0.145284	0.148027	0.150770	0.153512
5	0.164491	0.167920	0.171350	0.174779	0.178209	0.181638	0.185068	0.188498	0.191928
6	0.197422	0.201538	0.205655	0.209772	0.213889	0.218005	0.222123	0.226240	0.230357
7	0.230364	0.235168	0.239972	0.244776	0.249581	0.254386	0.259191	0.263996	0.268802
8	0.263316	0.268808	0.274301	0.279793	0.285286	0.290780	0.296273	0.301767	0.307261
9	0.296279	0.302460	0.308641	0.314823	0.321005	0.327187	0.333369	0.339552	0.345735
10	0.329253	0.336123	0.342994	0.349864	0.356735	0.363607	0.370479	0.377351	0.384224
11	0.362238	0.369798	0.377358	0.384918	0.392479	0.400040	0.407602	0.415164	0.422727
12	0.395234	0.403483	0.411733	0.419984	0.428235	0.436487	0.444739	0.452992	0.461246
13	0.428241	0.437181	0.446121	0.455062	0.464004	0.472947	0.481890	0.490834	0.499779
14	0.461258	0.470889	0.480520	0.490153	0.499786	0.509420	0.519054	0.528690	0.538327
15	0.494287	0.504609	0.514931	0.525255	0.535580	0.545906	0.556233	0.566561	0.576889
16	0.527326	0.538340	0.549354	0.560370	0.571387	0.582405	0.593425	0.604445	0.615467
17	0.560376	0.572082	0.583789	0.595498	0.607207	0.618918	0.630631	0.642344	0.654059
18	0.593437	0.605836	0.618236	0.630637	0.643040	0.655444	0.667850	0.680257	0.692666
19	0.626509	0.639601	0.652694	0.665789	0.678885	0.691984	0.705083	0.718185	0.731288
20	0.659591	0.673377	0.687164	0.700953	0.714744	0.728536	0.742330	0.756127	0.769925
21	0.692685	0.707164	0.721646	0.736129	0.750615	0.765102	0.779591	0.794083	0.808576
22	0.725789	0.740963	0.756140	0.771318	0.786498	0.801681	0.816866	0.832053	0.847242
23	0.758905	0.774774	0.790645	0.806519	0.822395	0.838274	0.854154	0.870038	0.885923
24	0.792031	0.808595	0.825162	0.841732	0.858304	0.874879	0.891457	0.908037	0.924619
25	0.825168	0.842428	0.859692	0.876958	0.894226	0.911498	0.928773	0.946050	0.963330
26	0.858316	0.876273	0.894233	0.912195	0.930161	0.948130	0.966102	0.984078	1.002056
27	0.891475	0.910129	0.928785	0.947446	0.966109	0.984776	1.003446	1.022120	1.040796
28	0.924645	0.943996	0.963350	0.982708	1.002070	1.021435	1.040804	1.060176	1.079552
29	0.957826	0.977874	0.997927	1.017983	1.038043	1.058107	1.078175	1.098246	1.118322
30	0.991017	1.011764	1.032515	1.053270	1.074029	1.094792	1.115560	1.136331	1.157107

Table shows interest on $100 compounded daily for N days at an annual rate of R. Table values can be generated using the formula $I = 100\left(1 + \frac{R}{365}\right)^N - 100$.

Example 7 Find the interest on $800 at 13% annually, compounded daily, for 28 days.

$$\$800 \div \$100 = 8$$

Find the number of $100 units in the principal. Find the 28 days row in Table 10–2. Move across to the 13% column and find the interest for $100.

$$8 \times \$1.002070 = \$8.02$$

Multiply the table value by 8, the number of $100-units.

The interest is $8.02.

Chapter 10 Compound Interest, Future Value, and Present Value

Table 10–2 shows the interest per $100 of principal since most of the table values for $1 of principal would round to $0.00. The formula for calculating daily interest is more cumbersome; thus, tables, scientific or financial calculators, or computers are generally used to calculate daily interest. The formula used to generate the

table is $I = \$100\left(1 + \dfrac{R}{365}\right)^N - 100$, where I is the interest, R is the annual rate,

and N is the number of days.

To verify the table value from Example 7 with the formula we would calculate

$I = \$100\left(1 + \dfrac{0.13}{365}\right)^{28} - 100$. Using a scientific calculator,

$\boxed{AC}$ 100 $\boxed{\times}$ $\boxed{(}$ 1 + .13 ÷ 365 $\boxed{)}$ $\boxed{x^y}$ 28 $\boxed{=}$ $\boxed{-}$ 100 $\boxed{=}$ ⟹ 1.002070144

If the $100 in the formula is replaced with any amount of principal, the interest can

be found without using tables. $I = P\left(1 + \dfrac{R}{365}\right)^N - P$. Find the compound

interest for $300 at 9% per year compounded daily for 45 days.

$$I = \$300\left(1 + \frac{0.09}{365}\right)^{45} - 300$$

$\boxed{AC}$ 300 $\boxed{\times}$ $\boxed{(}$ 1 + .09 ÷ 365 $\boxed{)}$ $\boxed{x^y}$ 45 $\boxed{=}$ $\boxed{-}$ 300 $\boxed{=}$

⟹ 3.346888494 or $3.35

Self-Check 10.1

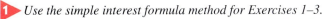

1 ▶ *Use the simple interest formula method for Exercises 1–3.*

1. Thayer Farm Trust made a farmer a loan of $1,200 at 16% for three years, compounded annually. Find the compound amount and the compound interest paid on the loan. Compare the compound interest with simple interest for the same period.

2. Maeola Killebrew invests $3,800 at 7%, compounded semiannually for two years. What is the future value of the investment and how much interest will she earn over the two-year period?

3. Carolyn Smith borrowed $6,300 at $8\frac{1}{2}$% for three years, compounded annually. What is the compound amount of the loan and how much interest will she pay on the loan?

2 ▶ *Use Table 10–1 for Exercises 4–8.*

4. First State Bank loaned Doug Morgan $2,000 for four years compounded annually at 8%. How much interest was Doug required to pay on the loan?

5. A loan of $8,000 for two acres of woodland is compounded quarterly at 12% for five years. Find the compound amount and the compound interest.

6. Compute the compound amount and the interest on a loan of $10,500 compounded annually for four years at 10%.

7. Find the future value of an investment of $10,500 if it is invested for four years and compounded quarterly at 8%.

Senate Plan vs. Current Spending: $961 Billion Less

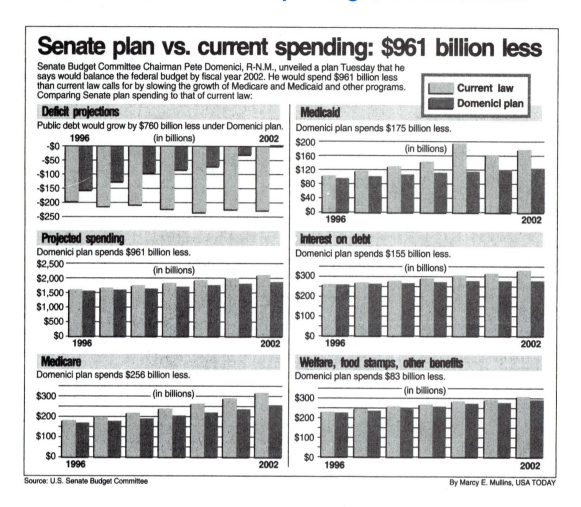

1. Describe the "Interest on debt" graph by describing what it compares and what time periods are shown.

2. According to the graph, what will be the current law interest on debt for the year 2000?

3. Under current law, what will the interest on debt be in 2002?

4. To produce interest of $250 billion on a simple interest loan at 7% for 1 year, what is the principal?

8. You have $8,000 which you plan to invest in a compound interest bearing instrument. Your investment agent advises you that you can invest the $8,000 at 8% compounded quarterly for three years or you can invest the $8,000 at $8\frac{1}{4}$% compounded annually for three years. Which investment should you choose to receive the most interest?

9. Find the effective interest rate for the loan described in Exercise 7. Use the Table Method.

10. What is the effective interest rate for a loan of $5,000 at 10%, compounded semiannually for three years? Use the simple interest formula method.

11. Ross Land has a loan of $8,500, compounded quarterly for four years at 6%. What is the effective interest rate for the loan? Use the table method.

Use Table 10–2 for Exercises 12–14.

12. Find the compound interest on $2,500 at $13\frac{1}{4}$% compounded daily by Leader Financial Bank for 20 days.

13. How much compound interest is earned on a deposit of $1,500 at 12% compounded daily for 30 days?

14. John McCormick has found a short term investment opportunity. He can invest $8,000 at 12.25% interest for 15 days. How much interest will he earn on this investment if the interest is compounded daily?

10.2	**Present Value**

 Find the present value based on annual compounding for one year

Find the present value using a $1.00 present value table

In the first part of this chapter we learned how to find the future value of money invested at the present time. Sometimes businesses and individuals need to know how much to invest at the present time to yield a certain amount at some specified future date. For example, a business may want to set aside a lump sum of money to provide pensions for employees in years to come. Individuals may want to set aside a lump sum of money now to pay for a child's college education or for a vacation. You can use the concepts of compound interest to figure the amount of money that must be set aside at present and compounded periodically to yield a certain amount of money at some specific time in the future. The amount of money set aside now is called **present value.**

▶ *Finding the Present Value Based on Annual Compounding for One Year*

Finding the present value of, say, $100, means finding the *principal* that we must invest today so that $100 is its future value. But we know that the future value of principal depends on the period interest rate and the number of interest periods. Just as calculating future value by hand is time consuming when there are many interest periods, so is calculating present value by hand. We use a present value table instead, which we turn to shortly. For now, we find present value based on the simplest case—annual compounding for one year. In this case, the number of interest periods is 1, and the period interest rate is the annual interest rate. Thus, in this simple case

$$\text{Future value} = \text{principal}(1 + \text{annual interest rate})$$

and

$$\text{Principal (present value)} = \frac{\text{future value}}{(1 + \text{annual interest rate})}$$

? HOW TO	**Find the Present Value Based on Annual Compounding for One Year**

Divide the future value by the sum of 1 and the annual interest rate.

$$\text{Present value (principal)} = \frac{\text{future value}}{1 + \text{annual interest rate}}$$

Example 1 Find the amount of money that Read and Wright Editorial Services needs to set aside today to ensure that $10,000 will be available to buy a new desktop publishing system in one year if the annual interest rate is 8% compounded annually.

$1 + 0.08 = \boxed{1.08}$ Convert the annual interest rate to a decimal and add to 1.

$\dfrac{\$10,000}{\boxed{1.08}} = \$9,259.26$ Divide the future value by 1.08 to get the present value.

An investment of $9,259.26 at 8% would have a value of $10,000 in one year.

Table 10–3   Present Value of $1.00

Periods	\multicolumn{11}{c}{Rate per Period}										
	1%	1.5%	2%	2.5%	3%	4%	5%	6%	8%	10%	12%
1	0.99010	0.98522	0.98039	0.97561	0.97087	0.96154	0.95238	0.94340	0.92593	0.90909	0.89286
2	0.98030	0.97066	0.96117	0.95181	0.94260	0.92456	0.90703	0.89000	0.85734	0.82645	0.79719
3	0.97059	0.95632	0.94232	0.92860	0.91514	0.88900	0.86384	0.83962	0.79383	0.75131	0.71178
4	0.96098	0.94218	0.92385	0.90595	0.88849	0.85480	0.82270	0.79209	0.73503	0.68301	0.63552
5	0.95147	0.92826	0.90573	0.88385	0.86261	0.82193	0.78353	0.74726	0.68058	0.62092	0.56743
6	0.94205	0.91454	0.88797	0.86230	0.83748	0.79031	0.74622	0.70496	0.63017	0.56447	0.50663
7	0.93272	0.90103	0.87056	0.84127	0.81309	0.75992	0.71068	0.66506	0.58349	0.51316	0.45235
8	0.92348	0.88771	0.85349	0.82075	0.78941	0.73069	0.67684	0.62741	0.54027	0.46651	0.40388
9	0.91434	0.87459	0.83676	0.80073	0.76642	0.70259	0.64461	0.59190	0.50025	0.42410	0.36061
10	0.90529	0.86167	0.82035	0.78120	0.74409	0.67556	0.61391	0.55839	0.46319	0.38554	0.32197
11	0.89632	0.84893	0.80426	0.76214	0.72242	0.64958	0.58468	0.52679	0.42888	0.35049	0.28748
12	0.88475	0.83639	0.78849	0.74356	0.70138	0.62460	0.55684	0.49697	0.39711	0.31863	0.25668
13	0.87866	0.82403	0.77303	0.72542	0.68095	0.60057	0.53032	0.46884	0.36770	0.28966	0.22917
14	0.86996	0.81185	0.75788	0.70773	0.66112	0.57748	0.50507	0.44230	0.34046	0.26333	0.20462
15	0.86135	0.79985	0.74301	0.69047	0.64186	0.55526	0.48102	0.41727	0.31524	0.23939	0.18270
16	0.85282	0.78803	0.72845	0.67362	0.62317	0.53391	0.45811	0.39365	0.29189	0.21763	0.16312
17	0.84438	0.77639	0.71416	0.65720	0.60502	0.51337	0.43630	0.37136	0.27027	0.19784	0.14564
18	0.83602	0.76491	0.70016	0.64117	0.58739	0.49363	0.41552	0.35034	0.25025	0.17986	0.13004
19	0.82774	0.75361	0.68643	0.62553	0.57029	0.47464	0.39573	0.33051	0.23171	0.16351	0.11611
20	0.81954	0.74247	0.67297	0.61027	0.55368	0.45639	0.37689	0.31180	0.21455	0.14864	0.10367
21	0.81143	0.73150	0.65978	0.59539	0.53755	0.43883	0.35894	0.29416	0.19866	0.13513	0.09256
22	0.80340	0.72069	0.64684	0.58086	0.52189	0.42196	0.34185	0.27751	0.18394	0.12285	0.08264
23	0.79544	0.71004	0.63416	0.56670	0.50669	0.40573	0.32557	0.26180	0.17032	0.11168	0.07379
24	0.78757	0.69954	0.62172	0.55288	0.49193	0.39012	0.31007	0.24698	0.15770	0.10153	0.06588
25	0.77977	0.68921	0.60953	0.53939	0.47761	0.37512	0.29530	0.23300	0.14602	0.09230	0.05882
26	0.77205	0.67902	0.59758	0.52623	0.46369	0.36069	0.28124	0.21981	0.13520	0.08391	0.05252
27	0.76440	0.66899	0.58586	0.51340	0.45019	0.34682	0.26785	0.20737	0.12519	0.07628	0.04689
28	0.75684	0.65910	0.57437	0.50088	0.43708	0.33348	0.25509	0.19563	0.11591	0.06934	0.04187
29	0.74934	0.64935	0.56311	0.48866	0.42435	0.32065	0.24295	0.18456	0.10733	0.06304	0.03738
30	0.74192	0.63976	0.55207	0.47674	0.41199	0.30832	0.23138	0.17411	0.09938	0.05731	0.00338

Table shows the lump sum amount of money that should be invested now so that the accumulated amount, A, will be $1 after a specified number of periods, N, at a specified rate per period, R. Table values can be generated using the formula $PV = \dfrac{\$1}{(1 + R)^N}$.

2 Finding the Present Value Using a $1.00 Present Value Table

If the interest in Example 1 had been compounded more than once a year, you would have to make calculations for each time the money was compounded. This would be a very time consuming process if there were a large number of compounding periods. Instead, you can use Table 10–3, which shows the present value of $1 at different interest rates for different periods.

Table 10–3 is used exactly like Table 10–1, which gives the future value of $1.00: Locate the value in the cell where the applicable periods row intersects the applicable rate-per-period column. This value is the present value of $1.00, so multiply this value by the desired future value.

Example 2 The Absorbant Diaper Company will need $20,000 in ten years to buy a new diaper edging machine. How much must the firm invest at the present if it receives 10% interest compounded annually?

$R = 10\%$ and $N = 10$ years.

Table value = 0.38554

> The money is to be compounded for ten periods, so we find periods row 10 in Table 10–3 and the 10% rate column to find the present value of $1.00.

$20,000 \times 0.38554 = \$7,710.80$

> Multiply the present value factor times the desired future value to find the amount that must be invested at the present.

Absorbant Diaper Company should invest $7,710.80 today to have $20,000 in ten years.

Self-Check 10.2

1. Compute the amount of money that should be set aside today to ensure a future value of $2,500 in one year if the interest rate is 11% annually, compounded annually.

2. How much money should Linda Bryan set aside today to buy printing equipment that costs $8,500 in one year? The current interest rate is 7.5% annually, compounded annually.

3. Ronnie Cox has just inherited $27,000. How much of this money should he set aside today to have $21,000 to pay cash for a Ventura Van which he plans to purchase in one year? He can invest at 7.9% annually, compounded annually.

4. Shirley Riddle has just received a $10,000 gift from her mother. She plans to make a major renovation to her home and have enough left to invest for one year at which time she plans to take a trip which is projected to cost $6,999. Current interest rates are 8.3% annually, compounded annually. How much does Shirley need to set aside today for her trip?

5. Rosa Burnett thinks she will need $2,000 in three years to make the down payment on a new car. How much must she invest today if she will receive 8% interest annually, compounded annually? Use Table 10–3.

6. Use Table 10–3 to calculate the amount of money that must be invested now at 6% annually, compounded quarterly, to obtain $1,500 in three years.

Chapter 10   Compound Interest, Future Value, and Present Value

353

7. Dewey Sykes plans to open a business in four years when he can retire from his present job. How much must he invest today to have $10,000 to invest in his small business when he retires? He has found that one bank will pay 10% annually, compounded quarterly.

8. Charlie Bryant has three children who will be college age in five more years. How much must he set aside today to have $20,000 for college tuition in five years if he can get a rate of 8% annually, compounded annually?

SELF-CHECK SOLUTIONS

Self-Check 10.1

1. $1,200 × (1 + 0.16) = $1,392 (first year)
$1,392 × (1.016) = $1,614.72 (second year)
$1,614.72 × (1 + 0.16) = $1,873.08 (third year)
                          compound amount
Compound interest = $1,873.08 − $1,200
                  = $673.08
Simple interest = $1,200 × 0.16 × 3 = $576

2. Period interest rate = $\frac{7\%}{2}$ = 0.035
$3,800 × (1 + 0.035) = $3,933 (first period)
$3,933 × (1 + 0.035) = $4,070.66 (second period)
$4,070.66 × (1 + 0.035) = $4,213.13 (third period)
$4,213.13 × (1 + 0.035) = $4,360.59 (last period)
Compound amount = $4,360.59
Compound interest = $4,360.59 − $3,800 = $560.59

3. $6,300 × (1 + 0.085) = $6,835.50 (first year)
$6,835.50 × (1 + 0.085) = $7,416.52 (second year)
$7,416.52 × (1 + 0.085) = $8,046.92 (last year)
Compound amount = $8,046.92
Compound interest = $8,046.92 − $6,300 = $1,746.92

4. Find periods row 4 (Table 10–1). Move across to the 8% rate column.
Table value = 1.36049
$2,000(1.36049) = $2,720.98 compound amount
$2,720.98 − $2,000 = $720.98 compound interest

5. 5 years × 4 quarters per year = 20 periods
12% ÷ 4 quarters = 3% per period
Table value = 1.80611 (Table 10–1)
$8,000(1.80611) = $14,448.88 compound amount
$14,448.88 − $8,000 = $6,448.88 compound interest

6. Find the table value for 4 periods and 10% per period.
Table value = 1.46410
$10,500 × 1.46410 = $15,373.05 compound amount
Interest = $15,373.05 − $10,500 = $4,873.05

7. 4 years × 4 quarters = 16 periods
8% ÷ 4 quarters = 2% per period
Table value = 1.37279
$10,500 × 1.37279 = $14,414.30

8. 8% quarterly; 12 periods at 2% per period
Table value = 1.26824
$8,000 × 1.26824 = $10,145.92
$8\frac{1}{4}$% annually
  $8,000 × 1.0825 = $8,660
  $8,660 × 1.0825 = $9,374.45
$9,374.45 × 1.0825 = $10,147.84
$8\frac{1}{4}$% annually is the better deal.

9. Compounded quarterly = 4 periods in year 1
$\frac{8\% \text{ annual}}{4}$ = 0.02 per period
Table value = 1.08243
Effective rate = 1.08243 − 1
              = .08243
              = 8.24%

10. Period interest rate = $\frac{10\%}{2}$ = 0.05
$5,000 × (1 + 0.05) = $5,250 (first period)
$5,250 × (1 + 0.05) = $5,512.50 (second period)
Compound interest = $5,512.50 − $5,000 = $512.50
Effective rate = $\frac{\$512.50}{\$5,000}$
              = 0.1025
              = 10.25%

11. Compounded quarterly = 4 periods in year 1
$\frac{6\%}{4}$ = 0.0125 per period
Table value = 1.06136
Effective rate = 1.06136 − 1
              = 0.06136
              = 6.14%

12. 20 days; $13\frac{1}{4}$% annual rate
Table value = 0.728536
$\frac{\$2,500}{\$100}$ = 25 $100-units
Compound interest = 25(0.728536)
                  = $18.21

13. 30 days; 12% annual rate
Table value = 0.991017

$$\frac{\$1,500}{\$100} = 15\ \$100\text{-units}$$

Compound interest = 15(0.991017)
= \$14.87

14. 15 days; 12.25% annual rate
Table value = 0.504609

$$\frac{\$8,000}{\$100} = 80\ \$100\text{-units}$$

Compound interest = 80(0.504609)
= \$40.37

Self-Check 10.2

1. Present value = $\dfrac{\$2,500}{1 + 0.11} = \dfrac{\$2,500}{1.11} = \$2,252.25$ **2.** $\dfrac{\$8,500}{1.075} = \$7,906.98$ **3.** $\dfrac{\$21,000}{1.079} = \$19,462.47$

4. $\dfrac{\$6,999}{1.083} = \$6,462.60$

5. 3 periods; 8% per period
Table value = 0.79383
\$2,000(0.79383) = \$1,587.66

6. $3 \times 4 = 12$ periods
$6\% \div 4 = 1\frac{1}{2}\%$ per period
Table value = 0.83639
\$1,500(0.83639) = \$1,254.59

7. $4 \times 4 = 16$ periods
$10\% \div 4 = 2\frac{1}{2}\%$ per period
Table value = 0.67362
\$10,000(0.67362) = \$6,736.20

8. 5 periods; 8% per period
Table value = 0.68058
\$20,000(0.68058) = \$13,611.60

CHAPTER 10 OVERVIEW

Section—Objective

Important Points with Examples

 **10.1 — 1** (page 340)

Use the simple interest formula to find the future value

Find the period interest rate Divide the annual interest rate by the number of interest periods per year.

$$\text{Period interest rate} = \frac{\text{annual interest rate}}{\text{number of interest periods per year}}$$

Find the future value using the simple interest formula method **Step 1** Find the first end-of-period principal: Multiply the original principal by the sum of 1 and the period interest rate.

First end-of-period principal = original principal $\times$ (1 + period interest rate)

Step 2 For each remaining period in turn, find the next end-of-period principal: Multiply the previous end-of-period principal by the sum of one and the period interest rate.

End-of-period principal = previous end-of-period principal

$\times$ (1 + period interest rate)

Step 3 Identify the last end-of-period principal as the future value.

Future value = last end-of-period principal

Find the compound interest Subtract the original principal from the future value.

Compound interest = future value − original principal

> Find the compound amount and compound interest on \$500 at 7% compounded annually for two years.
>
> \$500 $\times$ (1 + 0.07) = \$535 first period
> \$535 $\times$ (1 + 0.07) = \$572.45 last period
> Compound amount = \$572.45
> Compound interest = \$572.45 − \$500 = \$72.45

Find the compound amount (future value) and compound amount on $1,500 at 8% compounded semiannually for 2 years.

Number of interest periods = 2 × 2 = 4 periods

Period interest rate = $\dfrac{8\%}{2}$ = 4% or 0.04

$1,500 × (1 + 0.04) = $1,560 (first period)
$1,560 × (1 + 0.04) = $1,622.40 (second period)
$1,622.40 × (1 + 0.04) = $1,687.30 (third period)
$1,687.30 × (1 + 0.04) = $1,754.79 (fourth period)
Compound amount = $1,754.79
Compound interest = $1,754.79 − $1,500 = $254.79

 (page 342)

Find the future value using a $1.00 future value table

Step 1 Find the number of interest periods: Multiply the time period, in years, by the interest periods per year.

Interest periods = number of years × number of interest periods per year

Step 2 Find the period interest rate: Divide the annual interest rate by the number of interest periods per year.

$$\text{Period interest rate} = \dfrac{\text{annual interest rate}}{\text{number of interest periods per year}}$$

Step 3 Select the periods row corresponding to the number of interest periods.
Step 4 Select the rate-per-period column corresponding to the period interest rate.
Step 5 Locate the value in the cell where the periods row intersects the rate-per-period column. **Step 6** Multiply the original principal by the value from step 5.

Find the future value of $2,000 at 12% compounded semiannually for four years.

4 × 2 = 8 periods

$\dfrac{12\%}{2}$ = 6% period interest rate

Find periods row 8 in Table 10–1 and move across to the 6% rate column: 1.59385.

$2,000 × 1.59385 = $3,187.70 future value

Find the compound interest on $800 at 8% compounded annually for four years.

Find periods row 4 in Table 10–1.

Move across to the 8% rate column and find the compound amount per dollar of principal: 1.36049.

$800 × 1.36049 = $1,088.39 compound amount

$1,088.39   compound amount
− 800   principal
$288.39   compound interest

 (page 346)

Find the effective interest rate

Step 1 Using the simple interest formula method: Divide the interest compounded for the first year by the principal.

$$\text{Effective interest rate} = \dfrac{\text{interest compounded for first year}}{\text{principal}}$$

Step 2 Using the table method: Subtract $1.00 from the future value of $1.00 after one year, and remove the dollar sign.

$$\text{Effective interest rate} = \frac{\text{future value of \$1.00 after 1 year} - \$1.00}{\$1.00}$$

Jane earned $247.29 interest on an investment of $3,000 at 8% annually, compounded quarterly. Find the effective interest rate.

Using the simple interest formula method:

$$\text{Effective interest} = \frac{\$279.49}{\$3,000} = 0.08243 = 8.24\%$$ ~WRONG~

Using Table 10-1:

$$\text{Periods per year} = 4$$

$$\text{Rate per period} = \frac{8\%}{4} = 0.02$$

$$\text{Table value} = 1.08243$$

Effective interest rate = $1.08243 - 1.00 = 0.08243 = 8.24\%$

10.1 — 4 (page 347)

Find the interest compounded daily using a table

Step 1 Determine the amount of money the table uses as the principal. (A typical table principal is $1, $100, or $1,000.) **Step 2** Divide the loan principal by the table principal. **Step 3** Select the days row corresponding to the time period (in days) of the loan. **Step 4** Select the interest column corresponding to the interest rate of the loan. **Step 5** Locate the value in the cell where the interest column intersects the days row. **Step 6** Multiply the quotient from step 2 by the value from step 5.

Find the interest on a $300 loan borrowed at 13% compounded daily for 21 days.

Select the 21 days row of Table 10–2; then move across to the 13% rate column. The table value is 0.750615.

$$\frac{\$300}{100} \times 0.750615 = \$2.25$$

The interest on $300 is $2.25.

10.2 — 1 (page 351)

Find the present value based on annual compounding for one year

Divide the future value by the sum of 1 and the annual interest rate.

$$\text{Present value (principal)} = \frac{\text{future value}}{1 + \text{annual interest rate}}$$

Find the amount of money that must be invested to produce $4,000 in one year if the interest rate is 7% annually, compounded annually.

$$\text{Present value} = \frac{\$4,000}{1 + 0.07} = \frac{\$4,000}{1.07} = \$3,738.32$$

How much must be invested to produce $30,000 in one year if the interest rate is 6% annually, compounded annually?

$$\text{Present value} = \frac{\$30,000}{1 + 0.06} = \frac{\$30,000}{1.06} = \$28,301.89$$

10.2 — 2 (page 353)

Find the present value using a $1.00 present value table

Step 1 Find the number of interest periods: Multiply the time period, in years, by the number of interest periods per year.

Interest periods = number of years × number of interest periods per year

Step 2 Find the period interest rate: Divide the annual interest rate by the number of interest periods per year.

$$\text{Period interest rate} = \frac{\text{annual interest rate}}{\text{number of interest periods per year}}$$

Step 3 Select the periods row corresponding to the number of interest periods. **Step 4** Select the rate-per-period column corresponding to the period interest rate. **Step 5** Locate the value in the cell where the periods row intersects the rate-per-period column. **Step 6** Multiply the future value by the value from step 5.

Find the amount of money that must be deposited to ensure $3,000 at the end of three years if the investment earns 6% compounded semiannually.

$3 \times 2 = 6$ periods

$\dfrac{6\%}{2} = 3\%$ rate per period

Find periods row 6 in Table 10–3 and move across to the 3% rate column: 0.83748.

$\$3,000 \times 0.83748 = \$2,512.44$

The amount that must be invested now to have $3,000 in three years is $2,512.44

CHAPTER 10 REVIEW

Section 10.1

1. Calculate the compound interest on a loan of $1,000 at 8% compounded annually for two years.

2. Calculate the compound interest on a loan of $200 at 6% compounded annually for four years.

3. Calculate the compound interest on a 13% loan of $1,600 for three years if the interest is compounded annually.

4. Calculate the compound interest on a loan of $6,150 at $11\frac{1}{2}$% annual interest compounded annually for three years.

5. Maria Sanchez invested $2,000 for two years at 12% annual interest compounded semiannually. Calculate the interest she earned on her investment.

6. EZ Loan Company loaned $500 at 8% annual interest compounded quarterly for one year. Calculate the amount the loan company will earn in interest.

7. Use Table 10–1 to find the future value on an investment of $3,000 made by Ling Lee for five years at 12% annual interest compounded semiannually.

8. Use Table 10–2 to find the daily interest on $2,500 invested for 21 days at 12% compounded annually.

9. Consult Table 10–1 to find the interest on a loan of $10,000 for five years at 4%, compounded semiannually.

10. How much more interest is paid on the loan in Exercise 9 than if simple interest had been used?

Use Table 10–1 for Exercises 11–18. Find the compound interest on the following loans:

	Principal	Term (Years)	Rate of Compound Interest	Compound Interest	Compounded
11.	$2,000	3	3%	_____	Annually
12.	$3,500	4	10%	_____	Semiannually
13.	$ 800	2	6%	_____	Quarterly

14. Find the factor for compounding an amount for 25 periods at 8% per period.

15. Find the future value on an investment of $8,000 compounded quarterly for seven years at 8%.

16. Calculate the compound interest on a loan of $5,000 for two years if the interest is compounded semiannually at 12%.

17. Calculate the compound interest on a loan of $5,000 for two years if the interest is compounded quarterly at 12%.

18. An investment of $1,000 is made at the beginning of each year for two years, compounded semiannually at 10%. Find the compound amount and the compound interest at the end of the two years.

19. Mario Piazza was offered $900 now for one of his salon photographs or $1,100 in one year for the same photograph. Which would give Mr. Piazza a greater yield if he could invest the $900 for one year at 16% compounded quarterly? Use Table 10–1.

20. Find the effective interest rate for the loan described in Exercise 18.

21. Find the effective interest rate for the loan described in Exercise 17.

22. Use Table 10–2 to find the daily interest on an investment of $5,000 invested for 30 days at $13\frac{1}{2}$%.

23. Use Table 10–2 to find the amount of interest on $100 invested for ten days at 13% compounded daily.

24. Use Table 10–2 to find the compound interest and the compound amount on an investment of $24,982 if it is invested for 28 days at 12% compounded daily.

25. Use Table 10–2 to find the compound interest and the compound amount on an investment of $2,000 if it is invested for 21 days at 13% compounded daily.

26. Find the interest on an investment of $1,000 for 30 days if it is invested at an annual rate of 12% compounded monthly. Compare this interest to the interest earned on $1,000 for 30 days at an annual rate of 12% compounded daily. (Use Tables 10–1 and 10–2.)

27. Linda Boyd invests $2,000 at 8% compounded semiannually for two years and Inez Everett invests an equal amount at 8% compounded quarterly for 18 months. Use Table 10–1 to determine which investment yields the greater interest.

28. What is the effective interest rate of each investment in Exercise 27?

Section 10.2

29. How much money should Brienne Smith set aside today to have $5,000 in one year for an international trip? Today's annual interest rate is 7.9%.

30. Miranda Bolden wishes to have $8,000 one year from now to make a down payment on a lake house. How much should she invest at 9.5% annual interest to have her payment in one year?

In the following exercises, find the amount of money that should be invested (present value) at the stated interest rate to yield the given amount (future value) after the indicated amount of time. Use Table 10–3.

31. $1,500 in three years at 10%, compounded annually

32. $2,000 in five years at 10%, compounded semiannually

33. $1,000 in seven years at 8%, compounded quarterly

34. $3,500 in 12 years at 12%, compounded annually

35. $4,000 in two years at 12% annual interest compounded quarterly

36. $10,000 in seven years at 16% annual interest compounded quarterly

37. $500 in 15 years at 8% annual interest compounded semiannually

38. $800 in four years at 10% annual interest compounded annually

39. $1,800 in one year at 12% annual interest compounded monthly

40. $700 in six years at 8% annual interest compounded quarterly

41. Myrna Lewis wished to have $4,000 in four years to tour Europe. How much must she invest today at 8% annual interest compounded quarterly to have the $4,000 in four years?

42. Louis Banks was offered $15,000 cash or $19,500 to be paid in two years for a resort cabin. If money can be invested in today's market for 12% annual interest compounded quarterly, which offer should Louis accept?

43. An art dealer offered a collector $8,000 cash for a painting. The collector could sell the painting to an individual for $11,000 to be paid in 18 months. On the current money market, investments bring 12% annual interest compounded monthly. Which is the better deal for the collector?

44. If you were offered $700 today or $800 in two years, which would you accept if money can be invested at 12% annual interest compounded monthly?

45. Use Table 10–3 to calculate how much a family should invest now at 10% compounded annually to have a $7,000 down payment on a house in four years.

Challenge Problems

46. An investment of $2,000 is made at the beginning of each year for three years. The investment is compounded annually at 8%. Find the future value and the compound interest at the end of three years.

47. Your company plans to enter several short-term financing agreements. It is your assignment to compute interest for monthly compounding at the nominal annual rate of 8%. Construct an interest rate table showing the current principal and the interest earned for each of the twelve months for $1.00 compounded monthly. What is the effective rate of this financing agreement?

48. One real estate sales technique is to encourage customers or clients to buy today, because the value of the property will probably increase during the next few years. "Buy this lot today for $30,000. In two years, I project it will sell for $32,500." Let's see if this is a wise investment.

In two years the future value is projected to be $32,500. If the interest rate is 12%, compounded annually, what amount should you invest today to have the $32,500 in two years?

Using Table 10–3, the factor for 12% and two periods is 0.79719.

Present value = $32,500 × 0.79719 = $25,908.68

By investing only $25,908.68 today at 12% for two years, you will have the $32,500 needed to purchase the land. You have actually paid only $25,908.68 for the lot, a savings of $4,091.32 on the $30,000 price. Of course, there are always problems with waiting to buy.

a. What are some of the problems with waiting to buy land?

b. What are some of the advantages of waiting?

c. Lots in a new subdivision sell for $15,600. If you invest your money today in an account earning 8% quarterly, how much will the lot actually cost you in a year assuming the price does not go up? How much do you save?

d. (1) You have inherited $60,000 and plan to buy a home. If you invest the $60,000 today at 10% compounded annually, how much could you spend on the house in one year?

(2) If you intend to spend $60,000 on a house in one year, how much of your inheritance should you invest today at 10% compounded annually? How much do you have left to spend on a car?

1. Calculate the compound interest on a loan $2,000 at 7% compounded annually for three years.

2. Calculate the compound interest on a 14% annual interest loan of $3,000 for four years if interest is compounded annually.

3. Use Table 10–1 to find the interest on a loan of $5,000 for six years at 10% annual interest if interest is compounded semiannually.

4. Use Table 10–1 to find the compound amount on an investment of $12,000 for seven years at 12% annual interest compounded quarterly.

5. An investment of $1,500 is made at the beginning of each year for two years at 12% annual interest compounded semiannually. Find the compound amount and the compound interest at the end of two years.

6. Use Table 10–1 to find the compound interest on a loan of $3,000 for one year at 12% annual interest if the interest is compounded quarterly.

7. Find the effective interest rate for the loan described in Exercise 6.

8. Use Table 10–2 to find the daily interest on an investment of $2,000 invested at 14% for 28 days.

9. Use Tables 10–1 and 10–2 to compare the interest on an investment of $3,000 that is invested at 12% annual interest compounded monthly and daily for the month of April (30 days).

In the following exercises, find the amount of money that should be invested today (present value) at the stated interest rate to yield the given amount (future value) after the indicated amount of time.

10. $3,400 in four years at 8% annual interest compounded annually

11. $5,000 in eight years at 8% annual interest compounded semiannually

12. $8,000 in 12 years at 12% annual interest compounded annually

13. $6,000 in six years at 12% annual interest compounded quarterly

14. Jamie Juarez will need $12,000 in ten years for her daughter's college education. Her parents are willing to invest the necessary funds. How much must be invested today at 8% annual interest compounded semiannually, to have the necessary funds for college?

15. If you were offered $600 today or $680 in one year, which would you accept if money can be invested at 12% annual interest compounded monthly?

16. Derek Anderson plans to buy a house in four years. He will make an $8,000 down payment on the property. How much should he invest today at 6% annual interest compounded quarterly, to have the required amount in four years?

17. You have $2,000 to invest and have two options. Which of the two options will yield the greatest return on your investment?
    Option 1: 8% annual interest compounded quarterly for four years
    Option 2: $8\frac{1}{4}$% annual interest compounded annually for four years

18. If you invest $2,000 today at 8% annual interest compounded quarterly, how much will you have after three years? (Table 10–1)

19. If you invest $1,000 today at 12% annual interest compounded daily, how much will you have after 20 days? (Table 10–2)

20. How much money should Bryan Trailer Sales set aside today to have $15,000 in one year to purchase a forklift if the interest rate is 10.4%, compounded annually?

CHAPTER 11

ANNUITIES AND SINKING FUNDS

GOOD DECISIONS THROUGH TEAMWORK

With your team members, investigate the planning and saving required for a major vacation that is being planned by a couple in their fourth year of marriage, as a celebration for their tenth wedding anniversary. Choose a desirable location outside the United States for a one- to two-week romantic getaway. The couple will set aside $30 to $50 per month for the next six years. Team members should shop several institutions that offer sinking fund investment plans to determine which plan is the best choice.

List and discuss all categories of expenditures that must be allocated for this vacation. Note that prices may be lower during the off-season at certain resorts, a factor it may be necessary to consider depending upon your team's budget.

Using the figures compiled by your team, and adjusting for inflation, prepare a written report that outlines the destination, mode of travel, lodging accommodations, and activities. Include in the report the savings plan or program for accumulating the necessary funds. Present an oral report detailing your choices.

11.1 Future Value of an Annuity

▶ **1** *Find the future value of an ordinary annuity using the simple interest formula method*

▶ **2** *Find the future value of an ordinary annuity using a $1.00 ordinary annuity future value table*

▶ **3** *Find the future value of an annuity due using the simple interest formula method*

▶ **4** *Find the future value of an annuity due using a $1.00 ordinary annuity future value table*

11.2 Sinking Funds and the Present Value of an Annuity

▶ **1** *Find the sinking fund payment using a $1.00 sinking fund payment table*

▶ **2** *Find the present value of an ordinary annuity using a $1.00 ordinary annuity present value table*

So far we have discussed interest accumulated from one *lump sum investment*. But an individual or business may also make *periodic investments,* or payments, to a compound interest account. If the payment each period is the same, and the rate of interest does not change, the payment is called an **annuity** payment or **sinking fund** payment. The growing account is called an annuity or sinking fund. Retirement funds, saving for a college education or vacation, a company putting away money periodically now to pay for new equipment and buildings or to retire a bond debt in the future are all examples of an annuity or sinking fund.

11.1 Future Value of an Annuity

▶ **1** *Find the future value of an ordinary annuity using the simple interest formula method*

▶ **2** *Find the future value of an ordinary annuity using a $1.00 ordinary annuity future value table*

▶ **3** *Find the future value of an annuity due using the simple interest formula method*

▶ **4** *Find the future value of an annuity due using a $1.00 ordinary annuity future value table*

An annuity may be paid over a guaranteed number of periods, in which case the annuity is an **annuity certain.** Or the annuity may be paid over an uncertain number of periods, in which case the annuity is a **contingent annuity.** A mortgage payment is an annuity certain, whereas a life insurance premium is a contingent annuity.

We can also categorize annuities according to when payment is made. For an **ordinary annuity,** payment is made at the *end* of the period. For an **annuity due,** payment is made at the *beginning* of the period.

▶ **1** *The Simple Interest Basis of Annuity Future Value*

Finding the future value of an annuity is similar to finding the future value of a lump sum. The significant difference is that, for each interest period, more principal—the annuity payment—is added to the amount on which interest is earned. Nonetheless, the simple interest formula $I = PRT$ is still the basis of calculating interest.

HOW TO | Find the Future Value of an Ordinary Annuity Using the Simple Interest Formula Method

Step 1 Find the first end-of-period principal.

First end-of-period principal = annuity payment

Step 2 For each remaining period in turn, find the next end-of-period principal: **(a)** Multiply the previous end-of-period principal by the sum of 1 and the period interest rate. **(b)** Add the product from step 2a and the annuity payment.

End-of-period principal = previous end-of-period principal
$\times$ (1 + period interest rate) + annuity payment

Step 3 Identify the last end-of-period principal as the future value.

Future value = last end-of-period principal

Notice for an ordinary annuity, no interest accumulates on the annuity payment during the month in which it is paid, because the payment is made at the *end* of the period. For the first period, this means no interest accumulates at all.

Example 1 What is the future value of an annual ordinary annuity of $1,000 for three years at 8% annual interest?

The period interest rate is 0.08. The annuity is $1,000.

End-of-year = (previous end-of-year)(1 + 0.08) + 1,000

End of year 1 = $1,000.00   **No interest earned the first year.**

End of year 2 = $1,000.00 (1.08) + $1,000.00

= $1,080.00 + $1,000.00

= $2,080.00

End of year 3 = $2,080.00 (1.08) + $1,000.00

= $2,246.40 + $1,000.00

= $3,246.40

The future value is $3,246.40.

 Ordinary Annuity Future Value Tables

As you can see, calculating the future value of an ordinary annuity could become quite tedious if the number of periods was large. For example, a monthly annuity such as a savings plan, running for five years, would have 60 periods, and thus 60 calculation sequences. For this reason, most businesspeople rely on prepared tables or computers.

HOW TO	Find the Future Value of an Ordinary Annuity Using a $1.00 Ordinary Annuity Future Value Table

Step 1 Select the periods row corresponding to the number of interest periods.

Step 2 Select the rate-per-period column corresponding to the period interest rate.

Step 3 Locate the value in the cell where the periods row intersects the rate-per-period column.

Step 4 Multiply the annuity payment by the table value from step 3.

Future value = annuity payment × table value

Example 2 Use Table 11–1 to find the future value of a semiannual ordinary annuity of $6,000 for 5 years at 12% annual interest compounded semiannually.

5 years × 2 periods per year = 10 periods

$$\frac{12\% \text{ annual interest rate}}{2 \text{ periods per year}} = 6\% \text{ period interest rate}$$

Table 11–1 value for 10 periods at 6% is 13.181.

future value of annuity = annuity payment × table value

= $6,000 × 13.181

= $79,086

The future value of the ordinary annuity is $79,086.

Table 11–1 Future Value of $1.00 Ordinary Annuity

Periods					Rate per Period						
	2%	3%	4%	5%	6%	7%	8%	9%	10%	12%
1	1.000	1.000	1.000	1.000	1.000	1.000	1.000	1.000	1.000	1.000
2	2.020	2.030	2.040	2.050	2.060	2.070	2.080	2.090	2.100	2.120
3	3.060	3.091	3.122	3.153	3.184	3.215	3.246	3.278	3.310	3.374
4	4.122	4.184	4.246	4.310	4.375	4.440	4.506	4.573	4.641	4.779
5	5.204	5.309	5.416	5.526	5.637	5.751	5.867	5.985	6.105	6.353
6	6.308	6.468	6.633	6.802	6.975	7.153	7.336	7.523	7.716	8.115
7	7.434	7.662	7.898	8.142	8.394	8.654	8.923	9.200	9.487	10.089
8	8.583	8.892	9.214	9.549	9.897	10.260	10.637	11.028	11.436	12.300
9	9.755	10.159	10.583	11.027	11.491	11.978	12.488	13.021	13.579	14.776
10	10.950	11.464	12.006	12.578	13.181	13.816	14.487	15.193	15.937	17.549
11	12.169	12.808	13.486	14.207	14.972	15.784	16.645	17.560	18.531	20.655
12	13.412	14.192	15.026	15.917	16.870	17.888	18.977	20.141	21.384	24.133
13	14.680	15.618	16.627	17.713	18.882	20.141	21.495	22.523	24.523	28.029
14	15.974	17.086	18.292	19.599	21.015	22.550	24.215	26.019	27.975	32.393
15	17.293	18.599	20.024	21.579	23.276	25.129	27.152	29.361	31.772	37.280
16	18.639	20.157	21.825	23.657	25.673	27.888	30.324	33.003	35.950	42.753
17	20.012	21.762	23.698	25.840	20.213	30.840	33.750	36.974	40.545	48.884
18	21.412	23.414	25.645	28.132	30.906	33.999	37.450	41.301	45.599	55.750
19	22.841	25.117	27.671	30.539	33.760	37.379	41.446	46.018	51.159	63.440
20	24.297	26.870	29.778	33.066	36.786	40.995	45.762	51.160	57.275	72.052

Table values show the future value, or accumulated amount of the investment and interest, of a $1 investment at the beginning of a given number of periods at a given rate per period. Table values can be generated using the formula FV of $1 per period = $\left(\frac{(1 + R)^N - 1}{R}\right)$, when FV is the future value, R is the rate per period, and N is the number of periods.

To calculate the future value of an ordinary annuity or to verify the calculations using the formula $FV = P\left(\dfrac{(I + R)^N - 1}{R}\right)$, where FV is future value, P is the annuity payment, R is the rate per period, and N is the number of periods. The value in the parentheses represents the table value.

To verify the results of Example 2,

$$FV = 6000 \left(\frac{(1.06)^{10} - 1}{0.06}\right)$$

Make the calculations inside the parentheses first.

$\boxed{\text{AC}}$ 1.06 $\boxed{x^y}$ 10 $\boxed{=}$ − 1 $\boxed{=}$ $\boxed{\div}$ .06 $\boxed{=}$ $\boxed{\times}$ 6000 $\boxed{=}$ ⇒ 79084.76965 or \$79,084.77

The slight variation in the future value of the annuity is due to the increased accuracy when using full calculator values in calculations.

3 ▶ *Annuities Due*

Because an annuity due is paid at the *beginning* of each period, rather than the end, the annuity due payment earns interest throughout the period in which it is paid. To find the interest earned for any given period, the annuity payment is added to the previous accumulation and the sum is multiplied by the period interest rate. The future value of an annuity due, then, is greater than the future value of the corresponding ordinary annuity: Given the same number of periods, the same period interest rate, and the same annuity payment, the difference of the future values of an ordinary annuity and an annuity due is exactly one period's worth of interest on what amounts to the future value of the ordinary annuity.

HOW TO	**Find the Future Value of an Annuity Due Using the Simple Interest Formula Method**

Step 1 Find the first end-of-period principal: Multiply the annuity payment by the sum of 1 and the period interest rate.

First end-of-period principal = annuity payment × (1 + period interest rate)

Step 2 For each remaining period in turn, find the next end-of-period principal: **(a)** Add the previous end-of-period principal and the annuity payment. **(b)** Multiply the sum from step 2a by the sum of 1 and the period interest rate.

End-of-period principal = (previous end-of-period principal + annuity payment) × (1 + period interest rate)

Step 3 Identify the last end-of-period principal as the future value.

Future value = last end-of-period principal

Example 3 What is the future value of a quarterly annuity due of \$100 for 1 year at 10% annual interest compounded quarterly? Find the total investment and the total interest earned. The annuity is \$100; the period interest rate is:

$$\frac{10\% \text{ annual interest rate}}{4 \text{ periods per year}} = 2.5\% = 0.025 \text{ period interest rate}$$

End of quarter = (previous end-of-quarter + $100)(1 + 0.025)

End of quarter 1 = $100(1.025)   **The annuity earns interest during the first period.**

$\qquad\qquad = \$102.50$

End of quarter 2 = ($102.50 + $100)(1.025)

$\qquad\qquad = \$202.50(1.025)$

$\qquad\qquad = \$207.56$

End of quarter 3 = ($207.56 + $100)(1.025)

$\qquad\qquad = \$307.56(1.025)$

$\qquad\qquad = \$315.25$

End of quarter 4 = ($315.25 + $100)(1.025)

$\qquad\qquad = \$415.25(1.025)$

$\qquad\qquad = \$425.63$ (future value of annuity due)

Total investment = Investment per period $\times$ total periods

$\qquad\qquad = \$100 \times 4$

$\qquad\qquad = \$400$

Total interest earned = Future value $-$ total investment

$\qquad\qquad = \$425.63 - \$400$

$\qquad\qquad = \$25.63$

The future value of the annuity due is $425.63, the total investment is $400, and the total interest earned is $25.63.

 Annuity Due and the Ordinary Annuity Future Value Table

Because the future value of an annuity due is so closely related to the future value of the corresponding ordinary annuity, we can use Table 11–1 to find the annuity due future value. An annuity due accumulates interest once more than does the ordinary annuity, but has the same number of payments. Thus, we adjust Table 11–1 values by multiplying by the sum of 1 and the period interest rate.

 HOW TO | **Find the Future Value of an Annuity Due Using a $1.00 Ordinary Annuity Future Value Table**

Step 1 Select the periods row corresponding to the number of interest periods.
Step 2 Select the rate-per-period column corresponding to the period interest rate.
Step 3 Locate the value in the cell where the periods row intersects the rate-per-period column.
Step 4 Multiply the table value from step 3 by the sum of 1 and the period interest rate.
Step 5 Multiply the annuity payment by the product from step 4.

Future value = annuity payment $\times$ table value $\times$ (1 + period interest rate)

Example 4 Use Table 11–1 to find the future value of a quarterly annuity due of $2,800 for four years at 12% annual interest compounded quarterly.

$$4 \text{ years} \times 4 \text{ periods per year} = 16 \text{ periods}$$

$$\frac{12\% \text{ annual interest rate}}{4 \text{ periods per year}} = 3\% \text{ period interest rate}$$

The Table 11–1 value for 16 periods at 3% is 20.157.

Future value = annuity payment × table value × (1 + period interest rate)

$$= \$2,800 \times 20.157 \times 1.03$$

$$= \$58,132.79$$

The future value is $58,132.79.

To calculate the future value of an annuity due or to verify the calculations using a table value, use the formula $FV = P\left(\dfrac{(1 + R)^N - 1}{R}\right)(1 + R)$, where FV is future value, P is the annuity payment, R is the rate per period, and N is the number of periods. The value in the first set of parentheses represents the table value. To verify the results of Example 4,

$$FV = \$2,800\left(\frac{(1.03)^{16} - 1}{0.03}\right)(1.03)$$

Start by making the calculations in the first set of parentheses

$$\boxed{\text{AC}}\ 1.03\ \boxed{x^y}\ 16\ \boxed{=}\ \boxed{-}\ 1\ \boxed{=}\ \boxed{\div}\ .03\ \boxed{=}\ \boxed{\times}\ 1.03\ \boxed{=}\ \boxed{\times}\ 2800\ \boxed{=}\ \Rightarrow 58132.44567$$

Example 5 Sarah Smith is trying to decide which annuity plan she wants to use. She plans to invest a total of $8,000 over two-years time at 8% annual interest. Annuity One is a quarterly ordinary annuity of $1,000; interest is compounded quarterly. Annuity Two is a semiannual annuity of $2,000; interest is compounded semiannually. Annuity Three is a quarterly annuity due of $1,000; interest is compounded quarterly. Annuity Four is a semiannual annuity due of $2,000; interest is compounded semiannually. Which annuity yields the greatest future value?

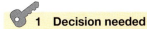

1 Decision needed

Which annuity yields the greatest future value?

2 Unknown facts

Future value of each annuity

3 Known facts

Annuity One: Ordinary annuity of $1,000 quarterly for two years at 8% annual interest compounded quarterly
Annuity Two: Ordinary annuity of $2,000 semiannually for two years at 8% annual interest compounded semiannually
Annuity Three: Annuity due of $1,000 quarterly for two years at 8% annual interest compounded quarterly
Annuity Four: Annuity due of $2,000 semiannually for two years at 8% annual interest compounded semiannually.

4 Relationships

Future value of ordinary annuity = annuity payment × Table 11–1 value
Future value of annuity due = annuity payment × Table 11–1 value × (1 + period interest rate)
Number of periods = years × periods per year

$$\text{Period interest rate} = \frac{\text{annual interest rate}}{\text{periods per year}}$$

5 Estimation

An annuity due yields a greater future value than a corresponding ordinary annuity, since the annuity payment earns interest during the period in which it is paid. So Annuity Three will be better than Annuity One, and Annuity Four will be better than Annuity Two.

6 Calculations

Annuity One
Number of periods = years × periods per year
$$= 2 \times 4$$
$$= 8$$

$$\text{Period interest rate} = \frac{\text{annual interest rate}}{\text{periods per year}}$$
$$= \frac{8\%}{4} = 2\%$$
$$= 0.02$$

Table value = 8.583
Future value = annuity payment × table value
Future value = ($1,000)(8.583)
$$= \$8,583$$

Annuity Two
Number of periods = years × periods per year
$$= 2 \times 2$$
$$= 4$$

$$\text{Period interest rate} = \frac{\text{annual interest rate}}{\text{periods per year}}$$
$$= \frac{8\%}{2} = 4\%$$
$$= 0.04$$

Table value = 4.246
Future value = annuity payment × table value
$$= \$2,000 \times 4.246$$
$$= \$8,492.00$$

Annuity Three
The number of periods and period interest rate are the same as those for Annuity One.
Future value = annuity payment × Table value × (1 + period interest rate)
$$= \$1,000 \times 8.583 \times 1.02$$
$$= \$8,754.66$$

Annuity Four
The number of periods and period interest rate are the same as those for Annuity Two.
Future value = annuity payment × table value × (1 + period interest rate)
$$= \$2,000 \times 4.246 \times 1.04$$
$$= \$8,831.68$$

7 Decision made

Annuity Four, with the larger annuity due payment, yields the greatest future value. Notice, too, that the ordinary annuity with the fewer periods per year yields the least future value of all four annuities. If the total investment is the same, the number of years are the same, and the annual rate of interest is the same, any annuity due yields a larger future value than any corresponding ordinary annuity. The annuity due with the largest payment is the most profitable, while the ordinary annuity paid most frequently is the most profitable ordinary annuity.

Back-to-School Shopping

Seven of 10 parents plan to shop for back-to-school items with their kids. What parents say they'll buy with the average $325 they expect to spend:

91% Clothing
90% General supplies
39% Text books
32% Computer supplies
16% Furniture/appliances
13% Electronics

Note: Could choose more than one.

Source: American Express survey

By Anne R. Carey and Marcy E. Mullins, USA TODAY

1. The Smiths have four children to send to school. Find the future value of an ordinary monthly annuity of $50 for 7 years at 5% annual interest compounded quarterly.

2. If the Smiths withdraw the money from the annuity at the end of 7 years, how many years will they be able to provide the $325 per year per child for back-to-school shopping?

3. Using the information in the graph, find the amount of money provided by the annuity for clothing and electronics.

4. If this graph were produced 10 years from now, what changes would you expect?

Slow-Moving States

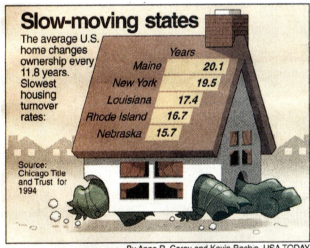

Slow-moving states

The average U.S. home changes ownership every 11.8 years. Slowest housing turnover rates:

	Years
Maine	20.1
New York	19.5
Louisiana	17.4
Rhode Island	16.7
Nebraska	15.7

Source: Chicago Title and Trust for 1994

By Anne R. Carey and Kevin Rechin, USA TODAY

1. The Vans currently own a home in Rhode Island. They wish to purchase a new home in 16 or 17 years without selling their current home. To save for the new down payment, they contribute $250 a quarter to an ordinary annuity for 16 years at 8% annual interest compounded semiannually. Find the amount of money they will have for the down payment.

2. If the Vans lived in Maine and saved for 20 years under the same conditions, how much money would they have for the down payment?

Self-Check 11.1

1 ▶ *Use the simple interest formula method for Exercises 1–4.*

1. Find the future value of an ordinary annuity of $3,000 annually for two years at 9% annual interest.

2. Len and Sharron Smith are saving money for their daughter, Heather, to attend college. They set aside an ordinary annuity of $4,000 annually for two years at 7% annual interest. How much will Heather have for college when she graduates from high school in three years?

3. Harry Taylor has a plan to pay an ordinary annuity of $5,000 annually for three years so that he can take a year away from work to study for a Master's degree in business. The annual rate of interest is 8%. How much will Harry have at the end of three years?

4. Scott Martin is planning to establish a small business to provide consulting services in computer networking. He is committed to an ordinary annuity of $3,000 annually at 8.5% annual interest. How much will Scott have to establish the business after three years?

2 ▶ *Use Table 11–1 for Exercises 5–9.*

5. Find the future value of an ordinary annuity of $6,500 semiannually for seven years at 10% annual interest compounded semiannually.

6. Pat Lechleiter pays an ordinary annuity of $2,500 quarterly at 8% annual interest compounded quarterly, to establish supplemental income for retirement. How much will Pat have available at the end of five years?

7. Latanya Brown established an ordinary annuity of $1,000 annually at 7% annual interest. What is the future value of the annuity after 15 years? How much will Latanya have invested of her own money during this period of time? By how much will her investment have grown?

8. You invest in an ordinary annuity of $500 annually at 8% annual interest. Find the future value of the annuity at the end of ten years. How much have you invested? How much interest has your annuity earned?

9. You invest in an ordinary annuity of $2,000 annually at 8% annual interest. What is the future value of the annuity at the end of five years? How much have you invested? How much interest has your annuity earned?

10. Make a chart comparing your results for Exercises 8 and 9. Use these headings: Years, Total Investment, Total Interest. What general conclusion might you draw about effective investment strategy?

3 ▶ *Use the simple interest formula method for Exercises 11–14.*

11. Find the future value of an annuity due of $12,000 annually for three years at 14% annual interest.

12. Bernard McGhee has decided to establish an annuity due of $2,500 annually for 15 years at 7.2% annual interest. How much is the annuity due worth after two years?

13. Find the future value of an annuity due of $7,800 annually for two years at 8.1% annual interest.

14. Find the future value of an annuity due of $400 annually for two years at 6.8% annual interest compounded annually.

4 ▶ *Use Table 11–1 for Exercises 15–18.*

15. Find the future value of a quarterly annuity due of $4,400 for three years at 8% annual interest compounded quarterly.

16. Find the future value of an annuity due of $750 semiannually for four years at 8% annual interest compounded semiannually.

17. Which annuity earns more interest: An annuity due of $300 quarterly for one year at 8% annual interest compounded quarterly, or an annuity due of $600 semiannually for one year at 8% annual interest compounded semiannually?

18. You have carefully examined your budget and determined that you can only manage to set aside $250 per year. So you set up an annuity due of $250 annually at 7% annual interest. How much of your own money will you have contributed after 20 years? What is the future value of your annuity after 20 years? How much interest will your money earn for you?

11.2 Sinking Funds and the Present Value of an Annuity

> **1** ▶ Find the sinking fund payment using a $1.00 sinking fund payment table
>
> **2** ▶ Find the present value of an ordinary annuity using a $1.00 ordinary annuity present value table

Businesses and individuals often use **sinking funds** to accumulate a desired amount of money by the end of a certain period of time to pay off a financial obligation, for a vacation or college fund, or to reach a specific goal, such as retiring a bond issue or paying for equipment replacement and modernization. Essentially, a sinking fund is payment into an ordinary annuity to yield a desired future value.

In general, you are finding the *future value of an annuity* when you know how much you can set aside per period at a given rate and you want to know how much you will have accumulated after a certain amount of time. You are finding the *sinking fund payment* when you know in advance how much future value you want after a certain amount of time at a given rate and you want to know how much you should set aside each period to reach that goal.

 ### Sinking Fund Payments

A sinking fund payment is made at the *end* of each period so a sinking fund payment is an ordinary annuity payment. These payments, along with the interest, accumulate over a period of time in order to provide the desired future value.

To calculate the payment required to yield a desired future value, we use Table 11–2.

Using Table 11–2 is similar to using Table 11–1: Locate the table value for the given number of periods and the given rate per period, and multiply by the desired future value.

Sinking fund payment = future value × Table 11–2 value.

Example 1 Use Table 11–2 to find the annual sinking fund payment required to accumulate $140,000 in 12 years at 8% annual interest.

12 years × 1 period per year = 12 periods

$$\frac{8\% \text{ annual interest rate}}{1 \text{ period per year}} = 8\% \text{ period interest rate}$$

The Table 11–2 value for 12 periods at 8% is 0.0526950.

$$\text{sinking fund payment} = \text{desired future value} \times \text{table factor}$$

$$= \$140,000 \times 0.0526950$$

$$= \$7,377.30$$

A sinking fund payment of \$7,377.30 is required at the end of each year for 12 years at 8% to yield the desired \$140,000.

A scientific calculator can be used to find the sinking fund payment using the formula $P = FV\left(\dfrac{R}{(1 + R)^N - 1}\right)$ where P is the sinking fund payment, FV is the future value of the sinking fund, R is the rate per period, and N is the number of periods. The value in the parentheses represents the table value. To verify the results of Example 1,

$$P = 140,000\left(\frac{0.08}{(1.08)^{12} - 1}\right)$$

Make the calculations inside the parentheses first.

$\boxed{\text{AC}}\ .08\ \boxed{\div}\ \boxed{(}\ 1.08\ \boxed{x^y}\ 12\ \boxed{-}\ 1\ \boxed{)}\boxed{=}\boxed{\times}\ 140000\ \boxed{=}$

Table 11–2 $1.00 Sinking Fund Payments

Periods	\multicolumn{7}{c}{Rate per Period}						
	1%	2%	3%	4%	6%	8%	12%
1	1.0000000	1.0000000	1.0000000	1.0000000	1.0000000	1.0000000	1.0000000
2	0.4975124	0.4950495	0.4926108	0.4901961	0.4854369	0.4807692	0.4716981
3	0.3300221	0.3267547	0.3235304	0.3203485	0.3141098	0.3080335	0.2963490
4	0.2462881	0.2426238	0.2390271	0.2354901	0.2285915	0.2219208	0.2092344
5	0.1960398	0.1921584	0.1883546	0.1846271	0.1773964	0.1704565	0.1574097
6	0.1625484	0.1585258	0.1545975	0.1507619	0.1433626	0.1363154	0.1232257
7	0.1386283	0.1345120	0.1305064	0.1266096	0.1191350	0.1120724	0.0991177
8	0.1206903	0.1165098	0.1124564	0.1085278	0.1010359	0.0940148	0.0813028
9	0.1067404	0.1025154	0.0984339	0.0944930	0.0870222	0.0800797	0.0676789
10	0.0955821	0.0913265	0.0872305	0.0832909	0.0758680	0.0690295	0.0569842
11	0.0864541	0.0821779	0.0780775	0.0741490	0.0667929	0.0600763	0.0484154
12	0.0788488	0.0745596	0.0704621	0.0675522	0.0592770	0.0526950	0.0414368
13	0.0724148	0.0681184	0.0670295	0.0601437	0.0529601	0.0465218	0.0356772
14	0.0669012	0.0626020	0.0585263	0.0546690	0.0475849	0.0412969	0.0308712
15	0.0621238	0.0578255	0.0537666	0.0499411	0.0429628	0.0368295	0.0268242
16	0.0579446	0.0536501	0.0496109	0.0458200	0.0389521	0.0329769	0.0233900
17	0.0542581	0.0499698	0.0459525	0.0421985	0.0354448	0.0296294	0.0204567
18	0.0509821	0.0467021	0.0427087	0.0389933	0.0323565	0.0267021	0.0179373
19	0.0480518	0.0437818	0.0398139	0.0361386	0.0296209	0.0241276	0.0157630
20	0.0454153	0.0411567	0.0372157	0.0335818	0.0271846	0.0218522	0.0138788
25	0.0354068	0.0312204	0.0274279	0.0240120	0.0182267	0.0136788	0.0075000
30	0.0287481	0.0246499	0.0210193	0.0178301	0.0126489	0.0088274	0.0041437
40	0.0204556	0.0165558	0.0132624	0.0105235	0.0064615	0.0038602	0.0013036
50	0.0155127	0.0118232	0.0088655	0.0065502	0.0034443	0.0017429	0.0004167

Table values show the sinking fund payment earning a given rate for a given number of periods so that the accumulated amount at the end of the time will be $1. The formula for generating the table values is $TV = \dfrac{R}{(1 + R)^N - 1}$ where TV is the table value, R is the rate per period, and N is the number of periods or payments.

2▶ *Present Value of an Ordinary Annuity*

An annuity allows you to make periodic payments that will accumulate with interest over a period of time to reach a future value. For comparative purposes a business or individual may want to know what lump sum investment with compound interest made now at the same rate for the same length of time would yield the exact same future value. The **present value of an annuity** is the lump sum that must be invested now to achieve the future value of the annuity started now.

To find the present value of an annuity, we use Table 11–3: Locate the table value for the given number of periods and the given rate per period, and multiply by the annuity payment.

Table 11–3 Present Value of a $1.00 Ordinary Annuity

Periods	\multicolumn{10}{c}{Rate per Period}
	2%	3%	4%	5%	6%	7%	8%	9%	10%	12%
1	0.980	0.971	0.962	0.952	0.943	0.935	0.926	0.917	0.909	0.893
2	1.942	1.913	1.886	1.859	1.833	1.808	1.783	1.759	1.736	1.690
3	2.884	2.829	2.775	2.723	2.673	2.624	2.577	2.531	2.487	2.402
4	3.808	3.717	3.630	3.546	3.465	3.387	3.312	3.240	3.170	3.037
5	4.713	4.580	4.452	4.329	4.212	4.100	3.993	3.890	3.791	3.605
6	5.601	5.417	5.242	5.076	4.917	4.767	4.623	4.486	4.355	4.111
7	6.472	6.230	6.002	5.786	5.582	5.389	5.206	5.033	4.868	4.564
8	7.325	7.020	6.733	6.463	6.210	5.971	5.747	5.535	5.335	4.968
9	8.162	7.786	7.435	7.108	6.802	6.515	6.247	5.995	5.759	5.328
10	8.983	8.530	8.111	7.722	7.360	7.024	6.710	6.418	6.145	5.650
11	9.787	9.253	8.760	8.306	7.887	7.499	7.139	6.805	6.495	5.938
12	10.575	9.954	9.385	8.863	8.384	7.943	7.536	7.161	6.814	6.194
13	11.348	10.635	9.986	9.394	8.853	8.358	7.904	7.487	7.103	6.424
14	12.106	11.296	10.563	9.899	9.295	8.745	8.244	7.786	7.367	6.628
15	12.849	11.939	11.118	10.380	9.712	9.108	8.559	8.061	7.606	6.811
16	13.578	12.561	11.652	10.838	10.106	9.447	8.851	8.313	7.824	6.974
17	14.292	13.166	12.166	11.274	10.477	9.763	9.122	8.544	8.022	7.102
18	14.992	13.754	12.659	11.690	10.828	10.059	9.372	8.756	8.201	7.250
19	15.678	14.324	13.134	12.085	11.158	10.336	9.604	8.950	8.365	7.366
20	16.351	14.877	13.590	12.462	11.470	10.594	9.818	9.129	8.514	7.469
25	19.523	17.413	15.622	14.094	12.783	11.654	10.675	9.823	9.077	7.843
30	22.396	19.600	17.292	15.372	13.765	12.409	11.258	10.274	9.427	8.055
40	27.355	23.115	19.793	17.159	15.046	13.332	11.925	10.757	9.779	8.244
50	31.424	25.730	21.482	18.256	15.762	13.801	12.233	10.962	9.915	8.304

Table values show the present value of a $1.00 ordinary annuity, or the lump sum amount that, invested now, yields the same compounded amount as an annuity of $1.00 at a given rate per period for a given number of periods. The formula for generating the table values is $TV = \dfrac{(1 + R)^N - 1}{R(1 + R)^N}$ where TV is the table value, R is the rate per period, and N is the number of periods.

> **Example 2** Use Table 11–3 to find the present value of a semiannual ordinary annuity of $3,000 for seven years at 12% annual interest compounded semiannually.

$$7 \text{ years} \times 2 \text{ periods per year} = 14 \text{ periods}$$

$$\frac{12\% \text{ annual interest}}{2 \text{ periods per year}} = 6\% \text{ period interest rate}$$

The Table 11–3 value for 14 periods at 6% is 9.295.

$$
\begin{aligned}
\text{present value of annuity} &= \text{annuity payment} \times \text{table factor} \\
&= \$3{,}000 \times 9.295 \\
&= \$27{,}885
\end{aligned}
$$

> **By investing $27,885 now at 12% interest compounded semiannually, you will accumulate after seven years the same amount of money as you would if you paid the annuity instead.**

To calculate the present value of an ordinary annuity or to verify the calculations using a table value, use the formula $PV = P\left(\dfrac{(1 + R)^N - 1}{R(1 + R)^N}\right)$, where PV is present value, P is the annuity, R is the rate per period, and N is the number of periods. The value in the parentheses represents the table value.

To verify the results of Example 2,

$$PV = 3000\left(\frac{(1.06)^{14} - 1}{0.06(1.06)^{14}}\right)$$

Make the calculations inside the parentheses first.

$\boxed{AC}\boxed{(}\boxed{(}1.06\boxed{x^y}14 - 1\boxed{)}\div\boxed{(}.06\boxed{\times}1.06\boxed{x^y}14\boxed{)}\boxed{=}\boxed{\times}3000\boxed{=}\Rightarrow$

27884.95178

Self-Check 11.2

1. What semiannual sinking fund payment would be required to yield $48,000 nine years from now? The annual interest rate is 6% compounded semiannually.

2. The Bamboo Furniture Company manufactures rattan patio furniture. It has just purchased a machine for $13,500 to cut and glue the pieces of wood. The machine is expected to last five years. If the company wants to establish a sinking fund to replace this machine, what annual payments must be made if the annual interest rate is 8%?

3. Ben and Susan Duke have a one-year-old daughter and are establishing a college fund. They want to save enough now to have her entire college expenses paid for at the time she enters college (17 years from now). If her college expenses are projected to be $35,000 for a two-year degree, what annual sinking fund payment should they make if the annual interest is 8%?

4. Michelle and Joe Hanover have a 12-year-old daughter and are now in a financial position to begin saving for her college education. What annual sinking fund payment will they need to make to have her entire college expenses available at the time she enters college six years from now? Her college expenses are projected to be $30,000 and the annual interest rate is 6%.

5. Bertha Looney recognizes the value of saving part of her income. She has set a goal to have $25,000 in cash available for emergencies. How much should she invest semiannually to have $25,000 in ten years if the sinking fund she has selected pays 8% annually compounded semiannually?

6. Stein and Company has established a sinking fund to retire a bond issue of $500,000, which is due in ten years. How much is the quarterly sinking fund payment if the account pays 8% annual interest compounded quarterly?

7. What is the present value of an annual ordinary annuity of $680 at 9% annual interest for 25 years?

8. Cindy Meziere plans to set aside $2,500 at the end of each year for two years at 8% annual interest to pay for her college tuition and expenses at a local community college. What lump sum should she invest today to achieve the same value at the end of two years?

9. Laura Kleinaitis is setting up an annuity for a memorial scholarship. She can set aside $3,000 at the end of each year for the next ten years and it will earn 7% annual interest. What lump sum would she need to set aside today at 7% annual interest to have the same scholarship fund available ten years from now?

10. William Farris, a nationally recognized philanthropist, set up an annuity by depositing $1,600 at the end of each year for ten years at 9% annual interest. The Farris Fund would be used to reward faculty for teaching, service, and research at a major two-year community/technical college. How much would Farris have to deposit today at an annual interest rate of 9% to have the same amount as the annuity yields after the ten years?

11. George and Kathy Miller have agreed to pay for their granddaughter's college education. Melanie will be ready to attend college seven years from now. George and Kathy are trying to decide whether to deposit $2,300 at the end of each year for the seven years into an annuity at 7% annual interest, or make a lump sum deposit now at 7% annual interest. What lump sum should be deposited now to have the same amount as the annuity after seven years?

12. Janice and Terry Van Dyke are investigating retirement. Since they have ten more years until retirement, they have decided to establish a quarterly ordinary annuity of $3,000 for the next ten years at 8% annual interest compounded quarterly. How much should they invest in a lump sum now at 8% annual interest compounded quarterly if they want to have the same amount as the annuity yields after ten years?

AROUND THE BUSINESS WORLD

From Russia with Blessings

Does blessed water really taste better? Yes, according to the Russian Orthodox Church. In its first private business deal since the Bolshevik Revolution, the church is marketing Saint Springs, a new bottled mineral water that costs about $1 for a 1.5-liter bottle. The water project is a joint venture among U.S. businessman John King, Russian bottler Rodniki, and the diocese of Kostroma, where the spring is located.

The water is clear, sweet-tasting, and metal free—which alone would make it noteworthy in Russia. But the big selling point is a blessing its spring and bottling plant have received from Russian Patriarch Alexei II.

(The water, however, is not used in liturgy.) Besides spiritual benefits, the church enjoys certain business advantages: It can get government approvals faster and isn't hounded by Russia's pervasive organized crime. While the church will not participate in the marketing of the product, it will get a cut of the profits to use for charitable works.

Saint Springs is a big seller among foreigners and hip, newly rich Russians. And King hopes eventually to sell the water to Russian communities in America. Says King, who retired from the plastics industry: "We aim to be the Evian of Russia."

Reprinted from August 22, 1994 issue of *Business Week* by special permission, copyright © 1994 by the McGraw-Hill Companies.

SELF-CHECK SOLUTIONS

Self-Check 11.1

1. End of year 1 = $3,000
   End of year 2 = $3,000(1.09) + $3,000
                 = $3,270 + $3,000
                 = $6,270
   The future value is $6,270.

2. End of year 1 = $4,000
   End of year 2 = $4,000(1.07) + $4,000
                 = $4,280 + $4,000
                 = $8,280
   Heather will have $8,280 for college.

3. End of year 1 = $5,000

End of year 2 = $5,000(1.08) + $5,000

= $5,400 + $5,000

= $10,400

End of year 3 = $10,400(1.08) + $5,000

= $11,232 + $5,000

= $16,232

Harry will have $16,232 at the end of three years.

4. End of year 1 = $3,000

End of year 2 = $3,000(1.085) + $3,000

= $3,255 + $3,000

= $6,255

End of year 3 = $6,255(1.085) + $3,000

= $6,786.68 + $3,000

= $9,786.68

Scott will have $9,786.68 after three years.

5. 7 years × 2 periods per year = 14 periods

$$\frac{10\% \text{ annual interest rate}}{2 \text{ periods per year}} = 5\% \text{ period interest rate}$$

The Table 11–1 value for 14 periods at 5% is 19.599.

Future value = annuity payment × table value

= $6,500 × 19.599

= $127,393.50

6. 5 years × 4 periods per year = 20 periods

$$\frac{8\% \text{ annual interest rate}}{4 \text{ periods per year}} = 2\% \text{ period interest rate}$$

The Table 11–1 value for 20 periods at 2% is 24.297.

Future value = $2,500 × 24.297

= $60,742.50

Pat will have $60,742.50 after five years.

7. The Table 11–1 value for 15 periods at 7% is 25.129.

Future value = $1,000 × 25.129

= $25,129

The future value is $25,129. Latanya will have invested 15 × $1,000, or $15,000, of her own money and will have received $10,129 in interest.

8. Table 11–1 value for 10 periods at 8% is 14.487.

$500 × 14.487 = $7,243.50

The annuity is worth $7,243.50 after ten years.

Your investment = $500 × 10 = $5,000

Your interest = $7,243.50 − $5,000 = $2,243.50

9. The Table value for five periods at 8% is 5.867.

$2,000 × 5.867 = $11,734

The future value of the annuity is $11,734.

Your investment = $2,000 × 5 = $10,000

Your interest = $11,734 − $10,000 = $1,734

10.

Years	Total Investment	Total Interest
Ten-year	$ 5,000	$2,243.50
Five-year	$10,000	$ 1,734

The ten-year investment earned more interest even though half as much money was invested. At the same period interest rate, investing for twice as long gives a better yield on your investment than investing twice as much for half as long.

11. End of year 1 = $12,000(1.14)

= $13,680

End of year 2 = ($13,680 + $12,000)(1.14)

= $25,680(1.14)

= $29,275.20

End of year 3 = ($29,275.20 + $12,000)(1.14)

= $41,275.20(1.14)

= $47,053.73

The future value is $47,053.73.

12. End of year 1 = $2,500(1.072)

= $2,680

End of year 2 = ($2,650 + $2,500)(1.072)

= $5,150(1.072)

= $5,552.96

The annuity is worth $5,552.96 after two years.

13. End of year 1 = $7,800(1.081)

= $8,431.80

End of year 2 = ($8,431.80 + $7,800)(1.081)

= $16,231.80(1.081)

= $17,546.58

The future value is $17,546.58.

14. End of year 1 = $400(1.068)

= $427

End of year 2 = ($427 + $400)(1.068)

= $827(1.068)

= $883.45

The future value is $883.45.

15. 3 years × 4 periods per year = 12 periods

$$\frac{8\% \text{ annual interest rate}}{4 \text{ periods per year}} = 2\% \text{ period interest rate}$$

The Table 11–1 value for 12 periods at 2% is 13.412.

Future value = $4,400 × 13.412 × 1.02

= $60,193.06

16. 4 years × 2 periods per year = 8 periods

$$\frac{8\% \text{ annual interest rate}}{2 \text{ periods per year}} = 4\% \text{ period interest rate}$$

The Table 11–1 value for eight periods at 4% is 9.214.

Future value = $750(9.214)(1.04)

= $7,186.92

17. *Quarterly annuity due*

1 year × 4 periods = 4 periods

$$\frac{8\% \text{ annual interest rate}}{4 \text{ periods per year}} = 2\% \text{ period interest rate}$$

The Table 11–1 value for 4 periods at 2% is 4.122.

Future value = $300 × 4.122 × 1.02 = $1,261.33

Semiannual annuity due

1 year × 2 periods per year = 2 periods

$$\frac{8\% \text{ annual interest rate}}{2 \text{ periods per year}} = 4\% \text{ period interest rate}$$

The Table 11–1 value for 2 periods at 4% is 2.040.

Future value = $600 × 2.040 × 1.04 = $1,272.96

The semiannual annuity yields more interest.

18. Your contribution = $250 × 20 = $5,000

The Table 11–1 value for 20 periods at 7% is 40.995.

Future value = $250 × 40.995 × 1.07 = $10,966.16.

Earned interest = $10,966.16 − $5,000 = $5,966.16

Self-Check 11.2

1. 9 years × 2 periods per year = 18 periods

$$\frac{6\% \text{ annual interest rate}}{2 \text{ periods per year}} = 3\% \text{ period interest rate}$$

The Table 11–2 value for 18 periods at 3% is 0.0427087.

Sinking fund payment = $48,000 × 0.0427087
= $2,050.02

2. 5 years × 1 period per year = 5 periods

$$\frac{8\% \text{ annual interest rate}}{1 \text{ period per year}} = 8\% \text{ period interest rate}$$

The Table 11–2 value for 5 periods at 8% is 0.1704565.

Sinking fund payment = $13,500 × 0.1704565
= $2,301.16

3. 17 years × 1 period per year = 17 periods

$$\frac{8\% \text{ annual interest rate}}{1 \text{ period per year}} = 8\% \text{ period interest rate}$$

The Table 11–2 value for 17 periods at 8% is 0.0296294.

Sinking fund payment = $35,000 × 0.0296294
= $1,037.03

4. 6 years × 1 period per year = 6 periods

$$\frac{6\% \text{ annual interest rate}}{1 \text{ period per year}} = 6\% \text{ period interest rate}$$

The Table 11–2 value for 6 periods at 6% is 0.1433626.

Sinking fund payment = $30,000 × 0.1433626
= $4,300.88

5. 10 years × 2 periods per year = 20 periods

$$\frac{8\% \text{ annual interest rate}}{2 \text{ periods per year}} = 4\% \text{ period interest rate}$$

The Table 11–2 value for 20 periods at 4% is 0.0335818.

Sinking fund payment = $25,000 × 0.0335818
= $839.55

6. 10 years × 4 periods per year = 40 periods

$$\frac{8\% \text{ annual interest rate}}{4 \text{ periods per year}} = 2\% \text{ period interest rate}$$

The Table 11–2 value for 40 periods at 2% is 0.0165558.

Sinking fund payment = $500,000 × 0.0165558
= $8,277.90

7. 25 years × 1 period per year = 25 periods

$$\frac{9\% \text{ annual interest rate}}{1 \text{ period per year}} = 9\% \text{ period interest rate}$$

The Table 11–3 value for 25 periods at 9% is 9.823.

Present value = $680 × 9.823
= $6,679.64

8. The Table 11–3 value for 2 periods at 8% is 1.783.

Present value = $2,500 × 1.783
= $4,457.50

9. The Table 11–3 value for 10 periods at 7% is 7.024.

Present value = $3,000 × 7.024
= $21,072

10. The Table 11–3 value for 10 periods at 9% is 6.418.

Present value = $1,600 × 6.418
= $10,268.80

11. The Table 11–3 value for 7 periods at 7% is 5.389.

Present value = $2,300 × 5.389
= $12,394.70

12. 10 years × 4 periods per year = 40 periods

$$\frac{8\% \text{ annual interest rate}}{4 \text{ periods per year}} = 2\% \text{ period interest rate}$$

The Table 11–3 value for 40 periods at 2% is 27.355.

Present value = $3,000 × 27.355
= $82,065.00

Section—Objective	Important Points with Examples

 (page 366)

Find the future value of an ordinary annuity using the simple interest formula method

Step 1 Find the first end-of-period principle.

First end-of-period principal = annuity payment

Step 2 For each remaining period in turn, find the next end-of-period principal: **(a)** Multiply the previous end-of-period principal by the sum of 1 and the period interest rate. **(b)** Add the product from step 2a and the annuity payment.

End-of-period principal = previous end-of-period principal
$$\times \,(1 + \text{period interest rate}) + \text{annuity payment}$$

Step 3 Identify the last end-of-period principal as the future value.

Future value = last end-of-period principal

Find the future value of an annual ordinary annuity of $2,000 for two years at 9% annual interest.

$$\text{End of year 1} = \$2,000$$
$$\text{End of year 2} = \$2,000(1.09) + \$2,000$$
$$= \$2,180 + \$2,000$$
$$= \$4,180$$

The future value is $4,180.

Find the future value of a semiannual ordinary annuity of $300 for one year at 9% annual interest compounded semiannually.

$$\frac{9\% \text{ annual interest rate}}{2 \text{ periods per year}} = 4.5\% = 0.045 \text{ period interest rate}$$

$$\text{End of period 1} = \$300$$
$$\text{End of period 2} = \$300(1.045) + \$300$$
$$= \$313.50 + \$300$$
$$= \$613.50$$

The future value is $613.50.

11.1 — 2 (page 367)

Find the future value of an ordinary annuity using a $1.00 ordinary annuity future value table

Step 1 Select the periods row corresponding to the number of interest periods. **Step 2** Select the rate-per-period column corresponding to the period interest rate. **Step 3** Locate the value in the cell where the periods row intersects the rate-per-period column. **Step 4** Multiply the annuity payment by the table value from step 3.

Future value = annuity payment × table value

Find the future value of an ordinary annuity of $5,000 semiannually for four years at 12% annual interest compounded semiannually.

$$4 \text{ years} \times 2 \text{ periods per year} = 8 \text{ periods}$$

$$\frac{12\% \text{ annual interest rate}}{2 \text{ periods per year}} = 6\% \text{ period interest rate}$$

The Table 11–1 value for eight periods and 6% is 9.897.

$$\text{Future value} = \$5,000 \times 9.987$$

$$= \$49,485$$

The future value is $49,485.

 (page 369)

Find the future value of an annuity due using the simple interest formula method

Step 1 Find the first end-of-period principle: Multiply the annuity payment by the sum of 1 and the period interest rate.

First end-of-period principal = annuity payment × (1 + period interest rate)

Step 2 For each remaining period in turn, find the next end-of-period principal: **(a)** Add the previous end-of-period principal and the annuity payment. **(b)** Multiply the sum from step 2a by the sum of 1 and the period interest rate.

End-of-period principal = (previous end-of-period principal
+ annuity payment) × (1 + period interest rate)

Step 3 Identify the last end-of-period principal as the future value.

Future value = last end-of-period principal

Find the future value of an annual annuity due of $3,000 for two years at 10% annual interest.

$$\text{End of year 1} = \$3,000(1.1)$$

$$= \$3,300$$

$$\text{End of year 2} = (\$3,300 + \$3,000)(1.1)$$

$$= \$6,300(1.1)$$

$$= \$6,930$$

Find the future value of a semiannual annuity due of $400 for one year at 8% annual interest compounded semiannually.

$$\frac{8\% \text{ annual interest rate}}{2 \text{ periods per year}} = 4\% = 0.04 \text{ period interest rate}$$

$$\text{End of period 1} = \$400(1.04)$$

$$= \$416$$

$$\text{End of period 2} = (\$416 + \$400)(1.04)$$

$$= (\$816)(1.04)$$

$$= \$848.64$$

The future value is $848.64.

 (page 370)

Find the future value of an annuity due using a $1.00 ordinary annuity future value table

Step 1 Select the periods row corresponding to the number of interest periods.
Step 2 Select the rate-per-period column corresponding to the period interest rate.
Step 3 Locate the value in the cell where the periods row intersects the rate-per-period column. **Step 4** Multiply the table value from step 3 by the sum of 1 and the period interest rate. **Step 5** Multiply the annuity payment by the product from step 4.

$$\text{Future value} = \text{annuity payment} \times \text{table value} \times (1 + \text{period interest rate})$$

> Find the future value of a quarterly annuity due of $1,500 for three years at 12% annual interest compounded quarterly.
>
> $$3 \text{ years} \times 4 \text{ periods per year} = 12 \text{ periods}$$
>
> $$\frac{12\% \text{ annual interest rate}}{4 \text{ periods per year}} = 3\% \text{ period interest rate}$$
>
> The Table 11–1 value for 12 periods and 3% is 14.192.
>
> $$\text{Future value} = \$1,500 \times 14.192 \times 1.03$$
>
> $$= \$21,926.64$$
>
> The future value is $21,926.64.

 (page 375)

Find the sinking fund payment using a $1.00 sinking fund payment table

Step 1 Select the periods row corresponding to the number of interest periods.
Step 2 Select the rate-per-period column corresponding to the period interest rate.
Step 3 Locate the value in the cell where the periods row intersects the rate-per-period column. **Step 4** Multiply the table value from step 3 by the desired future value.

$$\text{Sinking fund payment} = \text{desired future value} \times \text{table value}$$

> Find the quarterly sinking fund payment required to yield $15,000 in five years if interest is 12% compounded quarterly.
>
> $$5 \text{ years} \times 4 \text{ periods per year} = 20 \text{ periods}$$
>
> $$\frac{12\% \text{ annual interest rate}}{4 \text{ periods per year}} = 3\% \text{ period interest rate}$$
>
> The Table 11–2 value for 20 periods and 3% is 0.0372157.
>
> $$\text{Sinking fund payment} = 15,000 \times 0.0372157$$
>
> $$= \$558.24$$
>
> The required quarterly payment is $558.24.

 (page 377)

Find the present value of an ordinary annuity using a $1.00 ordinary annuity present value table

Step 1 Select the periods row corresponding to the number of interest periods.
Step 2 Select the rate-per-period column corresponding to the period interest rate.
Step 3 Locate the value in the cell where the periods row intersects the rate-per-period column. **Step 4** Multiply the table value from step 3 by the annuity payment.

$$\text{Present value} = \text{annuity payment} \times \text{table value}$$

Find the lump sum required for deposit today earning 8% annual interest compounded semiannually to yield the future value of a semiannual ordinary annuity of $2,500 at 8% annual interest compounded semiannually for 15 years.

$$15 \text{ years} \times 2 \text{ periods per year} = 30 \text{ periods}$$

$$\frac{8\% \text{ annual interest rate}}{2 \text{ periods per year}} = 4\% \text{ period interest rate}$$

The Table 11–3 value for 30 periods and 4% is 17.292.

$$\text{Present value} = \$2,500 \times 17.292$$

$$= \$43,230$$

The lump sum required for deposit today is $43,230.

CHAPTER 11 REVIEW

Section 11.1

Use Table 11–1 to complete the table below.

	Annuity Payment	Rate	Annual Interest	Years	Type of Annuity	Future Value of Annuity
1.	$1,400	12%	Compounded quarterly	5	Quarterly ordinary	_____
2.	$2,900	9%	Compounded annually	12	Annual ordinary	_____
3.	$ 125	24%	Compounded monthly	$1\frac{1}{2}$	Monthly annuity due	_____
4.	$ 800	7%	Compounded annually	15	Annual annuity due	_____

Use the simple interest formula method for Exercises 5 and 6.

5. Roni Sue deposited $1,500 at the beginning of each year for three years at an annual interest rate of 9%. Find the future value.

6. Find the future value if Roni Sue in Exercise 5 had deposited the money at the end of each year rather than at the beginning.

Use Table 11–1 for Exercises 7–12.

7. Barry Michael plans to deposit $2,000 at the end of every six months for the next five years to save up for a boat. If the interest rate is 12% annually compounded semiannually, how much money will Barry have in his boat fund after five years?

8. Sam and Jane Crawford had a baby in 1978. At the end of that year they began putting away $900 per year at 10% annual interest for a college fund. When their child is 18 years old in 1996, college costs for four years of college are estimated to be about $20,000 per year.
   a. How much money will be in the account when the child is 18 years old?
   b. Will the Crawfords have enough saved to send their child to college for 4 years?

9. Bob Paris is 46 years old when he opens a retirement income account paying 9% annually. He deposits $3,000 at the beginning of each year.
   a. How much will be in the account after ten years?
   b. When Bob retires at age 65, in 19 years, how much will be in the account?

10. A business deposits $4,500 at the end of each quarter in an account that earns 8% annual interest compounded quarterly. What is the value of the annuity in five years?

11. The Shari Joy Corporation decided to set aside $3,200 at the beginning of every six months to provide donation funds for a new Little League baseball field scheduled to be built in 18 months. If money earns 12% annual interest compounded semiannually, how much will be available as a donation for the field?

12. University Trailers is setting aside $800 at the beginning of every quarter to purchase a forklift in 30 months. The annual interest will be 8% compounded quarterly. How much will be available for the purchase?

Section 11.2

Use Table 11–2 to complete the table below.

	Desired Future Value	Annual Interest Rate	Years	Annual Sinking Fund Payment
13.	$ 240,000	6%	15	_____
14.	$3,000,000	8%	10	_____
15.	$ 50,000	12%	5	_____
16.	$ 45,000	4%	8	_____

Use Table 11–2 for the Exercises that follow.

17. How much must be set aside at the end of each six months by the Fabulous Toy Company to replace a $155,000 piece of equipment at the end of eight years if the account pays 8% annual interest compounded semiannually?

18. Tasty Food Manufacturers, Inc., has a bond issue of $1,400,000 due in 30 years. If they want to establish a sinking fund to meet this obligation, how much must be set aside at the end of each year if the annual interest rate is 6%?

19. Lausanne Private School System needs to set aside funds for a new mainframe computer. What monthly sinking fund payment would be required to amount to $45,000, the approximate cost of the computer, in $1\frac{1}{2}$ years at 12% annual interest compounded monthly?

20. Zachary Alexander owns a limousine that will need to be replaced in four years at a cost of $65,000. How much must he put aside each year in a sinking fund at 8% annual interest to be able to afford the new limousine?

21. Goldie's Department Store has a fleet of delivery trucks that will last for three years of heavy use and then need to be replaced at a cost of $75,000. How much must they set aside every three months in a sinking fund at 8% annual interest compounded quarterly to have enough money to replace the trucks?

22. Danny Lawrence Properties, Inc., has a bond issue that will mature in 25 years for $1,000,000. How much must the company set aside each year in a sinking fund at 12% annual interest to meet this future obligation?

23. Linda Zuk wants to save $25,000 for a new boat in six years. How much must be put aside in equal payments each year in an account earning 8% annual interest for Linda to be able to purchase the boat?

24. How much money would need to be set aside today at 10% annual interest compounded semiannually to have the same amount as a semiannual ordinary annuity of $500 for five years at 10% annual interest compounded semiannually?

25. What is the present value of an annual ordinary annuity of $3,400 at 5% annual interest for seven years?

26. You are starting an annual ordinary annuity of $680 for 25 years at 9% annual interest. What lump sum amount would have to be set aside today earning 9% annual interest to have the same amount accumulated as the annuity?

27. An annual ordinary annuity of $2,500 for five years at 8% annual interest is equivalent to what lump sum earning 8% annual interest for the same period of time?

28. Your parents are trying to get you to form the habit of investing part of your paycheck and have agreed to set aside a lump sum of money today earning 12% annual interest compounded quarterly that will have the same value after five years as an annuity you begin now and continue for five years. Your ordinary annuity requires you to pay $500 quarterly at an annual interest rate of 12% compounded quarterly. What lump sum will your parents set aside today?

29. Craig Campanella is committed to creating a scholarship fund to be available when he retires from the faculty in eight years. How much does he need to set aside today earning 10% annual interest compounded semiannually to have an amount equivalent to the future value of a semiannual ordinary annuity of $700 at 10% annual interest compounded semiannually?

30. Byron Spellacy has set the goal of accumulating $80,000 for his son's college fund which will be needed 18 years in the future. How much should he deposit each year in a sinking fund that earns 8% annual interest? How much should he deposit each year if he waits until his son starts school (at age six) to begin saving? Compare the two payment amounts.

CHAPTER 11 PRACTICE TEST

1. Use the simple interest formula method to find the future value of an ordinary annuity of $9,000 per year for two years at 15% annual interest.

2. Use the simple interest formula method to find the future value of an annuity due of $2,700 per year for three years at 11% annual interest.

3. What is the future value of an annuity due of $5,645 every six months for three years at 12% annual interest compounded semiannually?

4. What is the future value of an ordinary annuity of $300 every three months for four years at 8% annual interest compounded quarterly?

5. What is the sinking fund payment required at the end of each year to accumulate to $125,000 in 16 years at 4% annual interest?

6. What is the present value of an ordinary annuity of $985 every six months for eight years at 8% annual interest compounded semiannually?

7. Mike's Sport Shop deposited $3,400 at the end of each year for 12 years at 7% annual interest. How much will Mike have in the account at the end of the time period?

8. How much would the annuity amount to in Exercise 7 if Mike had deposited the money at the beginning of each year instead of at the end of each year?

9. How much must be set aside at the end of each year by the Caroline Cab Company to replace four taxicabs at a cost of $90,000? The current interest rate is 6% annually. The existing cabs will wear out in three years.

10. How much must Buddy Wilbur invest today to have an amount equivalent to investing $2,800 at the end of every six months for the next 15 years if interest is earned at 8% annually compounded semiannually?

11. Edward Spencer owns a lawn maintenance business. His riding lawnmower cost $850 and should last for six years. Edward wants to establish a sinking fund to buy a new mower. How much must he set aside at the end of each year at 12% annual interest to have enough money to buy the new equipment?

12. Larry and Penny want to know how much they must deposit in a retirement savings account today that would be equivalent to depositing $1,500 at the end of every six months for 15 years. The retirement account is paying 10% annual interest compounded semiannually.

13. Lawrence Kenneth wants to save $2,200 at the end of each year for 11 years in an account paying 7% annual interest. What is the future value of the annuity at the end of this period of time?

14. Amanda Ashley is saving for her college expenses. She sets aside $175 at the beginning of each three months in an account paying 12% annual interest compounded quarterly. How much will Amanda have accumulated in the account at the end of four years?

15. What is the present value of a semiannual ordinary annuity of $2,500 for seven years at 6% annual interest compounded semiannually?

16. How much will you need to invest today to have the same amount after 5 years as a quarterly ordinary annuity of $800 if both interest rates are 8% annually compounded quarterly?

CONSUMER CREDIT

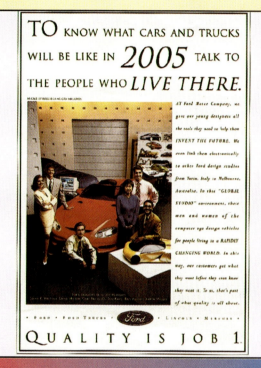

TO KNOW WHAT CARS AND TRUCKS WILL BE LIKE IN *2005* TALK TO THE PEOPLE WHO *LIVE THERE.*

QUALITY IS JOB 1.

GOOD DECISIONS THROUGH TEAMWORK

Many credit unions and some other types of lending institutions offer car loans in which interest is applied on a monthly basis to the unpaid balance. With your team members, select a low- to moderately-priced new car to purchase, and investigate current new car loan rates for a three-year loan and for a four-year loan at a local credit union. For each loan period, prepare a spreadsheet showing the beginning monthly balance, the portion of the payment applied to interest, the portion of the payment applied to the principal, and the ending monthly balance for each month of the loan period. Decide which option you would choose and state your reasons for choosing that option.

If you have access to an electronic spreadsheet, include in your report the total interest paid for the various options. Also, investigate the effects of increasing the monthly payments by $10 over the required payment.

CHAPTER 12 CONSUMER CREDIT

Many individuals and businesses make purchases for which they do not pay the full amount at the time of purchase. These purchases are paid for by paying a portion of the amount owed in regular payments. This type of loan or credit, by which many of us are able to purchase equipment, supplies, and other items we need in our businesses or personal lives, is called **consumer credit.**

In the preceding chapters, we discussed the interest to be paid on loans that are paid in full on the date of maturity of the loan. But loans are often handled in other ways as well. Many times loans are made so that the maker (the borrower) pays a given amount in regular payments. This means that the borrower does not have use of the full amount of money borrowed for the full length of time it was borrowed. Instead, a certain portion of it has to be paid back with each regular payment. Loans with regular payments are called **installment loans.**

There are two kinds of installment loans. Basic installment loans are loans in which the amount borrowed plus interest is repaid in a specified number of equal payments. Examples include bank loans and loans for large purchases such as cars and appliances. **Open-end loans** are loans in which there is no fixed number of payments—the person keeps making payments until the amount is paid off, and the interest is computed on the unpaid balance at the end of each payment period. Credit card companies and retail stores most often use the open-end type of loan.

In this chapter, we will consider both types of loans, as well as the annual percentage rate at which most such loans are made.

12.1 Installment Loans

▶1 *Find the installment price given the installment payment*

▶2 *Find the installment payment given the installment price*

Should you or your business take out an installment loan? Much depends on the interest you will pay and how it is computed. The interest associated with an installment loan is part of the charges referred to as **finance charges** or **carrying charges.** In addition to accrued interest charges, installment loans often include charges for insurance, credit-report fees, or loan fees. Under the truth-in-lending law, all of these charges must be revealed.

The Installment Price

The **cash price** is the price you pay if you pay all at once at the time of sale. If you pay on an installment basis instead, the **down payment** is a partial payment of the cash price at the time of sale. The **amount financed** is the total amount you pay in regular payments to pay off the loan. The **installment payment** is the amount you pay for each period, including interest, to pay off the loan. The **installment price** is the total paid, including all of the installment payments and the down payment.

 HOW TO | **Find the Installment Price**

Step 1 Find the total of the installment payments: Multiply the number of installment payments by the installment payment.

Total of installment payments = number of installment payments
$\times$ installment payment

Step 2 Add the down payment to the total of the installment payments

Installment price = total of installment payments + down payment

Example 1 A printer was purchased on the installment plan with a $60 down payment and 12 payments of $45.58. Find the installment price of the printer.

$$\text{Installment price} = \left(\begin{array}{c}\text{number of}\\\text{installments}\end{array}\right) \times \left(\begin{array}{c}\text{installment}\\\text{payment}\end{array}\right) + \text{down payment}$$

$$= \quad 12 \quad \times \quad \$45.58 \quad + \quad \$60$$

$$= \$546.96 + \$60$$

$$= \$606.96$$

The installment price is $606.96.

The Installment Payment

Since the installment price is the total of the installment payments plus the down payment, we can find the installment payment if we know the installment price, the down payment, and the number of payments.

HOW TO | **Find the Installment Payment**

Step 1 Find the total of the installment payments: Subtract the down payment from the installment price.

Total of installment payments = installment price − down payment

Step 2 Divide the total of installment payments by the number of installment payments.

$$\text{Installment payment} = \frac{\text{total of installment payments}}{\text{number of payments}}$$

Example 2 The installment price of a drafting table with built-in lighting was $627 for a 12-month loan. If a $75 down payment had been made, find the installment payment.

Total of installment payments = installment price − down payment

= $627 − $75 = $552

$$\text{Installment payment} = \frac{\text{total of installment payments}}{\text{number of payments}} = \frac{\$552}{12} = \$46$$

The installment payment is $46.

Sometimes the finance charge is given as a percent of the cash price. In such a case, you use the simple interest formula ($I = PRT$), with the cash price being the principal, the percent of interest charged being the rate per year, and the time being expressed in number of years or fraction of a year.

Example 3 Pyramid Realty can recarpet its office for $4,000 in cash. If they choose to pay for it in 24 monthly installment payments, a 12% annual finance charge will be assessed for the total amount for the entire 24 months. Find the amount of the finance charge, the installment price, and the monthly payment if no down payment is made.

$I = PRT$ **Compute the finance charge as simple interest.**

$I = \$4,000 \times 0.12 \times 2$

$I = \$960$ **The finance charge is $960.**

Total of monthly payments

= amount financed + finance charge

= $4,000 + $960

= $4,960 **The total of monthly payments is $4,960.**

$$\text{Monthly payment} = \frac{\text{total of monthly payments}}{\text{number of monthly payments}}$$

$$= \frac{\$4,960}{24} = \$206.67 \quad \text{(rounded to the nearest cent)}$$

The finance charge is $960, the installment price is $4,960, and the monthly payment is $206.67.

Self-Check 12.1

1. Find the installment price of a recliner bought on the installment plan with a down payment of $100 and six payments of $108.20.

2. Find the amount financed if a $125 down payment is made on a TV with a cash price of $579.

3. Supora Cook purchased a TV with surround sound and remote control on an installment plan with $100 down and 12 payments of $106.32. Find the installment price of the TV.

4. A queen-size bedroom suite can be purchased on an installment plan with 18 payments of $97.42 if an $80 down payment is made. What is the installment price of the suite?

5. Zack's Trailer Sales will finance a 16-foot utility trailer with ramps and electric brakes. If a down payment of $100 and eight monthly payments of $82.56 are required, what is the installment price of the trailer?

6. The cash price of a bedroom suite is $2,590. There is a 24% finance charge on the cash price, and 12 monthly payments. Find the monthly payment.

7. Find the monthly payment on a VCR with an installment price of $929, 12 monthly payments, and a down payment of $100.

8. The installment price of a teakwood extension table and four chairs is $625 with 18 monthly payments and a down payment of $75. What is the monthly payment?

9. An entertainment center is financed at a total cost of $2,357 including a down payment of $250. If the center is financed over 24 months, find the monthly payment.

10. A Hepplewhite sofa costs $3,780 in cash. Jaquanna Wilson will purchase the sofa in 36 monthly installment payments. A 13% finance charge will be assessed on the amount financed. Find the finance charge, installment price, and the monthly payment.

AROUND THE BUSINESS WORLD

Fund Facts

Mutual funds are basically investment pools. A fund company takes in money from many investors and buys securities such as stocks and bonds. Stock represents a share of ownership in a corporation; a bond is a loan to a corporation, government, or government agency. Fund investors share in any profits or losses on their collective portfolio, and the fund company takes a percentage of the fund's total assets to pay its operating expenses.

The arguments in favor of mutual funds over many other types of investments are powerful. For one thing, funds provide a level of diversification that few investors could achieve on their own. By investing in a stock mutual fund, you can own stock in hundreds of companies. That reduces the risk to your money, because if one or several stocks held by a fund stumble, it's unlikely to have a devastating effect on the overall portfolio. Most mutual funds also diversify across industries, insulating investors against a slump in any one field.

Professional managers make the day-to-day decisions about which securities to buy and sell, usually—but not always—in keeping with the fund's

stated objective. And fund investors can buy and sell shares in a fund quickly, often with just a phone call. Fund investors also avoid the high commissions that stockbrokers charge small investors who buy individual stocks.

But when you invest in mutual funds, you're taking a risk. Unlike bank deposits, which are insured up to certain limits, mutual funds put both your principal and any potential earnings at risk. Mutual funds rise and fall in value, their returns dependent partly on how well the markets as a whole are doing and partly on the shrewdness of the fund manager's investment decisions.

For that reason, picking funds that will consistently sit at the top of their categories is a difficult task. Unlike many of the products covered in the pages of *Consumer Reports* each month, mutual funds can be rated only on their historical performance. At best, that performance is a guide to how well a fund's managers have made decisions in the past. There's no guarantee that the same fund manager (or the manager's successors) will do as well in the future.

"Mutual Funds" Copyright 1995 by Consumers Union of U.S., Inc., Yonkers, NY 10703-1057. Reprinted by permission of CONSUMER REPORTS, May 1995.

Find the interest refund using the rule of 78

If an installment loan is paid entirely before the last payment is actually due, is part of the interest refundable? In most cases it is, but not at the rate you might hope. If you paid a 12-month loan in six months, you might expect a refund of half the total interest. However, this is not usually the case, because the portion of the monthly payment that is interest is not the same from month to month. In general, interest or finance charge refunds are made according to the **rule of 78.**

▶ *The Rule of 78*

Where does 78 come from in the rule of 78? Imagine that a loan is made for 12 months. We consider the principal to be divided into twelve equal parts and estimate that one part is paid each month. If interest accrues on the parts of the principal that are left to be paid, then interest accrues on all 12 parts for the first month; interest accrues only on 11 parts for the second month, on ten parts for the third month, and so on.

Month **1**   Interest accrues on **12** parts of principal
Month **2**   Interest accrues on **11** parts of principal
Month **3**   Interest accrues on **10** parts of principal
Month **4**   Interest accrues on **9** parts of principal
Month **5**   Interest accrues on **8** parts of principal
Month **6**   Interest accrues on **7** parts of principal
Month **7**   Interest accrues on **6** parts of principal
Month **8**   Interest accrues on **5** parts of principal
Month **9**   Interest accrues on **4** parts of principal
Month **10**   Interest accrues on **3** parts of principal
Month **11**   Interest accrues on **2** parts of principal
Month **12**   Interest accrues on **1** part of principal

The sum of all the parts accruing interest for a 12-month loan is $12 + 11 + 10 + 9 + 8 + 7 + 6 + 5 + 4 + 3 + 2 + 1$, or 78.

Thus, 78 equal parts accrue interest. The interest each part accrues is the same because the rate is the same and the parts are the same (each is $\frac{1}{12}$ of the principal). Since 78 equal parts each accrue equal interest, the interest each part accrues must be $\frac{1}{78}$ of the total interest for the one-year loan. So if all 12 monthly payments are paid early, say with three months remaining, then the interest that would have accrued in the tenth, eleventh, and twelfth months may be refunded. In the tenth month, three parts each accrue $\frac{1}{78}$ of the total interest, in the eleventh month, two parts each accrue $\frac{1}{78}$ of the total interest, and in the twelfth month, one part accrues $\frac{1}{78}$ of the total interest. So $3 + 2 + 1$ parts, or 6 parts each accrue $\frac{1}{78}$ of the total interest. Thus $\frac{6}{78}$ of the total interest must be refunded. The fraction $\frac{6}{78}$ is called the **refund fraction.**

All installment loans are not for 12 months, but the rule of 78 gives us a pattern that we can apply to loans of any length. We find the *numerator* of the refund fraction by adding the sequence numbers for the periods that a refund is due. For example, the numerator of the refund fraction for a six-month loan paid two months early would be $2 + 1$ or 3. We find the *denominator* by adding the sequence numbers for *all* the periods of the loan. The six-addend sum for a six-month loan is $6 + 5 + 4 + 3 + 2 + 1$, or 21. The refund fraction, then, is $\frac{3}{21}$.

Step 1 Find the period sequence numbers: Number the periods of the loan, so that the last period is 1, the next to the last is 2, and so on.

Step 2 Find the denominator of the refund fraction: Add the sequence numbers of all the periods.

Step 3 Find the numerator of the refund fraction: Add the sequence numbers of the periods for which an interest refund is due.

Step 4 Multiply the total interest by the refund fraction.

$$\text{Interest refund} = \text{total interest} \times \text{refund fraction}$$

Example 1 A loan for 12 months with a finance charge $117 is paid in full with four payments remaining. Find the amount of the finance charge (interest) refund.

$$\text{Refund fraction} = \frac{\text{sum of sequence numbers of payments remaining}}{\text{sum of all payment sequence numbers}}$$

$$= \frac{1 + 2 + 3 + 4}{1 + 2 + 3 + 4 + 5 + 6 + 7 + 8 + 9 + 10 + 11 + 12}$$

$$= \frac{10}{78}$$

$$\text{Refund} = \text{total finance charge} \times \text{refund fraction}$$

$$= \$117 \times \frac{10}{78}$$

$$= \$15$$

The finance charge refund is $15.

If there are, say, 24 periods in the loan, finding the refund fraction requires adding the numbers from 1 to 24. The greater the number of periods, the more tedious this adding becomes. But there is a shortcut.

Examine the following illustrations for finding *twice* the sum of consecutive numbers beginning with 1.

Add the numbers from 1 to 4 twice.
$$\begin{array}{r} 1 + 2 + 3 + 4 \\ + 4 + 3 + 2 + 1 \\ \hline 5 + 5 + 5 + 5 = 4 \times 5 = 20 \end{array}$$

Add the numbers from 1 to 5 twice.
$$\begin{array}{r} 1 + 2 + 3 + 4 + 5 \\ + 5 + 4 + 3 + 2 + 1 \\ \hline 6 + 6 + 6 + 6 + 6 = 5 \times 6 = 30 \end{array}$$

Add the numbers from 1 to 6 twice.
$$\begin{array}{r} 1 + 2 + 3 + 4 + 5 + 6 \\ 6 + 5 + 4 + 3 + 2 + 1 \\ \hline 7 + 7 + 7 + 7 + 7 + 7 = 6 \times 7 = 42 \end{array}$$

Do you see a pattern developing? In each case, twice the sum is the product of the largest number and 1 more than the largest number. Twice the sum of 1 to 7, then, we predict is $7 \times (7 + 1)$, or 7×8, or 56. Lets see if our prediction is correct:

$$\begin{array}{r} 1 + 2 + 3 + 4 + 5 + 6 + 7 \\ + 7 + 6 + 5 + 4 + 3 + 2 + 1 \\ \hline 8 + 8 + 8 + 8 + 8 + 8 + 8 = 7 \times 8 = 56 \end{array}$$

It is correct: *Twice* the sum of consecutive numbers beginning with 1 is the product of the largest number and 1 more than the largest number. But we are really interested not in *twice* the sum, but *only* the sum. So we divide twice the sum by 2, leaving only the sum.

Our shortcut for finding the sum of consecutive numbers beginning with 1 is: Multiply the largest number by 1 more than the largest number, and divide the product by 2. You may be interested to know that a young boy in elementary school discovered this shortcut in the late eighteenth century. He later went on to be one of the greatest mathematicians of all time. His name was Carl Friedrich Gauss (1777–1855).

HOW TO   **Find the Sum of Consecutive Numbers Beginning With One**

Multiply the largest number by 1 more than the largest number, and divide the product by 2.

$$\text{Sum of consecutive numbers} = \frac{\text{largest number} \times (\text{largest number} + 1)}{2}$$

Example 2   A loan for 36 months, with a finance charge of \$1276.50, is paid in full with 15 payments remaining. Find the finance charge to be refunded.

$$\text{Refund fraction} = \frac{\text{sum of sequence numbers of payments remaining}}{\text{sum of all payment sequence numbers}}$$

$$\text{Sum of the sequence numbers of 15 payments remaining} = \frac{15 \times (15 + 1)}{2}$$ The sum of consecutive numbers from 1 to 15.

$$= \frac{15 \times 16}{2}$$

$$= 120$$

$$\text{Sum of all 36 payment sequence numbers} = \frac{36 \times (36 + 1)}{2}$$ The sum of consecutive numbers from 1 to 36.

$$= \frac{36 \times 37}{2}$$

$$= 666$$

$$\text{Refund fraction} = \frac{120}{666} = \frac{20}{111}$$

Finance charge refund = finance charge × refund fraction.

$$= \$1{,}276.50 \times \frac{20}{111}$$

$$= \$230$$

The finance charge refund is \$230.

The calculations for the refund fraction in Example 2 can be further simplified by writing all the calculations in a complex fraction.

$$\text{Refund fraction} = \frac{\text{sum of sequence numbers of 15 payments remaining}}{\text{sum of all 36 payment sequence numbers}}$$

$$= \frac{\dfrac{15 \times (15 + 1)}{2}}{\dfrac{36 \times (36 + 1)}{2}}$$

$$= \frac{15 \times (15 + 1)}{2} \div \frac{36 \times (36 + 1)}{2}$$

$$= \frac{15 \times (15 + 1)}{2} \times \frac{2}{36 \times (36 + 1)}$$

$$= \frac{15 \times (15 + 1)}{36 \times (36 + 1)}$$

Compare this common fraction with the complex fraction we started with. The 2s in the denominators of the complex fraction are reduced. This pattern holds true for every refund fraction. For instance, we can apply this pattern to a refund fraction for eight months remaining on a 24-month loan paid in full.

$$\text{Refund fraction} = \frac{\text{sum of sequence numbers of eight payments remaining}}{\text{sum of all 24 payment sequence numbers}}$$

$$\text{Refund fraction} = \frac{8 \times 9}{24 \times 25} = \frac{72}{600} = \frac{3}{25}$$

Even though we use the terminology *refund fraction,* we can use a decimal equivalent of the fraction instead. In finding the decimal equivalent using a scientific or business calculator, we can use a continuous series of calculations. Remember, the fraction bar indicates division. Using the division symbol instead, we must enclose the denominator in parentheses. For instance, use a calculator to find $\dfrac{8 \times 9}{24 \times 25}$.

$$\boxed{AC}\; 8 \;\boxed{\times}\; 9 \;\boxed{\div}\; \boxed{(}\; 24 \;\boxed{\times}\; 25 \;\boxed{)} \;\boxed{=} \Rightarrow 0.12$$

Self-Check 12.2

 1. Find the refund fraction on an 18-month loan if it is paid off with eight months remaining.

2. Ted Davis took out a loan to purchase a computer. He originally agreed to pay off the loan in 18 months with a finance charge of $205. He paid the loan in full after 12 payments. How much finance charge refund should he get?

3. John Paszel took out a loan for 48 months, but paid it in full after 28 months. Find the refund fraction he should use to calculate the amount of his refund.

4. If the finance charge on a loan made by Marjorie Young is $1,645 and the loan is to be paid in 48 monthly payments, find the finance charge refund if the loan is paid in full with 28 months remaining.

5. Phillamone Berry has a car loan which refunds interest using the rule of 78 when loans are paid in full ahead of schedule. He is using an employee bonus to pay off his Taurus which is on a 42-month loan. The total interest for the loan is $2,397 and he has 15 more payments to make. How much finance charge will he get credit for if he pays the loan in full immediately?

12.3   Open-End Credit

 Find the unpaid balance using the unpaid balance method

 Find the average daily balance

Open-end loans are often called **revolving charge accounts.** While a person or company is paying off loans that person or company may also be adding to the total loan account by making a new purchase or otherwise borrowing money on the account.

For example, you may want to use your Visa card to buy new textbooks even though you still owe for clothes bought last winter. Likewise, a business may use an open-end credit account to buy a new machine this month even though it still owes the bank for funds used to pay a major supplier six months ago.

Nearly all open-end accounts are billed monthly. Interest rates are most often stated as annual rates compounded monthly. Therefore, interest accrued for the month will itself accrue interest the next month if it has not been paid. Interest on open-end credit accounts is figured according to the *unpaid balance method* or the *average daily balance method.*

▶ The Unpaid Balance Method

Using the unpaid balance method, interest accrues on the unpaid balance as of the first day of the monthly period, regardless of the charges or payments made to the account during the month. Interest is calculated by multiplying the unpaid balance on the first day of the monthly period by the monthly rate of interest.

$$I = P \times R \times T$$

Interest for 1 month = unpaid balance on first day $\times$ annual rate $\times \frac{1}{12}$ year

= unpaid balance on first day $\times$ monthly rate

For example, if the unpaid balance on the first day is $147 and the interest rate is $1\frac{1}{2}\%$ monthly, the interest for the monthly period is 147×0.015, or $2.21 rounded to the nearest cent.

To find the unpaid balance as of the first day of the monthly period, we begin with the unpaid balance as of the first day of the previous monthly period, add the previous monthly period's accrued interest, add purchases made during the previous monthly period, and subtract payments made during the previous monthly period.

HOW TO | **Find the Unpaid Balance Using the Unpaid Balance Method**

Step 1 Find the interest for the previous monthly period: Multiply the unpaid balance as of the first day of the previous monthly period by the monthly interest rate.

Interest = unpaid balance × monthly interest rate

Step 2 Find the total purchases and cash advances during the previous monthly period: Add all purchases or cash advances charged to the account during the previous monthly period.

Step 3 Find the total payments for the previous monthly period: Add all payments credited to the account during the previous monthly period.

Step 4 To the unpaid balance at the beginning of the previous monthly period, add the interest for the previous monthly period from step 1, add the total purchases and cash advances from step 2. Then subtract the total payments from step 3.

Unpaid balance at the beginning of the monthly period = unpaid balance at the beginning of previous monthly period + interest for previous monthly period + total purchases and cash advances during previous monthly period − total payments during previous monthly period

Example 1 Strong's Boxes has an open-end credit account at a local business supply store. On September 1, Strong's account had an unpaid balance of $150. During September, Strong's made purchases totaling $356.20 and a payment of $42.50. The supply store charges 1.7% interest per month on any unpaid balance. In October, Strong's made a payment of $200 and made purchases of $50. Find the unpaid balance on (a) October 1 and (b) November 1.

(a) Find the finance charge on the unpaid balance as of September 1.

Finance charge = previous unpaid balance × rate

= $150 × 0.017

= $2.55

October 1 unpaid balance = September 1 unpaid balance + interest for September 1 unpaid balance + September charges − September payments

= $150 + $2.55 + $356.20 − $42.50

= $466.25

(b) Find the finance charge on the unpaid balance as of October 1.

Finance charge = unpaid balance × rate

= $466.25 × 0.017

= $7.93

November 1 unpaid balance = October 1 unpaid balance + interest on October 1 unpaid balance + October charges − October payments

$$= \$466.25 + \boxed{\$7.93} + \$50 − \$200$$

$$= \$324.18$$

The October 1 unpaid balance is \$466.25. The November 1 unpaid balance is \$324.18.

 Average Daily Balance Method

Rather than basing interest on the unpaid balance as of the first day of the monthly period, many lenders determine the finance charge using the **average daily balance method.** In this method, the daily balances of the account are determined, and then the sum of these balances is divided by the number of days in the billing cycle. This average daily balance is then multiplied by the monthly interest rate to find the finance charge for the month.

 HOW TO | **Find the Average Daily Balance**

Step 1 Find the daily unpaid balance for each day in the monthly period
    a) Find the total purchases and cash advances for the day: Add all the purchases and cash advances charged to the account during the day.
    b) Find the total payments for the day: Add all the payments credited to the account during the day.
    c) To the previous daily unpaid balance, add the total purchases and cash advances for the day (from step 1a). Then subtract the total payments for the day (from step 1b).

        Daily unpaid balance = previous daily unpaid balance
                + total purchases and cash advances for the day
                                  − total payments for the day

Step 2 Add the unpaid balances from step 1 for each day, and divide the sum by the number of days in the monthly period.

$$\text{Average daily balance} = \frac{\text{sum of daily unpaid balances}}{\text{number of days in monthly period}}$$

 TIPS & TRAPS

When does the balance change? In most cases, if a transaction reaches a financial institution at any time during the day, the transaction is posted and the balance is updated at the end of the business day. Thus, the new balance takes effect at the beginning of the next day. **Calculations on the day's unpaid balance are made on the end-of-day amount.**

Example 2 Use the chart showing May activity in the Hodge's Tax Service charge account to determine the average daily balance and finance charge for the month. The bank's interest rate is 1.5% per month.

Date Transaction Posted	Transaction	Amount
May 1	Billing date	Balance $122.70
May 7	Payment	$ 25
May 10	Purchase (pencils)	$ 12
May 13	Purchase (envelopes)	$ 20
May 20	Cash advance	$ 50
May 23	Purchase (business forms)	$100

To find the average daily balance, we must find the unpaid balance for each day, add them, and divide by the number of days.

For the first six days, May 1–May 6, there is no activity, so the daily unpaid balance is the previous unpaid balance of $122.70. The sum of daily unpaid balances for these six days, then, is 122.70×6.

$$\$122.70 \times 6 = \$736.20$$

On May 7 there is a payment of $25, which reduces the daily unpaid balance.

$$\$122.70 - \$25 = \$97.70$$

The new balance of $97.70 holds for the three days (May 7, 8, and 9) until May 10.

$$\$97.70 \times 3 = \$293.10$$

Continue doing this until you get to the end of the cycle. The calculations can be organized in a chart.

Date	Daily Unpaid Balance	Number of Days	Partial Sum
May 1–May 6	$122.70	6	$ 736.20
May 7–May 9	97.70	3	293.10
May 10–May 12	109.70	3	329.10
May 13–May 19	129.70	7	907.90
May 20–May 22	179.70	3	539.10
May 23–May 31	279.70	9	2,517.30
		Total 31	$5,322.70

Now divide the sum of $5,322.70 by the 31 days.

$$\text{Average daily balance} = \frac{\text{sum of daily unpaid balances}}{\text{number of days}}$$

$$= \frac{\$5,322.70}{31} = \$171.70$$

To find the interest, multiply the average daily balance by the monthly interest rate of 1.5%.

$$\text{Finance charge} = \$171.70 \times 0.015$$

$$= \$2.58$$

The average daily balance is $171.70 and the finance charge is $2.58.

1. What is the finance charge on an unpaid balance of $275.69 if the interest rate per month is 2.3%

2. Find the new unpaid balance on an account with an interest rate of 1.6% per month if the previous unpaid balance was $176.95 and a payment of $45 was made.

3. Chang's grocery has an open-end credit account with Great China Wholesale Distributor. Interest is charged on the unpaid balance on the 15th of each month at a rate of 1.2%. On June 15 Chang's unpaid balance was $3,805. How much interest was charged?

4. Between June 15 and July 15, Chang charged $4,983 worth of merchandise and paid $7,000 on the account. What was Chang's unpaid balance on July 15?

5. How much interest was charged on July 15? What was the unpaid balance on August 15 if Chang made a payment of $500 on August 1 but charged $75 on the same day?

 6. Suppose the charge account of Strong's Boxes at the local supply store had a 1.8% interest rate per month on the average daily balance. Find the average daily balance if Strong's had an unpaid balance on March 1 of $128.50, a payment of $20 posted on March 6, and a purchase of $25.60 posted on March 20. The billing cycle ends March 31.

7. Using Exercise 6, find Strong's finance charge on April 1.

8. Make a chart to show the transactions for Rick's credit-card account in which interest is charged on the average daily balance. The cycle begins on May 4, and the cycle ends on June 3. The beginning balance is $283.57. A payment of $200 is posted on May 18. A charge of $19.73 is posted on May 7. A charge of $53.82 is posted on May 12. A charge of $115.18 is posted on May 29. How many days are in the cycle? What is the average daily balance?

9. Rick is charged 1.42% per period. What is the finance charge for the cycle?

10. What is the beginning balance for the next cycle?

12.4 Annual Percentage Rates

 Estimate the annual percentage rate using the constant ratio formula

 Find the annual percentage rate using a table

In 1969, the federal government passed the truth-in-lending law, which requires that a lending institution tell the borrower, in writing, what the actual annual rate of interest is as it applies to the balance due on the loan each period. This interest rate tells the borrower what the true cost of the loan is.

For example, if you borrowed $1,500 for a year and paid an interest charge of $165, you would be paying an interest rate of 11% annually on the entire $1,500. But if you paid the money back in 12 monthly installments of $138.75 [($1,500 + $165) ÷ 12 = $138.75], you would not have the use of the $1,500 for a full year. Instead, you would be paying it back in 12 payments of $138.75 each. Thus, you are losing the use of some of the money every month, but are still paying interest at the rate of 11% of *the entire amount*. This means that you are actually paying *more than* 11% interest. The true **annual percentage rate (APR)** is the effective interest rate discussed in Chapter 10. Applied to installment loans, the APR, or effective rate, is the annual simple interest rate you are actually paying on your unpaid balances. The APR can be calculated using a government-issued table, or estimated by a formula.

▶ *Using the Constant Ratio Formula*

You can use the **constant ratio formula** to estimate the annual percentage rate on any loan that is paid back in equal quarterly, monthly, or weekly installments. This formula gives a close approximation of the APR if the time of the loan is short. On loans made for ten years or more, this formula will not give a fair approximation of the APR.

? HOW TO | **Estimate the Annual Percentage Rate Using the Constant Ratio Formula**

Step 1 Substitute known values into the formula.

Approximate annual percentage rate

$$= \frac{2 \times \text{number of payments per year} \times \text{total interest}}{\text{amount financed} \times (\text{number of payments} + 1)}$$

$$\text{APR} = \frac{2NI}{P(N + 1)}$$

Step 2 Solve the formula for the unknown.

Example 1 A loan of $6,000, borrowed for three years, required interest of $1,440. Find the annual percentage rate if the loan was repaid in monthly installments.

Number of payments on the loan = 3 years × 12 payments per year = 36

Annual percentage rate

$$\text{APR} = \frac{2 \times \text{number of payments per year} \times \text{total interest}}{\text{amount financed} \times (\text{number of payments} + 1)}$$

$$\text{APR} = \frac{(2)(12)(\$1,440)}{(\$6,000)(36 + 1)} = 0.1556756, \text{ which rounds to } 0.156, \text{ or } 15.6\%$$

The approximate annual percentage rate is 15.6%. Thus, each month the borrower is paying approximately $\frac{15.6}{12}\%$ of the remaining balance in interest.

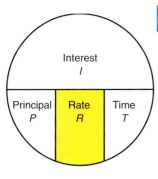

Compare the APR for Example 1 to the simple interest rate if the loan was repaid in a lump sum at the end of the 3 years.

$$R = \frac{I}{PT} = \frac{\$1,440}{\$6,000(3)} = \frac{\$1,440}{\$18,000} = 0.08 = 8\%$$

The loan rate could have been advertised as 8% based on the simple interest rate for the entire time of the loan.

The APR Table

While the formula provides a good approximation in many cases, the federal government issues annual percentage rate tables, which are used to find *exact* APR rates (within $\frac{1}{4}\%$, which is the federal standard). A portion of one of these tables, based on monthly payments, is shown in Table 12–1.

Table 12–1 Interest per $100 of Amount Financed

Number of Monthly Payments	APR (Annual Percentage Rate)															
	10.00%	10.25%	10.50%	10.75%	11.00%	11.25%	11.50%	11.75%	12.00%	12.25%	12.50%	12.75%	13.00%	13.25%	13.50%	13.75%
1	0.83	0.85	0.87	0.90	0.92	0.94	0.96	0.98	1.00	1.02	1.04	1.06	1.08	1.10	1.12	1.15
2	1.25	1.28	1.31	1.35	1.38	1.41	1.44	1.47	1.50	1.53	1.57	1.60	1.63	1.66	1.69	1.72
3	1.67	1.71	1.76	1.80	1.84	1.88	1.92	1.96	2.01	2.05	2.09	2.13	2.17	2.22	2.26	2.30
4	2.09	2.14	2.20	2.25	2.30	2.35	2.41	2.46	2.51	2.57	2.62	2.67	2.72	2.78	2.83	2.88
5	2.51	2.58	2.64	2.70	2.77	2.83	2.89	2.96	3.02	3.08	3.15	3.21	3.27	3.34	3.40	3.46
6	2.94	3.01	3.08	3.16	3.23	3.31	3.38	3.45	3.53	3.60	3.68	3.75	3.83	3.90	3.97	4.05
7	3.36	3.45	3.53	3.62	3.70	3.78	3.87	3.95	4.04	4.12	4.21	4.29	4.38	4.47	4.55	4.64
8	3.79	3.88	3.98	4.07	4.17	4.26	4.36	4.46	4.55	4.65	4.74	4.84	4.94	5.03	5.13	5.22
9	4.21	4.32	4.43	4.53	4.64	4.75	4.85	4.96	5.07	5.17	5.28	5.39	5.49	5.60	5.71	5.82
10	4.64	4.76	4.88	4.99	5.11	5.23	5.35	5.46	5.58	5.70	5.82	5.94	6.05	6.17	6.29	6.41
11	5.07	5.20	5.33	5.45	5.58	5.71	5.84	5.97	6.10	6.23	6.36	6.49	6.62	6.75	6.88	7.01
12	5.50	5.64	5.78	5.92	6.06	6.20	6.34	6.48	6.62	6.76	6.90	7.04	7.18	7.32	7.46	7.60
13	5.93	6.08	6.23	6.38	6.53	6.68	6.84	6.99	7.14	7.29	7.44	7.59	7.75	7.90	8.05	8.20
14	6.36	6.52	6.69	6.85	7.01	7.17	7.34	7.50	7.66	7.82	7.99	8.15	8.31	8.48	8.64	8.81
15	6.80	6.97	7.14	7.32	7.49	7.66	7.84	8.01	8.19	8.36	8.53	8.71	8.88	9.06	9.23	9.41
16	7.23	7.41	7.60	7.78	7.97	8.15	8.34	8.53	8.71	8.90	9.08	9.27	9.46	9.64	9.83	10.02
17	7.67	7.86	8.06	8.25	8.45	8.65	8.84	9.04	9.24	9.44	9.63	9.83	10.03	10.23	10.44	10.63
18	8.10	8.31	8.52	8.73	8.93	9.14	9.35	9.56	9.77	9.98	10.19	10.40	10.61	10.82	11.03	11.24
19	8.54	8.76	8.98	9.20	9.42	9.64	9.86	10.08	10.30	10.52	10.74	10.96	11.18	11.41	11.63	11.85
20	8.98	9.21	9.44	9.67	9.90	10.13	10.37	10.60	10.83	11.06	11.30	11.53	11.76	12.00	12.23	12.46
21	9.42	9.66	9.90	10.15	10.39	10.63	10.88	11.12	11.36	11.61	11.85	12.10	12.34	12.59	12.84	13.08
22	9.86	10.12	10.37	10.62	10.88	11.13	11.39	11.64	11.90	12.16	12.41	12.67	12.93	13.19	13.44	13.70
23	10.30	10.57	10.84	11.10	11.37	11.63	11.90	12.17	12.44	12.71	12.97	13.24	13.51	13.78	14.05	14.32
24	10.75	11.02	11.30	11.58	11.86	12.14	12.42	12.70	12.98	13.26	13.54	13.82	14.10	14.38	14.66	14.95
25	11.19	11.48	11.77	12.06	12.35	12.64	12.93	13.22	13.52	13.81	14.10	14.40	14.69	14.98	15.28	15.57
26	11.64	11.94	12.24	12.54	12.85	13.15	13.45	13.75	14.06	14.36	14.67	14.97	15.28	15.59	15.89	16.20
27	12.09	12.40	12.71	13.03	13.34	13.66	13.97	14.29	14.60	14.92	15.24	15.56	15.87	16.19	16.51	16.83
28	12.53	12.86	13.18	13.51	13.84	14.16	14.49	14.82	15.15	15.48	15.81	16.14	16.47	16.80	17.13	17.46
29	12.98	13.32	13.66	14.00	14.33	14.67	15.01	15.35	15.70	16.04	16.38	16.72	17.07	17.41	17.75	18.10
30	13.43	13.78	14.13	14.48	14.82	15.19	15.54	15.89	16.24	16.60	16.95	17.31	17.66	18.02	18.38	18.74
31	13.89	14.25	14.61	14.97	15.33	15.70	16.06	16.43	16.79	17.16	17.53	17.90	18.27	18.63	19.00	19.38
32	14.34	14.71	15.09	15.46	15.84	16.21	16.59	16.97	17.35	17.73	18.11	18.49	18.87	19.25	19.63	20.02
33	14.79	15.18	15.57	15.95	16.34	16.73	17.12	17.51	17.90	18.29	18.69	19.08	19.47	19.87	20.26	20.66
34	15.25	15.65	16.05	16.44	16.85	17.25	17.65	18.05	18.46	18.86	19.27	19.67	20.08	20.49	20.90	21.31
35	15.70	16.11	16.53	16.94	17.35	17.77	18.18	18.60	19.01	19.43	19.85	20.27	20.69	21.11	21.53	21.95
36	16.16	16.58	17.01	17.43	17.86	18.29	18.71	19.14	19.57	20.00	20.43	20.87	21.30	21.73	22.17	22.60
37	16.62	17.06	17.49	17.93	18.37	18.81	19.25	19.69	20.13	20.58	21.02	21.46	21.91	22.36	22.81	23.25
38	17.08	17.53	17.98	18.43	18.88	19.33	19.78	20.24	20.69	21.15	21.61	22.07	22.52	22.99	23.45	23.91
39	17.54	18.00	18.46	18.93	19.39	19.86	20.32	20.79	21.26	21.73	22.20	22.67	23.14	23.61	24.09	24.56
40	18.00	18.48	18.95	19.43	19.90	20.38	20.86	21.34	21.82	22.30	22.79	23.27	23.76	24.25	24.73	25.22
41	18.47	18.95	19.44	19.93	20.42	20.91	21.40	21.89	22.39	22.88	23.38	23.88	24.38	24.88	25.38	25.88
42	18.93	19.43	19.93	20.43	20.93	21.44	21.94	22.45	22.96	23.47	23.98	24.49	25.00	25.51	26.03	26.55
43	19.40	19.91	20.42	20.94	21.45	21.97	22.49	23.01	23.53	24.05	24.58	25.10	25.62	26.15	26.68	27.21
44	19.86	20.39	20.91	21.44	21.97	22.50	23.03	23.57	24.10	24.64	25.17	25.71	26.25	26.79	27.33	27.88
45	20.33	20.87	21.41	21.95	22.49	23.03	23.58	24.12	24.67	25.22	25.77	26.32	26.88	27.43	27.99	28.55
46	20.80	21.35	21.90	22.46	23.01	23.57	24.13	24.69	25.25	25.81	26.37	26.94	27.51	28.08	28.65	29.22
47	21.27	21.83	22.40	22.79	23.53	24.04	24.68	25.25	25.82	26.40	26.97	27.56	28.14	28.72	29.31	29.89
48	21.74	22.32	22.90	23.48	24.06	24.64	25.23	25.81	26.40	26.99	27.58	28.18	28.77	29.37	29.97	30.57
49	22.21	22.80	23.39	23.99	24.58	25.18	25.78	26.38	26.98	27.59	28.19	28.80	29.41	30.02	30.63	31.24
50	22.69	23.29	23.89	24.50	25.11	25.72	26.33	26.95	27.56	28.18	28.80	29.42	30.04	30.67	31.29	31.92
51	23.16	23.78	24.40	25.02	25.64	26.26	26.89	27.52	28.15	28.78	29.41	30.05	30.68	31.32	31.96	32.60
52	23.64	24.27	24.90	25.53	26.17	26.81	27.45	28.09	28.73	29.38	30.02	30.67	31.32	31.98	32.63	33.29
53	24.11	24.76	25.40	26.05	26.70	27.35	28.00	28.66	29.32	29.98	30.64	31.30	31.97	32.63	33.30	33.97
54	24.59	25.25	25.91	26.57	27.23	27.90	28.56	29.23	29.91	30.58	31.25	31.93	32.61	33.29	33.98	34.66
55	25.07	25.74	26.41	27.09	27.77	28.44	29.13	29.81	30.50	31.18	31.87	32.56	33.26	33.95	34.65	35.35
56	25.55	26.23	26.92	27.61	28.30	28.99	29.69	30.39	31.09	31.79	32.49	33.20	33.91	34.62	35.33	36.04
57	26.03	26.73	27.43	28.13	28.84	29.54	30.25	30.97	31.68	32.39	33.11	33.83	34.56	35.28	36.01	36.74
58	26.51	27.23	27.94	28.66	29.37	30.10	30.82	31.55	32.27	33.00	33.74	34.47	35.21	35.95	36.69	37.43
59	27.00	27.72	28.45	29.18	29.91	30.65	31.39	32.13	32.87	33.61	34.36	35.11	35.86	36.62	37.37	38.13
60	27.48	28.22	28.96	29.71	30.45	31.20	31.96	32.71	33.47	34.23	44.99	35.75	36.52	37.29	38.06	38.83

Table entries are the result of the calculations using the formula Interest = $100 × APR × $\dfrac{\text{number of monthly payments}}{12}$

Table 12–1 (continued)

Number of Monthly Payments	APR (Annual Percentage Rate)															
	14.00%	14.25%	14.50%	14.75%	15.00%	15.25%	15.50%	15.75%	16.00%	16.25%	16.50%	16.75%	17.00%	17.25%	17.50%	17.75%
1	1.17	1.19	1.21	1.23	1.25	1.27	1.29	1.31	1.33	1.35	1.37	1.40	1.42	1.44	1.46	1.48
2	1.75	1.78	1.82	1.85	1.88	1.91	1.94	1.97	2.00	2.04	2.07	2.10	2.13	2.16	2.17	2.22
3	2.34	2.38	2.43	2.47	2.51	2.55	2.59	2.64	2.68	2.72	2.76	2.80	2.85	2.89	2.93	2.97
4	2.93	2.99	3.04	3.09	3.14	3.20	3.25	3.30	3.36	3.41	3.46	3.51	3.57	3.62	3.67	3.73
5	3.53	3.59	3.65	3.72	3.78	3.84	3.91	3.97	4.04	4.10	4.16	4.23	4.29	4.35	4.42	4.48
6	4.12	4.20	4.27	4.35	4.42	4.49	4.57	4.64	4.72	4.79	4.87	4.94	5.02	5.01	5.17	5.24
7	4.72	4.81	4.89	4.98	5.06	5.15	5.23	5.32	5.40	5.49	5.58	5.66	5.75	5.83	5.92	6.00
8	5.32	5.42	5.51	5.61	5.71	5.80	5.90	6.00	6.09	6.19	6.29	6.38	6.48	6.58	6.67	6.77
9	5.92	6.03	6.14	6.25	6.35	6.46	6.57	6.68	6.78	6.89	7.00	7.11	7.22	7.32	7.43	7.54
10	6.53	6.65	6.77	6.88	7.00	7.12	7.24	7.36	7.48	7.60	7.72	7.84	7.96	8.08	8.19	8.31
11	7.14	7.27	7.40	7.53	7.66	7.79	7.92	8.05	8.18	8.31	8.44	8.57	8.70	8.83	8.96	9.09
12	7.74	7.89	8.03	8.17	8.31	8.45	8.59	8.74	8.88	9.02	9.16	9.30	9.45	9.59	9.73	9.87
13	8.36	8.51	8.66	8.81	8.97	9.12	9.27	9.43	9.58	9.73	9.89	10.04	10.20	10.35	10.50	10.66
14	8.97	9.13	9.30	9.46	9.63	9.79	9.96	10.12	10.29	10.45	10.67	10.78	10.95	11.11	11.28	11.45
15	9.59	9.76	9.94	10.11	10.29	10.47	10.64	10.82	11.00	11.17	11.35	11.53	11.71	11.88	12.06	12.24
16	10.20	10.39	10.58	10.77	10.95	11.14	11.33	11.52	11.71	11.90	12.09	12.28	12.46	12.65	12.84	13.03
17	10.82	11.02	11.22	11.42	11.62	11.82	12.02	12.22	12.42	12.62	12.83	13.03	13.23	13.43	13.63	13.83
18	11.45	11.66	11.87	12.08	12.29	12.50	12.72	12.93	13.14	13.35	13.57	13.78	13.99	14.21	14.42	14.64
19	12.07	12.30	12.52	12.74	12.97	13.19	13.41	13.64	13.86	14.09	14.31	14.54	14.76	14.99	15.22	15.44
20	12.70	12.93	13.17	13.41	13.64	13.88	14.11	14.35	14.59	14.82	15.06	15.30	15.54	15.77	16.01	16.25
21	13.33	13.58	13.82	14.07	14.32	14.57	14.82	15.06	15.31	15.56	15.81	16.06	16.31	16.56	16.81	17.07
22	13.96	14.22	14.48	14.74	15.00	15.26	15.52	15.78	16.04	16.30	16.57	16.83	17.09	17.36	17.62	17.88
23	14.59	14.87	15.14	15.41	15.68	15.96	16.23	16.50	16.78	17.05	17.32	17.60	17.88	18.15	18.43	18.70
24	15.23	15.51	15.80	16.08	16.37	16.65	16.94	17.22	17.51	17.80	18.09	18.37	18.66	18.95	19.24	19.53
25	15.87	16.17	16.46	16.76	17.06	17.35	17.65	17.95	18.25	18.55	18.85	19.15	19.45	19.75	20.05	20.36
26	16.51	16.82	17.13	17.44	17.75	18.06	18.37	18.68	18.99	19.30	19.62	19.93	20.24	20.56	20.87	21.19
27	17.15	17.47	17.80	18.12	18.44	18.76	19.09	19.41	19.74	20.06	20.39	20.71	21.04	21.37	21.69	22.02
28	17.80	18.13	18.47	18.80	19.14	19.47	19.81	20.15	20.48	20.82	21.16	21.50	21.84	22.18	22.52	22.86
29	18.45	18.79	19.14	19.49	19.83	20.18	20.53	20.88	21.23	21.58	21.94	22.29	22.64	22.99	23.35	23.70
30	19.10	19.45	19.81	20.17	20.54	20.90	21.26	21.62	21.99	22.35	22.72	23.08	23.45	23.81	24.18	24.55
31	19.75	20.12	20.49	20.87	21.24	21.61	21.99	22.37	22.74	23.12	23.50	23.88	24.26	24.64	25.02	25.40
32	20.40	20.79	21.17	21.56	21.95	22.33	22.72	23.11	23.50	23.89	24.28	24.68	25.07	25.46	25.86	26.25
33	21.06	21.46	21.85	22.25	22.65	23.06	23.46	23.86	24.26	24.67	25.07	25.48	25.88	26.29	26.70	27.11
34	21.72	22.13	22.54	22.95	23.37	23.78	24.19	24.61	25.03	25.44	25.86	26.28	26.70	27.12	27.54	27.97
35	22.38	22.80	23.23	23.65	24.08	24.51	24.94	25.36	25.79	26.23	26.66	27.09	27.52	27.96	28.39	28.83
36	23.04	23.48	23.92	24.35	24.80	25.24	25.68	26.12	26.57	27.01	27.46	27.90	28.35	28.80	29.25	29.70
37	23.70	24.16	24.69	25.06	25.51	25.97	26.42	26.88	27.34	27.80	28.26	28.72	29.18	29.64	30.10	30.57
38	24.37	24.84	25.30	25.77	26.24	26.70	27.17	27.64	28.11	28.59	29.06	29.53	30.01	30.49	30.96	31.44
39	25.04	25.52	26.00	26.48	26.96	27.44	27.92	28.41	28.89	29.38	29.87	30.36	30.85	31.34	31.83	32.32
40	25.71	26.20	26.70	27.19	27.69	28.18	28.68	29.18	29.68	30.18	30.68	31.18	31.68	32.19	32.69	33.20
41	26.39	26.89	27.40	27.91	28.41	28.92	29.44	29.95	30.46	30.97	31.49	32.01	32.52	33.04	33.56	34.08
42	27.06	27.58	28.10	28.62	29.15	29.67	30.19	30.72	31.25	31.78	32.31	32.84	33.37	33.90	34.44	34.97
43	27.74	28.27	28.81	29.34	29.88	30.42	30.96	31.50	32.04	32.58	33.13	33.67	34.22	34.76	35.31	35.86
44	28.42	28.97	29.52	30.07	30.62	31.17	31.72	32.28	32.83	33.39	33.95	34.51	35.07	35.63	36.19	36.78
45	29.11	29.67	30.23	30.79	31.36	31.92	32.49	33.06	33.63	34.20	34.77	35.35	35.92	36.50	37.08	37.66
46	29.79	30.36	30.94	31.52	32.10	32.68	33.26	33.84	34.43	35.01	35.60	36.19	36.78	37.37	37.96	38.56
47	30.48	31.07	31.66	32.25	32.84	33.44	34.03	34.63	35.23	35.83	36.43	37.04	37.64	38.25	38.86	39.46
48	31.17	31.77	32.37	32.98	33.59	34.20	34.81	35.42	36.03	36.65	37.27	37.88	38.50	39.13	39.75	40.37
49	31.86	32.48	33.09	33.71	34.34	34.96	35.59	36.21	36.84	37.47	38.10	38.74	39.37	40.01	40.65	41.29
50	32.55	33.18	33.82	34.45	35.09	35.73	36.37	37.01	37.65	38.30	38.94	39.59	40.24	40.89	41.55	42.20
51	33.25	33.89	34.54	35.19	35.84	36.49	37.15	37.81	38.46	39.17	39.79	40.45	41.11	41.78	42.45	43.12
52	33.95	34.61	35.27	35.93	36.60	37.27	37.94	38.61	39.28	39.96	40.63	41.31	41.99	42.67	43.36	44.04
53	34.65	35.32	36.00	36.68	37.36	38.04	38.72	39.41	40.10	40.79	41.48	42.17	42.87	43.57	44.27	44.97
54	35.35	36.04	36.73	37.42	38.12	38.82	39.52	40.22	40.92	41.63	42.33	43.04	43.75	44.47	45.18	45.90
55	36.05	36.76	37.46	38.17	38.88	39.60	40.31	41.03	41.74	42.47	43.19	43.91	44.64	45.37	46.10	46.83
56	36.76	37.48	38.20	38.92	39.65	40.38	41.11	41.84	42.57	43.31	44.05	44.79	45.53	46.27	47.02	47.77
57	37.47	38.20	38.94	39.68	40.42	41.16	41.91	42.65	43.40	44.15	44.91	45.66	46.42	47.18	47.94	47.71
58	38.18	38.93	39.68	40.43	41.19	41.95	42.71	43.47	44.23	45.00	45.77	46.54	47.32	48.09	48.87	49.65
59	38.89	39.66	40.42	41.19	41.96	42.74	43.51	44.29	45.07	45.85	46.64	47.42	48.21	49.01	49.80	50.60
60	39.61	40.39	41.17	41.95	42.74	43.53	44.32	45.11	45.91	46.71	47.51	48.31	49.12	49.92	50.73	51.55

Table entries are the result of the calculations using the formula Interest $= \$100 \times APR \times \dfrac{\text{number of monthly payments}}{12}$

Table 12–1 (continued)

Number of Monthly Payments	APR (Annual Percentage Rate)															
	18.00%	18.25%	18.50%	18.75%	19.00%	19.25%	19.50%	19.75%	20.00%	20.25%	20.50%	20.75%	21.00%	21.25%	21.50%	21.75%
1	1.50	1.52	1.54	1.56	1.58	1.60	1.62	1.65	1.67	1.69	1.71	1.73	1.75	1.77	1.79	1.81
2	2.26	2.29	2.32	2.35	2.38	2.41	2.44	2.48	2.51	2.54	2.57	2.60	2.63	2.66	2.70	2.73
3	3.01	3.06	3.10	3.14	3.18	3.23	3.27	3.31	3.35	3.39	3.44	3.48	3.52	3.56	3.60	3.65
4	3.78	3.83	3.88	3.94	3.99	4.04	4.10	4.15	4.20	4.25	4.31	4.36	4.41	4.47	4.52	4.57
5	4.54	4.61	4.67	4.74	4.80	4.86	4.93	4.99	5.06	5.12	5.18	5.25	5.31	5.37	5.44	5.50
6	5.32	5.39	5.46	5.54	5.61	5.69	5.76	5.84	5.91	5.99	6.06	6.14	6.21	6.29	6.36	6.44
7	6.09	6.18	6.26	6.35	6.43	6.52	6.60	6.69	6.78	6.86	6.95	7.04	7.12	7.21	7.29	7.38
8	6.87	6.96	7.06	7.16	7.26	7.35	7.45	7.55	7.64	7.74	7.84	7.94	8.03	8.13	8.23	8.33
9	7.65	7.76	7.87	7.97	8.08	8.19	8.30	8.41	8.52	8.63	8.73	8.84	8.95	9.06	9.17	9.28
10	8.43	8.55	8.67	8.79	8.91	9.03	9.15	9.27	9.39	9.51	9.63	9.75	9.88	10.00	10.12	10.24
11	9.22	9.35	9.49	9.62	9.75	9.88	10.01	10.14	10.28	10.41	10.54	10.67	10.80	10.94	11.07	11.20
12	10.02	10.16	10.30	10.44	10.59	10.73	10.87	11.02	11.16	11.31	11.45	11.59	11.74	11.88	12.02	12.17
13	10.81	10.97	11.12	11.28	11.43	11.59	11.74	11.90	12.05	12.21	12.36	12.52	12.67	12.83	12.99	13.14
14	11.61	11.78	11.95	12.11	12.28	12.45	12.61	12.78	12.95	13.11	13.28	13.45	13.62	13.79	13.95	14.12
15	12.42	12.59	12.77	12.95	13.13	13.31	13.49	13.67	13.85	14.03	14.21	14.39	14.57	14.75	14.93	15.11
16	13.22	13.41	13.60	13.80	13.99	14.18	14.37	14.56	14.75	14.94	15.13	15.33	15.52	15.71	15.90	16.10
17	14.04	14.24	14.44	14.64	14.85	15.05	15.25	15.46	15.66	15.86	16.07	16.27	16.48	16.68	16.89	17.09
18	14.85	15.07	15.28	15.49	15.71	15.93	16.14	16.36	16.57	16.79	17.01	17.22	17.44	17.66	17.88	18.09
19	15.67	15.90	16.12	16.35	16.58	16.81	17.03	17.26	17.49	17.72	17.95	18.18	18.41	18.64	18.87	19.10
20	16.49	16.73	16.97	17.21	17.45	17.69	17.93	18.17	18.41	18.66	18.90	19.14	19.38	19.63	19.87	20.11
21	17.32	17.57	17.82	18.07	18.33	18.58	18.83	19.09	19.34	19.60	19.85	20.11	20.36	20.62	20.87	21.13
22	18.15	18.41	18.68	18.94	19.21	19.47	19.74	20.01	20.27	20.54	20.81	21.08	21.34	21.61	21.88	22.15
23	18.98	19.26	19.54	19.81	20.09	20.37	20.65	20.93	21.21	21.49	21.77	22.05	22.33	22.61	22.90	23.18
24	19.82	20.11	20.40	20.69	20.98	21.27	21.56	21.86	22.15	22.44	22.74	23.03	23.33	23.62	23.92	24.21
25	20.66	20.96	21.27	21.57	21.87	22.18	22.48	22.79	23.10	23.40	23.71	24.02	24.32	24.63	24.94	25.25
26	21.50	21.82	22.14	22.45	22.77	23.09	23.41	23.73	24.04	24.36	24.68	25.01	25.33	25.65	25.97	26.29
27	22.35	22.68	23.01	23.44	23.67	24.00	24.33	24.67	25.00	25.33	25.67	26.00	26.34	26.67	27.01	27.34
28	23.20	23.55	23.89	24.23	24.58	24.92	25.27	25.61	25.96	26.30	26.65	27.00	27.35	27.70	28.05	28.40
29	24.06	24.41	24.27	25.13	25.49	25.84	26.20	26.56	26.92	27.28	27.64	28.00	28.37	28.73	29.09	29.46
30	24.92	25.29	25.66	26.03	26.40	26.77	27.14	27.52	27.89	28.26	28.64	29.01	29.39	29.77	30.14	30.52
31	25.78	26.16	26.55	26.93	27.32	27.70	28.09	28.47	28.86	29.25	29.64	30.03	30.42	30.81	31.20	31.59
32	26.65	27.04	27.44	27.84	28.24	28.64	29.04	29.44	29.84	30.24	30.64	31.05	31.45	31.85	32.26	32.67
33	27.52	27.93	28.34	28.75	29.16	29.57	29.99	30.40	30.82	31.23	31.65	32.07	32.49	32.91	33.33	33.75
34	28.39	28.81	29.24	29.66	30.09	30.52	30.95	31.37	31.80	32.23	32.67	33.10	33.53	33.96	34.40	34.83
35	29.27	29.71	30.14	30.58	31.02	31.47	31.91	32.35	32.79	33.24	33.68	34.13	34.58	35.03	35.47	35.92
36	30.15	30.60	31.05	31.51	31.96	32.42	32.87	33.33	33.79	34.25	34.71	35.17	35.63	36.09	36.56	37.02
37	31.03	31.50	31.97	32.43	32.90	33.37	33.84	34.32	34.79	35.26	35.74	36.21	36.69	37.16	37.64	38.12
38	31.92	32.40	32.88	33.37	33.85	34.33	34.82	35.30	35.79	36.28	36.77	37.26	37.75	38.24	38.73	39.23
39	32.81	33.31	33.80	34.30	34.80	35.30	35.80	36.30	36.80	37.30	37.81	38.31	38.82	39.32	39.83	40.34
40	33.71	34.22	34.73	35.24	35.75	36.26	36.78	37.29	37.81	38.33	38.85	39.37	39.89	40.41	40.93	41.46
41	34.61	35.13	35.66	36.18	36.71	37.24	37.77	38.30	38.83	39.36	39.89	40.43	40.96	41.50	42.04	42.58
42	35.51	36.05	36.59	37.13	37.67	38.21	38.76	39.30	39.85	40.40	40.95	41.50	42.05	42.60	43.15	43.71
43	36.42	36.97	37.52	38.08	38.63	39.19	39.75	40.31	40.87	41.44	42.00	42.57	43.13	43.70	44.27	44.84
44	37.33	37.89	38.46	39.03	39.60	40.18	40.75	41.33	41.90	42.48	43.06	43.64	44.22	44.81	45.39	45.98
45	38.24	38.82	39.41	39.99	40.58	41.17	41.75	42.35	42.94	43.53	44.13	44.72	45.32	45.92	46.52	47.12
46	39.16	39.75	40.35	40.95	41.55	42.16	42.76	43.37	43.98	44.58	45.20	45.81	46.42	47.03	47.65	48.27
47	40.08	40.69	41.30	41.92	42.54	43.15	43.77	44.40	45.02	45.64	46.27	46.90	47.53	48.16	48.79	49.42
48	41.00	41.63	42.26	42.89	43.52	44.15	44.79	45.43	46.07	46.71	47.35	47.99	48.64	49.28	49.93	50.58
49	41.93	42.57	43.22	43.86	44.51	45.16	45.81	46.46	47.12	47.77	48.43	49.09	49.75	50.41	51.08	51.74
50	42.86	43.52	44.18	44.84	45.50	46.17	46.83	47.50	48.17	48.84	49.52	50.19	50.87	51.55	52.23	52.91
51	43.79	44.47	45.14	45.82	46.50	47.18	47.86	48.55	49.23	49.92	50.61	51.30	51.99	52.69	53.38	54.08
52	44.73	45.42	46.11	46.80	47.50	48.20	48.89	49.59	50.30	51.00	51.71	52.41	53.12	53.83	54.55	55.26
53	45.67	46.38	47.08	47.79	48.50	49.22	49.93	50.65	51.37	52.09	52.81	53.53	54.26	54.98	55.71	56.44
54	46.62	47.34	48.06	48.79	49.51	50.24	50.97	51.70	52.44	53.17	53.91	54.65	55.39	56.14	56.88	57.63
55	47.57	48.30	49.04	49.78	50.52	51.27	52.02	52.76	53.52	54.27	55.02	55.78	56.54	57.30	58.08	58.82
56	48.52	49.27	50.03	50.78	51.54	52.30	53.06	53.83	54.60	55.37	56.14	56.91	57.68	58.46	59.24	60.02
57	49.47	50.24	51.01	51.79	52.56	53.34	54.12	54.90	55.68	56.47	57.25	58.04	58.84	59.63	60.43	61.22
58	50.43	51.22	52.00	52.79	53.58	54.38	55.17	55.97	56.77	57.57	58.38	59.18	59.99	60.80	61.62	62.43
59	51.39	52.20	53.00	53.80	54.61	55.42	56.23	57.05	57.87	58.68	59.51	60.33	61.15	61.98	62.81	63.64
60	52.36	53.18	54.00	54.82	55.64	56.47	57.30	58.13	58.96	59.80	60.64	61.48	62.32	63.17	64.01	64.86

Table entries are the result of the calculations using the formula Interest $= \$100 \times \text{APR} \times \dfrac{\text{number of monthly payments}}{12}$

HOW TO	Find the Annual Percentage Rate Using a per $100 of Amount Financed Table

Step 1 Find the interest per $100 of amount financed: Multiply the finance charge by $100 and divide by the amount financed.

$$\text{Interest per } \$100 = \frac{\text{finance charge} \times \$100}{\text{amount financed}}$$

Step 2 Find the row corresponding to the number of monthly payments. Move across the row to find the number closest to the value from step 1. Read up the column to find the annual percentage rate for that column. If the result in step 1 is exactly halfway between two table values, a rate halfway between the two rates can be used.

Example 2 Lewis Strang bought a motorcycle for $3,000, which was financed at $142 per month for 24 months. There was no down payment. Find the APR.

$$\begin{aligned}
\text{Total paid} &= 24 \times \$142 \\
&= \$3,408 \\
\text{Interest} &= \$3,408 - \$3,000 \\
&= \$408
\end{aligned}$$

$$\text{Interest per } \$100 = \frac{\text{Finance charge} \times \$100}{\text{amount financed}} = \frac{\$408 \times \$100}{\$3,000} = \$13.60$$

Find the row for 24 monthly payments. Move across to find the number nearest to $13.60. $13.60 is between $13.54 and $13.82. $13.60 − $13.54 = $0.06; $13.82 − $13.60 = $0.22. Thus, $13.60 is closer to $13.54. Move up to the top of that column to find the annual percentage rate, which is 12.50%.

 TIPS & TRAPS

Formulas often represent the result of several manipulations, so that fewer steps are required when using the final version of the formula.

Since Table 12–1 uses the finance change per $100 of the amount financed, the amount financed could first be divided by $100, then the finance charge would be divided by the result. Examine the manipulations.

$$\text{Finance charge} \div (\text{amount financed} \div 100)$$

$$\text{Finance charge} \div (\text{amount financed} \times \frac{1}{100})$$

$$\text{Finance charge} \div \frac{\text{amount financed}}{100}$$

$$\text{Finance charge} \times \frac{100}{\text{amount financed}}$$

$$\frac{\text{Finance charge} \times 100}{\text{amount financed}}$$

1. Use the constant ratio formula to estimate the annual percentage rate on a loan of $1,500 borrowed for two years with interest of $265. The loan is repaid in monthly payments. Round to the nearest tenth of a percent.

2. What is the estimated annual percentage rate on a loan of $3,800 borrowed for three years with interest of $518 if the loan is repaid in monthly payments? Round to the nearest tenth of a percent.

3. A loan of $2,750 is borrowed for 18 months and repaid in monthly payments. If the interest on the loan is $412, find the approximate annual percentage rate. Round to the nearest tenth of a percent.

4. Leon Griffin made a loan of $5,800 for 30 months and is repaying it in monthly payments. He is paying $1,215 interest on the loan. What is the approximate annual percentage rate for the loan? Round to the nearest tenth of a percent.

5. Alvin Ailey borrowed $3,715 for two years and is repaying it in monthly payments. If the loan company is charging $698 interest, estimate the annual percentage rate.

6. A fishing boat is purchased for $5,600 and financed for 36 months. If the total finance charge is $1,025, find the annual percentage rate using Table 12–1.

7. An air compressor costs $780 and is financed with monthly payments for 12 months. The total finance charge is $90. Find the annual percentage rate using Table 12–1.

8. Use Table 12–1 to find the APR for the loan in Exercise 3. Compare the rate from the table with the rate calculated using the formula.

9. Use Table 12–1 to find the APR for the loan in Exercise 4. Compare the rate from the table with the rate calculated using the formula.

10. Use Table 12–1 to find the APR for the loan in Exercise 5. Compare the rate from the table with the rate calculated using the formula.

11. Summarize and generalize the comparisons made in Exercises 8–10.

12.5 Home Mortgages

 Find the monthly mortgage payment and total interest

 Complete a monthly amortization schedule

The purchase of a home is one of the most costly purchases individuals or families make in a lifetime. Most individuals must borrow money to pay for the home. Home loans are generally referred to as **mortgages** because the lending agency requires that the home be held as **collateral.** If the payments are not made as scheduled, the lending agency can take possession of the home and sell it to pay against the loan.

As a home buyer makes payments on a mortgage, the home buyer builds equity in the home. The home buyer's **equity** is the difference of the expected selling price of a home (market value) and the balance owed on the home. A home may increase in value as a result of rising prices and average prices of other homes in the neighborhood. This increase in value also increases the owner's equity in the home.

A home buyer may select from several types of first mortgages. A **first mortgage** is the primary mortgage on a home and is ordinarily made at the time of purchase of the home. The agency holding the first mortgage has the first right to the proceeds up to the amount of the mortgage and settlement fees from the sale of the home if the homeowner fails to make required payments.

One type of first mortgage is the **conventional mortgage.** Money for a conventional mortgage is usually obtained through a savings and loan institution or a bank. These loans are not insured by a government program. Two types of conventional mortgages are the **fixed-rate mortgage** (FRM) and the **adjustable-rate mortgage** (ARM). The rate of interest on the loan for a fixed-rate mortgage remains the same for the entire time of the loan. Fixed-rate mortgages have several payment options. The number of years of the loan may vary, but 15- and 30-year loans are the most common. The home buyer makes the same payment (principal plus interest) each month of the loan. Another option is the **biweekly mortgage**. The home buyer makes 26 equal payments each year rather than 12. This method builds equity more quickly than the monthly payment method.

Another option for fixed-rate loans is the **graduated payments mortgage.** The home buyer makes small payments at the beginning of the loan and larger payments at the end. Home buyers who expect their income to rise may choose this option.

The rate of interest on a loan for an adjustable-rate mortgage may escalate (increase) or de-escalate (decrease) during the time of the loan. The rate of adjustable-rate mortgages depends on the prime lending rate of most banks.

Several government agencies insure that first mortgage loans will be repaid. Loans with this insurance include those made under the Federal Housing Administration (FHA) and the Veterans Administration (VA). These loans may be obtained through a savings and loan institution, a bank, or a mortgage lending company and are insured by a government program.

Interest paid on home loans is an allowable deduction on personal federal income tax under certain conditions. For this reason, many homeowners choose to borrow money for home improvements, college education, and the like, by making a home equity loan. This type of loan is a **second mortgage** and is made against the equity in the home. In the case of a loan default, the second mortgage lender has rights to the proceeds of the sale of the home *after* the first mortgage has been paid.

 ### The Monthly Mortgage Payment and Total Interest

The repayment of the loan in equal installments that are applied to principal and interest over a specific period of time is called the *amortization* of a loan. To calculate the monthly mortgage payment, it is customary to use an amortization table, a business or financial calculator that has this chart programmed into the calculator, or computer software. The amortization chart or schedule gives the factor that is multiplied by the dollar amount of the loan in thousands to give the total monthly payment including principal and interest. A portion of an amortization table is shown in Table 12–2.

Table 12–2 Monthly Payment per $1,000 of Amount Financed

Years Financed	Annual Interest Rate							
	8%	$8\frac{1}{2}$%	9%	$9\frac{1}{2}$%	10%	$10\frac{1}{2}$%	11%	$11\frac{1}{2}$%
10	12.14	12.40	12.67	12.94	13.22	13.50	13.78	14.06
12	10.83	11.11	11.39	11.67	11.96	12.25	12.54	12.84
15	9.56	9.85	10.15	10.45	10.75	11.06	11.37	11.69
17	8.99	9.29	9.59	9.90	10.22	10.54	10.86	11.19
20	8.37	8.68	9.00	9.33	9.66	9.99	10.33	10.67
22	8.07	8.39	8.72	9.05	9.39	9.73	10.08	10.43
25	7.72	8.06	8.40	8.74	9.09	9.45	9.81	10.17
30	7.34	7.69	8.05	8.41	8.78	9.15	9.53	9.91
35	7.11	7.47	7.84	8.22	8.60	8.99	9.37	9.77

Table 12–2 (continued)

Years Financed	Annual Interest Rate								
	12%	12½%	13%	13½%	14%	14½%	15%	15½%	16%
10	14.35	14.64	14.94	15.23	15.53	15.83	16.14	16.45	16.76
12	13.14	13.44	13.75	14.06	14.38	14.69	15.01	15.34	15.66
15	12.01	12.33	12.66	12.99	13.32	13.66	14.00	14.34	14.69
17	11.52	11.85	12.19	12.53	12.88	13.23	13.58	13.94	14.30
20	11.02	11.37	11.72	12.08	12.44	12.80	13.17	13.54	13.92
22	10.78	11.14	11.51	11.87	12.24	12.62	12.99	13.37	13.75
25	10.54	10.91	11.28	11.66	12.04	12.43	12.81	13.20	13.59
30	10.29	10.68	11.07	11.46	11.85	12.25	12.65	13.05	13.45
35	10.16	10.56	10.96	11.36	11.76	12.17	12.57	12.98	13.39

(?) HOW TO — **Find the Monthly Mortgage Payment Using a per-$1,000 Monthly Payment Table**

Step 1 Find the amount financed: Subtract the down payment from the purchase price.

Step 2 Find the $1,000-units of amount financed: Divide the amount financed (from step 1) by $1,000.

Step 3 Locate the table value for the number of years financed and the annual interest rate.

Step 4 Multiply the table value from step 3 by the $1,000-units from step 2.

$$\text{Monthly mortgage payment} = \frac{\text{amount financed}}{\$1,000} \times \text{table value}$$

Example 1 Lunelle Miller is purchasing a home for $87,000. Home Federal Savings and Loan has approved her loan application for a 30-year fixed-rate loan at 10% annual interest. If Lunelle agrees to pay 20% of the purchase price as a down payment, calculate the monthly payment.

The down payment is

$87,000 × 0.20 = $17,400

Calculate the amount to be financed.

$87,000 − $17,400 = $69,600

Determine how many thousands of dollars will be financed.

$69,600 ÷ $1,000 = 69.6

Use Table 12–2 to find the factor for financing a loan for 30 years with a 10% interest rate. This factor is 8.78.

Multiply the number of thousands times the factor.

69.6 × $8.78 = $611.09

The monthly payment of $611.09 includes the principal and interest.

Many times a person wants to know the total amount of interest that will be paid during the entire loan.

 **HOW TO** | **Find the Total Interest**

Step 1 Find the total of the payments: Multiply the number of payments by the amount of payment.

Step 2 Subtract the amount financed from the total of the payments.

Total interest = number of payments × amount of payment − amount financed

Example 2 Calculate the total interest paid on the loan in Example 1.

Total interest = number of payments × amount of payment − amount financed

$$= 30 \times 12 \times \$611.09 - \$69,600$$

$$= \$219,992.40 - \$69,600$$

$$= \$150,392.40$$

The total interest is $150,392.40.

The two examples show how to calculate the monthly payment and the total interest for a mortgage loan. There are other costs associated with purchasing a home. Lending companies require the borrower to pay *points* at the time the loan is made or closed. Payment of points is a one-time payment of a percent of the loan that is an additional cost of making the mortgage. One point is 1%, two points is 2%, and so on.

Other costs related to buying a home may include attorney fees, sales commissions, taxes, and insurance. Since the lending agency must be assured that the property taxes and insurance are paid on the property, the annual costs of these items may be pro-rated each year and added for that year to the monthly payment. These funds are held in escrow until the taxes or insurance payment is due, at which time the lending agency makes the payment for the home owner. These additional costs make the monthly payment more than just the principal and interest payment we found in Example 1.

Example 3 If the annual insurance premium for Lunelle's home is $923 and the annual tax on the property is $950, find the adjusted monthly payment that includes principal, interest, tax, and insurance.

$923 + $950 = $1,873   **Annual taxes and insurance needed in escrow**

$1,873 ÷ 12 = $156.08   **Monthly payment for taxes and insurance**

$611.09 + $156.08 = $767.17   **Adjusted monthly payment**

The adjusted monthly payment is $767.17.

Example 4 Qua Wau is trying to determine whether to accept a 25-year 9% mortgage or a 20-year 9% mortgage on the house he is planning to buy. He needs to finance $125,700 and has planned to budget $1,250 monthly for his payment of principal and interest. Which mortgage should Qua choose?

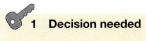

1 Decision needed | Which mortgage should Qua choose?

2 Unknown facts | Monthly payment and total cost for 25-year mortgage, and monthly payment and total cost for 20-year mortgage.

<table>
<tr><td>**3   Known facts**</td><td>Amount financed: $125,700</td></tr>
</table>

3 Known facts	Amount financed: $125,700
	Annual interest rate: 9%
	Monthly budget allowance: $1,250
4 Relationships	Total cost = monthly payment × 12 × years financed
	Number of $1,000-units of amount financed = amount financed ÷ $1,000
	Monthly payment = number of $1,000-units of amount financed × table value
5 Estimation	Since the 20-year mortgage is for less time, but the same interest rate as the 25-year loan, the total cost of the 20-year mortgage is less than the total cost of the 25-year mortgage.
6 Calculations	Number of $1,000-units financed = $125,700 ÷ $1,000

$$= 125.7$$

25-year Mortgage
The Table 12–2 value for 25 years and 9% is 8.40.

Monthly payment = number of $1,000-units financed × table value
$$= 125.7 \times 8.40$$
$$= \$1,055.88$$

Total cost = monthly payment × 12 × years financed
$$= \$1,055.88 \times 12 \times 25$$
$$= \$316,764$$

20-year Mortgage
The Table 12–2 value for 20 years and 9% is 9.00.

Monthly payment = number of $1,000-units financed × table value
$$= 125.7 \times 9.00$$
$$= \$1,131.50$$

Total cost = monthly payment × 12 × years financed
$$= \$1,131.50 \times 12 \times 20$$
$$= \$271,512$$

7   Decision made

Qua's budget of $1,250 monthly can cover either monthly payment. He would save $45,252 over the 20-year period if he chooses the 20-year plan. That is the plan he should choose. Other considerations that could impact his decision would be the return on an investment of the difference in the monthly payments if an annuity was started with the difference.

 The Amortization Schedule

Homeowners are often given an amortization schedule that shows the amount of principal and interest for each payment of the loan. With some loan arrangements, extra amounts paid with the monthly payment are credited against the principal, allowing for the mortgage to be paid sooner.

 HOW TO   **Complete a Monthly Amortization Schedule**

Step 1   For the first month:
   a) Find the interest portion of the first monthly payment: Multiply the original principal by the monthly interest rate.

Interest portion of the first monthly payment = original principal
× monthly interest rate

b) Find the principal portion of the monthly payment: Subtract the interest portion of the first monthly payment (from step 1a) from the monthly payment (not including taxes or insurance).

Principal portion of the first monthly payment = monthly payment
− interest portion of the first monthly payment

c) Find the first end-of-month principal: Subtract the principal portion of the first monthly payment (from step 1b) from the original principal.

First end-of-month principal = original principal
− principal portion of the first monthly payment

Step 2 For each remaining month in turn:

a) Find the interest portion of the monthly payment: Multiply the previous end-of-month principal by the monthly interest rate.

Interest portion of the monthly payment
= previous end-of-month principal × monthly interest rate

b) Find the principal portion of the monthly payment: Subtract the interest portion of the monthly payment (from step 2a) from the monthly payment (not including taxes or insurance).

Principal portion of the monthly payment = monthly payment
− interest portion of the monthly payment

c) Find the end-of-month principal: Subtract the principal portion of the monthly payment (from step 2b) from the previous end-of-month principal.

End-of-month principal = previous end-of-month principal
− principal portion of the monthly payment

Example 5 Complete the first two rows of the amortization schedule for Lunelle's mortgage.

First month

Interest = original principal × monthly rate

$$= \$69{,}600 \times \frac{0.1}{12}$$

$$= \$580.00$$

Principal portion of monthly payment = monthly payment (without insurance and taxes) − interest portion of monthly payment

$$= \$611.09 - \$580.00$$

$$= \$31.09$$

End-of-month principal = previous end-of-month principal − principal portion of monthly payment

$$= \$69{,}600 - \$31.09$$

$$= \$69{,}568.91$$

Key Interest Rates at a Glance

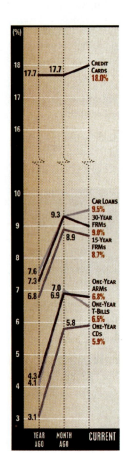

The table at left is a comparison of interest rates for April, 1995.

1. What do FRMs and ARMs stand for?

2. Describe the trend in interest rates from a year ago to a month ago, according to the graph.

3. Describe the trend in interest rates from a month ago to current, according to the graph.

4. According to the data in the table, would you have been better off buying a car one year ago or today, assuming you needed a loan to purchase the car? Explain.

Reprinted from the April 1995 issue of MONEY by special permission; copyright 1995, Time Inc.

Second month

$$\text{Interest portion} = \$69,568.91 \times \frac{0.1}{12}$$

$$= \$579.74$$

$$\text{Principal portion of monthly payment} = \$611.09 - \$579.74$$

$$= \$31.35$$

$$\text{End-of-month principal} = \$69,568.91 - \$31.35$$

$$= \$69,537.56$$

The first two rows of an amortization schedule for this loan are shown in the chart.

	Portion of Payment Applied to:		
Month	Interest [Previous End-of-Month Principal × Monthly Rate]	Principal [Monthly Payment − Interest Portion]	End-of-Month Principal [Previous End-of Month Principal − Principal Portion]
1	$580.00	$31.09	$69,568.91
2	$579.74	$31.35	$69,537.56

Computers are normally used to generate an amortization schedule that shows the interest and principal breakdown for each payment of the loan.

Self-Check 12.5

 1. Find the down payment and amount financed for a home that sells for $67,000. The down payment must be 15% of the selling price.

2. Find the monthly payment for the mortgage in Exercise 1 if it is financed for 25 years at $8\frac{1}{2}\%$.

3. Find the total interest for the mortgage in Exercise 1.

4. Stephen Black has just purchased a home for $155,000. Northridge Mortgage Company has approved his loan application for a 25-year fixed-rate loan at $9\frac{1}{2}\%$. Stephen has agreed to pay 18% of the purchase price as a down payment. Calculate the down payment, amount of mortgage, and monthly payment.

5. Find the total interest Stephen will pay if he pays the loan on schedule.

6. If Stephen Black could budget an additional $100 for housing could he reduce the number of years required to repay the loan to 20 years?

7. If Stephen made the loan for 20 years, how much interest would he save?

8. Make an amortization schedule for the first three months of Stephen's 25-year loan.

9. Calculate the interest paid and principal paid for the first two months of Stephen's loan if the loan is a 20-year loan, and find the principal owed at the end of the second month.

10. Justin Wimmer is financing $69,700 for a home at 8.5% interest with a 20-year fixed-rate loan. Calculate the interest paid and principal paid for the first two months of the loan, and find the principal owed at the end of the second month.

11. Heike Drechsler is financing $84,700 for a home in the mountains. The 17-year fixed-rate loan has an interest rate of 9%. Calculate the interest paid and principal paid for the first two months and the principal owed at the end of the second month.

12. Conchita Martinez has made a $210,300 loan for a home near Albany, New York. Her 20-year fixed-rate loan has an interest rate of $8\frac{1}{2}\%$. Calculate the principal paid and interest paid for the first two months of the loan, and find the principal owed at the end of the second month.

SELF-CHECK SOLUTIONS

Self-Check 12.1

1. $6 \times \$108.20 + 100 = \$749.20$ **2.** $\$579 - \$125 = \$454$ **3.** $12 \times \$106.32 + \$100 = \$1,375.84$

4. $18 \times \$97.42 + \$80 = \$1,833.56$ **5.** $8 \times \$82.56 + \$100 = \$760.48$ **6.** $\$2590 \times 24\% \times 1 = \$621.60$

$$\frac{\$621.60 + 2,590}{12} = \$267.63$$

7. $\dfrac{\$929 - \$100}{12} = \$69.08$ **8.** $\dfrac{\$625 - \$75}{18} = \$30.56$ **9.** $\dfrac{\$2,357 - \$250}{24} = \$87.79$

10. Finance charge $= \$3,780 \times 0.13 = \$491.40$

Installment price $= \$3,780 + \$491.40 = \$4,271.40$

Monthly payment $= \dfrac{\$4,271.40}{36} = \$118.65$

Self-Check 12.2

1. $\dfrac{\overset{4}{\cancel{8}}(\overset{1}{\cancel{9}})}{\underset{1}{\cancel{18}}(19)} = \dfrac{4}{19}$

2. $18 - 6 = 6$ months remaining

$\dfrac{\overset{1}{\cancel{6}}(7)}{\underset{3}{\cancel{18}}(19)} = \dfrac{7}{57}$

$\dfrac{7}{57} \times \$205 = \$25.18$

3. $48 - 28 = 20$ months remaining

$\dfrac{\overset{5}{\cancel{20}}(\overset{\cancel{7}}{\cancel{21}})}{\underset{\overset{\cancel{12}}{4}}{\cancel{48}}(\cancel{49})} = \dfrac{5}{28}$

4. $48 - 20 = 28$ months remaining

$\dfrac{\overset{1}{\cancel{7}}}{\cancel{28}(29)}{\underset{12}{\cancel{48}}(\cancel{49})} = \dfrac{29}{84}$

$\dfrac{29}{84} \times \$1,645 = \$567.92$

5. 15 months remaining

$\dfrac{\overset{5}{\cancel{15}}(\overset{8}{\cancel{16}})}{\underset{\overset{\cancel{14}}{7}}{\cancel{42}}(43)} = \dfrac{40}{301}$

$\dfrac{40}{301} \times \$2,397 = \$318.54$

Self-Check 12.3

1. $\$275.69 \times 0.023 = \$6.34$

2. $\$176.95 \times 0.016 = \$2.83$

$\$176.95 + \$2.83 - \$45$

$= \$134.78$

3. $\$3,805 \times 0.012 = \$45.66$

4. $3,805 + $45.66 + $4,983 - $7,000 = $1,833.66   **5.** $1,833.66 × 0.012 = $22.00
$1,833.66 + $22.00 + $75.00 - $500.00 = $1,430.66

6.   March 1–5: 5 × $128.50 = $642.50   **7.** $121.64 × 0.018 = $2.19
$128.50 - $20 = $108.50
March 6–19: 14 × $108.50 = $1,519.00
$108.50 + $25.60 = $134.10

March 20–31: 12 × $134.10 = $1,609.20
$642.50 + $1,519.00 + $1,609.20 = $3,770.70
$3,770.70 ÷ 31 = $121.64

8.

Date	Unpaid Balance	Number of Days	Total
May 4–May 6	$283.57	3	$850.71
May 7–May 11	$303.30	5	$1,516.50
May 12–May 17	$357.12	6	$2,142.72
May 18–May 28	$157.12	11	$1,728.32
May 29–June 3	$272.30	6	$1,633.80
31 days in cycle		31	$7,872.05

Average daily balance $= \dfrac{\$7,872.05}{31} = \$253.94$

9. Finance charge = $253.94 × 0.0142 = $3.61   **10.** $272.30 + $3.61 = $275.91

Self-Check 12.4

1. $\dfrac{2 \times 12 \times \$265}{\$1,500 \times (24 + 1)} = 17.0\%$ **2.** APR $= \dfrac{2 \times 12 \times \$518}{\$3,800 \times (36 + 1)} = 0.088 \text{ or } 8.8\%$

3. APR $= \dfrac{2 \times 12 \times \$412}{\$2,750 \times (18 + 1)} = 0.189 \text{ or } 18.9\%$ **4.** APR $= \dfrac{2 \times 12 \times \$1,215}{\$5,800 \times (30 + 1)} = 0.162 \text{ or } 16.2\%$

5. APR $= \dfrac{2 \times 12 \times \$698}{\$3,715 \times (24 + 1)} = 0.180 \text{ or } 18.0\%$ **6.** $\dfrac{\$1,025 \times \$100}{\$5,600} = \$18.30$

In the row for 36 months, move across to 18.29 (nearest to $18.30). The APR at the top of this column is 11.25%.

7. $\dfrac{\$90 \times \$100}{\$780} = \$11.54$

In the row for 12 months, move
across to 11.59 (nearest to 11.54).
The APR at the top of this column
is 20.75%.

8. $\dfrac{\$412 \times \$100}{\$2,750} = \$14.98$

In the row for 18 months, move across to 15.07
(nearest to 14.98). The APR at the top of this
column is 18.25%. Compare with 18.9% using
the formula.

9. $\dfrac{\$1,215 \times \$100}{\$5,800} = \$20.95$

In the row for 30 months, move across
to 20.90 (nearest to 20.95). The APR
at the top of this column is 15.25%.
Compare with 16.2% using the formula.

10. $\dfrac{\$698 \times \$100}{\$3,715} = \$18.79$

In the row for 24 months, move across
to 18.66 (nearest to 18.79). The APR
at the top of this column is 17.00%.
Compare with 18.0% using the formula.

11. The APR using the table value seems to be
consistently lower than the APR found by
using the formula.

1. Down payment = $67,000 \times 0.15 = \$10,050$
Amount financed = $\$67,000 - \$10,050 = \$56,950$

2. $\$56,950 \div \$1,000 = 56.95$
The Table 12–2 value for 25 years and $8\frac{1}{2}\%$ is 8.06.
Monthly payment = $56.95 \times \$8.06 = \$459.02$

3. Amount paid = $\$459.02 \times 12 \times 25 = \$137,706$
Total interest = $\$137,706 - \$56,950 = \$80,756$

4. Down payment = $\$155,000 \times 0.18 = \$27,900$
Amount of mortgage = $\$155,000 - \$27,900 = \$127,100$
The Table 12–2 value for 25 years and $9\frac{1}{2}\%$ is 8.74.
$\$127,100 \div \$1,000 = 127.1$
Monthly payment = $127.1 \times \$8.74 = \$1,110.85$

5. Total paid = $\$1,110.85 \times 12 \times 25 = \$333,255.00$
Interest paid = $\$333,255.00 - \$127,100 = \$206,155$

6. The Table 12–2 value for 20 years and $9\frac{1}{2}\%$ is 9.33.
$\$127,100 \div 1,000 = 127.1$
Monthly payment = $127.1 \times \$9.33 = \$1,185.84$
This monthly payment is only $74.99 more than the monthly payment for the 25-year loan. So, he could reduce the number of years required to repay the loan to 20 years.

7. Total paid = $\$1,185.84 \times 12 \times 20 = \$284,601.60$
Interest paid = $\$284,601.60 - \$127,100 = \$157,501.60$
Interest savings = $\$206,155.00 - \$157,501.60 = \$48,653.40$

8. *Month 1*

Interest portion of payment = $\$127,100 \times \dfrac{0.095}{12}$

$= \$1,006.21$

Principal portion of payment = $\$1,110.85 - \$1,006.21 = \$104.64$
End-of-month principal $\$127,100 - \$104.64 = \$126,995.36$
Month 2

Interest portion of payment = $\$126,995.36 \times \dfrac{0.095}{12}$

$= \$1,005.38$

Principal portion of payment = $\$1,110.85 - \$1,005.38 = \$105.47$
End-of-month principal = $\$126,995.36 - \$105.47 = \$126,889.89$
Month 3

Interest portion of payment = $\$126,889.89 \times \dfrac{0.095}{12}$

$= \$1,004.54$

Principal portion of payment = $\$1,110.85 - \$1,004.54 = \$106.31$
End-of-month principal = $\$126,889.89 - \$106.31 = \$126,783.58$

Month	Portion of Payment Applied to:		End-of-Month Principal
	Interest	Principal	
1	1,006.21	104.64	126,995.36
2	1,005.38	105.47	126,889.89
3	1,004.54	106.31	126,783.58

9. *Month 1*

Interest portion of payment = $\$127,100 \times \dfrac{0.095}{12}$

$= \$1,006.21$

Principal portion of payment = $\$1,185.84 - \$1,006.21 = \$179.63$
End-of-month principal = $\$127,100 - \$179.63 = \$126,920.37$

Month 2

$$\text{Interest portion of payment} = \$126,920.37 \times \frac{0.095}{12}$$
$$= \$1,004.79$$

Principal portion of payment = $1,185.84 − $1,004.79 = $181.05
End-of-month principal = $126,920.37 − $181.05 = $126,739.32

10. Find the monthly payment.

20 years at $8\frac{1}{2}$% gives a Table 12–2 value of 8.68.
$69,700 ÷ $1000 = 69.7
Monthly payment = 69.7 × $8.68 = $605.00
Month 1

$$\text{Interest portion of payment} = \$69,700 \times \frac{0.085}{12}$$
$$= \$493.71$$

Principal portion of payment = $605.00 − $493.71 = $111.29
End-of-month principal = $69,700 − $111.29 = $69,588.71
Month 2

$$\text{Interest portion of payment} = \$69,588.71 \times \frac{0.085}{12}$$
$$= \$492.92$$

Principal portion of payment = $605.00 − $492.92 = $112.08
End-of-month principal = $69,588.71 − $112.08 = $69,476.63

11. Find the monthly payment.

17 years at 9% gives a Table 12–2 value of 9.59.
$84,700 ÷ $1,000 = 84.7
Monthly payment = 84.7 × $9.59 = $812.27
Month 1

$$\text{Interest portion of payment} = \$84,700 \times \frac{0.09}{12}$$
$$= \$635.25$$

Principal portion of payment = $812.27 − $635.25 = $177.02
End-of-month principal = $84,700 − $177.02 = $84,522.98
Month 2

$$\text{Interest portion of payment} = \$84,522.98 \times \frac{0.09}{12}$$
$$= \$633.92$$

Principal portion of payment = $812.27 − $633.92 = $178.35
End-of-month principal = $84,522.98 − $178.35 = $84,344.63

12. Find the monthly payment.

20 years at $8\frac{1}{2}$% gives a Table 12–2 value of 8.68.
$210,300 ÷ $1,000 = 210.3
Monthly payment = 210.3 × 8.68 = $1,825.40
Month 1

$$\text{Interest portion of payment} = \$210,300 \times \frac{0.085}{12}$$
$$= \$1,489.63$$

Principal portion of payment = $1,825.40 − $1,489.63 = $335.77
End-of-month principal = $210,300 − $335.77 = $209,964.23
Month 2

$$\text{Interest portion of payment} = \$209,964.23 \times \frac{0.085}{12}$$
$$= \$1,487.25$$

Principal portion of payment = $1,825.40 − $1,487.25 = $338.15
End-of-month principal = $209,964.23 − $338.15 = $209,626.08

Section—Objective	Important Points with Examples

12.1 — 1 (page 391)

Find the installment price given the installment payment

Step 1 Find the total of the installment payments: Multiply the number of installment payments by the installment payment.

Total of installment payments = number of installment payments

× installment payment

Step 2 Add the down payment to the total of the installment payments.

Installment price = total of installment payments + down payment

> Find the installment price of a computer that is paid for in 24 monthly payments of $113 if a down payment of $50 is made.
>
> $$(24 \times \$113) + \$50 = \$2,712 + \$50 = \$2,762$$

12.1 — 2 (page 391)

Find the installment payment given the installment price

Step 1 Find the total of the installment payments: Subtract the down payment from the installment price.

Total of installment payments = installment price − down payment

Step 2 Divide the total of installment payments by the number of installment payments.

$$\text{Installment payments} = \frac{\text{total of installment payments}}{\text{number of payments}}$$

> Find the monthly payment on a computer if the cash price is $3,285. A 14% interest rate is charged on the cash price, and there are 12 monthly payments.
>
> $$\$3,285 \times 0.14 \times 1 = \$459.90$$
>
> Installment price = $3,285 + $459.90 = $3,744.90
>
> $$\text{Monthly payment} = \frac{\$3,744.90}{12} = \$312.08$$
>
> A computer has an installment price of $2,187.25 when financed over 18 months. If a $100 down payment is made, find the monthly payment.
>
> $$\$2,187.25 - \$100 = \$2,087.25$$
>
> $$\frac{\$2,087.25}{18} = \$115.96$$

12.2 — 1 (page 394)

Find the interest refund using the rule of 78

Find the interest refund using the rule of 78. **Step 1** Find the period sequence numbers: Number the periods of the loan, so that the last period is 1, the next to the last is 2, and so on. **Step 2** Find the denominator of the refund fraction: Add the sequence numbers of all the periods. **Step 3** Find the numerator of the refund fraction: Add the sequence numbers of the periods for which an interest refund is due. **Step 4** Multiply the total interest by the refund fraction.

Interest refund = total interest × refund fraction

Find the interest refund on a loan that has a total finance charge of $892 and was made for 24 months. The loan is paid in full with ten months (payments) remaining.

$$\text{Refund fraction} = \frac{\text{sum of sequence numbers of periods remaining}}{\text{sum of all period sequence numbers}}$$

$$= \frac{\text{sum of 1--10}}{\text{sum of 1--24}}$$

$$= \frac{55}{300} = \frac{11}{60}$$

$$\text{Refund} = \$892 \times \frac{11}{60} = \$163.53$$

Find the sum of consecutive numbers beginning with 1   Multiply the largest number by 1 more than the largest number, and divide the product by 2.

$$\text{Sum of consecutive numbers} = \frac{\text{largest number(largest number} + 1)}{2}$$

Find the interest refund on a loan with 10 payments remaining out of 24 payments if the total interest was $892.

$$\text{Refund} = \text{total interest} \times \frac{\text{sum of 1--10}}{\text{sum of 1--24}}$$

$$\text{Sum of 1--10} = \frac{10(11)}{2} = 55$$

$$\text{Sum of 1--24} = \frac{24(25)}{2} = 300$$

$$\text{Refund} = \$892 \times \frac{11}{60}$$

$$= \$163.53$$

12.3 — 1 (page 398)

Find the unpaid balance using the unpaid balance method

Step 1 Find the interest for the previous monthly period: Multiply the unpaid balance as of the first day of the previous monthly period by the monthly interest rate.

$$\text{Interest} = \text{unpaid balance} \times \text{monthly interest rate}$$

Step 2 Find the total purchases and cash advances during the previous monthly period: Add all purchases or cash advances charged to the account during the previous monthly period. **Step 3** Find the total payments for the previous monthly period: Add all payments credited to the account during the previous monthly period. **Step 4** To the unpaid balance at the beginning of the previous monthly period, add the interest for the previous monthly period from step 1, and add the total purchases and cash advances from step 2. Then, subtract the total payments from step 3.

Unpaid balance at the beginning of the monthly period
= unpaid balance at the beginning of previous monthly period
+ interest for previous monthly period
+ total purchases and cash advances during previous monthly period
− total payments during previous monthly period

> A charge account has an unpaid balance of $1,384.37 and the monthly interest rate is 1.75%. Find the interest.
>
> $$\$1,384.37 \times 0.0175 = \$24.23$$

To this account these transactions were made during the month: purchases of $23.85, $41.18, and $123.74; cash advance of $100.00; payment of $200.00. Find the unpaid balance.

$$\text{total purchase: } \$23.85 + \$41.18 + \$123.74 = \$188.77$$

$$\$1,384.37 + \$24.23 + \$188.77 + \$100.00 - \$200.00 = \$1,497.37$$

12.3 — 2 (page 400)

Find the average daily balance

Step 1 Find the daily unpaid balance for each day in the monthly period. **(a)** Find the total purchases and cash advances for the day: Add all the purchases and cash advances charged to the account during the day. **(b)** Find the total payments for the day: Add all the payments credited to the account during the day. **(c)** To the previous daily unpaid balance, add the total purchases and cash advances for the day (from step 1a). Then subtract the total payments for the day (from step 1b).

Daily unpaid balance = previous daily unpaid balance
+ total purchases and cash advances for the day − total payments for the day

Step 2 Add the unpaid balances from step 1 for each day, and divide the sum by the number of days in the monthly period.

$$\text{Average daily balance} = \frac{\text{sum of daily unpaid balances}}{\text{number of days in monthly period}}$$

> A credit card has a balance of $398.42 on September 14, the first day of the billing cycle. A charge of $182.37 is posted to the account on September 16. Another charge of $82.21 is posted to the account on September 25. The amount of a returned item ($19.98) is posted to the account on October 10 and a payment of $500 is made on October 12. The billing period ends on October 13. Find the average daily balance and finance charge if a monthly rate of 1.3% is assessed.
>
> | Date | Daily Unpaid Balance | Number of Days | Partial Sum |
> |---|---|---|---|
> | September 14–15 | $398.42 | 2 days | $ 796.84 |
> | September 16–24 | $580.79 | 9 days | $ 5,227.11 |
> | September 25–October 9 | $663.00 | 15 days | $ 9,945.00 |
> | October 10–11 | $643.02 | 2 days | $ 1,286.04 |
> | October 12–13 | $143.03 | 2 days | $ 286.06 |
> | | Total | 30 days | $17,543.07 |
>
> Average daily balance = $17,543.07 ÷ 30 = $584.77
> Finance charge = $584.77 × 0.013 = $7.60

12.4 — 1 (page 403)

Estimate the annual percentage rate using the constant ratio formula

Step 1 Substitute known values into the formula. **Step 2** Solve the formula for the unknown.

Approximate annual percentage rate

$$= \frac{2 \times \text{number of payments per year} \times \text{total interest}}{\text{amount financed} \times (\text{number of payments} + 1)}$$

Estimate the annual percentage rate for a loan of $13,850 that is repaid in 42 monthly installments. The interest for the loan is $2,382.20.

$$\text{Approximate APR} = \frac{2(12)(\$2,382.20)}{\$13,850(43)}$$

$$= 0.096 = 9.6\%$$

12.4 — 2 (page 404)

Find the annual percentage rate using a per $100 of amount financed table

Step 1 Find the interest per $100 of amount financed: Multiply the total finance charge by $100 and divide by the amount financed.

$$\text{Interest per \$100} = \frac{\text{total finance charge} \times \$100}{\text{amount financed}}$$

Step 2 Find the row corresponding to the number of monthly payments. Move across the row to find the number closest to the value from step 1. Read up the column to find the annual percentage rate for that column.

Find the annual percentage rate on a loan of $500 that is repaid in 36 monthly installments. The interest for the loan is $95.

$$\text{Interest per \$100} = \frac{\$95 \times \$100}{\$500} = \$19$$

In the row for 36 months, move across to 19.14 (nearest to 19). APR is at the top of the column, 11.75%.

12.5 — 1 (page 409)

Find the monthly mortgage payment and total interest

Find the monthly mortgage payment using a per $1,000 monthly payment table
Step 1 Find the amount financed: Subtract the down payment from the purchase price.
Step 2 Find the $1,000-units of amount financed: Divide the amount financed (from step 1) by $1,000. **Step 3** Locate the table value for the number of years financed and the annual interest rate. **Step 4** Multiply the table value from step 3 by the $1,000-units from step 2.

$$\text{Monthly mortgage payment} = \frac{\text{amount financed}}{\$1,000} \times \text{table value}$$

Find the total interest. Step 1 Find the total of the payments: Multiply the number of payments by the payment. **Step 2** Subtract the amount financed from the total of the payments.

$$\text{Total interest} = \text{number of payments} \times \text{payment} - \text{amount financed}$$

Find the monthly payment and the total interest for a home selling for $90,000 if a 10% down payment is made, payments are made for 30 years, and the annual interest rate is $10\frac{1}{2}\%$.

$$\$90,000 \times 0.1 = \$9,000 \text{ down payment}$$

$$\$90,000 - \$9,000 = \$81,000 \text{ mortgage amount}$$

$$\$81,000 \div \$1,000 = 81 \text{ \$1,000-units}$$

The table value for 30 years and $10\frac{1}{2}\%$ is 9.15

$$\text{Payment} = 81 \times \$9.15 = \$741.15$$

$$\text{Total interest} = \$741.15 \times 30 \times 12 - \$81,000 = \$266,814 - \$81,000$$

$$= \$185,814$$

12.5 — **2** (page 412)

Complete a monthly amortization schedule

Step 1 For the first month: **(a)** Find the interest portion of the first monthly payment: Multiply the original principal by the monthly interest rate.

Interest portion of the first monthly payment = original principal
$\times$ monthly interest rate

(b) Find the principal portion of the monthly payment: Subtract the interest portion of the first monthly payment (from step 1a) from the monthly payment (not including taxes or insurance).

Principal portion of the first monthly payment = monthly payment
− interest portion of first monthly payment

(c) Find the first end-of-month principal: Subtract the principal portion of the first monthly payment (from step 1b) from the original principal.

First end-of-month principal = original principal
− principal portion of the first monthly payment

Step 2 For each remaining month in turn: **(a)** Find the interest portion of the monthly payment: Multiply the previous end-of-month principal by the monthly interest rate.

Interest portion of the monthly payment = previous end-of-month principal
$\times$ monthly interest rate

(b) Find the principal portion of the monthly payment: Subtract the interest portion of the monthly payment (from step 2a) from the monthly payment (not including taxes or insurance).

Principal portion of the monthly payment = monthly payment
− interest portion of the monthly payment

(c) Find the end-of-month principal: Subtract the principal portion of the monthly payment (from step 2b) from the previous end-of-month principal.

End-of-month principal = previous end-of-month principal
− principal portion of the monthly payment

Complete an amortization schedule for three months of payments on a $90,000 mortgage at 8% for 30 years.

$$\text{Monthly payment} = \frac{\$90,000}{\$1,000} \times \text{table value}$$

$$= 90 \times 7.34$$

$$= \$660.60$$

Month 1

$$\text{Interest portion} = \$90,000 \times \frac{0.08}{12}$$

$$= \$600$$

$$\text{Principal portion} = \$660.60 - 600$$

$$= \$60.60$$

$$\text{End-of-month principal} = \$90,000 - \$60.60$$

$$= \$89,939.40$$

Month 2

$$\text{Interest portion} = \$89{,}939.40 \times \frac{0.08}{12}$$

$$= \$599.60$$

$$\text{Principal portion} = \$660.60 - \$599.60$$

$$= \$61.00$$

$$\text{End-of-month principal} = \$89{,}939.40 - \$61.00$$

$$= \$89{,}878.40$$

Month 3

$$\text{Interest portion} = \$89{,}878.40 \times \frac{.08}{12}$$

$$= \$599.19$$

$$\text{Principal portion} = \$660.60 - \$599.19$$

$$= \$61.41$$

$$\text{End-of-month principal} = \$89{,}878.40 - \$61.41$$

$$= \$89{,}816.99$$

Month	Portion of Payment Applied to		End-of-Month Principal
	Interest	Principal	
1	$600	$60.60	$89,939.40
2	$599.60	$61.00	$89,878.40
3	$599.19	$61.41	$89,816.99

CHAPTER 12 REVIEW

Section 12.1

1. Find the installment price of a pentium computer system bought on the installment plan with $250 down and 12 payments of $111.33.

2. A television set has been purchased on the installment plan with a down payment of $120 and six monthly payments of $98.50. Find the installment price of the television set.

3. Find the monthly payment on a water bed if the installment price is $1,050, the down payment is $200, and there are ten monthly payments.

4. A dishwasher sold for a $983 installment price with a down payment of $150 and 12 monthly payments. How much is each payment?

5. If the cash price of a refrigerator is $879 and a down payment of $150 is made, how much is to be financed?

6. What is the cash price of a chair if the installment price is $679, the finance charge is $102, and there was no down payment?

Use the rule of 78 to find the finance charge refund in each of the following.

	Finance Charge	Number of Monthly Payments	Remaining Payments	Interest Refund
7.	$ 238	12	4	
8.	$1,076	18	6	
9.	$2,175	24	10	
10.	$ 476	12	5	
11.	$ 896	18	4	
12.	$ 683	15	11	

Use the rule of 78 to solve the following problems.

13. The finance charge on a computer was $1,778. The loan for the computer was to be paid in 18 monthly payments. Find the finance charge refund if it is paid off in eight months.

14. Find the refund fraction on a 48-month loan if it is paid off after 20 months.

15. Becky Whitehead has a loan with $1,115 in finance charges, which she paid in full after 8 of the 18 monthly payments. What is her finance charge refund?

16. Lanny Jacobs made a loan to purchase a computer. Find the refund due on this loan with charges of $657 if it is paid off after paying 7 of the 12 monthly payments.

17. Alice Dubois charged $455 in finance charges on a loan for 15 months. Find the finance charge refund if she pays off the loan in full after ten payments.

18. Suppose you have borrowed money that is being repaid at $45 a month for 12 months. What is the finance charge refund after making eight payments if the finance charge is $105?

19. Find the finance charge refund on a 15-month loan with monthly payments of $103.50 if you decide to pay off the loan at the end of the tenth month. The finance charge is $215.55.

20. You have purchased a new stereo on the installment plan. The plan calls for 12 monthly payments of $45 and a $115 finance charge. After 9 months you decide to pay off the loan. How much is the refund?

21. If you purchase a fishing boat for 18 monthly payments of $106 and an interest charge of $238, how much is the refund after 10 payments?

22. The interest for an automobile loan is $2,843. The automobile is financed for 36 monthly payments and interest refunds are made using the rule of 78. How much interest should be refunded if the loan is paid in full with 22 months still remaining?

23. Find the interest on an unpaid balance of $265 with an interest rate of $1\frac{1}{2}\%$.

24. Find the finance charge on $371 if the interest charged is 1.4% of the unpaid balance.

25. Find the finance charge on a credit card with an unpaid balance of $465 if the rate charged is 1.25%.

26. Find the new unpaid balance on an account with a previous balance of $263.50, purchases of $38.75, a payment of $35, and a finance charge of 1.5% of the unpaid balance.

27. Find the new unpaid balance on an account with a previous balance of $155, purchases of $47.38, a payment of $20, and an interest charge of 1.8%.

28. A new desk for an office has a cash price of $1,500 and can be purchased on the installment plan with a 12.5% finance charge. The desk will be paid for in 12 monthly payments. Find the amount of the finance charge, the total price, and the amount of each monthly payment, if there was no down payment.

29. On June 1, the unpaid balance on a credit card was $174. During the month, purchases of $32, $14.50, and $28.75 are made. Using the unpaid balance method, find the unpaid balance on July 1 if the finance charge is 1.4% of the unpaid balance and a payment of $50 is made on June 15.

30. On August 1, the unpaid balance on a credit card was $206. During the month, purchases of $98.65 and a payment of $60 were made. Using the unpaid balance method and a finance charge of 1.5%, find the unpaid balance on September 1.

31. Use the following activity chart to find the unpaid balance on November 1. The billing cycle ended on October 31, and the finance charge is 1.5% of the average daily balance.

Date Posted	Activity	Amount
October 1	Billing date	Previous balance $426.40
October 7	Purchase	$ 41.60
October 10	Payment	$ 70
October 15	Purchase	$ 31.25
October 20	Purchase	$ 26.80

32. On January 1, the previous balance for Lynn's charge account was $569.80. On the following days, she made the purchases shown:
January 13 $38.50   jewelry
January 21 $44.56   clothing
On January 16, Lynn made a $50 payment. Using the average daily balance method, find the finance charge and unpaid balance on February 1 if the bank charges interest of 1.5% per month.

Section 12.4

Use the constant ratio formula to estimate the annual percentage rate for the following exercises. Round results to the nearest tenth of a percent.

33. Find the annual percentage rate on a loan of $1,500 for 18 months if the loan requires $190 interest and is repaid monthly.

34. Find the annual percentage rate on a loan that is repaid weekly for 25 weeks if the amount of the loan is $300. The loan requires $20 interest.

35. Find the annual percentage rate on a loan of $3,820 if the monthly payment is $120 for 36 months.

36. Find the annual percentage rate on a loan of $700 with 12 monthly payments. The loan requires $101 interest.

37. A vacuum cleaner was purchased on the installment plan with ten monthly payments of $10.50 each. If the cash price was $95 and there was no down payment, find the annual percentage rate.

Use Table 12–1 to find the annual percentage rate for the following.

38. A queen-size brass bed costs $1,155 and is financed with monthly payments for three years. The total finance charge is $415.80. Find the annual percentage rate.

39. A merchant charged $420 in cash for a dining room set that could be bought for $50 down and $40.75 per month for ten months. What is the annual percentage rate?

40. John Edmonds borrowed $500. He repaid the loan in 22 monthly payments of $26.30 each. Find the annual percentage rate.

41. An electric mixer was purchased on the installment plan for a down payment of $60 and 11 monthly payments of $11.05 each. The cash price was $170. Find the annual percentage rate.

42. A loan of $3,380 was paid back in 30 monthly payments with an interest charge of $620. Find the annual percentage rate to the nearest tenth of a percent.

43. A word processor was purchased by paying $50 down and 24 monthly payments of $65 each. The cash price was $1,400. Find the annual percentage rate to the nearest tenth of a percent.

44. A 6 × 6 color enlarger costs $1,295 and is financed with monthly payments for two years. The total finance charge is $310.80. Find the annual percentage rate.

Section 12.5

Hullett Houpt is purchasing a home for $97,000. He will finance the mortgage for 15 years and pay 11% interest on the loan. He makes a down payment that is 20% of the purchase price. Use Table 12–2 as needed.

45. Find the down payment.

46. Find the amount of the mortgage.

77600

47. If Hullett is required to pay two points for making the loan, how much will the points cost?

48. Find the monthly payment that includes principal and interest.

882.31

49. Find the total interest Hullett will pay over the 15-year period.

50. Calculate the monthly payment and the total interest Hullett would have to pay if he decided to make the loan for 30 years instead of 15 years.

739.53
188,630.80

51. How much interest can be saved by paying for the home in 15 years rather than 30 years?

52. Find the interest portion and principal portion for the first payment of Hullett's 15-year loan.

711.33
170.98

53. Make an amortization schedule for the first three payments of the 15-year loan in Exercise 49. 882.31

| | Portion of Payment Applied to: | | End-of-Month |
Month	Interest	Principal	Principal
1	711.33		
2			
3			

77,600 × $\frac{11}{12}$ = 711.33

54. Make an amortization schedule for the first three payments of the 30-year loan in Exercise 50.

| | Portion of Payment Applied to: | | End-of-Month |
Month	Interest	Principal	Principal
1	711.33	28.20	77571.80
2	711.07	28.46	77543.34
3	710.81	28.72	77514.62

55. Bob and Janice Malena need to finance $80,000 on their new home. After checking with several mortgage companies they have narrowed their choices to two options.

            Option 1: 20 year at 11%
            Option 2: 25 years at 10%

If the Malenas can budget for either monthly payment, which option do you recommend? Why?

CHAPTER 12 PRACTICE TEST

1. Find the finance charge on an item with a cash price of $469 if the installment price is $503 and no down payment was made.

2. An item with a cash price of $578 can be purchased on the installment plan in 15 monthly payments of $46. Find the installment price if no down payment was made. Find the finance charge.

3. A copier that originally cost $300 was sold on the installment plan at $28 per month for 12 months. Find the installment price if no down payment was made. Find the finance charge.

4. Use Table 12–1 to find the annual percentage rate for the loan in Exercise 3.

5. Use the constant ratio formula to estimate the annual percentage rate to the nearest tenth of a percent, for the copier in Exercise 3.

6. Use the constant ratio formula to estimate the annual percentage rate, to the nearest tenth of a percent, on a loan of $3,000 at 9% for three years if the loan had interest of $810 and was repaid monthly.

7. Find the interest on an unpaid balance of $165 if the monthly interest rate is $1\frac{3}{4}\%$.

8. Find the yearly rate of interest on a loan if the monthly rate is 2%.

9. Find the interest refunded on a 15-month loan with total interest of $72 if the loan is paid in full with six months remaining.

10. Find the annual interest rate on a loan of $1,600 for 24 months if $200 interest is charged and the loan is repaid in monthly payments.

11. Find the annual interest rate on a loan that is repaid weekly for 26 weeks if the amount of the loan is $1,075. The interest charged is $60.

12. Office equipment was purchased on the installment plan with 12 monthly payments of $11.20 each. If the cash price was $120 and there was no down payment, find the annual percentage rate.

13. Find the new unpaid balance on an account with a previous balance of $205.60, purchases of $67.38, a payment of $40, and a finance charge of 1.75%.

14. A canoe has been purchased on the installment plan with a down payment of $75 and ten monthly payments of $80 each. Find the installment price of the canoe.

15. Find the monthly payment when the installment price is $2,300, a down payment of $400 is made, and there are 12 monthly payments.

16. How much is to be financed on a cash price of $729 if a down payment of $75 is made?

17. Find the refund fraction on a four-year loan if it is paid off in 25 months.

18. The unpaid balance on a credit card at the beginning of the month is $288.93. During the month, purchases totaling $75.60 and one payment of $50 were made. Using the unpaid balance method and a finance rate of 1.9% per month, find the unpaid balance at the beginning of the next month.

19. Use the following activity chart to find the average daily balance and finance charge for July. The monthly interest rate is 1.75%. The billing cycle has 31 days.

Date Posted	Activity	Amount
July 1	Billing date	Previous balance $441.05
July 5	Payment	$75
July 16	Purchase	$23.50
July 26	Purchase	$31.40

20. Ginger Canoy has purchased a home for $122,000. She plans to finance $100,000 for 15 years at $9\frac{1}{2}\%$ interest. Calculate the monthly payment and the total interest. Use Table 12–2.

21. Make Ginger an amortization schedule for the first two months of the mortgage.

Month	Portion of Payment Applied to:		End-of-Month Principal
	Interest	Principal	
1			
2			

ANSWERS TO ODD-NUMBERED PROBLEMS

CHAPTER 1   REVIEW, p. 29

Section 1.1

1. four thousand, two hundred nine
3. three hundred one million, nine
5. 400
7. 9,000
9. 830
11. 30,000
13. 28,000,000,000
15. 4,000,000
17. 5,000
19. 10,000,000
21. 400
23. 700,000
25. 20
27. 35
29. 28
31. 30,787
33. 1,832
35. 5,773
37. 44,014
39. 310,000; 318,936
41. 22,000; 21,335
43. 2,600; 2,612
45. 230 items
47. 469 dolls
49. 671 points
51. 9,756
53. 1,865,741
55. 4,715,606
57. 5,322,571
59. 4,000; 4,072
61. 50,000,000; 56,539,090
63. 55,000; 55,632
65. 88 packages
67. 244 fan belts
69. 4,952,385
71. 782,878
73. 41,772
75. 6,938,694
77. 861,900
79. 16,500
81. 48,000
83. 30,000
85. 47,220,000
87. 162,000
89. 210,000; 254,626
91. 1,550,000; 1,495,184
93. 120 ribbons
95. 140 pieces
97. 45
99. 24
101. 77
103. 54 R 5
105. 7,000; 8805 R6
107. 249 packages
109. $12 average hourly wage
111. 75 cards
113. 20 pairs
115. $160
117. $8 per hour
119. 48 ounces

Section 1.2

121. five tenths
123. one hundred eight thousandths
125. two hundred seventy-five hundred-thousandths
127. seventeen and eight tenths
129. one hundred twenty-eight and twenty-three hundredths
131. five hundred and seven ten-thousandths
133. 0.135
135. 380
137. 1,700
139. $175
141. 1.246
143. 165.8312
145. $20.93
147. 376.74
149. 57.4525
151. 135.6
153. 419.103
155. 325.74
157. 2.3068
159. 0.001474
161. $88.96
163. $92.61
165. 193.41
167. 50.076
169. 21.2352
171. 275.8
173. 198.74
175. 27,300
177. 17,454
179. 370,000
181. $12,850.00
183. 0.15
185. 2.19
187. 8.57
189. 33.77
191. 1,559.79
193. 60.713.24
195. 8.572
197. 0.019874
199. 0.0018
201. 37.49298
203. 0.0178

205. $0.989 in thousandths

207.

INCOME		
	Gross income	$34,356
	Interest income	282
	Dividend income	455
Total		$35,093
EXPENSES	Living	$16,898
	Home maintenance	495
	Auto maintenance & repair	117
	Insurance premiums (medical, auto, home, life)	1,778
	Taxes (sales, income, FICA, real property, personal property)	11,130
	Medical (not covered by insurance)	450
	Planning investment	2,500
	Unspent income	1,725
Total		$35,093

CHAPTER 1   PRACTICE TEST, p. 37

1. five hundred three

3. 84,300

5. 80,000

7. 2,200; 2,117

9. 45,000; 41,032

11. 1,153 items

13. 30

15. 24.092

17. 224.857

19. 447.12

21. 89.82

23. 2,379.019

25. 179.24

27. $19.20

BUSINESS AND MATHEMATICS IN THE NEWS, p. 14

1. Ford F-series: 650,000; Chevy K/K pickup: 550,000; Ford Taurus: 400,000; Honda Accord: 370,000; Ford Ranger pickup: 340,000.

2. Ford F-series: 600,000; Chevy C/K pickup: 600,000; Ford Taurus: 400,000; Honda Accord: 400,000; Ford Ranger: 300,000; Ford Escort: 300,000; Toyota Camry: 300,000; Saturn: 300,000; Ford Explorer: 300,000; Dodge Caravan: 300,000. Approximation: 3,800,000

3. 3,807,079

4. Estimate was under by 7,079

5. Answers may vary. Some advantages: easier to work with rounded numbers; rounded numbers give a general idea of the trends in the numbers; easier to make estimations using rounded numbers.

CHAPTER 2

CHAPTER 2   REVIEW, p. 69

Section 2.1

1.

3.

5.

786	Date 5/10 19 XX
Amount $28.97	
To Jacqueline Voss	
For Office supplies	

Balance Forward	4307	21
Deposits		
Total	4307	21
Amount This Check	28	97
Balance	4278	24

7.

RECORD ALL TRANSACTIONS THAT AFFECT YOUR ACCOUNT

NUMBER	DATE	DESCRIPTION OF TRANSACTION	DEBIT (−)		√ T	FEE (IF ANY) (−)	CREDIT (+)		BALANCE 983	47
1213	3/10	Linens, Inc. laundry services	220	00					763	47
1214	3/10	Bugs Away extermination services	65	00					698	47
ATM	3/11	withdrawal	80	00					618	47
Dep	3/12						315	24	933	71

9.

Barter Home Repair		8212
302 Cannon Dr. Germantown, TN 38138	6/12 19 XX	87-278/840

PAY TO THE ORDER OF Alpine Industries $ 85.50

Eighty-five and 50/100 ———————— DOLLARS

Community First Bank
2177 Germantown Rd. South
Germantown, Tennessee 38138

MEMO building supplies   Your name

⑈035008217⑈

11.

RECORD ALL TRANSACTIONS THAT AFFECT YOUR ACCOUNT

NUMBER	DATE	DESCRIPTION OF TRANSACTION	DEBIT (−)		√ T	FEE (IF ANY) (−)	CREDIT (+)		BALANCE 876	54
234	5/3	Organic materials fertilizer	175	00					701	54
235	5/3	Klean Kuts chain saw	524	82					176	72
	5/15	Deposit					472	39	649	11

13. For Deposit Only
Valley Electric Coop
15-2713140
restricted endorsement

15. The electronic deposit is usually more convenient and safer since the funds are transferred directly from the employer's bank account to the employee's bank account. A disadvantage is that the employee does not actually see the amount deposited and should carefully compare the amount shown on the check stub with the amount deposited. Answers will vary.

Section 2.2

17. 0

19. Five checks

21. $4,975.50

23. 7/7

25. $12.50

27. 3

29. $2,571.37

31. 4/8

33. $5.83

35. 5

37. $3,485.73

39. 6/20

41.

RECORD ALL TRANSACTIONS THAT AFFECT YOUR ACCOUNT

NUMBER	DATE	DESCRIPTION OF TRANSACTION	DEBIT (−)		√ T	FEE (IF ANY) (−)	CREDIT (+)		BALANCE 1,034	10
Deposit	4/1	Payroll			√		850	00	1,884	10
Deposit	4/3	Payroll - Bonus			√		800	00	2,684	10
5374	4/3	First Union Mortgage Co.	647	53	√				2,036	57
5375	4/3	South Florida Utility	82	75	√				1,953	82
5376	4/5	First Federal Credit Union	219	95	√				1,733	87
5377	4/15	Banc Boston	510	48					1,223	39
Deposit	4/15	Payroll			√		850	00	2,073	39
5378	4/20	Northwest Airlines	403	21					1,670	18
5379	4/20	Auto Zone	18	97					1,651	21
ATM	5/4	Cordova Branch	100	00					1,551	21
	4/30	Service Fee	12	50	√				1,538	71
	4/30	Statement Reconciled								

REMEMBER TO RECORD AUTOMATIC PAYMENTS/DEPOSITS ON DATE AUTHORIZED.

43. Reconciled account register balance: $712.16

45. Reconciled account register balance: $398.43

47. Total assets 1996: $7,637;
total liabilities 1996; $65,422
Projected assets 1997: $90,830.50;
projected liabilities 1997; $60,644
1997 net worth: $30,186.50;
increase in net worth: $7,971.50

1.

3. Five checks   **5.** $142.38   **7.** $3,600

9. $1881.49   **11.** Reconciled account register balance: $1,589.10.

BUSINESS AND MATHEMATICS IN THE NEWS, p. 48

1. 72   **2.** 15   **3.** 146   **4.** 28

CHAPTER 3

CHAPTER 3   REVIEW, p. 118

Section 3.1

1. Answers will vary. $\frac{3}{5}$, $\frac{7}{9}$, $\frac{5}{8}$, $\frac{100}{301}$, $\frac{41}{53}$ proper

3. $20\frac{2}{3}$ **5.** 7   **7.** $8\frac{1}{2}$ **9.** $12\frac{2}{5}$ **11.** $14\frac{22}{25}$

13. $\frac{35}{6}$ **15.** $\frac{13}{3}$ **17.** $\frac{100}{3}$ **19.** $\frac{5}{8}$ **21.** $\frac{5}{6}$ **23.** $\frac{7}{8}$

25. $\frac{3}{8}$ **27.** $\frac{3}{4}$ **29.** $\frac{2}{5}$ **31.** $\frac{7}{9}$ **33.** $\frac{5}{6}$ **35.** $\frac{3}{5}$

37. $\frac{2}{3}$ **39.** $\frac{13}{24}$ **41.** $\frac{54}{72}$ **43.** $\frac{10}{12}$ **45.** $\frac{10}{15}$ **47.** $\frac{63}{77}$

49. $\frac{117}{143}$ **51.** $\frac{1}{7}$ of the employees   **53.** 48   **55.** 30   **57.** 168   **59.** $1\frac{2}{5}$

61. $1\frac{1}{15}$ **63.** $1\frac{7}{9}$ **65.** $1\frac{11}{24}$ **67.** $1\frac{13}{36}$ **69.** $11\frac{7}{8}$ **71.** $25\frac{1}{4}$

73. $23\frac{2}{5}$ **75.** $91\frac{5}{6}$ **77.** $154\frac{17}{42}$ **79.** 108   **81.** 29 yards   **83.** $\frac{1}{6}$

85. $\frac{1}{6}$ **87.** $\frac{7}{48}$ **89.** $3\frac{3}{10}$ **91.** $1\frac{1}{2}$ **93.** $3\frac{1}{12}$ **95.** $2\frac{1}{18}$

97. $42\frac{11}{15}$ **99.** $1\frac{29}{35}$ **101.** $12\frac{1}{6}$ **103.** $2\frac{3}{8}$ feet   **105.** $\frac{7}{32}$ **107.** $\frac{5}{18}$

109. $\frac{9}{20}$ **111.** $3\frac{1}{3}$ **113.** $2\frac{5}{8}$ **115.** $\frac{5}{9}$ **117.** $\frac{7}{18}$ **119.** $\frac{84}{125}$

121. $\frac{8}{49}$ **123.** $\frac{3}{41}$ **125.** $37\frac{1}{10}$ **127.** $74\frac{47}{48}$ **129.** $94\frac{2}{7}$ **131.** $48

133. $4,110   **135.** $\frac{8}{5}$ **137.** 4   **139.** $\frac{4}{13}$ **141.** $\frac{5}{8}$ **143.** 3

145. $\frac{10}{21}$ **147.** $\frac{1}{20}$ **149.** $3\frac{3}{4}$ **151.** $\frac{4}{7}$ **153.** 32 pieces   **155.** $7\frac{3}{4}$% total sales tax rate

157. $1\frac{1}{4}$ inches   **159.** 12 hours   **161.** $192 sale price   **163.** 4 full-length pieces

Section 3.2

165. 23%   **167.** 82%   **169.** 3%   **171.** 34%   **173.** 60.1%   **175.** 100%

177. 300%   **179.** 37%   **181.** 20%   **183.** 400%   **185.** 17%   **187.** 6%

189. 52%   **191.** 10%   **193.** 125%   **195.** 39%   **197.** 33.33%   **199.** 3%

201. 0.98   **203.** 2.56   **205.** 0.917   **207.** 0.005   **209.** 0.06   **211.** 0.36

213. 0.06   **215.** $\frac{1}{10}$ **217.** $\frac{3}{50}$ **219.** $\frac{89}{100}$ **221.** $\frac{9}{20}$ **223.** $2\frac{1}{4}$

225. $\frac{1}{3}$; $0.33\frac{1}{3}$ **227.** 12.5%; $\frac{1}{8}$ **229.** 80%, $\frac{4}{5}$ **231.** $P = 81$ **233.** $P = 25$ **235.** $R = 25\%$

237. $R = 33\frac{1}{3}\%$ **239.** $B = 400$ **241.** $P = 15.12$ **243.** $B = \$26,093.75$ **245.** $P = 1,134.24$ **247.** $P = 305.88$

249. $R = 250\%$ **251.** $P = 51.44$ **253.** $P = 24$ **255.** $P = 8.1$ **257.** $B = 30$ **259.** $B = 180$

261. $R = 97\%$ **263.** $R = 2\%$ **265.** $R = 200\%$ **267.** 32 customers   **269.** 2,270 people   **271.** 74% of the shareholders

273. 80% of the questions   **275.** 19.29% (approximately) of the rest-rooms   **277.** 26% (rounded) is *not* within the budgeted 25%   **279.** $1,212.50

281. $\frac{\$405}{\$1,625} = 0.249 = 25\%$. You should be able to afford the apartment.

$1,250 \times 25\% = \$1,250 \times 0.25 = \$312.50$

$\frac{\$375}{\$1,115} = 0.336 = 34\%$

CHAPTER 3   PRACTICE TEST, p. 127

1. $\frac{1}{6}$ **3.** $\frac{7}{16}$ **5.** $1\frac{19}{23}$ **7.** $5\frac{5}{6}$ **9.** $\frac{1}{4}$ has been unloaded; $\frac{1}{2}$ remains to be unloaded.

11. 24%   **13.** 60%   **15.** 37.5%   **17.** $P = \$72$ **19.** $R = 87\frac{1}{2}\%$
21. All 22 rooms   **23.** 90 employees   **25.** 56,600 automobiles

---

BUSINESS AND MATHEMATICS IN THE NEWS, p. 105

1. $2012.39

3. Yes, Joe should be concerned that he spent 50% of his health care cost for hospital care compared to 37% for the average American.

2. Since 6/25 = 24%, she spent the same as the average American.

CHAPTER 4

CHAPTER 4   REVIEW, p. 159

Section 4.1

1. Range: 14; Mean: 22; Median: 22; Mode: none
5. Range: $9.27; Mean: $8.42; Median: $5.53; Mode: $13.95
9. 795 students.
13. 2,531 students
17. 54.4%
21. Debt retirement
25. (b) Intervals of $10,000 are more appropriate because the data can be shown with fewer intervals than with (a).
29. Answers will vary. Beginning of school, middle of baseball season, too soon for winter sports
33. (b) 5°. The data can be adequately shown on a graph with 5° intervals.
37. 20%
41. $17,000 cost of lot with landscaping; 19.8%
45. 84°
49. Range: 32; Mean: 74.33; Median: 71; No mode

3. Range: $1.02; Mean: $1.44; Median: $1.46; Mode: $1.65
7. Range: $6.75; Mean: $40.34; Median: $40.75; Mode: none
11. 3,997 students
15. Period 5
19. 1995: $65,153; 1996; $68,324
23. Social projects and education costs
27. May, June, July

31. 70°

35. (c) Fluctuating

39. $153
43. 1,198 cars sold
47. Mail to former buyers, phone former buyers

1. 77	**3.** 29.5	**5.** 110	**7.** 165
9. $120	**11.** 33.3%	**13.** Labor: 135°; Materials: 120°; Overhead: 105°	**15.** Fresh flowers: $23,712; silk flowers: $17,892
17. (c) $5,000, other interval sizes would provide too many or too few intervals	**19.** Smallest: 250; greatest: 1,117	**21.** 1990, 1992, 1993	**23.** 1991, 1994, 1995

BUSINESS AND MATHEMATICS IN THE NEWS, p. 145

1. Year-end unemployment rates: line graph
USA's civilian workforce: circle graph
Median hourly wage for all workers: bar graph

3. White: 76%
Black: 11%
Hispanic: 9%
Other: 4%

5. The hourly wage earned by the most workers.

2. 131.7 million

4. The average of all the hourly wages.

CHAPTER **5**

Section 5.1

1. $P = \$120$	**3.** $P = 142$ feet	**5.** $I = \$2,025$	**7.** $P = 8s$	**9.** $P = 136$ inches

Section 5.2

11. $N = 7$	**13.** $A = 12$	**15.** $N = 17$
17. $N = 4$	**19.** $A = 24$	**21.** $x = 7$
23. $x = 11$	**25.** $A = 8$	**27.** $X = 7$
29. The number of cards sold is 9.	**31.** Five of each card were ordered.	**33.** The amount of money spent on supplies was $96.
35. 416 fan belts should be ordered.	**37.** The amount spent on groceries is $57.50.	**39.** Shaquita earns $8.75 each hour.
41. Molly earns $272.32 for 37 hours of work.	**43.** Wallpaper for the kitchen will cost $116.73.	**45.** The total weight of the shipment is 830 pounds.
47. Each shirt was reduced by $3.02.	**49.** There were 11 executive desks and 29 secretarial desks.	**51.** 280 headlights were purchased at a cost of $3,906. 720 taillights were purchased at a total cost of $5,436.

53. $100

1. $S = \$446$	**3.** $M = S - C$	**5.** $N = 11$
7. $A = 18$	**9.** $A = 5$	**11.** $N = 6$
13. The new salary is $285.	**15.** 130 containers are needed.	**17.** 116 ceramic cups and 284 plastic cups were sold. The value of the ceramic cups was $464. The value of the plastic cups was $994.

19. $27,200

1. 1,000 square feet
2. 1,600 square feet in Sevilla
   800 square feet in Hong Kong.

3. Given their budget and office space constraints, the company cannot afford these two cities. Renting 1,500 square feet in Hong Kong and Lima, Peru, would require a total of $215,235 per month for rent. The company should consider renting smaller offices (for example, 1,200 square feet in each city would cost $172,188) or consider expanding into lower-priced cities (for example, 1,500 square feet in Shanghai and Edmonton would rent for $147,765 per month).

CHAPTER 6

CHAPTER 6 REVIEW, p. 231

Section 6.1

1. $7,938
3. $53,872
5. $425
7. $141.75
9. $377 (gross earnings)
11. $493 (gross earnings)
13. $483.14
15. $316.02
17. $228.80
19. Regular Hours: 31;
    Regular Pay: $248;
    $1\frac{1}{2}$ OT Hours: 2;
    $1\frac{1}{2}$ OT Pay: $24;
    2 OT Hours: 4;
    2 OT Pay: $64;
    Gross Earnings: $336
21. Regular Hours: 40:
    Regular Pay: $270;
    $1\frac{1}{2}$ OT Hours: 9;
    $1\frac{1}{2}$ OT Pay: $91.13;
    2 OT Hours: 5;
    2 OT Pay: $67.50;
    Gross Earnings:
    $428.63
23. $40 (1 day's pay);
    $200 (5 days' pay)

25. $216.45
27. $486.15
29. $910
31. $400
33. $800
35. $7,800
37. $1,191.20
39. $334.64

Section 6.2

41. $0
43. $53
45. $19
47. $0
49. $98.38
51. FICA: $9.73; Medicare: $2.28
53. FICA: $1,488; Medicare: $348
55. FICA: $1,129.95; Medicare: $264.26
57. Withholding Tax: $0;
    FICA: $8.99;
    Medicare: $2.10;
    Total Deductions: $33.03;
    Net Earnings: $111.97
59. Withholding Tax: $0;
    FICA: $10.23;
    Medicare: $2.39;
    Total Deductions: $12.62;
    Net Earnings: $152.38
61. $117.50; $367.50

Section 6.3

63. $181.60
65. $378
67. $1,134; $1,076.76
69. $427.91

CHAPTER 6 PRACTICE TEST, p. 234

1. $354
3. $262.50
5. $126
7. $522
9. FICA: $22.40; Medicare: $5.24
11. $0
13. $221.27
15. FICA: $14.57; Medicare: $3.41;
    Withholding Tax: $17;
    Net Earnings: $174.90
17. FICA: $18.11; Medicare: $4.24;
    Withholding Tax: $11;
    Net Earnings: $258.82

19. FICA: $13.03; Medicare: $3.05;
Withholding Tax: $0;
Net Earnings: $194.05

21. $378

23. $0

BUSINESS AND MATHEMATICS IN THE NEWS, p. 207

1. 41–48 hours; increased approximately 2.5%

2. Approximately 10.2%

3. Answers may vary. As a salaried employee, you would not receive overtime pay. Considering the trends, this would be the least desirable choice. Hourly pay with time-and-a-half for overtime would be more desirable than piecework since producing more pieces doesn't result in more pay per piece.

CHAPTER 7

CHAPTER 7 REVIEW, p. 264

Section 7.1

1. $45

3. $25.50

5. $7.57

7. $102.50

9. $19.80

11. $94.50

13. $660 skirts; $1,480 jumpers; $2,140 total list price; $235.40 trade discount

15. $18

17. $6.13

19. $336.03

21. Trade Discount: $1.25; Net Price: $23.75

23. Trade Discount: $0.02; Net Price: $0.87

25. Trade Discount: $357; Net Price: $1,743

27. Complement: 96%; Net Price: $15.33

29. Complement: 94%; Net Price: $130.23

31. Complement: 89%; Net Price: $15.10

Section 7.2

33. 0.8(0.9); 0.72; $144

35. 0.8(0.85)(0.9); 0.612; $918

37. 0.85(0.95); 0.8075; $323

39. $3.42 net price

41. $852.86 total net price

43. 76.5%; 23.5%

45. 68.35%; 31.65%

47. 74.34%; 25.66%

49. 28%

51. 16.21%

53. 14.5%

55. $400 less 20% is the better deal.

57. $60 less $9.45 is the better deal.

59. $20 less discount series of 10/10/10 is the better deal.

Section 7.3

61. 3% discount

63. Yes

65. $5.40 cash discount

67. $1.40 cash discount; $68.60 net amount

69. a. $7 cash discount; $343 net amount
b. $3.50 cash discount: $346.50 net amount
c. $350 (no discount)

71. $13 cash discount; $637 net amount

73. $5,139.06 net amount

75. $824.74 credited to account June 12; $375.26 paid on July 2; $1,175.26 total paid

77. $824.74 credited to account; $325.26 outstanding balance

79. The purchaser

81. $711.97; $719.24; $726.50

1. $110 trade discount

3. $7.31 trade discount; $29.24 net price

5. $250 chair less 20% is the better deal

7. 0.684 net decimal equivalent

9. Receipt of goods

11. $1,080 net price

13. End of month

15. $2 cash discount

17. $392 net amount

19. $489.60 total net price

21. $618.56 amount credited to account; $276.44 outstanding balance

BUSINESS AND MATHEMATICS IN THE NEWS, p. 248

1. $20,750 to $22,000

3. Net price = $25,216.08 Trade Discount = 13% or $3,767.92

4. Accura: 12% to 14% Audi: 12% BMW: 16% to 18% Buick: 8% to 14%

2. 12% to 17%

5. Answers may vary. For example: the Mitsubishi. The cost factor of 80% to 90% means a trade discount to the dealer of 10% to 20% off the sticker price, giving more room to bargain on the price.

CHAPTER 8

CHAPTER 8   REVIEW, p. 296

Section 8.1

1. $75; 150%

3. 41; $82; 100%, 200%

5. $52.48; $90;48; 58%

7. $45.33; $53.33; 85%; 100%

9. Markup: $6; selling price: $21

11. Cost: $36; Rate of markup: 25%

13. Markup: $39.80; Rate of markup: 25.1%

15. Cost: $24; selling price: $36

17. Cost: $35.70; selling price: $51.00

19. Rate of markup: 31.62%; markup: $18.50

21. Cost: $14; markup: $21

23. $57; 56.14%; 35.96%

25. $0.44; 28.21%; 22%

27. $68.45; $95.83; 28.57%

29. $49.60; $74.40; 60%

31. $16.11; $2.84; 17.63%

33. 13.6%

35. 38.7%

37. Markdown: $38; Markdown rate: 10%

39. Markdown: $24.99; Markdown rate: 27.77%

41. Markdown: $50; Sale price: $199.99

43. Markdown: $19.75; Sale price: $59.25

45. First reduction: Markdown: $6.25; Sale price: $25 Second reduction: Markdown: $7.50; Sale price: $17.50

47. $0.54

49. $17.33 per pair

1. $7.16	**3.** $15.50	**5.** $22.68	**7.** $26.07	**9.** $126.75
11. 25%	**13.** $160	**15.** $48.74	**17.** $1.80	**19.** Cost: $15.75; markup: $29.25

BUSINESS AND MATHEMATICS IN THE NEWS, p. 287

1. Amount of markdown = $20.01
Percent of markdown = 25%

3. $68; $44.20

2. The total markdown from $80 to $40 is 50%. The markdown from $59.99 to $40.00 is 33%. 25% + 33% ≠ 50%.

4. 33% of $59.99 = $19.80. Actually $19.99 is closer to $33\frac{1}{3}$% of $59.99 (33% of $59.99 = $20.00). The advertiser may have approximated $33\frac{1}{3}$% with 33% to give the ad a neater appearance, or for convenience.

CHAPTER **9**

CHAPTER **9** **REVIEW, p. 331**

Section 9.1

1. $120	**3.** $2,252.52	**5.** $144	**7.** Interest: $1,923.75; Maturity value: $6,198.75	**9.** 15.5%
11. 12.5%	**13.** 15%	**15.** 3 years	**17.** 1.5 years	**19.** 2 years
21. 6 months	**23.** $500	**25.** $1,000	**27.** $1,500	**29.** $900
31. $\frac{7}{12}$ year	**33.** $\frac{4}{3}$ years	**35.** $\frac{1}{4}$ year	**37.**	**39.** $1,050

37. Circle diagram: Interest I over Principal P × Rate R × Time T

41. $20	**43.** $12	**45.** $16

Section 9.2

47. Ordinary time	**49.** 117 days	**51.** 261 days
53. 153 days	**55.** 167 days	**57.** 247 days
59. 163 days	**61.** Ordinary time: August 10; Exact time; August 8	**63.** Ordinary time: October 12; Exact time: October 11
65. Ordinary time: February 28 of the following year; Exact time: February 26	**67.** a. $105; b. $103.56; c. $105	**69.** a. $51.67; b. $51.29; c. $52
71. First State Bank	**73.** August 10, 1995	**75.** $1,909.50
77. $18.63	**79.** $22.64	**81.** $10,040.56

83. Rocky's Market Principal: $840; David's Art Gallery Principal: $2,550; Fortune Hardware Annual Rate: 7.6%; M. Converse & Son Annual Rate: 6.2%; Sun Twins Jai Alai Time: 75 days; Sun Coast Brokerage Time: 200 days
To protect themselves from data loss as described in this question, most financial institutions use a computerized backup system with storage either on disk or magnetic tape.

1. $210
9. $I = \$8,400$
3. 20% annually
11. $I = \$28.14$
5. 287 days
13. $665
7. 159 days
15. Time: 60 days; Interest: $21.25

17. $\frac{3}{4}$ year or 9 months
25. $169.01
19. 20% annually
27. $44.30
21. $462.50
23. $64

BUSINESS AND MATHEMATICS IN THE NEWS, p. 318

1. .5 years, 1 year, 2.5 years, 5 years
4. Interest rates were lower a year ago for all time periods shown in the graph.
2. 6.49% for a 5-year investment
3. 5-year

CHAPTER 10

CHAPTER 10   REVIEW, p. 358

Section 10.1

1. $166.40
9. $2,189.90
17. $1,333.85
3. $708.64
11. $185.46
19. $1,100 in one year is more than the yield on $900 invested today.
5. $524.95
13. $101.19
21. 12.55%
7. $5,372.55
15. $13,928.16
23. $0.36

25. $15.01 compound interest: $2,015.01 compound amount

27. The two-year investment yields the greater amount of interest.

Section 10.2

29. $4,633.92
37. $154.16
45. $4,781.07
31. $1,126.97
39. $1,592.55
33. $574.37
41. $2,913.80
35. $3,157.64
43. $11,000 in 18 months is better.

47.

Month	Rate	End of Month Balance
Jan.	0.006667	1.006667
Feb.	0.006667	1.013378
Mar.	0.006667	1.020135
Apr.	0.006667	1.026936
May	0.006667	1.033783
June	0.006667	1.040675
July	0.006667	1.047613
Aug.	0.006667	1.054597
Sept.	0.006667	1.061628
Oct.	0.006667	1.068706
Nov.	0.006667	1.075831
Dec.	0.006667	1.083004

1. $450.09 **3.** $3,979.30 **5.** $579.12 **7.** 12.55% **9.** Compounded monthly yields greater interest.

11. $2,669.55 **13.** $2,951.58 **15.** $680 in one year is better. **17.** Option 2 yields the greater return by $0.68. **19.** $1,006.60

BUSINESS AND MATHEMATICS IN THE NEWS, p. 350

1. The graph compares yearly changes in the interest on debt under current law and using the Domenici plan. The years shown are from 1996 to 2002.

2. Approximately $300 billion

3. Approximately $325 billion

4. $3,571 billion or 3 trillion, 571 billion

CHAPTER **11**

CHAPTER **11** REVIEW, p. 385

Section 11.1

1. $37,618 **3.** $2,730.03 **5.** $5,359.69 **7.** $26,362 **9.** (a) $49,681.11; (b) $150,478.86 **11.** $10,800.13

Section 11.2

13. $10,311.07 **15.** $7,870.49 **17.** $7,102.10 **19.** $2,294.19 **21.** $5,591.97
23. $3,407.89 **25.** $19,672.40 **27.** $9,982.50 **29.** $7,586.60

CHAPTER **11** PRACTICE TEST, p. 387

1. $19,350.00 end of second year **3.** $41,739.31 **5.** $5,727.50 **7.** $60,819.20 **9.** $28,269.88 **11.** $104.74

13. $34,724.80 **15.** $28,240

BUSINESS AND MATHEMATICS IN THE NEWS, p. 373

Back to School Shopping

1. $7,356.50 **2.** 5.7 Years **3.** Clothing: $6,694.42 electronics: $956.35 **4.** Answers will vary

Slow-Moving States

1. $70,665.48 **2.** $137,811.24

CHAPTER 12 REVIEW, p. 425

Section 12.1

1. $1,585.96   **3.** $85   **5.** $729

Section 12.2

7. $30.51   **9.** $398.75   **11.** $52.40   **13.** $571.87
15. $358.63   **17.** $56.88   **19.** $26.94   **21.** $50.11

Section 12.3

23. $3.98   **25.** $5.81   **27.** $185.17   **29.** $201.69   **31.** $462.62

Section 12.4

33. 16%   **35.** 8.5%   **37.** 23%   **39.** 21.50%   **41.** 20.50%   **43.** 14.25%

Section 12.5

45. $19,400   **47.** $1,552   **49.** $81,215.80   **51.** $107,415.00
53. Portion of Payment Applied to: **55.** Option 1 is recommended since it costs $19,824 less in interest.

Month	Interest	Principal	End-of-Month Principal
1	$711.33	$170.98	$77,429.02
2	$709.77	$172.54	$77,256.48
3	$708.18	$174.13	$77,082.35

CHAPTER 12 PRACTICE TEST, p. 429

1. $34   **3.** $336 installment price; $36 finance charge   **5.** 22.2%   **7.** $2.89

9. $12.60   **11.** 21.5%   **13.** $236.58   **15.** $158.33

17. $\frac{23}{98}$ **19.** $393.93 average daily balance; $6.89 finance charge   **21.** Portion of Payment Applied to:

Month	Principal	Interest	End-of-Month Principal
1	$791.67	$253.33	$99,746.67
2	$789.66	$255.34	$99,491.33

BUSINESS AND MATHEMATICS IN THE NEWS, p. 414

1. FRMs—Fixed-rate mortgages
ARMs—Adjustable-rate mortgages
3. Interest rates for 30-year FRMs, 15-year FRMs, one-year ARMs, and one-year T-Bills (Treasury bills) decreased. Interest rates for credit cards, car loans, and one-year CDs (certificates of deposit) increased.

2. All interest rates increased except credit cards, which stayed the same.
4. You would have been better off a year ago, when the rate for car loans was only 7.6%, compared to 9.5% currently.

GLOSSARY/INDEX

difference in the list price and the trade discount of the article, 238
    calculating using end-of-month terms, 252–253, 262
    calculating using ordinary dating terms, 250–252, 261
    calculating using receipt-of-goods terms, 253–254, 263
    freight terms and, 255–256
    net decimal equivalent and, 243–245, 261
    single discount equivalent and, 245–247, 261
    and trade discount series, 243
Nonsufficient funds (NSF) fee: a fee charged to your account when you write a check and do not have enough money in your account to cover it, 50
Nonterminating (or repeating), decimal: the quotient of a division that does not come out even, no matter how many decimal places it is carried to, 96
Nonzero digit: a digit that is not zero, 5
Numerator: the top term of a fraction or the number being divided, 82

Open-end loan: a loan in which there is no fixed number of payments—the borrower keeps making payments until the amount is paid off, and the interest is computed on the unpaid balance at the end of each payment period, 390, 398
    average daily balance method, 400–402, 422
    unpaid balance method, 398–400, 421–422
Ordinary annuity: annuity with payment made at end of periods, 366
Ordinary balance: the amount owed after a partial payment and partial cash discount are deducted, 254
Ordinary interest: interest that is calculated using 360 days to find the ratio per day, 313–316, 329
Ordinary time: 30 days per month regardless of the month of the year, 250, 261, 310-312, 328
Outstanding balance: the amount owed after a partial payment and partial cash discount are deducted, 254
Outstanding checks or deposits: checks or deposits that do not reach the bank in time to appear on the monthly statement, 50
Overtime rate: rate of pay for hours worked beyond 40 hours in a week (sometimes given for work on holidays), It must be at least 1.5 times the regular pay rate, 205

Partial cash discount: amount of cash discount allowed when partial payment is made, 254
Partial dividend, 10
Partial payment: payment that is eligible for a cash discount when the invoice is not paid in full, 254–255, 263

Partial product: the product of one digit of the multiplier and the multiplicand, 8
Partial quotient, 10
Payee: the person or company to whom a check is made out—the one who gets the money, 43, 319
Payor: the person or company issuing a check; also called the maker, 43
Payroll:
    deductions, 209–220
    employer's payroll taxes, 220–231
    gross pay, 204–209
Percent: a hundredth of a whole amount; a fraction with a denominator of 100; *percent* means *per hundred,* 98
    mixed, 98
    using the percentage formula, 102–107, 117
    writing as a number, 100–102, 116
    writing numbers as, 98–100, 116
Percentage: a portion of the base in a percentage problem, 214
Percentage formula, 117
Percentage method income: adjusted gross income after deducting a tax-exempt amount based on the withholding allowances claimed. This income is used in calculating income tax by the percentage method, 214
Perimeter: the distance around the edges of a square, triangle, rectangle, or other geometric shape, 169
Piecework rate: pay rate based on the amount of acceptable work done, 204
Place-value system: a system in which a digit has a value according to its place, or position, in a number, 2–3, 15
Point-of-sale, 41
Prepay and add: a shipping term that indicates that the seller pays the freight charges and then adds the cost to the invoice, 255, 263
Present value: the amount of money needed at present to yield, or earn, a specified amount at a future date, 351
    based on annual compounding for one year, 351–352, 357–358
    based on present value using a $1.00 present value table, 353, 358
Present value of an annuity: the lump sum amount that must be invested now to equal the future value of an annuity, 377
Prime number: a whole number larger than 1 that is divisible only by itself and 1, 88
Principal: the amount of money borrowed or invested, 306
Problem solving:
    decision key for, 6–7
    using equations, 183–190, 198
    with decimals, 15–22
    with fractions, 82–98
    with percents, 98–109
    with whole numbers, 2–12

Proceeds: the amount that the maker of a discounted note receives; proceeds = face value–discount, 319, 330, 331

Product: the answer, or result, in multiplication, 8

Promissory note: a legal document or instrument by which the borrower promises to repay a loan, 319

    simple discount notes, 319–320, 330

    third-party discount notes, 321–323, 331

Proper fraction: a fraction with a numerator smaller than a denominator, 83–84

Proportion: an equation in which both sides are fractions or ratios, 187

Quota: a specific amount of work to be completed; often a commission or bonus is earned if work exceeds quota, 208

Quotient: the answer, or result, of division, 10

Range or spread: the result when the smallest number is subtracted from the largest number in a group of numbers, 130–131, 154–155

Rate: a percent that indicates how the base and percentage are related; the percent or decimal or fractional equivalent of the percent that is charged or earned for the use of money, 102–103, 106–107, 117, 158, 302

Rate of change, 146, 158

Ratio: the comparison of two numbers by division that can also be written as a fraction, 146

Real property: land or anything permanently attached to the land, such as buildings and fences, 408

Receipt of goods (ROG) discount: sales terms in which the discount is determined from the day the goods are received instead of the invoice date, 253, 263

Reciprocals: two numbers that give a product of 1 when multiplied by each other, 7/8 and 8/7 are reciprocals, 94

Refund fraction: a fraction that shows what portion of the total finance charge has not been used at the time the loan is paid off, 394

Regular pay: earnings based on the hourly wage, 205

Relationships: equations and solving problems, 183–189

Remainder: the amount left over if division does not come out even, 10

Repeating decimal. *See* Nonterminating decimal

Restricted endorsement: occurs when the payee signs a check on the back and adds special instructions such as changing the payee or restricting the check for deposit only, 45

Returned check fee: a fee charged to your account when someone writes you a check without the funds to cover it and you deposit it in your account, 50

Returned check: a check returned to the payee because it was not honored by the maker's bank, 50

Revolving charge accounts: open-end loans, in which borrowers keep making payments at a stated rate of interest until the loan is paid off. Additional charges can be made at any time as long as they are below the credit limit, 398

Round, rounding: a procedure to find an estimated or approximate answer, 4–5

Rule of 78: a method used to calculate the refund due when a loan is paid off early, 394–397, 420–421

Salary: a set amount of money paid to an employee for work done during a specific time period, 204

Salary plus commission: a certain basic salary that is earned in addition to a commission on sales, 208

Second mortgage: a note whose holder has second rights to the proceeds from the sale of a home, 409

Selling price: the price at which merchandise is sold to consumers, 272

Semiannually: twice a year; 2 periods per year, 204

Semimonthly: twice a month, 24 periods in a year, 204

Service charge: a fee the bank charges for operation of a checking account, 50

Signature card: a record maintained by the bank which records the signature of persons authorized to make withdrawals from an account, 41

Simple discount rate: a discount note for which the simple interest was deducted from the face value of the note, 319

Simple interest: the amount of money paid or earned on a loan or investment of a lump sum for a specified period of time, 302

    finding the principal, rate, or time using the simple interest formula, 306–309, 327

    formula, 302–303, 326

    fractional parts of a year, 305–306

    maturity value of a loan, 303–305, 327

    tables, 316–317, 330

Single discount equivalent: a percent that is the complement of the percent form of the net decimal equivalent. It gives a net price that is equivalent to a net price resulting from applying a series of trade discounts, 245

Single discount rate: a term used to indicate that only one discount rate is applied to the list price, 239

    complements of, 240–241

    finding the net price using, 240

    finding the trade discount using, 239

Sinking fund: an annuity established at compound interest over a period of time to